Market research and analysis

Market research and analysis

DONALD R. LEHMANN
Columbia University

1979

RICHARD D. IRWIN, INC.   Homewood, Illinois   60430
Irwin-Dorsey Limited   Georgetown, Ontario   L7G 4B3

ISBN 0-256-02140-6
Library of Congress Catalog Card No. 78–61187

Printed in the United States of America

1 2 3 4 5 6 7 8 9 0 MP 6 5 4 3 2 1 0 9

Preface

A commonly asked question is, "Why write another marketing research book?" The answer is that, like most professors, the author somewhat egotistically believes he can cover the subject better than existing books and hopefully make some money at the same time. In writing this book, there was a strong inclination to do something radically different so that the value of the book would be obvious. In spite of this inclination the book may look fairly standard. The reason for this is that radical changes didn't seem to make the book more useful. Nonetheless, the book does have some unique features.

1. While there are descriptive sections, the basic writing style is instructive rather than encyclopedic. The reason for this is the assumption that most people need to follow a learning process in understanding marketing research which is more than just memorization of facts.

2. The author feels that the best way to learn the nuances of research is by doing some. He has found that a simple project (define a problem, make up a questionnaire, go get 150 respondents, analyze the data, and write a report) is the best learning experience in the course. Next to that, analysis of results seems to be the best way to increase understanding. For that reason, the analysis chapters contain studies already analyzed so the reader can see how inferences can be drawn from actual results.

3. A common data base involving 940 female heads of households' responses to a 1975 survey about usage of and attitudes toward foods is used throughout much of the book as an ongoing case example. This provides readers with the opportunity to view a large survey as it is analyzed by several methods and hence to compare the methods in a concrete situation.

4. The "fancy" analytical techniques are discussed mainly in words in the chapters. Mathematics are generally banished to appendixes. (How's that for market segmentation?)

5. Sample computer output from the SPSS program is reproduced in

the appendixes to the analysis chapters. This allows practice in interpreting essential results from actual output.

6.   The target reader is a user rather than a producer of marketing research. Still in order to be a good user, one must know enough about the subject to ask good questions. Hence the book will try to explain how or at least why many of the basic procedures are used.

7.   The writing style will be at times light. This is based on the assumptions that (a) some readers may not be passionately interested in the subject and need to be kept awake, (b) it is dangerous for an author to take himself too seriously, and (c) this book should help introduce the subject but cannot possibly say everything relevant about it.

In writing this book, the author has benefited greatly from both teaching executives and serving as a consultant. This real world exposure to people such as Larry Schecter at Pfizer and Aaron Straus at Best Foods has immeasurably improved both the style and the content selection.

The author also has many people in the academic world to thank. The careful and extensive reviews provided by Don Morrison at Columbia, Lyman Ostlund at Arizona, and Terry Shimp at South Carolina were both terrifically useful and a great favor. While the names are too numerous to mention, some other especially influential and helpful people have been Frank Bass and Edgar Pessemier at Purdue, John Farley, John Howard, and Mac Hulbert at Columbia, and Neil Beckwith at Wharton. Try as I might, however, I cannot blame them for any shortcomings of this book. Last but not least, the author wishes to thank his family for their patience. It will be nice to have something besides McDonald's for dinner.

Finally, having just completed my first textbook, I now understand why texts often seem cumbersome. Writing the first draft of a text is hard enough; revising it is about as much fun as running barefoot through a junkyard. Now only the market can tell whether the book will pay for the investment cost.

February 1979   DONALD R. LEHMANN

Contents

Chapter 7.   Nonsurvey research   183

Chapter 8.   Major research suppliers   208

Chapter 9.   Sampling in marketing research   252

PART ONE

Basic concepts

1

The role of marketing research

The term marketing research means different things to different people. For this book, the following definition seems best suited:

> Marketing research is the collection, processing, and analysis of information on topics relevant to marketing. It begins with problem definition and ends with a report and action recommendations.

This is purposely a broad definition and is intended to include the large variety of things done under the name of marketing research. One thing this definition excludes are marketing/sales gimmicks which masquerade as marketing research (e.g., the old opening gambit of many encyclopedia or real estate salespersons).

WHAT IS MARKETING RESEARCH?

In order to understand what marketing research is about, it is useful to understand where it comes from. Set in a business environment, marketing research is practically oriented. Aligned as it is with marketing, producing results which "sell" (are accepted) is very important. Yet in juxtaposition with this pragmatic framework is the connotation of research—scientific, scholarly, logical pursuit of truth. As will be seen, this juxtaposition leads to perpetual conflict between the demands of expediency and truth seeking.

As an applied field, marketing research has been a large importer of methodologies and concepts from other fields. These "benefactors" have included the following:

Psychology and sociology, from which most of the theories about how consumers think and process information have been drawn. Particularly relevant is the field of social psychology.

3

Microeconomics, from which utility theory and related concepts have been appropriated.

Statistics, from which most of the analytical procedures have been borrowed.

Experimental design, from which the fundamental concepts of testing and research design have largely been drawn.

As would be expected in such a hybrid field, the terminology also is drawn from separate areas, and learning the jargon can be a nontrivial barrier to understanding the subject (as the reader may already be aware).

The term "research" encompasses widely disparate approaches to gaining and analyzing information. Some of the major contrasts are as follows:

Orientation. This can range from tightly focused research (e.g., what would be the effect on sales of a 10 percent price cut) to very general, scholarly styled investigations (e.g., finding out what our customers think about when they use our product).

Formality. While most people associate research with studies which are structured with budgets, time schedules, and computerized analysis, both introspection and informal contacts with customers or salespersons are excellent ways to gain information.

Amount of data collection. Again a common stereotype of marketing research is that it involves extensive data collection, usually in the form of either an experiment or a survey. Not only are there many other kinds of data collection, but much of marketing research involves analysis of data which is already available.

Complexity of analysis. Research can include nothing more complicated than counts of the responses to a single question (i.e., how many people bought blue shirts) or "fancy" multivariate statistical procedures which simultaneously examine several variables in a variety of ways.

Marketing research and analysis is thus something of a hodgepodge of different approaches and heritages.

Another view of marketing research can be gained by viewing who it reports to and what the pay scale is. The results of surveys done every five years by the American Marketing Association (Twedt, 1975) appear in the table on page 5.

These results are hard to interpret because they are aggregated across many types of companies of vastly different sizes. They do point up two key results, however. First, marketing research is very likely to report to a general rather than a marketing manager which means it often functions in something of a watchdog capacity with respect to marketing. Second,

Position	1963	1968	1973
Immediate boss of marketing research director			
President, executive vice president, divisional vice president	23%	30%	45%
Sales/marketing management	54	54	46
Other	23	14	9
Average annual compensation (\$000)			
Marketing research director	\$13.7	\$19.5	\$24.6
Assistant director	10.9	15.7	20.0
Statistician	7.5	11.5	16.5
Senior analyst	9.6	13.6	16.3
Analyst	7.5	10.2	13.0
Junior analyst	5.7	7.6	12.7
Librarian	5.0	7.2	12.1
Clerical supervisor	5.7	7.0	13.6
Field work director	5.1	7.2	11.9
Interviewer	5.0	7.0	10.2
Clerical/tabulating	4.0	5.5	11.4

Source: Dik W. Twedt, "Six Trends in Corporate Marketing Research Show Budget, Productivity, Pay, and Opportunity Increases." Reprinted from *Marketing News*, published by the American Marketing Association, vol. 9 (March 14, 1975), p. 3.

there are a variety of jobs in research—with living wages. Actually the wages for those with advanced degrees at the "top" firms are noticeably higher than these, and it is possible to earn \$50,000 or above in the business.

The problems addressed by marketing research are as varied as its methods. Some of the most common include the following:

Forecasting. Forecasting sales is one of the most obvious tasks of marketing research. Unfortunately, how to get good forecasts is much less obvious.

Buyer analysis/segmentation. Studying buyers to find out what are the characteristics of users of different brands in order to more efficiently allocate resources (i.e., advertising dollars) is another common type of research.

Choice processes and information processing. Studying how buyers get information and make choices is probably the most common form of "basic" research done in marketing.

Factor choice/testing. The focus of a large portion of marketing research is selecting among different combinations and levels of the various factors which make up the marketing mix: price, advertising level and copy, promotion, packaging, and so forth.

It is also interesting to realize how the research business differs in various situations. Consumer package goods research often involves large sample surveys or experiments as well as frequently employing multivariate statistical procedures. Industrial marketing research is much more likely to use existing data or small samples of key accounts along with relatively simple analytical procedures. Research in the developing nations is most likely to be a struggle to collect reliable data. The "moral" of this discussion, then, is that marketing research is many things to many people.

WHY DO MARKETING RESEARCH?

When asked why someone would do marketing research, the obvious answer is to learn something which will help make better decisions. Put differently, by reducing uncertainty about the way the market operates, we can improve the odds of making good decisions. While learning something is clearly the main reason for doing research, the following variety of other reasons also contribute:

Tradition. As is the case with any organization, patterns of behavior become established. A budget allocated to research is a budget that will be spent. While marketing research typically is a very weak competitor in the bureaucratic battles for funds, it does have a certain permanence.

To gain agreement. Often research is used not to influence the person who orders the research (who has already made a decision) but as a supporting document to gain support for the decision within the organization. Here research serves both a legitimization and a quality control function.

To prepare a defense in case of failure. Research serves as a defense in case a decision goes awry. While there is a fairly low limit to the number of blunders a person can be associated with and still be employed, it is a lot easier to explain a decision if you can produce a report which said it was the right one.

To stall. One of the best ways to delay a decision is to postpone it by ordering that it be studied.

Legal. An increasing amount of research is related to legal issues such as claim substantiation. Also deceptive advertising complaints to the FTC have created a growing demand for marketing research studies.

PR/advertising. Research often serves as the basis for advertising claims (e.g., "seven of ten doctors . . ."). Here its role is to convince consumers of either the truth of a particular claim or of the trustworthiness and high-mindedness of the company in general.

WHO DOES MARKETING RESEARCH?

The people who do marketing research are a widely disparate group. There are no marketing research schools, no certification exams, and very few schools where even a marketing research major exists. Hence the academic backgrounds of those in research tend to be varied, with psychology and statistics the two most common courses of study of those in research. Many people enter research on rotational assignments from line marketing positions. Hence it may be somewhat surprising that there is considerable colleagueality among members of the research business. Job movement between suppliers (companies that provide research services to other companies for a fee), advertising agencies, and marketing companies is common.

The research function is traditionally a staff function. In the past, this has been synonomous with dead-end jobs and a certain lack of respect. Recently this has begun to change as job mobility and integration have increased. Still in many organizations, research is something of a stepchild.

HOW COMPANIES GET RESEARCH DONE

Where research is done is also interesting and occasionally surprising to the uninitiated. Few companies have the staff to actually do data collection. Even General Foods with a corporate marketing research staff of just under 200 does not usually become involved in the data collection or mechanical analysis phases of research. Rather most companies contract data collection to a host of supplier companies ranging from large, well-known firms with offices in many major cities to small job shops with fewer than ten people. While advertising agencies often serve as a vehicle for getting research done, typically they serve as conduits to the same suppliers. The suppliers in turn may subcontract out data collection work to a network of field supervisors. Similarly, computer analysis is often handled by outside firms. Hence data collection and analysis involves a whole series of subcontractors who work on various parts of a job.

To get a feel for the size of the research business, consider a study by Honomichl (1974). The major research companies in terms of U.S. dollar volume (in millions) were as follows:

A. C. Nielsen ($55.3). Its major marketing research service is a retail audit service for consumer package goods sales. The general public is acquainted with Nielsen because of its audience ratings of TV shows.

SAMI ($18.5). A Nielsen competitor and subsidiary of Time, Inc., SAMI offers as its main service a warehouse withdrawal monitoring service.

American Research Bureau ($16.0).   This Control Data subsidiary specializes in broadcast (radio and TV) audience measurement.

Market Facts ($12.6).   Largely packaged goods oriented, Market Facts offers market test services in various cities, a diary panel, and a mail panel in addition to custom research.

IMS International ($11.1).   The dominant researcher in the pharmaceutical area, IMS International offers audits and doctor panels among their services. Worldwide, they are second only to Nielsen in revenue.

Audits and Surveys ($9.0).   This firm, as the name suggests, does both store audits and large-scale surveys.

Burke International ($8.9).   Located in Cincinnati, Burke is a large custom research firm perhaps best known for its Burke scores which are used to test TV ads.

Immarco ($5.5).   Its subsidiary, Audience Studies, Inc. (ASI), is well known for its TV commercial and magazine advertising testing.

National Analysts ($4.9).   A Philadelphia based division of Booz, Allen, and Hamilton, the two divisions of National Analysts specialize in survey research.

Daniel Yankelovich, Inc. ($4.8) (now Yankelovich, Skelly, and White).   Better known for its political polls, this firm specializes in custom survey research.

Some of the other large research firms include the following:

Opinion Research Corporation	Oxtoby Smith
Chilton Research	National Family Opinion
Starch INRA Hopper	Home Testing Institute
MRCA	NPD
Louis Harris	

These are all substantial firms. Yet in a relative sense, they are small. Proctor and Gamble's annual advertising budget would more than pay for all of the services of all of these firms for a year. Similarly R&D budgets typically dwarf marketing research spending. This fact more than anything else typifies the position of research—an important activity with a limited budget.

WHAT RESEARCH DOES NOT DO

Research can possibly best be understood in terms of what it can't do. The following two major things research cannot do:

Make decisions.   Research's role is not to make decisions. Rather research takes data on a confusing/uncertain market and rearranges it into a different form which hopefully makes the market more understandable and consequently good decisions easier. Realistically, however, researchers often make recommendations which become the decision after the appropriate approval is gained.

Guarantee success.   Research at best can improve the odds of making a correct decision. Anyone who expects to eliminate the possibility of failure by doing research is both unrealistic and likely to be disappointed. The real value of research can be seen over the long run where increasing the percentage of good decisions should be manifested in improved bottom-line performance.

THE APPROACH OF THIS BOOK

Many people argue that marketing research is more of an art than a science. Actually it probably most resembles a craft in that it requires both adherence to some basic principles and some skill gained from experience. This book will approach the topic by attempting to explain the methods most commonly used: what they are, how they work, and what their weaknesses are. As much as possible, the book will be user oriented and stress practicality over purity.

In the interest of practicality, it is important to recognize that there are other useful references available to anyone interested in the subject.

Peterson (1976) reported the ten books most frequently mentioned as vital to marketing practitioners by a sample of 70 "distinguished marketing researchers." These books included the following:

1. Ferber, ed., *Handbook of Marketing Research* (New York: Mc-Graw-Hill, 1974). This book is worth its high price ($38.50) for the heavy user.
2. Green and Tull, *Research for Marketing Decisions,* 3d ed. (Englewood Cliffs, N.J.: Prentice-Hall, 1975). This is a competitive text which is very useful if the reader has reasonable experience and quantitative skill.
3. Boyd and Westfall, *Marketing Research: Text and Cases,* 3d ed. (Homewood, Ill.: Irwin, 1972). This "standard" text was revised to become Boyd, Westfall, and Stasch (1977).
4. Banks, *Experimentation in Marketing* (New York: McGraw-Hill, 1965).
5. Kotler, *Marketing Management* (Englewood Cliffs, N.J., Prentice-Hall, 1972). Kotler's 2d edition has a lot of valuable information relevant to marketing research (more so than the abbreviated 3d edition).
6. Payne, *The Art of Asking Questions* (Princeton, N.J.: Princeton University Press, 1951).
7. Ferber, *Market Research* (New York: McGraw-Hill, 1949). This is the "classic" in the field.

8. *Statistical Abstract of the United States*.
9. Nie, et al., *Statistical Package for the Social Sciences* (New York: McGraw-Hill, 1975). This is a canned program package for computer users.
10. Cox and Enis, *The Marketing Research Process* (Pacific Palisades, Calif.: Goodyear, 1972).

In addition to these, the following books are also relevant to a variety of research issues:

1. Tull and Albaum, *Survey Research: A Decisional Approach* (New York: Intext, 1973).
2. Tull and Hawkins, *Marketing Research* (New York: Macmillan, 1976).
3. Churchill, *Marketing Research* (Hinsdale, Ill.: Dryden, 1976).
4. Schoner and Uhl, *Marketing Research* (New York: Wiley, 1975).
5. Kotler, *Marketing Decision Making: A Model Building Approach* (New York: Holt, Rinehart and Winston, 1971).
6. Campbell and Stanley, *Experimental Designs for Research* (Chicago: Rand-McNally, 1966).
7. Zaltman and Burger, *Marketing Research,* (Hinsdale, Ill.: Dryden, 1975).
8. Shaw and Wright, *Scales for the Measurement of Attitude* (New York: McGraw-Hill, 1967).
9. Kerlinger, *Foundations of Behavioral Research,* 2d ed. (New York: Holt, Rinehart and Winston, 1973).
10. Sellitz, *Research Methods in Social Relations* (New York: Holt, Rinehart and Winston, 1959).

The point of listing these books is not to convince you to use another book. Rather, the purpose is to list some of the sources where additional information and different perspectives are available. The rest of this book will then provide a *Layman's* (no one spells my name correctly) view of marketing research.

BIBLIOGRAPHY

Banks, Seymour. *Experimentation in Marketing.* New York: McGraw-Hill, 1965.

Boyd, Harper W., Jr., and Westfall, Ralph. *Marketing Research: Text and Cases,* 4th ed. Homewood, Ill.: Irwin, 1972.

Campbell, Donald T., and Stanley, Julian C. *Experimental Designs for Research.* Chicago: Rand McNally, 1966.

Churchill, Gilbert A. *Marketing Research.* Hinsdale, Ill.: Dryden, 1976.

Cox, Keith K., and Enis, Ben M. *The Marketing Research Process.* Pacific Palisades, Calif.: Goodyear, 1972.

Ferber, Robert, ed. *Handbook of Marketing Research.* New York: McGraw-Hill, 1974.

————. *Market Research.* New York: McGraw-Hill, 1949.

Green, Paul E., and Tull, Donald S. *Research for Marketing Decisions,* 4th ed. Englewood Cliffs, N.J.: Prentice-Hall, 1978.

Honomichl, Jack J. "Research Top Ten: Who They Are and What They Do." *Advertising Age,* vol. 45 (July 15, 1974). (Material adapted with permission from the July, 1974 issue of *Advertising Age.* Copyright 1974 by Crain Communications, Inc.)

Kerlinger, Fred N. *Foundations of Behavioral Research.* 2d ed., New York: Holt, Rinehart and Winston, 1973.

Kotler, Philip. *Marketing Decision Making: A Model Building Approach.* New York: Holt, Rinehart and Winston, 1971.

————. *Marketing Management,* 2d ed. Englewood Cliffs, N.J.: Prentice-Hall, 1972.

Nie, Norman H.; Hull, C. Hadlai; Jenkins, Jean G.; Steinbrenner, Karin; and Bent, Dale H. *Statistical Package for the Social Sciences.* New York: McGraw-Hill, 1975.

Payne, Stanley L. *The Art of Asking Questions.* Princeton, N.J.: Princeton University Press, 1951.

Peterson, Robert A. "The JMR Book Review in Transition." *Journal of Marketing Research,* vol. 13 (May 1976), p. 205. (Material reprinted from *Journal of Marketing Research* published by the American Marketing Association.

Schoner, Bertram, and Uhl, Kenneth P. *Marketing Research.* New York: Wiley, 1975.

Sellitz, Claire. *Research Methods in Social Relations.* New York: Holt, Rinehart and Winston, 1959.

Shaw, Marvin E., and Wright, Jack M. *Scales for the Measurement of Attitude.* New York: McGraw-Hill, 1967.

Statistical Abstract of the United States. Department of Commerce, published annually.

Tull, Donald S., and Albaum, Gerald S. *Survey Research: A Decisional Approach.* New York: Intext, 1973.

————, and Hawkins, Del I. *Marketing Research.* New York: MacMillan, 1976.

Twedt, Dik W. "Six Trends in Corporate Marketing Research Show Budget, Productivity, Pay, and Opportunity Increases." *Marketing News,* vol. 9 (March 14, 1975), p. 3. (Material reprinted from *Marketing News,* published by the American Marketing Association.)

Zaltman, Gerald, and Burger, Philip C. *Marketing Research.* Hinsdale, Ill.: Dryden, 1975.

2 _____

The value of information

This chapter deals with the question of what is the value of information. Clearly there are many decisions where the situation is sufficiently clear so that no additional information is likely to change the decision and hence the value of information is very small. (For example, if the boss asks if you'd like to get coffee, the answer is, "How much?") On the other hand, some decisions cry out for information which may not be available at any price. (For example, secret information about the price of Polaroid stock six months in the future would be crucial to the decision whether to buy or sell the stock.) More likely, however, is a situation where information will improve the odds of making a good decision (such as getting a better measure of market potential for a new product).

The concept of the odds of making a good decision is crucial to the concept of the value of information. Assume that a decision maker is faced with a tough decision—one where there are two choices and each one seems about equally likely to be correct. For example, by relying on experience the decision maker might be able to increase the odds of choosing the correct action from 50 : 50 to 60 : 40. By collecting the best available information, the odds might be increased from 60 : 40 to 80 : 20 in favor of making the correct decision. Hence the value of information in this case comes in increasing the chance of the correct decision from three out of five to four out of five. Information is not perfect (there is still a one in five chance of making a wrong decision), and in fact it is possible that we will make the wrong decision after collecting information whereas we would have made the correct decision without the information. Still over the long run, one is clearly better off with information than without it whenever there is uncertainty about the consequences of alternative decisions.

Another point worth making is that unless a decision changes as the result of information, then the information has no value in this context.

12

This truism has two separate levels of meaning. First, unless the manager is willing to change his/her mind based on data, then the data is an unnecessary expense. Second, if all the decisions after information collection are to go and the prior decision was also to go, the information has no value. For example, it could be relatively obvious that we wish to enter a market. If we collected further information, we might better pinpoint the size of the market but we would be so unlikely to find an inadequate market that for the purpose of the enter/not enter decision, the information would not be worth anything. This leads to two other key points. In general, information is most useful in cases where (1) we are most unsure what to do and (2) where there are extreme values (either huge losses or profits) which would be extremely important if they came to pass. What collecting information really does is lower the odds you will go ahead with a flop or, conversely, fail to proceed with a success. Exactly how much information is worth depends on the following three basic things:

1. The amount the odds of making the correct decision increase when the information is collected and used.
2. The relative benefit (profitability) of the alternative decisions.
3. The cost of the information.

This chapter will proceed by first presenting a formal framework for making "logical" decisions: decision analysis. Next, the decision analysis framework will be extended to provide a quantification of the value of information. Finally, some "real-world" considerations in assessing the role of information in marketing will be discussed.

DECISION ANALYSIS

The term decision analysis refers to a logical framework for choosing among alternative courses of action. Much has been written on the subject (Assmus, 1977; MaGee, 1964; Raiffa, 1968; Schlaiffer, 1959) including a fairly readable recent book by Jones (1977). The framework is typically visualized in terms of a tree diagram (Figure 2–1). The typical method of constructing such a tree is as follows:

1. First delineate the possible courses of action.
2. Next, list the possible results ("states of nature") of each course of action.
3. Third, estimate the payoff (usually in monetary terms) of each possible combination of courses of action and results.
4. Assign the probabilities to the different possible results for each given course of action.
5. Finally, select the course of action which seems to lead to the most desirable results.

14

FIGURE 2–1
Basic decision tree

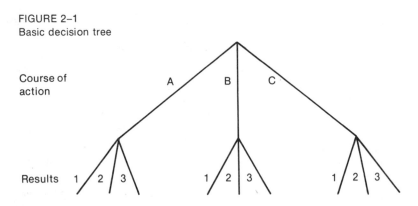

Course of
action

Results

Example

To see how decision analysis is used, consider the following problem: The XYZ Transportation Company, which specializes in freight deliveries, is considering a new rate on its New York to Boston route. (For the moment, assume that government regulations such as the Interstate Commerce Commission rules do not apply.) In the past, there has been a two-tier pricing system for 1-pound packages: $20 for "first class" which guarantees next-day delivery, and $10 for "regular" which typically takes two to three days. We are now considering instituting a same-day delivery service at the price of $30 or $40 (we have a thing about prices in $10 increments and will consider no other prices—boss's orders). After some preliminary analysis, we decide that one of three possible results is likely to occur if we price at $30: getting 100, 60, or 20 new packages per day. Similarly, if we price at $40, we can get either 50, 30, or 5 new packages per day.

Also at the new prices, we expect some of our present customers to "trade up" to the new service. At the $30 price, we think either 20 or 30 packages per day will be sent same-day instead of first class, whereas at $40, either 10 or 20 will move to same-day.

The daily cost of setting up and running the new service will be $700. The variable costs to send a package by the three classes of service are: $18 for same-day, $12 for first class, and $8 for regular. What should we do?

Even though this is a fairly simple situation, the data is sufficiently extensive to make analyzing the decision in one's head fairly complicated. Hence to provide a structure to the decision-making process, one could quite logically begin by drawing a tree to represent the situation (Figure 2–2).

Having delineated the situation faced by identifying (a) the courses of

FIGURE 2–2
Package pricing decision tree

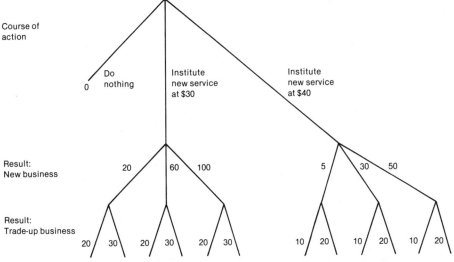

Course of
action

0   Do   Institute   Institute
     nothing new service   new service
             at $30   at $40

Result: 20   60 100   5   30 50
New business

Result:
Trade-up business
          20 30   20 30   20 30   10 20   10 20   10 20

action and (*b*) the possible results (outcomes), one would now proceed to estimate (*c*) the monetary consequences of each of the possible results. Consider the value of a single new piece of business at the $30 price. Since XYZ gets $30 and it costs them $18, they gain $12 for each new piece of business. Similarly for everyone who "trades up," they make $12 instead of $20 − $12 = $8 for a net gain of $4. Hence for the result of 20 new packages plus 20 "trade-ups" they would make incrementally 20 × $12 + 20 × $4 = $320 per day. When the fixed cost of $700 per day is figured in, the incremental profit becomes $320 − $700 = −$380. (Note here that we are using the incremental profit compared with doing nothing. We could also have calculated actual profit but chose incremental because, quite frankly, the numbers are smaller.) Similarly one can get the profit results for each of the profit combinations (Table 2–1).

Having identified the profit implications of the various results, the next step is to estimate the relative likelihoods of the different possible results. This is typically done by assigning probabilities to each of the possible branches of the tree. These probabilities may be based on survey results, experience in analogous situations, or expert judgment. In the present situation, assume that the probabilities of the different possible levels of new business for the $30 price are 20 units, .2; 60 units, .5; and 100 units, .3. Also assume the trade-up business probabilities are 20 units, .6; and 30 units, .4. For the $40 price, the probabilities of new business are 5 units,

TABLE 2–1
Profit results given different market results

Course of action; new service price	Result: New business	Result: Trade-up business	Incremental daily profit*
None	—	—	0
$30	20	20	320 − 700 = −380
		30	360 − 700 = −340
	60	20	800 − 700 = 100
		30	840 − 700 = 140
	100	20	1,280 − 700 = 580
		30	1,320 − 700 = 620
40	5	10	250 − 700 = −450
		20	390 − 700 = −310
	30	10	800 − 700 = 100
		20	940 − 700 = 240
	50	10	1,240 − 700 = 540
		20	1,380 − 700 = 680

* For the $30 price, incremental profit is $12 × New Business + $4 × Trade-up business − $700; whereas for $40, incremental profit is $22 × New business + $14 × Trade-up business − $700.

.2; 30 units, .6; and 50 units, .2. The trade-up business probabilities are 10 units, .5; and 20 units, .5. The decision tree can then be redrawn with the appropriate probabilities[1] and profits (Figure 2–3).

In order to estimate the probability of a particular profit for a given course of action, simply multiply the probabilities of the results which must occur to produce the profit result. For example, an incremental profit of −380 requires 20 new packages and 20 trade-ups. The probability of the result of 20 new and 20 trade-up packages for a $30 price is thus .2 × .6 = .12.

We can thus see that each course of action produces a distribution of possible profits, with probabilities attached to them (Table 2–2). Hence the decision about which course of action to take has been converted to a decision as to which distribution of results is more appealing. Several

[1] The "appropriate" probabilities are called conditional probabilities. The probability of trade-up business being 20 when new business is 20 might well be different from the probability that trade-up business would be 20 if new business were 100. (This could happen if one believed that the service would either be a big success all around or a consistent failure.) Hence the probability of 20 units of trade-up business could depend/be conditional on the level of new business. For the sake of simplicity, however, this example assumes the trade-up business achieved will be unrelated to/independent of the level of new business.

FIGURE 2–3
Package pricing decision tree with probabilities and profits

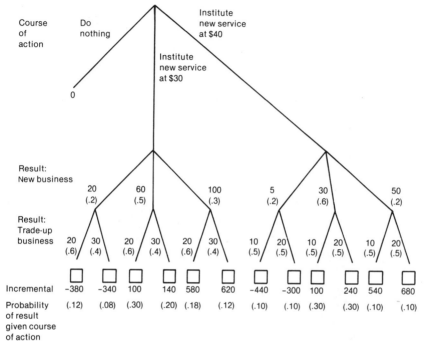

TABLE 2–2
Profit distributions for three possible courses of action

Course of action	Incremental profit	Probability of profit
Do nothing	0	1.0
Institute new service at $30	−380	.12
	−340	.08
	100	.30
	140	.20
	580	.18
	520	.12
Institute new service at $40	−450	.10
	−310	.10
	100	.30
	240	.30
	540	.10
	680	.10

selection procedures are possible. Three of the most common are as follows:

1. Choose that decision which guarantees the best result if everything goes wrong. This criterion (known as minimax) is the most conservative procedure and leads to very conservative decisions—in this case, doing nothing since both the other decisions could lose money and doing nothing would keep profits constant.

2. Choose the decision which gives the chance for the best possible result. This is the gamble strategy (called maximax) which explains why people are willing to buy lottery tickets—they are willing to expect to lose a little money on the chance they will earn a lot. Since the $40 price offers the greatest potential gain ($680 if 50 packages are generated and 20 trade-up), the new service would be instituted at a $40 price under this criterion.

3. Choose that course of action which provides the largest expected monetary reward. This is the criterion most often associated with decision trees (although not necessarily the best one). It requires calculating the expected monetary consequences of each of the possible courses of action by "weighting" the possible monetary results by their probabilities of occurrence. In the present example, this involves the following:

   a. Do nothing = $0.
   b. Institute the new service at $30 (Table 2–3).
   c. Institute the new service at $40 (Table 2–4).

Hence under this criterion we would expect to make $164 per day net incremental profit by instituting the service at the $30 price, and since this is the maximum of the three possibilities, we would choose to institute the new service at $30.

TABLE 2–3
Expected profit of $30 price

Result: New business	Trade-up business	(A) Increment in daily profit: $IP|R$	(B) Probability of result: $P(R)$	(A) × (B)
20	20	−380	.12	$ −45.60
	30	−340	.08	−27.20
60	20	100	.30	+30.00
	30	140	.20	+28.00
100	20	580	.18	+104.40
	30	620	.12	+74.40
				$ 164.00

TABLE 2–4
Expected profit of $40 price

Result: New business	Trade-up business	(A) Increment in daily profit: $IP|R$	(B) Probability of result: $P(R)$	(A) × (B)
5	10	−450	.10	$−45.00
	20	−310	.10	−31.00
30	10	100	.30	+30.00
	20	240	.30	+72.00
50	10	540	.10	+54.00
	20	680	.10	+68.00
				$ 148.00

Summary of the problems with using decision trees

Decision analysis has been around for a long time, and its pros and cons are fairly well known (MaGee, 1964; Villani and Morrison, 1976). There are a number of problems inherent in using decision trees. They are discussed in this section.

Specifying the alternative courses of action and their consequences. In many situations the alternatives are fairly clear-cut. For example, the phone company's choices in raising pay-phone charges were/are pretty much limited to 15 cents, 20 cents, or 25 cents, given the equipment already in place. Similarly a product manager at some stage may be faced with a choice between launching a new product nationally or regionally, test marketing it, doing further tests or refinements, or dropping it. What makes things complicated is the possible responses of competition or, as is becoming more important, regulatory bodies or lobbying groups. Since these responses can affect both the results (i.e., if the rate case finds against the phone company, they can't charge 25 cents) and their profitability (beating back consumer or competitive challenges is expensive), these potential responses can greatly complicate the tree. Even in the example used in this chapter, we would expect some probability that the rate would not be approved by the appropriate regulatory agency and a good likelihood that competition would react to the new service in some way. These would in turn lead to further actions by XYZ, Inc. In short, a series of courses of action and results are needed to realistically represent most decisions.

Finally, it is important to recognize that for a "real" problem, no single tree is drawn. Rather a first-cut tree is constructed to select those alternatives which seem most promising. Then the other branches of the tree are dropped and those which are retained are refined, sometimes by collecting data, until the "best" decision emerges.

Estimating possible results and their probabilities. There are three basic sources of the possible results of a decision and their probabilities: logic/deduction, past experience/empirical evidence, and subjective estimates.

1. Logic/deduction. In certain very simple situations, it is possible to deduce the probabilities of the results from the situation. For example, the probability of a head on the flip of a coin, a 7 on the roll of two dice, or a full house in a game of poker can be deduced from the situation and a few basic rules of probability and statistics (although students have a disarming tendency to do so incorrectly on tests). Unfortunately in most marketing research situations, this method is not applicable.

2. Past experience/empirical evidence. Past experience is one source of estimates of the possible results and their probabilities. When Proctor and Gamble introduces a new soap or American Can a new container, they have a pretty sound idea of possible sales levels because they have introduced so many similar products in the past. Similarly data analysis is often performed and sales levels forecast based on models using variables such as GNP, market growth rate, and so forth. The models in turn can be used to formally generate the probabilities of different results. Unfortunately the past data and analyses rarely seem perfectly compatible with the situation under consideration. Hence the analysis of past data typically only serves as a basis for subjective estimates of the possible results and their probabilities.

3. Subjective estimates. In the absence of hard data, a manager must make guesses about what the results will be. While these guesses should be based on as much analysis and experience as possible, they still involve some subjectivity. It is this subjectivity which to many people causes the greatest consternation over the use of decision analysis.

The first major issue in obtaining subjective estimates of the possible results and their probabilities is to decide from whom to collect the estimates. Aside from the obvious—finding someone who is knowledgeable, honest, and willing to provide estimates—knowing exactly who to talk to is something of an art. One obvious source is salespersons who are in direct contact with buyers and hence hopefully (but not always actually) in tune with the market. Another source is so-called experts, both within and outside the organization. Since the responsibility for the decision under consideration will ultimately fall on someone, however, it is appropriate to involve the person or persons (i.e., the product manager) whose evaluation depends on the decision in estimating possible results and their probabilities. (A side benefit of this is that those people who give estimates will be involved in the analysis and hence more committed to the results. This benefit can, of course, turn into a cost if individuals involved give false probabilities in order to affect the outcome of the analysis.)

The second major issue in assessing the possible results and their probabilities is how to obtain them. This turns out to be a very tricky task, since most people don't understand probability concepts (Tversky and Kahneman, 1974). The most obvious approach is to directly ask an individual to list the possible results and their probabilities of occurring. Unfortunately, many people (and especially nonquantitatively oriented managers) don't respond well to such direct assessments of probabilities, and when they do respond, they often are inaccurate. Hence a variety of devices are employed to get the probabilities less directly.

The most commonly used gambit to elicit probabilities involves asking an individual to indicate various levels which sales will exceed with a certain likelihood. For example, the individual might be asked to indicate—

1. What level will sales exceed 90 percent of the time (for example, 5,000 units).
2. What level will sales exceed 50 percent of the time (for example, 10,000 units).
3. What level will sales exceed only 10 percent of the time (for example, 20,000 units).

By using the answers to these questions, a researcher can develop an entire distribution of possible results (Figure 2–4).

FIGURE 2–4
Derived distribution of possible sales levels

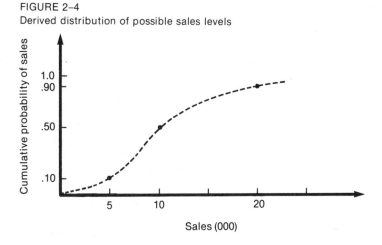

Alternatively, a researcher may ask a key individual to first list some possible results. Then the researcher can ask the individual to indicate their relative likelihood of occurrence (from which probabilities of the results can be deduced). Detailed discussion of methods for eliciting results and their probabilities is beyond the scope of this book. For further reading, see Hogarth, 1975; Jones, 1977; Sarin, 1978; Savage, 1971; Winkler, 1967a,b. Suffice it to say that elicitation of accurate probabilities is a doable but not a trivial task.

Considerable opposition exists to using subjective probabilities. This comes from two basic schools of thought. The first position of opposition is that anything based on subjective probabilities is essentially worthless. Assuming the person making the estimates has experience, the subjective estimates will in fact be based on data (experience in analogous situations, etc.). The difference between subjective and data-based estimates (which should be and typically are subjectively adjusted) is thus not as great as it at first appears. The other major opposition to using subjective probabilities is that since they are not perfectly accurate or easy to obtain, they are not worthwhile. Development of the probabilities of results is a nontrivial task. It is, however, solvable. It should also be noted that it is possible to see if the decision is sensitive to changes in the probabilities. For example, if we would go ahead with a decision if the probability of success were .5 (our best guess), see if we would also go ahead if the probability is .4 (a more pessimistic figure). If the decision is still go, we can be more confident that we are pursuing the best course of action. If on the other hand the decision changes, it indicates that we might wish to commit some resources to estimating the probability of success more accurately in order to increase the odds of making the correct decision.

Assessing the monetary consequences of the different combinations of courses of action and results. While this is possibly the easiest of the problems to deal with, it is by no means trivial. For example, estimating future costs of production given changes in energy costs, raw material prices, and so forth, is very difficult. Hence the monetary consequences are really estimates whose effect on the decisions should usually be checked at least by sensitivity analysis if not by incorporating multiple monetary results and attendant probabilities into the decision tree.

Choosing an appropriate criterion. The most obvious criterion to apply is expected monetary value. Indeed, this is a good criterion to use only in the case of repetitive decisions which are independent of each other and are not so large as to affect the organization greatly depending on the results. The independence notion is rarely true, since the condition of the general economy alone dictates that either most things go well or many go sour together. Also, unfortunately, in many cases the decision will have sufficiently large impact that it will affect the organization, or at least the subpart of it with which the decision maker is associated. For example, certain possible results may seriously damage the financial position of the company and hence decisions leading to these will typically be avoided in going concerns.

Another barrier to the expected value criterion is individual behavior. Since turning a profitable product into an unprofitable one may lead to being fired whereas doubling profits may only lead to a 10 percent raise, the personal consequences of the results may be asymmetric and hence the expected value criterion inappropriate. In short, individuals may be understandably more cautious (risk averse) than is implied by the expected value criterion.

It is possible to develop a formula which translates the different monetary results into utilities and then to compute expected utilities. A more pragmatic approach, however, is to calculate the expected value and simply check to see if any of the likely results of the indicated decision are sufficiently bad to cause reconsideration and possibly a change to a less risky decision. It is also sometimes appropriate to check other decisions which result in lower expected values to see if there is a possible result under these decisions which is so desirable that it is worth going against averages.

Summary

Having spent considerable time pointing out the weaknesses of decision trees, it is important to indicate that they still are useful devices. Their major advantage is that they create structure in what appear to be largely unstructured situations. It seems far more constructive to have people debating the likely results in sales of a decision rather than arguing whether they like the decision or not. (Such discussions are also more likely to be based on facts than on political clout or debating skills.) There is also some evidence which suggests that breaking a decision into small parts leads to better decisions (e.g., Armstrong, 1975). Decision trees also provide an indication of what key uncertainties exist. If the expected value criterion is used, it provides a very useful starting point for deciding what to do. In short, given an uncertain world, decision trees are a useful device for structuring a problem and getting an indication (relatively quickly and inexpensively) of what is the best decision to make. Since managers are ultimately judged more by results than by method, however, it is the managers' prerogative to make choices any way they choose.

VALUE OF INFORMATION: QUANTITATIVE ASSESSMENT

Before investing time and money in collecting information about a decision, most people make a judgment (at least implicitly) as to whether the information will be worth the trouble. Consider, for example, an individual choosing a new dishwasher. That person may already have a choice in mind (e.g., I have a GE now that I bought from Store A and it worked well, so I will buy a GE there next time). In deciding whether to gather more information (e.g., read *Consumer Reports,* shop around, etc.), several major considerations exist as follows:

1. Under what kind of time pressure is the individual? (For example, is the present dishwasher flooding the kitchen or just getting old? How much "free" time does the individual have?)
2. How easy is it to collect more information? (For example, does the individual subscribe to *Consumer Reports,* live in an area where shopping is easy, etc.?)
3. What is the cost of a bad decision? (For example, what is the cost of buying another new machine, cost of a service contract, etc.?)
4. How different are the available alternatives? (For example, does which brand is bought make much difference in terms of either length of like or quality of service?)
5. How likely is it that more information will change the decision? (For example, if the individual is fairly certain that he or she will buy a GE at Store A, then more information is probably irrelevant.)

Of these considerations, 1 and 2 are related to the cost of information, 3 and 4 to the relative results of the alternative decisions, and 5 to the relative odds of making a good decision with and without more information. If a sample of people were asked whether they would collect information in a set of situations/scenarios, we would expect more of them to collect information when (a) the cost of information were low, (b) there was a noticeable difference among alternatives, and (c) they felt a relative high degree of uncertainty about which decision alternative to select.

While the preceeding seems sensible, it does not directly produce a quantitative assessment of the value of additional information. In order to get a quantitative assessment, one procedure uses decision trees. The procedure has three basic steps:

1. Build a decision tree for the situation assuming current information. Then calculate the optimal decision and its expected value $(EV|CI)$.
2. Build a decision tree for the situation assuming that additional information were available. Then calculate the optimal decision given the additional information and its expected value $(EV|AI)$.
3. Estimate the expected value of additional information (EVAI) as $EVAI = EV|AI - EV|CI$. Hence the value of information is the expected improvement in profit which would result if the information were obtained.

Example

A more complete discussion of the methodology appears in the Appendix to this chapter. However, for illustrative purposes a simpler example will be used here. Assume an individual is trying to decide whether to put money in the bank (and end up with $50) or to buy a stock (which will end up worth either $10 or $80). If the individual buys the stock, it seems equally likely it will be worth $10 or $80 given current information. Hence we get the picture in Figure 2–5. The expected values of the two decisions are as follows:

$$\text{Put money in the bank:} \quad \$50(1.0) = \$50$$
$$\text{Buy the stock:} \quad \$10(.5) + \$80(.5) = \$45$$

Hence given current information, we would put the money in the bank and EV|CI = $50.

FIGURE 2–5
Decision tree with current information

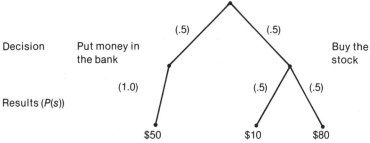

Now assume we could get a research report on the stock which would be either unfavorable (in which case the probability the stock value would be $10 increases to .66) or favorable (in which case the probability that the stock value would be $10 decreases to .26). Also assume that we expect the probability of an unfavorable report is .60. We can represent the choices given this additional information by Figure 2–6.

FIGURE 2–6
Decision tree with additional information

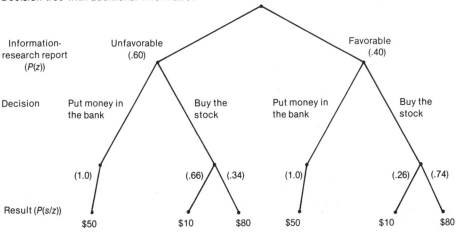

The result of the two decisions under the two possible research reports are determined as follows:

Unfavorable report:

Put money in the bank: $50(1.0) = $50
Buy the stock: $10(.66) + $80(.34) = $33.80

Favorable report:

Put money in the bank: $50(1.0) = $50
Buy the stock: $10(.26) + $80(.74) = $61.80

Hence given an unfavorable report, we would, not surprisingly, put the money in the bank and make $50; while given a favorable report we would buy the stock and expect to make $61.80. Since 60 percent of the time we expect an unfavorable report, the expected value given additional information is given by

$$EV|AI = \$50(.60) + \$61.80(.40)$$
$$= \$54.72$$

Thus the expected value of the additional information (in this case the research report) is

$$EVAI = EV|AI - EV|CI$$
$$= \$54.72 - \$50.00$$
$$= \$4.72$$

This approach is relatively easy to extend to more complex situations. The problem in applying the approach comes in obtaining reasonable estimates for the monetary results which are possible, the prior probabilities of these results, the probabilities of the various possible results of additional information, and the probabilities of each of the actual results given the information. In many situations, these probabilities are hard to deduce even with considerable effort. For this and other reasons, it is often useful to calculate an upper limit on the value of additional information.

In order to calculate the upper limit on the value of information, two steps are employed:

1. Calculate the optimal decisions given perfect information (that is, the decision which you would make if you knew what the result would be in advance) and its expected value (EV|PI).
2. Calculate the expected value of perfect information (EVPI) as EVPI = EV|PI − EV|CI.

Returning to the example in Figure 2–5, we see that if the stock value would go to $10, we would want our money in the bank (and make $50); while if the stock value would go to $80, then we would want to buy stock (and make $80). Since half the time the stock value will be $10 and half the time $80,

$$EV|PI = \$50(.5) + \$80(.5)$$
$$= \$65$$

Hence

$$EVPI = EV|PI - EV|CI$$
$$= \$65 - \$50$$
$$= \$15$$

Hence the most we would be willing to pay for information would be $15. If someone offered to sell us research for $20, we would politely decline their offer no matter how good their forecasting record was.

Limitations on quantitatively assessing the value of information

The methodology just described for quantitatively evaluating the value of information, once learned, is relatively simple to apply. Its conceptual use is widespread. Yet its application in a formal sense is limited. There are several reasons for this limited use. They are as follows:

Difficulty in application.   It is possible to argue that the technique is not used because it is perceived to be hard to apply. This argument is, however, both largely incorrect and self-serving. The cost of using such procedures is fairly low, and its lack of use must be even lower, indicating other explanations are needed.

The expected value criterion does not apply.   This limitation is an important one. For a small firm, operating on an expected value basis ignores the very real problem of bankruptcy. Similarly the job security of an individual may require avoidance of bad results more than attainment of spectacular results.

Prima facie decisions.   Many apparent decisions may in fact be preordained. This can be due to the fact that the situation dictates the decision (i.e., if I'm a small firm producing a commodity, I may have to match price cuts). Alternatively, it may be that political realities dictate a decision. (We may all know that the idea is dumb, but if it is the boss's pet idea, we may prefer to have the market test tell the boss so.)

Company policy.   In many cases, it is company policy to proceed in a certain manner. For example, it may be policy to test commercials on samples of 100 in Albany, New York. Hence the value of information is not the issue—the only feasible course of action is to proceed. (It is of course possible to argue that the company policy is in need of revision. While this may make you a star, it is more likely to make you unpopular, unemployed, or both.)

INFORMATION NEED AND VALUE INFLUENCES

Having spent considerable effort on assessing the value of information, we concluded it is the improvement in profit which would occur if the information were available. The value of information is related to several factors. They are as follows:

The accuracy of obtainable information. Obviously the more accurate the information, the greater its value.

The cost (both dollar and time) of information. Data already on hand or contracted for is relatively costless, while collecting new data is both costly and time consuming.

The ability and willingness to accept information and act accordingly. The more receptive management is to information, the greater is the value of the information.

The lack of clarity over what the right answer is. The more obvious the decision, the less the need for information.

The extreme results and their consequences. The more serious the extreme results are, the greater the need for information.

The degree of risk aversion both on a company and personal level. The greater the risk aversion, the greater the information need. On a personal level, getting the right information may protect one to some extent in case the decision is bad. (At least we can blame luck or some other factor rather than lack of diligence.)

Competitive reaction to information gathering in terms of (a) "jamming" the information and (b) being given more time to plan a counterattack. Competitors will often do their best to destroy the information value of data collection, especially test market where tripling advertising, cutting price, and offering large trade deals to fill the channels of distribution are only a few of the common gambits. The motivation for this is to feed you bad information and hence make it harder for you to make the right decision. Also the more time you spend gathering data, the more obvious it becomes to competitors what you are planning to do and the more time they have to react to it.

Company policy. Company policy often dictates the "need" for information collection.

The need to gain agreement. Information collection is perhaps most important in that it facilitates the establishment of reasonable agreement among the many parties to a decision about the availability of the decision and the way to proceed.

The need to stall/build momentum. Often a decision is sufficiently controversial that people look for a way to postpone it. Hence opponents of a position who feel open opposition is unwise can and do line up in favor of gathering more data, a much less risky position. By the same logic, supporters of a proposal who believe they do not have sufficient support to push the proposal through at the present may suggest getting data (a "pilot" study) to determine feasibility as a means of getting a toe in the door.

SUMMARY

The formal determination of the value of information can be a fairly tricky task. Nonetheless the concept of comparing the value of information with its cost is a useful step. In doing so, it is essential to define both benefits and costs broadly enough to take into account the positions and proclivities of the various parties to the decision. Based on the assumption that at least occasionally one will find information of positive value (a hoped-for result if those individuals in market research positions are to continue to eat), the rest of this book is devoted to alternative means of collection, analyzing, and utilizing information.

PROBLEMS

1. Assume you were considering changing the formulation of a food product by substituting one ingredient for an existing one. (*a*) List the concerns you would have. (*b*) Draw a decision tree to represent the problem.
2. What do you think would be the value of additional information in each of the following situations:
   a. A decision by P&G about whether to market Tide next year.
   b. A decision about which style dial to put on GE dishwashers this year.
   c. A decision whether or not to drill an oil well.
   d. A decision to launch a new packaged goods product.
   e. A decision to change the format of a ballet company's performances.
3. Bernie C. owns an ice truck. He sells ice cream on his lunch hour. When the weather is good, hot, and humid, he can net about $120 per day at the beach, or about $60 per day if he sells ice cream around his home. When the weather is poor, cold, and rainy, his net at the beach is about $15 per day, and at home about $25 per day.
   In this area, there is a 20 percent chance of fair weather (and therefore an 80 percent chance of poor weather).
   a. What should Bernie do?
   b. How much should Bernie pay for a perfect forecast?
   c. How much should Bernie pay for an 80 percent reliable weather forecasting service? (Probability of forecast matching weather is .8.)
4. Draw a decision tree which would help the phone company assess the effect of raising the price of pay-phone calls above 10 cents.

5. In considering three different positioning strategies for Slurp, a new soft drink, I assume one of three possible market conditions can occur. These will influence the profits as follows:

Market condition			
I	II	III	Position
12	14	18	Conservative
16	12	12	Moderate
4	8	30	Flaky

My subjective estimates of the probabilities of the three market conditions are .5, .3, and .2 respectively.
(1) With no other information, what should I do?
(2) What is the most I would pay for information about which market condition will occur?
(3) A firm proposes to test what market condition will exist. It traditionally is right 80 percent of the time. When it is wrong, it is equally likely that anything else can happen. How much is this firm's research worth to me?

6. Assume demand for a machine I rent/lease is as follows:

Demand (units)	Probability
200	.05
220	.05
240	.10
260	.15
280	.20
300	.25
320	.15
340	.05

The item costs me $80 and I can rent it for $120. (a) How many should I stock? (b) What is EVPI. (c) If you were legally committed to stock 300, what would EVPI be?

7. Assume that I had a brilliant concept for a new product. It is company policy to test products sequentially. I estimate the probabilities of this idea passing each screen given that it passes the previous screens are as follows:

Stage	P (pass)	Cost
Initial screen	.5	1,000
Concept test	.8	10,000
Product test	.5	30,000
Economic analysis	.4	10,000
Test market	.5	400,000

If I pass the test-market stage, I will roll out nationally (fixed cost = $4,000,000) with three possible results: failure (net profit of $1,000,000), so-so (net profit $5,000,000), and success (net profit of $14,000,000). The probabilities of these three results are .4, .4, and .2 respectively

a. What is my expected profit if I begin the process and proceed unless screened out.

b. What is the expected value of perfect information?

c. Assuming you had passed the concept test, what is the expected profit in proceeding?

8. I am considering changing my package design for Munch, my best selling dog food. I suspect one of three market conditions will exist. The expected profits associated with each of the possible results are as follows:

	Market condition		
Packaging	A	B	C
Old	10	10	4
New	12	7	5

The probabilities of occurrence of the three market conditions are .5 for A, .3 for B, and .2 for C.

a. With no other information, what should I do?

b. What is the most I would pay for information about the future market condition?

c. My market research department has proposed a test to determine which market condition will hold. Its characteristics can be described as follows:

Market condition	Probability of test result given market condition		
	X	Y	Z
A	.8	.1	.1
B	.2	.7	.1
C	.2	.1	.7

What is the value of this test?

BIBLIOGRAPHY

Armstrong, J. S., et al. "The Use of the Decomposition Principle in Making Judgments." *Organizational Behaviour and Human Performance,* vol. 14 (1975), pp. 257–63.

Assmus, Gert. "Bayesian Analysis for the Evaluation of Marketing Research Expenditures: A Reassessment." *Journal of Marketing Research,* vol. 14 (November 1977), pp. 562–68.

Hogarth, Robin M. "Cognitive Processes and the Assessment of Subjective Probability Distributions." *Journal of the American Statistical Association,* vol. 70 (June 1975), pp. 271–89.

Jones, J. Morgan. *Introduction to Decision Theory.* Homewood, Ill.: Irwin, 1977.

MaGee, John F. "Decision Trees for Decision Making." *Harvard Business Review,* vol. 42 (July–August 1964), pp. 126–38.

Raiffa, Howard. *Decision Analysis: Introductory Lectures on Choices under Uncertainty.* Reading, Mass.: Addison-Wesley, 1968.

Sarin, Rakesh Kumar. "Elicitation of Subjective Probabilities in the Context of Decision Making." *Decision Sciences,* vol. 9 (January 1978), pp. 37–48.

Savage, L. J. "Elicitation of Personal Probabilities and Expectations." *Journal of the American Statistical Association,* vol. 66 (December 1971), pp. 783–801.

Schlaiffer, Robert. *Probability and Statistics for Business Decisions.* New York: McGraw-Hill, 1959.

Tversky, Amos, and Kahneman, Daniel. "Judgment under Uncertainty: Heuristics and Biases." *Science,* vol. 185 (September 1974), pp. 1124–31.

Villani, Kathryn E. A., and Morrison, Donald G. "A Method for Analyzing New Formulation Decisions." *Journal of Marketing Research,* vol. 13 (August 1976), pp. 284–88.

Winkler, R. L. "The Quantification of Judgment: Some Methodological Suggestions." *Journal of the American Statistical Association,* vol. 62 (December 1967), pp. 1105–20.

———. "The Assessment of Prior Distributions in Bayesian Analysis." *Journal of the American Statistical Association,* vol. 62 (September 1967), pp. 776–800.

———— APPENDIX 2–A ————

AN EXAMPLE OF EXPECTED INFORMATION VALUE CALCULATIONS

Assume a supplier of parts to automotive manufacturers just developed a new van accessory. Tooling and other fixed costs would be $3,000,000. Sales would be through an established distribution channel, and the price to the distributors would be $110. The variable costs per unit are $70. Analysis indicates four possible levels of sales:

Sales (s)	Probability of market result: P(s)
5,000	.4
50,000	.2
100,000	.2
200,000	.2

Questions:

1. With no other information, should the company market the accessory?
2. What is the most the company should pay for information about likely sales?
3. A firm specializing in projecting sales for products based on a scale which characterizes products as winners, also-rans, or losers offers to do research for the company. Based on their claims and discussions with former clients, their accuracy is estimated to be expressed as in Table 2A–1. How much is this survey worth?

TABLE 2A–1
Probability of test result given actual sales $P(z|s)$

	Test result (z)		
Sales (s)	Winner	Also-ran	Loser
5,000	.2	.2	.6
50,000	.3	.6	.1
100,000	.6	.2	.2
200,000	.7	.2	.1

Decision with no further information

The decision of what to do with no further information can be addressed by means of the decision tree approach of the previous section. First convert sales to profit figures:

$$\text{Profit} = \text{Sales} (110 - 70) - 3,000,000$$

Hence we have the following:

Sales (s)	Monetary profit given sales: M(s)	Probability of result: P(s)
5,000	−2,800,000	.4
50,000	−1,000,000	.2
100,000	+1,000,000	.2
200,000	+5,000,000	.2

Next compute an expected value given current information (EV|CI) by multiplying the profit given result times the probability of the results for each of the four results and summing the results:

$$EV|CI = \sum_{\substack{\text{all results}}} (\text{profit result}) \cdot P(\text{result})$$
$$= \Sigma M(s)P(s)$$
$$= (-2,800,000)(.4) + (-1,000,000)(.2)$$
$$\quad + (1,000,000)(.2) + (5,000,000)(.2)$$
$$= -1,120,000 - 200,000 + 200,000 + 1,000,000$$
$$= -120,000$$

Since $-120,000$ is less than zero (which I could achieve by not marketing the accessory), my decision on an expected value basis would be not to go ahead at the present time. Still the possibility of making $5,000,000 is sufficiently intriguing that I may not want to completely drop the idea.

The expected value of perfect information (EVPI)

The key to deciding whether to drop the concept or not is to find out *in advance* what market result I am facing. Obviously it is impossible for nonmystics or those who are not friends of the Delphic Oracle to know the results in the future. Still it is a useful step to calculate the value of such perfect information.

The concept of getting perfect information is that one would know what sales were going to be in advance but could not alter them. (In other words, you would be omniscient but not omnipotent.) Therefore what a decision maker would do would be to proceed whenever the profit were positive and not proceed (and hence have a zero rather than a negative profit) whenever the profit would be negative. This is equivalent in poker to knowing what cards the opponents hold: you drop if they will beat you, and stay if you will beat them (assuming no successful bluffing can be done). The expected profit given perfect information (EV|PI) would then be

$$EV|PI = \sum_{\substack{\text{all results} \\ \text{where profit} \\ \text{is negative}}} P(s)(0) + \sum_{\substack{\text{all results} \\ \text{where profit} \\ \text{is positive}}} P(s)M(s)$$

In this case, that becomes

$$EV|PI = (.4)(0) + (.2)(0) + (.2)(1,000,000) + (.2)(5,000,000)$$
$$= 1,200,000$$

The expected value of perfect information then is the *net* difference between the expected profit given perfect information and the expected profit under the optimal decision given current information:

$$EVPI = EV|PI - EV|CI$$

In this case, this becomes

$$EVPI = 1,200,000 - 0$$
$$= 1,200,000$$

(Notice that we subtract 0 rather than a $-120,000$ since under current information, the optimal policy is not to proceed.)

EVPI thus is an upper bound on the amount we would be willing to pay for additional information. If a firm offered to do a $2,000,000 study for us, we can reject it out of hand since in expected value terms even perfect information is only worth $1,200,000. We also would be very leary of proposals close in cost to the EVPI, since most information is far from perfect.

Expected value of additional information (EVAI)

The concept of the expected value of additional information is, like EVPI, a net value concept. EVAI is the difference between the expected profit given the additional information and the expected profit given current information. Calculating EVAI requires estimating the expected value given additional information, which in turn requires quantifying how accurate the information is likely to be.

To see this problem more clearly, it is useful to construct a decision tree to represent the situation (Figure 2A–1). In order to make a decision, we must attach monetary values to each of the results and probabilities to each of the branches of the trees. The monetary values are known and some probabilities are easily attached (Figure 2A–2). Thus we see that we should either do the study or not sell the accessory. Unfortunately to analyze the results of doing the study, we need two sets of probabilities: the probabilities of the study results $(P(z))$ and the probabilities of the sales given the study results $(P(s|z))$. There are two basic approaches to getting these:

Directly estimate them. It may in some cases be possible to directly estimate $P(z)$ and $P(s|z)$ based on experience. This is the exception rather than the rule, however.

Indirectly estimate them. In many cases it is not very easy to estimate the $P(s_i|z_j)$ and especially the $P(z_j)$ (as in the given example). However, $P(z_j|s_i)$ values may be more easily estimated. The method for transposing the $P(z_j|s_i)$ values into $P(z_j)$ and $P(s_i|z_j)$ values is based on something called Bayes theorem.

Bayes theorem is the result of the penchant of an English vicar for playing with probability theory. Its use has become synonomous to many with incorporating subjective probabilities in analysis (as well as so many four-letter words on the part of students that the good vicar would wonder

FIGURE 2A–1
Decision tree including additional information

Courses of action

Not sell the accessory

Sell the accessory now

Do the study

0

Study result

1 (winner)

2 (also-ran)

3 (loser)

Course of action

Not sell the accessory

Sell the accessory

Not sell the accessory

Sell the accessory

Not sell the accessory

Sell the accessory

Sales*

A B C D

A B C D

A B C D

A B C D

* A = 5,000
  B = 50,000
  C = 100,000
  D = 200,000

FIGURE 2A–2
Decision tree with known probabilities

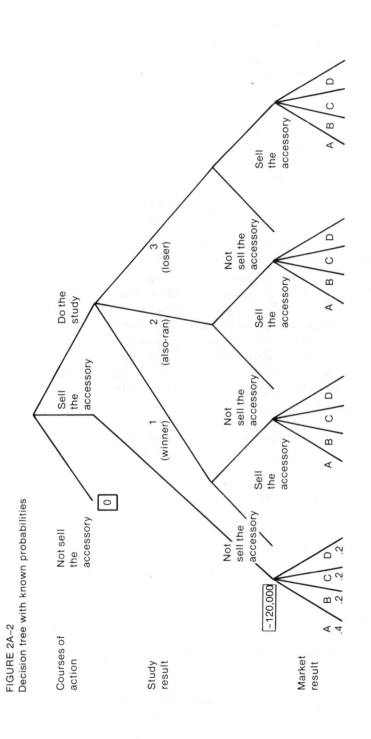

what he had wrought). Nonetheless, the concept is simple enough that it can be applied fairly easily (if somewhat cumbersomely).

The basic notion is that the probability of a sales level given a test result is the probability of a sales level *and* the test result divided by the probability of the test result:

$$P(s_i|z_j) = \frac{P(z_j \cap s_i)}{P(z_j)} = \frac{P(\text{sales level and test result})}{P(\text{test result})}$$

By clever manipulation, this converts to

$$P(s_i|z_j) = \frac{P(s_i)P(z_j|s_i)}{P(z_j)}$$

The secret then is to calculate $P(z)$ since the $P(z|s)$'s are already known. The procedure followed has three basic steps. First we construct a table as follows: Since we know that $P(z_j \cap s_i) = P(s_i)P(z_j|s_i)$, we can use the information originally given to calculate a table of the joint probability of a particular test result and a particular market result. Returning to the numerical example, the $P(\text{test result 1 and sales of 5,000})$ is calculated by $P(\text{sales of 5,000}) \cdot P(\text{test result 1}|\text{sales of 5,000}) = (.4)(.2) = .08$. Similarly we compute all the numbers in the table down through $P(\text{sales of } 200,000 \text{ and test result 3}) = (.2)(.1) = .02$. We now have Table 2A–2 which represents all possible combinations of test results and sales levels.

TABLE 2A–2
Joint probability of test result and sales level: $P(z_j \cap s_i)$

		Test result (z)		
Sales (s)		1	2	3
5,000	....	.08	.08	.24
50,000	....	.06	.12	.02
100,000	....	.12	.04	.04
200,000	....	.14	.04	.02

The next step is to calculate the probability of the different test results—$P(z)$. Since a test-market result must occur in conjunction with one of the four sales levels, we can get $P(z)$ by simply summing numbers down the column of the previous table:

$$P(z_j) = \sum_{\text{all } i} P(z_j \cap s_i)$$

Hence we get Table 2A–3.

TABLE 2A–3
$P(z_j)$

	Test result (z)		
Sales (s)	1	2	3
5,000	.08	.08	.24
50,000	.06	.12	.02
100,000	.12	.04	.04
200,000	.14	.04	.02
$P(z_j)$	.40	.28	.32

The final step is to calculate the probabilities of the market given test results. This is done by using

$$P(s_i|z_j) = \frac{P(s_i \cap z_j)}{P(z_j)}$$

For example, the probability of a sales level of 5,000 given test result 1 is

$$\frac{P(\text{sales of 5,000 and test result 1})}{P(\text{test result 1})} = \frac{.08}{.40} = .20$$

Similarly I can calculate all elements[2] $P(s_i|z_j)$ (Table 2A–4). We can now attach all the necessary probabilities to the decision tree as in Figure 2A–3.

TABLE 2A–4
$P(s_i|z_j)$

	Test result (z)		
Sales (s)	1	2	3
5,000	.20	.29	.75
50,000	.15	.43	.06
100,000	.30	.14	.13
200,000	.35	.14	.06
	1.00	1.00	1.00

---

[2] In this case by dividing each element in the $P(z_j \cap s_i)$ table by its column sum.

FIGURE 2A–3
Decision tree with computed probabilities

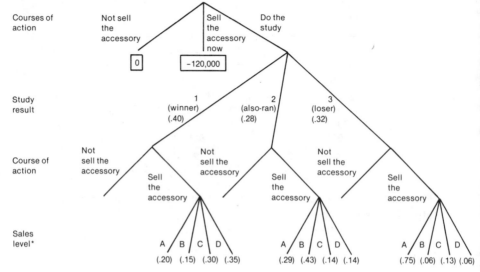

* A = 5,000
  B = 50,000
  C = 100,000
  D = 200,000

The next step is to calculate the expected values of the decisions given the test results so we can determine optimal decision based on the test information.

Test result 1:

Expected profit given do not sell the accessory = 0

$$\begin{aligned}
\text{Expected profit given sell} &= (.20)(-2,800,000) + .15(-1,000,000) \\
&\quad + .30(+1,000,000) + .35(+5,000,000) \\
&= -560,000 - 150,000 + 300,000 + 1,750,000 \\
&= +1,340,000
\end{aligned}$$

Hence given a test result of 1, we would go ahead.

Test result 2:

Expected profit given do not sell the accessory = 0

$$\begin{aligned}
\text{Expected profit given sell} &= (.29)(-2,800,000) + .43(-1,000,000) \\
&\quad + .14(1,000,000) + .14(5,000,000) \\
&= -812,000 - 430,000 + 140,000 + 700,000 \\
&= -402,000
\end{aligned}$$

Given this test result, we will not market the accessory.

Test result 3:

Expected profit given do not sell the accessory = 0

Expected profit given sell = $(.75)(-2,800,000) + .06(-1,000,000)$
$+ .13(1,000,000) + .06(5,000,000)$
$= -2,100,000 - 60,000 + 130,000 + 300,000$
$= -1,730,000$

Here we also do not market the accessory. (Actually since result 2 indicated not to market and result 3 suggests a lower chance for success than 2, we could have saved ourselves the calculation time.)

We are now (finally) ready to calculate the expected value given additional information. Returning to the tree, we have Figure 2A–4. The ex-

FIGURE 2A–4
Expected profit—Consequences of additional information

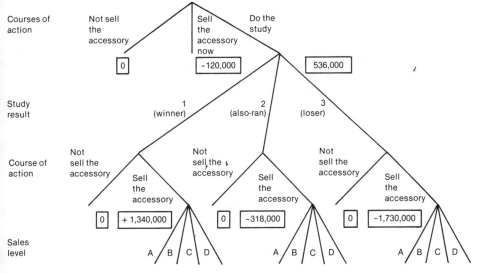

pected value given additional information is the weighted sum of the expected profit of the *optimal* decision given each of the test results:

$$EV|AI = .40(1,340,000) + .28(0) + .32(0) = \$536,000$$

We now calculate the value of additional information as the net increase in expected profit given the information:

$$EVAI = EV|AI - EV|CI$$
$$= \$536,000$$

What this means is that if the cost of this particular study is less than $536,000, we should go ahead with the study. If the study's costs are greater, however, we should not do the study. While this process may seem tedious, it is actually quite straightforward (Figure 2A–5). It is also

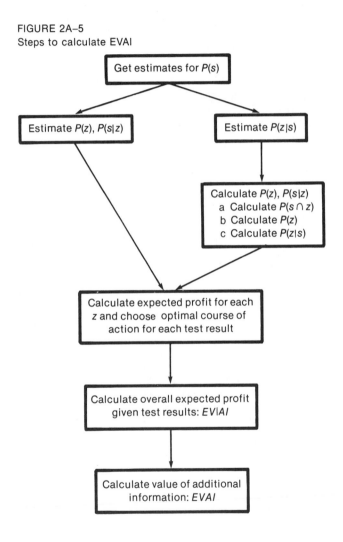

FIGURE 2A–5
Steps to calculate EVAI

possible to convert these steps to a series of matrix operations. (See D. H. Mann, "A Matrix Technique for Finite Bayesian Decision Problems," *Decision Sciences,* vol. 3 [October 1972], pp. 129–36.)

Some comments on the methodology

In reviewing the methodology just presented, two points seem worth emphasis. First, the conclusions are only as good as the input data. Since suppliers will tend to be overly optimistic in their presentation of the accuracy of their service in predicting results, it is often necessary to "tone down" these predictions. Put differently, it is desirable to do sensitivity analysis by varying the input values—$P(z)$, $M(s)$, and $P(z|s)$—to see if the decision would change. If the decision is relatively sensitive to small changes in these input values, then it is often worth reconsidering the input values. A final point can be made concerning the relationship between information value and the accuracy of additional information. Since the accuracy of additional information is measured by $P(z|s)$, we can see how information value could be related to the $P(z|s)$ values for a hypothetical three equally likely states of nature, three test-result case. Perfect information would look like the following:

$P(z|s)$

	Test result (z)		
Sales level (s)	1	2	3
A	1	0	0
B	0	1	0
C	0	0	1

In other words, the test results will be a perfect match with the sales level. Information of no value, on the other hand, would appear as follows:

$P(z|s)$

	Test result (z)		
Sales level (s)	1	2	3
A	.33	.33	.33
B	.33	.33	.33
C	.33	.33	.33

Put differently, if the test result is independent of the sales level, then the test results will have no information value. Clearly the closer the situation is to the perfect information case (especially for extreme/serious market results), the greater will be the value of the information.

3 _____

Research design

This chapter attempts to give a verbal overview of the process of research design. Discussions of research design often appear to be a series of platitudes and caveats which, if taken together, would void almost all research actually done. Nowhere is the conflict between "scientific" and real-world considerations more apparent than in the selection of a research design. To be purely scientific is so costly that research becomes more of a cost than a benefit; to ignore sound research design may cut costs drastically but also cuts the value of the research to zero (or even negative if the results are sufficiently misleading). The key to research design, then, is to make an intelligent compromise between scientific correctness and easy doability.

The research process can be viewed as a series of eight steps; the first five of which are design phases:

1. Problem definition.
2. Statement of hypotheses.
3. Selection of type of research.
4. Selection of test instrument.
5. Development of a plan of analysis.
6. Data collection.
7. Analysis.
8. Drawing conclusions.

This chapter proceeds by briefly discussing each of these eight steps (Figure 3–1). More detailed discussions appear in ensuing chapters.

PROBLEM DEFINITION

The most important phase of any research is the definition of the problem to be addressed. In spite of this, there is a tendency to spend very

FIGURE 3-1

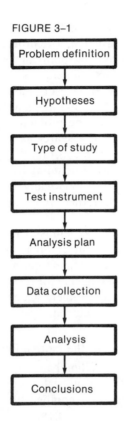

Problem definition

↓

Hypotheses

↓

Type of study

↓

Test instrument

↓

Analysis plan

↓

Data collection

↓

Analysis

↓

Conclusions

little time on this issue. Partially due to the pressure of busy schedules, partially because people assume that the stated problem is the real one, and partially from a reluctance to appear foolish by asking such a naive question as, "What is the real problem?" a large percentage of research turns out to be of little or no value.

It is very easy to assume that the stated problem is the real one. If someone asks if a particular analysis can be performed (e.g., a regression analysis of price on sales), it is very easy to answer this technical question rather than inquire why you want to do the analysis (e.g., to set the price on a new product, choose a promotion plan for an existing product, or evaluate the decisions of a product manager). Put differently, the stated problem is usually the tip of the real problem iceberg (a mixed metaphor, but hopefully an informative one); its relation to the real issue is often quite small.

The moral of this discussion is to continually probe to uncover the real problem. In a large percentage of cases where practitioners feel that researchers have produced useless results, the source of this feeling was the unwillingness or inability of the practitioner and the researcher to jointly define and comprehend the problem. The problem can range from making a particular decision to providing political ammunition for convincing someone that a particular course of action is useful (and if it fails, at least logical), giving a learning experience or sense of prestige to the person whose budget is being tapped, or simply using up a budget so it isn't cut next year. It is not unusual for the problem definition to change in the mind of the person paying for the research as a study is in the field. Hence it is strongly advisable to ask the question. "What is the real problem?" several different times and ways (including by observing what the person paying for the research is both personally interested in and rewarded for by the organization), and then put the agreed-upon problem in writing.

A key element in defining a problem is distinguishing a problem symptom from a problem situation. Put differently, it is easy to spend one's effort stopping a runny nose rather than treating the flu which is causing it. This occurs because the person asking for research often states the symptom rather than the underlying problem. Consider, for example, the following situations which have occurred:

1. *Stated problem:* To improve the motivation of the sales force.

   Real problem: Sales were falling below quotas. As it turned out, the cause was a combination of a quality control problem in the company's product and aggressive competitive activities. Motivation was a symptom of the situation, not a cause.

2. *Stated problem:* To use regression analysis to forecast sales.

   Real problem: A textile manufacturer was interested in developing a forecasting system for its many lines of fabrics and patterns. As it turned out, business was so volatile that regression analysis (or any other mechanical forecasting system) proved to be of limited value.

3. *Stated problem:* To study the relationship between price and sales for an ethical drug market.

   Real problem: A pharmaceutical manufacturer was considering introducing a drug in the market. A key concern was what price it could charge for it, which was the result of someone's suggestion that a very high price could be set since prescriptions were insensitive to price. Investigation of the relation between the price of existing drugs and sales indicated that the higher priced goods were in fact the major sellers, hence suggesting a high price was appropriate. Further study, however, indicated that the high price/high sales brands were the first to enter the product category as well as the most highly rated by doctors. Hence studying the historical data relating price to sales was at best of little value and at worst misleading.

4. *Stated problem:* To evaluate methods of forecasting sales of a major new durable.

   Real problem: A major manufacturer was in the process of developing a new durable for a potentially large but undeveloped market. The manufacturer needed to decide (*a*) whether to continue with development, (*b*) what particular features of the product would be most appealing and hence should be developed further by the R&D/engineering department, and (*c*) what level of sales to plan for. While describing different forecasting methodologies is interesting, it does not solve the basic problems facing the manufacturer.

5. *Stated problem:* To find out what consumers think of a company's advertising.

   Real problem: A company faced a possible cease and desist order from the Federal Trade Commission concerning their advertising. The problem was to collect evidence (*a*) which showed whether the ads were in fact having a measurable and inappropriate affect on consumer perceptions of the product (obviously the "right" answer was no), and (*b*) which would be admissible and persuasive in legal proceedings. The outcome was a national probability sample done by Gallup which surveyed consumers and became a key element in the company's defense. Knowing that the real problem was legal rather than informational led to a different approach to data collection, analysis, and result presentation.

A key related issue is, "When must the results be available?" This is another question to which the first answer is typically unrealistic (i.e., yesterday), and some thought must be given to deciding what the real deadline is.

It is possible to spend so much time defining the problem that nothing is accomplished. It also may be uncomfortable for someone in a staff position or consultancy role to probe a "superior." Hence there is a limit to how long the "What is the problem?" game can be played. (Some people cover up inability or unwillingness to proceed by stalling with general questions.) Nonetheless, problem definition should receive more attention than it typically does.

STATEMENT OF HYPOTHESES

Scientific method

The basic procedure which underlies most research is called the scientific method. Borrowed (or misappropriated, depending on your point of view) from the physical sciences, it can be seen as the following four phases:

Statement of hypotheses. These are essentially prior conceptions about the way things are (i.e., blue-eyed people have blond hair, market share and advertising are positively related, etc.).

Data collection. In this phase, data is collected to see if the prior conceptions are correct.

Comparison of data with hypothesized (expected) results.

Rejection or acceptance of hypotheses.

The thrust of this approach is based on the notion of predicting results which are falsifiable by data. A hypothesis which cannot be disproven is not useful. For example, I could have a theory (hypothesis) that the stock market will go up whenever the general interest rate falls. To test this, I would look at whether the market goes up the *next* time the general interest rate falls. If the market does not go up, I reject my theory as false. On the other hand, one could have a "theory" that the general interest rate sometimes influences the stock market. Unless I define when is "sometimes," there is no way to falsify this assertion, and hence it is a bad hypothesis.

Type of study

Deciding on hypotheses first requires understanding of the type of research being done. The most common categorization ranges from exploratory (which assumes no preconceived notions) to causal (which assumes a very specific preconception of how one or more variables influence one or more other variables). A useful categorization is exploratory, descriptive, and causal.

Exploratory. This is a study which is designed to find out enough about a problem to usefully formulate hypotheses. It stems from general problem descriptions such as finding out how consumers make decisions about life insurance. Typically such studies have few if any formal hypotheses and use "soft" methods such as in-depth interviews, focus groups, or employee testing.

Descriptive. Descriptive studies are part way along the continuum from exploratory to causal. These studies assume that relevant variables are known (for example, for life insurance purchase, income, age, family status, and risk aversion). Hypotheses are of the general type: x and y are related (e.g., life insurance purchase is related to age). Results tend to be profiles of purchasers versus nonpurchasers, and so forth.

Causal. These are the most demanding type of study. They assume that not only do we know what are the relevant variables but that we know (hypothesize) how they affect each other. Hence we are concerned with two basic problems:

1. Confirming or disproving the hypothesized relationships, and
2. If the hypotheses are so specific that the mathematical form of the

relationship between variables is known (e.g., $Y = a + bx$), estimating the parameters and strength of the relationship.

Exploratory research is very important in that it prevents preconceived notions from excluding potentially useful results. It is easy for a researcher or brand manager to forget that they are not typical consumers. Pure exploratory research, however, is almost never done. By selecting who to get data from and the general form of that information, a researcher betrays his/her preconceptions about the problem. Also though exploratory research is useful for generating ideas (hypotheses), it typically fails to be a good basis for decision making. The results of exploratory research also often defy statistical analysis. Hence there is substantial pressure to make research less exploratory and more causal.

Stating hypotheses

In stating hypotheses, we are really explicitly stating our preconceptions about the way the market we are concerned with works. While the hypotheses can be simply prejudices or hunches, they are more appropriately based on prior research or existing theories. It is possible and often useful to state hypotheses quite explicitly. (For example, H_0: A 10 percent increase in advertising will generate an 8 percent increase in brand mentions.) Such explicitivity is not necessary, however, and often is a symptom of pseudoscientification. If the strongest reasonable guess you have is that increasing advertising will increase brand mentions, then your hypotheses should state that.

Stating hypotheses has two major advantages. First, it translates a problem statement into a series of assertions (questions) which can be addressed with data, and hence essentially largely determines the research designed by specifying the data needed. Second, being forced to make implicit notions explicit is a healthy exercise which often leads to modifications of opinions even without data collection. It is possible to overly bureaucratize the hypothesis-generating process by demanding such things as a formal hypothesis for every question asked and a significance test and cutoff level in advance of data collection. In such a case, the form of hypotheses may become more important than the substance to the detriment of the research. Still, with the caveat of avoiding foolish rigor, explicit (as opposed to formal) statements of hypotheses are very beneficial.

SELECTION OF TYPE OF STUDY

The hypotheses dictate the data needed. Selection of the type of study provides the means for obtaining it. Actually the selection of type of study involves several choices which will be discussed in this section.

Using existing versus new data

Before spending the time, money, and effort to collect data, it is useful to see if usable data is already available. Existing data is more widespread and useful than most people realize, and should be considered first.

Method of collection

Assuming new data is required (and can be justified in terms of a cost/benefit analysis), the following alternatives are available: observation, questioning, and simulation.

Observation. One of the most obvious ways to collect data is to simply observe behavior. This can be done in a natural setting (where people are allowed to go about their "normal" business) or a controlled (laboratory) situation. This can also be done either unobtrusively so that people are unaware they are being observed (i.e., with hidden cameras) or obtrusively with either personal or mechanical observation.

The advantage of directly observing behavior is that one can directly obtain information which is "bottom line"—did they buy our brand, use the coupon, read the point-of-purchase ad? The disadvantages are first that it can be costly (try following an individual around with a videotape camera to observe a typical shopping trip or a salesperson to see which accounts s/he calls on). Second, the fact that a person is being observed may affect the behavior which is directly exhibited. (I rarely beat my kids in public, and always support socially desirable causes.) There is also a very important indirect effect on behavior of any obtrusive measurement method. By focusing an individual's attention on a particular aspect of behavior, the individual may think about it more consciously, which may in turn cause a behavior change. Hence measurement methods may be every bit as important agents of change as advertising or price promotions, and consequently care should be taken to be sure that the behavior being monitored is typical of the real world and not an artifact of the data collection process.

Questioning. By far the most widely recognized method of collecting data is questioning. (Who hasn't been asked to fill out some survey at one time or another?) Market research is equivalent in many people's minds to survey research. Even when observation studies are done, it is common to supplement them with a questionnaire.

One advantage of surveys is they are generally much less expensive than observation. They also can cover areas which are not subject to direct observation such as awareness, attitudes, and intentions. The major disadvantage of questions is that the responses may not be accurate. This can be true because of either a simple memory error (what brand of gas did I buy last?) or a conscious attempt to distort the facts (most people won't admit to being "against" ecology, good nutrition, etc.). In fact, the tendency to present socially desirable responses is a major problem with survey research. There are also some common results, such as the over-statement of intentions (of those who say they definitely will buy some-thing in the next six months, typically less than half do) which make interpreting survey responses difficult.

Simulation.   One type of study which is very different is that which falls under the broad title "simulation." Simulation studies are not di-rected toward collecting data but rather at using existing (past) data and models to project the answer to "what if" questions. Based on a model of a situation (i.e., Sales = 2.73 + 4.12 advertising + log (percent distribu-tion) + · · ·), the results are projected for different hypothetical situa-tions; hence "simulating" actual results. While simple models can be solved analytically, many of these models are sufficiently complex to defy easy analytical solution. In these situations, results are simulated over many trials, usually by means of a computer program. It is these large-scale computer models that are typically associated with the term simulation.

The advantage of these models is that they can be directed toward answering managerial questions without collecting new data. The disad-vantage is that if the model is faultily constructed or the past data which was used to calibrate the model is no longer relevant, the results will be misleading. Unfortunately there is no mechanism built into simulation (or to any other projection method, for that matter) which will enable the user to know a priori when the results are bad. In general, simulation models are not used to generate marketing research data.

Control of stimuli

A major issue in selecting a type of study is to decide which stimuli, if any, the subjects will be exposed to in the course of the data collection process. This in turn depends on how tightly focused the problem defini-tion is. For example, a study designed to assess the impact of different copy executions for an advertising strategy or a study intended to test the effectiveness of different selling pitches by the sales staff often leads to a controlled situation in which subjects are exposed to one or more prede-termined ads or selling pitches. On the other hand, loosely defined prob-lems are much less likely to require control and hence experiments. In short, situations (*a*) where subjects must be exposed to certain stimuli and (*b*) where the researcher controls the stimuli to which they are exposed call for experiments.

The simplest form of an experiment is to keep all controllable variables constant except one and see how varying this one affects another key variable/behavior (i.e., show respondents different prices for the same product and see if their buying intentions or behavior change). Many more complex designs exist, and a complete treatment of these is beyond the scope of this book. In deciding how to set up an experiment, however, two basic points are relevant:

1. Be logical, thorough, and careful.
2. If your confidence in your logic is limited, consult a good reference on experimental design such as Campbell and Stanley (1966).

Who will be sampled

A key question in any study is who will be studied. If an industrial company has four major clients, then a sample of all those four clients is often in order. For a consumer package good, however, there are obviously too many customers to include all in a study, and hence we must choose a sample to represent them. The question of who will be sampled really breaks down into the following four separate but related issues:

1. Who is the target population? This question requires specification of who are the subjects from whom you desire information (e.g., our five largest accounts, female heads of households between 21 and 39).
2. How many will be sampled? This question deals with trading off accuracy, which requires making the sample large, against cost constraints, which lead to making the sample smaller.
3. How will the subjects be contacted? While a variety of means exist for contacting target subjects, the vast majority of studies use either personal contact, phone contact, or mail.
4. How will sample points be selected from the target population? Another budget constrained decision, the choice of sample points ranges from pure random selection (which is usually very expensive and almost never employed) through methods designed to ensure representation of key groups (e.g., stratified or quota samples) to convenience sampling procedures.

Who will do the work

One of the first questions addressed is who will do the work. The answer is overwhelmingly a supplier/outside contractor. Next the question of who will work on it both from the company and the supplier (a critical factor which is often overlooked) must be addressed.

How much will be spent

The amount of money to be spent has a (the) critical effect on the type of study chosen (i.e., budgets of $10,000 exclude complex field experiments). While in theory the amount of money budgeted should be the result of an analysis of the likely value of information, in practice it is more likely to be a predetermined figure.

SELECTION AND DESIGN OF TEST INSTRUMENT

The term "test instrument" is used here to signify the method by which data is actually secured. Hence for a lab experiment involving placement of chips into piles to indicate the relative importance of attributes, the chips serve as the test instrument.

In the case of a survey, one issue which arises is that of direct versus indirect questions. Indirect may sometimes "trick" respondents into giving a more truthful answer about touchy subjects (i.e., the projective technique of asking what does your neighbor think about . . .). Another issue is whether to use aided/structured versus unaided/open-ended questions. Structured response questions get results which are easier for analysis, while unaided have less measurement effect built in but tend to be dominated by the verbal respondents and those with strong positions on the issues involved. The overall format of the questionnaire, the order of questions, and length are among numerous other issues which must be considered in designing a questionnaire.

One potential hazard of designing a test instrument is that it can become a catchall for many different individuals' research needs. Nice-to-know questions are interesting but usually not worth their cost. Questionnaires designed by committee are usually long and disparate ones. While it is obviously desirable to piggyback questions on a study if the cost is low, the point is often reached where the costs are substantial and some brave soul must say "Enough," lest the instrument become so cumbersome that it no longer serves its original purpose.

ANALYSIS PLAN

Before data is actually collected, an analysis plan should be developed. Since most commercial research is done on a tight timetable, all relevant analyses should be prespecified. A side benefit of this prespecification is that it allows one to check to see if the data being collected is adequate for the form of analysis planned. This cuts down considerably on the after-the-fact "why didn't we . . ." questions.

It is also important to specify in advance what levels in the results lead to what actions. Prespecifying these "action standards" prevents a lot of agonizing over what the results mean as people with different desires interpret the results to suit their positions. While it is important not to overlook unexpected events which affect the results of a study, it is also important to have predetermined decision cutoffs.

54

An example of a situation requiring predetermined action standards is the introduction of a new food product in test market. The key decision is whether to introduce the product nationally, and the key piece of information needed is what level of sales the product would attain nationally. Because the first months of sales will largely be pipeline (wholesale and retail trade stocking up), factory shipments are a poor indicator of sales. Hence an indicator of retail sales (e.g., Nielsen) is needed.

In order to develop action standards, the national share needed to achieve a satisfactory rate of return must be calculated (assume it is 8 percent). Next, characteristics of the test market must be considered. These include advertising levels (likely to be higher than normal), prices (likely to be lower than normal), and so forth, which might be thought to affect market share (assume an inflation of 1 percent). Hence a 9 percent share in the test market is needed to indicate profitability. The resulting action standards might thus be:

Test-market share	Decision
12% or more	Expand aggressively
10–12%	Limited expansion
8–10%	Continue to test
Under 7%	Reevaluate the product

A final point concerning analysis is that the availability and requirements of analytical routines (mainly computer programs) must be considered. If the planned analyses require certain forms of data, then that data must be included in the test instrument. Similarly the availability of analytical procedures will influence which analyses are planned; only rarely is it worth developing a new procedure for a single application.

DATA COLLECTION

The data collection phase is one which typically is a period of waiting for the researcher. Having specified what is to be done, s/he sits back and lets the supplier work. This can be a mistake. Keeping in touch with the supplier both helps quality control and gives insights which often are unavailable from the summarized results. Also the data collection phase is an opportunity to try out and debug the analytical procedures needed when the data becomes available.

It is crucial to pretest a procedure before going to a big sample. At the very least, researchers should subject themselves and a few convenient subjects to the process. It is amazing how many poor questions can be screened out this way. It is also desirable to run a pilot of 50–100 typical subjects. Thus the pilot tests whether the procedure works on subjects in the target population and whether the data has any variability. (If everyone answers a question the same way, it is probably not worth asking.) While a pilot test has both time and monetary costs associated with it, its benefits usually far exceed its costs.

ANALYSIS AND INTERPRETATION

This analysis phase is in one sense the least interesting part of most research. The analyses prespecified by the analysis plan are simply (assuming computer gremlins are absent) carried out and the results reported. While the results may suggest further analyses, carrying out such analysis is the exception rather than the rule.

Interpretation of the results is rarely literal. For example, 40 percent of a sample may say they remembered a given ad. While this sounds good in absolute terms, it is not clear what it would translate into in dollar sales. The key to interpretation is to gather information on a previously used scale. For example, assume in the past I ran 34 similar studies in which an ad was actually used and sales as well as ad recall were measured. These results could be portrayed graphically as in Figure 3–2. Given this back-

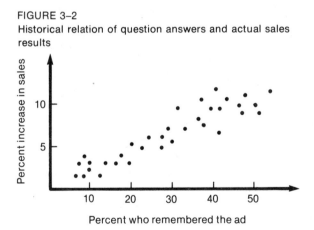

FIGURE 3–2
Historical relation of question answers and actual sales results

ground, a 40 percent favorable rating seems likely to produce between a 6 percent and 11 percent increase in sales. Hence we might interpret the 40 percent recall as an indication that the ad, if run, would produce an 8 percent increase in sales.

So important is the calibration issue that design of the basic elements of the test instrument should almost always be restricted to previously used methods. Even such seemingly innocuous changes as going from five to six-point intentions scales make interpretation of the results difficult (are 20 percent "top box" responses on a five-point scale the same as 17 percent "top box" responses on a six-point scale?). Similarly to know 70 percent of respondents are satisfied with our brand is not very informative unless I know what percent are satisfied with our major competitors. In short, absolute values in research are usually misleading. It is only by examining measured values relative to either historical data or concurrently gathered measures of competitive products that useful interpretations can be made.

The process of reconciling results with prior conceptions is very interesting. Whenever analysis of data conflicts with strongly held preconceptions, the natural inclination is to question the data, the analysis, or both. This is a healthy reaction since innumerable biases may creep into a study and errors in analysis, both conceptual and computational/programming, are far from uncommon. Still at some point, a manager must be willing to give up preconceptions or information collection loses its real value and becomes a bureaucratic ceremonial exercise. The art of using marketing research is to know when that point has been reached.

CONCLUSIONS

The final step of a well-ordered research process is drawing conclusions. The ex post value of the conclusions depends on how well they assist in resolving the problem. Unfortunately much research ends up by concluding (a) that the problem needs to be modified, (b) that the data doesn't address the problem, or (c) that more research is needed. (This is the favorite conclusion of both academic research and reports from consultants for obvious reasons.)

THE TYPICAL APPROACH

The approach just outlined is a series of logical steps occurring in sequence. In practice, this approach is more goal than reality. In the first place, the sequence is typically attacked iteratively with problem definition, statement of hypothesis, selection of type of study, sample definition, and analysis plan all considered almost simultaneously. While not pure in an academic sense, this approach has much to recommend it when there are time and money constraints as well as established company procedures for certain types of research. What is often disastrous, however, is when the sequence is used out of order. For example, assume that using a particular analytic procedure is the goal of the study (i.e., "I want to do a market segmentation study using multidimensional scaling"). This is appropriate for basic research but certainly not for applied research. The effect of such bad priorities, where the analytical procedure dictates problem definition, is generally the production of research which is read and then appropriately filed but which does nothing which aids management. Put differently, it is perfectly reasonable to build a data collection method or analytical technique into a study to assess its value for this and future problems, but it is generally wasteful to build a major study around a technique. This is especially true of fancy multivariate techniques, which make good "add-ons" but should rarely be used in the absence of more standard techniques which serve as the "fail safe" in case the fancy techniques fail to uncover anything interesting.

The typical approach, then, is to see what approaches are feasible, given multiple constraints such as the following:

1. Time (a two-month deadline eliminates many approaches).
2. Budget ($3,000 does not lend itself to probability samples and personal interviewing).
3. Standard practice (standard procedures have big edges in that they are easier to interpret because of comparability to past results and easier to communicate because of familiarity).

The culmination of any good research design is a time-line summarizing when different stages will be completed. This time-line is often/typically constructed with the ending date given (i.e., "we expect a report on March 1"). While it is possible to use elaborate CPM or Pert Chart procedures, the example in Figure 3–3 of the process for a survey is more typical. Notice that is common to do several activities in parallel (simultaneously). Also notice that the entire process was scheduled for five

FIGURE 3–3

Completion date	Duration (weeks)	Task
February 1	4	Finalization of problem and data needs (hypothesis statements)
March 1	4	1. Development of questionnaire (test instrument) 2. Selection of sampling plan 3. Analysis plan
April 1	4	Pilot test and tabs
April 15	2	1. Revision of questionnaire 2. Final analysis of plan 3. Payment of federal taxes
June 1	6	Field work
June 15	2	Data coding, punching, and initial tabs
July 1	2	1. Complete analysis 2. Initial ("top-line") results produced
July 15	2	Final report presented

months, indicating the need to plan well in advance. While this can be cut, the tendency to save six weeks by eliminating the pilot test stage is probably the worst bargain imaginable. It is also worth pointing out that large projects usually have built-in evaluation/exit points. These points provide the option to discontinue the research once the results become sufficiently clear without spending the entire budget.

AN EXAMPLE

This section describes a project which will serve as a point of reference for the entire book. The subject of the project was the nutritional knowledge, attitudes, and practices of U.S. households (Lehmann, 1976). The project was undertaken for two basic reasons: (a) the issue was interesting and important and (b) a budget was available to spend on it.

Obviously a variety of approaches are available for studying this problem. A variety of constraints, however, largely dictated the following design:

1. A budget ceiling of $10,000.
2. A single principal researcher with no staff.
3. A five-month time frame in which to complete the research.
4. The principal researcher's familiarity with survey methodology and fondness for large data sets and multivariate procedures.

Given these constraints, the resulting design should have been no surprise. A series of notions about how nutritional knowledge would affect behavior were considered. Changes in behavior and perceptions were also deemed important pieces of data. To gather data, a survey of 1,200 female heads of households was undertaken. These respondents were chosen from an existing mail panel (thus guaranteeing both demographic information and a high response rate as well as removing the sample selection, mailing, and data punching jobs from the principal researcher). The analysis plan was to establish a simple question-by-question tabulation as the basic report for wide dissemination and to play with "fancy" techniques both to understand the determinants of weekly food expenditures and to see how various foods, nutrients, and parts of the body were perceived to relate to each other. A pilot test of 100 was also included, and it resulted in one major change in the questionnaire. While the results came in late (so much for the time line), the study provided some interesting findings, some of which will be discussed later.

SUMMARY

Research design is the crucial stage of research. As will be seen later in this book, many of the issues raised here have been well delineated and the alternative solutions examined. The six keys to a good research design are common sense, logic, knowledge of the problem, attention to detail, effort, and luck. No matter how good the first five elements, nature can provide surprises or changes (i.e., oil embargoes) which invalidate well-designed research.

PROBLEMS

1. Assume you had eight packages of a certain product and knew one had been short-weighted. Design the most efficient scheme for using a balancing scale (assume each use of the scale is expensive) to find the short-weighted package. (This is a classic logic problem.)
2. Mr. Smart has just been assigned the task of recommending a way to test the effect of shelf facings (2 versus 3 versus 4) and promotions (5 cents, 10 cents, and 20 cents discounts) on Slop-out, a new toilet bowl cleaner and sterling silver wash. Suggest three alternative approaches, list their pros and cons, and make a recommendation.
3. Estimating the effect of advertising on sales is a key problem in marketing. (a) Suggest some alternative research designs for addressing this problem and (b) indicate why this problem is so elusive.
4. Assume you wanted to monitor food consumption patterns of 20–25-year-olds in the United States. What could be done?
5. A certain school points proudly to the average salaries of its graduates (highest in the country) and claims this proves it is the best program. What counterarguments might be made?
6. Assume you wanted to know whether attitude change preceeded or followed behavior change for a new food product. What would you do?
7. Is it possible to prove causality? To disprove it?

BIBLIOGRAPHY

Campbell, Donald T., and Stanley, Julian C. *Experimental Designs for Research.* Chicago: Rand McNally, 1966.

Lehmann, Donald R. "Nutritional Knowledge, Attitudes, and Food Consumption Patterns of U.S. Female Heads of Households." Columbia University Graduate School of Business, Research Paper No. 121, 1976.

4

Sources of information

The purpose of this chapter is to delineate the various sources of information available for marketing research. As will be seen, there are enough sources that keeping up with them is a full-time job. The extent of the job is such that most larger firms establish research libraries. A user of research should be careful to support a good library and librarian. Beyond that and keeping up in spare time, making friends with the librarian is probably the best way to keep informed about available information. The rest of this chapter is intended to point out what are some of the most important sources of information.

INFORMAL SOURCES

It may seem strange to begin a discussion of sources of information for research by considering informal sources. Yet much useful information can be gained from introspection, discussions with acquaintances, and listening to consumer comments and complaints. By carefully considering how you and other people in the office behave, one can learn a lot about a market. Admittedly these results are not projectable to the market as a whole given the small, biased sample used. What the results of informal research are useful for is getting ideas. These ideas can either be applied directly or submitted to more formal research for substantiation or rejection. Given the cost of informal research, any good idea which emerges is a bargain.

A side benefit of conducting informal research is that it forces researchers and managers to address problems directly, rather than simply considering the information that is filtered through various reports. One often feels that many of the bad management and research decisions which are made could be avoided if someone had taken the simple step of directly talking to customers and/or looking at the problem from the customer's point of view.

INTERNAL DATA

A major source of data is information available within the company. Sales records by territories, factory shipments, and marketing programs are all typically available. The problem comes in getting them in a form which is relevant for marketing. A discussion of some of the major problems follows.

Responsibility for data gathering is diffuse

Much of the data available is gathered for accounting purposes. This implies that many of the profit figures, for example, will be based on fully allocated costs, and hence may not be directly usable for abandonment decisions. It is also not unlikely to find production, sales, and profit figures all measured in slightly different time frames (as well as in some conflict with each other). In short, since much of the data is not gathered for marketing research purposes, it is often in a form which requires adjustment before it is useful. It also tends to be at variance with external measures such as those obtained from sales audits by firms such as Nielsen.

More data is available than you know about

Few companies have accurate filing systems on the information and research which has already been completed. Decentralized management and product management systems may be excellent for increasing incentives but are inefficient in terms of conveying information. It is not uncommon for essentially the same study to be done in two or more regions as well as at the corporate staff level. Hence it is advisable to have a central information clearing house in a large company. Failing that, it is usually a good investment to have occasional lunches with people outside your immediate group to find out what's going on elsewhere in the company.

The data is overly aggregated

In order to investigate a variety of issues (i.e., advertising's effect on sales), it is desirable to have data as disaggregated as possible (i.e., sales by regions, districts, or even individual consumers). Yet much of the data collected is available in summary form only (i.e., national sales and advertising figures). Hence analyses which could be performed if the original data were accessible are often precluded by the retention of only aggregate information.

Report formats are rigid

Most of the data available is in the form of periodic reports. These reports typically are imposing collections of tables, typically in the form of computer output. These reports might, for example, break sales by region and income category. If someone wanted sales broken by educational background, this would entail a special report, a time delay, and a budget outlay even if it were possible. Hence many of the reports serve more to fill up empty shelves than to help make decisions.

Yet in spite of these problems, internal data and past research reports are very useful forms of information. It is also possible to use internal data to generate the equivalent of primary data. For example, any company which bills its accounts on a periodic basis, such as a utility, can use its own billing records to set up a sample of accounts to act as a panel for monitoring customer behavior over time. One such panel has been set up by AT&T, which monitors a sample of both business and residential customers on a monthly basis. (Since the billing system is already in place, the marginal cost of such a system should be relatively low.) Hence given some modest ingenuity, internal data can be put to use effectively.

LIBRARY/SECONDARY SOURCES

Probably the most underutilized source of information is the library (both the company's, if a good one exists, and the public library). There seem to be two principle reasons for this. First, knowing something is in a library does not make finding it in an up-to-date form easy. Second, there is a feeling that each problem is sufficiently different to require special research (i.e., "that may be true for toothpaste, but we're talking about mouthwash"). The first point can best be addressed by getting to know a research librarian. The second point is true, but only to a point—surely something about toothpaste purchase behavior is relevant to mouthwash purchase behavior, at least to the extent that it suggests the kind of research which might be useful. This section will therefore proceed to suggest some of the most useful secondary sources.

Trade associations

Trade associations often maintain extensive information on sales and profits. In addition, they often keep a file on reported research dealing with their industry. Finally, a few actually collect data from consumers, such as the Textile Manufacturers Association which maintains a panel who report their clothing purchases. For a list of associations, see Fisk and Pair (1977). Another useful source of basic information is The Conference Board.

General business publications

In addition to specific industry-oriented publications (e.g., *Progressive Grocer, Steel, Chemical and Engineering News,* etc.) a variety of general publications often carry useful information. Among the most useful are: *Advertising Age, Business Week, Forbes, Fortune, Industrial Marketing,* and *Sales Management.* Also, the *Wall Street Journal* and *New York Times* newspapers provide additional sources of general information. In addition to these publications, two sets of handbooks contain useful information. The Dartnell Corporation series of handbooks includes *Advertising Manager's Handbook, Direct Mail and Mail Order Handbook, Marketing Managers Handbook,* and *Sales Promotion Handbook.* The McGraw-Hill Handbook Series includes *Handbook of Advertising Management, Handbook of Marketing Research,* and *Handbook of Modern Marketing.*

Academic publications

A variety of "professional" journals exist which contain articles of value for marketing research. These journals provide a means of communication both between academics (usually the theoretically/ quantitatively oriented ones) and other academics and between academics and practitioners. Those most directed toward practitioners include *Harvard Business Review, Journal of Marketing, Journal of Advertising Research,* and *Journal of Retailing.* The more theoretically/methodologically oriented include *Journal of Consumer Research* and *Journal of Marketing Research.*

Annual reports

Annual reports provide substantial companywide information. Each company is now also required to provide information about its various lines of business annually in a form known as a 10-K report. These reports are filed with the Securities Exchange Commission and are available upon request from the company. As line of business reporting becomes more firmly established, the results of general divisions (e.g., pet foods) can be monitored from public data. Since this type of reporting, in addition to being expensive, provides some useful competitive information, it is not surprising that companies are not eager to comply with this requirement.

Government publications

Perhaps the most common source of information is the U.S. government. Since your taxes already have paid for it, it is strongly advisable to gather any possible benefit from the various government offices. Most of the data is aggregate in nature (product rather than brand, region rather than individual oriented). Its major value is often in assessing market potential.

Department of Commerce/Bureau of Census. The single most useful publication is the *Statistical Abstract of the United States.* This book contains tables of statistical data on income, sales by product categories, and so on. It also provides references to other sources and hence serves as an excellent starting point in any data collection process. Another useful reference guide is *Measuring Markets: A Guide to the Use of Federal and State Statistical Data.* Also see *Current Survey Statistics Available from the Bureau of Census.*

Much of the useful data available comes from the Commerce Department/Bureau of Census. Hence making contact with someone there is a wise move. Some of the most useful sources you are likely to be guided to include the following:

Survey of Current Business. Over 2,500 indicators are reviewed, including commodity prices, real estate, labor force, employment, earnings, foreign trade, and various raw material industries. In addition, a verbal review of the current situation and other articles are included. The data reported here is summarized every two years in *Business Statistics.*

Census of Business (economic censuses). For purposes of reporting, similar companies are grouped together by means of a Standard Industrial Classification (SIC) coding system. This system is described in detail by the *Standard Industrial Classification Manual.* The grouping method is based on the principal product or service the company produces. Consequently, companies with multiple product lines and those companies that are vertically integrated are difficult to classify, as are many companies which end up in miscellaneous categories. Classification is done first by major groups (two-digit SIC code), then by subgroups which are broadly defined industries (three-digit SIC code), and then by specific industry (four-digit SIC code). For example, Major Group 34 is Fabricated Metal Products, Group 344 is Fabricated Structural Metal Products, and Industry 3442 is metal doors, sash frames, molding, and trim.

Censuses of the following areas are prepared: Retail Trade, Wholesale Trade, Selected Service Industries, Construction Industries, Manufacturers, Mineral Industries, and Transportation. For example, the census of manufacturers is a production-oriented report geared to measuring number of establishments, output, costs, value added, and wages. Reports are also available both on a product basis in the industry series (e.g., Fabricated Structural Metal Products SIC Group 344) and on a regional basis in the Area Series (e.g., New Jersey). Data is collected by mail canvass on employment, payrolls, man-hours, inventories, capital expenditures, and costs of materials, resales, fuels, electricity, and contract work. In addition, the *Annual Survey of Manufacturers* surveys 65,000 firms to update this data and also collects information on type of fuel consumed, supplemental labor costs, quantity of electricity, gross value of fixed assets, and rental payments. An excellent summary of available reports is provided in *Mini-Guide to the 1972 Economic Census*. It is also possible to obtain some of the raw data in the form of "public use" tapes.

Current industrial reports. These are the periodically updated production statistics for the various product classifications (SIC codes). For example, in April 1976 a report on the "Pulp, Paper and Board" industry was issued based on a sample of 650 firms.

Current business reports. These reports summarize business in different areas. Monthly retail trade by product category is a widely used form of this report.

County business patterns. These documents report data on employment and payroll for type of business (two- and four-digit SIC codes) and by geographic area (states, counties, and SMSAs—Standard Metropolitan Statistical Areas) as well as for total United States.

Census data. The census of individual households done every ten years provides a wealth of consumer data on a regional basis. The 1970 data was reported in a series of six "counts." The information available is summarized in the *The 1970 Census and You*. The following are the key points:

1. In addition to the questions everyone answered, two other sample questionnaires (the "long forms") went to 15 percent and 5 percent of the total population.
2. Data is reported for various areas, including the following:
   a. Total United States.
   b. States.
   c. Counties.
   d. Congressional districts.
   e. Minor civil divisions (MCDs) such as towns and precincts in 29 states, census county divisions in the other 21.
3. Also data is broken by statistical areas:
   a. SMSAs (standard metropolitan statistical areas).
   b. Urbanized areas (center city plus urban fringe).
   c. Unincorporated places (rural areas of 1,000 inhabitants or more).
   d. Census tracts (subdivision of SMSAs averaging 4,000 inhabitants).
   e. Enumeration districts (EDs averaging 800 people).
   f. Block groups (equivalent of EDs in 145 large metropolitan areas averaging 1,000 inhabitants).
   g. Blocks (subdivisions of block groups in cities 50,000 or greater plus a few others, averaging 100 people).
4. Both summary reports ("counts") and raw data are available. (Use of raw census data, however, often proves to be difficult.)

The census data is very useful for assessing potential by area. In spite of the massive effort entailed, however, it is not a true census in the sense of being completely accurate. Interviewing cheating is a factor, and so is the desire of some people to provide false data. (For example, since welfare depends on the presence of a male head of household, there is an obvious incentive to falsify those responses.) Hence it is unfair to deify the census results or castigate other results too harshly which are at slight variance with census results.

Other government sources

Department of Labor. The *Monthly Labor Review* provides data on employment, wages, and consumer price indexes.

Department of Agriculture. The Agriculture Department has monthly and special publications as well as such annual reports as *Agricultural Statistics, Crop Production,* and *Crop Values.*

Department of Health, Education, and Welfare. HEW provides data on population in the monthly *Vital Statistics Report* and the annual *Vital Statistics of the United States* and data on education in the annual *Digest of Educational Statistics.*

Federal Reserve System. The monthly *Federal Reserve Bulletin* reports on financial indicators such as interest rates, funds flows, and national income data. Each of the 12 Regional Federal Reserve banks also puts out periodic reports.

Other sources: Businesses

Thomas Register of American Manufacturers contains information on products manufactured and services rendered by company including brand names.

Standard Rate and Data Service publishes advertising rates and data for periodicals, direct mail, network, spot radio and TV, newspaper, and transit. Also newspaper circulation is audited annually. In addition to rates, the newspaper and spot radio and TV reports include data by state, city, county, and metropolitan area on population, spendable income, retail sales, farm population, and farm income.

Other sources on media include *Ayer Directory of Publications, Standard Periodical Directory,* and *TV Factbook.*

Morton Reports gives over 500 industry fact reports. These reports cost about $100–$200 per industry and go into some detail in describing an industry. Some other companies which provide industry reports include Frost and Sullivan, Predicasts, Information Source, and Find/SVP.

Other sources: Consumers

Sales Management Survey of Buying Power gives data for cities, counties, metropolitan areas, states, and total United States on population, number of households, per capita income, retail sales in total and nine categories, plus indices of buying power and sales activities.

Editor and Publisher Market Guide profiles 1,500 newspaper markets in terms of a variety of standard measures (population, housing, transportation facilities, salaries, number employed) as well as other measures such as principal industries, utility meters, temperature, shopping days, and retail outlets.

A Guide to Consumer Markets contains census information plus population, prices, employment, and so forth, on statewide or larger regional unit bases. Ownership of durables and spending by categories, often cross-tabbed by income, age, and so forth, are given.

Rand McNally Commercial Atlas and Marketing Guide contains population figures plus 40 statistics on each county in the United States.

United Nations Statistical Yearbook is a source of international statistical data.

General comments

Obviously there are a variety of sources of information which may be useful for specific problems. The key is to know which are relevant. Guides to data sources are available. Two useful ones are as follows:

Business Periodicals Index, a cross-indexed source of 150 major business periodicals.

Encyclopedia of Business Information Sources.

Finding the data is not the only problem, however. The accuracy of the data is often questionable, government sources included. Most of the data sources are good for relative comparisons (comparing current sales with last year's). On the other hand, almost no source (the census included) is perfectly accurate in an absolute sense. For example, accurately measuring the unemployment rate requires assumptions about how to compute the total labor force, what to do about so-called underemployment (e.g., a Ph.D. working as a waiter), and so forth. Also, frequently apparently accurate statistics are really gross approximations. For example, the number of umbrellas bought in the United States could be estimated based on a sample of 1,000 in Buffalo, New York, and then projected to the United States as a whole. When the data is reported, however, the numbers take on a permanence and aura of truth which their estimation rarely justifies. Hence care must be taken not to interpret reported data as perfectly accurate.

PURCHASING PRIMARY INFORMATION:
SUPPLIER SERVICES

Most library data reports measurable statistics (units, dollars, etc.). When subjective data (attitudes, satisfaction measures, etc.) is needed, secondary sources are often inadequate. Similarly the difficulty in reconciling secondary data with internal data often leads companies to seek data on their own. There are two general types of sources: those which provide information about businesses and those which provide information about customers/consumers. An example of the business-oriented supplier is Dun and Bradstreet's Market Identifier service. This service keeps track of business enterprises in terms of location, number of employees, sales, and so forth. This data is very useful for market potential determination of products which are oriented to business customers.

The remainder of this chapter will deal with the types of outside supplier services available to a firm. While these general types are applicable to industrial as well as consumer products, use of these methods is most evident in consumer product companies. These methods receive more detailed discussion in later chapters. The basic types of information include observation, audits, panels, experiments, omnibus surveys, special surveys, "soft" methods, and models/simulations.

Observation

Suppliers can be contracted to actually observe customers, either directly or by the use of some mechanical device such as Nielsen's TV audiometer which keeps track of the TV shows a family watches (or at least tunes in).

Audits

Two basic types of audits are common. The first is store audits, where products movement is monitored on a retail basis, made "famous" by A. C. Nielsen. This type of audit simply uses store records on beginning and ending inventory plus purchases to calculate retail sales. The other type of audit is a middleman audit, such as SAMI's warehouse withdrawal monitoring system. Here sales are estimated based on shipments from warehouses to retail stores. Occasionally a final consumer audit is also made where researchers go into the house and audit what is on the shelves, sometimes called a pantry audit. Since this method has the unfortunate tendency to measure what was bought and not used, and is quite expensive, it is not widely used.

Panels

Continuous reporting panels. Many companies maintain panels of individuals who agree to report all their purchases of a certain category of products such as groceries, clothing, and so forth. These panels allow tracking of brand, size, and quantity purchased over time. This allows both the continuous monitoring of shares by brand, size, and so forth, and the identification of which brands compete most closely. The problems with continuous reporting panels are unfortunately fairly severe (Boyd and Westfall, 1960; Sudman, 1964). Yet in spite of these problems, panels are widely used and useful.

Panel membership bias. The panel recruitment process is one which produces a high level of nonparticipation. A 10 percent or smaller recruitment rate is typical. Reporting every bottle of catsup purchased by brand, size, store, price, whether it was on special, whether a coupon was used, and so forth, is an activity in which most people refuse to participate. While the people who are eventually included in the panel are typically matched to the general population in terms of obvious characteristics such as age and income, there is a nagging worry that the same motivation which led someone to join the panel would cause them to behave differently from those "normal" people who refused.

False reporting. The reporting forms are sufficiently complex that a variety of shortcuts may be appealing to the respondents. One obvious way to shorten the task is to simply fail to report some purchases. Alternatively, it is convenient to report multiple purchases of a single brand and size or to report more purchases of the brand immediately previously reported. Finally there is the real problem of forgetting and either failing to report a purchase or reporting it incorrectly.

Panel aging and dropouts. A problem all panels struggle with is aging. A panel with the right average age in 1980 will be on average about ten years too old in 1990 if no one drops out. Hence it is important to continually update the panel by adding members both to keep the average age down and to replace respondents who for one reason or another (moving, loss of interest, death) depart from the panel.

Panel conditioning. The mere fact that an individual is reporting purchases of a product is likely to make the person think more carefully about the product. Hence being on the panel may create an expert consumer whose behavior no longer is representative of consumers in general.

Getting the data in shape for analysis. The problems involved in transforming the returned forms into computer-ready data are legion. As such, the chance for error is great.

Special-purpose panels. In order to avoid the aging, conditioning, and other problems with existing panels as well as to collect data on subjects not covered by existing panels, it is possible to set up a special-purpose panel to gather data. The two main problems with this approach are as follows:

Recruitment of panel members is expensive both in terms of effort and money.

The dropout rate may be a problem (Sobol, 1959). For example, in one study a special phone panel was established to monitor sales of a new car over an 18-month period in five measurement waves. In spite of the strong "guarantee" of the supplier that dropouts would be 5 percent or at most 10 percent per wave, the actual dropout rate was nearly 20 percent per wave. Hence by wave 5, less than half the original panel members remained (Farley, Katz, and Lehmann, 1978). Since dropouts were, as expected, less interested in new cars, this dropout problem led to a biased sample in later waves which required some gyrations to overcome (or at least reduce).

Standby panels. In order to insure a large response rate, it is possible to utilize panels of people who have previously agreed to provide information on any subject. Background information such as age, income, and so on, is maintained on these panel members. The most common form of the standby panel is the mail panel. These panels are often maintained in units of 1,000, each of which is intended to be representative of the total United States in terms of age, region of the country, and so on. Two major problems with this approach are the low recruitment rate and the under-representation of minority groups.

The low recruitment rate. Typically fewer than one in ten people will agree to serve on a stand-by panel. Those who do obviously are more interested in filling out questionnaires and hence are at least in one aspect atypical of the general population. They are also relatively literate. (Illiterates have slight problems with six-page mail questionnaires.)

The underrepresentation of minority groups. Mail panels typically underrepresent minority groups such as Blacks and Spanish-Americans. The minority members included tend to be older. Hence for some purposes, these panels are seriously (no pun intended) biased.

Experiments

An obvious source of information is experiments. These come in two basic types: laboratory and field.

Laboratory. Laboratory experiments are the epitome of tightly controlled experiments. Here essentially all the stimuli the respondent is exposed to can be controlled. Hence the effect of a single variable (e.g., a particular ad) can be assessed. The disadvantage of a lab setting is its lack of realism, and the resulting likelihood that lab results will differ from field results, usually in the form of being more dramatic. For this reason, absolute results are generally recalibrated according to the past correspondence between lab results and subsequent field results.

Field. The opposite of a lab experiment, a field experiment is the ultimate in realism but the worst in terms of control. To be effective, it is important to insure that (1) the controlled variable did in fact vary according to the design and (2) that other things which influence the results did not change concurrently (i.e., when the ads shown were changed, the prices did not also change). While sometimes one of these problems occurs in a lab experiment, at least one and often both will inevitably occur in a field experiment.

In constructing these polar extreme types of experiments, it is important to realize that intermediate services are available. One of the best known is a controlled store test where "real" shoppers in a real store are exposed to an experiment (e.g., changes in shelf facings or prices). Such tests are designed to achieve most of the control of a lab experiment plus most of the realism of a field setting. Another important distinction is between controlled and natural experiments. In a controlled experiment, the subjects are assigned to a "treatment" by the researcher. For example, if you were testing three prices, you could assign every third person to a particular price setting. By contrast, in a natural experiment, respondents are allowed to select (naturally) their own treatment. For example, if I were interested in assessing the effect of education on job choice, I could try to control the situation by assigning subjects to educational levels. This, however, would be both grossly expensive and morally questionable. Hence an alternative is to simply observe how job choice and education correlate in a sample of individuals. The problem with this (natural) approach is that the education level is likely to be related to a set of variables such as parents' education and income, attitude toward school, IQ, and so on, which also influence job choice. Hence a natural experiment is cheap in terms of data collection but expensive in terms of the analysis required to deduce correctly the effect of the treatment variable on the criterion. (Survey data, the mainstay of current marketing research, is basically treated as a series of natural experiments when it is analyzed.)

Omnibus surveys

Surveys are one way of collecting data, and in marketing research unfortunately sometimes thought of as the only way. Several companies prepare massive (syndicated) surveys, usually annually, which collect data on a variety of topics such as background (age, income, etc.), media exposure (magazines read, TV shows viewed), and product ownership. For a fee, a company can buy into such a survey. In addition, a company can add a few special questions of its own. The advantage is that by cooperating with others, the costs are shared and hence lower for each of the participants. The disadvantages are:

1. The timetable for the survey is rigid and may not match the decision-making process.
2. The number and type of questions a company may add are very limited.

Special surveys

Custom-designed surveys are a widely available supplier service. These surveys are much more flexible than syndicated surveys. Among their disadvantages are the requirements (both time and monetary) of sample selection and questionnaire design. Actually these surveys can be conducted in a variety of ways, including by personal interviews, mail surveys, or phone interviews.

"Soft" methods

A variety of soft methods of data collection are available from suppliers. At one time in-depth interviewing, where a psychologist extensively probed individual subjects in a one-to-one situation, was a very common form of data collection. More recently, focus groups have been used where a leader directs a group of respondents through a discussion of a particular topic. Focus group interviews depend tremendously on the skill of the leader, and focus group services are provided both by the larger suppliers and small shops of as few as two to three people. What the soft methods have in common is that they are typically first-stage research designed to generate hypotheses and used before one of the six previously discussed methods or are used when the results of another method seem incomprehensible.

Models/simulations

At the polar extreme from focus groups are the collection of models which are formal/mathematical descriptions of a situation. These models are typically the result of analysis of some form of data plus a theory and are calibrated to answer "what if?" questions. (For example, "What if I increase price 10 percent?") What is available to a potential user is typically a general description of the model plus the model's answers to a series of questions.

Actually models are at least as much users of data as sources of data. Typically they require one of the other forms of input data (panel, special survey, etc.) for calibration. Only after this data is available and analyzed do the models become sources of information.

Summary

It is important to remember that these are not necessarily competing sources of data. For example, it is possible to use multiple forms concurrently (e.g., during a field experiment having a special-purpose panel to monitor the results). Similarly services can appear which are mixtures of these eight basic services. Since all these services have been available in the past and continue to be purchased, one must conclude that the market has shown them to be of some value (although for some procedures, there may be more trial than repeat use). The point of this section has not been to promote one type over another but rather to delineate some of the major alternative sources of data which exist.

THE COMPANY AS RESEARCHER: DEALING WITH SUPPLIERS

Even in the largest companies, data collection is rarely carried out by company personnel. Rather the company will subcontract the work to "suppliers." Hence most marketing research work involves dealing with suppliers. This section is designed to acquaint readers with some of the major issues in supplier selection and monitoring. It is important to remember, however, that the responsibility for the study and hence a good part of the burden of design and interpretation should rest with the company, not the supplier.

Selecting a supplier

Probably the key decision a company researcher makes is which suppliers to employ. A variety of considerations are relevant for this decision.

Reputation of the supplier. The supplier's reputation is important for lending credibility to the results. Even if firm XYZ, Inc., can do a better job, a study by Gallup or Nielsen will have more "clout" with the average person. This is important when the study is designed to have impact on someone who is not knowledgeable about marketing research suppliers and practices.

Technical competence of the supplier. The technical competence of a supplier should always be assessed. Many suppliers who are good at basic studies do not possess the personnel or computer capability to do complex analyses. Those who profess to possess such capabilities may have one technician who is supposed to oversee all "fancy" analysis, or even an outside consultant who serves as a hired gun on technical matters.

Experience of the supplier. General experience is very important in doing good marketing research. Often overlooked however is experience in a particular type of research. It is generally advisable to avoid paying a supplier's development costs to learn about a new type of analysis if an experienced alternative supplier is available.

Costs. The instinct to cut costs is essentially sound. A little price shopping is desirable. After a point, however, cost cutting may be false economy. Suppliers are in business to make a profit and can only be squeezed so far before they lower the quality of the results by hidden methods such as cutting the number of callbacks or time spent on the project or obvious methods such as cutting sample size or pretests.

Reliable delivery schedule. Most suppliers require approximately the same amount of time for a given project. Still checking to make sure the supplier consistently delivers on time is advisable.

Project director. The person who will be project director is the key to the success of a project. An experienced director with sufficient time, interest, and knowledge is a quantum improvement over an inexperienced, harrassed, or uninterested one.

Project specification

It is to the benefit of both the company and the supplier to formally prespecify the dimensions of the project to be undertaken. Many companies have adopted standard research request forms. While these forms range from one-page summaries to fairly extensive forms (General Foods has a thick manual which details to suppliers how to prepare studies and what the "terms and conditions" of employment are), the following are essential elements:

1. Problem definition.
2. Methodology of data collection, including both method and sampling plan.
3. Analysis plan.
4. Report format.
5. Budget.
6. Time schedule.

Quality control

Checking up on suppliers is advisable. Without being a complete stickler, it is advisable to monitor what is going on by such activities as spending a day in the field and keeping in contact with the supplier during the course of the study. This both helps ensure attention to the project and tends to give insights into what happened which are unavailable from the summary report.

There are two basic methods of employing suppliers. One is to request bids on a project. This requires either (*a*) well-defined specs, which might be prematurely drawn, or (b) loosely defined specs, which can lead to widely disparate proposals and hence comparisons of very different approaches to a problem. The other approach is to deal over time with a small number of suppliers (e.g., two to four). This strategy has the advantage of economies of scale in the sense that the time spent by the supplier in understanding the company's business is greatly reduced, especially if the supplier assigns a permanent account representative to the client. Also dealing consistently with a given supplier makes comparability of results across studies somewhat easier. The disadvantage of this approach is that new ideas/approaches may be overlooked and that research may become stereotyped. This approach also may raise cost by making the supplier take his business for granted.

At this point a few words can be said about academic suppliers. With the exception of those who have genuine businesses established, academics are typically relatively understaffed. Hence they are relatively poor at meeting deadlines and giving polished presentations. On the other hand, they are witty, have low overhead, and occasionally have novel ideas. If one can put up with their occasional lapses into academic jargon, they are often useful in helping specify research design or analytical procedures. Basically they are complementary to rather than replacements for "real" suppliers. (This commercial was brought to you by your local chapter of the Hire/Employ Local Professors Association.)

SUMMARY

This chapter has attempted to delineate different sources of information which are available to a company. In order to be an intelligent user of such sources of information, it is important to understand how data is collected and how it can be analyzed. This book therefore next turns to the question of how data is collected. It proceeds by first discussing some essentials of measurement methods (Chapter 5). Next both survey (Chapter 6) and nonsurvey (Chapter 7) procedures are described. Finally, a limited description of some of the major available supplier services is provided (Chapter 8).

PROBLEMS

1. Discuss the appropriateness of a continuous panel versus a revolving panel (new respondents each wave) for monitoring.
   a. Advertising awareness.
   b. Brand-switching patterns.
   c. Attitude toward a brand.
2. What were U.S. dishwasher sales in 1978? Compare several sources and explain the disparity.

76

3. Where would you go to find out information about the PVC business?
4. What would you do to estimate the growth rate of microwave oven sales in the United States?

BIBLIOGRAPHY

Agricultural Statistics. Washington, D.C.: Department of Agriculture, published annually.

Annual Survey of Manufacturers. Washington, D.C.: Department of Commerce, Bureau of the Census, published annually.

Ayer Directory of Publications. Philadelphia: Ayer Press, published annually.

Barton, Roger, ed. *Handbook of Advertising Management.* New York: McGraw-Hill, 1970.

Boyd, Harper W., Jr., and Westfall, Ralph L. *An Evaluation of Continuous Consumer Panels as a Source of Marketing Information.* Chicago: American Marketing Association, 1960.

Britt, Steuart H. *Marketing Managers Handbook.* Chicago: Dartnell, 1973.

————, and Shapiro, Irwin A. "Where to Find Marketing Facts," *Harvard Business Review,* vol. 40 (September–October 1962), pp. 44–50 and 171–78.

Buell, Victor, ed. *Handbook of Modern Marketing.* New York: McGraw-Hill, 1970.

Business Statistics. Washington, D.C.: Department of Commerce, Bureau of the Census, published biannually.

Census of Business. Washington, D.C.: Department of Commerce, Bureau of the Census, 1977.

Crop Production. Washington, D.C.: Department of Agriculture, published annually.

Crop Values. Washington, D.C.: Department of Agriculture, published annually.

Current Survey Statistics Available from the Bureau of the Census. Washington, D.C.: Department of Commerce, Bureau of the Census, 1975.

Digest of Educational Statistics. Washington, D.C.: Department of Health, Education, and Welfare, published annually.

Editor and Publisher Market Guide. New York: The Editor and Publisher Co., published annually.

Farley, John U.; Katz, Jerrold P.; and Lehmann, Donald R. "Impact of Different Comparison Sets on Evaluation of a New Subcompact Car Brand." *Journal of Consumer Research,* vol. 5 (September 1978), pp. 138–42.

Federal Reserve Bulletin. Washington, D.C.: Federal Reserve, published monthly.

Ferber, Robert, ed. *Handbook of Marketing Research.* New York: McGraw-Hill, 1974.

Fisk, Margaret, and Pair, Mary Wilson, eds. *Encyclopedia of Associations.* 11th ed. Detroit: Gale Research, 1977.

Garry, Leon, ed. *Standard Periodical Directory.* 4th ed. New York: Oxbridge, 1973.

A Guide to Consumer Markets. New York: The Conference Board, published annually.

Harvey, Joan, ed. *Statistics—Europe: Sources for Social, Economic, and Market Research.* 3d ed. Beckenham, Kent, England: CBD Research Ltd., published monthly.

Hodgson, Richard S. *Direct Mail and Mail Order Handbook.* 3d ed. Chicago: Dartnell, 1976.

Measuring Markets: A Guide to the Use of Federal and State Statistical Data. Washington, D.C.: Department of Commerce, 1974.

Mini-Guide to the 1972 Economic Census. Washington, D.C.: Department of Commerce, Bureau of the Census, 1973.

Monthly Labor Review. Washington, D.C.: Department of Labor, published monthly.

Morton Reports. Merrick, New York: Morton Research, published annually.

The 1970 Census and You. Rev. ed. Washington, D.C.: Department of Commerce, Bureau of the Census, 1975.

Rand-McNally Commercial Atlas and Marketing Guide. Chicago: Rand-McNally, published annually.

Riso, Ovid, ed. *Sales Promotion Handbook.* 6th ed., Chicago: Dartnell, 1973.

Sales Management Survey of Buying Power. New York: Bill Brothers, published bimonthly.

Sobol, M. "Panel Mortality and Panel Bias." *Journal of the American Statistical Association,* vol. 54 (1959), pp. 52–68.

Standard Industrial Classification Manual. Washington, D.C.: Office of Statistical Standards, 1967.

Stansfied, Richard H. *Advertising Manager's Handbook.* Chicago: Dartnell, 1969.

Statistical Abstract of the United States. Washington, D.C.: U.S. Department of Commerce, Bureau of the Census, published annually.

Sudman, Seymour. "On the Accuracy of Recording of Consumer Panels." *Journal of Marketing Research,* vol. 2 (May 1964), pp. 14–20, and (August 1964), pp. 69–88.

Survey of Current Business. Washington, D.C. Department of Commerce, Bureau of Economic Analysis, published monthly.

TV Factbook. 2 volumes. Washington, D.C.: Television Digest, Inc., 1975.

Thomas Register of American Manufacturers. New York: Thomas, published annually, 11 volumes.

United Nations Statistical Yearbook. New York: United Nations, published annually.

Vital Statistics of the United States. Washington, D.C.: Department of Health, Education, and Welfare, published annually.

Vital Statistics Report. Washington, D.C.: Department of Health, Education, and Welfare, published monthly.

Wasserman, Paul; Olive, Betsy Ann; Allen, Eleanor; Georgi, Charlotte; and Woy, James, eds. *Encyclopedia of Business Information Sources.* 3d ed. Detroit: Gale Research, 1976.

Wasson, Chester R. "Use and Appraisal of Existing Information." In *Handbook of Marketing Research,* pp. 2–11 to 2–25. Edited by Robert Ferber. New York: McGraw-Hill, 1974.

_____ PART TWO

Collecting information and preparing for analysis

5

Measurement and scaling

This chapter deals with the general issues of measurement and the specific issues of question and scale design in survey research. In discussing the topic, some of the fundamental concepts of social science research are relevant. While these concepts will be introduced, however, this book is positioned as an applied and analytically oriented book. Hence those with strong interests in measurement should consult another source to fill out their study of measurement fundamentals. This chapter begins by describing the basic types of scales and what analyses can be performed on the different types of scales. Next some fundamental concepts in measurement (e.g., validity, bias) are described, as are a series of data collection issues. Finally, a typology of errors which can occur in a study is presented.

SCALES AND SCALE TYPES

The notion of measurement assumes that there is something worth measuring. The "thing" to be measured (e.g., an attitude toward a supplier, favorite color, or sales) is referred to here as a construct. Many constructs are fairly complex and multifaceted (e.g., one's attitude toward Japanese restaurants selling liquor on Sundays includes feelings toward Japanese, restaurants, liquor, etc.). Nonetheless, in order to arrive at a "bottom-line" statement about such constructs, there is a strong tendency to convert/simplify these constructs into a single scale or series of scales, usually quantitative ones.

In many cases, the underlying construct may in fact be numerical (e.g., sales). In other cases, the construct is measured numerically because this proves to be a useful way to represent the construct. While quantification of some constructs such as attitude may lose some of the subtleties of the concept, the advantages of a quantitative representation for purposes of analysis and interpretation often outweigh the costs. One motivation for the quantification of a construct is the desire to convert a problem to a form where current computer technology and programs can deal with it. Hence for better or worse (and in general for better), constructs are converted to quantitative scales.

Several schemes for classifying data have been proposed, most notably by Coombs (1964) and Stevens (1946, 1952). In this book, the commonly used four-part classification will be followed: nominal (categorical), ordinal, interval, and ratio.

Nominal (categorical)

The simplest scale type is a nominal scale. A nominal scale simply refers to arbitrarily assigning a number to different response categories. The scale number has meaning only as an index: it has no meaning in and of itself. Some obvious examples of nominal scales include social security numbers and the numbers on basketball players' jerseys. Put differently, there is no obvious relation between the quantity of the construct being measured and the numerical value assigned to it (e.g., the picture in Figure 5–1A).

Ordinal

The next type of scale is an ordinal scale. In an ordinal scale, the higher the number, the more (or less) the construct exists. The absolute size of the number, however, has no meaning nor do the differences between two scale values. Consider the most common form of an ordinal scale, a ranking. If the ranking is based on intelligence, we know that the subject ranked first is more intelligent (at least according to our ranking method) than the person ranked second, but we have no idea how much smarter s/he is. A graphical example of an ordinal scale is shown in Figure 5–1B.

Interval

An interval scale is a scale where differences (intervals) between scale values have meaning, but the absolute scale values are not meaningful. A good example of an interval scale is the fahrenheit temperature scale. The difference between 41 degrees and 40 degrees is the same as the difference between 8 degrees and 9 degrees. The origin (0 degrees), however, has no particular meaning. All we can say is that 0 degrees is colder than 1 degree and warmer than −1 degree. Hence 100 degrees is not twice as hot as 50 degrees. An interval scale can be represented as a straight line which does not pass through the origin (Figure 5–1C). The units of measure of interval

FIGURE 5–1

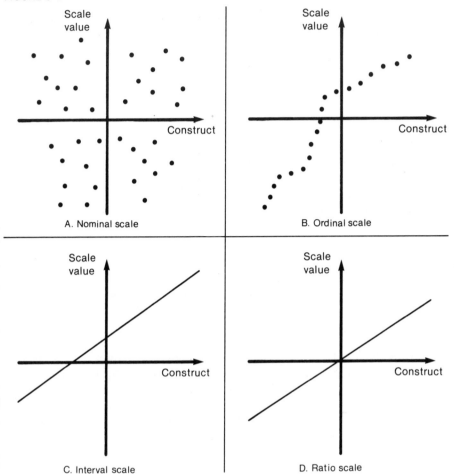

scales (and hence the slope of the line) can be different, as both fahrenheit and centigrade temperatures are interval scales.

Ratio

The highest order scale is a ratio scale. A ratio scale, as the name implies, is one where the ratio between scale values is meaningful. A ratio scale is one where the 0 value indicates the absence of the construct; put differently a ratio scale is an interval scale with a natural origin. A good example of this type of scale is money, where $100 is twice as much as $50. Graphically, a ratio scale would appear as a straight line through the origin (Figure 5–1D).

THE EFFECT OF SCALES ON ANALYSIS

The previous section discussed scale types in a fairly abstract way. One could appropriately wonder what difference scale types make. The answer is that scale types directly affect the type of analysis which can be usefully performed. Put differently, if you plan to do a particular type of analysis, you better have data which is appropriate.

Nominal scales

Nominal scales are useful only for computing frequencies. Hence for a scale which indicates color preference with 1 = blue, 2 = red, 3 = green, and 4 = yellow, it is possible to compute the percent of the people in a sample who like each of the four colors. Other calculations, such as the average value, are meaningless.

Ordinal scales

In addition to computing frequencies, ordinal scales allow medians, percentiles, and a variety of other order statistics to be utilized.

Interval scales

While the first two scale types are called nonmetric, interval and ratio scales are called metric. The presence of an interval scale allows computation of means and standard deviations, the use of parametric statistical tests, and the computation of product-moment correlations between two intervally scaled variables. This in turn allows the application of such "fancy" techniques as regression, discriminant, and factor analysis. In short, interval scales are highly desirable in that they allow the use of most of the analytical tools common to statistics and marketing research.

Ratio scales

Ratio scales allow, in addition to the analysis permitted by interval scales, some specialized calculations such as a geometric mean or the coefficient of variation. They are also meaningful when multiplied together, something which is desirable in certain models.

The practical significance of scale type is fairly clear. Higher order scales can be subjected to more analytical procedures and hence are easier to analyze. On the other hand, getting a higher order scale requires more effort on the part of the subject. Hence choosing scale type involves a trade-off between putting the burden on the respondent and putting the burden on the analyst. While no general solution is apparent, an interval scale is usually the chosen alternative in applied marketing research. It also is important to understand that some constructs are inherently only nominally scaled (e.g., eye color) and attempts to get them measured on higher order scales (e.g., degree of blueness) may be foolish.

EXAMPLES

This section will provide some examples of scales used in marketing research in general and surveys in particular. The coverage is intended to be useful but not necessarily complete. Nonetheless, the vast majority of types of questions used in market research studies are discussed here.

Nominal scales

Multiple choice. One of the most obvious ways to get a nominally scaled measure of a construct is to get a respondent to check a single answer from a set of alternatives. This type question (known to students as multiple guess) is of the following general form:

```
Which of the following terms best describes inizlots?
_____A   Riboflavit.
_____B   Ordils and humspiels.
_____C   Octiviniginianus.
_____D   All of the above.
_____E   B on alternate Tuesdays.
_____F   None of the above.
```

For quantification purposes, one would typically assign a 1 to the first answer (riboflavit), a 2 to the second (ordils and humspiels), and so forth so the "none of the above" response would be coded as a 6. These numbers would only indicate which response category was chosen, not how much of the construct was present. Some marketing research examples of multiple choice questions are as follows:

```
Region: Where do you live?

_____      _____       _____       _____
 East       Midwest       South         West
(=1)         (=2)         (=3)          (=4)
```

(Notice this is a poor question because the regions are not clearly defined for the respondent.)

Marital status: What is your marital status?

Single	Married	Divorced, separated	Widowed
(=1)	(=2)	(=3)	(=4)

Occupation: What is your occupation?

Lawyer	Teacher	. . .
(=1)	(=2)	

Brand choice/used: Which brand of soft drink did you last buy?

Coke	7-Up	Pepsi	other
(=1)	(=2)	(=3)	(=4)

The categories used may be either supplied in advance to the respondent (aided) or coded after the respondent gives a verbal/written answer (unaided). In general, the aided/structured approach is easier for both the respondent and the analyst.

Yes-no (binary). Measures which have only two possible values are typically nominal scales. Some examples are:

Ownership: Do you own a color TV?

Yes	No
(=1)	(=2)

Awareness: Have you heard of new Znarts cereal?

Yes	No
(=1)	(=2)

Trait association (adjective checklist): Please indicate which of the following descriptions apply to these products. Check as many descriptions as you feel apply to each product.

	Descriptions			
Product	Necessary	Fun	Useless	Good investment
Color TV				
Snowmobile				
Life insurance				

Ordinal scales

Forced ranking.   The most obvious ordinal scale is a forced ranking:

Please rank the following five brands in terms of your preference by marking a 1 next to your most preferred brand, a 2 next to your second most preferred brand, and so forth:

        Coke _____
        Pepsi _____
        7-Up _____
        Dr. Pepper _____
        Fresca _____

Paired comparison.   Paired comparisons are essentially a means of generating an ordinal scale without asking the respondent to consider all the alternatives simultaneously. Rather, respondents only choose the more preferred (or heavier or prettier, or any other characteristic you wish to measure) of two alternatives at a time. Converting the previous question involving five soft drinks into a paired comparison framework, there are ten pairs:

        Coke, Pepsi
        Coke, 7-Up
        Coke, Dr. Pepper
        Coke, Fresca
        Pepsi, 7-Up
        Pepsi, Dr. Pepper
        Pepsi, Fresca
        7-Up, Dr. Pepper
        7-Up, Fresca
        Dr. Pepper, Fresca

The derived scale value for each brand is simply the number of times that the brand was preferred in comparisons involving it. The advantage of this method is that each individual decision made is as simple as possible. The method also allows for intransitivity (i.e., preferring Coke to Pepsi, Pepsi to Dr. Pepper, and Dr. Pepper to Coke) which is an advantage in uncovering choice processes but a disadvantage in that it sometimes raises questions about data quality which we may prefer to have hidden. The major disadvantage with paired comparisons is that they become quite cumbersome with many alternatives. If there are 15 alternatives, there are 105 paired comparisons required, quite a lot of trouble to get an ordinal scale. Because of their cumbersome nature, complete paired comparisons are rarely used except in pilot studies or laboratory situations.[1]

---

[1] A modification of this approach, called triads, where respondents pick the most and least alternative from triples has also been used. Since it only works for certain numbers of alternatives and saves space but not respondent effort, this approach is almost never used in marketing research.

Semantic scale. A semantic scale obtains responses to a stimulus in terms of semantic categories. For example, we could ask:

Do you like yogurt?				
Dislike extremely (=1)	Dislike (=2)	Neutral (=3)	Like (=4)	Like extremely (=5)

Respondents are instructed to check the category which best describes their feelings. Since they choose the category on the basis of the words (semantics) attached to it, this is a semantic differential scale. The scale is ordinal but not interval. For example, it is not clear what is the relation between the difference between like and neutral and the difference between dislike and dislike extremely (Myers and Warner, 1968; Dickson and Albaum, 1977).

Summated (Likert). A likert scale is an extension of a semantic scale in two ways. Rather than measure a construct in a single item, a series of items are used to measure the construct and a summed score is calculated. Second, the scales are traditionally calibrated so that a neutral response is coded "0." (This difference is, however, unimportant.) For example, attitude toward yogurt might be assessed by several questions:

Do you like the taste of yogurt?				
	x			
Dislike strongly (−2)	Dislike (−1)	Neutral (0)	Like (+1)	Like strongly (+2)
Is yogurt a healthful food?				
		x		
Extremely not healthful (−2)	Not healthful (−1)	Neutral (0)	Healthful (+1)	Extremely healthful (+2)
Do you feel your friends like yogurt?				
x				
Dislike strongly (−2)	Dislike (−1)	Neutral (0)	Like (+1)	Like strongly (+2)

In this case, the summed score would be $-1 + 0 + (-2) = -3$, which indicates a negative attitude toward yogurt.

Others. There are a variety of other ordinal scales. One is the Guttman scale, which is really designed to order statements but is rarely used in marketing research. Another is the Q-sort technique which is designed to cluster either respondents or alternatives. This works in several steps:

1. A set of items to be sorted are chosen. (Traditionally about 100 items have been used.)
2. Subjects are required to sort the items (usually represented by cards) into piles (traditionally 11) which represent degrees on a scale such as aesthetic beauty, value for the money, and so on.
3. The results are used to indicate similarity among either subjects (by seeing how closely subjects agree on the sorting results) or items (by seeing which items are consistently sorted into the same pile).

Unfortunately this technique is so unwieldy that it too is almost never used in large-scale marketing research. It is sometimes used in small sample studies, usually as a basis for structuring a large-scale study.

Interval scales

Equal appearing interval. Thurstone proposed that an interval scale measure of an overall attitude could be constructed by a series of steps: (*a*) first, at least 100 statements related to the overall attitude are chosen. (*b*) Next, a set of judges rate the statements in terms of their favorability from 1 to 11. (*c*) The 10–20 statements which get the most consistent ratings are selected, and they are assigned the median value from the 1–11 scale given them by the judges. (*d*) Subjects indicate which of the statements they agree with (*e*) Attitude scores are the sum of the scale values in (*c*) for the statements that the subject checked. Given the difficulty in applying this technique it is almost never used.

Bipolar adjective. The bipolar adjective scale is a revision of the semantic scale with the express hope that the subjects will respond to it by giving intervally scaled data. Rather than attaching a description to each of the response categories, only the two extreme categories are labeled:

Dislike extremely					*Like extremely*
1	2	3	4	5	6

Since the scale points are equally far apart both physically and numerically, it can be assumed that the responses will be intervally scaled. Two points are worth making here. The first is that many people find this argument wanting and argue that at best the scale is somewhere in between an interval and an ordinal scale. Secondly, when respondents are asked to rate on both bipolar adjective and semantic scales, the results are typically practically identical. In fact both types are commonly referred to as semantic differential scales (Osgood, Suci, and Tannenbaum, 1957). Hence for practical purposes, either scale is about equally good to use if intervally scaled data is needed.

It is also possible to get people to respond on a continuous scale:

Very bad ———————————————— *Very good*	

and then actually measure (usually with an optical scanner) the exact position on the scale. This is generally agreed to be an intervally scaled measure. However, since results using these continuous scales are essentially identical to bipolar adjective scales, they are almost never worth using.

Equal width interval. Another way to generate intervally scaled data is to ask respondents to indicate into which category they fall when the categories are quantitative groupings of equal size. Hence the following scale is only ordinal:

None	1–2	3–15	16–99	100 or more

while this scale is "good" (intervally scaled):

0–4	5–9	10–14	15–19	. . .

While the practical difference is small, the second approach to grouping responses has a slight advantage and no obvious cost associated with it if likely responses are fairly evenly distributed. When the vast majority of responses are likely to be 0 or 1–2, however, the unequal sized categories are more useful.

At this point three questions usually arise. The first is how many scale points to use. The key issue, however, is the ability of respondents to make discriminations on the construct. The finer the discriminations the respondent makes, the more scale points are appropriate. For individual level analysis, six or more scale points are usually sufficient to account for respondents' discriminatory abilities (Lehmann and Hulbert, 1972). Obviously for aggregate analysis, even fewer are needed. Hence most scales should use between four scale points (for phone surveys, intercept inter-

views, low commitment situations) and eight (for committed and knowledgeable respondents).

The second major question is whether there should be an odd or even
number of scale points. Arguments can be made on either side of the
issue. Proponents of odd numbers argue that the presence of a neutral
point allows respondents who are neutral to quickly and easily indicate so.
Proponents of even numbers argue that the neutral vote is a cop-out, that
the respondent is really leaning one way or the other, and that using an
even number forces the respondent to reveal which way s/he is leaning.
While in general this author prefers even numbers, the differences in
results between well-done studies using, for example, five and six scale
points are essentially unnoticeable.

A third question has to do with whether a scale should be balanced or
not. Consider these examples of balanced and unbalanced scales:

How do you rate the writing style of this book?				
Poor	Average	Good	Very good	Excellent
Very poor	Poor	Neutral	Good	Very good

In the first case, the responses are stacked toward the positive. While this
may be beneficial to the ego, it probably biases the results unfairly since
the midpoint of the scale is "good" and many respondents will consider
the position and not the semantic cues. On the other hand, balanced
scales often produce highly skewed results so that almost all the responses fall in one half of the scale. For example, this typically happens
when subjects rate the importance of a list of attributes. In this case,
almost no respondents are willing to say that an attribute is unimportant.
Hence an unbalanced scale is occasionally used to increase dispersion of
the responses. Unless there is a particular reason, however, balanced
scales are typically employed.

Law of comparative judgment.   Paired comparison judgments can be
converted into intervally scaled data by means of Thurstone's law of
comparative judgment. Two basic assumptions are required: (a) a group
of respondents are homogeneous (in agreement) with respect to their ratings of the alternatives, and (b) individuals are uncertain about their feelings toward each alternative and respond with some random component
toward it. Based on these and some interesting manipulations, an interval
scale is obtained. This technique is interesting (see Appendix 5–A) but very
infrequently used in marketing research.

Dollar metric (graded paired comparison).   An interesting way to generate an interval scale is an extension of the paired comparison method
known as the dollar metric (Pessemier, 1963). This method works by

getting paired comparison judgments of both which brand is preferred and the amount (in dollars) by which it is preferred. Returning to the example involving the five brands of soft drinks, the responses could be as follows:

Which brand do you prefer?	How much extra would you be willing to pay to get your more preferred brand?
Coke, Pepsi	2¢
Coke, 7-Up	8¢
Coke, Dr. Pepper	5¢
Coke, Fresca	12¢
Pepsi, 7-Up	6¢
Pepsi, Dr. Pepper	3¢
Pepsi, Fresca	10¢
7-Up, Dr. Pepper	3¢
7-Up, Fresca	4¢
Dr. Pepper, Fresca	7¢

By summing the values when a brand is being compared, a preference scale can be generated. Here we have

$$\text{Coke: } 2 + 8 + 5 + 12 = 27$$
$$\text{Pepsi: } -2 + 6 + 3 + 10 = 17$$
$$\text{7-Up: } -8 + (-6) + (-3) + 4 = -13$$
$$\text{Dr. Pepper: } -5 + (-3) + 3 + 7 = 2$$
$$\text{Fresca: } -12 + (-10) + (-4) + (-7) = -33$$

Hence we have an intervally scaled measure of preference. For a variety of reasons, this does not directly represent the actual strength of preference between brands. It is possible, however, to transform this scale into a predicted market share for each brand.[2]

---

[2] This is done by first converting the $ metric scale to a 0 to 1 adjusted scale where Coke becomes a 1, Fresca a 0, and the rest of the brands in between. The formula for this is

$$\frac{\$\text{ metric scale value}_i + |\text{Smallest scale value}|}{\text{Range of scale values}} = \frac{\text{Scale value} + 33}{60}$$

The predicted share is given by

$$\text{Predicted share}_i = \frac{(\text{adjusted score}_i)^K}{\text{Sum of (adjusted score}_j)^K \text{ for all } j \text{ brands}}$$

The K value is a constant (usually between 2 and 6) determined by trial and error so that the predicted share matches the actual share as closely as possible. The effect of K is to increase the predicted share of the first choice brand and to reduce the predicted shares of the less preferred brands.

Ratio scales

Direct quantification.   The simplest way to obtain ratio scaled data is to ask directly for quantification of a construct which is ratio scaled. For example:

How many dress shirts do you own?   _____

How old are you?   _____

The problem with this approach is the respondent probably doesn't know (i.e., how many dress shirts do you own) or want to reveal (e.g., age) what the exact answer is. Consequently instead of upgrading from an intervally to ratio scaled answer, you may end up with no answer at all. Hence direct quantification tends to be used only in pilot/small-scale surveys.

Constant sum scale.   A very popular device in marketing research is the so-called constant sum scale. Respondents are given a number of points (if the process is conducted in person, chips or other physical objects are often used) and told to divide them among alternatives according to some criteria (e.g., preference, importance, aesthetic appeal). Since respondents are told to allocate chips in a ratio manner (if you like brand A twice as much as brand B, assign it twice as many chips, etc.), then the results are presumably ratio scaled.

For example, I might ask for ten points to be allocated among three brands:

$$
\begin{array}{ll}
A \ldots\ldots\ldots & 2 \\
B \ldots\ldots\ldots & 3 \\
C \ldots\ldots\ldots & 5 \\
\hline
& 10
\end{array}
$$

At least two problems exist with this approach. First, respondents may mess up the allocation by not using ten points, necessitating recalculation by the analyst. Hence some time is often required to teach the approach to respondents. Secondly, determining the appropriate number of points/ chips to use requires trading off between rounding error if too few are used and fatigue/frustration/refusal problems if too many are used. Still the approach is quite useful.

Delphi procedure.   The Delphi procedure is a modification of the constant sum scale designed to produce agreement among judges. For a more thorough discussion, see Appendix 5–B.

Reference alternative.   Sometimes called fractionation, this approach seeks a ratio scale by having respondents compare alternatives to a reference alternative. Respondents are instructed to indicate how alternatives compare to the reference alternative on some criterion such as preference by putting down a number half as large if the alternative is half as preferred, and so on:

```
Reference alternative X = 100
Alternative  A  _____
Alternative  B  _____
Alternative  C  _____
```

A respondent might then assign 50 to A, 250 to B, and 130 to C. In essence, this is a paired-comparison type method where respondents only consider two alternatives at once. Unfortunately choice of the reference alternative has been found to influence the results, necessitating rotating the reference alternative to remove this effect. Since this approach is somewhat more cumbersome vis-a-vis a constant sum scale, the constant sum scale is typically used rather than the reference alternative approach.

BASIC CONCEPTS

There is a long tradition in measurement, especially in the psychological literature (see Torgerson, 1958; Thurstone, 1959). From this literature come two major terms which relate to measurement: validity and reliability. From statistics come the terms biased, efficient, and consistent. While these terms themselves have no great value, the ideas they represent are quite important.

Validity

The term "valid" is essentially synonymous with the word "good." In fact, the term is loosely used in conversation as a synonym by many people. This is unfortunate, since it causes purists to be unbearably uncomfortable and occasionally leads to important misunderstandings. Actually there are a variety of subclasses of validity. Four of the most common types of validity are construct validity, content validity, convergent validity, and predictive validity.

Construct validity.   Construct validity refers to the ability of a measure to both represent the underlying construct (concept) and to relate to other constructs in an expected way. This is a fairly amorphous term and really says that a measure has construct validity if it behaves according to existing theory. Given the relative paucity of good theory in marketing, this type of validity rarely receives much attention in applied marketing research.

Content validity.   Content validity refers to the logical appropriateness of the measure used. For example, one might argue that observing how much a person eats of a vegetable on his/her plate is a measure of the person's liking of the vegetable. This has logical appeal (often called face validity), and hence the measure would appear to have content validity. (Actually the amount eaten might depend on how hungry the person was or some other variable.) Content validity also refers to the inclusiveness in the measure of all relevant aspects of the construct. Hence a content valid measure of your opinion of this book should include your opinion of its topic, style, format, and so on. In order to achieve content validity, constructs often must be measured by more than one item.

Convergent validity. A measure has convergent validity if it follows the same pattern as other measures of the same construct. For example, three different measures of attitude would be said to have convergent validity if they were highly correlated with each other. A related concept is concurrent validity, which occurs when a measure is highly correlated with known values of the underlying construct.

Predictive validity. Predictive validity is the most pragmatic form of validity. In the narrow sense of the term, the predictive validity of a measure is the ability of the measure to relate to other measures in a known/predicted way. Taken in its loosest form, predictive validity is synonymous with predictive usefulness/accuracy. In the extreme, predictive accuracy is the engineering (as opposed to scientific) view which says if a measure is useful in prediction, then use it regardless of whether we can explain why it works. To take an extreme example, assume I predicted sales of a new product by multiplying the number of letters in the name by the weight of a package. Assume somehow this turned out to be predictive of sales. While the measure has no construct or content validity, it "works" and is predictively valid. Most people smirk at this point and argue they would never use such a foolish measure. Consider the following: Would you use it if it worked ten times in a row? How about 100 times? The point is that at some stage, the predictive accuracy of a measure will outweigh the prior theories and can in fact lead to the development of new theories. (If this were not true, it would imply we already perfectly understood the world, which is both scary and untrue.)

Reliability

A measure is said to be reliable if it consistently obtains the same result. Hence a scale which measured a weight and got 90.10 pounds, 89.95 pounds, 90.06 pounds, and 89.98 pounds in four trials would be quite reliable (the spread/range is only .15 pounds) even if the true weight were 100 pounds. Conversely, a second scale which produced weights of 95 pounds, 103 pounds, 92 pounds, and 109 pounds would be less reliable than the first even if in the sense of being closer to the true value it was better. Reliability is thus synonymous with repetitive consistency.

Two basic operational approaches exist to measuring reliability: test retest and alternative forms.

Test retest. By applying the same measure to the same subjects at two different points in time, we can compare the two measures and see how closely they match and hence what the test-retest reliability is. This is a common approach in areas such as educational testing. Using test-retest reliability as an indicator of "true" reliability makes some fairly strong assumptions. First, it assumes that the measurement process has no affect on the subject. Second, it assumes the subject's opinion/behavior has remained constant over the time period between the two measures. Since at least one of these assumptions are likely to be violated, test-retest comparisons are imperfect measures of reliability.

Alternative forms. The alternate forms approach to measuring reliability assumes that equivalent measuring devices (forms) are available. By applying two or more equivalent forms to the same subjects and checking the consistency of the results, a measure of reliability can be obtained. Unfortunately this measure depends at least as much on the degree of equivalency of the alternative forms as on the true reliability of the measure.

Unbiased/biased

The term "biased" as used in marketing research has nothing to do with holding offensive personal opinions or prejudices. The term bias is borrowed from statistics, and a biased measurement is one where we expect the measured result to be different from the true value of the construct/variable. Hence a person who consistently underestimates how long a task will take gives biased estimates. Similarly the "reliable" scale of the previous section which kept measuring the 100-pound weight at about 90 pounds would also be called biased. Actually a biased measure can be very useful if the extent of the bias can be assessed. For example, if the temperature control on an oven consistently reliably registers 50 degrees warmer than the actual oven temperature, it is fairly simple to adjust the control to achieve the desired temperature. Similarly, panels may be biased in that they overreport purchases of a certain brand, but if one looks at purchases of the brand over time, then the results can be very useful for signaling changes in sales.

Efficient

Another term borrowed from statistics, a procedure is said to be efficient if it gets the maximum possible information from a given sample size. In measurement terms, a simple scale may be just as accurate a measuring device as a more elaborate setup and hence would be chosen because of its superior efficiency.

Consistent

The third major statistical term relevant here, "consistency" refers to the ability of a statistic to tend toward the true value of the construct/variable as more data is gathered. In measurement terms, a measure would be consistent if averaging repeated measures produced a result which approached the true value as the number of measures averaged increased.

So what?

The terms and issues just discussed are important to someone who decides to specialize in measurement theory and methods. To the applied researcher or manager, however, the terms often are either foreboding or used merely as advertising slogans. (For example, "We have a valid study which. . . .") Therefore it is useful to translate these concepts into some action suggestions. At least six suggestions are relevant:

1. Select only those variables to measure which make logical sense in the context of the problem being studied.
2. Use measures which seem logically appropriate to the construct/variable to be measured.
3. Use measures which are reliable.
4. Use variables which produce similar results over related measurement methods. (If the response obtained depends heavily on the measurement method employed, chances are the information being collected is a response to the measurement method and not the construct.)
5. Use measures which are as easily usable by researcher and respondent as possible.
6. Use measures which prove to be useful in a pragmatic way (i.e., if a variable proves to be a good predictor of a key variable, use it; if a variable doesn't seem to be related to any other variables, save your effort and don't measure it.)

OTHER ISSUES

Individual versus group-level study

Most of the measurement and scale discussion presented here is directed at accurately estimating an individual's scale value. In marketing, one typically is interested in group/average behavior for decision purposes (at least in consumer marketing). One advantage of this is that averaging out results tends to cover up problems in scale type. Averages are intervally scaled even if the original scale is binary. Moreover, if you're lucky, averages reduce some measurement and response style problems as well.

There are, however, two disadvantages to grouping respondents/data points. The first is that the respondents are implicitly assumed to be homogeneous, a sometimes fallacious assumption. For example, if some people like tea hot and some cold, the average preferred temperature for tea would be lukewarm. While this suggests an interesting marketing strategy ("Try Blahz, the room temperature tea"), the strategy is likely to be a disaster. Hence making sure that only homogeneous data points are grouped is an important but nontrivial task.

The second disadvantage deals with the operational problem of comparing responses of different people on nonobjective questions such as attitudes. Consider the following two respondents:

	Very bad							Very good
				Respondent 1				
A	1	2	3	④	5	6	7	8
B	1	2	3	4	5	⑥	7	8
C	1	2	3	4	5	6	7	⑧
D	1	2	3	4	5	⑥	7	8
E	1	2	3	④	5	6	7	8
F	1	2	3	4	5	6	7	⑧
				Respondent 2				
A	1	②	3	4	5	6	7	8
B	1	2	③	4	5	6	7	8
C	1	2	3	④	5	6	7	8
D	1	2	③	4	5	6	7	8
E	1	②	3	4	5	6	7	8
F	1	2	3	④	5	6	7	8

In considering the response to A, there are at least three pieces of information in the "4" given by respondent 1: the absolute value of the response (indicating a slightly negative attitude), the position relative to a typical response (lower, indicating a negative attitude), and the difference between "4" and a typical response (two scale points). If we believe that only relative responses matter, we could *normalize* the data to obtain only relative responses. Alternatively, if we believe both the typical response and the amount of spread a respondent uses in answering is not meaningful, we can *standardize* the data to remove both effects (see Appendix 5–C). If we standardized the answers of both respondents, we would argue that both respondents view the six alternatives identically. Without any adjustment, respondent 1 appears to be favorable toward all but A and E, while respondent 2 thinks all the alternatives are bad. What you believe about the meaning of a response thus has a lot to say about how data are grouped and analyzed.

Direct versus indirect probing

Another major issue involves whether information should be gathered directly or in a more circuitous manner. The simplest way to gather data is the obtrusive, direct method where the subject is aware of being studied and is directly asked the question at hand. This method works quite well most of the time.

The straightforward approach runs into trouble, however, when respondents either have a reason to hide their feelings (as in the case of certain antisocial attitudes) or can't really express their feelings accurately. In these cases, indirect methods are often employed. Here, rather than asking a person what they personally do or think, the subject may be asked how friends or neighbors think or behave. The assumptions underlying this approach are that (*a*) neighbors behave the same way and (*b*) I will be more honest in revealing my neighbors' behavior patterns than my own. Another indirect method is the projective technique. Here a subject is given a vague task and the response then is used to deduce the subject's feelings. This technique takes many forms, including sentence completion (e.g., "people who eat Znarts are _____"), scenario/cartoon (interpretation known as TATs (thematic apperception test), and word association (e.g., "What word do you associate with Znarts?"). Possibly the best-known projective technique is the Rorschach Inkblot Test. Interesting as these techniques are, however, they are used almost exclusively in small scale or pilot studies in marketing research. Anyone interested in using projective techniques should consult another source, such as Kassarjian (1974).

Soft (survey) versus hard (observed) data

The distinction between survey and hard data appears to be quite great. Yet on closer inspection, there are more similarities than most people notice. First, much so-called hard data is estimated/projected/fudged. (Do you really believe anyone knows exactly how many dishwashers were sold in the United States last year?) Also, with the exception of mechanical recording devices (which are far from foolproof themselves), a person gathers data either by interpreting written reports (e.g., audits) or by actually asking a question. Hence this data is subject to many of the same sources of error (misinterpretation, expectation, etc.) as survey data.

A more meaningful distinction is between objective data (for which a right answer exists and is measurable directly) and subjective data (for which the right answer, if it exists, is not precisely measurable). For example, the number of cars I own is objective data while my attitude toward public education is subjective. In measuring an objective variable, both survey and hard methods are applicable. For example, to measure how many cars I own, one could (*a*) ask me, (*b*) check the motor vehicle registration list, or (*c*) observe how many cars are parked at my house at night. The survey method may produce a wrong answer if I decide to hide the true number of cars owned for whatever reason. On the other hand, checking the auto registration lists may fail because (*a*) you have registered a car in another state or not at all, or (*b*) the auditor makes a mistake. Similarly observing how many cars are at home at night may (*a*) spot a neighbor's cars, or (*b*) fail to spot a car which is in a body shop for repairs. The point, therefore, is that survey data is not as inferior to hard data as it at first appears to be.

Share data

One of the key measures used by marketers is market share. Yet calculations of share are very imprecise. The biggest problem in defining share is in answering the question, "Share of what?" For example, should you compute Sugar Pops' share of presweetened cereals, ready-to-eat cereals, or cereals in general? Secondly, you must decide, "Share on what basis—dollars, unit sales, net weight, or number of servings?" Even having settled on a market definition and a measurement basis, the share measures are subject to all the sources of error that any other objective variable faces. In short, share measures are rarely as objective and accurate as their numbers (e.g., 32.7 percent) seem to indicate.

AN ERROR TYPOLOGY

Having discussed measurement methods and problems, it is useful to recall some of the major sources of error which affect research. These sources of error, here divided into five major categories, go far beyond measurement issues (Hulbert and Lehmann, 1975). Their purpose, therefore, is to put measurement issues "in their place" (see Figure 5–2).

Researcher

The following variety of errors in marketing research are directly traceable to the researcher: myopia, inappropriate analysis, misinterpretation, and communication.

Myopia. Research results can be reduced in value if the wrong questions are asked. This is usually a manifestation of poor problem definition and hypothesis specification.

Inappropriate analysis. There are two major ways a researcher can err in performing analysis. The first is an error of omission: failing to perform what would be a meaningful analysis. The second is an error of commission: performing an analysis for which the data is not suited.

FIGURE 5–2
Sources of errors

General source	Type

I. Researcher/user	Myopia (wrong question)
	Inappropriate analysis
	Misinterpretation
	  Mistaken
	  Researcher expectation
	Communication

II. Sample	Frame (wrong target population) Process (biased method) Response (biased respondents)

III. Measurement process	Conditioning
	Process bias
	Recording
	  Interpretation (mistaken)
	  Carelessness
	  Fudging

IV. Instrument	Individual scale item
	  Rounding
	  Truncating
	  Ambiguity
	Test instrument
	  Evoked set
	  Positional (order)

V. Respondent	Response style
	  Consistency/inconsistency
	  Boasting/humility
	  Agreement (yea saying)
	  Acquiescence
	  Lying
	  Extremism/caution
	  Socially desirable
	Response
	  Mistakes
	  Uncertainty
	  Inarticulation

Misinterpretation. The two kinds of misinterpretation errors are quite different. A mistaken interpretation can be the result of poor training, inability to understand the results of the analysis performed because of a technical deficiency, or just a bad day (even we brilliant researchers occasionally make an error in judgment due to time pressure, fatigue, carelessness, poor eyesight, etc.). On the other hand, misinterpretation may be the result of researcher expectation. When one has a strong prior feeling about the results of a study for either logical or emotional reasons, it is usually possible to find some result which supports this prior feeling. Hence the interpretation may be unduly influenced by prior opinions.

Communication. Even the most competent researcher has a serious problem in communicating results. Often the users of research are unable to correctly perceive the results because of technical deficiencies, strong prior opinions, or a general distrust of or dislike for research. Also the technically competent researcher is frequently unable to translate results into a form which is understandable by intelligent, decision-oriented managers.

Sample

Since most data collection is partial in nature, the selection of who to analyze can greatly influence the results. There are at least three basic types of sampling error: frame, process, and response.

Frame. In studying a particular problem, an early decision must be made concerning who are the relevant subjects/respondents. For example, in studying the market for TV video games, one could target on male heads of households. Since others in the family, especially children, influence this decision, the target population would be defined too narrowly. Alternatively, it is possible to design the target population so broadly that the "frame" includes many irrelevant people. Hence matching the sampling frame to the appropriate population is very important, and erring by having too narrow a frame is especially disastrous.

Process. Once the frame is chosen, a process must be chosen for selecting respondents. If, for example, a list is chosen as the source of respondents, it can be too broad and include people not in the target population. (The National Association of Retired Persons has been trying to get me to join since I was 29 which, unless they know something I don't, is just a bit too premature.) This is wasteful but not necessarily destructive. On the other hand, the process may be so narrow that it excludes important segments of the target population.

Response. Even with a good frame and process, the sample may be unrepresentative. This is because many people will fail to respond to research inquiries. Response rates are rarely about 70 percent and sometimes as low as 10 percent or less. If the nonrespondents have different characteristics than respondents, then the results can be badly distorted. One general tendency is for both old people and poor people to respond less than other groups. Also people with strong opinions about the subject in question are more likely to respond. An example of this is the recent surveys about school priorities undertaken in New Jersey. Under both court and legislative mandates to find out what localities want in a "thorough and efficient" education, many districts mailed questionnaires to all residents in their towns. With response rates of 10 percent or less in many localities, it is hard to argue convincingly that the results are projectable to the community at large. This nonresponse problem is typically greatest when either recruitment for extended tasks (e.g., panel member-ship) or mail surveys are used.

Measurement process

The measurement process itself is an important determinant of re-sponses and hence a potential source of error. Some of the major charac-teristics of the measurement process are conditioning, process bias, and recording.

Conditioning.   Data collection processes are outside stimuli which can condition/affect responses. By exposing a subject to a problem, the sub-ject's attention will be drawn to the problem and hence the subject may behave differently. This is an especially serious problem when the subject is questioned several times.

Process bias.   Respondents often are motivated by the data collec-tion process as a "game" and respond to beat the game. The best-known example of this problem is interviewer bias, where the presence of the interviewer leads the respondents to respond to please (or occasionally, to irritate or surprise) the interviewer. An example of this is that when the interviewer is identified as working for a particular company, the respon-dent often tends to give answers favorable to the company in order to please the interviewer. Also the physical surroundings (e.g., a bright, cheerful, air-conditioned room) can affect the respondent's overall at-titude and hence responses.

Recording.   The process of recording a response is subject to many possible sources of error. The most obvious error of this type, mistaken interpretation, is usually associated with an interviewer misinterpreting a verbal response. This error can also occur when gremlins infest mechan-ical recording devices. A related form of error is due to simple careless-ness where the interviewer or recording device records the wrong answer due to sloppiness. A third type of recording problem is fudging. Here answers are recorded without measurement to speed up the data collec-tion or make life easier for the respondent and interviewer. Given crafty interviewers, this source of error is quite hard to detect.

Instrument

The particulars of the questions/measures themselves have a strong influence on responses. Two basic sources of these problems exist: the individual question/scale and the test instrument.

The individual question/scale.   One problem with questions is that the response categories given often truncate responses. Multiple answer questions tend to limit the respondents' consideration to the listed alterna-tives even if an "all other" category is included. (Filling out an "other" response is more trouble than checking one of the listed alternatives and also may connote that the respondent is somehow different/weird.) In quantitatively scaled questions (e.g., rate how well you like brussels sprouts on a six-point scale from 1 = dislike somewhat to 6 = like somewhat), especially strong feelings cannot be expressed and are hence truncated. (On the brussels sprouts scale, my true feelings are about -8, but being a good subject, I would circle a 1.)

Another major scale problem is rounding error. Given a multiple choice question, a respondent will tend to choose the answer which is closest to his/her true response. The classic example is a numerical scale. For example, if I truly feel about brussels sprouts 3.4 on a six-point scale, I would round off my response to the closest digit (3) and hence the rounding error would be .4. Similarly if I were asked, "Are you going to vote in the next election?" and I were 60 percent sure I would, I would have to round my response to "yes" (100 percent certain) or "no" (no chance at all of voting).

A final type of problem is ambiguity. Ambiguity can occur because the underlying construct to be measured and the question are not perfectly congruent. For example, in order to measure attitude toward the environment one might ask, "Should pollution control standards on automobiles be relaxed?" An affirmative answer would presumably indicate a relatively low environmental concern. Unfortunately, it could also indicate a great concern for jobs or for increasing the use of coal to conserve petroleum reserves and limit nuclear reactor development. Hence the match between the construct and the question is imperfect. Another source of ambiguity is confusion about the meaning of the particular combination of words used to define the question. Both gross lack of understanding due to poor vocabulary skills on the part of either the question writer or the respondent or more subtle different nuances in meanings resulting from different cultural backgrounds can lead the respondent to answer a different question than the researcher wished answered.

The test instrument. The instrument (questionnaire) itself has an effect on the response. The items discussed bring to mind an evoked set of thoughts and standards of comparison which the respondent uses to determine his response. For example, if one designed a questionnaire concerning such leisure time activities as bridge, chess, backgammon, cribbage, and football, football would on an exertion or risk of injury scale probably be rated at the maximum. If on the other hand football were being compared with rugby, sword fighting, and motorcycle racing, it probably would be rated more moderately in terms of exertion or injury risk. In short the responses depend on the bases of comparison which the test instrument (questionnaire) establishes.

The position (order) of items is also important. This is true at both the macro level (question order) and micro level (order of responses within question). At the micro level, the response category in the first possible position tends to get an inordinate number of responses simply because it is convenient to use. At the macro level, the position of an item in the test affects both the attentiveness of the respondent (one tends to be pretty casual about answering the 141st life-style question) and the frame-of-reference which the previous questions have imparted.

Respondent

Ultimate control over the quality of data is in the hands of the subject/respondent. This control is exercised in two major ways: response style and the response.

Response style.   The way a respondent approaches the data collection process influences the responses obtained. Responses may be as much the result of the respondent's response style as his/her true feelings/behavior. A variety of such styles may exist, including the following:

Consistency/inconsistency.   Many respondents give answers to questions under the assumption that their answers to the questions should be what they perceive to be consistent even if their feelings or behavior is not (i.e., if I have previously indicated that I am in favor of equal rights, I "should," to be consistent, also indicate support of programs such as the ERA). Similarly some respondents give inconsistent responses to appear interesting to the researcher.

Boasting/humility.   Respondents may overstate their position (e.g., income, possessions) in order to appear superior. There also is the tendency in some individuals to state that "I can do anything better than you!" Alternatively, some humble souls may understate their accomplishments out of some form of humility. (An excellent example of this is available to anyone who plays golf and attempts to subjectively establish a handicap with three other players.)

Agreement.   Some respondents have a tendency to be "yea-sayers," responding positively to most questions. (Do you like to swim? Yes. Do you like to sit on the beach? Yes. Do you like to stay home? Yes.)

Lying.   Respondents are not unlikely to knowingly falsify data. While some may be pathological lyers, most probably lie out of self-interest. One need only observe a few individuals filling out tax returns to notice this tendency. Also respondents will give answers they think are "right" in order to get a possible reward—a free product, a trip, and so on.

Extremism/caution.   Some respondents tend to use extreme responses on scaled questions (i.e., 1's and 5's on a 1–5 scale), while others may use more moderate (i.e., 2's and 4's) responses. The tendency toward caution is generally correlated with cynical and/or highly educated people who do not believe in absolutes.

Socially desirable.   Many respondents feel uncomfortable admitting to unusual behavior or attitudes. As a consequence, their answers reflect as much what they perceive to be the desirable answer as they do their own true responses.

Response. The respondent is the source of the following three other errors:

Inarticulation. In responding to a question (especially an open-ended one), a respondent may be unable or unwilling to accurately articulate a response.

Mistakes. Even sincere respondents can make errors by marking the wrong response carelessly, especially if they are not committed to the task. Also for many questions, there is a strong tendency to give a particular answer because, for example, a brand has become synonymous with the product category. (What soft drink did you last have? Coke. What kind of facial tissue do you use? Kleenex.)

Uncertainty. All the above sources of error are theoretically controllable. Yet even perfect control of these (the impossible dream of researchers) would not guarantee perfect data. Individuals are often not sure exactly what their true feelings are or actual behavior has been. This underlying source of measurement error is irreducible.

Controlling errors

A general comment about control of errors is in order. Setting aside for the moment researcher and sampling errors, we can view the measured response as a sum of the true response plus the possible errors:

$$\text{Measured value} = \text{True value} + \text{Measurement process errors} \\ + \text{Instrument errors} + \text{Respondent errors}$$

While it would be nice and convenient to assume that all the sources of error will cancel out, this ostrich-like approach is pure polyanna. In order to make the measured value closer to the true value, there are a variety of fairly obvious methods available, such as precise wording, which should reduce ambiguity errors and possible general fatigue by making the task easier.

Still three points remain:

1. Reducing one type of error will often increase another.
2. Some random error remains no matter what you do.
3. As an individual progresses through a test situation (experiment, questionnaire, etc.), the experience will change him/her by both conditioning and fatigue.

The purpose of these three points is not to discourage efforts to reduce error but rather to indicate that error reduction is a vexing, complex problem. Fortunately, if one is concerned with relative rather than absolute values, many of these sources of error will tend to cancel out.

SUMMARY

Having read (or at least turned the pages of) this chapter, someone may pose the question, "Can a few simple notions be taken from this chapter?" Put more crudely, "What good is all this?" This section is an attempt to respond to that question.

Sources of error

There are a vast number of sources of error which *cannot* be simultaneously reduced. Many of these sources of error depend on researcher, sample, or respondent and are beyond the control of the measurement process.

Measurement theory

A variety of concepts have been advanced which are desirable characteristics of measurement. Though the terms are formidable, the concepts are largely intuitive. Good measures are ones which produce good estimates of the constructs and which are useful in terms of relating to other measures.

Scale types

There are four basic scale types: nominal (categorical), ordinal, interval, and ratio. Whenever possible, intervally scaled data should be obtained since it allows the more powerful statistical tools (e.g., regression analysis) to be applied. It is possible to use nonmetric data in calculations such as correlations and means. The problem is that some error is introduced by using nonintervally scaled data such as rankings in these calculations which we have classified as "inappropriate application." As long as the data is ordinally scaled (monotonic), these calculations are in general not so badly distorted that they need be abandoned. While the results of such calculations are not appropriate for fine tuning, they certainly are useful for getting a general notion about the results.

Typical scales

In spite of the variety of scales available, a surprisingly small number form the mainstay of market research data. The following are the most commonly used:

Nominal (categorical):
1. Multiple choice (e.g., region, occupation, brand chosen).
2. Yes–no (e.g., ownership, awareness).

Ordinal:

Forced ranking (e.g., brand preference).

Ordinal–interval:

Semantic differential/bipolar adjective (e.g., attitudes, opinions).

Ratio:

1. Direct quantification (e.g., number of people in household).
2. Constant sum scale.

PROBLEMS

1. How would you determine—
   a. How important nutrition was to consumers in their choice of food?
   b. What process consumers follow in selecting a brand of gasoline for their car?
   c. How many pairs of slacks a sample of consumers own?
   d. What consumers feel is the effect of television advertising on children?
2. Write a dollar metric question to assess preference for brands of washing machines.
3. Assume you had to predict the likely winner of the next presidential election based on a single poll two weeks before the election. A good sample has already agreed to participate.

   Assume you are to ask two questions: (*a*) will you vote and (*b*) who will you vote for. Describe:
   a. The exact form of the response scale.
   b. Exactly (mathematically) how you would go about making your prediction.
4. List the major control variables a survey/question designer has at his/her disposal (e.g., number of scale points).
5. Suggest how the control variables in your answer to Problem 4 relate to the sources of error in Figure 5–2.

BIBLIOGRAPHY

Coombs, Clyde H. *A Theory of Data.* New York: Wiley, 1964.

Dickson, John, and Albaum, Gerald. "A Method for Developing Tailormade Semantic Differentials for Specific Marketing Content Areas." *Journal of Marketing Research,* vol. 14 (February 1977), pp. 87–91.

Hulbert, James, and Lehmann, Donald R. "Reducing Error in Question and Scale Design: A Conceptual Framework." *Decision Sciences,* vol. 6 (January 1975), pp. 166–73.

Kassarjian, Harold H. "Projective Methods." In *Handbook of Marketing Research,* pp. 3–85 to 3–100. Edited by Robert Ferber. New York: McGraw-Hill, 1974.

Lehmann, Donald R., and Hulbert, James. "Are Three-Point Scales Always Good Enough?" *Journal of Marketing Research,* vol. 9 (November 1972), pp. 444–46.

Myers, James H., and Warner, W. Gregory. "Semantic Properties of Selected Evaluation Adjectives." *Journal of Marketing Research,* vol. 4 (November 1968), pp. 409–13.

Osgood, C.; Suci, G.; and Tannenbaum, P. *The Measurement of Meaning.* Urbana, Ill.: University of Illinois Press, 1957.

Pessemier, Edgar A. *Experimental Methods of Analyzing Demand for Branded Consumer Goods with Applications to Problems in Marketing Strategy.* Bulletin No. 39. Pullman, Wash.: Washington State University Bureau of Economic and Business Research, June 1963.

Robinson, John P., and Shaver, Philip R. *Measures of Social Psychological Attitudes,* rev. ed. Ann Arbor, Mich.: Institute of Social Research, 1973.

Stevens, S. S. "Mathematics, Measurement, and Psychophysics." In *Handbook of Experimental Psychology,* edited by S. S. Stevens. New York: Wiley, 1962.

———. "On the Theory of Scales of Measurement." *Science,* vol. 103 (June 7, 1946), pp. 677–80.

Thorndike, Robert L., ed. *Educational Measurement.* Washington, D.C.: American Council on Education, 1971.

Thurstone, L. L. *The Measurement of Value.* Chicago, University of Chicago Press, 1959.

Torgerson, W. S. *Theory and Methods of Scaling.* New York: Wiley, 1958.

_____ APPENDIX 5–A _____

LAW OF COMPARATIVE JUDGMENT

The law of comparative judgment requires that several subjects (or one subject at several points in time) perform paired comparisons on a set of alternatives.

Consider the following example:

Number of times column item
preferred to row item (n = 200)

	A	B	C	D
A	—	40	80	130
B	160	—	140	180
C	120	60	—	150
D	70	20	50	—

We next compute the pecent of time each alternative is preferred to each other alternative. (Note that 50 has been put on the diagonal. This is unnecessary but traditional and has no effect on the result.)

Percent of time column item
preferred to row item

	A	B	C	D
A	50	20	40	65
B	80	50	70	90
C	60	30	50	75
D	35	10	25	50
	225	110	185	280

We can see that D is most preferred followed by A, C, and B (D > A > C > B). To convert this to an interval scale, we will assume the following:

1. Respondents have the same preferences on some underlying interval scale.
2. Respondents are equally uncertain about the alternatives and draw their preference feelings from a normal distribution (Figure 5A–1).

FIGURE 5A–1

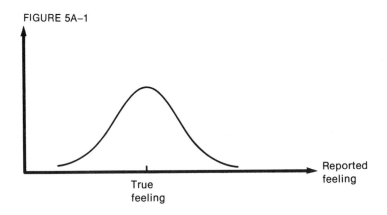

Since preferences are stochastic, it is possible that a respondent will say B is preferred to A when in fact A is "truly" preferred to B. The number of times this occurs is an indication of how far apart the alternatives are on the underlying scale. The trick of the law of comparative judgment is to deduce the underlying scale from the preference data.

Consider the preference distribution for A and B (Figure 5A–2). The percent of the time A is preferred to B depends on (a) the difference in their preferences $P_A - P_B$ and (b) the amount of uncertainty in their pref-

FIGURE 5A–2

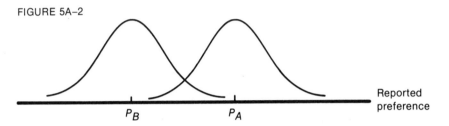

erences. Since the reported feelings toward A and B are assumed to be normally distributed and independent, the difference between them will also be normally distributed with mean $P_A - P_B$ and

$$\text{Standard deviation} = \sqrt{S_A^2 + S_B^2} = S \sqrt{2}$$

since we assume S_A and S_B are equal (Figure 5A–3). If we knew P_A, P_B, and S, we could get the percent of the time that A should be preferred to B

FIGURE 5A–3

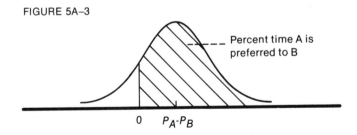

from the standard normal table. Here we reverse that procedure, taking the percent of the time A is preferred to B to the table and deducing how far apart A and B are in standard deviations. For example, since A is preferred to B 80 percent of the time, we estimate A is .84 standard deviations above B on the preference scale. Similarly, we fill in an entire table of estimates of the number of standard deviations between pairs of alternatives:

Standard deviations apart

	A	B	C	D
A	0	−.84	−.25	.39
B	.84	0	.52	1.28
C	.25	−.52	0	.67
D	−.39	−1.28	−.67	0
	.70	−2.64	−.40	2.34

Since the column sums are measured in units (standard deviations) of the underlying preference distribution, the results form an interval scale. (Actually a normalized interval scale, since the scale values sum to zero.)

This clever approach is perhaps most useful because of its two major assumptions. The formalized homogeneity assumption which is used in many calculations but usually hidden or ignored is bothersome as it should be. The random response notion is basic to the concept of measurement. Hence even if the technique is not used, its two major assumptions require attention in analysis of any type of survey data.

_____ APPENDIX 5–B _____

THE DELPHI PROCEDURE

The Delphi procedure is designed to produce a consensus ratio-scaled evaluation of alternatives among a set of judgments. It is most commonly used in evaluating budget priorities. To see how it works, consider the following example:

Assume three trustees were assigned to allocate funds ($100) to four projects. At step 1, each would be asked to allocate the $100 among the four projects:

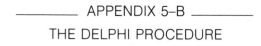

	Trustee		
Project	A	B	C
I	40	20	15
II	10	30	50
III	20	15	10
IV	30	35	25
	100	100	100

Someone then collates the responses from the three trustees and computes the average allocation for each project. Each trustee is then given a copy of both the original allocation and the average, and asked to modify the original allocation. For example, Trustee A would receive a form such as

Project	Original allocation	Average allocation	New allocation
I	40	25	
II	10	30	
III	20	15	
IV	30	30	___
	100	100	100

By repeating the process several times, presumably agreement (or at least near agreement) can be reached. The big advantage of this technique is that it can be used for individuals who are distant geographically or who have difficulty discussing allocations amicably. It also downplays the importance of slick verbal presentations in obtaining allocations. On the other hand, several problems exist. First, participants must be sufficiently committed that they respond honestly but not so fanatical that they refuse to budge (having participated in three such studies, I found that the game could be brought to a conclusion by adopting the mean as my response by wave 3). Second, shrewd respondents can influence results by a modified "bullet-vote" technique, where they inflate the allocation to their pet project and reduce it to their main competitors, thereby biasing the averages and hopefully (from their point of view) the final solution. Finally, there is the implicit assumption that either the average is right (very democratic but often false) or that agreement is an end in itself (which it can become, given especially strident arguments). Hence the technique is very specialized and not useful for most marketing research purposes.

_____ APPENDIX 5–C _____

NORMALIZING AND STANDARDIZING

Normalizing

Normalizing is the process of removing the mean (average) from a series of responses:

$$\text{Normalized } X = \text{Original } X - \text{Mean } X$$
$$X_N = X - \bar{X}$$

Example:

Given:

$$X$$

4
6
8
6
4
8

Thus $\overline{X} = 6$, and we get

$$X_N = X - \overline{X}$$

−2
0
+2
0
−2
+2

Standardizing

Standardizing is the process making the mean 0 and the standard deviation 1 for a series of responses:

$$\text{Standardized } X = \frac{\text{Original } X - \text{Mean } X}{\text{Standard deviation of } X}$$

$$X_S = \frac{X - \overline{X}}{S_X}$$

Example:

Given:

$$X$$

4
6
8
6
4
8

$$\overline{X} = 6$$

and

$$S = \sqrt{16/5} = \sqrt{3.2} = 1.79$$

Thus

$$X_s$$

$$-1.12$$
$$0$$
$$+1.12$$
$$0$$
$$-1.12$$
$$+1.12$$

Applications

There are two basic applications of normalizing and standardizing. One is by variable across people to indicate which people are relatively high or low on the variable. The other is by person across response. This approach obtains on the individual level the relative responses to a series of questions. It is also possible to double standardize by standardizing first by person across variables and then across people by variable. The purpose of all these transformations is to convert data to a form which is more useful for comparative purposes. The danger is that both normalizing and standardizing cause the loss of information (the absolute values of the variables) which may be useful. Hence decisions concerning normalizing or standardizing should be made only if (a) a firm grasp of the problem and (b) an assumption about the meaning of the absolute level of a response are available.

6

Survey design and execution

Surveys are the mainstays of most marketing research. Even when other methods such as experiments are used, a survey is often also employed. The reason for this is that surveys are relatively easy and cheap to administer. They are also the only known way to get measures of thoughts and attitudes. The disadvantage with surveys is that reported behaviors are often inaccurate. In spite of occasional (make that constant) problems, however, surveys remain an integral part of research.

This chapter proceeds by describing some of the choices and problems involved in developing a questionnaire. Next choice of survey method is discussed. Finally, some issues of pretesting and control are addressed.

One final point is in order. The best way to learn about surveys and their problems is to become involved in them. Especially useful is assuming the role of a personal interviewer so problems such as refusal to cooperate, don't know responses, and bad respondents become real. Filling out a few questionnaires will also help hone your skills.

CONTENT

The first subject to be considered is the content of the questionnaire. The correct starting point here is to review the problem and the hypotheses which have been developed. Additionally, assumptions about how consumers behave are important in structuring the data collection process (Appendix 6–D).

There is also a danger that too little information will be collected. This is especially true when the final version of the questionnaire is frozen before pilot tests or respondent interviews. On the other hand, it is very common to end up with an unwieldy document, especially if the "wouldn't it be nice to know" mentality dominates questionnaire construction. Another sure way to generate a massive incoherent questionnaire is to allow everyone in the neighborhood to put in a few questions. This questionnaire-by-committee approach may solve many individuals' data needs for no apparent additional cost (the something-for-nothing syndrome), but chances are the results will be sufficiently cumbersome or muddled that even the original sponsor of the research will be unsatisfied.

Addressing the specific content question, this section gives a typology of data which are often used in marketing research studies of individuals.

Background characteristics

Demographics:
  Age
  Sex
  Marital status
  Household size
  Number of children
  Region
  Degree of urbanization

Socioeconomics:
  Income
  Education
  Occupation

Basic ownership:
  Appliances
  Home (own or rent)
  Automobiles

Media exposure:
  TV
  Print

These characteristics often are useful predictors of product usage rates at least for segmenting purposes, but poor predictors of brand choice (i.e., Hunt's versus Heinz Catsup) or individual consumer behavior.

General characteristics

Personality. A variety of general personality variables have been applied in marketing studies for many years (Gottlieb, 1959; Robertson and Myers, 1969). The hope is to find an enduring general characteristic of a person which relates to many aspects of behavior. Generally these variables have been fairly weak predictors of consumer behavior. Massy, Frank, and Lodahl (1968) found both background and personality variables together account for less than 10 percent of the variation in brand choice.

In his summary, Kassarjian (1971) reviews several basic psychological theories: Freudian, social theory, stimulus-response, trait and factor theories, and self-concept. Some general personality instruments which have been used in marketing research (typically of the trait or factor theory type) include the following:

Gordon Personal Profile, used by Tucker and Painter (1961) and Kernan (1968).

Edwards Personal Preference Scale, made famous in marketing by the 1960s controversy over whether you could tell a Ford owner from a Chevy owner (Evans and Roberts, 1962). (Answer: Not very well, unless of course you observe what car they drive.)

Thurstone's Temperament Scale used by Kamen (1964) and Westfall (1962).

California Personality Inventory, used for innovativeness and opinion leadership studies by Robertson and Myers (1969) and Bruce and Witt (1970), topics also investigated by King and Summers (1970) and Darden and Reynolds (1974). Also considerable work has been done on self-concept in general (Birdwell, 1968; Grubb and Hupp, 1968) and self-confidence and risk taking in particular (Cox and Bauer, 1964; Barach, 1969; Venkatesan, 1968), as well as inner-other directedness (Kassarjian and Kassarjian, 1966).

Some other scales which have been used include

McClosky Personality Inventory
Dunette Adjective Checklist
Borgatta Personality Scale
Strong Vocational Interest Bank
Rokeach's Values
Cattell's 16 Personality Factor Inventory.

In spite of all this effort the predictive power of these general variables has been low, typically around 5–10 percent of the total variation available to be explained. Both Kassarjian (1971) and Jacoby (1971) point out that given the purposes for which general personality scales were developed, the low predictive power for brand choice decisions is quite reasonable. Product class choice seems more promising as a subject for personality variable prediction (Alpert, 1972; Bither and Dolich, 1972; Greeno, Sommers and Kernan, 1973). Still personality variables are generally of little value.

General activities/attitudes/opinions/interests. Generally known as life-style or psychographic measures, these variables are still general characteristics but logically more closely related to product choice than personality scales such as dominance-compliance, and so forth. Exactly where to draw the line between personality, life-style, and product-related variables is somewhat unclear. Nonetheless, most researchers agree that dominance-compliance is a personality trait, love of the outdoors a life-style (attitude) variable, and time spent playing tennis is a product-use variable (at least if the product I'm studying is a tennis racket). Hence we will classify a life-style variable as something more general than a product-related variable and something more product oriented than a personality trait. Life-style variables come in two major types: activities and attitudes.

Activities. Measures of the actual involvement in various activities such as sports, crafts, watching TV, reading magazines, and so forth.

Attitudes. Opinions about life in general, institutions (e.g., credit, education, churches), particular issues (e.g., welfare programs), as well as activities (e.g., baking from scratch) and interests (i.e., reading).

Tremendous effort has been involved in using life-style measures (see Wells, 1974; Plummer, 1974; Reynolds, 1973; Hustad and Pessemier, 1971). A major inventory of life-style questions is that used extensively by Market Facts, reported by Wells and Tigert (1971). Reliability of life-style measures has been investigated and found to be reasonably good (see Pessemier and Bruno, 1971; Villani and Lehmann, 1975). Moreover, several companies have used life-style segmentations as the basis for developing marketing strategy (e.g., White Stag used life-style analysis to reposition their entire clothing product line). Yet here again the predictive results have often been disappointing in spite of some reported successes. One thing which is true (and not at all surprising) is that the closer the life-style variables are to product variables, the better they are as predictors. An excellent review of psychographics is provided by Wells (1974)—"must" reading if you are interested in using these variables.

Product and brand usage

Typically the key variable for marketing decisions is actual brand choice. Hence considerable effort is devoted to measuring both product class and brand choice. Common variables include the following:

1. Usage rate of the product class as a whole.
2. Brand used/planned to use. This includes brand bought last time, time before last, and planned to buy next time.
3. Quantity purchased.
4. Time between purchases.

Determinants of brand choice

A number of variables have been hypothesized to be determinants (or antecedents) of choice. Some of the most widely used are as follows:

1. Awareness of the product class in general and particular brands.
2. Awareness of advertising.
3. Knowledge/understanding of the brand.
4. Perception/rating of brands on specific attributes. (For example, in the case of toothpaste, ratings of Crest, Colgate, etc., on attributes such as decay prevention, tooth whitening, etc.).
5. Importance of product attributes.
6. Satisfaction with present product.
7. Perceived risk in using the product.

Contextual/situational variables

A variety of contextual/situational variables influence product and brand choice (Belk, 1975). Hence a purchase of a sofa may depend on where it will be used (basement versus formal living room), who will use it (kids versus guests), and amount of wear you expect it to suffer. These variables break into two basic types:

Usage situation. This includes place used, alternatives, time of day, social visibility, heaviness of usage, and so forth.

Influence of others (children, spouse, etc.) on the decision.

TYPE OF QUESTION

The type of question asked to uncover a particular piece of information is an important consideration in any survey. In discussing this issue, it is useful to recall the measurement, question, and respondent sources of error delineated in the previous chapter (Figure 5–2).

In attempting to choose a type of question to minimize the cumulative effect of these sources of error, the following variety of decisions must be made.

Open- versus closed-end questions

Data can be gathered in either open- or closed-end forms. Consider the following examples:

In the case of the brand choice question, since the major brands are well known, the reason for an open-ended question is unclear. Its only advantage is that users of off-brands might not feel as conspicuous as they would if they were relegated to the "other" (translation: they must be a weirdo) category. On the other hand, for an established product category the number of people in the "other" category should be negligible and both the respondent (because it's easier to check a space than write a

---

Open end: What brand of toothpaste do you use most often? _____
Closed end: Please indicate which brand of toothpaste you use most often:
Aim   _____
Colgate   _____
Crest   _____
Other (please specify) _____
Open end: Why do you choose a particular brand of toothpaste? _____
Closed end: Please indicate the importance of the following attributes in se-
    lecting a toothpaste:

	Very unim- por- tant			Very im- por- tant
Decay	1	2	3	4	5
Price	1	2	3	4	5
Tooth whitening	1	2	3	4	5

---

word) and the analyst (because the data is precoded) will find the closed-end format better.

In the case of the question relating to reason for brand choice, the closed-end question requires more careful consideration. To be successful, we must first assume that the decision rests on attributes and their relative importances. Secondly, we must assume that the relevant attributes are known and included in the questionnaire. Actually for many product categories this is a fairly believable assumption, but it does require the researcher to have either knowledge of the product or past research data. It also is important to notice that the open-end question is not without problems, since such incisive answers as "to put on my toothbrush" and "for brushing my teeth" are likely responses.

A serious general problem with open-ended questions is that the extent of the response depends on the glibness and interest of the respondent. Hence the open-end answers are the result of opinionated, glib respondents and may not be representative of the total population. (This is especially true of political surveys.) Also open-end questions do not produce direct comparisons between competing attributes (i.e., the relative importance of two attributes), and the relative importance must be inferred from the percent of the time each of the attributes is mentioned. While generalizations are dangerous, it is usually true that open-end questions should be restricted to the following:

1. Exploratory studies from which closed-end questions will be formed.
2. Pilot tests where they can be used to pick up missing relevant data by allowing the respondent to report it.

3. Small sample studies of especially articulate respondents or respondents who are being surveyed by special interviewers.
4. As a final catchall question to (a) pick up any missing data ideas the respondent holds or (b) provide the respondent a chance to voice his/her opinion on a subject of interest. (Many people will put up with a certain amount of pain and suffering if they have the feeling that somehow their opinion will be listened to.)

An example of the value of an open-end question occurred in a study of soft drink preference. After ranking eight soft drinks on a set of pre-specified attributes, respondents were asked to list other attributes which were important to their choice. Several respondents listed "after taste" (which they apparently distinguished from the included variable "flavor") and "packaging" (which since all soft drinks were served cold in 12-ounce pop-top cans suggested that some people got their jollies by looking at the designs on the cans—possibly a result of spending the summer in West Lafayette). Since this was a multiwave study, these attributes were included in a subsequent wave of data collection.

Direct versus indirect

In asking a question, the researcher must decide whether to ask the question directly or indirectly. The indirect method assumes that an individual will not accurately respond to a direct question because of—

Inability to understand the question if it is asked directly (e.g., would you characterize your decision style as sophisticated or routinized?).

Inability to answer the question (e.g., you might not know how long you spend eating each day).

Unwillingness to provide the accurate response because of social pressure (e.g., nutrition is important, etc.). A favorite gambit for avoiding this problem is a projective technique where instead of asking directly, the question is phrased in terms of the person's reference group, such as "my neighbors." The assumption here is that you are more willing to expose undesirable traits if they are not personally attributed to you. The disadvantage is that you assume neighbors are similar (how many of your neighbors do you exactly match?), which guarantees some error in the results.

The direct method, on the other hand, assumes that the respondent can and will try to respond accurately. While indirect methods may be necessary for complex social issues or unstructured problems, most of the questions in marketing research are sufficiently straightforward that direct questions will do most of the time. The indirect method is also somewhat condescending since it assumes (a) the respondent isn't too bright or honest and (*b*) that the respondent can be easily tricked. Actually most normal respondents will try to respond honestly if given that opportunity, but may be offended by "games." Incidentally, the "best" respondents tend to be those who have normal profiles (high school or college graduates with a job, etc.) or grammar school students (whose interest in filling out questionnaires is remarkable). Experts (especially MBAs or market researchers) are typically poor respondents since they spend time evaluating the questionnaire, making helpful suggestions, and trying to figure out what tricks have been employed, not to mention protesting the format.

Aided versus unaided

A final issue is whether the responses should be aided or unaided. This is really a variation of the open- versus closed-end question theme which deals with how much information to give the respondent. A common example of this problem is the question of whether to measure aided or unaided advertising recall. Actually several levels of "aidedness" can be envisioned:

1. Have you heard anything lately?
2. Have you heard any ads lately?
3. Have you heard any motor oil ads lately?
4. Have you heard any ads for Mobil lately?
5. What is Mobil 1's main advantage?
6. Who claims their oil will add to your gas's mileage?

Depending on what you want the percentage who are aware of Mobil 1's claim that it adds to gas mileage to be, you can use the first two (likely response less than 1 percent), the third (probably about 10 percent), or the specified aided versions 4–6, where the recall may be more than half. Which you use depends on what you want: top of the mind (short-term memory) recall or to know if someone has stored in memory the message. Actually for most studies, it is not the absolute value but the changes over time which matter, so that the real problem is to keep using the same scale over time.

PHRASEOLOGY

Choosing a set of words to convey a construct is at best a difficult task. Words are imprecise, and most individuals' knowledge of their meanings even fuzzier. By being overly detailed, you run the risk of creating fatigue and boredom. Also many individuals typically try to answer questions without looking at the directions (just like putting together a tool or a toy without using the directions, it seems so much easier that way). On the other hand, vague phrasing can create problems in interpreting the re-

124

sponse. (For example, I could respond affirmatively to "Do you like Rolls Royce?" either because I like it but have no intention of buying it given my cash position, or to indicate I am considering buying it.) Hence the solution is to be "just right" in terms of detail.

Two procedures are very important in getting good wording for a question. First, give up on the notion that the first draft of a questionnaire is the final one. During revisions, continually see if respondents (a) answered, (b) answered with some reasonable dispersion, and (c) seemed to understand the question. Second, the translation practices used in going from one language to another can be employed in a modified fashion. (In translating questions from one language to another, it is advisable to have one person translate the question from the first language to the second and a second translator translate the translated question back to the original language. Only when the retranslated question matches the original is the question used.) Here a researcher writes a question and a respondent then assesses what the researcher really wanted to know. Only when the researcher's problem matches the data the respondent thinks s/he is supposed to give is the question accepted. Some general tips include the following:

Be direct. Don't ask, "May I know your age?" since the correct answer is yes or no. Ask, "What is your age?"

Avoid slang and fancy/polysyllabic wording. For example, use "like" instead of "appreciate."

When rating products, specify their use/purpose. Rating products without use/situation specification can be very hard for the respondent and misleading to the researcher.

RESPONSE FORMAT

Response format determination has three main aspects: repeat measures, scale type, and provision for don't knows and refusals.

Repeat measures

A fundamental issue in the format is whether a single scale or multiple items will be used to measure a construct. The advantage to the multiple item approach is that it increases the reliability of the measure of the construct. Using multiple items may help cancel out some errors which are idiosyncratic to a particular item, although this is more of an assumption/hope than a proven fact in most cases. One disadvantage is that the presentation of multiple measures may either irritate the respondent (who then could retaliate by giving poor quality responses) or convince the respondent that the survey is a consistency test and bias the responses accordingly. The main disadvantage is that it takes time and space for multiple measures which means either extending the question-naire with the effect of increasing both cost and respondent fatigue or eliminating other items from the survey. In most marketing research stud-ies where the focus is on group rather than individual behavior, the choice between a few reliable measures and many relatively unreliable measures is usually resolved in favor of many unreliable measures. One reason for this is that if respondents are assumed to be homogeneous, then average values can be calculated, and the averaging process creates a reliable statistic.

Scale type

The scale type (nominal, ordinal, interval, ratio) used depends on (a) the analysis desired and (b) the amount of effort obtainable from the respondents. Most questions should be gathered on interval scales when at all possible. One interesting point concerns the choice between rank-ings (i.e., "please rank the following brands with 1 being your most pre-ferred . . .") and ratings (i.e., "please indicate how well you like each of the following scales by circling a 1 if you strongly dislike it, a 6 if you strongly like it, or somewhere in between depending on how well you like the brand"). Rankings (ordinally scaled) are usually harder to obtain than ratings and produce more refusals, bad data (i.e., incomplete rankings), and so forth. The reason for choosing a ranking over a rating is to prevent ties. Hence if it is important to know what *the* first choice brand is, rankings may be required. Otherwise, ratings will usually suffice.

Provision for don't knows and refusals

The don't know/refusal response is a difficult problem. In some cases it is a legitimate answer (e.g., "Do you know what the term compactness means in numerical topology?"). In other cases, it is a convenient cop-out to avoid answering taxing or unpleasant questions. For example, I might wish to get a person's perception of a brand even though they had never used it to either assess its image or see if there were a reason for the nonuse.

The key decision, therefore, is whether to formally provide the respon-dent with the "don't know" response or not. (You can be sure some respondents will leave questions blank anyway.) If the "don't know" response is meaningful data, it should usually be used as a response category even though some respondents will use it as an easy out. If "don't know" is an unusual response, however, providing a "don't know" response will generally reduce the quality of the data. In any event, provision for "don't knows" needs to be made in the coding phase of analysis.

General suggestions

Ask simple, not complex questions. A question such as

> Do you own a summer house and a snowmobile?
> Neither _____
> Summer house only _____
> Snowmobile only _____
> Both _____

is generally inferior to

> Which of the following do you own?
>
> Summer house _____   _____
>   Own   Do not own
> Snowbile   _____   _____
>   Own   Do not own

Use nontechnical language. Too many studies go to the field in a form which is useful to engineering but meaningless to customers. For example, in one study concerning a major purchase item, a group of nontechnically trained respondents were exposed to product features developed and named by the R&D group. While the terms used were precise (e.g., response time in milliseconds, frame buffer, etc.), the typical respondent simply didn't know (or much care) what the technical features were and hence the responses were of limited value.

Group questions of similar types together. It is possible to ask questions in the following manner:

	Dislike very much				Like very much
How well do you like yogurt?	1	2	3	4	5	6
	Very infre- quently				Very fre- quently
How often do you watch TV?	1	2	3	4	5	6

However, it is often more efficient to get this information by combining the questions into a series of agree-disagree questions:

Please indicate your degree of agreement with the following statements:

	Disagree strongly					Agree strongly
I like yogurt	1	2	3	4	5	6
I watch TV frequently	1	2	3	4	5	6

Use mutually exclusive and exhaustive categories for multichoice questions. On the technical level, this means the following scale is bad: 1–10, 10–20, 20–30, while this scale is good: 0–9, 10–19, 20–29, 30–39, and so forth. On the more general level, it means you should take care to (a) specify all reasonable responses and (b) make it clear when only one answer is desired.

When appropriate, use objective rather than subjective scales for key constructs. It is possible to measure TV viewing on subjective scales such as "none" to "a great deal" or on agree-disagree scales. As long as TV viewing is not a key question, this is probably good enough. If a question is central, however, a quantitative scale is better:

How much TV do you watch on a typical weekday night?

None	Less than ½ hour	½–1 hour	1–2 hours	2–3 hours	More than 3 hours

---

While this scale requires the researcher to know a priori something about typical amounts of TV viewing, the scale may actually be easier for the respondent to use than a vague agree-disagree type question.

Avoid unbalanced scales. It is possible to have respondents answer on scales such as poor, satisfactory, good, very good, and excellent. This is occasionally necessary when the items being rated are all presumed to be fairly good in order to increase the dispersion of the answers. In general, however, a balanced scale (e.g., very poor to very good) is preferable.

Rate brands attribute by attribute. When brand ratings are to be obtained, it is possible to rate all the brands on one attribute at a time or a single brand on all the attributes. The former approach is better in that it reduces a respondent's tendency to "halo" ratings by responding only to overall feeling about the brand rather than the particular attribute in question. Hence this is bad:

Please rate Crest on the following attributes.

	Very poor				*Very good*
Decay prevention	____	____	____	____	____
Price	____	____	____	____	____
Tooth whitening	____	____	____	____	____

While this is better:

Please rate the following brands in terms of decay prevention.

	Very poor				*Very good*
Aim	____	____	____	____	____
Crest....................	____	____	____	____	____
Colgate	____	____	____	____	____

Be careful of the order in which a set of alternatives are presented. Since items in the first position tend to get a disproportionate number of mentions due to heightened visibility, it is often useful to put a weak alternative in this position to force respondents to look further in the list when the responses are of the multiple choice type. Some people like to randomly order lists, and others use alphabetical order. If the question asks the respondent to rate a series of alternatives on some criteria, the first alternative serves as a reference point. For this reason some people try to put a neutral/typical alternative first on the assumption it will be rated in the middle of the scale and hence leave room for both more positive and negative responses. While the order bias cannot be removed on an individual question, it is possible to reduce its effect on average responses by rotating the order of the responses. This could be done for three brands (A, B, and C) by giving each third of the sample a different format:

Format 1	*Format 2*	*Format 3*
A	B	C
B	C	A
C	A	B

Don't worry too much about the physical format for scaled questions.   A variety of response formats can be used for scale questions. Some of the most popular are as follows:

Other scales have also been used. (Many researchers have used 3– to 7–point "smile" scales with pictures ranging from a sad to a happy face when questioning children.) Fortunately the choice of format is usually more a matter of aesthetic opinion than practical importance.

Try to get relative ratings.   Absolute ratings of brands are interesting (i.e., brand X is "good"—average 4 on a five-point scale) but often disguise information. (If competitive brands Y and Z rate 4.5 and 4.7, 4.0 is pretty bad, while if the other brands rate 3.5 and 3.7, brand X is in good shape.)

SEQUENCE

The order in which questions are placed is often very important. The early questions set the "tone" of the survey by creating the mental set the respondent uses to produce answers. This is true in terms of both content and interest. For example, a series of early questions on symphony orchestra music might serve to (a) lead the consumer to assume that the subject matter was music preference and hence answer accordingly or (b) increase (or decrease) the subject's interest and consequently the likelihood the respondent will complete the questionnaire. In fact maintaining interest is one of the largest problems in many surveys. While some topics are inherently more interesting than others, proper format (including plenty of white space) and sequencing can do a lot to maintain the respondent's concentration. Some issues include placement of hard questions, placement of prying/offensive or experimental questions, variety of format, and branching.

Placement of hard questions

Many surveys have two or three key questions which are particularly difficult (e.g., preference rankings from 1–20 of 20 TV shows or suppliers). When these questions are placed at the very beginning of a study, they may convince a subject that the study is overly difficult and hence lead to a refusal to participate. On the other hand, placing these questions last will confront tired respondents with a difficult task, leading to either refusals or poor quality data. The best solution is often to put them fairly early but interspersed with easy questions. Hence many surveys will begin with a simple "warm-up" question or two (the marketing research equivalent of "What color is the White House?"), then go to the real questions.

FIGURE 6–1
Flow diagram of question branching

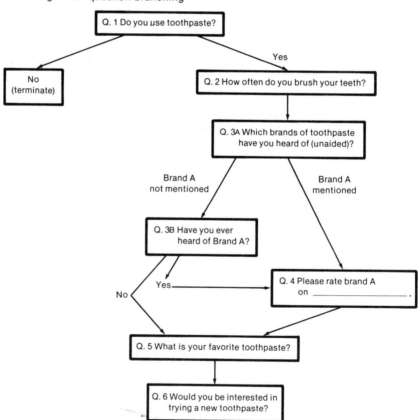

Placement of prying/offensive or experimental questions

There is no place to hide questions which people don't want to answer (including income). Typically, however, a survey will still have some value without these responses. Hence it is often·advisable to put these questions toward the end in order to avoid contaminating the other responses.

Variety of format

In order to keep respondents alert, it is useful to vary the format somewhat throughout the questionnaire. Hence when gathering data on a large number of variables of the same type (e.g., 150 life-style measures), some people choose to break up the section into parts (e.g., three parts of 50 each) and intersperse the parts with other questions. It is not clear, however, that this type of variety markedly improves data quality.

Branching

In many questionnaires, the questions to be asked depend on the answer to previous questions. One piece of advice is not to branch unless absolutely necessary. If branching is needed, it is useful to first set up a diagram to summarize the flow, such as Figure 6–1. Translating this into questionnaire form, we get Figure 6–2. As can be seen from this example, even simple branching instructions can be hard to follow. Some become so elaborate that they can quickly get out of hand.

A related issue is whether you can ask someone to rate a product which they have not actually used. Some people believe in "branching" around such questions to avoid burdening the respondent. An alternative approach is to ask everyone to rate a product whether they have heard of it or not. The rationale for this is they have perceptions of the brand which may explain their nonuse. (e.g., I can rate bank robbing as risky without doing it.) Since I can also ask (preferably later to cut down on refusals) whether the product has been used, I have the option of looking at only those people who use the product anyway. This strong-arm approach hence may get additional information while avoiding branching instructions and is typically preferable if the respondents can reasonably be expected to have some knowledge of or attitude toward the product in question.

TYPE OF SURVEY

This section focuses on methods of collecting data from individuals. The choice of how to collect survey data is typically viewed as the choice

FIGURE 6–2

---

1. Do you use toothpaste?

    _____Yes (go to question 2)
    _____No (terminate)

2. How often do you brush your teeth?

    _____   _____   _____   _____   _____

    Rarely   Weekly   A few times   Daily   More than
                         a week   once per day

3a. What brands of toothpaste have you heard of?

    _____

    _____

    _____

    If brand A is not mentioned—

3b. Have you heard of brand A?

    _____ Yes (go to question 4)
    _____ No (go to question 5)

4. Please rate brand A in terms of its sex appeal.

    Very   *Very*
    ordinary   *sexy*

       1   2   3   4   5

5. What is your favorite toothpaste?

    Aim _____
    Colgate _____
    Crest _____
    Ultra Bright _____
    Other (please specify) _____

6. Would you be interested in trying a new toothpaste?

    Very   *Very*
    uninterested   *interested*

       1   2   3   4   5

---

between the big three: personal, mail, and phone interviews. Here, seven major methods will be discussed:

1. Personal (in home) interviews.
2. Telephone interviews.
3. Mail surveys.
4. Drop-off, callback.
5. Panels.
6. Group interviews.
7. Location interviews.

Personal interviews

The view of marketing research in the general public is likely to consist of a mental picture of an interviewer asking questions of an individual and recording the responses on a clipboard (Figure 6–3). Indeed, the personal interview is a major tool of marketing research. Like all the survey approaches, it has both advantages and disadvantages.

FIGURE 6–3

Advantages

Relatively complex presentations can be shown to subjects in conjunction with questioning (e.g., samples of different packages, mock-ups of a new machine).

Depending on what answer a respondent gives to a particular question, the interviewer can then branch to the next appropriate question. Branching instructions are often quite complex. (For example, if it's Tuesday and the person answered "2" to question 31, go to question 34. If not, ...") While complex branching could theoretically be done with other designs, in practice only telephone surveys also do this as "standard practice."

Respondents can be asked to give responses other than multiple choice type. For example, respondents could be asked to sort cards containing the names of different brands into piles based on some criterion.

The presence of the interviewer can help convince the respondent to answer questions s/he might otherwise leave blank. Alternatively, the interviewer may be able to deduce the answer to questions such as annual income based on cues such as the size of the house, type of furniture, and so forth.

Disadvantages

The presence of the interviewer may influence the responses. This influence may be the result of the interviewer's opinions showing or the respondent giving those answers which s/he perceives will meet with approval from another human being.

Since the interviewer often is required to interpret the response and assign it to a predesignated category, there is a serious potential problem of errors in interpretation caused either because of the selective perception of the interviewer based on personal opinions or expectations of the likely response, or simply essentially random error in recording the answer.

There is a strong possibility of interviewer cheating. The firms which offer personal interviewing services generally bid on a potential job based on the number of completed interviews. Once they get a job, there is a very obvious incentive to get the interviews completed as quickly as possible. This incentive is likely to be transferred from the project director to the interviewers, often very directly by means of a pay schedule which is based on the number of completed interviews. Hence it is very common for interviewers to "help out" a respondent by filling in some answers without asking the questions, and not uncommon for an interviewer to dummy up an entire questionnaire. (For example, they might play act: "If I lived at 1182 Maple Avenue, how would I respond?"). Besides dealing with a reputable firm, or more drastically, doing the interviewing yourself, the only alternative is to check up on the interviewers. Calling back 20 percent of the respondents and asking four to five questions to see if the responses match is a common practice. Unfortunately even this process is inexact since the demographics may be relatively easily guessed by the interviewer and attitudes are subject to change over time. The shrewd interviewer who asks the objective questions and a few of the subjective ones and then fills out the rest is especially difficult to catch. Since the respondent may be reluctant to "rat" on the interviewer, even asking what the interviewer did may fail to uncover the cheating. In short, interviewer cheating is a difficult problem to control.

Costs. Personal interviews are in general the most expensive way to collect data from individual respondents. Costs can range from about $10 per completed interview for relatively short questionnaires (those requiring about 5 minutes to complete) with simple instructions and sample designs to $100 or more for longer questionnaires (requiring 45 minutes to one hour to complete) and "hard to get" respondents such as top executives or ghetto dwellers. For a typical half-hour questionnaire (six to eight pages) and a sample consisting of typical consumers, the cost tends to be about $25–$50 per completed interview. If two-way cable TV ever becomes a reality, however, this figure may be significantly reduced.

Response rate.   The response rate to personal interviews obviously depends on many factors including the sample chosen, the length of the questionnaires, the number of callbacks, the reward offered, and the competence of the interviewer. Nonetheless, typical response rates run between 50 and 80 percent.

Telephone interviews

Phone interviewing is essentially a low cost form of personal interviewing. As such, it shares many of the pros and cons of personal interviewing.

Advantages

Like personal interviews, phone interviews may follow fairly elaborate branching patterns.

The phone interviewer may help "prod" the respondent to answer questions.

Some individuals are more likely to answer a phone than to let a stranger enter their house, especially in high crime areas and in the evening when interviewing of people who work during the day is normally done.

It can be completed quickly.   Phone interviews on a topic can be ready for analysis faster than personal interviews.

It can be done from a single location.   By using WATS lines, all the interviewing can be conducted from a central location, simultaneously increasing control and reducing travel time.

Interviewer bias is reduced somewhat since the interviewer is not physically present.

Disadvantages

The questions must be asked without any visual props such as actual packages or pictures of products.

People may well respond differently to phone interviews than they do to personal interviews or in fact than they actually feel. In general, a person responding to a phone interview will probably concentrate less than when responding to a personal interview.

The responses are limited in that complex response scales (such as a constant sum scale) are not practically usable. Also it is rare for a phone interview to exceed 30–45 minutes in duration.

As in the case of personal interviews, there is the opportunity for the interviewer to exert influence either overtly or subconsciously, misperceive the answer given, or outright cheat.

Unless the person you are trying to contact has a phone, you can't get them. This is an especially serious problem when phone books are the source of the sample, since in areas like southern California up to 30 percent of the phones are unlisted. Fortunately, studies have shown that for many responses, nonlisted phone owners are very similar to listed phone owners. However, unlisted phones are most common among the young or the very old, the poor or the very rich. The use of a technique called Random Digit Dialing which, as the name implies, dials numbers randomly and then includes the person answering the phone in the sample, circumvents the problem of listed phone owners only being available. Random Digit Dialing does have the disadvantage of generating a lot of worthless responses (numbers not in service, businesses, and other people outside the target population). Also, those with unlisted numbers may not respond even if you call them. After all, they have their number unlisted to keep from getting nuisance calls. In fact, some people have been known to complain bitterly to the phone company, who they believe has given out their number. Nothing, however, helps with the problem of reaching individuals without phones. Since for most products, people without phones account for a very small share of the business, this is fortunately more of a theoretical than a practical problem.

Costs. Compared to personal interviews, phone interviews are relatively inexpensive. Although costs vary depending on the length of the interview, and so forth, costs for a completed interview tend to run between $5 and $10. This low cost is partly due to the existence of WATS (Wide Area Telephone Service) lines which allow unlimited calling from a particular area to another area for a fixed monthly charge. Hence WATS lines allow interviewers in a central location to do interviewing essentially anywhere, thus eliminating the need for travel and for numerous interviewers. Phone interviews also eliminate the costs associated with travel between interviews, which is a part of personal interviewing costs.

Response rate. The response rate of phone surveys is usually slightly below that of personal interviews, ranging from 40–75 percent.

Mail surveys

The third of the "big three" methods of obtaining responses from individuals is the mail survey. This method provides a clear contrast with both personal and phone surveys (see Figure 6–4).

FIGURE 6–4
A comparison of three survey methods

Characteristic	Personal	Mail	Phone
Usable length	Good	Fair	Poor-fair
Suitability for complex questions	Good	Poor	Fair
Minimization of process bias	Poor	Good	Fair
Cost per completed interview	High	Low	Low
	($25–$50)	($5–$10)	($5–$10)
Speed	Moderate	Slow	Fast
		(6 weeks)	

Advantages

The respondent is allowed to work at his/her own pace in completing the questions.

No interviewer is present to bias or misinterpret the responses.

With adequate instructions, fairly complicated scales (e.g., ten points) can be used to gather responses.

By receiving the responses directly, the possibility of interviewer cheating is essentially eliminated. (If you allow a firm to collect the responses for you, they could potentially "doctor" them to improve the response rate.)

Disadvantages

There is no one present to prod the respondent to complete the questions. This leads to greater numbers of partially completed questions and also to a higher rate of discontinuance in the middle of the survey (or for that matter, before the start).

No one is available to help interpret instructions or questions. This can lead to both confusion and frustration on the part of the respondent.

There is a nontrivial chance the survey will be treated as another piece of junk mail and appropriately filed (discarded).

Since most mail lists are at least one to two years old, many people on the list will have moved and hence many of the respondents will be unreachable. Unlike the case in personal and phone interviews, however, this will not be immediately obvious.

Most mail surveys are left open three to four weeks, although the bulk of responses come in during the first two weeks. This means that mail surveys may take a little longer to complete than personal or phone interviews if the latter are fully expedited.

Respondents tend to be slightly more up-scale (higher income, education, etc.) than nonrespondents.

Cost. The cost of mail surveys is similar to that of phone surveys, ranging from \$5 to \$10 per completed interview. An example of the cost basis for a single mailout is approximately as follows:

Stamp	13¢
Envelope	10
Return envelope and stamp	23
Cover letter	10
Questionnaire (6 pages)	20
Name label	5
	81¢

While labor increases this cost, the cost base is still very low when compared to a personal interview. As in the case of phone, very short (ten questions or fewer) surveys are even less expensive.

Response rate. The response rate of mail surveys varies widely and is currently the subject of considerable research. The lower bound can be close to zero if too much is asked of the respondent. For example, direct-mail solicitations typically get 1 percent or smaller responses. On the other hand, some interesting surveys with artful cover letters have received 50–60 percent responses. Somewhere in the middle of these two extremes lies the most likely result. For example, one survey which was six pages long, focusing on durable goods ownership plus demographics, and containing no incentive other than a cover letter penned by yet another fictitious research director produced a response rate of 20 percent out of 100,000 mailed questionnaires.

Drop-off callback

A procedure designed to include the best aspects of several methods, drop-off callback involves dropping off a questionnaire (usually after asking the respondent a few initial questions) and then returning to pick it up sometime later. This strategy allows the respondent to complete the questionnaire on his/her own time and yet has the advantage of an interviewer to build initial commitment and "check up" on the responses. This technique has been used extensively for super-long questionnaires which often run over 100 pages and take several hours to complete (Pessemier, DeBruicker, and Hustad, 1971; Lovelock et al., 1976).

Panels

One way to collect data is to utilize a group of individuals who have already agreed to participate. This approach includes both using commercially available panels and instituting and maintaining your own panel. There are really three major types of panels. The first is the diary panel in which members agree to record their purchases of a variety of products in terms of brand, price, size, and so forth. M.R.C.A. and N.P.D. maintain well-known panels of this type. A second type of panel is one in which individuals' behavior is monitored by some device which does not require panel member participation. Nielsen's audiometer, which records data on television viewing among participating households for the famous Nielsen TV ratings, is the prime example of this type. Monitored panels could be totally unobtrusive by basing them on credit card receipts, utility bills, and so forth. The third type of panel is simply a list of a set of individuals who agree to answer questionnaires. The mail panels of Market Facts, NFO (National Family Opinion), and Home Testing Institute (HTI) are examples of the third type of panel. While the particulars of the panels obviously are important, some general comments about panel usage are appropriate.

Advantages

The response rate among panel members is extremely high. Even for mail panels, the response rate to four- to six-page questionnaires is usually 70–80 percent.

For established panels, a great deal of other information such as demographics is already available on each of the respondents.

Using a panel is "easy" since the sample design issue is already taken care of.

Disadvantages

At least in one aspect, panel members are clearly not typical individuals. Recruitment is difficult with typically 10 percent or fewer of the individuals agreeing to participate. Hence panel members tend to be "questionnaire freaks."

Panels have a tendency to age. Hence as time passes, either the average age increases or the panel must be "rolled over" by the addition of younger panel members.

Most mail panels, including those designed to represent all segments of the population, tend to underrepresent both minority groups and low education levels. (Someone who can't read will hardly be likely to fill out six-page questionnaires.)

Being in a panel tends to "condition" respondents. Someone who has filled out three questionnaires about a product or seen the name of an unfamiliar product may tend to behave differently by, for example, spending more time considering the product or trying the unfamiliar product as a result of being made aware of it. Hence care must be taken that panel members' responses have not been conditioned by prior questionnaires or information collection.

Response rate. The response rates of panels are very high ranging from 70 to 80 percent for the mail panels to close to 100 percent for mechanical observation panels such as Nielsen.

Cost. Costs vary greatly depending on the panel in question. Six-page questionnaires sent to standby mail panels tend to cost about $10 per completed interview. Ongoing panels generally require a yearly subscription at a price from $50,000 to $150,000.

Group interviews

Group interviews are widely used in marketing research. They are essentially a combination of "cheap" personal interviews and self-administered questionnaires. A leader administers a questionnaire to a group of individuals at one time in a single location. This technique can be very economical, especially when used with church or community groups.

Location interviews

One of the least expensive ways to collect survey data is to station an interviewer in a central ("high traffic") location. The interviewer then "accosts" unsuspecting individuals and attempts to convince them to participate in the study. One of the most common forms of this type of study is shopping center intercept interviews. In such studies, the interviewer may conduct the interview on the spot as a personal interview. Alternatively the interviewer will lead the respondent to a separate area where the respondent may be treated to either a self-administered, personal, or group interview. Usually the separate area will contain some type of demonstration, either of a product or of advertising.

PRETEST

The stage in the research process which is most likely to be squeezed out due to cost/time pressures is the pretest. This is unfortunate, since a pretest is also the stage in which fundamental problems in a survey can be corrected. There are an incredible number of disasters around which a pretest of 50–100 "real" subjects would have prevented. Pretests allow checking to see (a) whether there are a disproportionate number of nonresponses to particular questions, (b) whether the questions discriminate (respondents give different answers), and (c) whether the respondents seem to understand the questions.

Pretests can also be used to convert open-ended questions to categories for the final study. There is also no shame in multiple pretests, especially if convenience samples are used at most of the stages. A questionnaire which does not change between initial drafting and field execution is probably one which has not been carefully examined.

QUALITY CONTROL IN THE FIELD

Quality control while the study is in the field is very important. Interviewers are motivated to get completed interviews and will tend to help respondents by either suggesting answers or by simply filling in sections of the survey to ease the burden on the respondent. In order to control this, checking is required. Typically this is done by recontacting 15–20 percent of the sample and asking (a) if they were in fact interviewed and (b) some questions to which the answers should not have changed. By comparing answers to these questions between the original and follow-up surveys, grossly disparate response patterns can be seen which can be used to eliminate both the respondent and the interviewer.

EXAMPLES

Examples of surveys can be misleading since there is no such thing as a typical survey. Nonetheless, Appendices 6–A to 6–C present three examples worth studying: typical commercial survey, nutritional survey, and educational needs survey.

Typical commercial survey

Appendix 6–A presents a survey which represents the typical format of a commercial study done by personal interviewing about a product category with several different brands (Katz, 1974). With the exception of the income categories, it is a good model/starting point for such a study. The pupose of each of the product-related questions is to measure the following:

1. Unaided recall of brands.
2. Unaided advertising recall of brands.
3–5. Purchase.
6. Aided recall.
7. Opinion/attitude.
8. Ever tried.
9. If repeat purchase.
10. Advertising recall.
11. Copy point recall (unaided).
12. Copy point recall (aided).
13. Brand ratings on attributes.
14–16. Size and style used.

The classification questions measure:

1–3. Price change perceptions.
  4. TV viewing.
  5. Age.
  6. Household size.
  7. Income.

Nutritional survey

Appendix 6–B presents the questionnaire which serves as a basis for discussion throughout much of the rest of this book. It was administered to a mail panel and hence by contrast is more structured than the personal interview survey of Appendix 6–A. (It also is academic rather than commercial in purpose and hence less tightly focused.) The questions were as follows:

Section I:
    1–8   Food shopping habits
    9–10 Food attribute importance
  11–14 Personal food consumption
    15   Change in household consumption.

Section II:
Nutritional information sources and perceived needs.

Section III:
Background (over and above already-collected demographics).

Section IV:
Life-style.

Section V:
Knowledge and perception of foods.

As an aside, it is useful to remember that this questionnaire, imperfect as it is, went through five revisions including a field pretest. The pretest found a serious problem in the wording of the final three questions which caused 20 percent of the sample to refuse to answer the section. Consequently the wording of question 2, section V, was changed from "Please indicate which of the nine functions of the body listed below are aided by consuming whole milk, beef, tomatoes, and enriched bread by putting a check in the appropriate box" to "For each of the nine body functions listed down the side of the page, please indicate which of the four foods contribute *importantly* to the function. *Check as many or as few* of the foods as you think apply to each function." This seemingly small change greatly reduced the nonresponse and hence again demonstrated the value of a pretest. As a further aside, the last three questions were added (*a*) to replicate questions on a study done for the FDA and (*b*) to serve as input for the use of multidimensional scaling algorithms. Since the scaling procedures basically recovered the four basic food groups, the value of these questions is questionable after the fact.

Educational needs survey

The questionnaire in Appendix 6–C was sent to all homes in a regional New Jersey school district in order to assess community feelings about education. The process was mandated by a law called "T and E" (Thorough and Efficient) which was passed by the state legislature, after the State Supreme Court invalidated the property tax as a basis for school support on the grounds that it did not provide for thorough and efficient education in poorer districts.

SUMMARY

Survey design is an art requiring balancing various sources of error and costs. It is important to recognize that many sources of error are beyond the control of the researcher such as the respondent's lack of interest in the subject and resulting lack of care in filling out the survey. Survey execution requires effort and care. In short, survey design and execution is an area where additional effort improves results. The desire to "get on with it" so that data can be analyzed and decisions made is understandable, but unless held in check is often counterproductive.

PROBLEMS

1. Evaluate the questionnaire in Appendix 6–A.
2. Evaluate the questionnaire in Appendix 6–B.
3. Evaluate the questionnaire in Appendix 6–C.
4. Assume you were designing a phone survey to find out how consumers choose a new appliance.
    a. Design the flow of the questionnaire (similar to Figure 6–3).
    b. Would you have a screening question?
    c. If your client were General Electric, how would the survey change?
    d. If your client were White-Westinghouse, how would the survey change?
5. Which type of survey (personal, phone, mail) would you use to get—
    a. Opinions about political issues.
    b. Ratings of a new product.
    c. Ratings of a new product concept.
    d. Priority rankings of 15 goals.
6. List ten things that you could do *wrong* in a survey.

BIBLIOGRAPHY

Alpert, Mark I. "Personality and the Determinants of Product Choice." *Journal of Marketing Research,* vol. 9 (February 1972), pp. 89–92.

Bailar, Barbara; Bailey, Leroy; and Stevens, Joyce. "Measures of Interviewer Bias and Variance." *Journal of Marketing Research,* vol. 14 (August 1977), pp. 337–43.

Barach, Jeffrey A. "Advertising Effectiveness and Risk in the Consumer Decision Process." *Journal of Marketing Research,* vol. 6 (August 1969), pp. 314–20.

Belk, Russell W. "Situational Variables and Consumer Behavior." *The Journal of Consumer Research,* vol. 2 (December 1975), pp. 157–64.

Birdwell, Al E. "A Study of the Influence of Image Congruence on Consumer Choice." *Journal of Business,* vol. 41 (January 1968), pp. 76–88.

Bither, Steward W., and Dolich, Ira J. "Personality as a Determinant Factor in Store Choice." *Proceedings,* Third Annual Conference, Association for Consumer Research, 1972, pp. 9–19.

Blair, Ed.; Sudman, Seymour; Bradburn, Norman M.; and Stocking, Carol. "How to Ask Questions about Drinking and Sex: Response Effects in Measuring Consumer Behavior." *Journal of Marketing Research,* vol. 14 (August, 1977), pp. 316–21.

Blankenship, A. B. *Professional Telephone Surveys.* New York: McGraw-Hill, 1977.

Bogart, Leo. "No Opinion, Don't Know, and Maybe No Answer." *Public Opinion Quarterly,* vol. 31 (Fall 1967), p. 332.

Bruce, Grady D., and Witt, Robert E. "Personality Correlates of Innovative Buying Behavior." *Journal of Marketing Research,* vol. 7 (May 1970), pp. 259–60.

Cahalan, Don. "Correlates of Respondent Accuracy in Denver Validity Survey." *Public Opinion Quarterly,* vol. 32 (Winter 1968–69), pp. 607–21.

Cannell, Charles F.; Oksengerg, Lois; and Converse, Joan M. "Striving for Response Accuracy: Experiments in New Interviewing Techniques." *Journal of Marketing Research,* vol. 14 (August 1977), pp. 306–15.

Cox, Donald F., and Bauer, Raymond A. "Self-Confidence and Persuasibility in Women." *Public Opinion Quarterly,* vol. 28 (Fall 1964), pp. 453–66.

Darden, William R., and Reynolds, Fred D. "Backward Profiling of Male Innovators." *Journal of Marketing Research,* vol. 11 (February 1974), pp. 79–85.

Erdos, Paul. *Professional Mail Surveys.* New York: McGraw-Hill, 1970.

Evans, Franklin B. "Ford versus Chevrolet: Park Forest Revisited." *Journal of Business,* vol. 41 (October 1968), pp. 445–59.

———. "Psychological and Objective Factors in the Prediction of Brand Choice." *Journal of Business,* vol. 32 (October 1959), pp. 340–69.

———, and Roberts, Harry V. "Fords, Chevrolets, and the Problem of Discrimination." *Journal of Business,* vol. 36 (April 1963), pp. 242–49.

Ferber, Robert. *The Reliability of Consumer Reports of Financial Assets and Debts.* Urbana, Ill.: Bureau of Economic and Business Research, University of Illinois, 1966.

Frankel, Martin R., and Frankel, Lester R. "Some Recent Developments in Sample Survey Design." *Journal of Marketing Research,* vol. 14 (August 1977), pp. 280–93.

Gottlieb, Morris J. "Segmentation by Personality Types," In *Advancing Marketing Efficiency,* pp. 148–58. Edited by Lynne H. Stockman. Chicago: American Marketing Association, 1959.

Greeno, Daniel W.; Sommers, Montrose S.; and Kernan, Jerome B. "Personality and Implicit Behavior Patterns." *Journal of Marketing Research,* vol. 10 (February 1973), pp. 63–69.

Grubb, Edward L., and Hupp, Gregg. "Perception of Self, Generalized Stereotypes, and Brand Selection." *Journal of Marketing Research,* vol. 5 (February 1968), pp. 58–63.

Hagburg, Eugene C. "Validity of Questionnaire Data: Reported and Observed Attendance in an Adult Education Program." *Public Opinion Quarterly,* vol. 32 (Fall 1968), p. 453.

Herriot, Roger A. "Collecting Income Data on Sample Surveys: Evidence from Split-Panel Studies." *Journal of Marketing Research,* vol. 14 (August 1977), pp. 322–29.

Hustad, Thomas P., and Pessemier, Edgar A. "Segmenting Consumer Markets with Activity and Attitude Measures." Institute Paper No. 298. Lafayette, Ind.: Krannert Graduate School of Industrial Administration, Purdue University, 1971.

Jacoby, Jacob. *Handbook of Questionnaire Construction.* Cambridge, Mass.: Ballinger Publishing, 1976.

———. "Personality and Innovation Proneness." *Journal of Marketing Research,* vol. 8 (May 1971), pp. 244–47.

Kamen, Joseph M. "Personality and Food Preferences." *Journal of Advertising Research,* vol. 4 (September 1964), pp. 29–32.

Kassarjian, Harold H. "Personality and Consumer Behavior: A Review." *Journal of Marketing Research,* vol. 8 (November 1971), pp. 409–19.

———, and Kassarjian, Waltraud M. "Personality Correlates of Inner- and Other-Direction." *Journal of Social Psychology,* vol. 70 (June 1966), pp. 281–85.

Katz, Jerrold P. "An Examination of Sample Survey Research in Marketing in the Context of a Buyer Behavior Model." Ph.D. dissertation, Columbia University, 1974.

Kernan, Jerome. "Choice Criteria, Decision Behavior, and Personality." *Journal of Marketing Research,* vol. 5 (May 1968), pp. 155–64.

King, Charles W., and Summers, John O. "Overlap of Opinion Leadership Across Consumer Product Categories." *Journal of Marketing Research,* vol. 7 (February 1970), pp. 43–50.

Kuehn, Alfred A. "Demonstration of a Relationship between Psychological

Factors and Brand Choice." *Journal of Business,* vol. 36 (April 1963), pp. 237–41.

Lovelock, Christopher H.; Stiff, Ronald; Cullwick, David; and Kaufman, Ira M. "An Evaluation of the Effectiveness of Drop-Off Questionnaire Delivery." *Journal of Marketing Research,* vol. 13 (November 1976), pp. 358–64.

McKenzie, J. R., "An Investigation into Interviewer Effects in Market Research." *Journal of Marketing Research,* Vol. 14 (August 1977), pp. 330–36.

Massy, William F.; Frank, Ronald E.; and Lodahl, Thomas M. *Purchasing Behavior and Personal Attributes.* Philadelphia: University of Pennsylvania Press, 1968.

Payne, Stanley L. *The Art of Asking Questions.* Princeton, N.J.: Princeton University Press, 1951.

Pessemier, Edgar A., and Bruno, A. "An Empirical investigation of the Reliability and Stability of Selected Activity and Attitude Measures." *Proceedings,* Annual Conference, Association for Consumer Research, 1971, pp. 389–403.

Pessemier, Edgar; DeBruicker, Stewart; and Hustad, Thomas, "The 1970 Purdue Consumer Behavior Research Project." Lafayette, Ind.: Purdue University, 1971.

Plummer, Joseph T. "The Theory and Uses of Life Style Segmentation." *Journal of Marketing,* vol. 38 (January 1974), pp. 33–37.

Pressley, Milton M., ed. *Mail Survey Response: A Critically Annotated Bibliography.* Greensboro, N.C.: Faber, 1976.

———, and Tullar, William L. "A Factor Interactive Investigation of Mail Survey Response Rates from a Commercial Population." *Journal of Marketing Research,* vol. 14 (February 1977), pp. 108–11.

Reynolds, Fred D. *Psychographics: A Conceptual Orientation,* Research Monograph No. 6. Athans, Ga.: College of Business Administration, University of Georgia, 1973.

Robertson, Thomas S., and Myers, James H. "Personality Correlates of Opinion Leadership and Innovative Buying Behavior." *Journal of Marketing Research,* vol. 6 (May 1969), pp. 164–68.

Spaeth, Mary A. "Recent Publications on Survey Research Techniques." *Journal of Marketing Research,* vol. 14 (August 1977), pp. 403–09.

Torgerson, Warren S. *Theory and Methods of Scaling.* New York: Wiley, 1958.

Tucker, William T., and Painter, John. "Personality and Product Use." *Journal of Applied Psychology,* vol. 45 (October 1961), pp. 325–29.

Venkatesan, M. "Personality and Persuasibility in Consumer Decision Making." *Journal of Advertising Research,* vol. 8 (March 1968), pp. 39–45.

Villani, Kathryn E. A., and Lehmann, Donald R. "An Examination of the Stability of AIO Measures." *Proceedings,* Fall Conference, American Marketing Association, 1975, pp. 484–88.

Walsh, T. C. "Selected Results from the 1972–73 Diary Surveys." *Journal of Marketing Research,* vol. 14 (August 1977), pp. 344–52.

Wells, William D. "Psychographics: A Critical Review." *Journal of Marketing Research,* vol. 12 (May 1975), pp. 196–213.

———, *Life Style and Psychographics.* Chicago: American Marketing Association, 1974.

———, and Tigert, Douglas J. "Activities, Interests, and Opinions." *Journal of Advertising Research,* vol. 2 (August 1971), pp. 27–35.

Westfall, Ralph. "Psychological Factors in Predicting Product Choice." *Journal of Marketing,* vol. 26 (April 1962), pp. 34–40.

Commercial personal interview survey*

DO NOT WRITE IN THIS SPACE

Study #	(1-3) X05
Respondent #	(4-7)
Area Code	(8-9)
Questre. Type	10-5
Card #	11-1

Respondent's Name _____

Address _____

City, State _____ Zip Code _____

Telephone # _____

(Area Code _____)

Interviewer's Name _____

City _____ State _____

Date _____

PRODUCT ONE

1. First, when you think of product 1 what brands come to mind? Any others? (CIRCLE BELOW BY ORDER OF MENTION)

2. What brands of product 1 have you seen or heard advertised recently? Any others? (CIRCLE BELOW BY ORDER OF MENTION)

3. The last time you bought product 1 what brand did you buy? (CIRCLE BELOW)

4. What other brands have you bought in the last two months? (CIRCLE BELOW)

5. And what brand do you buy most often? (CIRCLE BELOW)

6. Have you ever heard of _____ product 1? (CIRCLE BELOW)

INTERVIEWER: CIRCLE UNDER Q.6 "YES", EACH BRAND MENTIONED IN Q.1 THROUGH Q.5 THEN ASK Q.6 FOR EACH BRAND NOT YET CIRCLED "YES".

ASK Q.7 AND Q.8 FOR EACH BRAND CIRCLED UNDER Q.6 "YES".
7. Everything considered, what is your overall opinion of _____? Would you say it is one of the Best, Very Good, Good, Fair or Poor? (CIRCLE BELOW)

8. Have you ever tried _____ product 1 (CIRCLE BELOW)

11-3	Q.1 Come to mind			Q.2 Advertised		Q.3,4,5 – Brand buying			Q.6 Heard Of		Q.7 Overall Opinion						Q.8
	1st	2nd	Others	1st	Others	Q.3 Last	Q.4 Others	Q.5 Most	Yes	No	One of The Best	Very Good	Good	Fair	Poor	No Opinion	Tried
Brand E	12-1	14-1	16-1	18-1	20-1	22-1	24-1	26-1	28-1	30-1	32-1	-2	-3	-4	-5	X	45-1
Brand F	-2	-2	-2	-2	-2	-2	-2	-2	-2	-2	33-1	-2	-3	-4	-5	X	-2
Brand B1	-3	-3	-3	-3	-3	-3	-3	-3	-3	-3	34-1	-2	-3	-4	-5	X	-3
Brand B2	-4	-4	-4	-4	-4	-4	-4	-4	-4	-4	35-1	-2	-3	-4	-5	X	-4
Brand B3	-5	-5	-5	-5	-5	-5	-5	-5	-5	-5	36-1	-2	-3	-4	-5	X	-5
Brand G	-6	-6	-6	-6	-6	-6	-6	-6	-6	-6	37-1	-2	-3	-4	-5	X	-6
Brand A	-7	-7	-7	-7	-7	-7	-7	-7	-7	-7	38-1	-2	-3	-4	-5	X	-7
Brand R	-8	-8	-8	-8	-8	-8	-8	-8	-8	-8	39-1	-2	-3	-4	-5	X	-8
Brand P	-9	-9	-9	-9	-9	-9	-9	-9	-9	-9	40-1	-2	-3	-4	-5	X	-9
Brand H	-0	-0	-0	-0	-0	-0	-0	-0	-0	-0	41-1	-2	-3	-4	-5	X	-0
Brand I	13-1	15-1	17-1	19-1	21-1	23-1	25-1	27-1	29-1	31-1	42-1	-2	-3	-4	-5	X	47-1
Brand U	-2	-2	-2	-2	-2	-2	-2	-2	-2	-2	43-1	-2	-3	-4	-5	X	-2
Other	-3	-3	-3	-3	-3	-3	-3	-3	-3	-3		44-45						-3

9. (FOR EACH BRAND BELOW CIRCLED IN Q. 8, ASK:) Have you tried _____ just once or more than once? (CIRCLE BELOW)

10. (FOR EACH BRAND BELOW CIRCLED IN Q. 6, ASK:) Have you seen or heard of any advertising recently for _____ product 1 (CIRCLE BELOW)

11. (FOR EACH BRAND BELOW CIRCLED IN Q.10, ASK:) a) Please describe exactly what you saw in the advertising for _____ product 1 (RECORD BELOW)
b) What else did you see? (INTERVIEWER: PROBE FOR AS MUCH DETAIL AS POSSIBLE, RECORD BELOW)

INTERVIEWER: IF ANY OF THE Brand B PRODUCTS ARE TO BE ASKED ABOUT IN Q. 10-11, SIMPLY ASK ABOUT Brand B WITHOUT MENTIONING THE TYPES

	Q.9 Tried		Q.10	Q. 10, 11 Advertising — Q. 11 a, b Exactly what was seen
	Once	More than once		
Brand B1	48-3	49-3	50-3	51- _____ 52- _____
Brand B2	-4	-4		53- _____ 54- _____
Brand B3	-5	-5		55- _____ 56- _____
Brand G	-6	-6	-6	57- _____ 58- _____
Brand A	-7	-7	-7	59- _____ 60- _____
Brand P	-9	-9	-9	61- _____ 62- _____

12. Different brands of product 1 say and show different things in their advertising. I'm going to read you some of these things, and I'd like you to tell me which brand's advertising I am describing. (DO NOT READ BRANDS - CIRCLE OR WRITE IN BRANDS MENTIONED BY RESPONDENT)

	Brand B	Brand G	Brand A	Brand P	Other (SPECIFY EXACTLY)	Don't Know
a. Advertising Copy 1	14-3	-6	-7	-9	15-	X
b. Advertising Copy 2	16-3	-6	-7	-9	17-	X
c. Advertising Copy 3	18-3	-6	-7	-9	19-	X
d. Advertising Copy 4	20-3	-6	-7	-9	21-	X
e. Advertising Copy 5	22-3	-6	-7	-9	23-	X
f. Advertising Copy 6	24-3	-6	-7	-9	25-	X
g. Advertising Copy 7	26-3	-6	-7	-9	27-	X
h. Advertising Copy 8	28-3	-6	-7	-9	29-	X
i. Advertising Copy 9	30-3	-6	-7	-9	31-	X

ASK Q.13 FOR EACH BRAND LISTED BELOW THAT WAS CIRCLED IN Q.6.

13. Now, I'd like your opinion of a few brands of product 1 on some of their specific features. For example, would you say that _____ product 1 is one of the best, very good, good, fair or poor on Attribute 1? (CIRCLE BELOW AND REPEAT EACH FEATURE FOR EACH BRAND CIRCLED IN Q.6)

ATTRIBUTE ONE

	One of the best	Very good	Good	Fair	Poor	Have no opinion
Brand E	36-1	2	3	4	5	X
Brand F	6	7	8	9	0	Y
Brand B	37-1	2	3	4	5	X
Brand A	6	7	8	9	0	Y
Brand P	38-1	2	3	4	5	X
Brand H	6	7	8	9	0	Y
Brand I	39-1	2	3	4	5	X

ATTRIBUTE TWO

	One of the best	Very good	Good	Fair	Poor	Have no opinion
Brand E	40-1	2	3	4	5	X
Brand F	6	7	8	9	0	Y
Brand B	41-1	2	3	4	5	X
Brand A	6	7	8	9	0	Y
Brand P	42-1	2	3	4	5	X
Brand H	6	7	8	9	0	Y
Brand I	43-1	2	3	4	5	X

ATTRIBUTE THREE

	One of the best	Very good	Good	Fair	Poor	Have no opinion
Brand E	44-1	2	3	4	5	X
Brand F	6	7	8	9	0	Y
Brand B	45-1	2	3	4	5	X
Brand A	6	7	8	9	0	Y
Brand P	46-1	2	3	4	5	X
Brand H	6	7	8	9	0	Y
Brand I	47-1	2	3	4	5	X

14. As you probably know there are   size 1   and size 2 units of product 1.   About how many size 1 units   did your family use last month?

RECORD # UNITS_____(64–65) IF NONE, CIRCLE: Y

15. About how many   size 2 units of product 1 did your family use last month?

RECORD # UNITS_____(66–67) IF NONE, CIRCLE: Y

16. For the next few questions, please tell us how often you buy different kinds of product 1.   Your answer should be either frequently, occasionally, seldom or never.
For example, how often do you buy.........(CIRCLE)

		Frequently	Occasionally	Seldom	Never
		68–1	69–1	70–1	71–1
a.	Kind 1	–2	–2	–2	–2
b.	Kind 2	–3	–3	–3	–3
c.	Kind 3	–4	–4	–4	–4
d.	Kind 4				
e.	Product 1 on special price, coupon, cents-off, or on some other special deal	–5	–5	–5	–5

CLASSIFICATION

1. Please think for a moment about your purchase of product 1 in the past six months. In general, do you seem to be buying....(CIRCLE BELOW)

2. And what about your purchase of product 2 in the past six months? In general, do you seem to be buying....(CIRCLE BELOW)

	Q.1 Product 1	Q.2 Product 2
More expensive brands	72-1	73-1
Less expensive brands or	2	2
The same priced brands that you have always bought	3	3
(DO NOT READ) Don't know	X	X

3. Generally speaking, in the next six months do you expect the price of products such as product 1, product 2, etc. ....(CIRCLE BELOW)

Go up some	74-1	Don't know (DO NOT READ)	X
Go down some or	(2)		
Remain the same	3		

4. In terms of a typical seven-day week, how much television do you watch at different times of the day and night? For example, during the day before 5 pm, do you watch a lot of TV, or none at all? Now in the evening.....(REPEAT FOR EACH OF THE THREE REMAINING TIME PERIODS - CIRCLE BELOW)

11-1
CONT'D

	A Lot	A Little	None	(DO NOT READ) Don't Know
During the day before 5 PM	63-1	64-1	65-1	-9
Between 5 and 7:30 PM	-2	-2	-2	-0
Between 7:30 and 11 PM	-3	-3	-3	-X
After 11 PM	-4	-4	-4	-Y

66-X

5. Which of these age groups are you in? (CIRCLE NUMBER UNDER THE GROUP)

	Under 25	25 - 34	35 - 44	45 - 54	Over 54
67	-1	-2	-3	-4	-5

6. How many members of your family are living at home now, including yourself? (CIRCLE)

68	-1	-2	-3	-4	-5	-6+

7. And to help us tabulate your answers, what is your total family income per year before taxes? (CIRCLE NUMBER TO LEFT OF GROUP)

69-1	Under $3,000	-4	$7,500 - $10,000	
-2	$3,000 - $5,000	-5	$10,000 - $15,000	70-
-3	$5,000 - $7,500	-6	Over $15,000	71-

156

Nutritional questionnaire

<u>SECTION I - FOOD AND SHOPPING HABITS</u>

1. Please check to indicate what portion
   of the food shopping for your household
   you do personally . . . .
   - [ ] None of it
   - [ ] Less than half of it
   - [ ] About half of it
   - [ ] Most of it
   - [ ] All of it

2. About how many times PER WEEK
   do you shop for food? · · · · · · · · · · · · · · · ·
   - [ ] Less than once a week
   - [ ] Once a week
   - [ ] 2 - 4 times a week
   - [ ] 5 or more times a week

3. a) Do you prepare a shopping list before you go to the store?

   [ ] YES - Continue   [ ] NO - Skip to Question 4

   b) About what portion of the items that are
      purchased at the grocery store or super-
      market are on your shopping list? . . . .
      - [ ] None of them
      - [ ] Some of them
      - [ ] About half of them
      - [ ] More than half
      - [ ] Almost all of them

4. Approximately how much money
   is spent on food for your
   household in an average <u>week</u>? . . . .
   - [ ] Under $15
   - [ ] $15 - $29
   - [ ] $30 - $44
   - [ ] $45 - $60
   - [ ] Over $60

5. Approximately how much different
   is the amount you now spend on
   food each week as compared to one
   year ago at this time? . . . .
   - [ ] Spend at least $10 less than last year
   - [ ] $5 - $10 less than last year
   - [ ] About the same as last year
   - [ ] $5 - $10 more than last year
   - [ ] Over $10 more than last year

6. When you buy staple products (i.e. canned soup,
   ketchup, etc.), how many brands and sizes do you
   usually consider? (CHECK ONLY ONE) . . . .
   - [ ] Only 1 or 2
   - [ ] Many brands, one size
   - [ ] Many sizes, one brand
   - [ ] Many brands and sizes

7. Which <u>one</u> of the following <u>best</u> describes the way you shop for food?   (CHECK ONLY <u>ONE</u>)

   - [ ] I actively seek information about food in terms of nutritional value, price, etc.
   - [ ] I sometimes try new foods because of new information, but generally buy the same foods
   - [ ] The food I buy is almost always the same, and I spend very little time thinking about it

8. Have you, or any members of your immediate family, ever used food stamps?

   - [ ] Never
   - [ ] Used to, but do not use them now
   - [ ] We are presently using them

National Family Opinion, Inc. (f.)

50739

9. When deciding which foods to serve, how important are the following considerations? Indicate the degree of importance for each either by checking under the heading that describes your feelings, or by checking a box in between the headings that describe your feelings if your feelings fall somewhere between the headings.

	VERY IMPORTANT		SOMEWHAT IMPORTANT		NOT VERY IMPORTANT
Variety..	☐	☐	☐	☐	☐
Taste..	☐	☐	☐	☐	☐
Other family members' preferences..............	☐	☐	☐	☐	☐
Diet restrictions..............................	☐	☐	☐	☐	☐
Price..	☐	☐	☐	☐	☐
Availability at stores where you normally shop.	☐	☐	☐	☐	☐
Ease of preparation............................	☐	☐	☐	☐	☐
Habit (past eating patterns)...................	☐	☐	☐	☐	☐
Advertised specials............................	☐	☐	☐	☐	☐
Nutritional value..............................	☐	☐	☐	☐	☐

10. When you are deciding which brand of a particular food to purchase in the store, how much attention do you pay to the following?

	Pay a Great Deal Of Attention	Pay Some Attention	Pay Little or No Attention
Brand name....................................	☐	☐	☐
Number of servings............................	☐	☐	☐
Net weight or volume..........................	☐	☐	☐
Total price...................................	☐	☐	☐
Amount of ingredients.........................	☐	☐	☐
Unit price....................................	☐	☐	☐
List of ingredients...........................	☐	☐	☐
Nutritional value.............................	☐	☐	☐
Recipes.......................................	☐	☐	☐
Food additives and preservatives.............	☐	☐	☐
Date of manufacture or expiration............	☐	☐	☐

11. Please check below to indicate how many times per week you, <u>personally</u>, eat each of the following meals.

	Never	1 - 2	3 - 4	5 - 6	Everyday
Breakfast....................	☐	☐	☐	☐	☐
Lunch........................	☐	☐	☐	☐	☐
Dinner.......................	☐	☐	☐	☐	☐

12. How many snacks do you, <u>personally</u>, have in a typical day?

None.........................	☐
One..........................	☐
Two..........................	☐
Three or more...............	☐

50739

13. How much food do you can yourself?

☐ None   ☐ A small amount   ☐ A large amount

14. How often do you personally consume each of the following?

	Never	A Few Times A Year	1 - 2 Times A Month	Weekly	Several Times A Week	Once A Day	More than Once A Day
Canned fruit	1 ☐	2 ☐	3 ☐	4 ☐	5 ☐	6 ☐	7 ☐
Fresh fruit	☐	☐	☐	☐	☐	☐	☐
Bread	☐	☐	☐	☐	☐	☐	☐
Rice	1 ☐	2 ☐	3 ☐	4 ☐	5 ☐	6 ☐	7 ☐
Butter	1 ☐	2 ☐	3 ☐	4 ☐	5 ☐	6 ☐	7 ☐
Margarine	☐	☐	☐	☐	☐	☐	☐
Cheese	☐	☐	☐	☐	☐	☐	☐
Ice cream	1 ☐	2 ☐	3 ☐	4 ☐	5 ☐	6 ☐	7 ☐
Whole milk	1 ☐	2 ☐	3 ☐	4 ☐	5 ☐	6 ☐	7 ☐
Skim milk or low fat milk	☐	☐	☐	☐	☐	☐	☐
Snack foods (potato chips, pretzels, etc.)	☐	☐	☐	☐	☐	☐	☐
Desserts	1 ☐	2 ☐	3 ☐	4 ☐	5 ☐	6 ☐	7 ☐
Alcoholic beverages (beer, wine, liquor)	1 ☐	2 ☐	3 ☐	4 ☐	5 ☐	6 ☐	7 ☐
Soft drinks	☐	☐	☐	☐	☐	☐	☐
Fish	☐	☐	☐	☐	☐	☐	☐
Cold cereal	1 ☐	2 ☐	3 ☐	4 ☐	5 ☐	6 ☐	7 ☐
Frozen vegetables	1 ☐	2 ☐	3 ☐	4 ☐	5 ☐	6 ☐	7 ☐
Fresh vegetables	☐	☐	☐	☐	☐	☐	☐
Canned vegetables	☐	☐	☐	☐	☐	☐	☐
Poultry	1 ☐	2 ☐	3 ☐	4 ☐	5 ☐	6 ☐	7 ☐
Beef (hamburger or stew meat)	1 ☐	2 ☐	3 ☐	4 ☐	5 ☐	6 ☐	7 ☐
Beef (steak or roast)	☐	☐	☐	☐	☐	☐	☐
Pork	☐	☐	☐	☐	☐	☐	☐
Tuna fish	1 ☐	2 ☐	3 ☐	4 ☐	5 ☐	6 ☐	7 ☐
Frozen dinners	1 ☐	2 ☐	3 ☐	4 ☐	5 ☐	6 ☐	7 ☐
Hot dogs	☐	☐	☐	☐	☐	☐	☐
Coffee or tea	☐	☐	☐	☐	☐	☐	☐
Pasta (pizza, spaghetti, etc.)	1 ☐	2 ☐	3 ☐	4 ☐	5 ☐	6 ☐	7 ☐
Food at "fast food" restaurant (i.e. McDonald's, etc.)	1 ☐	2 ☐	3 ☐	4 ☐	5 ☐	6 ☐	7 ☐
Food at regular restaurants	1 ☐	2 ☐	3 ☐	4 ☐	5 ☐	6 ☐	7 ☐

National Family Opinion, Inc. Ⓕ

50739

15. How has the <u>amount your household consumes</u> of each of the following food categories <u>changed</u> in the past year?

	Much Less	Somewhat Less	About The Same	Somewhat More	Much More
Canned fruit............................	☐	☐	☐	☐	☐
Fresh fruit.............................	☐	☐	☐	☐	☐
Bread..................................	☐	☐	☐	☐	☐
Rice...................................	☐	☐	☐	☐	☐
Butter.................................	☐	☐	☐	☐	☐
Margarine..............................	☐	☐	☐	☐	☐
Cheese.................................	☐	☐	☐	☐	☐
Ice cream..............................	☐	☐	☐	☐	☐
Whole milk.............................	☐	☐	☐	☐	☐
Skim milk or low fat milk.............	☐	☐	☐	☐	☐
Snack foods (potato chips, pretzels, etc.)....................	☐	☐	☐	☐	☐
Desserts...............................	☐	☐	☐	☐	☐
Alcoholic beverages (beer, wine, liquor).....................	☐	☐	☐	☐	☐
Soft drinks............................	☐	☐	☐	☐	☐
Fish...................................	☐	☐	☐	☐	☐
Cold cereal............................	☐	☐	☐	☐	☐
Frozen vegetables......................	☐	☐	☐	☐	☐
Fresh vegetables.......................	☐	☐	☐	☐	☐
Canned vegetables......................	☐	☐	☐	☐	☐
Poultry................................	☐	☐	☐	☐	☐
Beef (hamburger or stew meat).........	☐	☐	☐	☐	☐
Beef (steak or roast).................	☐	☐	☐	☐	☐
Pork...................................	☐	☐	☐	☐	☐
Tuna fish..............................	☐	☐	☐	☐	☐
Frozen dinners........................	☐	☐	☐	☐	☐
Hot dogs...............................	☐	☐	☐	☐	☐
Coffee or tea..........................	☐	☐	☐	☐	☐
Pasta (pizza, spaghetti, etc.)........	☐	☐	☐	☐	☐
Food at "fast food" restaurants (i.e. McDonald's, etc.)...........	☐	☐	☐	☐	☐
Food at regular restaurants...........	☐	☐	☐	☐	☐

SECTION II - NUTRITIONAL INFORMATION

1. How much information about nutrition have you gained from each of the following sources?

	None	Very Little	Some	Quite A Bit	A Tremendous Amount
Books	☐	☐	☐	☐	☐
Magazines	☐	☐	☐	☐	☐
Labels on the packages food comes in	☐	☐	☐	☐	☐
Your mother	☐	☐	☐	☐	☐
Other family members	☐	☐	☐	☐	☐
Friends	☐	☐	☐	☐	☐
Doctors	☐	☐	☐	☐	☐
TV programs	☐	☐	☐	☐	☐
TV advertisements	☐	☐	☐	☐	☐
Newspapers	☐	☐	☐	☐	☐
Your own experience	☐	☐	☐	☐	☐
Courses in school	☐	☐	☐	☐	☐

2. In the past year, have you read book(s) about any of the following? . . . .

	NO	YES
Dieting	☐	☐
Nutrition	☐	☐
Cooking	☐	☐

3. Assume the Federal Government were about to launch a major nutrition education campaign aimed at adults. Which of the following forms would you prefer the campaign to take?

1 ☐ Column in the newspapers
2 ☐ TV special
3 ☐ Special edition of a prominent magazine
4 ☐ Government brochure
5 ☐ Extension courses
6 ☐ Workshops
7 ☐ Public Service TV announcements
8 ☐ Information on packages
9 ☐ Information in TV advertisements
11 ☐ Don't Care

4. If a service were to become available which provided specific information about the nutritional value of the brands offered in your local supermarkets, how much would you be willing to pay per week to subscribe to it?

1 ☐ Nothing
2 ☐ 10¢ - 19¢
3 ☐ 20¢ - 49¢
4 ☐ 50¢ - 99¢
5 ☐ $1 - $2
6 ☐ Over $2

5. Have you ever had a formal nutrition course in any of the following? . . . .

	NO	YES
High School	☐	☐
College	☐	☐
Adult Education/Workshop	☐	☐

SECTION III - BACKGROUND INFORMATION

1. Please indicate if any members of your household are on any of the following special diets:

CHECK HERE IF NO MEMBERS OF YOUR HOUSEHOLD ARE ON A DIET ☐

	Self-imposed	Doctor's Orders
Low cholesterol	1 ☐	1 ☐
Low fat/calorie	2 ☐	2 ☐
Diabetic	3 ☐	3 ☐
Low salt	4 ☐	4 ☐
Vegetarian	5 ☐	5 ☐
Low triglyceride	6 ☐	6 ☐

2. How often do you smoke?

☐ Never
☐ Occasionally
☐ Regularly, but light (less than 1 pack of cigarettes each day)
☐ Regularly (one pack of cigarettes a day)
☐ Heavily (more than 1 pack each day or equivalent)

3. Which of the following types of vitamin pills do you personally take?

1 ☐ None
2 ☐ Multiple
3 ☐ Vitamin C
4 ☐ Vitamin G
5 ☐ Vitamin B-12 Complex
6 ☐ Vitamin A
7 ☐ Iron

National Family Opinion, Inc. (f.)

50739

4. How much time do you spend
    watching TV on an average
    day? . . . .

    ☐ None
    ☐ Less than 1 hour
    ☐ 1 - 2 hours
    ☐ 3 - 4 hours
    ☐ Over 4 hours

5. How has <u>your family income</u>
    changed in the last year? . . .

    ☐ Gone down a lot
    ☐ Gone down a little
    ☐ Stayed about the same
    ☐ Gone up a little
    ☐ Gone up a lot

6. How has your household size
    changed in the past year? . . .

    ☐ Decreased by two or more
    ☐ Decreased by one
    ☐ Stayed the same
    ☐ Increased by one
    ☐ Increased by
       two or more

SECTION IV - GENERAL ATTITUDE INFORMATION

Please indicate how much you agree or disagree with each of the following statements by checking a box
under the heading that best describes your feelings.

	STRONGLY AGREE	SOMEWHAT AGREE	NEITHER AGREE NOR DISAGREE	SOMEWHAT DISAGREE	STRONGLY DISAGREE
People need to eat meat to be healthy.........	☐	☐	☐	☐	☐
A high level of consumption is necessary to maintain a high standard of living........	☐	☐	☐	☐	☐
I am personally more conscientious in conserving energy than I was 3 years ago.....	☐	☐	☐	☐	☐
The government should be more active in giving information about nutrition to consumers..	☐	☐	☐	☐	☐
I expect things to get better for my family next year................................	☐	☐	☐	☐	☐
I feel the need for more information about nutrition................................	☐	☐	☐	☐	☐
All people would have better diets if there were fewer mouths to feed................	☐	☐	☐	☐	☐
All cold cereals are about the same nutritionally............................	☐	☐	☐	☐	☐
Health is more important than money..........	☐	☐	☐	☐	☐
I get more exercise than the average person...	☐	☐	☐	☐	☐
We entertain at home more than the average family...................................	☐	☐	☐	☐	☐
I am healthier than the average American......	☐	☐	☐	☐	☐
I consider myself better informed about nutrition than the average American.......	☐	☐	☐	☐	☐
National brands of food are a better buy than local brands........................	☐	☐	☐	☐	☐
Life is going well for me....................	☐	☐	☐	☐	☐
Prices of food are so high that my nutrition is suffering..............................	☐	☐	☐	☐	☐
Television advertising has an adverse effect on diets because it encourages people to eat "junk" foods.........................	☐	☐	☐	☐	☐
I am heavier than I should be.....'..........	☐	☐	☐	☐	☐
I would be willing to eat less if the food were sent to the poor <u>in the United States</u>	☐	☐	☐	☐	☐

SECTION IV - GENERAL ATTITUDE INFORMATION (Continued) Please continue to indicate how much you agree or disagree with each of the following statements by checking a box under the heading that best describes your feelings.

	STRONGLY AGREE	SOMEWHAT AGREE	NEITHER AGREE NOR DISAGREE	SOMEWHAT DISAGREE	STRONGLY DISAGREE
America has a responsibility to share our agricultural abundance with hungry people in poor countries as well as home in the United States...............................	☐	☐	☐	☐	☐
The United States Government should pass laws which would encourage and reward the farmer for full scale production...................	☐	☐	☐	☐	☐
The children in our household have a large influence on what we eat....................	☐	☐	☐	☐	☐
Filling out this questionnaire has made me think about things which will change the types of foods I buy........................	☐	☐	☐	☐	☐

SECTION V - FOOD OPINIONS This final section deals with food opinions. I am asking questions about how you feel about certain types of foods. It would be quite unusual for a person to know the correct answers to every one of these questions. However, your feelings are very important to me, and I would like you to answer every question even if you have to guess.

1. Please answer the following questions by checking TRUE, FALSE, or DON'T KNOW.

	True	False	Don't Know
Hamburger contains substantially more protein per ounce than do soy beans..	☐	☐	☐
Pasta is high in cholesterol.....................................	☐	☐	☐
Poultry are more efficient than cattle as producers of protein...	☐	☐	☐
A large amount of one vitamin is sufficient to overcome deficiencies of other vitamins...............................	☐	☐	☐
Beans and rice together are a low-protein meal...................	☐	☐	☐
Eating a variety of foods from the supermarket will ensure a balanced diet.......................................	☐	☐	☐
The cost of the vitamins needed to meet 100% of the minimum daily requirements is less than 10¢ per day..........	☐	☐	☐
Food coloring additives create hyperactivity in children.........	☐	☐	☐
Sugar causes cavities in children...............................	☐	☐	☐
Whole wheat bread is healthier than enriched white bread........	☐	☐	☐

2. For each of the nine body functions listed down the side of the page, please indicate which of the four foods contribute importantly to the function. Check as many or as few of the foods that you think apply to each function.

	Whole Milk	Beef	Tomatoes	Enriched Bread
Eyes are aided by:...........................	1 ☐	2 ☐	3 ☐	4 ☐
Teeth and bones are aided by:................	☐	☐	☐	☐
Muscle tissue is aided by:...................	1 ☐	2 ☐	3 ☐	4 ☐
Repair of body tissues is aided by:.........	1 ☐	2 ☐	3 ☐	4
Blood cells are aided by:....................	☐	☐	☐	☐
Fighting infection is aided by:.............	1 ☐	2 ☐	3 ☐	4
Nervous system is aided by:.................	1 ☐	2 ☐	3	4 ☐
Skin is aided by:...........................	☐	☐	☐	☐
Proper growth of children is aided by:......	1 ☐	2 ☐	3 ☐	4 ☐

3. For each of the nutrients listed down the side of the page, <u>check as many or as few of</u> the four foods (whole milk, beef, tomatoes, enriched bread) that you think contain <u>a lot of</u> the nutrients.

	Whole Milk	Beef	Tomatoes	Enriched Bread
There is a lot of <u>Vitamin A</u> in:..................... 1 ☐	1 ☐	1 ☐	1 ☐
There is a lot of <u>Thiamin (Vitamin B₁)</u> in:........ 2 ☐	2 ☐	2 ☐	2 ☐
There is a lot of <u>Riboflavin (Vitamin B₂)</u> in:..... 3 ☐	3 ☐	3 ☐	3 ☐
There is a lot of <u>Niacin</u> in:...................... 4 ☐	4 ☐	4 ☐	4 ☐
There is a lot of <u>Vitamin C</u> in:.................... 5 ☐	5 ☐	5 ☐	5 ☐
There is a lot of <u>Vitamin D</u> in:.................... 6 ☐	6 ☐	6 ☐	6 ☐
There is a lot of <u>Protein</u> in:..................... 7 ☐	7 ☐	7 ☐	7 ☐
There are a lot of <u>Carbohydrates</u> in:.............. 8 ☐	8 ☐	8 ☐	8 ☐
There is a lot of <u>Fat</u> in:......................... 9 ☐	9 ☐	9 ☐	9 ☐
There are a lot of <u>Calories</u> in:..................10 ☐	10 ☐	10 ☐	10 ☐
There is a lot of <u>Iron</u> in:.......................11 ☐	11 ☐	11 ☐	11 ☐
There is a lot of <u>Calcium</u> in:....................12 ☐	12 ☐	12 ☐	12 ☐

4. And finally, I would like you to match certain foods with others. <u>Check as many or as few</u> of the four (4) foods (whole milk, beef, tomatoes, enriched bread) that you think have <u>a lot of</u> the same benefits to the body as each of the 14 foods listed down the side of the page.

	Whole Milk	Beef	Tomatoes	Enriched Bread
<u>Oatmeal</u> provides a lot of the same benefits as:....... 1 ☐	2 ☐	3 ☐	4 ☐
<u>Fish</u> provides a lot of the same benefits as:.......... ☐	☐	☐	☐
<u>Rice</u> provides a lot of the same benefits as:.......... ☐	☐	☐	☐
<u>Navy beans</u> provide a lot of the same benefits as:..... 1 ☐	2 ☐	3 ☐	4 ☐
<u>Chicken</u> provides a lot of the same benefits as:....... 1 ☐	2 ☐	3 ☐	4 ☐
<u>Potatoes</u> provide a lot of the same benefits as:....... ☐	☐	☐	☐
<u>Eggs</u> provide a lot of the same benefits as:.......... ☐	☐	☐	☐
<u>Macaroni</u> provides a lot of the same benefits as:...... 1 ☐	2 ☐	3 ☐	4 ☐
<u>Pork and Lamb</u> provide a lot of the same benefits as:.. 1 ☐	2 ☐	3 ☐	4 ☐
<u>String beans</u> provide a lot of the same benefits as:... ☐	☐	☐	☐
<u>Carrots</u> provide a lot of the same benefits as:........ ☐	☐	☐	☐
<u>Bananas</u> provide a lot of the same benefits as:........ 1 ☐	2 ☐	3 ☐	4 ☐
<u>Peanut butter</u> provides a lot of the same benefits as:. 1 ☐	2 ☐	3 ☐	4 ☐
<u>Cottage cheese</u> provides a lot of the same benefits as: 1 ☐	2 ☐	3 ☐	4 ☐

National Family Opinion, Inc. (f.)   50739

_____ APPENDIX 6–C _____

Educational needs survey*

Dear Resident:

Everyone in our seven Northern Valley communities has feelings and opinions about the schools today. Since the schools are supported out of public tax monies, we believe that everyone has a right to state his or her opinion. Often, these opinions are not expressed. This is why we are asking for your help.

At present, the schools in the Northern Valley are involved in a "needs assessment." Briefly, this is an attempt on the part of your school board and administrators to find out what the community expects of its schools. Once we have some information about what the community expects, we can look critically at our schools and see if we are meeting the expressed "needs" of the community.

Representatives from each of the seven communities in the Northern Valley have devoted a considerable number of hours in developing the first phase of this needs assessment project. Community representatives included parents, students, teachers, administrators, and board members. The Committee recognizes that only thirty-seven opinions do not sufficiently reflect the feelings of the community which the schools serve. Therefore, it is most important that we have a response from you. We need to know what you think the schools should be doing. The information you give will assist us in our efforts to improve the schools through the setting of clear goals and priorities.

While the questions on the following pages focus upon the schools, many of the items deal with responsibilities shared with parents and the community, such as discipline and motivation to learn.

We realize that you may not have had recent direct contact with your schools. However, we would appreciate your responses, giving us the benefit of your best feeling right now as you see your schools. Because we value all opinions, we would appreciate your answers to all of the questions whether or not you have children in the schools.

Your responses to the questions which follow will serve as one important source of information for our planning. Students and teachers will also be involved in providing information for this assessment. Results will be shared with the public.

After you have finished answering the questions, please refold the two question sheets so as to show the address of the Educational Planning Committee, and mail it . . . no postage needed . . . by *November 1, 1976.*

The Committee needs a large response in order to make the best use of this information. Please help! Thank you.

* Reprinted with permission of Northern Valley Regional High School District, Bergen County, N.J., Educational Planning Committee and Office of Curriculum and Instruction, *Valley-wide Goals/Needs Survey, 1976.*

INSTRUCTIONS

There are two questions about each statement:

a. To what extent *does* the condition *actually exist* in your schools?
b. To what extent *should* the condition *exist* in your schools?

You have the opportunity to respond to *both* the *elementary and high school* programs.

As you respond to each statement use the numbers 1, 2, 3, *or* 4 as described on the scale below:

Actually exists	Not at all	To a slight extent	To a moderate extent	To a large extent
	1 —————— 2 —————— 3 —————— 4			
Should exist	Not at all	To a slight extent	To a moderate extent	To a large extent

Use a "?" if you have no opinion or no basis of knowledge upon which to make a judgment regarding a particular item.

Use 1, 2, 3, 4 *or* ? on *each* of the four lines following each statement.

	Elementary school		*High school*	
	Actually exists	*Should exist*	*Actually exists*	*Should exist*
Example: Discipline in our schools is appropriate and reasonable.	3	4	?	4

A scale has been printed on each page for your reference when responding to the items.

Thank you for your cooperation.

In order to make the best use of the information you provide, it would be most helpful if you would respond to the following:

In which town do you live? _____

Do you have any children currently enrolled in the public schools?
(Please circle *a, b, c, or d.*)
  a. Yes, kindergarten through 8th grade.
  b. Yes, high school (9–12).
  c. Both *a* and *b*.
  d. No.

Instructions continued

	Actually exists	Not at all	To a slight extent	To a moderate extent	To a large extent
		1 ———	2 ———	3 ———	4
	Should exist	Not at all	To a slight extent	To a moderate extent	To a large extent

	Elementary school		High school	
Please put 1, 2, 3, 4 *or* ? on each blank line	Actually exists	Should exist	Actually exists	Should exist
1. The goals of our schools are clearly stated.	———	———	———	———
2. Our schools carefully assess the desires and needs of the community they serve.	———	———	———	———
3. Our schools have an adequate preschool program.	———	———	Not applicable	
4. Our schools have an adequate kindergarten program.	———	———	Not applicable	
5. Our elementary schools adequately prepare a student for high school.	———	———	Not applicable	
6. Our schools adequately prepare a student for college.	———	———	———	———
7. Our schools provide adequate training for students who do not intend to go to college.	———	———	———	———
8. Our schools have educational programs which meet the individual needs of all students whether they be fast, average, or slow learners.	———	———	———	———
9. Our schools give adequate attention to the teaching of basic intellectual skills (reading, writing, and arithmetic).	———	———	———	———
10. Health and safety education is offered at all levels.	———	———	———	———
11. Our schools have a good program in art education.	———	———	———	———
12. Our schools have a good English program.	———	———	———	———
13. Our schools have a good music program.	———	———	———	———
14. Our schools have a good mathematics program.	———	———	———	———
15. Our schools have a good home economics program.	———	———	———	———
16. Our schools have a good industrial arts program.	———	———	———	———
17. Our schools have a good physical education program.	———	———	———	———
18. Our schools have a good foreign language program.	———	———	———	———
19. Our schools have a good social studies program.	———	———	———	———
20. Our schools have a good science program.	———	———	———	———
21. Our schools help students deal effectively with ecological and environmental problems.	———	———	———	———
22. Our schools provide cultural experiences such as art, drama, and music.	———	———	———	———

Instructions continued

	Actually exists	Not at all	To a slight extent	To a moderate extent	To a large extent
		1 ————————	2 ————————	3 ————————	4
	Should exist	Not at all	To a slight extent	To a moderate extent	To a large extent

		Elementary school		High school	
Please put 1, 2, 3, 4 *or* ? on each blank line.		Actually exists	Should exist	Actually exists	Should exist
23.	Effective guidance and counseling are readily available to each student.	___	___	___	___
24.	Our extracurricular activities support or complement the overall goals of the schools.	___	___	___	___
25.	Our schools' extracurricular activities are designed to include the entire student body.	___	___	___	___
26.	Our school buildings and equipment are used efficiently, such as for summer school and community events.	___	___	___	___
27.	Individual differences among students are accepted and encouraged.	___	___	___	___
28.	Individualized instruction is provided for each student.	___	___	___	___
29.	Student ideas and suggestions are considered and used.	___	___	___	___
30.	Students are encouraged to be independent thinkers.	___	___	___	___
31.	Students are encouraged to behave responsibly.	___	___	___	___
32.	Our schools help students develop self-respect.	___	___	___	___
33.	Students learn to communicate effectively.	___	___	___	___
34.	Teaching students to be good problem solvers is emphasized.	___	___	___	___
35.	Students are encouraged to be concerned about other people.	___	___	___	___
36.	Students are encouraged to respect property.	___	___	___	___
37.	Discipline in our schools is appropriate and reasonable.	___	___	___	___
38.	Students are encouraged to be open to new ideas and different points of view.	___	___	___	___
39.	Our schools help students prepare for continual change.	___	___	___	___
40.	Students enjoy going to our schools.	___	___	___	___
41.	Students are encouraged to develop and use good study habits.	___	___	___	___
42.	Our schools help to prepare students for parenthood and family living.	___	___	___	___
43.	Our schools encourage students to make good use of leisure time.	___	___	___	___

Instructions concluded

	Actually exists	Not at all	To a slight extent	To a moderate extent	To a large extent
		1 ————	2 ————	3 ————	4
	Should exist	Not at all	To a slight extent	To a moderate extent	To a large extent

	Elementary school		High school	
Please put 1, 2, 3, 4 *or* ? on each blank line.	Actually exists	Should exist	Actually exists	Should exist
44. Our schools display a readiness for constructive change.	———	———	———	———
45. Our schools handle problems promptly.	———	———	———	———
46. Our schools communicate effectively with all segments of the community.	———	———	———	———
47. The reporting procedure used in the school system gives parents a clear understanding of their child's progress.	———	———	———	———
48. Our schools cooperate with the community in seeking solutions to problems of mutual concern.	———	———	———	———
49. Our schools develop in students a desire for continued learning.	———	———	———	———

50. In the space below, please write any comments or suggestions you may wish to make regarding the needs of our schools.

Elementary	*High school*

Additional space on next page.

This form has been designed in such a way that you can refold it, showing the address of the Educational Planning Committee, and mail it . . . no postage needed.

Reprinted with permission of Northern Valley Regional High School District, Bergen County, N.J., Educational Planning Committee and Office of Curriculum and Instruction, Valleywide Goals/Needs Survey, 1976.

——————— APPENDIX 6–D ———————

SOME CONCEPTS OF CUSTOMER BEHAVIOR

The purpose of this Appendix is to briefly outline some notions of how consumers behave. These concepts influence both data collection and analysis strategies. To really understand customer/consumer behavior, one would need (*a*) insight, (*b*) several consumer behavior courses, (*c*) experience, and (*d*) luck. What this Appendix does is to provide some of the flavor of customer behavior theory so that users of research can better specify what they want and producers of research can more.efficiently supply it.

One final warning. This Appendix is not written in the style of a social scientist. Careful definition of terms, detailed development of theories, and so forth, will not be found here. Rather the approach will be engineering oriented. The reasons for using this impure approach are twofold. First, the user of marketing research doesn't need to understand the intricacies of behavioral theory. (Second, this author doesn't know the intricacies of behavioral theory.)

MAJOR INFLUENCES

The way a consumer behaves is subject to a wide variety of influences. These influences affect decisions concerning whether to buy, what to buy, how much to buy, when to buy, and why and how to buy. Some of the most important influences are contextual/situational, personal characteristics, and influences of other people.

Contextual/situational

The importance of context in the buying process is often overlooked to the detriment of both research and decision making. An extreme example is that consumers will behave very differently under emergency (e.g., the toilet bowl cracks) than they will under "normal" circumstances. Less obvious situation differences are also important. Coffee drunk in the morning may serve a different purpose than coffee drunk during midafternoon, and hence the coffee a particular consumer chooses (or the products with which coffee competes) at one time may not be the same as they are at another time because of the changed context. The most appropriate way to define choice alternatives is in terms of a usage situation (e.g., something to wake you up in the morning, which includes coffee, a pill, jogging, etc.) rather than apparently competing products (brands of coffee, tea, etc.). A key to improving research is to indicate to respondents the context in which the researcher is interested, rather than allowing the consumer to pick a context (or worse, several contexts) and then try to guess what s/he was thinking of after the fact. For a review of the role of situational variables in marketing, see Belk (1975).

Personal characteristics

As opposed to situational variables, personal characteristics are widely used in marketing research as explanations for behavior. These come in many categories, including the following.

1. Personality measures.
2. Personal values.
3. Life-styles/psychographics.

4. Demographics (age, marital status, household size, stage in life cycle, etc.).
5. Socioeconomic measures (income, education, occupation, etc.).
6. Shopping habits/patterns (where shop, how frequently, etc.).

Of these categories, shopping habits is probably the most overlooked and yet may be the most important. For example, if I shop at a particular hardware store, the brand of paint I buy will be whatever brand that store carries. In fact, many product and brand choice decisions can be explained by shopping patterns.

Influences of other people

Since few choices are made in a vacuum, purchasers often consider other people's opinions in making a decision. Other people are considered in two basic ways: the ubiquitous other and fellow sufferers.

The ubiquitous other. One influence on choice is the perception of how the choice will be perceived by others, particularly peers. The notion of social mores influencing attitude is built directly into some attitude models (Ryan and Bonfield, 1975).

Fellow sufferers. Often the choice made by one consumer has a direct effect on others. This is true of many consumer goods in terms of other family members (i.e., I may buy the toothpaste, but the other members suffer if it is ineffective or bad tasting). In such circumstances, the purchaser may be acting as an agent for other family members who have dictated the choice ("Get me Brand X or else!"), attempting to do what is best for the other members, or participating in a bargaining/trade-off game. (For example, "We had hamburger last night, so I get to choose tonight.") For a more detailed discussion of family members' influences, see Davis (1971).

The fellow sufferer concept is at least as relevant to industrial marketing as it is to consumer marketing. Most purchases affect several people and often several units within the organization. Hence consideration of multiple opinions is standard practice, especially by purchasing agents who want to keep their job.

A PREFERENCE DEVELOPMENT MODEL

The most common way to view consumer preference development is in terms of a hierarchical model. These models range from the simplified type (Lavidge and Steiner, 1961) to the very detailed (Howard and Sheth, 1969). The essential stages in such models are awareness, comprehension, evaluation, preference formation, usage, and reevaluation.

Awareness

The first stage in preference development is becoming aware of the existence of a product or service. Developing such awareness (and hopefully interest) is the objective of most introductory advertising. Word-of-mouth conversations also are a common source of initial awareness.

Comprehension

The next major stage deals with the development of a firm understanding of what the product can be used for and how it works. This may occur because the consumer becomes interested and seeks information from stores, friends, and so forth, or because enough advertising/promotional effort is employed that the consumer comprehends even if s/he is not initially interested.

Evaluation

Assuming the consumer's interest is sufficiently whetted, the next stage is for the consumer to evaluate the product. While this evaluation is sometimes gestalt (e.g., Pet Rock), for many products this evaluation requires that (*a*) the relevant attributes of the product and (*b*) the relevant alternatives be identified. Then the consumer uses the relevant attributes to evaluate the various alternatives. The most common model is the multi-attribute formulation

$$\text{Attitude} = \sum_{\substack{\text{relevant} \\ \text{attributes}}} W_i B_i$$

where
B_i = the amount of the attribute
W_i = the importance of the attribute

Preference formation

The logical extension of evaluation is preference formation. This stage implies that consumers, having evaluated the relevant alternatives on the relevant attributes, store a simplified preference score for purposes of future decision making.

Usage

Not every preference score is translated into action. A variety of problems including budget constraints (e.g., I really prefer a blue-grey Rolls

Royce, but . . .), availability, and so forth, often intervene between preferences and choice. Then too, the evaluation phase may produce the conclusion that the product is not worth trying.

Reevaluation

If a product is actually used, the consumer has the opportunity to reevaluate it. Sometimes this can be done objectively, but often the consumer cannot make an objective evaluation. In these situations, contextual variables strongly effect the evaluation. (I still remember the brand of beer I tried in a warm 16-ounce can one morning when all other provisions ran out, and to this day the taste of that brand is repugnant.)

Hierarchical models are a very useful tool for understanding and monitoring how choice decisions are made. These models are not deterministic: some people may reach one stage (e.g., awareness) and never enter the next stage (e.g., comprehension). Similarly information provided by ads is perceived selectively (or sometimes screened out entirely), and hence the consumer may not hear exactly what the advertisers think they are saying. Also, many individuals deviate from the learning process approach and jump directly into latter stages such as use (give me a free sample and I'll try almost anything). Still if one had to place a bet, they would probably bet that a brand which received higher awareness would also reach higher comprehension and so forth. Hence monitoring the various stages of these models provides a clue to the eventual success or failure of a product.

CHOICE RULES

Having discussed hierarchical models and in a previous chapter multiattribute models, one can get the impression that most decision making involves sequential information processing and rational deliberation. This is an appealing but potentially false impression. Actually a consumer's approach to thinking about a product can be classified into several categories. The typology can be seen to be closely related to the work of Howard and Sheth (1969), Newell and Simon (1972), and Howard (1977), as well as Alexis, Haines, and Simon (1968), Hansen (1972), and Hugues and Ray (1974). The four basic categories are as follows:

1. Basic learning.   3. Limited processing.
2. Extensive processing.   4. Rule following.

Basic learning

Basic learning typically occurs when an individual is first confronted with a new brand. In this stage, the (potential) consumer is concerned with defining what the product is, what it is a substitute or complement for, and how it can be used. As such, it is largely a screening state which decides which, if any, of the other approaches will be employed.

Extensive processing

Much of the recent consumer behavior research done in marketing has focused on the issue of what model individuals use when choosing among a set of alternatives. This is often called the concept attainment or limited problem solving approach. A large percentage of this research has dealt with what has become known as a class of "multiattribute models" (Mazis and Ahtola, 1975; Bettman, Capon, and Lutz, 1975). A popular form of these models formulated to explain multiple object situations (Wilkie and Pessemier, 1973) is of the general form:

$$A_i = \sum_{j=1}^{n} |B_{ji} - I_j|^k W_j$$

where

A_i = attitude toward brand i
B_{ji} = belief about brand i on attribute j
W_j = importance weight of attribute j
n = number of relevant attributes
k = constant, usually 1 (city block) or 2 (Euclidean)
I_j = ideal level of attribute j

and has been called additive linear compensatory. An interesting variation on these models has been proposed in microeconomic theory (Lancaster, 1966; Ratchford, 1975).

In addition to the general finding that multiattribute models predict attitude and/or choice reasonably well (Wilkie and Pessemier, 1973), some disquieting results have emerged. These include the following:

1. A variety of conceptual and methodological issues involving the operationalization of these models (Cohen, Fishbein, and Ahtola, 1972) have been raised.
2. The importance weights have failed to add much in terms of predictive power to beliefs-only models (i.e., Bass, Pessemier, and Lehmann, 1972; Beckwith and Lehmann, 1973), even when ingenious procedures for determining the weights are employed (Srinivasan and Shocker, 1973; Pekelman and Sen, 1974; Zeleny, 1976).
3. The ideal points have failed to be predictively viable vis-a-vis the assumption that more is better.
4. The large intercorrelations among the attributes suggest that the respondents may be following a response style which is more related to

their overall liking of the brand than their true opinion about its standing on the attributes (Beckwith and Lehmann, 1975).

These shortcomings, when combined with the promotion of other models such as multiplicative compensatory (Einhorn and Gonedes, 1971; Bettman, 1974; Wright, 1975), have led researchers to investigate other models. Many alternative models have been proposed as representative of how consumers combine evaluations of a brand on a set of attributes (Wright, 1975; Bettman, 1976). These models can be divided into two subcategories. The first category involves extensive processing without potential shortcuts. This category includes the usual additive, compensatory models, as well as multiplicative models of the form

$$A_i = \prod_{j=1}^{n} (B_{ji} - I_j)^{W_j}$$

The second subcategory of extensive processing models assumes that while a consumer may consider many alternatives and attributes, s/he will attempt to do so efficiently in order to obtain a good choice relatively easily. These rules in general do not guarantee the globally optimum choice of a compensatory model but rather help find a good (close to optimal) choice quickly. At least seven such models have been proposed:

1. *Lexicographic/sequential.* An individual compares alternatives on attributes in order of their importance until one with a noticeable advantage emerges.
2. *Conjunctive.* A consumer rejects alternatives whenever they fall below a certain minimum value on any of the relevant attributes.
3. *Disjunctive.* A consumer accepts any alternative which is above the minimum acceptable value on the dimensions.
4. *MAXIMAX.* Choice of an alternative is proposed to be based on the relative importance of the attributes on which the alternative is best.
5. *MAXIMIN.* Choice is dependent on which alternative has the least important worst aspect.
6. *Sequential elimination (Russ, 1971; Tversky, 1972).* Alternatives are eliminated on first the most important, then the second most important attribute, and so forth, if they fail to meet the acceptable minimum value on each attribute until a single alternative remains.
7. *Standard of comparison.* Here individuals retain information about the best brand and compare any new brand with this brand. This method cuts down on the number of alternatives considered but not necessarily the number of attributes.

Some attempts to deduce which of these processing models consumers use, notably the cognitive algebra studies (Bettman, Capon, and Lutz,

1975), are very interesting and promising as are the experiments of Russo and Rosen (1975), Jacoby (1975), Bettman and Jacoby (1976), and Jacoby, Chestnut, Weigl, and Fisher (1976). Yet the likelihood of findings generalizations seems small for several reasons:

1. The linear compensatory model is a good approximation of most of the other models and given the noise in nonexperimental data is often indistinguishable predictively (Dawes and Corrigan, 1974).
2. The type of model used probably varies by product class, person, situation, and time. Hence any attempt to find "the" model is doomed to failure.
3. If many individuals are not currently employing complex processing models, attempting to fit them with such models may produce biased results (Nakanishi and Bettman, 1974).

Limited processing

Limited processing of information is common among most "routine" purchases. As used here, limited processing means processing with only one or two attributes and usually very few brands involved. It is assumed this processing occurs when the choice is made, which may be either at home as the shopping list is made out or at the point of purchase. Consumers reduce their choice problem to a limited form based on prior knowledge and more complex processing, the need to limit decision making to a small number of alternatives, or the need to consider only a few attributes. In short, they pass the multiattribute phase.

Probably the most common form of such behavior is the choice among brands of frequently purchased products. Many individuals will have in mind a set of two to four acceptable alternatives and will then buy the least expensive brand available. Here, processing will be limited to the price dimension.

Limited processing behavior is probably more common than extensive processing. The set of two to four acceptable brands may well have been determined by extensive processing, but the consumer has now moved "beyond" such models. While extensive processing models may predict behavior well, they are not being employed and hence their predictive power is deceiving.

Preexisting rule

The ultimately simple form of choice behavior (and probably the most common) is the situation where choice is based on a preexisting rule. (This might be called routinized behavior or concept utilization.) The rule may be deterministic ("I always have Coke with lunch") or stochastic ("I have Coke with probability .6, 7-Up with probability .2, etc.). These rules may change over time. Nonetheless, the essential characteristic is that at a given point in time, an individual makes a choice without processing any information at all.

Extensive processing models have considerable appeal. They are the epitome of rational behavior and seem to be what consumers "ought" to use. Yet simple introspection would suggest that people employ complex processing in at most a few decisions per day. Hence the rest of the day's decisions are made on the basis of simplified rules for determining behavior.

Most of the so-called stochastic models of behavior fall in the category of preexisting rules. While some are simple (Lehmann, 1976) and others more complex (Kuehn, 1962; Massy, Montgomery, and Morrison, 1970; Ehrenberg, 1972; Bass, 1974; Herniter, 1973, 1974), most of these models implicitly assume that none or very little information processing occurs during a certain period of time. Rather, choice follows a predetermined pattern which includes a random component.

Approach switching

The approach consumers use to evaluate alternatives is determined by a number of factors. These factors include the importance of the decision, the complexity of the products, time pressure, experience, the evaluation proneness of the decision makers, the number of brands, and the level of market activity. While at some time consumers may use extensive processing, in general they will tend over time toward routinized or limited processing decision making.

SUMMARY

This Appendix has briefly outlined some basic notions about consumer behavior. These notions have been directed toward understanding individual consumer behavior. Since much of marketing deals with consumers as groups rather than individuals, a fair question to ask is why consider individual behavior at all. The answer is that in studying individual behavior, notions of how consumers in general behave may emerge which can then be used to make marketing decisions. The most important point of this appendix is that different groups of consumers behave different ways and hence that different strategies may be needed for altering behavior of different consumer segments. The corrolary to this is that researchers should seriously investigate the role of individual, or at least group, differences.

PROBLEMS

1. Create *simple* process models showing the major variables or factors useful in describing or explaining the purchase and use of the following products or services:
   a. Orange juice consumed by a family.
   b. Women's cosmetics.
   c. Household furniture.
   d. Life insurance policy.
   e. Fashion merchandise purchased by a buyer for a large department store chain.

   In each case indicate what implications your model has for planning marketing strategy by a company marketing the product or service.

2. It has been argued that awareness is a worthless variable to measure. On what basis could such an argument be made? What are the counterarguments?

3. Most buyer behavior research deals with evaluation before a brand is bought. What evaluation process, if any, is followed once a brand is bought?

4. It can be argued that product class choice and allocation of total budget is more important than brand choice. How would you investigate families' decisions concerning the amount of dollars to devote to recreation?

5. Some researchers argue that essentially all purchases are group decisions. How does this impinge on the models discussed in this appendix? How would you model family decision making?

BIBLIOGRAPHY

Alexis, Marcus; Haines, George H.; and Simon, Leonard. "Consumer Information Processing: The Case of Women's Clothing." *Proceedings*, Fall Conference, American Marketing Association, 1968, pp. 197–205.

Bass, Frank M. "The Theory of Stochastic Preference and Brand Switching." *Journal of Marketing Research*, vol. 11 (February 1974), pp. 1–20.

———; Pessemier, Edgar A.; and Lehmann, Donald R. "An Experimental Study of Relationships between Attitudes, Brand Preference, and Choice." *Behavioral Science*, vol. 17 (November 1972), pp. 532–41.

Beckwith, Neil D., and Lehmann, Donald R. "Halo Effects in Multiattribute Attitude Models: An Appraisal of Some Unresolved Issues." *Journal of Marketing Research*, vol. 13 (November 1976), pp. 418–21.

———, and Lehmann, Donald R. "The Importance of Differential Weights in Multiple Attribute Models of Consumer Attitude." *Journal of Marketing Research*, vol. 10 (May 1973), pp. 141–45.

———, and Lehmann, Donald R. "The Importance of Hal Effects in Multi-

Attribute Attitude Models." *Journal of Marketing Research,* vol. 12 (August 1975), pp. 265–75.

Belk, Russell, W. "Situational Variables and Consumer Behavior." *The Journal of Consumer Research,* vol. 2 (December 1975), pp. 157–64.

Bettman, James R. "Data Collection and Analysis Approaches for Studying Consumer Information Processing." In *Advances in Consumer Research,* vol. 4, pp. 342–48. Edited by William Perreault. Chicago: Association for Consumer Research, 1976.

———. "A Threshold Model of Attribute Satisfaction Decisions." *The Journal of Consumer Research,* vol. 1 (September 1974), pp. 30–35.

———. "Information Processing Models of Consumer Behavior." *Journal of Marketing Research,* vol. 7 (August 1970), pp. 370–76.

———; Capon, Noel; and Lutz, Richard J. "Cognitive Algebra in Multi-Attribute Attitude Models." *Journal of Marketing Research,* vol. 12 (May 1975), pp. 151–64.

———; Capon, Noel; and Lutz, Richard J. "Multiattribute Measurement Models and Multiattribute Theory: A Test of Construct Validity." *The Journal of Consumer Research,* vol. 1 (March 1975), pp. 1–15.

———, and Jacoby, Jacob. "Patterns of Processing in Consumer Information Acquisition." In *Advances in Consumer Research,* vol. 3, pp. 315–20. Edited by Beverlee B. Anderson. Chicago: Association for Consumer Research, 1976.

———, and Kakkar, Pradeep. "Effects of Information Presentation Format on Consumer Information Acquisition Strategies." *Journal of Consumer Research,* vol. 3 (March 1977), pp. 233–40.

———, and Zins, Michel A. "Constructive Processes in Consumer Choice," working paper, University of California Los Angeles and Universite de Quebec, Chicoutimi and University Laval, February 1977.

Blattberg, Robert; Buesing, Thomas; Peacock, Peter; and Sen, Subrata. "Who Is the Deal Prone Consumer?" In *Advances in Consumer Research,* pp. 57–62. Edited by H. Keith Hunt. Ann Arbor: Association for Consumer Research, 1977.

Cohen, Joel B.; Fishbein, Martin; and Ahtola, Olli T. "The Nature and Uses of Expectancy-Value Models in Consumer Attitude Research." *Journal of Marketing Research,* vol. 9 (November 1972), pp. 456–60.

Davis, Harry L. "Measurement of Husband-Wife Influences in Consumer Decision Making." *Journal of Marketing Research,* vol. 8 (August 1971), pp. 305–12.

Dawes, R. M., and Corrigan, Bernard. "Linear Models in Decision Making." *Psychological Bulletin,* vol. 81 (February 1974), pp. 95–106.

Ehrenberg, A. S. C. *Repeat-Buying: Theory and Application.* Amsterdam and London: North-Holland, 1972.

Einhorn, Hillel, J., and Gonedes, Nicholas J. "An Exponential Discrepancy Model for Attitude Evaluation." *Behavioral Science,* vol. 16 (March 1971), pp. 152–57.

Engel, James F.; Kollat, David T.; and Blackwell, Roger D. *Consumer Behavior.* 2d ed. New York: Holt, Rinehart and Winston, 1973.

Fishbein, Martin. "Attitude and the Prediction of Behavior." In *Readings in Attitude Theory and Measurement,* pp. 477–92. Edited by Martin Fishbein. New York: Wiley, 1967.

Givon, Moshe, and Horsky, Dan. "Application of a Composite Stochastic Model of Brand Choice." Working Paper Series #7633, Graduate School of Management, University of Rochester, 1977.

———. "Market Share Models as Approximators of Aggregated Heterogeneous Brand Choice Behavior." Working Paper Series #7711, Graduate School of Management, University of Rochester, 1976.

Green, Richard; Mitchell, Andrew; and Staelin, Richard. "Longitudinal Decision Studies Using a Process Approach: Some Results from a Preliminary Experiment." In *Contemporary Marketing Thought,* pp. 461–66. Edited by Barnett A. Greenberg and Danny N. Bellenger. Chicago: American Marketing Association, 1977.

Haines, George H. "Process Models of Consumer Decision Making." In *Buyer/Consumer Information Processing,* edited by G. David Hughes and Michael L. Ray. Chapel Hill: University of North Carolina Press, 1974.

———. "Process Models of Consumer Decision Making." Paper presented at the Association for Consumer Research Workshop in Information Processing, University of Chicago, 1972.

Hansen, Flemming. *Consumer Choice Behavior: A Cognitive Theory.* New York: Free Press, 1972.

Herniter, Jerome D. "A Comparison of the Entropy Model and the Hendry Model." *Journal of Marketing Research,* vol. 11 (February 1974), pp. 21–29.

———. "An Entropy Model of Brand Purchase Behavior." *Journal of Marketing Research,* vol. 10 (November 1973), pp. 361–75.

Horowitz, Bertrand, and Kolodny, Richard. "Line of Business Reporting and Security Prices: An Analysis of an SEC Disclosure Rule." *Bell Journal of Economics,* vol. 8 (Spring 1977), pp. 234–49.

Howard, John A. *Consumer Behavior: Application of Theory.* New York: McGraw-Hill, 1977.

———, and Sheth, Jagdish N. *The Theory of Buyer Behavior.* New York: Wiley, 1969.

———. *Marketing Management: Analysis and Planning.* Homewood, Ill.: Irwin, 1963.

Hughes, G. David, and Ray, Michael L. eds. *Buyer/Consumer Information Processing.* Chapel Hill: University of North Carolina Press, 1974.

Jacoby, Jacob. "Perspectives on a Consumer Information Processing Research Program." *Communication Research,* vol. 2 (July 1975), pp. 203–15.

———, Chestnut, Robert W.; Hoyer, Wayne D.; Sheluga, David A.; and Donahue, Michael J. "Psychometric Characteristics of Behavioral Process Data: Preliminary Findings on Validity and Reliability." In *Advances in Consumer Research,* vol. 5, pp. 546–54. Edited by J. Keith Hunt. Ann Arbor: Association for Consumer Research, 1978.

———; Chestnut, Robert W.; Weigl, Karl C.; and Fisher, William. "Prepurchase Information Acquisition: Description of a Process Methodology, Research Paradigm, and Pilot Investigation." In *Advances in Consumer Research,* vol. 3, pp. 306–14. Edited by Beverlee B. Anderson. Chicago: Association for Consumer Research, 1976.

Krugman, Herbert E. "The Impact of Television Advertising: Learning without Involvement." *The Public Opinion Quarterly,* vol. 29 (Fall 1965), pp. 349–56.

Kuehn, Alfred A. "Consumer Brand Choice as a Learning Process." *Journal of Advertising Research,* vol. 2 (December 1962), pp. 10–17.

Lancaster, Kelvin J. "A New Approach to Consumer Theory." *Journal of Political Economy,* vol. 74 (April 1966), pp. 132–57.

Lavidge, Robert J., and Steiner, Gary A. "A Model for Predictive Measurements of Advertising Effectiveness." *Journal of Marketing,* vol. 25 (October 1961), pp. 59–62.

Lehmann, Donald R. "Post Purchase Product Reevaluation." Working paper, Columbia University Graduate School of Business, 1978.

———. "Consumer Rule Following and Rule Switching Behavior: Theory and Implications." Working paper, Columbia University Graduate School of Business, 1978.

———. An Empirically Based Stochastic Model." *Journal of Business Research,* vol. 4 (November 1976), pp. 347–56.

———. "Television Show Preference: Application of a Choice Model." *Journal of Marketing Research,* vol. 8 (February 1971), pp. 47–55.

———, and O'Shaughnessy, John. "Difference in Attribute Importance for Different Industrial Products." *Journal of Marketing,* vol. 38 (April 1974), pp. 36–42.

Lilien, Gary L. "A Modified Linear Learning Model of Buyer Behavior." *Management Science,* vol. 20 (March 1974), pp. 1027–36.

Luce, R. Duncan. *Individual Choice Behavior.* New York: Wiley, 1959.

Massy, William F.; Montgomery, David B.; and Morrison, Donald G. *Stochastic Models of Buying Behavior.* Cambridge: M.I.T. Press, 1970.

Mazis, Michael B., and Ahtola, Olli T. "A Comparison of Four Multi-Attribute Models in the Prediction of Consumer Attitudes." *The Journal of Consumer Research,* vol. 2 (June 1975), pp. 38–52.

Nakanishi, Masao; and Bettman, James R. "Attitude Models Revisited: An Individual Level Analysis." *The Journal of Consumer Research,* vol. 1 (December 1974), pp. 16–21.

Newell, Allen, and Simon, Herbert A. *Human Problem Solving.* Englewood Cliffs, N.J.: Prentice-Hall, 1972.

Nicosia, Francesco. *Consumer Decision Processes: Marketing and Advertising Implications.* Englewood Cliffs, N.J.: Prentice-Hall, 1966.

Payne, John W. "Task Complexity and Contingent Processes in Decision Making." *Organizational Behavior and Human Performance,* vol. 16 (December 1975), pp. 479–91.

———, and Easton Ragsdale, E. K. "Verbal Protocols and Direct Observation of Supermarket Shopping Behavior: Some Findings and a Discussion of Methods." In *Advances in Consumer Research,* vol. 5, pp. 571–77. Edited by J. Keith Hunt. Ann Arbor: Association for Consumer Research, 1978.

Pekelman, Dov, and Sen, Subrata K. "Mathematical Programming Models for the Determination of Attribute Weights." *Management Science,* vol. 20 (April 1974), pp. 217–29.

Pessemier, Edgar A. *Experimental Methods of Analyzing Demand for Branded Consumer Goods with Applications to Problems in Marketing Strategy.* Bulletin #39. Pullman, Wash.: Washington State University Bureau of Economic and Business Research, June 1963.

———; Burger, Philip; Teach, Richard; and Tigert, Douglas. "Using Laboratory Brand Preference Scales to Predict Consumer Brand Purchases." *Management Science,* vol. 17 (February 1971), pp. B371–B385.

Phillips, Lynn W., and Sternthal, Brian. "Age Differences in Information Processing: A Perspective on the Aged Consumer." *Journal of Marketing Research,* vol. 14 (November 1977), pp. 444–57.

Pollay, Richard W. "The Structure of Executive Decisions and Decision Times." *Administrative Science Quarterly,* vol. 15 (December 1970), pp. 459–71.

Ratchford, Brian T. "The New Economic Theory of Consumer Behavior: An Interpretive Essay." *The Journal of Consumer Research,* vol. 2 (September 1975), pp. 65–75.

Rosenberg, M. J. "Cognitive Structure and Attitudinal Affect." *Journal of Abnormal and Social Psychology,* vol. 53 (November 1956), pp. 367–72.

Rothschild, Michael L., and Houston, Michael J. "The Consumer Involvement Matrix: Some Preliminary Findings." In *Contemporary Marketing Thought,* pp. 95–98. Edited by Barnett A. Greenberg and Danny N. Bellenger. Chicago: American Marketing Association, 1977.

Russ, Frederick A. "Consumer Evaluation of Alternative Product Models." Ph.D. dissertation, Carnegie-Mellon University, 1971.

Russo, J. Edward. "Eye Fixations Can Save the World: A Critical Evaluation and a Comparison between Eye Fixations and Other Information Processing Methodologies." In *Advances in Consumer Research,* vol. 5, pp. 561–70. Edited by H. Keith Hunt. Ann Arbor: Association for Consumer Research, 1978.

———. "The Value of Unit Price Information." *Journal of Marketing Research,* vol. 14 (May 1977), pp. 193–201.

———, and Rosen, Larry D. "An Eye Fixation Analysis of Multi-Alternative Choice." *Memory and Cognition,* vol. 3 (May 1975), pp. 267–76.

Ryan, Michael J., and Bonfield, E. H. "The Fishbein Extended Model and Consumer Behavior." *The Journal of Consumer Research,* vol. 2 (September 1975), pp. 118–36.

182

Scott, Jerome E., and Wright, Peter. "Modeling an Organizational Buyer's Product Evaluation Strategy: Validity and Procedural Considerations." *Journal of Marketing Research,* vol. 13 (August 1976), pp. 211–24.

Srinivasan, V., and A. D. Shocker. "Linear Programming Techniques for Multidimensional Analysis of Preferences." *Psychometrika,* vol. 38 (September 1973), pp. 337–69.

Tversky, Amos. "Elimination by Aspects: A Theory of Choice." *Psychological Review,* vol. 79 (July 1972), pp. 281–99.

Wilkie, William L., and Pessemier, Edgar A. "Issues in Marketing's Use of Multi-Attribute Attitude Models." *Journal of Marketing Research,* vol. 10 (November 1973), pp. 428–41.

Winter, Frederick W. "Laboratory Measurement of Response to Consumer Information." Faculty Working Papers, #227. Urbana-Champaign, Ill.: College of Commerce and Business Administration, University of Illinois, January 1975.

Wright, Peter. "Consumer Choice Strategies: Simplifying Optimizing." *Journal of Marketing Research,* vol. 12 (February 1975), pp. 60–67.

———. "The Harassed Decision Maker: Time Pressures, Distractions, and Use of Evidence." *Journal of Applied Psychology,* vol. 59 (October 1974), pp. 555–61.

———, and Weitz, Barton. "Time Horizon Effects on Product Evaluation Strategies." *Journal of Marketing Research,* vol. 14 (November 1977), pp. 429–43.

Zeleny, Milan. "The Attribute-Dynamic Attitude Model (ADAM)." *Management Science,* vol. 23 (September 1976), pp. 12–26.

7

Nonsurvey research

There are numerous approaches other than surveys for collecting marketing research data. The purpose of this chapter is to outline four such alternatives and their pros and cons.

QUALITATIVE METHODS

Survey research as discussed in this book has been largely directed toward generating quantitative measures of constructs for the purpose of aiding understanding of the market and hence decision making. The only means discussed so far for ascertaining what is important and therefore worth quantifying, however, is open-ended questions. Since structured questions presuppose that the relevant responses are known and the only issue is their relative frequency, they are not amenable to first-cut analysis of a problem. Qualitative methods, on the other hand, provide such a starting point and hence are largely useful prior to the use of structured surveys. Several qualitative methods are available and three will be discussed here—introspection/brainstorming, depth interviews, and focus group studies.

Introspection/brainstorming

Usually overlooked or downplayed by marketing research, some introspection about the problem in question is very useful. While no one can logically argue that brand managers, marketing researchers, or their associates and spouses are typical consumers, they are both consumers and (at least hopefully) fairly knowledgeable about the product/service in question. They also are observers of how others behave. Hence "insiders" should have a fairly good notion about the product/service under investigation and may be able to list such things as alternative product uses, attributes important to the selection process, and so forth. While such "results" may not be perfectly projectable, they are an extremely useful starting point for further research. Introspection also has the potential to generate a genuinely new idea, something which rarely results from standard surveys.

Depth interviews

Depth interviews consist of probing questions being directed at a single subject by a single interviewer. These interviews often last over one hour and require a highly trained (and hence highly paid) interviewer. The purpose of a depth interview is to continually probe responses so that superficial responses (e.g., "I use brand X because it is pretty") are translated into more specific responses (e.g., "I have a thing about pink and brand X's wrappers are pink").

Depth interviews were borrowed from psychology and during the 50s enjoyed considerable popularity. People like Ernest Dichter specialized in probing respondents to uncover basic motives (which incidentally often proved to be Freudian/sexual in nature). Recently depth interviews have fallen from favor in marketing research.

Focus group studies

Focus group interviews have appeared as the successor to depth interviews for the extensive probing of customers. Focus groups are really open discussions between six to ten people with the focus provided by a trained moderator. These sessions typically cost about $1,000 each. The moderator's role is to gently direct the group to discuss items of interest to the buyer of such research, probing what appear to be superficial answers and moving on when a topic seems to be exhausted.

Focus groups, including some of the best ones, are often conducted by single entrepreneurs operating out of their living rooms, although major firms such as National Analysts have considerable experience in conducting focus group sessions. Focus groups can be used for a variety of purposes (Calder, 1977):

To generate hypotheses about the way consumers think or behave.

To structure questionnaires by uncovering relevant questions and appropriate response categories.

To overcome reticence on the part of subjects to respond. The group setting often encourages participants to say things they would not say in a one-to-one setting. This can result because of a "safety in numbers" effect or the snowballing/egging-on which occurs in group situations.

To generate or evaluate new ideas for products or product uses.

To find explanations for results of other studies.

Focus group sessions are handled in many different ways. However, a common approach when the focus is brand preference and use is to have members of the group progress through three stages. First, group members discuss products they use for a particular situation/need with very little intervention by the moderator. Second, the members are guided to discuss how they rate alternative products. Finally, the moderator probes their feelings in order to uncover why they favor some products over another.

Focus groups are very flexible tools. One advantage of them is that they allow much greater probing than even relatively detailed questionnaires. Because they are flexible, they can take advantage of unexpected responses and probe areas previously thought unimportant. Also, people in the group may egg each other on so they will say things they never would say individually. Sensitive subjects such as birth control are often probed in focus group sessions. Moreover, a variety of interesting questions which are not amenable to structured question format may be asked. In fact, the session is basically one big open-ended question. Finally, since the entire session is usually recorded, analysts can review the results several times before drawing any conclusions.

The problems with focus groups are also numerous. First, the process is heavily dependent on the moderator's ability to direct the discussion. A poor leader or group selection will make the results relatively useless. Second, bad group dynamics (one loud mouth, etc.) can greatly reduce the value of the results. Third, interpreting the results requires considerable skill. A corrolary to this is the buyer of research who does not observe a focus group either in person or on tape may lose much of the value of the session. Finally, focus groups are not useful for projecting to total markets (Bellinger, Bernhardt, and Goldstucker, 1976).

On balance, then, focus groups have a valuable role to play in understanding the market. On the other hand, they are not useful for producing quantitative projections. For this reason, many researchers will use a focus group as a first step in a research strategy which later includes large-scale surveys and quantitative analysis.

OBSERVATIONS

Direct observation of behavior is a very important tool. Its major advantage is that in many circumstances it is the most accurate way to measure overt behavior. In some cases observation is the only way to measure behavior due to either unwillingness (bank robbers are unlikely to recount their actions very accurately) or inability (ever asked a two-year-old something?) on the part of a consumer to report past behavior. Its major disadvantages are (a) it cannot be used to measure thoughts, preferences, and so forth, and (b) it can be fairly costly. Actually, several types of observation methods exist. Some of the major choices to be made include scope of observation, degree of control over the setting, direct versus indirect, observer (human versus mechanical), and obtrusiveness of observer (known versus hidden observer).

Scope of observation

An observation can be highly structured if the key behavior is well established in advance. For example, in observing soap purchase at a given store, it is possible to observe only (a) brand purchased and (b) length of time to make the choice. Alternatively an observation could attempt to record all aspects of behavior, including number of packages examined, number of people talked to, and so forth. The degree of structure in the observation has a great deal to do with the problem definition. A vague problem definition and exploratory research (e.g., "let's see how people buy soap") tend to call for all inclusive observation, while a tight problem definition (e.g., "measure the relation between brand bought and time spent shopping") leads to much more structured and less extensive observations.

Degree of control over the setting

In observing behavior, there is a choice between observing behavior in a natural setting (where observation is fairly difficult) and a more controlled situation (where observation and control of extraneous and desired influences is easier but behavior may be more artificial). Not surprisingly, controlled observation is usually both less expensive and less realistic.

Direct versus indirect

Most observational methods involve directly measuring behavior. A variety of indirect methods have been employed. One example involved newspaper readership in New York City. Surveys consistently showed that the New York Times was the paper of choice even though the Daily News was clearly a larger seller. Given the large social pressure to give the "right" answer (the Times), one enterprising researcher decided to check the garbage cans of a number of residents. In addition to some fairly unpleasant items, the researcher found a preponderance of the Daily News.

A more common indirect method is a pantry audit to measure food purchase behavior. By literally going through a kitchen and recording what is on the shelves, an estimate of food shopping and consumption patterns can be made. It is only an estimate, however, since the items will be on the shelf because they were bought but not consumed, which tends to occur with rarely used or bad tasting foods at least as often as popular/ commonly used ones. A final example of indirect observation research is the Nielsen TV ratings. By attaching a recording device to TV sets, the programs that are on can be monitored. Whether they are being watched or slept through, however, is unknown. In fact, any audit is a form of indirect observation. Hence almost all accounting data (sales records, inventories, etc.) involve observations and, except in the case of physical audits, usually indirect observations.

Observer (human versus mechanical)

The choice between human and mechanical observations usually depends on which is easier to utilize in a given situation. When choosing between human and mechanical observation, the accuracy of mechanical observation must be contrasted with the less accurate but often more insightful human observations. One form of human observation is to have a subject of observation also serve as an observer. This *participant observer* then records both his/her own behavior as well as that of other participants.

By contrast, one form of mechanical response observation is physiological measures. A pupilometer is a device which attaches to a person's head that measures interest/attention by the amount of dilation in the pupil of the subject's eye. A galvinometer measures excitement by means of the electrical activity level in a subject's skin. Obviously the subject is acutely aware of such observation because of the equipment involved. These "unnatural" measurement devices have in some cases accurately measured level of response and helped predict reaction to an ad. They are, however, very specialized in their application.

Obtrusiveness of observer (known versus hidden observer)

The choice between hidden and revealed observers depends on how differently the researcher believes the subject will behave if it is known that the subject is being observed. One can imagine all kinds of modified behavior in which the subject attempts to appear more logical, and so forth, than he/she/it really is (Webb et al., 1966). In many cases, however, this source of bias is likely to be fairly small.

The question of obtrusiveness also raises myriad legal and ethical questions concerning protection of subjects. Many situations require that formal subject consent forms be signed by the subjects in advance. Moreover, whenever subjects are exposed to a manipulation (e.g., a mock-up ad, etc.) it is important to "debrief" the subjects at the end of the observation by explaining the purpose of the manipulation to them. The debriefing is especially crucial when one or more of the manipulations involve false information. The principles of consent and debriefing apply both to observational and experimental settings.

In summary, then, observation is really a broad category involving a variety of techniques. Examples are found in Figure 7–1. It is important to remember that observations can be used as complements to surveys or other methods. In fact, most experiments involve both observations and surveys to ascertain the effect of the experiment.

EXPERIMENTS

In order to make decisions concerning price, advertising, and so forth, a manager is concerned with how these factors influence sales and profits. In order to do this, the manager wants to know how prices affect sales in a causal way. In other words, the manager wants to know if the price is increased 10 cents a package, what will happen to sales. The obvious way to get the answer is to raise the price 10 cents and see what happens. This straightforward experimental approach has two problems. First, most experiments have unforseen problems which make direct causal interpretation difficult. Secondly, causality and certainty are not synonyms. Even if I know that a price increase will cause sales to drop, the amount of the decrease will not be known with certainty. Put differently, the best one can hope for is an estimate of the effect of price on sales with a fairly narrow range of uncertainty. Still experiments often offer the best hope of isolating the effects of decision variables on key outcomes.

Design

The logic underlying a simple experiment is fairly straightforward. Assume a company is considering changing advertising strategy from copy A to copy B. They could do the following:

1. Expose subjects to copy B.
2. Measure attitude toward the product after exposure.

This seems logical except for one point. Attitude after exposure needs to be compared with something. An attitude after exposure of 4 may sound good, but if the attitude before exposure was 4.5, it may indicate an impending disaster. The basic choices for standards of comparison are as follows:

1. Attitude before exposure to copy B.
2. Attitude after exposure to copy A.

FIGURE 7-1
Some examples of observational methods

Method	Characteristics				
	Scope (structured versus extensive)	Degree of control (natural versus controlled)	Directness (direct versus indirect)	Observer (human versus mechanical)	Obtrusiveness (known versus hidden observation)
Hidden camera	Extensive	Either	Direct	Mechanical	Hidden
Store clerk with check list	Structured	Natural	Direct	Human	Known
Physiological measurement (galvinometer, etc.)	Structured	Controlled	Direct	Mechanical	Known
Pantry audit	Structured	Natural	Indirect	Human	Known
Nielsen TV ratings	Structured	Natural	Indirect	Mechanical	Known
Participant observer	Extensive (usually)	Either	Direct	Human	Either

Comparing attitude after exposure to copy B with (2) gives an indication of whether copy A or copy B is better. Hence we could design the following two treatments to test whether copy A or copy B is more effective:

	Treatment	
	1	2
Premeasure of attitude	x	x
See copy A	x	
See copy B		x
Postmeasure of attitude	x	x

Assume the results (a bigger number indicates more favorable attitude) were as follows:

	Treatment	
	1	2
Premeasure	10	10
Postmeasure	15	13

We can thus see that copy B appears effective in an absolute sense but not as effective as copy A in a relative sense.

Alternatively we might have been concerned about the possible effect of the premeasure on the results. Then we could have designed the following four treatments:

	Treatment			
	1	2	3	4
Premeasure of attitude	x(10)	x(10)		
See copy A	x		x	
See copy B		x		x
Postmeasure of attitude	x(15)	x(13)	x(14)	x(15)

The reason for including treatments 3 and 4 is the possibility that the premeasure could influence the results by heightening awareness of the product and hence either receptivity to or resistance to the ads. By measuring the effect of the copy both with and without premeasures, we can attribute any difference between the results as the effect of the premeasure.

If, as before, one only looks at treatments 1 and 2, it appears that copy A (15) is more effective than copy B (13). Looking at treatments 3 and 4, on the other hand, it appears that copy B (15) is more effective than copy

A (14). In this case, the premeasure seems to have improved the effect of copy A by one (15 − 14), while the premeasure reduced the effect of copy B by two (13 − 15). However, in removing the possible effect of the premeasure in treatments 3 and 4, we also have removed the check which indicated that the groups exposed to treatments 3 and 4 had the same initial attitudes. To put it bluntly, we're not sure which ad is better.

If you are now somewhat confused as to what the effect of copy A versus copy B is, good. The seemingly simple problem of measuring which ad is better is actually considerably harder to solve than it appears at first. While using experiments is an obvious approach, the choice of (a) which experiment to run and (b) how to interpret the results can be fairly difficult.

At this point three things should be apparent. First, the design stage depends heavily on logic and is essentially the process of deciding which factors (variables) could influence the results so that the effect of each one can be separately isolated by either manipulation or control. Second, the number of factors which could possibly influence the results is enormous and hence choosing the most important for designing treatments and controlling and monitoring other variables which could influence results is crucial. Finally, one must be very careful in interpreting the results since the differences may not be statistically significant. For this reason, interpretation of the results of an experiment almost always involves a statistical analysis, usually analysis of variance (see Chapter 13).

Formal experimental designs

In the previous section, the basic notion of what an experiment is has been introduced. In this section, some examples of experimental designs will be shown. Before proceeding, however, it is useful to adopt the following definitions:

Factor: A variable which is explicitly controlled as a part of the experiment (e.g., price, advertising, copy, etc.).

Levels: The values a factor is allowed to take on (e.g., prices of $100, $200, and $300; advertising copy A or B).

Treatment: The combined levels of the factors to which an individual is exposed (e.g., price of $200 and advertising copy A).

Control group: Subjects who are exposed to no treatment.

Measurement: Recording of a response of the respondent by any means (observation, survey, etc.).

Problems with experiments.   A variety of things may happen during an experiment which can influence the results. Some of the most common of these contaminants follow.

Exogenous occurrences (history). During many experiments (and especially field experiments), an event occurs outside the control of the researcher (e.g., an oil embargo, a strike, a new product introduction). This event influences the measured results and makes it hard to estimate the treatment effect.

Changes over time (maturation). Over the course of an experiment, the subjects change. Aside from the obvious fact that respondents age over a period of time, they also can become more expert consumers, tired, or even better off financially.

Effect of the experiment (testing/conditioning). The fact that an experiment is being conducted often has an important effect on the subjects. Even prior measurement can, by alerting the subjects to the topic of the study, cause them to change their behavior. Hence even a measurement can be considered to be a factor.

Instrument variability. Any change in the measuring instrument (e.g., changing the number of scale points on a questionnaire, changing the inventory method from Fifo to Lifo in measuring profits) can produce a change in the results due to the instrument rather than the treatment. Hence it is advisable to keep the measuring device as constant as possible.

Noncomparability of groups (selection). In many field or natural experiments, the subjects are assigned to groups after the treatment occurs. In such cases, it is not unusual for the subjects who "selected" the treatment (e.g., read the latest *Sales Management*) to differ from those who were not exposed to the treatment in some unmeasured way (e.g., interest in reading, desire/need to keep current on topics, etc.) which could affect the results.

Lost subjects (mortality). Over the course of an experiment, subjects inevitably drop out (e.g., individuals can get tired, move; businesses can fold or get new management teams who are less hospitable to the research). If these dropouts differ from the retained subjects (which they often do), then the results are affected.

Single-factor designs. These designs differ in the amount of attention they pay to the various measurement problems of experiments (maturation, experiment effect, etc.).

After-only without control group. This, the simplest design, selects a single group of subjects, exposes them to a treatment (X), and then takes a measurement (O). For example, a group of purchasing agents might be sent to a training program and then their performance measured. Since there is no premeasure or control group, it is impossible to tell if performance improved or deproved, and hence this design is essentially worthless. Graphically this can be described as

Group 1 . . . . X O

Before-after without control group. This adds a premeasure to the after-only design:

Group 1 .... O_1 X O_2

After-only with a control group. This design requires two groups: one exposed to the treatment and one which is not.

Group 1 .... X O_1
Group 2 .... O_2

This design is often used post hoc when exposure to a treatment (e.g., an ad) is monitored after the fact. The effect of the treatment is given by $O_1 - O_2$.

Before-after with one control group

Group 1 .... O_1 X O_2
Group 2 .... O_3 O_4

Here the effect of the treatment is given by $(O_2 - O_1) - (O_4 - O_3)$. The control group is used to estimate the maturation and testing effects.

Four-Group, Six-Study

Group 1 (experimental) .... O_1 X O_2
Group 2 (control) .... O_3 O_4
Group 3 (experimental) ....   X O_5
Group 4 (control) .... O_6

This design attempts to simultaneously measure both the effect of the treatment (X) and the effect of the premeasurement (O_1 and O_3) on the results. The effect of the treatment X is estimated as

$$\frac{(O_2 - O_4) + (O_5 - O_6)}{2}$$

and the effect of the premeasure as

$$\frac{(O_2 - O_5) + (O_4 - O_6)}{2}$$

Several-factor designs. Designs involving the monitoring of two or more factors are very common. The basic idea of such experiments is to simultaneously assess the effects of varying levels on several factors.

Factorial design. The most complete information can always be obtained by means of a full factorial design. A full factorial design requires exposing two or more subjects to each of the various possible combinations of the factors. The results allow estimation of the effect of each level

TABLE 7-1
A three-factor factorial design example:
All possible treatments

Advertising strategy	Package design	Colors
A	I	Red
A	I	Green
A	I	Orange
A	II	Red
A	II	Green
A	II	Orange
A	III	Red
A	III	Green
A	III	Orange
B	I	Red
B	I	Green
B	I	Orange
B	II	Red
B	II	Green
B	II	Orange
B	III	Red
B	III	Green
B	III	Orange
C	I	Red
C	I	Green
C	I	Orange
C	II	Red
C	II	Green
C	II	Orange
C	III	Red
C	III	Green
C	III	Orange
D	I	Red
D	I	Green
D	I	Orange
D	II	Red
D	II	Green
D	II	Orange
D	III	Red
D	III	Green
D	III	Orange

for each factor as well as the interaction (synergy) between each combination of factor levels. Consider for a moment a problem involving in-store testing of four advertising strategies (A, B, C, D), three packages (I, II, III), and three colors (red, green, orange). There are $4 \times 3 \times 3 = 36$ combinations possible (see Table 7–1). To implement a full factorial design I need at least 36 stores. In order to estimate interactions (e.g., the unique effect of putting package design III and red color together), 72 stores (2 per possible treatment) are needed. Factorial designs are thus essentially two things:

1. The best in terms of information attainable since all possible combinations are examined, and
2. The most expensive to implement.

Finding 36 stores which are both comparable and willing to participate in an experiment is often impossible; and even if it were possible, it is a highly unmanageable experiment. Hence researchers tend to use less than full factorial designs. These designs, such as the so-called fractional factorial designs (Holland and Cravens, 1973; Green, 1974), require substantially less data than a full factorial design.

There are a massive number of nonfull factorial designs which are commonly used. All of these designs involve a "trick": in order to simplify the problem, we assume something about the way the influencing variables affect the dependent variable. Some of the most common are as follows:

1. *Independent factor testing.*   In this method, we assume the factors (influencing variables) all affect the dependent variable separately. Hence we can separately use four stores to check on the effect of advertising, three stores to check packaging, and three stores to check color for a total of ten instead of 36 stores.
2. *Orthogonal designs.*   If it is possible to assume that certain interactions do not occur (e.g., advertising and color do not interact), subsets of the factorial array can often be used to estimate the direct effects of the influencing variables.
3. *"Logical" designs.*   In many cases, it is relatively easy to eliminate several combinations as either infeasible technically (for example, a machine which is inexpensive, has high output, and produces high-quality products), unappealing intuitively (plain packaging with a high fashion appeal item), or infeasible politically (e.g., company policy is to produce high quality products; the boss likes TV advertising, etc.). Hence we can reduce many apparent factorial problems to testing of a small number of feasible combinations.
4. *Latin square.*   Latin square designs apply when two factors are involved. For example, in studying three package designs, we may wish to use actual store testing. We may also feel that store sales change over time due to seasonal demand variation. Since recruiting stores is very difficult, we attempt to use as few as possible. The Latin square "trick" is twofold. First, assume (a) that there is no interaction between the factors (often a reasonable assumption) and (b) that there is no carry-over effect; that is, sales in one period do not influence sales in the next. Then use only three stores over three time periods by cycling each package through each store (Table 7–2). This allows estimation of both the time effect and the package design effect. A major problem with Latin square designs when one factor is time is

TABLE 7–2
Latin square design

Time	Store		
	1	*2*	*3*
1	A	B	C
2	B	C	A
3	C	A	B

where
A = package design A
B = package design B
C = package design C

the no-carry-over assumption, which is clearly inappropriate for any product which either can be stockpiled (e.g., canned fruit) or satisfies a demand for a long time period (e.g., a car).

Summary. Developing an ability to design successful experiments requires a combination of logic, perseverance, and experience (plus a nontrivial amount of luck). Cookbook approaches are useful only in formulating a basic design. Still in designing an experiment, there are a variety of considerations including the following:

Always have a control group or result to serve as a baseline since absolute results are usually meaningless.

Choose a criterion variable which is both measurable and translatable to market results. The variable chosen to be measured during an experiment has to be both readily measurable and relevant. Awareness may be measurable but not closely related to market results; actual sales in stores are impractical to measure. For this reason, intermediate measures such as attitude are often used.

Calibrate before the experiment so that the translation from the experimental criterion variable (e.g., attitude) to the likely market result (e.g., share) is well established.

Carefully consider all factors which might influence results including decision variables (price, advertising, etc.), personal characteristics (age, income, values, etc.), media exposure, product usage, and exogenous influences (competitive activity, general economic conditions, etc.). Then separate these into the following:

1. Those which will be ignored.
2. Those which will be controlled for (meaning each treatment group will be matched in terms of these variables).

3. Those which will be monitored to see if they were important after the fact.
4. Those which will be manipulated in the design.

Be careful not to assume that the result of a one-shot treatment (e.g., price, ad copy) will be repeated with multiple exposure. Competitive reaction and boredom will both tend to affect results if a marketing program is continued over time. On the other hand, several exposures to certain promotions may be necessary before the promotion has an impact.

If you want to measure the effect of a particular factor/variable, make sure that it (a) varies (if I only expose subjects to regular cigarettes, I can't assess the effect of filters on preference) *and (b) varies in such a way that its variation is not perfectly related to the variation of other factors.* If all low price products were also late entries in the market, it is impossible to know whether their share is a function of late entry or price.

Be aware that the experiment itself may influence behavior by, for example, heightening awareness on the part of respondents. Even the time of day at which the experiment occurs may influence the results. (Postlunch studies about food will differ from prelunch studies, etc.)

Laboratory experiments

Most people's notion of experiments comes from the natural sciences where laboratories are used to tightly control conditions. In lab experiments we can control the angle at which a marble hits a wall to find out the angle of incidence equals the angle of reflection. Lab experiments are also commonly used in dealing with animals, and many psychologists are especially fond of rats. Unfortunately consumers and businesses are both more likely to realize they are being observed and to refuse to participate than a marble or a rat. (Only on New Year's Eve do most people get sufficiently interested in cheese to crawl through a maze to get it.) In fact, lab experiments are difficult to use for a number of reasons including the following:

"Normal" people may refuse to participate, leaving the sample stocked with "weirdos."
Those people who participate may be more likely to game-play than respond normally.
There may be such a tremendous number of variables of interest that a manageable design for separating all their effects is impossible. As-

sume you believed there were eight key variables, each with three possible levels. This would produce $3^8 = 6,561$ possible combinations and hence potential treatments. Unless simplifying assumptions can be made so that less than full factorial designs are employed, this is an essentially hopeless situation.

Lab conditions may be sufficiently different from the "real world" that laboratory results do not accurately reflect real-world results. Often this is a difference of degree, not kind, however. For example, in a lab setting everyone may see the test ad, while if the same ad ran on television, only 20 percent of viewers might see it with the other 80 percent busy sleeping, talking, reading, getting a snack, or going to the bathroom. Hence it is especially crucial in the case of lab experiments to calibrate the results so that a given lab result can be translated into a useful prediction of market results.

An example. An example of a laboratory experiment concerning soft drink preference (Bass, Pessemier, and Lehmann, 1972) is instructive. This experiment involved 264 students and secretaries (your basic convenience sample) who participated in a study over a three-week period. Part of the study involved filling out questionnaires at four points during the three-week period. The other basic part of the experiment consisted of subjects selecting soft drinks on 12 occasions. All soft drinks were in 12-ounce cans and served cold. The eight soft drinks themselves were selected to reflect two dimensions: flavor and calories (Figure 7–2). As

FIGURE 7–2
Brands in soft drink experiment

Calories	Flavor	
	Cola	Lemon-Lime
Nondiet	Coke Pepsi	7-Up Sprite
Diet	Tab Diet Pepsi	Like Fresca

part of the experiment, subjects were denied the opportunity to purchase Coke on the fifth occasion. The purpose of this was to see if those who had bought Coke in the previous period would switch to the most similar brand, Pepsi. The results are in Table 7–3. The obvious conclusion from this is that the majority of individuals did indeed switch to Pepsi when Coke was out of stock.

TABLE 7–3
Percent switching from coke to each brand

	Coke	7-Up	Tab	Like	Pepsi	Sprite	Diet Pepsi	Fresca	Sample (n)
Average switching in periods 1–2, 2–3, 3–4 ..	48	16	2	6	15	6	2	5	239
Period 4–5 switching	x	22	2	3	53	13	3	5	64

Field experiments

Field experiments are the opposite of lab experiments on the realism scale. By moving the experiment to the real world, many of the problems based on the artificial nature of lab experiments are reduced. As a corollary, field experiments tend to be concerned with aggregate and objective data (such as sales) rather than individual and subjective data (such as attitudes, etc.).

In solving the artificiality problem, field experiments pay a heavy price. One of the major detriments is cost in terms of money, time, and aggravation. Field experiments such as test markets in two cities run budgets of $500,000 routinely and require a minimum of six months to complete.

The other major problem with field experiments is the lack of control. I can show an ad on TV but I can't control who watches it. Similarly I can cut price 5 cents but can't control competitive activity. It would be hard to tell the effect of a price cut if simultaneously one competitor introduced a new product, a second dropped an old product, a third ran a major coupon special, and a fourth doubled advertising. Such events often happen without planning, but companies are likely to do anything possible to confuse test markets in order to deny useful information to their competitors.

Natural experiments

The standard view of an experiment is the situation in which a researcher assigns subjects to treatments in either a random or systematic manner. While this is possible in lab experiments, it is difficult in field settings. (How do I convince Mr. Smith of 123 Maple Street that he must watch channel 7 at 7:30 Monday night?) The concept of a natural experiment is to allow subjects to choose which treatment they receive. For example, some people will have been exposed to ads and some not. To measure the effect of an ad, we simply observe (after the fact) the difference in behavior between those who happened to see the ad and those who did not see it. Put differently, performing a natural experiment is treating data as though it were the output of an experiment.

The advantage of a natural experiment is that the artificial nature of a controlled experiment is circumvented. The disadvantage is that interpretation becomes a serious problem. Often the characteristic which led the subject to select a particular treatment is related to the criterion variable. Put differently, an important covariate may exist. For example, those who saw an ad may have been exposed to the ad because they sought it out and hence their likelihood of buying the product after the ad is greater not because of the effect of the ad but because of greater prior interest. Still post hoc experimentation is a very useful tool.

An example. To see how a natural experiment works, consider the issue of which media, TV or magazine, is more effective in increasing perceived knowledge of a new small car. It is possible to design either a lab or field experiment and control advertising exposure to examine the effect of advertising exposure on perceived knowledge. Such experiments, however, tend to be either unrealistic or expensive.

An alternative approach is to examine the perceived knowledge of subjects based on their actual exposure. In this case, subjects were asked their perceived knowledge (on a ten-point scale) of a new car both before and after the presentation of a major introductory campaign. The subjects were also asked to report which magazines they read and which television shows they viewed. By using the actual media plan, a potential advertising exposure measure was established (Lehmann, 1977). While this measures potential rather than actual exposure (I may read a magazine and skip the ads), this objective measure seemed preferable to self-reported advertising exposure, which can be expected to be both inaccurate and contaminated by attitudes. Based on the advertising exposure measures, 622 subjects were divided into nine categories. Next the average change in perceived knowledge was calculated for each of the nine possible combinations of TV and magazine advertising exposure. The average changes and number of subjects in each cell are shown in Table 7–4.

TABLE 7–4

Magazine advertising exposure	TV advertising exposure		
	Low	Medium	High
Low	1.68 (72)	1.32 (74)	1.90 (61)
Medium	1.19 (66)	1.50 (78)	1.61 (65)
High	1.89 (58)	2.30 (84)	2.70 (64)

Source: Donald R. Lehmann, "Responses to Advertising a New Car," *Journal of Advertising Research,* vol. 17 (August 1977), p. 25.

Ignoring issues of statistical significance and "fancy" anaytical procedures, these results seem to indicate three interesting findings:

1. More exposure generally means a larger increase in perceived knowledge. The exception to this is the low-low group.
2. Both TV and magazine advertising seem to contribute (at approximately equal levels) to increased knowledge. Since the budget was split about 50 : 50, this suggests (albeit weakly) that both media were about equally effective.
3. Even low-exposure people became noticeably more knowledgeable, presumably due to word of mouth discussion, and so forth.

A major problem exists with these results. The problem (common to all natural experiments) is that other variables are uncontrolled. Hence it is possible that, for example, all high-income people are in the high magazine–low TV exposure cell. Hence the results in this cell could be as much or more attributable to the effect of income (and its covariates, such as education) as to advertising exposure. This problem of uncontrolled variables which are related to the measured/key variables—often called covariates—makes simple analysis of the results dangerous. Dealing with covariates requires analytical procedures (such as the brilliantly named analysis of covariance, which is essentially multiple regression) beyond the scope of this chapter. It is interesting to note, however, that in this case employing "sophisticated" analytical procedures to control for the effect of these covariates left the findings essentially the same.

MATHEMATICAL MODELING

Mathematical modeling is often considered to be separate from marketing research. Models are commonly relegated to management science groups, which in turn are maintained as tokens which assure someone that "we really want to do things right." This banishment is partially deserved, since many modelers and models are sufficiently obtuse and/or naive that they are fairly useless. Nonetheless, models have a useful role to play in marketing research. The purpose of this short section is primarily to suggest that models are appropriate for use in marketing research.

Model development requires both theory and data. Hence during the development stage, models are a user rather than a source of data. Once developed, however, models can be used to generate data under various "what if" scenarios. As such they are essentially used as market simulators.

Probability models

The ancestral roots of many models of market behavior lie in a collection of probabilistic models (Massy, Montgomery, and Morrison, 1970).

These models were originally developed at the individual consumer level to explain brand choice, and can be classified into three major categories: zero-order models, first-order (Markov) models, and second- and higher-order models.

Zero-order models. These models maintain that absent any disturbance in the market, a consumer's likelihood of purchasing each of a set of brands is fixed. Hence if there are three brands and my probabilities of choosing the three brands are .7, .2, and .1, I could simulate a particular future purchase by drawing a random number and accordingly assigning a brand choice. While this would not exactly match individual behavior, aggregating across people might well approximate total/average behavior.

First-order (Markov) models. Probably the most "famous" probabilistic models involve the assumption that purchase last period gives some information about likely purchase next period. These models were very widely used in the early 1960s; and even though they fell into disfavor, examining a Markov model is instructive.

Consider the following situation. A brand currently has a 20 percent market share. There are only two sources of business: retaining people who bought the brand last time and getting people who bought some other brand last time to try the brand this time. Assuming I project a 70 percent retention rate among current users and a 25 percent trial rate among current nonusers, what will the brand's period share be?

To see what would happen, I can draw a tree which represents possible purchase patterns (Figure 7–3). Next we observe that there are only two

FIGURE 7–3

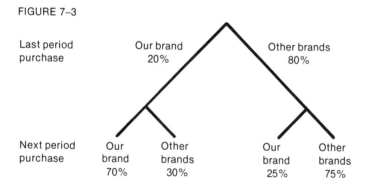

Last period purchase	Our brand 20%		Other brands 80%	
Next period purchase	Our brand 70%	Other brands 30%	Our brand 25%	Other brands 75%

sources of business: "repeaters" and "switch-inners." We expect to get (Old buyer share) · (percent remaining loyal) = 20 percent · 70 percent = 14 percent of the market from repeat buyers. Similarly we expect to get (Buyers of other brands) · (percent switch-in) = 80 percent · 25 percent = 20 percent of the market from switch-ins. Thus we would project a 14 percent + 20 percent = 34 percent share for next period. This kind of projection is both interesting in its own right and informative in that it clearly indicates the two possible sources of business: repeat business (loyal customers) and triers. It also suggests how, by varying the repeat and switch-in rates, that market share is likely to be altered. The methodology can be easily extended to multiple periods and more than three brands. Unfortunately, multiperiod extensions tend to be unreliable.

Second- and higher-order models.   Second- and higher-order models assume that purchase next period is related to not only purchase in the last period but also in the period before that, and so forth. The best known of these models are "learning models" of the type presented by Kuehn (1962). Actually learning is a somewhat misleading term, since the individual consumer is not learning anything by using the product; rather the researcher is learning about the consumer's preferences as more evidence is collected.

Marketing mix models

A large variety of models are available which attempt to tie marketing decision variables to actual market results. Currently one of the most widely considered of these models is the Hendry System (Butler and Butler, 1970, 1971; Kalwani and Morrison, 1977). Based on the twin notions that (*a*) choice among brands is dependent on attributes of the brands and (*b*) consumers are maximally uncertain about choice between similar brands, this system for evaluating marketing decisions is being utilized at a number of leading companies including General Foods and Lever Brothers.

A variety of other models have received considerable attention (Montgomery and Weinberg, 1973). Some of these are the following:

1. ADBUDG, developed by John Little (1970) to aid in budgeting advertising.
2. N. W. AYER's program for evaluating consumer packaged goods' introductory campaigns (Claycamp and Liddy, 1969).
3. BRANDAID, a program for evaluating marketing mix strategies (Little, 1972).
4. CALLPLAN, for allocation of salesperson's time (Lodish, 1971) to accounts.
5. DETAILER, for allocating selling effort across products and over time (Montgomery, Silk, and Zaragoza, 1971).
6. GEOLINE, a program for sales territory realignment (Hess and Samuels, 1971).
7. MEDIAC, for selecting advertising media (Little and Lodish, 1969).
8. SPRINTER III for projecting and analyzing introductory test market results for frequently purchased consumer products (Urban, 1970).

These models and their successors as well as in-company designed models provide another major tool for marketing researchers. Recent renewed interest in modeling (Bass, 1975; Herniter, 1974, 1975) suggests these models may become more central to marketing research in the future.

SUMMARY

A variety of approaches are available for collecting data. None is always best, and all have some value. The purpose of this chapter has been to briefly introduce some alternatives to surveys. The real issue, however, is not which method is best, but rather for a given problem, which combination of methods is most likely to contribute to the solution of the problem. The choice of method(s) may depend on the ability to translate study results into action based on experience with the approach. However, the choice of method should not be based on a prior doctrinaire notion of what is the "right" way to do research.

PROBLEMS

1. Assume I ran an experiment and got the following results:

	Treatment				
	1	2	3	4	5
Premeasure	x(10)		x(11)	x(9)	x(10)
Exposure to ad			x		x
Exposure to cents off coupon	x	x			x
Postmeasure	x(14)	x(13)	x(13)	x(11)	x(16)

   a. Estimate the effects of the ad and the coupon.
   b. What assumptions did you make in (a)?
   c. Change one of your assumptions and see if the results change.
2. The market research department of brand A ran an experiment involving a promotion and got the following results:

First purchase	Second purchase	
	A	B
Test group		
A	.90	.10
B	.15	.85
Control group		
A	.80	.20
B	.15	.85

Assuming brand A has a 20 percent share currently, interpret the results.

3. Write down a model of how you think people go about buying beer.

4. Get a group of friends together. Have them discuss beer purchasing. Summarize the discussion.

5. The sales levels in each of the two weeks following distribution of cents-off redeemable coupons were as follows:

	Sales after distribution	
Coupon	1st week	2d week
5¢ off one package	20	0
10¢ off on purchase of second package	50	10
10¢ off one package	40	40
20¢ off one package	90	70

The coupon distributions were made several months apart to allow the effects of previous coupons to die out before the next coupon was distributed.

What can you conclude about the difference in sales due to the coupons?

6. In the Yuk market, there are two major brands: Awful and Bad. Currently their shares are 40 percent and 30 percent respectively. Traditionally, the percentage of people who repeat purchase these brands from one period to the next has been 80 percent and 70 percent respectively. Also, 80 percent of the users of minor brands in one period purchase a minor brand in the following period. If a minor brand purchaser in a previous period does not buy a minor brand, s/he is equally likely to purchase Awful and Bad. Similarly purchases of Awful, who are not repeat purchasers, are equally likely to purchase Bad or a minor brand. However, purchasers of Bad that don't repeat purchase are twice as likely to buy Awful as any of the minor brands. What will be the market shares next period?

7. Assume you have 100 samples of a particular product which you wish to measure the ignition point of given different air temperature and humidity conditions. How would you proceed?

8. You have been assigned to find out which of three advertising campaigns, which of three package designs, and which of four names are best for a particular new detergent. How would you proceed given—

    a. A budget of $5,000 and one month.

    b. A budget of $30,000 and three months.

    c. A budget of $500,000 and one year.

BIBLIOGRAPHY

Banks, Seymour. *Experimentation in Marketing.* New York: McGraw-Hill, 1965.

Bass, Frank M. "The Theory of Stochastic Preference and Brand Switching." *Journal of Marketing Research,* vol. 11 (February 1974), pp. 1–20.

———; Pessemier, Edgar A.; and Lehmann, Donald R. "An Experimental Study of Relationships between Attitudes, Brand Preference, and Choice." *Behavioral Science,* vol. 17 (November 1972), pp. 532–41.

Bellenger, Danny N.; Bernhardt, Kenneth L.; and Goldstucker, Jac L. *Qualitative Methods in Marketing.* Chicago: American Marketing Association, 1976.

Butler, David H., and Butler, B. F. *Hendro Dynamics, Fundamental Laws of Consumer Dynamics,* chap. I. Monograph, The Hendry Corporation, August 1970.

———, and Butler, B. F. *Hendro Dynamics: Fundamental Laws of Consumer Dynamics,* chap. II. Monograph, The Hendry Corporation, 1971.

Calder, Bobby J. "Focus Groups and the Nature of Qualitative Marketing Research." *Journal of Marketing Research,* vol. 14 (August 1977), pp. 353–64.

Campbell, Donald T., and Stanley, Julian C. *Experimental Designs for Research.* Chicago: Rand-McNally, 1966.

Claycamp, Henry J., and Liddy, Lucien E. "Prediction of New Product Performance: An Analytical Approach." *Journal of Marketing Research,* vol. 4 (November 1969), pp. 414–420.

Green, Paul E. "On the Design of Choice Experiments Involving Multifactor Alternatives." *Journal of Consumer Research,* vol. 1 (September 1974), pp. 61–68.

Herniter, Jerome D. "A Comparison of the Entropy Model and the Hendry Model." *Journal of Marketing Research,* vol. 11 (February 1974), pp. 21–29.

———. "An Entropy Model of Brand Purchase Behavior." *Journal of Marketing Research,* vol. 10 (November 1973), pp. 361–75.

Hess, Sidney W., and Samuels, Stuart A. "Experiences with a Sales Districting Model: Criteria and Implementation." *Management Science,* vol. 18 (December 1971), pp. P41–P54.

Holland, Charles W., and Cravens, David W. "Fractional Factorial Experimental Designs in Marketing Research." *Journal of Marketing Research,* vol. 10 (August 1973), pp. 270–76.

Kalwani, Manohar U., and Morrison, Donald G. "A Parsimonious Description of the Hendry System." *Management Science,* vol. 23 (January 1977), pp. 467–77.

Kerlinger, Fred N. *Foundations of Behavioral Research,* 2d ed. New York: Holt, Rinehart and Winston, 1973.

Kuehn, Alfred A. "Demonstration of a Relationship between Psychological Factors and Brand Choice." *Journal of Business,* vol. 36 (April 1963), pp. 237–41.

Lehmann, Donald R. "Responses to Advertising a New Car." *Journal of Advertising Research,* vol. 17 (August 1977), pp. 23–32.

Little, John D. C., "BRANDAID: An On-Line Marketing-Mix Model." Working Paper No. 586-72. Alfred P. Sloan School of Management, M.I.T., 1972.

———, "Models and Managers: The Concept of a Decision Calculus." *Management Science,* vol. 16 (April 1970), pp. B466–B485.

———, and Lodish, Leonard M. "A Media Planning Calculus." *Operations Research,* vol. 17 (January–February 1969), pp. 1–35.

Lodish, Leonard M. "CALLPLAN: An Interactive Salesman's Call Planning System." *Management Science,* vol. 18 (December 1971), pp. P25–P40.

Massy, William F.; Montgomery, David B.; and Morrison, Donald G. *Stochastic Models of Buying Behavior.* Cambridge: M.I.T. Press, 1970.

Montgomery, David B.; Silk, Alvin J.; and Zaragoza, Carlos E. "A Multiple-Product Sales Force Allocation Model." *Management Science,* vol. 18 (December 1971), pp. P3–P24.

———, and Weinberg, Charles B. "Modeling Marketing Paenomena: A Managerial Perspective." *Journal of Contemporary Business,* vol. 2 (Autumn 1973), pp. 17–43.

Sellitz, Claire. *Research Methods in Social Relations.* New York: Holt, Rinehart and Winston, 1959.

Urban, Glen L. "SPRINTER Mod. III: A Model for the Analysis of New Frequently Purchased Consumer Products." *Operations Research,* vol. 18 (September–October 1970), pp. 805–54.

Webb, Eugene J.; Campbell, Donald T.; Schwartz, Richard D.; and Sechrest, Lee. *Unobtrusive Measures.* Chicago: Rand-McNally, 1966.

8

Major research suppliers

The purpose of this chapter is to expose readers to the real data sources—suppliers. The number of suppliers is enormous. What this chapter does, therefore, is to concentrate on the major sources, especially those which apply to consumer packaged goods. The reasons for this focus are (*a*) research suppliers have concentrated on packaged goods, and hence their services are fairly extensively developed, and (*b*) the information on them is widely available. Also, by examining the services offered by these suppliers, an understanding can be reached of the kinds of services that are perceived as valuable.

It is important to understand that this chapter is not an endorsement or advertisement. Many excellent suppliers are not discussed here. Moreover, the information is presented largely as it is given to prospective clients by the suppliers themselves. Hence editorializing is minimized. Suffice it to say that there are enough war stories around so that before using one of these services, it makes sense to talk to some past users.

A. C. NIELSEN

As the largest research supplier (1975 sales topped $200 million), the choice of A. C. Nielsen for the first topic is obvious. Nielsen's specialty is syndicated services, meaning it signs up clients in advance for a period of time (i.e., one year) and provides a service to a number of clients simultaneously. Nielsen offers numerous services which are described in this section.

Retail audits

By far the biggest part of the Nielsen portfolio are their auditing services. There are four major reporting groups:

Food (grocery products).

Drugs (toiletry and proprietary drugs).

Mass merchandiser (discount stores).

Alcoholic beverages.

The heart of the system is in-store audits. Every two months an auditor (there are over 500 of them) arrives at each store in the sample and records——

Beginning inventory.

Ending inventory.

Purchases.

Price at date of audit plus special prices (if any).

Distribution (if stocked and levels).

Deals (factory packs).

Local advertising.

Displays.

Total sales (all products).

In addition, major media advertising (newspaper, magazines, network TV, and spot TV) is also monitored. Hence for each brand, sales are estimated as shown in Figure 8–1. The results are then aggregated across stores to form regional and national statistics which are reported bimonthly. The standard areas and breakdowns are shown in Figure 8–2. Breakdowns are available on any other level the client requires (i.e., his/her own sales district), albeit at lesser precision and greater cost. While the accuracy of national share data is quite good, the accuracy of regional and other special breakdowns is much lower.

The audit period actually runs over several weeks. Auditing begins about two weeks before the end of the bimonthly period and continues two weeks after the next one starts. Hence the auditing cycle looks like the following:

bruary–March period

	First (prior) audit				Second (post) audit		
	Jan. 10,	Jan. 11,	. . . ,	Feb. 12	Mar. 10,	Mar. 11, . . . ,	Apr. 12
ore group 1	x				x		
ore group 2		x				x	
ore group 3			·			·	
·							
·			·		·		
·				·		·	
re group n				x			x

FIGURE 8-1

Principles of Nielsen retail index auditing ("Alpha" brand of spot remover—3 ounces in Super X Market)

	For June–July	
	Packages	Value
Inventory:		
May 30	114	
July 30	93	
Change	21	
Purchases:		
From manufacturer (1 order)	12	$ 3.72
From wholesalers (4 orders)	48	15.00
Total	60	$18.72
Consumer sales:		
Packages	81	
Price, per package		$ .39
Dollars, total		31.59
Adv. 1 2 3 4 5		
✗ 7 8 9		
Display X		Selling price, 39¢
		Special price, 35¢

Source: A. C. Nielsen Company, *Nielsen Retail Index Services,* 1975. Reprinted with permission.

Sales in the February–March bimonthly period are thus a "smoothed" average of sales January 10–March 10, January 11–March 11, and so forth, through February 12–April 12. This average can be an annoying problem in certain modeling endeavors, especially in estimating the effectiveness of advertising and promotion (Shoemaker and Pringle, 1977).

The sample used for the audit is a set panel of stores. Stores are recruited and induced to participate based on (*a*) an appeal for cooperation in the spirit of learning, (*b*) information provided to the stores about trends in business[1], and (*c*) monetary compensation (an above the table payment).

Until 1976, 1,600 stores were included in the grocery index. These stores were grouped into five categories and selected disproportionately to reflect the sales volume accounted for by 5 store types rather than just their number—see Figure 8–3. In early 1976, the sample of stores was changed (*a*) to reflect changes in the market and (*b*) to cut cost. The new sample of 1,300 stores (fewer stores means less cost) differed mainly in

---

[1] Examples include the annual reviews of retail grocery store trends and retail drugstore trends which report a variety of sales and distribution statistics.

Data breakdowns available

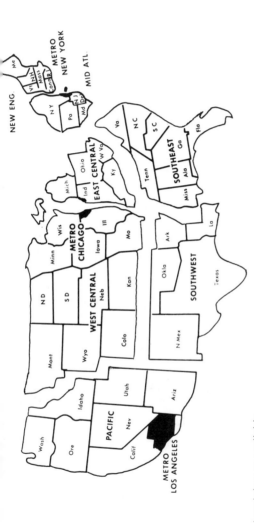

Territory	Client areas		County sizes	Brand, type, and size	Store types	
					Drug	Grocery
New England	1	10	Metro New York	All other brands	Chain (4 or more)	Chain (4 or more)
Metro New York	2	11	Metro Chicago	Private label:	Independents	Independents
Mid. Atlantic	3	12	Metro Los Angeles	D	Large ($300M and over)	Large (over $500M)
East Central	4	13	A counties	C	Medium ($150M to $300M)	Chain and large combined
Metro Chicago	5	14	B counties	B	Small (under $150M)	Medium ($100 to $500M)
West Central	6	15	C counties	A		Small (under $100M)
South East	7	16	D counties	Client brand		
South West	8	17				
Metro Los Angeles	9	18				
Rem. Pacific						

Source: A. C. Nielsen Company, *Nielsen Retail Index Services, 1975.* Reprinted with permission.

FIGURE 8–3
Demonstration of disproportionate sampling concept (national NFI sample used as an example)

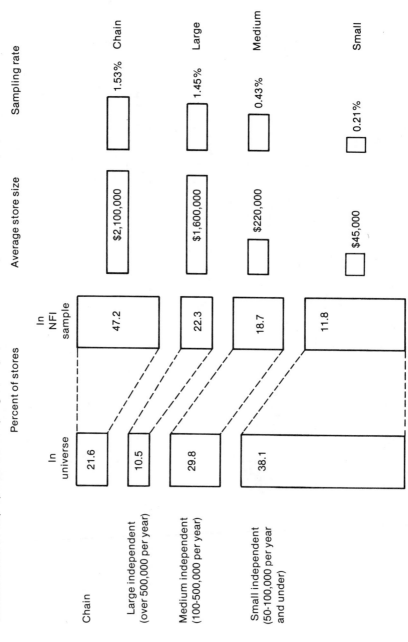

that A&P stores were now included, and many "ma and pa" stores were eliminated. For a single two-month period, both the old and new stores were monitored. This was supposed to provide a means of assurance that the sample change did not affect the results. For most brands, the national results were in fact stable (i.e., the share in the old sample was 29.1 versus 28.9 in the new sample). For some brands, however, national shares changed by three or four points. Since a difference of this size means a lot in terms of profits (and jobs retained or lost), a big question arose as to which share was correct.

The information collected by the audits is reported to clients in a variety of ways, with cost depending on the way the reports are made. Basic reports are computerized sheets on which are included the following:

1. Industry sales,
2. Market share of—
   a. Client.
   b. Major competitors.
   c. Family brands (i.e., A&P).
   d. An "all other" category.

Supplemental reports break the results by region, distribution (based both on the percent of stores carrying the product and on a weighted percent which reflects total volume of stores in which the brand is carried, often called ACV-all commonity volume), advertising (absolute level and share), displays, special prices, deals, and so forth.

Costs vary widely depending on the reports required. The ball-park annual cost for one product category is in the high five figures (i.e., $60–$90,000).

Other services

Neilsen has many other services built around the basic auditing service. These include the following:

Test marketing services: Major markets.   Thirty-two cities are available for special audits during introductory campaigns with audits available on a monthly, ad hoc basis. The cities are shown in Table 8–1. In addition to audits, Nielsen also does consumer surveys (usually by phone) including standard awareness, trial, and usage data such as shown in Figure 8–4.

Data markets.   In five smaller cities, Nielsen not only collects data but will handle the actual placement of products in stores for clients. The cities are Boise, Idaho; Green Bay, Wisconsin; Portland, Maine; Savannah, Georgia; and Tuscon, Arizona.

214

TABLE 8-1
Nielsen major markets

	Percent of U.S. population (Jan. 1, 1976)	Percent of U.S. grocery sales (1975)	Percent of U.S. drug sales (1975)
Metro areas			
New York	7.5	6.9	5.9
Los Angeles	4.7	4.9	5.8
Chicago	3.6	3.4	4.8
Other areas with population larger than 2.0% of U.S.:			
Philadelphia	3.6	3.7	3.2
Baltimore–Washington, D.C.	3.2	3.2	4.3
Boston	3.2	3.2	2.8
Detroit	2.9	3.1	3.7
San Francisco–Oakland	2.3	2.6	3.2
Cleveland	2.1	2.3	1.9
Pittsburgh	2.0	1.8	1.7
Areas with populations between 1.9% and 1.0% of U.S.:			
Dallas–Ft. Worth	1.5	1.6	1.6
Miami–Ft. Lauderdale	1.4	1.8	1.9
Minneapolis–St. Paul	1.4	1.3	1.2
St. Louis	1.4	1.4	1.3
Atlanta	1.3	1.4	1.3
Cincinnati	1.3	1.2	1.1
Houston	1.3	1.5	1.2
Indianapolis	1.3	1.1	1.4
Seattle–Tacoma	1.1	1.3	1.3
Kansas City	1.0	.9	.9
Memphis	1.0	.9	.7
Milwaukee	1.0	.9	.8
Portland, Or.	1.0	1.2	1.0
Areas with populations under 1.0% of U.S.:			
Buffalo	.9	.9	.9
Denver	.9	.9	1.0
Nashville	.8	.9	.8
Phoenix	.8	.9	.9
Sacramento–Stockton	.8	.9	1.2
Birmingham–Anniston	.7	.7	.6
Charlotte	.7	.7	.7
Grand Rapids–Kalamazoo	.7	.8	.6
Louisville	.7	.6	.6
Albany–Schenectady–Troy	.6	.7	.5
Oklahoma City	.6	.6	.5
Omaha	.6	.5	.6
San Antonio	.6	.6	.5
Jacksonville	.5	.5	.7
Rochester	.4	.5	.5
Total major market areas	61.4	62.3	63.6

Source: Reprinted with permission of A. C. Nielsen Company, New York, 1978.

FIGURE 8–4
"Hypothetical" major market interview

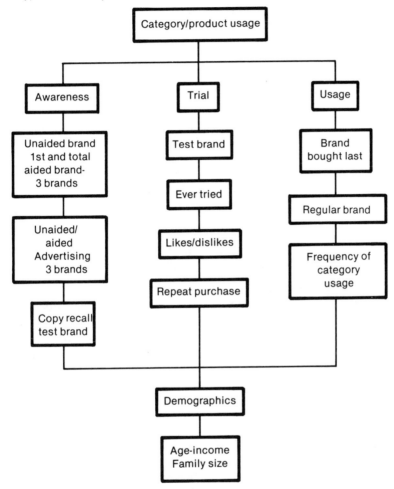

Source: Reprinted with permission of A. C. Nielsen Company, New York, 1978.

Custom audits.   If you're willing to pay, Nielsen will audit just about
anything.

Intelligence.   A service designed to alert clients to new products as
they are introduced and how they do in their early stages.

Media research.   Perhaps the most famous of Nielsen services is the
Nielsen ratings of TV shows. These ratings are based on two samples
which are queried differently. The first sample is queried automatically by phone lines via an electronic device called a Storage Instan-
taneous Audimeter (SIA). These devices are attached to the TV, and

record what channel was turned on at what time. The second sample is monitored by a less sophisticated electronic device (Recordimeter) plus a diary (Audilog). This log allows conclusions to be drawn about who (age, sex, etc.) was watching a given show.

Nielsen Clearing House. More of a marketing than a marketing research service, Nielsen offers to do the work on redeeming store coupons by collecting redeemed coupons and simultaneously paying retailers and billing manufacturers, as well as reporting on the results.

Neodata. This is essentially a magazine label printing business employing over 1,000 people and producing over 350 million labels per year.

Petroleum Information Corporation. An information service on oil and gas production of US and Canadian wells.

Worldwide. Nielsen has divisions in 21 foreign countries, mainly in Europe.

SAMI

A subsidiary of Time, Inc., SAMI is a Nielsen competitor in the audit business. SAMI differs from Nielsen in that its audits are done at the wholesale rather than retail level. Specifically, warehouse withdrawals are monitored every four weeks. Results are then reported to the owners of the warehouses (food operators) and to individual manufacturers. Food operators receive reports every 12 weeks, while manufacturers may get reports every 4 weeks.

The basic SAMI data

Food operators' cooperation is solicited by promising (*a*) information and (*b*) cash. Currently 36 markets which account for about three fourths of total U.S. food sales are used. These markets are centered around major cities. The operators include chains, wholesalers, health and beauty aid rack operators, and frozen food warehousers. For example, in 1975 the participating operators in the Cincinnati/Dayton/Columbus area were the following:

A&P	March
Big Bear	Redi-Frog
Columbus Merchandise	Scot Lad
Creasey	Super Food Services
Fisher Foods	Super-Value
Kroger	White Villa
Liberal Markets	

Typically the operators included account for about 80 percent of the volume in the area. Hence one problem is obvious with SAMI (or Nielsen or any other auditing service, for that matter): if a product tends to do better (or worse) in the nonincluded areas or with the nonincluded operators, the SAMI report will be misleading at least as an absolute measure.

The product categories monitored by SAMI fall into four major categories:

1. *Dry grocery—food.*   Over 200 product categories including pancake mix, croutons, and canned shrimp are included.
2. *Refrigerated and frozen foods.*   About 80 categories including frozen pies, butter, and refrigerated pastries are monitored.
3. *Dry grocery—nonfood.*   About 75 categories from housecleaning compounds (e.g., scouring pads) and household supplies (e.g., cellophane tape, furniture polish, and insect repellents) to laundry supplies (e.g., liquid bleach), paper products (e.g., paper towels, aluminum foil), and soaps (e.g., bath additives, dishwasher detergents) are available.
4. *Health and beauty aids.*   The major categories include baby needs, deodorants, first aids, hair care needs, oral hygiene, proprietary remedies, shaving needs, and skin care aids. The 50 specific categories include roll-on deodorants, antacids, and suntan lotions.

In addition to these basic SAMI reports, in 1976 a new service called SARDI (*SA*MI *R*etail *D*istribution *I*ndex) was instituted. SARDI is based on the assumption that if a retail store makes a withdrawal of a product from a central warehouse during a given time period (usually four weeks), then the retail store stocks/distributes the products. By arranging with each food operator to provide store-by-store withdrawal data for a sample of retail stores (over 5,000 in total), an index of distribution is obtained.

Basic reports

Reports are made available to both food operators and manufacturers. The basic reports are as follows:

Food operators

Executive Review.   This report provides information on sales of the individual operator and the total market by product groups (Figure 8–5).

Item Detail Report.   Sales data in units (usually cases) by individual item (Figure 8–6).

Exception Report: Zero.   Items carried by at least three other operators but not by the operator receiving the report. This report is designed to alert operators to trends which they may have overlooked.

FIGURE 8-5. Food operator's Executive Review

SAMI 0000

ON PAGE		TOTAL MEASURED MARKET — VOLUME			FOOD OPERATOR — VOLUME			FOOD OPERATOR — SHARE OF MARKET		
		4 WK	12WK	52 WK	4 WK	12 WK	52 WK	4 WK	12 WK	52 WK
GRAND TOTAL	DOL	133W	400W	1.432W	11389M	34167M	128W	8.5%	8.5%	8.6%
	CAS	15394M	46182M	201W	1.350M	4.050M	20127M	8.8%	8.7%	10.0%
TOTAL GROCERY	DOL	103W	310W	1.169W	9.372M	28116M	105W	9.0%	9.0%	8.9%
	CAS	11854M	35562M	154W	991M	2.973M	16181M	8.3%	8.4%	10.5%
BABY FOOD 100	DOL	1.525M	4.575M	17741M	120M	360M	1534M	7.9%	7.8%	8.6%
	CAS	302M	906M	3.812M	15.000	45.000	257M	5.0%	5.0%	6.7%
CEREAL BABY FOOD 103	DOL	65.000	195M	735M	5.027	15.081	60.000	7.7%	7.7%	8.2%
	CAS	28.000	84.000	380M	2.450	7.350	34.500	8.8%	8.7%	9.1%
LESS THAN 3 PRIVATE LABELS										
JUICE BABY FOOD 104	DOL	123M	369M	1.434M	8.625	25.875	114M	7.0%	7.0%	8.0%
	CAS	27.117	81.351	356M	1.947	5.841	29.642	7.2%	7.1%	8.3%
LESS THAN 3 PRIVATE LABELS										
FORMULA BABY FOOD 105	DOL	385M	1.156M	4.143M	39.311	117M	480M	10.2%	10.5%	11.6%
	CAS	41.116	123M	303M	4.317	12.951	34.845	10.5%	10.5%	11.5%
STRAINED BABY FOOD 106	DOL	607M	1.822M	7.145M	46.163	138M	600M	7.6%	7.5%	8.4%
	CAS	144M	433M	1.922M	11.000	33.000	172M	7.9%	7.6%	9.8%
LESS THAN 3 PRIVATE LABELS										
JUNIOR BABY FOOD 107	DOL	330M	991M	4.138M	19.509	58.500	269M	5.9%	5.9%	6.5%
	CAS	59.091	177M	825M	3.653	10.959	56.500	6.2%	6.1%	6.9%
LESS THAN 3 PRIVATE LABELS										
MISC. BABY FOOD 199	DOL	13.640	40.920	144M	1.214	3.642	9.535	8.9%	8.9%	6.6%
	CAS	2.590	7.770	29.589	233	699	2.604	9.0%	9.0%	8.8%
BAKING MIXES 200	DOL	2.061M	6.183M	20191M	150M	450M	1.488M	7.3%	7.2%	7.4%
	CAS	267M	801M	2.738M	20.000	60.000	265M	7.6%	7.4%	9.7%
DESSERT BAKING MIXES 201	DOL	1.257M	3.771M	12514M	86.000	260M	838M	6.9%	6.8%	6.7%
	CAS	129M	389M	1.518M	11.000	33.000	125M	8.5%	8.4%	8.2%
PRIVATE LABEL	DOL	75.420	226M	798M	22.248	66.500	206M	29.6%	29.1%	25.8%
	CAS	9.963	29.889	98.901	2.977	8.931	25.771	29.9%	29.9%	26.1%
PVT LABEL $ SHARE OF F O VOL								25.9%	25.6%	24.6%
PIECRUST MIX 203	DOL	135M	408M	974M	9.134	27.204	61.000	6.9%	6.7%	6.3%
	CAS	17.307	51.921	133M	1.209	3.627	9.627	7.0%	7.0%	7.2%
PRIVATE LABEL	DOL	8.112	32.336	596M	1.014	5.042	24.516	12.5%	15.6%	4.1%
	CAS	1.128	3.384	68.760	130	490	9.025	11.5%	14.5%	13.1%
PVT LABEL $ SHARE OF F O VOL								11.1%	18.5%	40.1%

M = (x)00 000   W = 000 000

SAMI 0000

MARKETING AREA   ISSUE 119   REPORT NUMBER 119   PERIOD COVERED   INITIAL PERIOD   PAGE

FOOD OPERATOR ITEM DETAIL REPORT

PERIOD COVERED: AUG 02 - OCT 24, 1975   INITIAL PERIOD: OCT 26 - NOV 22, 1974   3508-08

	SIZE	PACK PER CASE	TOTAL MEASURED MARKET — CASE VOLUME 12 WEEKS	52 WEEKS	DOLLAR SHARE CATEGORY 12 WEEKS	52 WEEKS	FOOD OPERATOR CASE VOLUME 12 WEEKS	52 WEEKS	SHARE OF CASE VOLUME 12 WEEKS	52 WEEKS	UPC CONSUMER PACKAGE CODE	FOOD OPERATORS SHIPPING	NEW ITEM IN MARKET PERIOD ENDING
DETERGENTS													
TOTAL - DETERGENTS, HEAVY DUTY			46,228	640M	100.0%	100.0%	4,840	42,039	10.5%	6.6%		8	
TOTAL - PRIVATE LABEL			10,960	125M	20.8%	17.7%	3,877	24,342	35.4%	19.4%		8	
TOTAL - BOLD			1,165	16,099	3.1%	3.0%	36	848	3.1%	5.3%		8	
BOLD DETERGENT	20 OZ	24	242	3,199	.6%	.6%		145	.0%	4.5%	0-37000-90010	6	
BOLD DETERGENT	49 OZ	10	200	2,389	.5%	.4%			.0%	.0%	0-37000-90020	4	
BOLD DETERGENT 10C	49 OZ	10	289	4,212	.8%	.8%	12	237	4.2%	5.6%		7	
BOLD DETERGENT	84 OZ	6	409	6,232	1.1%	1.1%	24	466	5.9%	7.5%	0-37000-90030	*	
BOLD DETERGENT 25C	84 OZ	6	25	67	.1%	.0%			.0%	.0%		8	0411N
TOTAL - CHEER			2,153	24,802	5.2%	4.3%	60	1,315	2.8%	5.3%		8	
CHEER DETERGENT	20 OZ	24	248	4,677	.6%	.8%	19	90	.0%	1.9%	0-37000-90210	5	
CHEER DETERGENT	49 OZ	10	450	6,441	1.1%	1.1%		659	4.2%	10.2%	0-37000-90220	6	
CHEER DETERGENT 10C	49 OZ	10		5	1.0%	.0%			.0%	.0%		0	
CHEER DETERGENT	96 OZ	6	428	5,240	1.0%	.9%	22	394	5.1%	7.5%		8	
CHEER DETERGENT	17 1/2 OZ	3	1,027	8,439	2.5%	1.4%	19	172	1.9%	2.0%	0-37000-90240	8	0411N
TOTAL - WISK			7,207	96,956	16.0%	15.4%	142	3,429	2.0%	3.5%		8	
WISK DETERGENT LIQUID	16 OZ	24	477	11,361	1.1%	1.8%	47	516	9.9%	4.5%	0-11111-27024	8	
WISK DETERGENT LIQUID	32 OZ	12	1,887	16,801	4.2%	2.6%	7	440	.4%	2.6%	0-11111-27012	8	
WISK DETERGENT LIQUID 6C	32 OZ	12	327	10,065	.8%	1.6%	12	356	3.7%	3.5%		6	
WISK DETERGENT LIQUID 10C	32 OZ	12	96	2,026	.2%	.3%			.0%	.0%		*	
WISK DETERGENT LIQUID	64 OZ	6	907	5,450	2.0%	.9%	5	318	.6%	5.8%	0-11111-27006	6	
WISK DETERGENT LIQUID 12C	64 OZ	6	166	2,584	.4%	.4%			.0%	.0%		4	
WISK DETERGENT LIQUID 25C	64 OZ	6		10	.0%	.0%			.0%	.0%		0	
WISK DETERGENT LIQUID	128 OZ	4	536	13,339	1.2%	2.2%	59	600	11.0%	4.5%	0-11111-27005	8	0411D
WISK DETERGENT LIQUID 25C	128 OZ	4	2,345	21,451	5.1%	3.4%	6	614	.3%	3.3%		8	
WISK DETERGENT LIQUID 50C	128 OZ	4	466	13,869	1.0%	2.2%	6	585	1.3%	4.2%		6	
TOTAL - DASH			2,344	32,050	6.2%	5.9%	84	1,465	3.6%	4.6%		8	
DASH DETERGENT	24 OZ	24	499	310	.0%	.1%		240	.0%	.0%	0-37000-90310	0	
DASH DETERGENT	50 OZ	12	503	6,139	1.3%	1.2%	17		3.4%	3.9%	0-37000-90320	8	0411N
DASH DETERGENT 10C	50 OZ	12	122	6,842	1.3%	1.2%	19	367	3.8%	5.4%		6	
DASH DETERGENT 10 OZ BONUS	50 OZ	12		1,603	.3%	.3%			.0%	.0%		*	
DASH DETERGENT	157 OZ	4	37	859	.2%	.2%			.0%	.0%	0-37000-90330	8	
DASH DETERGENT 30C	157 OZ	4	504	6,730	1.3%	1.7%	21	306	4.2%	4.5%		8	
DASH DETERGENT	20 LB	2	679	9,567	1.8%	1.7%	27	552	4.0%	5.8%	0-37000-90340	8	
TOTAL - POWER PLUS			2,004	27,281	3.9%	4.4%	108	1,219	5.4%	4.5%		8	
POWER PLUS DETERGENT	84 OZ	6	249	3,666	.6%	.6%	11	224	4.4%	6.1%		8	

M=000   W=000,000

Source: © 1976 Selling Areas-Marketing, Inc., a subsidiary of Time, Inc. Reprinted by permission.

FIGURE 8-7. Top 500 report for food operators

MARKET   ISSUE 126-128   GROCERY   **RANK FOR** — RANKED ON $ **PAGE 1**

PERIOD COVERED APR 10 – JUL 02. 1976
INITIAL PERIOD JUL 05 – AUG 01. 1975

Item	Item Size	Pack Per Case	Rank 12 Week	Rank 4 Week	Rank 52 Week	Vol 12 Week	Vol 4 Week	Vol 52 Week	UPC Consumer Package Code	Food Oper. Ship	Start Issue
COLONIAL SUGAR CANE	5 LB	12	1	1	1	74.108	27.070	263.054	0-37000-40010	***	
CRISCO SHORTENING	48 OZ	12	2	4	2	31.204	9.239	131.489	0-37000-91220	6	
TIDE DETERGENT	49 OZ	10	3	2	4	38.937	13.485	132.406	0-37000-91220	6	
DOMINO SUGAR GRANULATED	5 LB	12	4	3	3	29.991	12.106	153.202	0-49200-04625	4	
STAR-KIST TUNA CHK LT	6 1/2	48	5	7	5	10.444	3.457	49.288	0-79100-00280	6	
WHITE GOLD SUGAR CANE	5 LB	12	6	5	30	20.562	9.277	41.838		***	122
KRAFT MAYONAISE	32 OZ	12	7	41	7	19.250	2.985	73.897	0-37600-13872	6	
SPAM LUNCH MEAT	12 OZ	24	8	9	9	11.702	3.526	39.440		6	
VAN CAMP BEANS W PORK	16 OZ	48	9	6	10	16.491	6.481	59.426	0-43000-70403	6	
MAXWELL HOUSE COF ELC PRK BAG	1 LB	12	10	8	8	12.603	4.034	57.279	0-43000-79480	6	
MAXWELL HOUSE COF INS	10 OZ	18	11	11	16	4.583	1.374	16.251	0-27000-86064	6 •	
SNOWDRIFT SHORTENING	48 OZ	12	12	10	6	14.369	5.239	70.696	0-27000-00404	6	
CRISCO OIL	48 OZ	8	13	42	13	17.756	3.571	63.571	0-43000-70300	6	
MAXWELL HOUSE COF REG BAG	1 LB	12	14	14	15	10.620	3.393	47.639	0-43000-70300	6	
BLUE PLATE MAYONAISE	32 OZ	12	15	12	11	15.507	5.656	61.596	0-27000-50123	6	
TIDE DETERGENT 25C	84 OZ	6	16	81	110	15.277	2.163	23.080		***	
MAXWELL HOUSE COF INS	6 OZ	24	17	23	17	4.001	1.198	17.694	0-43000-79420	6	
TIDE DETERGENT	20 OZ	24	18	18	18	12.840	4.483	53.048	0-37000-92100	6	
HUNT KETCHUP	32 OZ	12	19	13	22	17.005	6.936	65.986	0-27000-38258	6	
PAMPERS DIAPER TDLR	12 CN	18	20	21	27	6.276	2.127	23.019	0-37000-65641	7	
GODCHAUX SUGAR CANE	5 LB	12	21	221	23	11.406	1.000	39.697		***	
ARMOUR STAR SSG VIENNA	5 OZ	48	22	17	21	8.479	3.190	35.057	0-46000-01113	6	
OLE DIZ CHARCOAL BRIQUETS	10 LB	5	23	15	88	28.497	12.072	54.979	0-37000-60111	6	
PET MILK TALL	141/2	48	24	20	19	11.190	4.072	49.211	0-24000-01656	6	
CHARMIN TISSUE WHITE 4S	4 CN	24	25	28	20	8.939	2.954	38.929	0-44600-00103	6	
DEL MONTE TUNA CHK LT	6 1/2	48	26	38	31	5.920	1.583	21.168	0-37000-65351	5	
CLOROX BLEACH	64 OZ	8	27	33	26	37.739	11.851	149.747	0-42000-13100	5	
PAMPERS DIAPER DAY EX-SRBT	24 CN	12	28	29	36	8.507	1.870	18.278	0-37000-44010	7	
NORTHERN TISSUE WHITE 4S	4 CN	24	29	24	29	8.317	3.126	32.864	0-41259-21602	6	
PRINGLES POTATO CHIPS	9 OZ	18	30	27	60	8.332	3.229	23.510	0-36000-55850	6	
BAMA MAYONAISE	32 OZ	12	31	16	12	11.856	5.685	65.245	0-50000-01011	6	
HI DRI TOWEL ASST	1 CN	30	32	22	44	10.649	4.449	34.747		***	
CARNATION MILK TALL	141/2	48	33	31	24	9.242	3.501	44.398	0-24000-00410	6	
CHEF WAY OIL VEGETABLE	48 OZ	6	34	34	28	20.135	7.758	80.621	0-39400-00000	5	
DEL MONTE CATSUP JUG	32 OZ	12	35	32	40	12.702	4.969	46.509	0-37000-65111	6	
SHOWBOAT BEANS W PORK	141/2	24	36	44	106	20.530	6.497	52.089		5	
PAMPERS DIAPER DAYTIME	30 CN	12	37	45	32	4.429	1.396	19.645	0-28000-30090	7	
EAGLE BRAND MILK	15 OZ	24	38	25	47	7.933	3.667	28.633		6	
TASTERS CHOICE COF FR DR	8 OZ	18	39	46	35	2.071	.642	9.637		6	
DOUBLE Q SALMON PINK	8 OZ	48	40	76	41	2.570	.569	9.898	0-43000-70301	6	
MAXWELL HOUSE COF DRP BAG	1 LB	12	41	51	43	6.202	1.811	27.024	0-37000-65521	6	
PAMPERS DIAPER OVERNITE	12 CN	18	42	55	42	5.078	1.542	20.369	0-37000-91230	6	
TIDE DETERGENT	84 OZ	6	43	30	37	8.689	3.938	38.078		5	119

Source: © 1976 Selling Areas-Marketing, Inc., a subsidiary of Time, Inc. Reprinted by permission.

FIGURE 8-8. (SAMI Retail Distribution Index)

FOOD OPERATOR:

ISSUES COVERED: 123 - 125

CATEGORY: PIZZA FROZEN

% ACV DISTRIBUTION
A - 12WK MAX DIST 04/09/76

MARKET AREA:

PERIOD COVERED: 01/17/76 - 04/09/76

REPORT TYPE: STORE SIZE-$MILLIONS AND POPULATION DENSITY

DESCRIPTION	SIZE	PACK PER CASE	TOTAL MARKET	FOOD OPER	TOTAL MARKET STORE SIZE-$MILLIONS				POPULATION DENSITY			
					OVER 4 MIL	2-4 MIL	1-2 MIL	UNDER 1 MIL	CENTRL CITY	OTHER CENTRL	REMAIN METRO	NON METRO
PIZZA FROZEN		A	99	100	100	100	100	74	100	99	100	100
CELESTE		A	99	97	100	100	86	74	100	99	99	100
CELESTE FZ PIZZA CHEESE	20 OZ	12 A	93	97	99	92	50	74	100	97	96	100
CELESTE FZ PIZZA CHS-BAMB	8 OZ	12 A	74	0	74	80	43	0	65	80	74	63
CELESTE FZ PIZZA SAUSAGE	23 OZ	12 A	56	91	56	58	50	74	53	46	62	25
CELESTE FZ PIZZA SAUS-BAMB	9 OZ	12 A	62	97	61	66	36	0	65	79	57	35
CELESTE FZ PIZZA HMBGR-BAMB	9 1/4	12 A	22	69	24	17	36	0	0	47	17	0
CELESTE FZ PIZZA PEPPERONI	21 OZ	12 A	1	0	0	0	50	0	0	0	1	9
CELESTE FZ PIZZA PPRNI-BAMB	8 1/4	12 A	13	74	9	26	0	0	0	22	12	0
CELESTE FZ PIZZA DELUXE	26 OZ	12 A	35	0	36	34	50	26	18	25	38	81
CELESTE FZ PIZZA DELUXE	10 OZ	12 A	97	97	98	100	36	0	100	99	96	91

Data not available. To avoid disclosure, this symbol is used under all key accounts where only one food operator distributes the item. It also appears through out the report wherever back data is not available.

This report is confidential and is not available to the public. It has been distributed on a restricted basis pursuant to contract by Selling Areas-Marketing, Inc. for the sale and confidential use of the limited number of persons designated in such contract. All persons with access to this report, whether authorized or unauthorized are subject to liability for any unauthorized use, reproduction, publication or divulgence of this report or any portion thereof.

FIGURE 8-9. SAMI Standard Dollar Report

SAMI

MANUFACTURER NON-CONTRACT
CONTRACT NO.
MARKET AREA

CATEGORY COFFEE. REGULAR
ISSUE NUMBER 116
CURRENT 4 WK. PERIOD 07/05/75 - 08/01/75

UNITS DOLLAR VOLUME
CASE VOLUME
PERIOD COVERED 07/30/74 - 08/01/75

STANDARD DOLLAR REPORT	ITEM SIZE	PACK PER CASE	AVG SHELF PRICE	MEASURED CASE VOLUME 4 WEEKS	MEASURED CASE VOLUME 52 WEEKS	MEASURED DOLLAR SALES 4 WEEKS	MEASURED DOLLAR SALES 52 WEEKS	DOLLAR SHARE OF BRAND 4 WEEKS	DOLLAR SHARE OF BRAND 52 WEEKS	DOLLAR SHARE OF CATEGORY 4 WEEKS	DOLLAR SHARE OF CATEGORY 52 WEEKS	LG PKG PRC WEEKS	NEW IN/DROP ITEM MARKET ENDING
YUBAN COFFEE ALL PURPOSE	2 LB	12	2.068	675	6.204	16.752	190.655	30.611%	21.999%	1.197%	.971%	*	
YUBAN COFFEE REGULAR	2 LB	12	2.710	46	.377	1.496	12.447	2.734%	1.436%	.107%	.063%	*	
YUBAN COFFEE DRIP	2 LB	12	2.700	35	2.572	1.134	84.937	2.072%	9.801%	.081%	.432%	7	
YUBAN COFFEE ELECTRAMATIC	1 LB	24	1.374	232	3.918	7.648	130.937	13.975%	15.108%	.546%	.667%	6	
YUBAN COFFEE ELECTRAMATIC	2 LB	12	2.130	767	10.544	19.600	325.775	35.815%	37.590%	1.401%	1.658%	6	
FOLGERS				14.405	193.431	446.064	5.916.015	100.000%	100.000%	31.874%	30.116%	8	
FOLGERS COFFEE REG	8 OZ	24	.721	26	.410	450	7.052	.101%	.119%	.032%	.036%	8	
FOLGERS COFFEE REG	1 LB	24	1.297	2.385	22.585	74.262	710.901	16.645%	12.017%	5.305%	3.619%	* 8	
FOLGERS COFFEE REG	2 LB	12	2.604	1.039	24.027	32.469	747.589	7.297%	12.637%	2.230%	3.806%	8	
FOLGERS COFFEE DRIP	3 LB	8	3.821	1.448	20.109	44.262	589.614	9.923%	9.966%	3.163%	3.001%	8	
FOLGERS COFFEE DRIP	1 LB	24	1.300	1.529	14.073	47.717	443.029	10.697%	7.489%	3.410%	2.255%	8	
FOLGERS COFFEE DRIP	2 LB	12	2.624	826	15.670	26.013	485.829	5.832%	8.212%	1.859%	2.473%	8	
FOLGERS COFFEE FINE	3 LB	8	3.801	1.116	13.365	33.932	394.721	7.607%	6.672%	2.425%	2.009%	8	
FOLGERS COFFEE FINE	1 LB	24	1.287	259	2.606	7.999	82.444	1.793%	1.394%	.572%	.420%	5	
FOLGERS COFFEE FINE	1 LB	12	2.599	89	1.691	2.776	53.292	.622%	.901%	.198%	.271%	* 8	
FOLGERS COFFEE ELECTRIC PRK	1 LB	24	1.306	2.574	24.814	80.672	778.244	18.085%	13.155%	5.765%	3.962%	8	
FOLGERS COFFEE ELECTRIC PRK	2 LB	12	2.599	1.181	28.425	36.832	882.427	8.257%	14.916%	2.632%	4.492%	8	
FOLGERS COFFEE ELECTRIC PRK	3 LB	8	3.796	1.933	25.656	58.694	740.873	13.158%	12.523%	4.194%	3.771%	8	
HIGH POINT				874	6.487	32.051	239.690	100.000%	100.000%	2.290%	1.220%	6	
HIGH POINT COF DRIP DECAF	1 LB	24	1.535	261	2.300	9.616	85.685	30.002%	35.748%	.687%	.436%	8	0214N
HIGH POINT COF DRIP DECAF	2 LB	12	3.048	124	757	4.536	27.666	14.152%	11.542%	.324%	.141%	5	0214N
HIGH POINT COF EL PERK DECAF	1 LB	24	1.535	275	2.081	10.133	77.278	31.615%	32.241%	.724%	.393%	8	0214N
HIGH POINT COF EL PERK DECAF	2 LB	12	3.024	214	1.349	7.766	49.061	24.230%	20.469%	.555%	.250%	7	0214N
CHASE SANBORN				583	21.733	17.951	653.726	100.000%	100.000%	1.283%	3.328%	4	
CHASE SANBORN COF REG	2 LB	12	2.576	224	8.193	6.923	249.779	38.566%	38.209%	.495%	1.272%	4	
CHASE SANBORN COF DRIP	2 LB	12	2.596	98	3.288	3.053	96.177	17.007%	14.712%	.218%	.490%	4	
CHASE SANBORN COF ELC PRK	2 LB	12	2.546	261	10.252	7.975	307.770	44.426%	47.079%	.570%	1.567%	4	
FRENCH MARKET				4	18	62	280	100.000%	100.000%	.004%	.001%	*	
FRENCH MARKET COF CHIC REG	1 LB	12	1.292	4	18	62	280	100.000%	100.000%	.004%	.001%	*	0314N
OLD JUDGE				1.847	33.829	54.275	1.060.584	100.000%	100.000%	3.878%	5.399%	6	
OLD JUDGE COFFEE REG	1 LB	24	1.304	299	6.418	9.360	203.224	17.246%	19.162%	.669%	1.035%	5	
OLD JUDGE COFFEE REG	2 LB	12	2.332	474	6.389	13.205	199.850	24.330%	18.843%	.944%	1.017%	6	
OLD JUDGE COFFEE REG	3 LB	8	3.822	59	2.510	1.804	77.465	3.324%	7.304%	.129%	.394%	*	
OLD JUDGE COFFEE DRIP	1 LB	24	1.303	127	1.892	3.972	59.711	7.318%	7.630%	.284%	.304%	*	

★ASTERISK INDICATES 3 OR LESS FOOD OPERATOR SHIPPING

Exception Report: Penetration.   Items which the operator has a share of at least three times his all-commodity volume share.

Top 500.   The top 500 items in each category in terms of dollar volume are reported (Figure 8–7).

SARDI.   Product distribution is reported for the operator and for the total market. This report points up products which are moving in the market but not stocked by the particular food operator or vice versa (Figure 8–8).

Manufacturers

Sales (Standard Dollar Report).   Sales are reported for the brand in total and by type and size for each of the market areas (Figure 8–9).

Distribution.   A SARDI report indicating distribution in each market area by (*a*) key accounts (chains, etc.) and (*b*) store type (size and location).

Brand Trend Report.   These reports show changes in sales versus a year ago.

Ranking Report.   This report ranks the products in a particular category based on sales.

Other services

In addition to the basic reports, SAMI has a variety of special services. These include the following:

New product service.   This service monitors new product activity on a product-by-product and market-by-market basis.

Scan service.   Provides basic information to a manufacturer on a product category in which he is not currently engaged. This is designed to help manufacturers consider entry decisions.

MRCA

The Market Research Corporation of America is very different from either Nielsen or SAMI. Its basic approach is to collect data from consumers by panel methods. It has four major services: national consumer panel, menu census, textile panel, and household cleaning and laundry census.

National consumer panel

The consumer panel maintained by MRCA consists of 7,500 households who by diary report on purchases of essentially the same packaged goods that Nielsen and SAMI monitor. These diaries are returned weekly. (Maintenance of such a system is a monumental task, and problems have occurred with the data.) Respondents report on all individual purchases in terms of brand, size, price, quantity, if bought on deal, and store. In addition demographic, attitudinal, and psychographic information are also

FIGURE 8–10

ACTUAL PURCHASE RECORD - MARGARINE

N.C.P. Family: #46141 - Product Class: 34 - Size: 00100

	DAY OF PURCHASE	TYPE	UNITS	DEAL	PRICE	OUTLET	WEIGHT
MAZOLA	7-7	02	1	X	$.36	13	1.00
MAZOLA	8-4	02	1		.43	12	1.00
IMPERIAL	8-8	00	1	X	.36	60	1.00
GOLD O'CORN	8-9	02	1		.35	12	1.00
GOLD O'CORN	9-19	02	1	X	.35	12	1.00
NUCOA	9-21	00	1		.30	12	1.00
GOLD O'CORN	9-22	02	1	X	.35	01	1.00
MIRACLE	9-26	00	1		.35	12	1.00
FLEISCHMANN'S	9-28	02	1	X	.33	12	1.00
FLEISCHMANN'S	10-6	02	1	X	.35	12	1.00
GOLD O'CORN	10-12	02	1		.35	60	1.00
GOLD O'CORN	10-13	02	1		.35	12	1.00
GOLD O'CORN	11-2	02	1		.35	12	1.00
GOLDEN GLOW	11-15	03	1	X	.35	12	1.00
GOLD O'CORN	11-24	02	1		.35	60	1.00
GOLDEN GLOW	11-27	03	1	X	.35	12	1.00
FLEISCHMANN'S	12-7	02	1	X	.34	12	1.00
GOLD O'CORN	12-15	02	1	X	.35	12	1.00
FYNE SPREAD	12-20	00	2		.35	12	2.00

Source: Market Research Corporation of America, *National Consumer Panel Diary*, p. 1.

maintained on the sample. A typical purchase record is shown in Figure 8–10. Basic data is reported biweekly (both for total United States and regions). The data reported are the following:

1. Total product category sales (in units such as pounds and/or dollars).
2. Number of households buying.
3. Brand shares in the category.

In addition, the panel data is available for a variety of analyses which rely on the individual level data. These include the following:

1. Segmentation studies of heavy versus light buyers, buyers of different brands, and so forth, in terms of demographics and attitudes.
2. Brand-switching studies.
3. Price-sensitivity and deal-proneness studies.

One of the main uses of panel data is to monitor a new product roll-out and to project eventual sales and share. By monitoring trial to establish an eventual trial level and repeat to estimate eventual repeat/loyalty, the ultimate share of a new product can be forecast.

Menu census

As an additional service, 4,000 members of the basic 7,500 member panel are queried about what they typically eat. The households report for a period of 14 days by filling in a daily menu diary. The information includes the following:

1. Every food dish served at home plus time of day served.
2. Food eaten away from home.
3. Items added to a dish.
4. How item was served (main dish, dessert, etc.).
5. Who prepared the meal.
6. Who ate the meal.
7. Leftovers.
8. Cooking fats and oils used as frying agents; flour used for dusting.
9. Brand name of packaged products used and type (ready-to-eat, canned, etc.).
10. How the dish was cooked.
11. Recipes used.

In addition to actual food usage and preparation, other data includes the following:

1. Diet status of household members.
2. Attitudes, interests, and opinions about homemaking.
3. Demographic data (already available).

Five basic reports are produced:

1. Usage of each of 5,000 items in terms of—
   a. Households who used each at least once.
   b. Total number of times served.
2. Usage of 400 food categories broken down by—
   a. Demographics of the household.
   b. Diet status of family members.
   c. Meal characteristics (which meal, etc.).
3. Correlation of usage of the 400 food categories with 30 psychographic scales.
4. Trends in usage of 5,000 items between last two menu censuses.
5. Food eaten away from home.

Many clients also request special reports. The cost of the base service is somewhere near $150,000 with special reports extra. In spite of the cost, many of the major food manufacturers purchase this service.

Textile panel

Based on a panel of 7,500 households, this service collects information on clothing purchases similar to the way the consumer panel collects food purchases. For each purchase, the following data is gathered:

1. Clothing characteristics:
   - *a.* Type.
   - *b.* Fiber.
   - *c.* Knit/woven.
   - *d.* Color/pattern.
   - *e.* Brand.
   - *f.* Size.
   - *g.* Age of wearer.
   - *h.* Age of buyer.
   - *i.* Whether the clothing is imported or domestic.
   - *j.* If the clothing is permanent press.
2. Purchase characteristics:
   - *a.* Price.
   - *b.* Type of outlet.
   - *c.* Quantity bought.
   - *d.* Date.
   - *e.* If bought on sale.
   - *f.* If bought for a gift.
   - *g.* If it was a catalog sale.
3. Buyer characteristics:
   - *a.* Age.
   - *b.* Sex.
   - *c.* Household income.
   - *d.* City size.
   - *e.* Occupation.
   - *f.* Household size.
   - *g.* Number of children.

The diary itself is a 15-page marathon. Cost of the service is substantial. The charge to each client just for developing a complete computer system to analyze the data runs about $60,000.

Household cleaning and laundry census

Begun in 1975, this service is similar to the menu census. The first census in 1975–76 used 2,000 members of the national household panel. The data for this service includes the following:

1. Home cleaning (14 consecutive days per household):
   - *a.* Kind of activity:

    (1) Dusting.
    (2) Waxing/polishing.
    (3) Stain removal.
    (4) Sweeping/vacuuming.
    (5) Washing/scouring.
  b. Product(s) used (brand and type).
  c. Identity of item or surface cleaned.
  d. Room in which activity occurred.
  e. Date, time of activity.
  f. Age/sex of "doer."
  g. Time required.
  h. Equipment used.
2. Dishwashing (14 consecutive days per household):
  a. Product(s) used.
  b. Automatic dishwasher or manual.
  c. Kinds of items washed.
  d. Meal (or occasion) identity.
  e. Date, time of activity.
  f. Time required.
  g. Dish-drying method.
  h. Age/sex of dishwasher.
3. Laundering (seven consecutive days):
  a. For each load (machine or hand wash):
    (1) Soap/detergent used (brand, type, quality).
    (2) Additives used (brand, type).
    (3) Water temperature, level, type.
    (4) Water hardness score.
    (5) Cycle setting.
    (6) Age of launderer.
  b. For each item laundered:
    (1) Identification of garment/item.
    (2) Presence/kind of stain (pretreatment product?).
    (3) Permanent/durable press.
    (4) Knit or woven.
    (5) Fiber content.
    (6) Color/pattern.
    (7) Age of wearer (apparel).
    (8) How dried.
    (9) Ironed?

The cost of subscribing to this service is just over $100,000 per year.

MARKET FACTS

In turning to Market Facts, we come to a company which specializes in custom rather than standard research. This is a "full-service" company which will engage in just about any stage of research from design through data collection and analysis. It uses a variety of data collection devices including the following:

Controlled store tests.

Test-market audits.

Central location research.

Personal interviewing.

Local telephone interviewing.

WATS line interviewing.

Executive interviewing.

Qualitative (focus group sessions and in-depth interviews).

Its major "capital good" is its consumer mail panel. The panel contains over 60,000 U.S. households (plus another 13,000 in Canada). It is balanced to match national statistics on the basis of geographic region, annual household income, population density and degree of urbanization, and age of panel member. Background data on each panel member is available in terms of demographics, psychographics, ownership, purchase or intent-to-buy over 200 consumer goods, use of credit and catalogs, and participation in 64 leisure-time sports and hobbies. Cost of using the sample varies with sample size, specific characteristics demanded, and length of survey. However, a six-page survey of 1,000 members should cost in the $10,000–15,000 range without analysis (the client receiving a clean data deck and tab run only).

In addition to consumer product research, Market Facts offers research services in the following areas:

Industrial marketing.

Pharmaceutical and medical.

Housing.

Retail location.

Transportation and travel.

Employee benefit planning.

Urban and real estate studies.

NPD

NPD maintains a consumer panel which many companies feel is the best available. The panel consists of 13,000 households broken into 29 local markets. About 50 product categories are monitored (Figure 8–11). Diaries are filled out daily and are collected each month. Panel members are automatically eliminated every four to five years to reduce panel bias

FIGURE 8–11
Sample of products monitored by NPD diary

DIARY PAGE

PERSONAL AND HOUSEHOLD PRODUCTS PURCHASED (in alphabetical order)

17 — Antiperspirants, Deodorants — (Underarm)
2 — Cleaning Cloths — All Purpose
3 — Cups, Disposable
16 — Creme Rinse and Hair Conditioners
17 — Deodorants, Antiperspirants — (Underarm)
3 — Diapers (cloth and disposable types)
    Diaper Liners
2 — Facial Tissue
5 — Games, Toys, Puzzles, Hobby Kits, etc.
17 — Hair Coloring Products
16 — Hair Creme Rinse and Conditioners
16 — Hair Shampoo
17 — Hair Sprays
2 — Handkerchiefs, paper (see Facial Tissue)
3 — Napkins, paper
4 — Needlework and Crafts

16 — Powder — Body (All Types)
4 — Patterns — For Sewing, Knitting, Crocheting
3 — Pre-Moistened Towelettes
17 — Sanitary Napkins, Tampons
16 — Shampoo — Hair
17 — Tampons
2 — Toilet Tissue
16 — Toothpaste, Toothpowder, Tooth Polish
2 — Towel Holders
3 — Towelettes, Pre-Moistened
2 — Towels, paper
5 — Toys, Games, Puzzles, Hobby Kits, etc.
4 — Underwear — Men's & Boys

FOOD PRODUCTS PURCHASED (in alphabetical order)

11 — Bacon — Other Breakfast Meats
6 — Baked Beans — Pork & Beans
    Hot Dogs & Beans, etc.
9 — Bar Mixes (see Cake Mixes)
15 — Bars, Squares, and Wafers (Meal and Snack)
15 — Bran or Bran Germ
9 — Brownie Mixes
8 — Cake and Pastry Fillings
9 — Cake Mixes
9 — Cake Mixes/Baking Mixes — Other
10 — Cat Food
15 — Cereals (either Hot or Cold)
6 — Chili Sauce
13 — Coffee — All Types
9 — Cookie Mixes
7 — Corn Chips & Curls, Other Corn Snacks
13 — Creamers — Non-Dairy (including Powdered,
    Frozen and Refrigerated Creamers)
9 — Cupcake Mixes
8 — Custards, Custard Pudding
8 — Dessert Mixes
12 — Dinners, Side Dishes (Packaged Dry Mix)
10 — Dog and Cat Food
9 — Doughnut Mixes
14 — English Muffins — Fresh, Refrigerated or
    Frozen
10 — Flour
9 — Frostings
7 — Frozen Main Dish Items, Entrees, Dinners
8 — Fruit (Individual Snack Sizes)
8 — Gelatin, Gelatin Salads, Gelatin Desserts
15 — Granola

11 — Meat Extenders, Substitutes
14 — Muffins, English — Fresh Refrigerated or Frozen
10 — Oils — for Cooking, Salad, etc.
10 — Pet Food
7 — Pizza-Frozen, Refrigerated, Dry-Mix & Take-Out
12 — Potatoes — Fresh, Instant, Frozen
7 — Potato Chips, other Potato Snacks
7 — Pretzels
8 — Puddings — All Types (including Pie Fillings)
8 — Ready-to-Eat Pudding, Fruit, Gelatin, etc.
    (Individual Snack Sizes)
10 — Shortening
6 — Sloppy Joe Sauce and Mixes
7 — Snack Items — Non Frozen/Non Refrigerated
14 — Soft Drinks — Carbonated
11 — Soups — Include Canned, Dry and Bouillon
11 — Soy Proteins
6 — Spaghetti Sauce
13 — Stuffing/Dressing
9 — Sweet Roll Mixes/Coffee Cake Mixes
6 — Tomato Products (Paste, Puree, etc.)
12 — Vegetables (Frozen)
15 — Wheat Germ
9 — Whipped Cream and Whipped Topping
14 — Wines
8 — Yogurt

Source: NPD Research. *American Shoppers Panel Diary.* Floral Park, N.Y., April, 1977.

due to aging (maturation) and conditioning. Participating in the panel costs in the $25,000–$40,000 range for one category for one year. In addition to collecting data, NPD specializes in several categories of analysis:

Market structure analyses.   Analyses of general purchase characteristics, demographic characteristics, sales by outlet, brand loyalty, brand mixing, and price/deal response.

New product evaluation. Forecasts of sales based on test markets using trial and repeat data.

CREST report (Chain Restaurant Eating-out Share Trend). This service uses a quarterly diary panel of 10,000 families reporting eating habits for a two-week period. Data collected include the following:

Amount spent.

Where spent.

What meals.

Activity before and after meal.

Products purchased.

Day of week.

Demographics.

Cost of this service is between $12,500 and $25,000 to a food service company, and about $25,000 to a food manufacturer or distributor.

ESP model. In addition to the panel, NPD has a model called ESP, which is designed to forecast eventual sales based on concept and product use tests. It is a simulation model which costs about $20,000 for the combination of a mail concept test ($1,000), a product use test ($11,000), and the model itself ($7,500). This model is based on the work of Eskin (1973).

NATIONAL FAMILY OPINION (NFO)

NFO specializes in phone and mail consumer panels. The key element in most of their research is their consumer family sample. This includes 150,000 families, 70,000 in 70 matched, balanced panels of 1,000 each designed to represent the total United States.

This panel is matched based on population density, age of homemaker, annual family income, and family size. (The matching is done one variable at a time, however, so it may be that a disproportionate number of the poor people are also old.) In addition, the usual demographics are maintained for each panel member. (Like many of the research operations, headquarters are far from New York City to escape high overhead costs—in this case in Toledo, Ohio.) A large portion of NFO's business involves mail or phone (via WATS lines) surveys of panels drawn from this base. As such, it competes heavily with both Market Facts and HTI.

In addition to one-shot surveys, NFO also constructs special-purpose panels from its 150,000 family sample. Recruitment is usually done by phone. Diaries are then sent by mail over the period of a test market. The dropout rate for the panel tends to run between 30 and 40 percent (an obvious source of potential bias). A sample format is shown in Figure 8–12.

FIGURE 8–12
Sample NFO special-purpose diary

···MARKET   RESEARCH   THROUGH   REPRESENTATIVE   HOUSEHOLDS··

National Family Opinion, Inc.   **A**

POST OFFICE BOX 474
TOLEDO, OHIO 43654

99900

Dear Homemaker,

Thank you for agreeing to help with our diary type study which will last for
several months. Here is your first diary in this series, for the next two
weeks:

> MONDAY, FEBRUARY 10 through SUNDAY, FEBRUARY 23

During this two-week period, please record in your diary (on the inside pages)
each time you, or any member of your family purchase any of the following:

      COFFEE - both regular and instant. Please be sure to include
           all purchases made -- including decaffeinated coffees.

      JAMS, JELLIES and PRESERVES.

      LAUNDRY DETERGENTS -- (liquid, powder, flakes, tablets) --
           all detergents bought for family laundry.

HERE ARE A FEW INSTRUCTIONS TO HELP YOU IN COMPLETING YOUR DIARY:

    Each time you return from shopping, complete a line in the diary
    for each different type and brand bought. Only items EXACTLY ALIKE
    and bought at the SAME TIME should be reported on the same line
    in your diary.

    Write in the DATE bought.

    Write in SIZE, NUMBER BOUGHT and TOTAL PRICE paid.

    Indicate if a SPECIAL OFFER was used.

    Check to indicate the type of store where the purchase was made.

Near the end of the two-week reporting period, I'll be writing again. At
that time I'll send you a postage-paid envelope for returning this diary,
as well as the next diary in the series.

Thanks again for your help with this study!

                Sincerely, *Carol*

MEMBER OF AMERICAN MARKETING ASSOCIATION TOLEDO CHAMBER OF COMMERCE

Source: National Family Opinion, Inc. New York, 1975.

FIGURE 8–12 (continued)

Monday, FEBRUARY 10 through Sunday, FEBRUARY 23

COUPONS RECEIVED

DATE REC'D	FOR WHICH OF THE DIARY PRODUCTS? Please write in.	BRAND NAME:	HOW RECEIVED? ✓ OR WRITE IN:				
			By Mail	From Ad	From Pkg.	Friend	Other

☐ NONE RECEIVED

SAMPLES RECEIVED

DATE REC'D	FOR WHICH OF THE DIARY PRODUCTS? Please write in.	BRAND NAME:	HOW RECEIVED? ✓ OR WRITE IN:				
			By Mail	From Ad	From Pkg.	Friend	Left at Door	Other

☐ NONE RECEIVED

COFFEE

DATE BOUGHT	Copy complete BRAND NAME from package	TYPE: (✓) ONE — Instant / Ground	Is it Decaffeinated? YES NO	IF INSTANT, does label say "freeze-dried"? YES NO	IF GROUND COFFEE, check (✓) to indicate TYPE OF GRIND — Regular / Drip / Fine / Electric / Other	SIZE: # lbs. or # of oz.	NUMBER BOUGHT	HOW MUCH DID YOU PAY? Don't include taxes. TOTAL PRICE PAID	WAS THIS A SPECIAL PRICE OR OFFER? YES NO — IF YES, DESCRIBE OFFER: Coupon Used / Cents Off / Combination deal / Store Special / Other-describe	TOTAL AMOUNT SAVED (if any)—value of special offer, cents off, value of coupon, etc.	WHERE BOUGHT? Supermarket / Independent Grocery / Other-describe

☐ NONE BOUGHT

JAM, JELLY, PRESERVES, FLAVORED REFRIGERATED SPREADS, MARMALADE, FRUIT BUTTER, etc.

DATE BOUGHT	Copy complete BRAND NAME from package	KIND OF PRODUCT (jam, jelly, preserves, flavored refrigerated spread, marmalade, fruit butter, etc.)	FLAVOR (copy from the label - such as "raisin cinnamon", "grape", "strawberry", "fruit-nut", etc.)	TYPE OF PACKAGE — Jar / Tub / Other	SIZE: # lbs. or # of oz.	NUMBER BOUGHT	HOW MUCH DID YOU PAY? Don't include taxes. TOTAL PRICE PAID	WAS THIS A SPECIAL PRICE OR OFFER? YES NO — IF YES, DESCRIBE OFFER: Coupon Used / Cents Off / Combination deal / Store Special / Other-describe	TOTAL AMOUNT SAVED (if any)—value of special offer, cents off, value of coupon, etc.	WHERE BOUGHT? Supermarket / Independent Grocery / Other-describe

☐ NONE BOUGHT

LAUNDRY DETERGENTS - liquid, powder, flakes, or tablets

DATE BOUGHT	Copy complete BRAND NAME from package	FORM: Liquid / Powder or Flakes / Tablets or Packets / Other, specify:	Is it mainly for use in COLD water? YES NO	Does it have active ENZYME ingredients? YES NO	SIZE: in lbs., ounces, quarts, pints, etc.	NUMBER BOUGHT	HOW MUCH DID YOU PAY? Don't include taxes. TOTAL PRICE PAID	WAS THIS A SPECIAL PRICE OR OFFER? YES NO — IF YES, DESCRIBE OFFER: Coupon Used / Cents Off / Combination deal / Store Special / Other-describe	TOTAL AMOUNT SAVED (if any)—value of special offer, cents off, value of coupon, etc.	WHERE BOUGHT? Supermarket / Independent Grocery / Other-describe

☐ NONE BOUGHT

National Family Opinion, Inc.

The data is typically analyzed in terms of (*a*) brand switching, (*b*) trial level tracking, and (*c*) repeat purchase level tracking, pretty much the standard approach. NFO also provides a predictive model for eventual sales called TRAC.

HOME TESTING INSTITUTE (HTI)

The third of the big mail panel maintainers, HTI, maintains a sample of 30,000 primary and 55,000 backup families. Custom samples are drawn from this overall sample. A large part of their business is special mail surveys. In addition, HTI provides (as do Market Facts and NFO) a low-cost cooperative mailing service called Insta-vue. Each client produces a short questionnaire the size of a single computer card. A packet of the cards are then mailed to a sample for relatively small cost. (A sample of 5,000 costs about $1,500; 30,000 between $5,000 and $6,000.)

In addition to mail surveys, HTI maintains a WATS interviewing facility. This facility can be used for either general population phone interviews or phone interviews to member of the family panel.

AUDITS AND SURVEYS

As the title suggests, Audits and Surveys concentrates its efforts in two major areas. The major services are as follows:

Survey Division.   This division specializes in in-home interviews. The top officers—Solomon Dutka, Lester Frankel, and Irving Roshwalb—are well known in the field. They have a field force of 8 full-time regional field supervisors and 150 local supervisors linked to over 2,500 interviewers. Quality control procedures include 20 percent validation by WATS interviews.

Test Audit Division.   A custom audit service designed to monitor market tests.

National Total-Market Audit.   A standard retail audit service gathering sales, inventory, and distribution on a bimonthly basis. In addition to the usual food products, automotive products, electrical products, tobacco products, photographic products, health and beauty aids, household products, and writing instruments are monitored.

National Restaurant Market Index.   This audit queries about 6,000 commercial restaurants. Information gathered includes the following:

Total sales.
Number of employees.
Usage of specific foods.
Equipment used.

Data is broken down by the following five types of restaurants:
Drugstores serving food.
Hotel/motel restaurants.
Drive-ins.
Counter service.
Table service.

Retail Census of Product Distribution. Based on a sample of 40,000 outlets, this service is intended to monitor brand-by-brand distribution in a variety of product categories.

Brand Name Store Search. An in-store search of 5,000 stores for names which sound, look, or mean the same thing as a proposed or existing brand name. The search focuses mainly on the product category in question, and is designed to avoid future questions of trademark infringement.

Selling Areas Distribution Index (SADI). Designed as a complement to SAMI data, this is a bimonthly survey of 2,375 supermarkets in 28 of the SAMI markets. The data collected includes distribution, facings, shelf price, displays and location, and promotional activity for various products.

National Sportsman's Consumer Audit. This is an annual survey of 5,000 men 15 or older. Data includes degree of participation in boating, bowling, camping, fishing, golf, skiing, and tennis, as well as products used. Interviewing is done by phone, and the cost of a report is about $5,000 for a single category.

Product pickup. This is a service in which field representatives buy "the next item available for sale." The products are then sent to the client, who can use the products to determine shelf age, package appearance and content, and product content.

Negro Market Index. Every two months, food and drug chains located in heavily black sections of 42 metropolitan areas are audited in the usual (sales, inventory, distribution) way.

The Center for Behavioral Research Surveys. This is a survey division focusing on noncommercial projects for government groups, universities, and so forth.

Controlled city tests. This service includes actually conducting a controlled city test.

SIMMONS

Simmons is primarily oriented toward profiling magazine audiences. The 1976–77 survey focused on 67 publications: 60 magazines, 5 newspapers*, and 2 supplements.†

American Baby
American Home
Atlantic Magazine
*Barron's
Better Homes & Gardens
Boating
Business Week
Car & Driver
Cosmopolitan
Cycle
Esquire
Family Circle
†Family Weekly
Field & Stream
Flying
Forbes
Fortune
Girl Talk
Glamour
Golf
Golf Digest
Good Housekeeping
Harper's Magazine
House & Garden
House Beautiful
Ladies' Home Journal
Mademoiselle
McCall's
Mechanix Illustrated
Money
Ms.
*National Enquirer
National Geographic
*National Observer

Natural History
Newsweek
New York
New Yorker
*New York Times (weekday)
†New York Times Magazine
Oui
Outdoor Life
Parent's Magazine
Penthouse
People
Playboy
Popular Mechanics
Popular Photography
Popular Science
Psychology Today
Reader's Digest
Redbook
Road & Track
Saturday Review
Scientific American
Skiing
Sport
Sports Afield
Sports Illustrated
Stereo Review
Time
TV Guide
U.S. News & World Report
Viva
Vogue
*The Wall Street Journal
Woman's Day

Source: W. R. Simmons and Associates Research. *1976/77 The Study of Selective Markets and the Media Reaching Them*, New York © 1977.

A large personal interview survey is performed with 15,000 households (adults age 18 and over). High-income households are sampled disproportionately.

In addition to magazine readership, data collected include the following:

Twenty-two demographic variables:

Sex.
Age.
Employment.
Index of social position.
Position in household and parental status.
Education.
Occupation.
Individual employment.
Size of company in which employed.
Marital status.
Race.
Household income.
Age of household head.
Occupation of household head.
Sources of nonemployment income.
Presence of children/teenagers in household.
Number of children/teenagers in household.
Home ownership and value.
Locality type.
Geographic region.
County size.
Type of dwelling.

Product usage and ownership for over 100 products, many of them durables ranging from food products and clothing to electric shavers, cars, boats and second homes.

TV viewing and radio listening data (collected separately).

The demographics, product data, and TV viewing data are collected over a 15-month period (Figure 8–13).

STARCH

Starch is best known for its Starch Message Report. This report attempts to measure the impact of ads in magazines and newspapers. Between 100 and 150 men and 100–150 women over age 18 are interviewed. Only individuals who have read at least some part of the magazine issue being studied are used as respondents. For each ad studied, respondents are classified in terms of—

1. Nonreader (does not remember reading the ad).
2. Noted reader (remembers reading the ad).
3. Associated reader (remembers the brand or advertiser).
4. Read most (read more than half the ad).

FIGURE 8–13
Simmons time schedule

Field interviewing:
    Print media and product data .... Nov. 1975–Aug. 1976
    Television and radio audience data .... Jan. 1977–Feb. 1977
Report and computer tape delivery
Print media data (4 volumes) .... Nov. 1976–Dec. 1976
    Vol. 1—General Demographic Characteristics
    Vol. 2—Demographic Cross-Tabulations
    Vol. 3—Reach and Frequency
    Vol. 4—Net Unduplicated Average Issue Audiences
Marketing data (19 volumes) .... Dec. 1976–Apr. 1977
Television and radio data (2 volumes) .... Apr. 1977
    Vol. 5—Television and Radio Audiences
    Vol. 6—Television and Radio Reach and Frequency
Intermedia comparisons (1 volume) .... Apr. 1977

Source: W. R. Simmons and Associates Research. *1976/77, The Study of Selective Markets and the Media Reaching Them,* New York © 1977.

The data is summarized for each individual ad and also each ad is compared with other ads in the same issue in terms of both raw readership scores and readership/cost ratios.

AMERICAN RESEARCH BUREAU (ARBITRON)

A subsidiary of Control Data, ARB specializes in measuring media (radio and TV) audiences on a local basis. Data is collected on a regional basis. It is grouped, among other ways, according to a measure called ADI (area of dominant influence). The basis for this breakdown is areas where media (radio and TV stations) reach from the ''center'' of the area. Hence a county is included in the area from which the majority of its radio or television programs are broadcast.

Data is collected by means of a diary. The steps followed are as follows:

1. Preplacement letter.
2. Placement phone call.
3. Diary mailed.
4. Presurvey call.
5. Midsurvey reminder call.

Respondents receive 25 cents or 50 cents per diary. The consent rate is 85 percent; and of those consenting, 65 percent return usable diaries. Names are drawn from the list maintained by Metro-Mail of households with listed telephone numbers.

The sample size varies depending on the size of the market. The approximate sizes are as follows:

Market rank (by size)	Metro area sample size	Total survey area sample size
1–4	2,000	2,400
4–30	1,200	1,500
31–50	700	850
51–75	575	700
76+	450	550

For radio, every person age 12 or older is sent a diary. The diary covers one week with a page for each day of the week.

A major use of this data is in evaluating advertising alternatives. In each area, audience is esimtated in 15-minute blocks of time. For each 15 minutes, the following are calculated:

1. Average *number* of persons listening.
2. Average *rating* (average number/population of area).
3. Metro *share* (shares of viewing audience).
4. *Cume persons* (number of persons who listen during at least some part of the time period, often called Reach).
5. *Cume ratings* (cume persons/population).

These numbers are used to derive several key figures:

1. Gross impressions (Average number of persons × Number of spots of a given ad aired during the time period).
2. Cost per thousand (CPM = Cost/1,000 gross impressions).
3. Gross rating points (Average rating × Number of spots).
4. Frequency (gross impressions/cume persons).

The data is also used to rank stations and programs based on audiences. The makeup of station audiences is available in terms of age and sex. The television data is essentially the same as the radio data. Its diary is a bit more structured (Figure 8–14), but other than that the two services are basically twins.

In addition to the radio and TV ratings, Arbitron also does a broad range of custom research, mainly surveys.

ADTEL

AdTel is a division of Booz, Allen, and Hamilton. It maintains special panels in four cities in the United States. For completing weekly diaries, panel members receive points which are redeemable for products in an

FIGURE 8–14
ARB TV diary

Leaving this portion of the page open will assist you in keeping the diary.

What TV stations (channels 2-83) can you receive clearly enough for viewing on this set? (Fill in below)

Channel Number	Station Call Letters	City	Channel Number	Station Call Letters	City

Accurate station identification is very important. Please use both the station call letters and channel number in your viewing entries.

MALE HEAD OF HOUSE	FIRST NAME ONLY:
FEMALE HEAD OF HOUSE	FIRST NAME ONLY:

OTHER FAMILY MEMBERS
NAMES

3

6:00 A.M.

WEDNESDAY

TIME QUARTER HOURS	TV SET OFF	TV SET ON	STATION TUNED IN CALL LETTERS	STATION TUNED IN CHAN. NO.	NAME OF PROGRAM	AGE → SEX →	M	F							VISITORS	VISITORS	VISITORS
6:00- 6:14																	
6:15- 6:29																	
6:30- 6:44																	
6:45- 6:59																	
7:00- 7:14																	
7:15- 7:29																	
7:30- 7:44																	
7:45- 7:59																	
8:00- 8:14																	
8:15- 8:29																	
8:30- 8:44																	
8:45- 8:59																	
9:00- 9:14																	
9:15- 9:29																	
9:30- 9:44																	
9:45- 9:59																	
10:00-10:14																	
10:15-10:29																	
10:30-10:44																	
10:45-10:59																	
11:00-11:14																	
11:15-11:29																	

Source: Arbitron Television Research, *Diary of Television Viewing,* November 3, 1976.

80-page catalog. These panels of 2,000 have an important special feature: they are in matched subpanels of 1,000 whose TV sets are in a split cable setup. (The cities are isolated so that a large percentage of the homes subscribe to cable services.) This cable is designed to allow ads to be changed during regular programs, and changed differently for the two halves of the sample. The major advantage of this is that two different ads (or an ad versus no-ad design) can actually be run on regular TV and the effects monitored by the panel data. (This is the equivalent of a split-run print test.)

In addition to the basic TV cable test, AdTel also offers the opportunity to test promotions and other marketing strategies. Also, by working with Market Audits (another subsidiary of Booz, Allen, and Hamilton), controlled store tests are run in the AdTel markets. Distribution is available in stores accounting for over 85 percent of all commodity volume in the markets on as little as three weeks' notice. A shelf display might be introduced for under $2,000 per market. A recent price list is shown in Figure 8–15.

FIGURE 8–15
Charges for AdTel services

	One AdTel market with cut-ins	One AdTel market without cut-ins*
Basic AdTel service (includes diary panel service, 4-week period summary reports, and TV cut-ins when specified):		
One-year service	$85,000	$50,000
Six months service	50,000	35,000
Pretest diary data:		
Per four-week period	1,000	1,000
Additional cost items:		
Controlled store distribution	(Cost quotes available upon	
Retail sales audits	receipt of specifications)	
Telephone tracking		
Special analyses/sales models		

* This price structure is available only for selected categories as designated by AdTel.
Source: AdTel, Inc. "How to Test and Measure the Sales Effectiveness of Television Advertising and Consumer Promotion." New York, 1978.

NATIONAL ANALYSTS

Another subsidiary of Booz, Allen, and Hamilton, National Analysts specializes in custom attitude and behavior research. It is a large user of focus group methodology and has a variety of services, such as the following:

1. Concept generation studies.
2. Package design studies.
3. Factor testing (price, design).

4. Concept/prototype tests.
5. Market positioning and segmentation.

IMS

IMS is to the pharmaceutical industry what Nielsen is to the packaged goods business. Actually, much of IMS's business is in countries other than the United States. Its major audit services, mostly quarterly, include the following:

Sales Analysis.   A report of sales to both drugstores (1,600) and hospitals (450). This service is based on purchase invoices.

Audatrex.   A panel of 700 physicians who furnish a copy of each prescription they write.

Laboratory.   Four hundred hospitals' and 200 nonhospital laboratories' purchase invoices are audited. Both chemicals (reagents) and supplies (beakers, etc.) are monitored.

Federal Government Contract Awards.

Hospital Disease and Therapeutic Index (HDTI).   Case history reports of 525 hospital-based physicians which focus on use of antibiotics.

Hospital Record Study.   From statistical study of over 220 hospitals in the United States, Canada, and Puerto Rico called the Professional Activity Study, a sample is drawn to produce a report on patient type, diagnosis, and surgical procedures followed.

Hospital Supplies.   Medical/surgical supplies used by 400 hospitals.

National Detailing Audit.   Every month, 1,000 physicians report on detailing (sales calls by pharmaceutical company representatives) over a two-week period.

National Journal Audit.   An audit of advertising in 3,500 medical journals broken down by product and therapeutic category advertised (a tough thing to do for many multiple-use drugs).

National Mail Audit.   Reports of 300 doctors and pharmacists on mail advertising received.

National Prescription Audit.   A biweekly audit of the prescriptions filled by 800 retail pharmacies in terms of product name, dosage, strength, quantity price, payment method, and source of prescription.

Animal and Poultry.   Report on pharmaceuticals, biologicals, diagnostic aids, and feed additives purchased in the United States for animals and poultry. One hundred fifty therapeutic categories are measured. A sample of 1,400 channels of distribution (livestock supply stores, feed stores, cooperative supply stores, feed mills, drugstores, veterinarians, feedlots, and producers) is used.

Laboratory Tests. A semiannual audit of the laboratory logs of 200 nonfederal government general hospitals.

Toiletry and Beauty Aids. A monthly audit based on purchase invoices of 1,200 drugstores, proprietary stores, and discount houses.

In addition to audits, IMS's Lea-Meudota research group conducts general market research. Its specialties include a monthly phone interview with 360 physicians, product image surveys of 100 physicians in a specialty, ad recall surveys of 30 physicians, and inventory checking of a panel of over 1,200 pharmacies.

BURKE

Burke Marketing Research is one of the major suppliers of research and perhaps the largest custom research supplier. In addition to the United States, Burke operates in 11 foreign countries: Argentina, Brazil, Canada, Denmark, France, Germany, Italy, Japan, Mexico, Sweden, and United Kingdom. In the United States, the primary services provided are as follows:

Phone interviewing. Burke has central interviewing facilities in 34 cities around the country, in addition to a National WATS center at the Cincinnati headquarters. Interviewers are both full and part time, but work exclusively for Burke.

Personal interviews. In addition to the standard door-to-door interview, Burke provides Central Location Studios (labs) in shopping centers, and in-store interviewing in shopping centers in New York, Florida, Michigan, and Colorado. Shopping center intercept interviews are performed in 30 cities.

Mail surveys.

Group discussions.

Concept tests.

Product tests. Both studio and in-home tests are provided.

In addition to standard awareness, attitude trial, and usage studies, Burke does a large amount of advertising research. Preproduction copy tests using forced exposures are provided for TV, print, and radio ads. Day-after phone recall surveys are then conducted. Many companies use the "Burke Scores" as a measure of commercial effectiveness.

DUN AND BRADSTREET

Dun and Bradstreet's Marketing Services Division provides a variety of basic services. The most widely used is the Dun's Market Identifiers

(DMI). This service is based on a data bank of over 4,000,000 businesses in the United States and Canada. The companies are grouped according to four-digit SIC codes. For example, there were 7,130 Truck Rental and Leasing firms (SIC code 7513), 2,919 Metal Door, Sash and Trim firms (SIC code 3442), and 27 firms mining Bauxite and Aluminum Ore (SIC code 1051).

The main use of this service has been for industrial marketers to estimate market potentials. The data is also used to help define sales ter-

FIGURE 8–16
Dun and Bradstreet basic marketing facts

Identification:
    1. Name of establishment.
    2. D-U-N-S number.
    3. D-U-N-S number of headquarters.
    4. D-U-N-S number of parent.

Classification:
    5. Headquarters.
    6. Branch.
    7. Subsidiary.
    8. Manufacturing or nonmanufacturing location.
    9. Single or multiple location.

Location:
   10. Street address.
   11. Mailing address (if different).
   12. Zip code.*
   13. City.
   14. County code.
   15. SMSA code.†
   16. State (or province).
   17. Telephone number.
   18. Area code.

Products or services:
   19. Primary line of business (SIC).
   20. Up to five secondary SICs.

Size:
   21. Sales volume.
   22. Employees at this location.
   23. Total employees.

Financial strength:
   24. Net worth.‡
   25. Credit rating.‡

Other:
   26. Year the business started.
   27. Chief executive (and title).

* First three digits of zip code denote sectional center.
† Standard metropolitan statistical area.
‡ Credit and net worth data available only to subscribers to the D & B Credit Service at an additional charge.
Source: Dun and Bradstreet, Inc., *Dun's Market Identifiers*, © 1976.

ritories and to pinpoint particularly good prospects as well as to provide a mailing list of potential customers. On each business a list of 27 variables are maintained (Figure 8–16). A customer selects the type of business s/he is interested in (typically described by geographic area and/or SIC code, but also sometimes by a variety of measures such as sales volume or employment size). The customer then receives anything from the name of the businesses which pass the screen to a complete profile of each of the companies based on the 27 available variables, depending on how much he is willing to pay.

SOME OTHER MAJOR SUPPLIERS

Space limitations make it impossible to adequately cover even the companies already discussed. Also, by the time you read this changes will have occurred, in prices if nothing else. Hence the purpose of this chapter was as much to indicate the kinds of services available from suppliers as to detail what services leading suppliers offer. Some of the big names left out were as follows:

1. The general survey conductors:
    a. Gallup, Gallup-Robinson.
    b. Yankelovich, Skelly and White.
    c. Louis Harris.
    d. Opinion Research Corporation.
2. Erdos and Morgan (a specialist in mail surveys).
3. Chilton Research.
4. Oxtoby-Smith.
5. Crossley Surveys.
6. Data Development.
7. Pulse (a competitor of Arbitron in audience measurement).
8. M.S.A. (Marketing Science Associates).
9. A.S.I. (Audience Studies, Inc.) a division of Immarco (one of the largest research suppliers) specializing in TV commercial testing in theater and home settings.
10. Doane (a major supplier of agricultural product data from their panels of feedlot operators, farmers, etc.).
11. Miller Agricultural Research.
12. The "Tab Houses" specializing in analysis rather than data collection, such as OPOC and Datatab.
13. Erhart-Babic (a specialist in custom audits and in-store research).
14. Walker Research (a major supplier of personal interview surveys).
15. Elrick and Lavidge.
16. Bruskin (best known for its monthly omnibus AIM survey).

17. Aulino-Baen.
18. AHF.

SUMMARY

This chapter has attempted to outline some of the major types of services available from suppliers. In using suppliers, it is important to note that performance should be carefully evaluated (Mayer, 1967). While most of the major suppliers are honest, they are under time and profit pressures which suggest continued involvement (but not harassment) on the part of the client is generally advisable from a quality control as well as an information perspective. Also in using suppliers, be careful to check out exactly what is going on—this chapter is not gospel and did not attempt to list the many criticisms each of the services have encountered.

One final point concerns the use of "other brands." A variety of small research shops exist. Some are very competent. The disadvantages of using a small operator are (a) they will have to do more subcontracting, (b) they usually do not have the same experience base as larger operators, and (c) the results are less impressive to the average reader of the report if s/he has never heard of the company. On the other hand, small companies often have novel approaches to problems which may be particularly useful.

PROBLEMS

1. Why do you think companies, including big ones like General Foods, hire suppliers rather than gathering and analyzing data themselves?
2. For each of the following problems, suggest the likely research approach(es) and at least two potential suppliers:
    a. Estimating the effect of a proposed TV advertising copy for shampoo.
    b. Estimating eventual sales of a new food product now in test market.
    c. Evaluating the appeal of various hypothetical product designs for a dishwasher.
    d. Understanding how consumers approach the decision to purchase a house.
    e. Studying the use of a new drug by physicians.
    f. Measuring the closeness of competition between two food products.
3. Interpret the following audit share data, assuming you were brand manager for Znarts:

		Brand share by store				
Total U.S.	*Brand*	*A&P*	*Finast*	*Grand Union*	*Other chains*	*Others*
18%	Znarts	12%	18%	17%	21%	16%
25	A	19	28	32	25	28
18	B	21	18	15	20	16
28	C	31	30	26	24	28
4	Other	3	3	5	4	10
5	Private label	15	3	5	6	2
100%						

4. Assume you were monitoring sales in a region and found the following results concerning market share:

SAMI	Jan.– Feb. 1978	Mar.– Apr. 1978	May– June 1978	July– Aug. 1978	Sept.– Oct. 1978	Nov.– Dec. 1978	Jan.– Feb. 1979
Audit data	29%	29%	28%	30%	32%	31%	30%
Panel data	29	28	27	28	31	29	33

   a. Is anything happening?

   b. If so, what might be the explanation for the data?

5. Assume you switched suppliers for audit data and overlapped suppliers for one period. The estimated shares were as follows:

	Jan.– Feb. 1978	Mar.– Apr. 1978	May– June 1978	July– Aug. 1978	Sept.– Oct. 1978	Nov.– Dec. 1978	Jan.– Feb. 1979	Mar.– Apr. 1979	May Jun 19
Old supplier	29.2	28.7	26.9	27.3	28.3	27.9	28.1	27.0	—
New supplier	—	—	—	—	—	—	—	29.2	30.

   a. Are we better or worse off than we were one year ago in May–June (and by how much)?

   b. What do you expect to happen to share next period (July–August)?

   c. Suggest how you might estimate what sales in July–Aug. 1978 would have been under the new supplier.

6. Which brand is doing better?

Brand	Percent of Distribution ACV	(Sales units)
A	70%	18,000
B	90	23,000

7. Assume I wanted to know how much a new brand would cannibalize sales of an existing brand. What research methods might be employed?

8. Explain the calculations of reach, frequency, and gross rating points. How accurate do you think the calculations are and what does this accuracy depend on? Under what circumstances would each be the appropriate objective to maximize in setting a media advertising schedule?

9. Given the following breakdown on sterling silver flatware purchase by magazine readership (see the accompanying table), how would you go about constructing a magazine advertising schedule?

AVERAGE ISSUE AUDIENCE

FLATWARE - PLACE SETTINGS PERSONALLY PURCHASED, AMOUNT SPENT AND PURPOSE OF PURCHASE IN LAST YEAR
TOTAL ADULTS

(IN THOUSANDS)

	US TOTAL	AMERICAN BABY	AMERICAN HOME	BARRON'S	BETTER HOMES & GARDENS	BUSINESS WEEK	CAR AND DRIVER	COSMOPOLITAN	ESQUIRE	FAMILY CIRCLE	FAMILY WEEKLY	FIELD & STREAM	FORBES	FORTUNE	GIRL TALK	GLAMOUR
RATING	149056	1871	4446	1054	24743	3837	3180	9498	4634	20908	18451	10061	1773	1661	1320	7256
	100.0	1.3	3.0	.7	16.6	2.6	2.1	6.4	3.1	14.0	12.4	6.7	1.2	1.1	.9	4.9
' FLATWARE RLING, ER PLATE, NLESS)																
AST YEAR	11233	**102	591	**39	2590	383	*261	956	544	2242	1648	682	174	154	**107	847
CT COMP	7.5	5.5	13.3	3.7	10.5	10.0	8.2	10.1	11.7	10.7	8.9	6.8	9.8	9.3	8.1	11.7
INDEX	100	73	177	49	140	133	109	135	156	143	119	91	131	124	108	156
RATING	100.0	.9	5.3	.3	23.1	3.4	2.3	8.5	4.8	20.0	14.7	6.1	1.5	1.4	1.0	7.5
SETTINGS GHT THAN 8	4088	**50	*260	**9	1001	*95	**139	319	*219	765	654	*226	**54	*104	**39	324
CT COMP	2.7	2.7	5.8	.9	4.0	2.5	3.4	3.4	4.7	3.7	3.5	2.2	3.0	6.3	3.0	4.5
INDEX	100	100	215	33	148	93	126	126	174	137	130	81	111	233	111	167
RATING	100.0	1.2	6.4	.2	24.5	2.3	2.7	7.8	5.4	18.7	16.0	5.5	1.3	2.5	1.0	7.9
	5173	**33	*244	**17	1031	*204	**118	454	*227	926	644	345	**65	**36	**50	396
CT COMP	3.5	1.8	5.5	1.6	4.2	5.3	3.7	4.8	4.9	4.4	3.5	3.4	3.7	2.2	3.8	5.5
INDEX	100	51	157	46	120	151	106	137	140	126	100	97	106	63	109	157
RATING	100.0	.6	4.7	.3	19.9	3.9	2.3	8.8	4.4	17.9	12.4	6.7	1.3	.7	1.0	7.7
R MORE	1972	**18	**87	**13	557	**84	**33	*182	**98	551	*350	**112	**55	**15	**19	**127
CT COMP	1.3	1.0	2.0	1.2	2.3	2.2	1.0	1.9	2.1	2.6	1.9	1.1	3.1	.9	1.4	1.8
INDEX	100	77	154	92	177	169	77	146	162	200	146	85	238	69	108	138
RATING	100.0	.9	4.4	.7	28.2	4.3	1.7	9.2	5.0	27.9	17.7	5.7	2.8	.8	1.0	6.4
NT SPENT S THAN $40	6889	**66	*288	**8	1427	*189	**191	560	349	1247	901	352	*106	*112	**48	469
CT COMP	4.6	3.5	6.5	.8	5.8	4.9	6.0	5.9	7.5	6.0	4.9	3.5	6.0	6.7	3.6	6.5
INDEX	100	76	141	17	126	107	130	128	163	130	107	76	130	146	78	141
RATING	100.0	1.0	4.2	.1	20.7	2.7	2.8	8.1	5.1	18.1	13.1	5.1	1.5	1.6	.7	6.8
OR MORE	4343	**36	*303	**31	1163	195	**69	396	*196	995	748	330	*69	*42	**59	378
CT COMP	2.9	1.9	6.8	2.9	4.7	5.1	2.2	4.2	4.2	4.8	4.1	3.3	3.9	2.5	4.5	5.2
INDEX	100	66	234	100	162	176	76	145	145	166	141	114	134	86	155	179
RATING	100.0	.8	7.0	.7	26.8	4.5	1.6	9.1	4.5	22.9	17.2	7.6	1.6	1.0	1.4	8.7

*PROJECTION RELATIVELY UNSTABLE BECAUSE OF SMALL SAMPLE BASE: USE WITH CAUTION
**NUMBER OF CASES TOO SMALL FOR RELIABILITY: SHOWN FOR CONSISTENCY ONLY

W. R. SIMMONS & ASSOCIATES RESEARCH
a division of Stanton-Grudin-Chook Inc.
1976/77

10. Assess the effect of the 80-cents-off coupon run by Wisk in the second four-week period of the following data compiled by AdTel from their panel:

	Period							
	1	2	3	4	5	6	7	8
Total share	4.7	6.4	16.5	10.6	5.4	4.6	4.5	4.8
Deal share	.7	3.3	11.7	7.9	1.8	.6	1.2	1.9
Nondeal share	4.0	3.1	4.8	2.7	3.6	4.0	3.3	3.9

11. Interpret the following data based on a two-year (July 1969–July 1971) AdTel study. The data is the percent of Brand Buyers Total Furniture Polish Volume accounted for by their favorite brand.

Favorite brand	Favorite brand share of total purchases
Lemon Pledge...................	41.5%
Regular Pledge.................	34.4
Favor	34.1
Behold	32.7
Pride	31.1
Jubilee	30.2
Old English	28.8
Endust.........................	22.9

Source: Reprinted with permission from AdTel, Inc., New York.

12. Interpret these two tables taken from AdTel results. What other data sources could be used to collect such data?

Deal loyalty	Ajax	Comet	Total Scouring Cleanser
Brand buyers purchasing 50% or more of brand volume on deal	27.1%	17.1%	15.9%
Volume accounted for by buyers purchasing 50% or more of brand volume on deal	20.1	9.9	11.5
Brand buyers purchasing 80%, or more of brand volume on deal	17.7	9.1	5.1
Volume accounted for by buyers purchasing 80% or more of brand volume on deal	10.6	3.4	2.9

Source: Reprinted with permission from AdTel, Inc., New York.

Combination buying patterns among heavy/light brand buyers of scouring cleanser (equivalent units bought during two-year period)

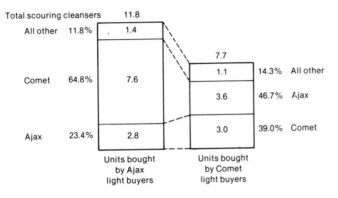

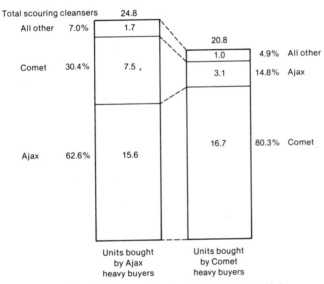

Source: Reprinted with permission from AdTel, Inc., New York.

BIBLIOGRAPHY

"A. C. Nielsen Company." Northbrook, Ill.: A. C. Nielsen, 1976.

"Concept Testing." Toledo, Ohio: National Family Opinion, 1975.

"Description of Methodology." New York: American Research Bureau, 1975.

"ESP." Floral Park, N.Y.: National Purchase Diary Panel, 1977.

Eskin, Gerald J. "Dynamic Forecasts of New Product Demand Using a Depth of Repeat Model." *Journal of Marketing Research,* vol. 10 (May 1973), pp. 115–29.

"Facts about CMP II." Chicago: Market Facts, 1976.

"The Facts of SAMI and SARDI." New York: Selling Area Marketing, 1976.

Green Book. New York: American Marketing Association, New York Chapter, published annually.

"How Arbitron Measures Radio." New York: American Research Bureau, 1974.

"How to Test and Measure the Sales Effectiveness of Television Advertising and Consumer Promotion." New York: AdTel, 1973.

"How to Use SAMI." New York: Selling Area Marketing, 1976.

Mayer, Charles S. "Evaluating the Quality of Market Research Contractors." *Journal of Marketing Research,* vol. 4 (May 1967), pp. 134–41.

"MRCA Reporting Systems." Chicago: Market Research Corporation of America.

"The National Consumer Panel." Chicago: Market Research Corporation of America.

"The National Consumer Textile Panel." Chicago: Market Research Corporation of America.

"National Household Cleaning and Laundry Census." Chicago: Market Research Corporation of America.

"The National Household Menu." Chicago: Market Research Corporation of America.

"NFO Consumer Family Sample." Toledo, Ohio: National Family Opinion, 1976.

"Nielsen Data Markets." Northbrook, Ill.: A. C. Nielsen, 1976.

"Nielsen Major Market Service." Northbrook, Ill.: A. C. Nielsen, 1976.

"Nielsen Retail Index Services." Northbrook, Ill.: A. C. Nielsen, 1975.

"SAMI Corporate Development Information Systems." New York: Selling Area Marketing, 1976.

"Sample Food Operator Reports." New York: Selling Area Marketing, 1976.

"Selective Markets and the Media: Reaching Them." New York: Simmons Media Studies.

"Sharpening Marketing Decisions with Diary Panels." Floral Park, N.Y.: National Purchase Diary Panel, 1975.

Shoemaker, Robert, and Pringle, Lew. "Problems in Using Nielsen Audit Data as a Measure of Bi-Monthly Sales." Unpublished working paper, Carnegie-Melon University, 1977.

"Sixteen Stages for Complete Marketing Planning." Northbrook, Ill.: A. C. Nielsen, 1976.

"Test Marketing and the Custom-Designed National Family Opinion Consumer Purchase Diary Panel." Toledo, Ohio: National Family Opinion, 1976.

"Understanding and Using Radio Audience Estimates." New York: American Research Bureau, 1976.

"Why Buy Industrial Marketing Research?" New York: Market Facts, Inc.

9

Sampling in marketing research

Sampling is fundamental to most human behavior. When trying a new food, a person will typically eat one or two bites and then form an opinion. Similarly a reader of this book will often sample several passages in order to make a decision about whether to continue reading. Yet somehow sampling in marketing research has achieved an aura of mystery and even science, due only in part to the quantitative formulations of the effects of employing various sampling procedures. While one approach to making sampling decisions is to call in a high priest (read Ph.D. in statistics), for most common situations a few basics plus some common sense will suffice. The purpose of this chapter is to introduce such basics. More detailed treatments are found in Hansen, Hurwitz, and Madow (1953); Deming (1960); Cochran (1963); Kish (1965); and Sudman (1976).

IS A SAMPLE REALLY NEEDED?

Often a researcher will be faced with a situation where someone has suggested that a sample should be taken. Before dashing out to begin interviews, however, a good researcher will do two things. First, the researcher will ask, "What is the problem?" Since the first response will often be something like, "To find out what people think of _____," the question will then be repeated until the researcher is satisfied that the "real" problem has been found. (For example, "A decision must be made about which of two package designs to use.") At this point the researcher should then evaluate whether information gained by sampling anything will help solve the problem. Assuming the conclusion is that a sample would be useful, the researcher then will proceed to the second step—finding out if there is an easier way to solve the problem. While the odds are low that the exact information needed exists, the odds are not so low that information is available which would be "good enough" to at least

252

solve part of the problem. There also may be an easier way than a formal sample to make the decision (e.g., ask someone who seems to have a good head for that type of decision). Only then "should" the researcher worry about what type of sample to take. (However, political realities within an organization being what they are, if the boss or company policy says "sample," the best response is often "How many?")

THE BASIC ISSUES OF SAMPLE DESIGN

The basic issues of sample design are really twofold. The first is that the sample should be representative of the population of interest in terms of the key responses. A sample does not have to be typical of the general population or even the part of the population under study in terms of other characteristics. While one would expect a sample which had the same average income, age, and so forth, as the population of interest to be representative in terms of purchase behavior, it may not be. Conversely, a sample can be very different demographically and still be representative of some types of behavior. Obviously a sample which is similar to the population under study is in general more likely to be representative in terms of key responses than one which is not.

The second basic issue of sampling has to do with nonresponse. Even the best designed sampling plans encounter nonresponse (the person/ sample point designated by the sample plan cannot be located or refuses to cooperate) and partial nonresponse (the respondent does not provide complete response to all questions). In the "real world," the handling of nonresponses often is much more important than the particular sampling plan chosen.

In order to cover the major aspects of sampling in a systematic way, the remainder of this chapter will proceed to address the following issues:

1. Who is the target population (frame)?
2. What method (process) will be used to elicit responses?
3. How many will be sampled?
4. How will the sampling points be selected?
5. What will be done about nonresponse?

WHO IS THE TARGET POPULATION?

The target population, or frame, is that part of the total population (universe) to which the study is directed. For example, for a company selling automobiles in the United States, the universe could be the entire U.S. population plus foreign visitors, and the frame might be people aged 18 or over. Alternatively, the focus could be on relatively well-off individuals, and hence the target might be those with annual incomes above

$20,000. Choice of a target population which is too large leads to the collection of data from people whose responses are meaningless. For example, car preferences of eight-year-olds, assuming they are relatively uninfluential in family auto purchase decisions, are irrelevant. On the other hand, choice of an overly narrow frame will tend to exclude potentially useful responses. For example, focusing on males aged 25–49 may cover the majority of a market but will undoubtedly exclude some important segments. The choice of a target population, then, requires balancing between including irrelevant sampling points and excluding relevant ones.

Screening questions

Many interviews begin by screening the respondents. The basis of screening may be visual (e.g., age, make of car, whether they just bought a particular product) or verbal (asking a screening question such as, "Do you smoke?"). Screening questions are used to avoid interviewing individuals not in the target population. Only those subjects who "qualify" are then presented with the full survey.

WHAT METHOD WILL BE USED?

Part of the job of designing a sampling plan is to specify how the data will be collected. This means that for a survey a choice must be made between phone, personal, mail, and so forth. Since the choice of the method of data collection often influences the type of sample to be drawn, the method used is an integral part of the sample determination process.

HOW MANY WILL BE SAMPLED?

The decision about how many to sample can be very complex. An entire branch of Bayesian statistics is devoted to this issue (Schlaifer, 1959). For the practical marketing researcher, however, four major considerations are paramount: statistical precision, credibility, company policy (generally accepted practice), and financial constraints.

Statistical precision

The larger the sample size, the more confident the researcher can be that the results are representative of the things being measured. In general, the precision of a sample is related to the square of the sample size. (By precision, we mean the level of uncertainty about the value of the construct being measured.) In other words, to double the precision of an estimate, the sample must be four times as large.

Once the sample is drawn, the level of precision is already determined. If the level of precision needed can be specified ahead of time, however, it is possible to determine the minimum required sample size. This sample size refers to the number of usable responses, not the number of individuals in the target sample. (e.g., If you expect a 50 percent response rate, the number in the target sample will be twice the number of usable responses needed, assuming equal response rates in all segments.)

Averages. Consider the problem of estimating average income of U.S. households from a sample. As you may recall from statistics (but undoubtedly do not; see Appendix 9–A), the average income generated by the sample ($\overline{X}$) is the best guess of the average income of U.S. households. However, the sample $\overline{X}$ may not exactly equal the population average due to idiosyncracies of the sample. The most accurate statement that can be made is that the true mean is within some range about $\overline{X}$. In order to quantify this range, two important facts are used:

1. The sample mean ($\overline{X}$) is approximately normally distributed.

2. The standard deviation of the sample mean is the standard deviation calculated in the sample divided by the square root of the sample size:

$$s_{\bar{X}} = \frac{s}{\sqrt{n}}$$

Using these two facts, it is possible to construct a range (known to statistics students as a *confidence interval*) into which the true mean will fall with a given level of certainty (known to statistics students as a *confidence level*). This range is given by

Range in which true mean falls = Sample mean $\pm z_\alpha \dfrac{s}{\sqrt{n}}$

where Z_α is a constant drawn from a standard normal table which depends on the level of confidence desired (Figure 9–1). For example, the commonly used 95 percent confidence interval (range in which we are 95 percent sure that the true mean falls) is given by

$$\overline{X} \pm 1.96 \frac{s}{\sqrt{n}}$$

Hence if we took a sample of 400 households in the United States and measured their average income as \$15,172 and the standard deviation of their income as 6,216, the 95 percent confidence interval for true household average income in the United States would be

$$15,172 \pm 1.96 \left(\frac{6,216}{\sqrt{400}}\right) = 15,172 \pm 609$$
$$= \text{between } 14,563 \text{ and } 15,781$$

The precision of this estimate was determined by the sample size (n), the standard deviation (s), and the confidence level desired.

FIGURE 9–1
Estimating the true mean from a sample mean

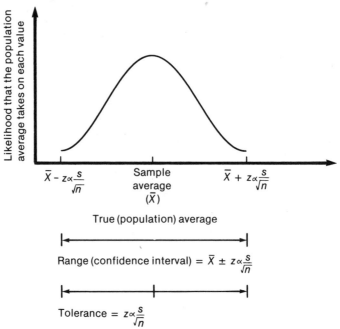

A slight variation on this formula can be used to determine necessary sample size in advance. First, decide on an acceptable confidence level. Second, estimate the standard deviation of income(s) in the target population. (In order to be "conservative" and guarantee the sample size is adequate, make sure this is a generous estimate.) This can be done either objectively (from a prior or special small sample) or subjectively (in other words, a guess). One useful method for estimating the standard deviation is to first estimate the range of the distribution and then divide by 6. Next solve the following formula for the necessary sample size n:

$$\text{Tolerance level acceptable} = z_\alpha \frac{s}{\sqrt{n}} \tag{9.1}$$

For example, assuming S were 3,000, the tolerance acceptable were 100, and we wanted to be 95 percent sure that we would be within the tolerance, we then get

$$100 = 1.96 \frac{3,000}{\sqrt{n}}$$

$$\therefore \sqrt{n} = 1.96(30)$$

and

$$n = 3,457.44 \Rightarrow 3,458$$

(We can't sample fractional people, and 3,457 won't give quite enough precision.) Hence if we sample 3,458 people, we can estimate the mean within ± 100.

Proportions.   A similar approach can be used to estimate the value of a proportion. Assume, for example, we wish to estimate the proportion of our accounts who also buy from a major competitor. If we take a sample of our accounts and calculate the proportion of them who also buy from the competitor (p), the proportion is approximately normally distributed. The proportion of our accounts who buy from the competitor thus can be estimated by a confidence interval:

$$p \pm z_\alpha \sqrt{\frac{p(1-p)}{n}}$$

For example, assume we sample 400 of our 30,000 accounts and find that 32 percent also buy from our competitor. The 95 percent confidence interval for the percent of all our accounts who buy from the competitor is given by

$$\text{Range of true proportion} = \text{Sample proportion} \pm z_\alpha \sqrt{\frac{p(1-p)}{n}}$$
$$= 32 \text{ percent} \pm 1.96 \sqrt{\frac{(32)(68)}{400}}$$
$$= 32 \text{ percent} \pm 4.6 \text{ percent}$$
$$= \text{range from 27.4 percent to 36.6\%}$$

As in the case of the mean, this formula can be used to estimate the necessary sample size in advance. In this case, the required sample size can be derived from the following:

$$\text{Tolerance} = z_\alpha \sqrt{\frac{p(1-p)}{n}} \qquad (9.2)$$

Assuming we wanted to be accurate within 3 percent at the 95 percent confidence interval, this reduces to

$$3 = 1.96 \sqrt{\frac{p(1-p)}{n}}$$

If we have a prior notion of p, we then proceed to plug it in. If, for example, we thought p were about 10 percent, then we would get

$$3 = 1.96 \sqrt{\frac{(10)(90)}{n}}$$

or

$$\sqrt{n} = 1.96 \frac{30}{3} = 19.6$$

Therefore

$$n = 384.16 \Rightarrow 385$$

Alternatively, we could adopt the "conservative" procedure and assume p were 50 percent. (This produces the maximum sample size needed for a given tolerance. Actually any p between .3 and .7 produces fairly similar results.) In this case, we would obtain

$$3 = 1.96 \sqrt{\frac{(50)(50)}{n}}$$

or

$$\sqrt{n} = 1.96 \frac{50}{3}$$

Therefore

$$n = 1,067.1 \Rightarrow 1,068$$

Notice that this result produces the "magic" sample size of between 1,000 and 1,500 which is characteristic of most national samples. In fact, this size national sample is chosen with just such notions of precision in mind.

Finite population correction. Both of the previous procedures apply to a situation where the target population is essentially infinite. This is the case of most consumer goods studies. When the sample gets large in relation to the target population (over 10–20 percent of its size), however, these formulas will over estimate the required sample. Assuming sample points are expensive, the finite sample size correction factor should be employed. (The correction factor accounts for the fact that when the sample size n approaches the population size N, the uncertainty about the population average drops to zero.) This correction would convert the two formulas for determining sample size to the more accurate

$$\text{Numerical tolerance} = z_\alpha \frac{s}{\sqrt{n}} \sqrt{\frac{N - n}{N - 1}} \qquad (9.3)$$

where N is the size of the target population.

$$\text{Percent tolerance} = z_\alpha \sqrt{\frac{p(1 - p)}{n}} \sqrt{\frac{N - n}{N - 1}} \qquad (9.4)$$

Credibility

Since the purpose of gathering data is to provide information someone else will use, it is important to have a credible sample size. Statistical issues aside, 100 is a sine qua non and 1,000 a magic cutoff among many users of research. Since marketing research is part marketing, a wise researcher takes this into account.

Company policy (generally accepted practice)

Many companies develop a sampling pattern over time which becomes a standard operating procedure. (For example, for a new product 200 interviews are gathered in the Albany area during test marketing.) While these policies (written or unwritten) usually have a logical basis, a different sample size may be better. Unless the sample is woefully inadequate, however, attempts to change the policy may prove more quixotic than useful (not to mention politically unwise, since your boss may have established the precedent).

Financial constraints

When all the scientific talk subsides, someone always asks how much money is available for the study. If this is known, the easiest way to calculate the sample size is to take the budget (SP), subtract the fixed costs of the study (EN) plus any dinners, trips, or expenses we can charge to it (D) and then divide by the variable cost of a sample point or interview (IT). This leads to the very scientific formula:

$$n = \frac{SP - EN - D}{IT}$$

This formula is in reality every bit as important in determining sample size as those relating to the statistical precision of the results.

WHO WILL BE SAMPLED?

In deciding who will be sampled, the first issue is to see if some list or other organized breakdown (e.g., geographic) of the target population exists. If not, location sampling or random digit dialing are probably the only alternatives. In this section, however, we will assume some list or breakdown is available.

One commonly drawn distinction in sampling is between probabilistic and purposive samples. In probabilistic samples, each member of the target population has a fixed (often equal) probability of being a member of the target sample. Purposive samples, on the other hand, place greater importance on some segments of the target population and consequently are drawn to "overrepresent" these important segments. Some of the major sampling approaches include simple random sampling, nth name (systematic) sampling, stratified sampling, universal sampling (census), convenience sampling, quota sampling, cluster sampling, sequential and replicated sampling, and multistage sampling.

Simple random sampling

The best known and most "democratic" form of selecting the sample points to be contacted is random. This method basically assures every individual in the target population has an equal chance of being drawn. This is done by using a random number table to generate n (the desired number to sample) random numbers between 1 and the number of names on the list. The individuals with numbers corresponding to the random numbers then become the target sample. This method is equivalent to the classic lottery where names are placed in a hat and drawn out "randomly."

Random samples have many nice properties. They are not, however, the most efficient (either logically or in a statistical estimation sense) procedure for many situations. For example, a random sample of 20 could contain all nonsmokers, with the resulting average opinions about the dangers of cigarettes seriously distorted. While such inhospitable results are relatively rare, they do occur (especially in small samples). For that reason, some of the subsequent procedures which guarantee the correct proportion of smokers and nonsmokers are sometimes more efficient in representing the target population (i.e., get a closer estimate of the true population value for a given sample size). In spite of this, however, random is a word close to motherhood and apple pie in the ears of many laypersons. One reason for this is that most of the statistical formulas used assume a random sample was taken. For that reason, random samples are often taken (or other sampling plans described as random) in order to gain credibility for the study. In fact, some researchers have been known to keep drawing random samples until the sample drawn looks good in terms of its characteristics. The resulting sample, however, is obviously neither very efficient in a practical sense nor truely random in a statistical sense.

nth name (systematic)

An nth name sample is in effect a poor person's random sample. The procedure here is to generate target sample points by picking an arbitrary starting point and then picking every nth person in succession from a list. For example, if I wished to draw a target sample of 30 from a target population of 1,200, I might arbitrarily select the 11th individual (a number between 1 and 40) as a starting point and then individuals 51, 91, 181, . . . , 1,181 as my 30 target sample points.

The major problem with nth name procedures occurs if there is a cycle in the data which is related to the interval between respondents. Especially obvious would be an nth name sample of daily sales of a particular store. If I took a seventh name sample, I would hit the same day of the week every time. If the day were Sunday and blue laws closed the store on Sundays, this would be especially unfortunate. While such obvious cycles rarely occur, occasionally a more subtle relation does appear. Assuming no cyclical problems, however, nth name samples turn out to be more efficient (give a more reliable estimate of some variable) than random samples when the underlying list used is logically ordered.

The major advantage of nth name sampling is its ease vis-a-vis random sampling. First, a set of random numbers does not have to be generated. Second, these random numbers do not have to be matched with individual respondents. Since some lists contain over 50 million households on computer tapes, matching is inefficient unless the random numbers are arranged in order, and even then the length of time to scan the tapes and pull off the names and addresses or phone numbers of the designated individuals is longer than in an nth name sample. For this reason, most consumer phone and mail surveys are based on nth name designs.

Stratified

For many studies, the target population can be divided into segments with different characteristics. In this case the information about the segments (strata) can be used to design the sampling plan. Specifically, separate sampling plans can be drawn for each of the stratum. This guarantees that each stratum will be adequately represented, something which random sampling does not. (It is possible, albeit unlikely for a random sample to fail to contain adequate representation of a particular segment of the population.)

Assuming different samples are drawn from each stratum, the mean and standard deviation of a variable in the entire target population can then be estimated as follows:

Let

N_i = size of the ith stratum

n_i = sample size in the ith stratum

N = size of the total target population

n = total sample size

w_i = weight of the estimate of the ith stratum = $\dfrac{N_i}{N}$

k = number of stratum

s_i = standard deviation in the ith stratum

$\bar{x}_i$ = mean in ith stratum

Then

$$\bar{x} = \sum_{i=1}^{k} w_i \bar{x}_i \tag{9.5}$$

$$s_{\bar{x}} = \sqrt{\sum_{i=1}^{k} w_i^2 s_{\bar{x}_i}^2} = \sqrt{\sum_{i=1}^{k} w_i^2 \frac{s_i^2}{n_i}} \qquad (9.6)$$

For proportions, the formulas become

$$p = \sum_{i=1}^{k} w_i p_i \qquad (9.7)$$

and

$$s_p = \sqrt{\sum_{i=1}^{k} w_i^2 \frac{p_i(1 - p_i)}{n_i}} \qquad (9.8)$$

Stratified sampling actually encompasses two approaches: proportionate (where the number sampled in each stratum is proportional to the size of the stratum) and disproportionate (where the number sampled is based on something other than the sample size).

Proportionate stratified sampling. For proportionate stratified sampling, the sample size of each stratum (n_i) is given by the proportion of the population that falls into that stratum (N_i/N). The standard deviation of the estimate of the mean becomes

$$s_{\bar{x}} = \sqrt{\sum \left(\frac{N_i}{N}\right)^2 \frac{s_i^2}{n_i}}$$

And since $n_i = \frac{N_i}{N} \cdot n$

$$s_{\bar{x}} = \sqrt{\frac{\sum w_i s_i^2}{n}} \qquad (9.9)$$

Consider the hypothetical situation (Table 9–1) where beer consumers were divided into four segments (strata) on the basis of demographics. A proportionate sample would then be drawn with sample size in each stratum proportional to the size of the sample:

$$n_i = \frac{N_i}{N} \cdot n$$

Hence a proportionate sample of size 200 would consist of 80, 60, 40, and 20 people respectively from the four strata.

Now assume a proportionate sample of 200 were drawn from the target population and the results in Table 9–1 were obtained. Thus my estimate of overall average beer consumption would be

$$\begin{aligned}
\bar{x} &= .4(20) + (.3)(10) + (.2)(15) + (.1)(6) \\
&= 8 + 3 + 3 + .6 \\
&= 14.6
\end{aligned}$$

Similarly, using the general formula (9.6):

TABLE 9–1
An example of proportionate stratified sampling

Stratum	Size of stratum	Stratum sample size $\left(= \dfrac{N_i}{N} \cdot n\right)$	Average beer consumption	Standard deviation of beer consumption
1	8,000	80	20	4
2	6,000	60	10	4
3	4,000	40	15	5
4	2,000	20	6	2
	20,000	200		

$$s_{\bar{x}} = \sqrt{(.4)^2 \frac{4^2}{80} + (.3)^2 \frac{4^2}{60} + (.2)^2 \frac{5^2}{40} + (.1)^2 \frac{2^2}{20}}$$
$$= \sqrt{.032 + .024 + .025 + .002}$$
$$= \sqrt{.083} = .288$$

Alternatively, the shortcut formula (9.9) gives

$$s_{\bar{x}} = \sqrt{\frac{.4(4)^2 + .3(4)^2 + .2(5)^2 + .1(2)^2}{200}}$$
$$= \sqrt{\frac{6.4 + 4.8 + 5.0 + .4}{200}}$$
$$= .288$$

Disproportionate sampling. A proportionate sample is designed to give each individual in the target population an equal chance of being included. Disproportionate samples, on the other hand, are "undemocratic" since some strata are deemed more important than others. A disproportionately large part of the sample is then obtained from these important strata.

The reasons for disproportionate sampling are multiple. One obvious reason is that certain segments of the population may be considered key for marketing strategy and hence a researcher will want a relatively large number of sample points in these segments, while at the same time other strata may be sufficiently important potentially that they cannot be totally ignored. Another reason for disproportionate sampling is that the costs of sampling across strata may be quite different. Hence a fixed budget dictates both logically and statistically that a relatively large proportion of the sample be drawn from the relatively "cheap" to question strata.

There also is a statistical reason for sampling disproportionately. If the goal is to produce the most reliable estimate possible, the optimal sample size drawn from each stratum depends on both the size of the stratum and the variance within the stratum. Taking an extreme example, assume one segment exists with average consumption of 3 and standard deviation of 4, and another exists with average consumption of 320 and standard deviation of 0. In this case, a single observation from the second stratum will produce all the information available from the stratum (the mean of 320) and all other sample points in this stratum will be redundant. Hence all of the sample except one should be drawn from the first segment if the goal is to produce the minimum variance (most reliable) estimate of the overall mean.

The general formula for optimal sampling to minimize total variance of the estimate is

$$n_i = \frac{w_i s_i}{\sum\limits_{i=1}^{k} w_i s_i} \cdot n \tag{9.10}$$

and the resulting standard error of the mean

$$s_{\bar{x}} = \sqrt{\frac{\left(\sum\limits_{i=1}^{k} w_i s_i\right)^2}{n}} \tag{9.11}$$

(The interested reader can prove this is a special case of the general formula 9.6.)

Returning to our beer (example, that is), we can find the optimal sample allocations as follows:

$$
\begin{aligned}
n_1 &= \frac{.4(4)}{.4(4) + .3(4) + .2(5) + .1(2)} \cdot 200 \\
&= \frac{1.6}{4.0} \cdot 200 \\
&= 80
\end{aligned}
$$

Similarly we can see

$$
\begin{aligned}
n_2 &= 60 \\
n_3 &= 50 \\
n_4 &= 10
\end{aligned}
$$

It is important to notice that this procedure requires knowing the standard deviations in each stratum in advance. Since the true standard deviations are never deducible, we substitute either subjective estimates of the sample or the results of a prior study.

Assuming we now proceeded to take another survey of size 200 according to the disproportionate approach, the results might be as follows:

Size strata	Size of sample	Mean	Standard deviation
8,000	80	20	4
6,000	60	10	4
4,000	50	15	5
2,000	10	6	2

Average beer consumption would then be, as before:

$$\bar{x} = .4(20) + .3(10) + .2(15) + .1(6)$$
$$= 14.6$$

The standard deviation would be

$$s_{\bar{x}} = \sqrt{\frac{[4(4) + .3(4) + .2(5) + .1(2)]^2}{200}}$$
$$= \sqrt{\frac{4^2}{200}} = \sqrt{.08}$$
$$= .283$$

In this case, the standard deviation is only slightly (less than 2 percent) smaller under the disproportionate sampling plan, a surprisingly typical result. In fact, unless the standard deviations of the strata are very different, disproportionate sampling does very little to the variance estimate. For example, if 50 were sampled from each of the four strata, the standard deviation of the mean would be (assuming the estimates of the mean and standard deviations were unchanged):

$$s_{\bar{x}} = \sqrt{.4^2 \frac{4^2}{50} + .3^2 \frac{4^2}{50} + .2^2 \frac{5^2}{50} + .1^2 \frac{2^2}{50}}$$
$$= \sqrt{\frac{5.04}{50}} = \sqrt{.1008}$$
$$= .317$$

The point, therefore, is that for most marketing surveys, sampling disproportionately to get the most reliable estimates is not very useful. Since it is both troublesome and a source of headaches for certain types of analysis, such "scientific" sampling is rarely employed purely to reduce overall variance in estimates. The major reason for using a stratified sample, therefore, is to ensure adequate representation of key subgroups of the target population.

Stratified samples often are applied to situations where more than one variable serves as a basis for stratification. For example, I might be interested in a consumer product which appealed primarily to middle-aged

TABLE 9–2
Stratified sampling plan

	Age group		
Income level	Under 30	30–50	51 and over
Under $10,000	50	50	50
$10,000–$20,000	50	200	100
$20,001–$30,000	100	400	100
Over $30,000	200	500	200

$$\boxed{2,000}$$

high-income consumers. Given a budget which allowed for a sample of 2,000, a stratified sampling plan might look like Table 9–2.

Universal sampling (census)

In most consumer surveys, it is obviously overly expensive to survey all possible customers. In industrial surveys, on the other hand, there may be only 30–40 important customers. In these situations sampling all the important customers is both logically and statistically desirable. It is important to note, however, that a true census is almost never obtained.

Convenience

The cheapest form of sample design is referred to as a convenience sample. This translates to using any warm body that is available. It is very popular in academic research (remember reading about samples of 56 college sophomores?) but also has a useful place in "real" research. While their projectability is very questionable, convenience samples are extremely useful for hypothesis generation and initial pilot testing of surveys.

Quota

A quota sample is based on the preconceived notion that certain individual characteristics must be adequately represented if the sample is to be projectable. It is essentially a compromise between a stratified and a convenience sample. For example, a firm may want the opinions of at least 30 housewives between the ages of 40 and 55. Hence a quota sample may be generated by having the interviewer collect data from the first 30 women who fall into that category who agree to participate. Such a procedure obviously does not make the quota sample as good as a random sample, but it does guarantee that in terms of some obvious characteristics the sample will represent the target population. The question of whether such a sample is a "good enough" approximation to a more elaborate design is an open question. The fact that quota samples are widely used indicates that for at least some purposes, some relatively intelligent researchers think they are.

Cluster samples

Cluster samples are exactly what the name implies, samples gathered in clusters. The basic motivation for cluster sampling is cost reduction. In the case of personal interviews, giving each interviewer a series of addresses leads to a large amount of travel time, even when an elaborate scheduling mechanism is employed. In order to cut this travel time (or to draw a sample when no list is available), a common approach is to draw samples in clusters. This means that areas (blocks, for example) are selected and then interviewers are instructed to get several interviews from the same block. This type of cluster sampling is commonly known as area sampling. Cluster samples can also be drawn from lists. An example of this type of sampling is sampling all people whose names begin with a set of randomly selected letters.

Sequential and replicated versus single samples

The sampling plans discussed to this point all assume a single sample is taken. Two alternative approaches are possible. One is to take several smaller samples simultaneously. Such replicated samples (e.g., 10 samples of 100) have some advantages over a single sample of equal size. They are, however, rarely used in marketing research.

The other alternative sampling approach is sequential. In this method, a small sample is drawn and the results analyzed. If the results are sufficiently clear, a decision is made and the rest of the sample is not drawn. If not, another sample is drawn subsequently. This approach offers potential economy by possibly reducing sample size. (Some of this economy is lost if any economies of scale exist in data collection.) On the other hand, this approach takes longer in calendar time than a one-shot study. Given the usual time pressure and fear of competitive reaction most market researchers face, sequential sampling is also rarely employed.

Multistage samples

In practice many sample designs are really a mix of several approaches to sampling. National consumer surveys involving personal interviews usually begin by first selecting a set of locations (counties or SMSA's) purposively to ensure representation of different areas. A second stage selects locations within the areas (blocks), often randomly. The third or final stage is to select individual households on the block which may be done randomly, systematically (e.g., go to the third house on the left), or on a convenience basis. The resulting sample tends to be both representative and reasonably efficient. By contrast, a purely random sample of U.S. households is much less efficient and essentially never employed.

Sources of lists

Many of the sample designs require a list of the target population. While this may seem to be a simple requirement, finding a good list is rarely a trivial task. Lists are notorious for containing outdated information. Given the large fraction of people (and businesses) who move each year, this is partially inevitable. Add in copying mistakes, list inflation (the longer the list, the higher price it commands), duplicate names, and less-than-annual updates, and the portion of usable names on many lists drops to 50 percent.

There are several major sources for consumer lists. Magazine subscriptions form a well-known basis, as do organization membership lists and credit cards. Professional associations are another common source of lists. Lists are available for just about anything, however, including everything from agricultural agents to zoologists. Lists of industrial concerns are also legion. Often based on trade association memberships, these lists cover almost every imaginable business. Lists are also available for associations such as PTAs.

A major focal point for such lists is the Direct Mail Advertising Association. A variety of companies compile "lists of lists" (catalogs). For example, Fritz Hofheimer's 1977 catalog contained almost 20,000 lists with list lengths ranging from one (a corrugated fiberboard coffin manufacturer) to 25,632,000 mail-order buyers (you too may well be on that list). Costs vary, but generally a list can be obtained for between $30 and $90 per thousand names.

In keeping track of households, the obvious "best" source is the U.S. census. Since this data is generally unavailable, some number of years out of date, and according to some not all that reliable anyway especially in rural and ghetto areas, alternatives have been produced. Two major firms have mailing lists of over 50 million households. In addition to addresses, the most recent census data available is coded into each household so that median income and age of the neighborhood, among other variables, are available as a basis for selectively pulling samples. Reuben H. Donnelley (cousin of R. A. Donnelley of yellow pages fame and son of Dun and Bradstreet) maintains a list based on merging a list based on telephone books with the auto registration lists of the various states. (States sell these lists to help defray costs of registration.) Metro Mail's list is based solely on telephone directories. Not surprisingly, the services of both these companies are more widely used for direct-mail solicitation than for research.

THE PROBLEM OF NONRESPONSE

Even the best planned samples of researchers and statisticians generate many nonrespondents. A major issue, therefore, is what bias does this nonresponse bring into the sample? Put differently, how much of the result is attributable to which sample points responded? Obviously the lower the response rate, the more nervous one tends to become about the representativeness of the sample. While doubling sample size may make the results seem more believable, it does nothing to reduce response bias. Actually the response bias has two major parts: noncoverage and nonresponse.

Response bias

Noncoverage. Most methods of obtaining samples have an inherent noncoverage element. Personal interviews are not useful for surveying people in remote areas due to cost and in areas where door-to-door interviews are banned by local ordinance. Mail questionnaires will not be filled out by illiterates or when the occupant moves. Phone questionnaires can only contact those with phones, excluding about 10 percent of the homes.

If phone books are used as the source of names, only those with listed numbers are covered. Since as many as 30 percent of the phones are unlisted in areas such as poor neighborhoods and the west coast, this can be a severe problem.

Nonresponse. The nonresponse bias is another problem. This bias can occur when a target subject cannot be found. In addition to those who are unable to respond, there are those people who are not at home. A classic example of a question which would be biased by the not-at-home problem is, "What do you do during the evening?" Taking an evening survey would yield a disproportionately high proportion of "stay at home" responses since those who don't stay at home are nonrespondents. A final category of nonresponse is refusals. A person may refuse to participate because of fear for personal safety (would you open the door at night for a stranger with a clipboard?), desire to protect privacy, lack of interest in the subject, time pressure, or a general dislike for marketing research or business. Insomuch as any of these nonrespondents would have responded differently to the questions asked, the results are biased. In fact, respondents to mail surveys tend to be somewhat more upscale: younger, richer, better educated, than the total population.

Given the risk of nonresponse bias, the obvious solution is to minimize the nonresponse rate. A plethora of devices are used to increase the response rate. To understand how they work, consider the following typology of potential respondents:

1. Happy to respond (15 percent).
2. Willing to be convinced to respond with modest effort (50 percent).
3. Can be bought at a high price (15 percent).
4. No way to make them respond (10 percent).
5. Not even covered by the process (10 percent).

Looking at this typology we see that category 1 is pretty much guaranteed. (It is possible to destroy even these respondents, however, with an especially arduous and confusing questionnaire or experiment.) On the other hand, people in categories 4 and 5 are practically unattainable. Given limited budgets, category 3 is usually conceded as well. That means the effort is usually placed on category 2 people. It also means that response rates tend to run from a low of 10–20 percent to a high of around 70 percent of the population of interest.

Determinants of response rate

A variety of factors influence the response rate. The effects of those factors under the control of the researcher have been studied extensively, especially in mail surveys (Kanuk and Berenson, 1975; Linsky, 1975; Houston and Ford, 1976). These factors include interest, length, opening gambit, incentives/bribery, format, advance notice, callback/follow-up, and overall.

Interest. The greater the interest, the lower the portion of nonrespondents. In fact, interest is probably the major determinant of response rate. Unfortunately, interest is largely inherent in the topic (most people would rather answer a questionnaire about food or sports than about caskets). Nonetheless, tedious surveys dampen enthusiasm, and clever design (use of white space, pictures, etc.) may increase interest.

Length. The longer the interview, questionnaire, or experiment appears, the less likely someone is to begin it. The longer it takes to complete, the better chance there is the respondent will either terminate the survey or leave large numbers of questions unasnwered. (These partial nonresponses pose a particularly difficult problem for complex forms of data anaysis such as regression analysis.) Length also obviously increases fatigue noticeably. While an amazing number of questions can be asked, typically a small number will suffice. Still response rates are remarkably constant for 8- to 20-page questionnaires. The cost of length, then, is more likely to be in lowered respondent quality than lowered response rate.

Opening gambit.   The opening which invites the individual to participate is very important. Aside from the appearance of the interviewer or
questionnaire (or the sound of the interviewer's voice in the case of phone
interviews), the first two or three sentences must grab the prospective
respondent much like the beginning of an ad. Appeals of many types are
useful, including mercy ("I'm a poor college student . . ."), self-interest
("your opinion will count"), or duty ("you should express your views").
Guarantees of anonymity are useful in persuading reluctant individuals to
participate, as are the "right" credentials for the interviewer or survey
company. Use of the person's name to get a personal touch tends to
increase the response rate. In mail surveys, better responses are obtained
by using a personalized letter, a return envelope with postage paid, and
"classy" format. Other variables such as the color of the questionnaire
seem to have little effect.

Incentives/bribery.   The most blatant (and expensive) way to increase
sample size is to buy respondents. This is commonly done by a monetary
inductment. Sometimes this inducement is offered in advance to "shame"
the individual into responding. A typical bribe in mail surveys is to include a small amount of money (25 cents or $1) when the questionnaire is
mailed. This is designed to increase both commitment and response rate,
and even though it is usually a pittance on a per hour basis, it often helps.
One problem with bribery is that the respondents may be more likely to
give responses they think you want to hear rather than true answers.

While modest monetary inducements help with some respondents, they
do very little for those who can only be bought for a high monetary price.
On the other hand, "end around" strategies may prove more successful
than monetary rewards. For example, aesthetic appeals (stamps, pictures,
etc.) may induce some to participate when money would fail. Similarly
offering to give a small sum to a favorite charity or church is often a
successful inducement. In addition, some phenomenal successes have
been achieved with gimmick rewards (who could refuse a Mickey Mouse
ring or a yo-yo?). In general, however, incentives are not overly effective.
In a study involving a survey about durable goods, three versions were
sent to groups of 400 each: version one had just a cover letter, version two
some mint coins (monetary), and version three some very appealing-
looking stamps (aesthetic). Alas when the results came back, there was
essentially no difference in the response rates, and certainly not enough to
justify anything except the plain cover letter approach.

Format.   Using adequate white space on a mail survey or breaks in a
personal interview helps keep the respondent fresh. Essentially the format
must make it easy (both in appearance and in fact) for the respondent to
respond.

Advance notice.   In order to secure cooperation, it is common to give
advance notice (by phone, postcard, or letter) of the impending study.
This is often useful in increasing both response rate and quality.

Callback/follow-up. Many individuals in the sample may not be home when the company makes the first attempt to contact a potential respondent. If no subsequent attempt is made to reach the individual, response rates to personal interviewing may dip below 50 percent. If on the other hand elaborate callback plans involving six to eight callbacks at different times of the day and week (or follow-up plans, in the case of a mail study) are employed, response rates may reach 80 percent. Two or three callbacks is a fairly standard procedure.

Overall. In getting a higher response rate, the cost per completed interview usually increases. This higher response rate is obtained not by magic but by work: more follow-ups, and so forth. The obvious question is, "Where does the trade-off between response rate and the cost/sample size occur?" The answer to this depends on the purpose of the study.

If the researcher is interested in studying the process/psychological phenomena on an individual level, biased samples may suffice. (How else could we publish articles based on 149 college sophomores in course X, etc.?) Similarly the relations among variables as measured by correlations may not be sensitive to modestly biased samples. When a study is interested in estimating levels (e.g., average income), however, nonresponse bias becomes a serious problem. (I would prefer a sample of 500 and a 60 percent response rate to a sample of 800 and a 35 percent response rate ceteris paribus for estimating certain facts and opinions.)

The problem of dropouts

In any study where the respondents are contacted repeatedly, a certain percentage drop out between waves. This percentage ranges from less than 5 percent in specially designed panels or experiments to 25 percent in some multiwave phone surveys. Since dropouts are typically different in some way from respondents (at least in terms of interest in the study), this makes subsequent analysis difficult. The two basic approaches are to use only those individuals who respond to all waves (and hence waste the other responses) or use all the responses and run the risk of measuring the differences between people rather than changes over time.

Weighting to account for nonresponse

There are two basic sources of bias in the final sample. The first is noncoverage by the process of the target population and the second is the nonrespondents being different in some important way from the respondents. The problem is that to assess the bias, the characteristics of nonrespondents must be known.

One way to treat the nonresponse bias is to logically (subjectively) adjust the results. Consider, for example, a mail survey which attempted to find a number of people who would be interested in buying a new product. There was a 30 percent response rate, and of the respondents 40 percent said they would buy the product. One estimate for the percent of the population who would be interested in buying (which incidentally, would greatly overstate actual buying) would thus be 40 percent. On the other hand, we could assume that the other 70 percent did not return the survey because they were not interested in the product. In that case, the appropriate estimate would be 40 percent × 30 percent = 12 percent. Actually, the number would probably lie somewhere in between 12 percent and 40 percent, but the 12 percent is likely to be a more accurate estimate than the 40 percent.

One interesting approach for dealing with a nonresponse problem was developed by Politz and Simmons (Ackoff, 1953). This procedure is designed to estimate results without callbacks and to overcome the not-at-home bias. The procedure accomplishes this by asking respondents to classify themselves in terms of how often they are home (and hence available to be questioned). Assume, for example, that respondents classified themselves according to three categories: at home 80 percent of the time, 50 percent of the time, and 20 percent of the time. If we call at random, we would expect to get 80 percent of group 1, 50 percent of group 2, and 20 percent of group 3, and hence overrepresent group 1 respondents. This overrepresentation is corrected by weighting each respondent in the group by the inverse of their likelihood of being home. (That is, weight each group 1 respondent by 1/.8 = 1.25, each group 2 respondent by 1/.5 = 2, and each group 3 respondent by 1/.2 = 5.) This effectively corrects the sample by removing the at-home bias in the original sample.

Another approach to nonresponse is to do a follow-up study on nonrespondents. Hopefully nonrespondents reached on the second try will be similar to respondents. If the nonrespondents are somehow different, however, the problem is which result to believe. Consider another example, this one a mail survey of 100,000 which had a 20 percent response rate. A subsequent phone follow-up study of 1,500 initial nonrespondents revealed a pattern of slight differences based on 1,000 respondents (a 67 percent response rate). The weights given to the two samples can vary greatly depending on whether you think the 1,000 respondents to the follow-up represent (a) the 70 percent of the individuals who did not respond, (b) 67 percent of the 70 percent, or (c) just themselves. Assuming the original 20,000 were given weights of 1 each, the respective weights given to the follow-up respondents would be (a) 70, (b) 46.66, and (c) 1. Since the first alternative essentially means the first study was largely worthless, this is very unappealing. In fact, because of the problems in deciding on appropriate weights and the problems of incorporating unequal weights into subsequent analysis, the nonresponse bias is often ignored. Fortunately as long as the bias is small, this is an acceptable alternative. Still the problem of potential nonresponse bias and how to deal with it makes increasing the response rate a very important goal.

SAMPLE DESIGN EXAMPLES

The Literary Digest poll

One of the classic examples of an unfortunate choice of sample involved the 1936 U.S. presidential election. Prior to the election, *The Literary Digest,* then among the most prestigious magazines in the country, predicted that Alf Landon would beat Franklin Roosevelt. Since FDR beat Landon in a landslide (for you trivia buffs, Landon carried only Maine and Vermont), this prediction seriously damaged the magazine's reputation.

The seeds of the disastrous prediction were sewn in the sampling plan. In the first phase, the magazine mailed cards to 10 million subscribers and asked those who would be willing to participate to return the card along with a phone number. About 2.3 million responded. A random sample was then drawn from those who agreed to participate. The problem was that the sample was biased. The popular version of this story suggests the problem was noncoverage based on the assumption that both subscribers to *The Literary Digest* and those who had telephones tended to be Republicans. Another explanation is that those who responded to the initial request were more committed/interested in the election and those who were interested were Republicans (Bryson, 1976). Whichever is true, it is clear that a response bias affected the results.

The nutrition study

The nutrition study previously referred to required that a sample be drawn. Given a budget of about $9,000, this made personal interviews too costly to get a "reasonable" sample size (800–1,000). On the other hand, phone interviews were deemed inappropriate because of the length of the survey (it takes about 30 minutes to complete). That left, in order to get broad geographic and demographic coverage, mail.

The choice then boiled down to a choice between a special mail-out and use of a mail panel. The mail panel has inherent bias in its makeup. In the case of this study, one would expect panel members to be relatively well-organized and systematic shoppers. A "blind" mail-out, on the other hand, could be expected to get a relatively low response rate for this eight-page questionnaire. Nonetheless, a university cover letter and a good list could probably achieve as many respondents for the same cost. In this case, however, convenience in terms of both a panel having already collected socioeconomic variables (age, income, etc.) and not having the hassle involved in drawing a special sample (stuffing envelopes, etc.) favored the mail panel. As usual, convenience won out. The survey was mailed to an NFO panel of 1,000 which was designed to match national percentages of age, region, and income. An additional 200 surveys were mailed to the lowest income members of a second panel in order to increase representation of lower income groups. 940 questionnaires were returned by the time the survey closed four weeks after the initial mailing. As is typically done, the sample was described in terms of some basic demographics (Table 9–3). The sample did succeed in increasing low-

TABLE 9–3
Demographic characteristics of the sample (by percent)

	Sample	U.S.
Respondent's age:		
Under 30	19.7	23.8
30–39	17.4	20.7
40–49	18.6	20.7
50–59	19.7	18.6
60 and over	24.6	16.6
Household income:		
Under 6,000	32.9	19.3
6,000–9,999	16.9	19.9
10,000–14,999	21.5	25.5
15,000–19,999	13.9	16.7
20,000 and over	14.8	18.6
Family size:		
2	44.1	36.1
3	20.3	21.4
4	17.0	19.7
5 or more	19.6	22.8
Race:		
White	96.8	
Other	3.2	
Population density:		
Rural	18.9	15.3
2,500–49,999	11.4	11.3
50,000–499,999	19.0	18.4
500,000–1,999,999	23.3	24.6
2,000,000 and over	27.3	30.4
Education:		
Attended grade school	3.4	
Grade school graduate	4.5	
Attended high school	14.0	
High school graduate	42.1	
Attended college	19.7	
College graduate	13.4	
Graduate school	2.6	
No answer	.2	

income respondents but left the sample relatively old and rural. Similarly blacks were badly underrepresented.

CONCLUSION

This chapter has outlined the most widely used means of obtaining a sample. In doing so, the advantages and disadvantages of each have been

276

briefly discussed. For those who wish to really know about sampling, this chapter is only a sketchy introduction. Anyone who began this chapter hoping to find the "right" way should by now be disillusioned. There is no simple way to make sampling decisions. Cost, reliability of the results, and convenience all affect the choice of a sample design. Often a smaller, more costly sample may be preferred because of lower nonresponse bias or increased interviewer control. Similarly, the method of data collection used and the method of choosing sampling points are closely related. Worrying about statistical niceties will improve the quality of the results as well as making them more credible. Most serious errors in sample design, however, turn out to be errors in logic, not statistics.

PROBLEMS

1. Evaluate the quality of the sample in the nutrition study in Table 9–3.
2. Draw a random sample of 20 from a list of 83 potential respondents. (Hint: Use a table of random numbers.)
3. Assume that a customer's purchase probabilities of buying three brands (A, B, and C) are .7, .2, and .1 respectively. (a) Using a table of random numbers, simulate ten purchases. (b) Simulate ten more purchases. (c) How representative are (a) and (b) of the customer's true purchase behavior?
4. Assume you were to take a sample of five customers for Junk, Inc. Which customers would you sample and why?

Capital district customer list of Junk, Inc.

	Customer	Location	Age	Business annually
1.	W. Rockhead	Albany, N.Y.	42	$110,000
2.	S. Blitz	Albany, N.Y.	24	32,000
3.		Albany, N.Y.	35	271,000
4.		Albany, N.Y.	57	14,000
5.		Albany, N.Y.	62	42,000
6.		Albany, N.Y.	21	5,000
7.		Albany, N.Y.	61	19,000
8.		Troy	35	41,000
9.		Troy	27	15,000
10.		Troy	51	7,000
11.		Troy	23	4,000
12.		Saratoga	34	37,000
13.		Saratoga	41	60,000
14.		Saratoga	42	15,000
15.		Schenectady	51	80,000
16.		Schenectady	41	14,000
17.		Schenectady	27	21,000
18.		Schenectady	35	87,000
19.		Schenectady	61	59,000
20.		Schenectady	58	8,000

5. Assume you had been retained to take a national sample of 1,000 to gauge opinions about food additives. Set up a plan to do personal interviewing.
   a. Use states as a starting point and draw ten at random.
   b. Use states as a starting point and draw ten randomly with the probability of inclusion proportional to their population.
   c. Set up a purposive plan for drawing states.
   d. Which of (a), (b), or (c) seems better?
   e. How would you go about sampling within states?
6. Assume you were going to set up a sample of 100 four-year colleges to monitor trends in undergraduate education. Which 100 would you choose?
   a. Assume cooperation is no problem.
   b. Develop a contingency procedure in the event of a refusal.
7. A mail survey produces a 43 percent response rate. Discuss potential nonresponse bias and what could be done to (a) assess it and (b) correct for it.
8. How many people in the United States must I sample to estimate preference in a two-way presidential race within 1 percent at the 95 percent confidence level?
9. Two years ago average consumption of fingles was 23 slops/slurp. The standard deviation of fingles consumption was .6. I feel that fingle consumption has about doubled and would like a new estimate on it. If I wish to be within .2 slops/slurp, how many people do I need to sample?
10. Assume you were in charge of setting up a panel to monitor introduction of a new breakfast food. How would you proceed? (Hint: Indicate how you would select panel members and what characteristics you would control for to help insure its representativeness.)
11. Given the following situation:

Group (stratum)	Size	Standard deviation of bottles of beer consumed
A	2,000	4
B	4,000	1
C	6,000	4
D	8,000	3
E	2,000	2

   a. How should I sample 600 people to minimize the variance of the estimate of average beer consumption?
   b. If I sample and get the following results:

Group	Sample size	Average beer consumption	Standard deviation
A	100	5	4.5
B	100	1	.8
C	100	12	4.1
D	200	2	2.9
E	100	3	1.8

    (1)   What is your estimate of average beer consumption?

    (2)   What is your standard deviation of this estimation?

12.   Two lists of names commonly used for obtaining samples are as follows:

    (1)   Vehicle registration lists

    (2)   Telephone directory lists.

    a.   How would you draw a simple random sample from each list?

    b.   What statistical biases would you expect if your population of interest were "all U.S. households?"

    c.   What could you do to reduce these biases?

13.   You wish to estimate the average consumption of caviar in the United States by interviewing a sample of 1,000 households drawn from the population of 100 million households. The research firm has proposed a stratified sample, which will "save you money." They said that they would "oversample the high income and urban areas where the caviar consumption variance is larger." What does this mean? In what sense does it save you money? Why would they "oversample" these groups?

14.   Recent studies by the Advertising Research Foundation have suggested that about 5 to 10 percent of field interviews are not actually conducted with the respondent, and that another 30 percent of the reported interviews contain substantial inaccuracies. What can be done to reduce the risk of such interviewer "cheating" or "bias"?

15.   In assessing the market for a new consumer durable, your boss plans to do a national survey using personal interviews and a probability sample. Discuss the advisability of such a course of action and suggest some feasible alternatives.

BIBLIOGRAPHY

Ackoff, Russel L. *The Design of Social Research.* Chicago: University of Chicago Press, 1953.

Armstrong, J. Scott, and Overton, Terry S. "Estimating Nonresponse Bias in Mail Surveys." *Journal of Marketing Research,* vol. 14 (August 1977), pp. 396–402.

Brown, Stephen W. and Coney, Kenneth A. "Comments on 'Mail Survey Premiums and Response Bias.'" *Journal of Marketing Research,* vol. 14 (August 1977), pp. 385–87.

Bryson, Maurice C. "The Literary Digest Poll: Making of a Statistical Myth." *The American Statistician,* vol. 30 (November 1976), pp. 184–85.

Catalog of Mailing Lists. Mineola, N.Y.: Fritz S. Hofheimer, Inc., 1977.

Cochran, W. G. *Sampling Techniques.* 2d ed. New York: Wiley, 1963.

Deming, W. E. *Sampling Design in Business Research.* New York: Wiley, 1960.

Ferber, Robert. "Research by Convenience." *Journal of Consumer Research,* vol. 4 (June 1977), pp. 57–58.

Forsythe, John B. "Obtaining Cooperation in a Survey of Business Executives." *Journal of Marketing Research,* vol. 14 (August 1977), pp. 370–73.

Goodstadt, Michael S.; Chung, Linda; Kronitz, Reena; and Gaynoll Cook. "Mail Survey Response Rates: Their Manipulation and Impact." *Journal of Marketing Research,* vol. 14 (August 1977), pp. 391–95.

Hansen, M. H.; Hurwitz, W. N.; and Madow, W. G. *Sample Survey Methods and Theory.* New York: Wiley, 1953.

Houston, Michael J., and Ford, Neil M. "Broadening the Scope of Methodological Research on Mail Surveys." *Journal of Marketing Research,* vol. 13 (November 1976), pp. 397–402.

————, and Nevin, John R. "The Effects of Source and Appeal on Mail Survey Response Patterns." *Journal of Marketing Research,* vol. 14 (August 1977), pp. 374–78.

Kanuk, Leslie, and Berenson, Conrad. "Mail Surveys and Response Rates: A Literature Review." *Journal of Marketing Research,* vol. 12 (November 1975), pp. 440–53.

Kish, Leslie. *Survey Sampling.* New York: Wiley, 1965.

Landon, E. Laird, Jr., and Banks, Sharon K. "Relative Efficiency and Bias of Plus-One Telephone Sampling." *Journal of Marketing Research,* vol. 14 (August 1977), pp. 294–99.

Linsky, Arnold S. "Stimulating Responses to Mailed Questionnaires: A Review." *Public Opinion Quarterly,* vol. 39 (Spring 1975), pp. 82–101.

McGinnis, Michael A., and Hollon, Charles J. "Mail Survey Response Rate and Bias: The Effect of Home versus Work Address." *Journal of Marketing Research,* vol. 14 (August 1977), pp. 383–84.

Pessemier, Edgar; DeBruicker, Stewart; and Hustad, Thomas. "The 1970 Purdue Consumer Behavior Research Project." Lafayette, Ind.: Purdue University, 1971.

Reingen, Peter H., and Kernan, Jerome B. "Compliance with an Interview Request: A Foot-in-the-Door, Self-Perception Interpretation." *Journal of Marketing Research,* vol. 14 (August 1977), pp. 365–69.

Rich, Clyde L. "Is Random Digit Dialing Really Necessary?" *Journal of Marketing Research,* vol. 14 (August 1977), pp. 300–305.

Schlaifer, Robert. *Probability and Statistics for Business Decisions.* New York: McGraw-Hill, 1959.

Sudman, Seymour. *Applied Sampling.* New York: Academic Press, 1976.

Walker, Bruce J., and Burdick, Richard K. "Advance Correspondence and Error in Mail Surveys." *Journal of Marketing Research,* vol. 14 (August 1977), pp. 379–82.

Whitmore, William J. "A Reply on 'Mail Survey Premiums and Response Bias.'" *Journal of Marketing Research,* vol. 14 (August 1977), pp. 388–90.

—————— APPENDIX 9–A ——————

REVIEW OF PROBABILITY AND STATISTICS

The purpose of this Appendix is to briefly summarize/review some basic concepts of probability and statistics.

PROBABILITY

Probability is a concept dealing with the likelihood (degree of certainty) that a series of events will occur. It is quantified on a scale from 0 (meaning the event definitely will not occur) to 1 (meaning the event definitely will occur).

Basic concept

A basic method for determining the probability an event will occur is to calculate the ratio of the number of ways the event can occur to the number of things that can possibly happen (assuming all things that can happen are equally likely):

$$P(A) = \frac{N(A)}{N(S)} = \frac{\text{No. of ``favorable'' outcomes}}{\text{No. of possible outcomes}} \qquad (9A.1)$$

Hence if I put five different names into a hat, the probability that I pull out a particular name is $1/5$. Similarly, if I draw a card from a standard deck of 52 cards, the probability the card is a heart is $13/52 = 1/4$.

Some simple formulas

In computing probabilities involving more than one result, the following three rules are particularly useful:

1. Probability of either of two events occurring

$$P(\text{either } A \text{ or } B) = P(A) + P(B) - P(\text{both } A \text{ and } B)$$

or

$$P(A \cup B) = P(A) + P(B) - P(A \cap B) \qquad (9A.2)$$

For example, assume I were interested in the probability that a card drawn from a standard deck of 52 was either a heart or an ace. I could solve the problem brute force by counting the cards which satisfy the requirement (the 13 hearts plus the ace of spades, clubs, and diamonds for a total of 16) and getting the probability from equation (9A.1):

$$P(\text{heart or ace}) = \frac{N(\text{hearts or aces})}{N(\text{cards})} = \frac{16}{52}$$

Alternatively, I could use equation (9A.2):

$$P(\text{heart or ace}) = P(\text{heart}) + P(\text{ace}) - P(\text{ace of hearts})\cdot$$
$$= \frac{13}{52} + \frac{4}{52} - \frac{1}{52} = \frac{16}{52}$$

The logic of equation (9A.2) can best be seen from Figure 9A–1, called a Venn diagram: If I simply add the areas of A and B, I will double count the

FIGURE 9A–1
Venn diagram of two possible events

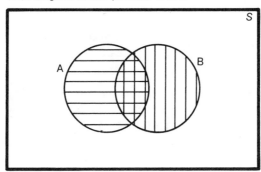

area in both A and B. In the previous example, this would count the ace of hearts twice. Hence to get the area inside A or B, I add the area in A to the area in B and then subtract the overlap between A and B.

When $P(A \cap B)$ is 0, A and B have no overlap and are said to be mutually exclusive. An example of this is tens and jacks. The $P(\text{ten} \cap \text{jack}) = 0$.

2. Probability of two events both occurring

$$P(A \cap B) = P(A)[P(B|A)] \qquad (9A.3)$$

This is the basic method for calculating the probability of a sequence of events occurring. In words, it says that the probability of getting a Ph.D. is

P(Ph.D.) $= P$(finish high school)[P(finish college|
finished high school)][P(finish Ph.D.|finish college)]

$P(B|A)$ means the probability B will occur given that A has occurred. When $P(B|A) = P(B)$, then A and B are said to be independent. (Put differently, this means that knowing A occurred gives no information about whether B will occur.) Consider the following two examples:

P(ace|heart)
P(ace|"honor"—a ten, jack, queen, king, or ace)

In the first case, P(ace|heart) $= \frac{1}{13}$ since one of the 13 hearts is the ace. Here aces and hearts are independent. In the second case, however, P(ace|"honor") $= \frac{4}{20} = \frac{1}{5} \neq \frac{1}{13}$, and hence aces and honors are clearly not independent.

3. Conditional probability. There is also a variation on (9A.3), known as conditional probability:

$$P(B|A) = \frac{P(A \cap B)}{P(A)} \tag{9A.4}$$

This is simply a rewrite of (9A.3). It says, for example, that

$$P(\text{ace}|\text{heart}) = \frac{P(\text{ace} \cap \text{heart})}{P(\text{heart})} = \frac{\dfrac{1}{52}}{\dfrac{13}{52}} = \frac{1}{13}$$

Methods for calculating the number of ways an event can occur. In calculating the number of ways events can occur, the following formulas are sometimes useful. The formulas use two definitions:

Definition: $a! = (a)(a - 1)(a - 2) \cdot \cdot \cdot (2)(1)$ (9A.5)

(this is called "a factorial") for example, $5! = (5)(4)(3)(2)(1) = 120$.

Definition: $\begin{pmatrix} a \\ b \end{pmatrix} = \dfrac{a!}{(a - b)!b!}$ (9A.6)

For example,

$$\begin{pmatrix} 5 \\ 3 \end{pmatrix} = \frac{5!}{2!3!} = \frac{(5)(4)(3)(2)(1)}{[(2)(1)][(3)(2)(1)]} = 10$$

Assume there are M possible outcomes. The question often arises how many distinct ways can I draw a sample of size N. This problem depends on how I define distinct and how I draw the sample.

Case A. *Sample drawn with replacement, order matters:*

$$M^N \tag{9A.7}$$

In this approach, I draw an outcome from my "hat" with M outcomes in it, then replace the outcome. I also will agree that getting A, B on the first two draws is *not* the same as getting B, A (order matters). In this case, there are M possible outcomes on the first draw, M more on the second, and so forth, so the possible outcomes become

$$(M)(M)(M) \cdots (M) = M^N$$

As an example, consider drawing three cards with replacement from a deck of 52. The number of possible outcomes is $(52)(52)(52) = 52^3$.

Case B. *Sample drawn without replacement, order matters:*

$$\frac{M!}{(M - N)!} \tag{9A.8}$$

In this case I do not replace the item each time I draw an outcome. Hence there are M possible choices for the first draw, $(M - 1)$ possible choices for the second draw, $(M - 2)$ possible choices for the third draw, and so forth. Hence the number of possible draws is

$$(M)(M - 1)(M - 2) \cdots (M - N + 1) = \frac{M!}{(M - N)!}$$

This case is often called permutations. Now the number of ways I can draw three cards from a deck of 52 is $(52)(51)(50) = 132,600$.

Case C. *Sample drawn without replacement, order does not matter:*

$$\frac{M!}{(M - N)!N!} \tag{9A.9}$$

In this case, I assume that not only do I not replace the drawn outcome in the "hat" but I also don't care in what order the cards come (the case in five-card draw poker).

To see the logic of this, consider the draw: AH, $2D$, $3C$. This is one of the $(52)(51)(50)$ possible draws. However, AH, $2D$, $3C$ is (if order doesn't matter) indistinguishable from

$$
\begin{array}{ccc}
AH, & 3C, & 2D \\
3C, & AH, & 2D \\
3C, & 2D, & AH \\
2D, & AH, & 3C \\
2D, & 3C, & AH
\end{array}
$$

Hence there are six ways each of the possible outcomes can be rearranged. This means that we have overcounted by a factor of 6 and the "answer" should be

$$\frac{(52)(51)(50)}{6} = \frac{52!}{49!(3!)} = \binom{52}{3}$$

This case is often called combinations.

Using these formats, we can generate two basic probability procedures. Assume there are g distinct outcomes in a population of size S:

Outcome	Number of events	Sample result
1	N_1	n_1
2	N_2	n_2
.	.	.
.	.	.
.	.	.
g	$\underline{N_g}$	$\underline{n_g}$
	N	n

The probability of a sample result with N_1 outcomes of the first type, N_2 of the second type, and so forth, can be found from two formulas:

With replacement: Multinomial

$$P(n_1, n_2, \ldots, n_g) = \frac{n!}{n_1!, n_2!, \ldots, n_g!} P_1{}^{n_1} P_2{}^{n_2} \cdots P_g{}^{n_g} \qquad (9A.10)$$

where

$$P_1 = \frac{N_1}{N}$$

$$P_2 = \frac{N_2}{N}$$

$$\cdot$$

$$\cdot$$

$$\cdot$$

$$P_g = \frac{N_g}{N}$$

Without replacement: Hypergeometric

$$P(n_1, n_2, \ldots, n_g) = \frac{\binom{N_1}{n_1} \binom{N_2}{n_2} \cdots \binom{N_g}{n_g}}{\binom{N}{n}} \qquad (9A.11)$$

PROBABILITY DISTRIBUTION

The basic notion of a probability distribution is to indicate the relative lilelihood of different possible outcomes. When there are a discrete (finite, manageable) number of possible outcomes (e.g., number of days it rains

FIGURE 9A–2
Discrete probability distribution

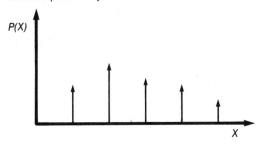

this week), the distribution attaches a probability to each of the possible outcomes, as is indicated in Figure 9A–2. Here

$$\sum_{\substack{all \\ outcomes}} P(X) = 1$$

When the outcomes are continuous (e.g., the diameter of a part can be infinitely many sizes), the relative likelihood of different outcomes is given by a density function (Figure 9A–3). Here $\int_{-\infty}^{+\infty} f(X)\, dX = 1$. Also here, the probability of a particular result (e.g., $P(X) = 3.12471\ldots$) is 0.

FIGURE 9A–3
Continuous probability distribution

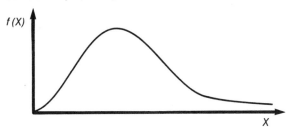

SUMMARY STATISTICS

The most comprehensive information about possible occurrences is contained in the complete probability distribution or density function.

Since these can be fairly unwieldy, however, measures are calculated which summarize the information contained in the distribution. The first group of measures concerns the notion of a "typical" response. Three measures are commonly calculated:

Mode: The most likely result.

Median: The result which lies exactly at the middle of the distribution (i.e., the score of the 49th student from a class of 99).

Mean: The average (expected) result.

Of these three measures, the mean is the most widely used. It is calculated by

Discrete distribution *Continuous distribution*

$$E(X) = \mu = \sum_{\substack{all \\ X}} XP(X) \qquad \mu = \int_{-\infty}^{+\infty} Xf(X)dX \qquad (9A.12)$$

The second group of measures deals with the dispersion/"fatness" of the distribution. These measures indicate the uncertainty inherent in the outcome. The most typical measure is the variance (σ^2):

Discrete distribution *Continuous distribution*

$$E(X - \mu)^2 = \sigma^2 \qquad\qquad \sigma^2 = \int_{-\infty}^{+\infty} (X - \mu)^2 f(X)dx \quad (9A.13)$$

$$= \sum_{\substack{all \\ X}} ((X - \mu)^2 P(X))$$

$$= \Sigma X^2 P(X) - \mu^2$$

$$= E(X^2) - \mu^2$$

(N.B.: Variance $(a - bX) = b^2$ variance X.) Actually, the square root of the variance, $\sigma = \sqrt{\sigma^2}$, is the most commonly used measure of dispersion. This is called the standard deviation.

Two other measures are occasionally calculated. These are as follows:

Skewness. $\dfrac{E(X - \mu)^3}{\sigma^3}$. If this equals zero, then the distribution is said to be symmetric (see Figure 9A–4).

FIGURE 9A–4
Skewness

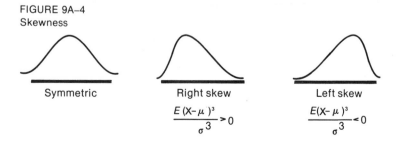

Symmetric	Right skew	Left skew
	$\dfrac{E(X-\mu)^3}{\sigma^3} > 0$	$\dfrac{E(X-\mu)^3}{\sigma^3} < 0$

Kurtosis. $\dfrac{E(X - \mu)^4}{\sigma^4}$. This is a measure of the height of the peak in a distribution, and is rarely used.

COMMONLY USED DISTRIBUTIONS

While an immense number of distributions exist, a small number turn out to be especially useful in marketing research. Some of these are binomial, poisson, normal (Gaussian), Student's t, chi-square, and F distributions, as well as some special distributions.

Binomial

The binomial is a discrete distribution which indicates the probability of X "successes" out of n trials. The key to the binomial is that it represents a situation in which there are (a) n independent trials and (b) exactly two possible outcomes. (This makes it a special case of the multinomial.) Its probability distribution is given by

$$P(X) = \binom{n}{X} p^X (1 - p)^{n-X}$$

where p = probability of success on a given trial. Also

$$\mu = np$$
$$\sigma = \sqrt{np(1 - p)}$$

It turns out that the binomial can be approximated by other distributions:

1. For p close to 0 or 1, the binomial is similar to the poisson.
2. For p close to .5 or for large n, the binomial is close to the normal.

Poisson

Another major discrete distribution is the poisson. It is often viewed as the distribution of the number of successes in a given time period. Its density function is given by

$$P(X) = \frac{\lambda^X e^{-\lambda}}{X!}$$

Its mean and standard deviation are

$$\mu = \lambda$$
$$\sigma = \sqrt{\lambda}$$

For large λ, the poisson becomes approximately normal.

Normal (Gaussian)

The normal distribution is the standard bell-shaped symmetric curve which recurs in many situations. It is continuous, and its density function is given by

$$f(X) = \frac{1}{2\pi\sqrt{\sigma}} \, e^{-\frac{1}{2}\left(\frac{X-\mu}{\sigma}\right)^2}$$

where

μ = the mean
σ = the standard deviation

This is such a mess mathematically that calculations of probabilities are impossible. In order to estimate probabilities (e.g., the probability a part will be between 80 and 85 mm in length), a "scale model" approach is used. The approach is to convert to the standard normal distribution

FIGURE 9A–5
Standard normal distribution

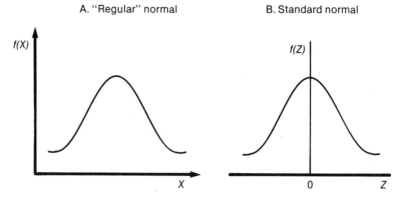

A. "Regular" normal   B. Standard normal

where $\mu = 0$ and $\sigma = 1$ and then look up the answer in a table (Figure 9A–5). The conversion is achieved by

$$Z = \frac{X - \mu}{\sigma}$$

For example, assume I were interested in obtaining the probability that a certain part were between 80 and 85 mm. If $\mu = 81$ and $\sigma = 1$, this means the shaded area in Figure 9A–6. Now from the table, the area from 0 to -1 standard deviation is about .34. Similarly the area from 0 to $+4$ is

FIGURE 9A–6
Example of conversion to standard normal

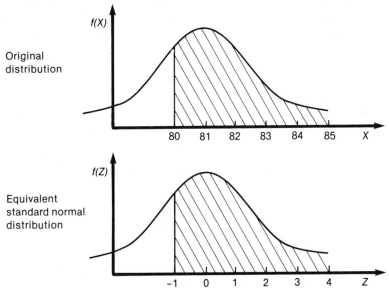

about .5. Hence the probability the part is between 80 and 85 mm is .5 + .34 = .84.

Student's t

The Student's t is another bell-shaped distribution which is slightly "fatter" than the normal. Its density function is also a "mess." (Since it was developed by the employee of an Irish brewery named Gosset, who used the pen name Student, its "sloppiness" is understandable.) Fortunately, the function is tabled so the density function is not used. The mean and standard deviation of the t distribution are given by

$$\mu = 0$$
$$\sigma = \sqrt{\frac{\nu}{\nu - 2}}$$

For large ν, the t distribution is approximately normal.[1]

---

[1] The t distribution is often expressed as the ratio of a standard normal to a chi-square: $t = \dfrac{X}{\sqrt{y/\nu}}$ where X is standard normal and y is chi-square with ν degrees of freedom.

Chi-square (χ^2)

The chi-square distribution is the distribution of a sum of squared in-dependent standard normal variables.[2] Its density function is also un-wieldy. Its mean and standard deviation are given by

$$\mu = v$$
$$\sigma = \sqrt{2v}$$

For large v, the chi-square distribution is approximately normal.

F distribution

The F distribution is the ratio of two chi-square variables.[3] Its density function is too messy to bother writing since it also is tabled. One interest-

FIGURE 9A–7

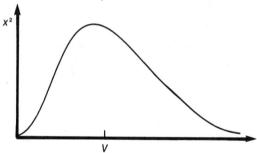

A. Chi-square distribution

B. F distribution

---

[2] $\chi^2 = \displaystyle\sum_{i=1}^{v} X_i^2$ where X_i is standard normal.

[3] $F = \dfrac{\dfrac{X_1}{v_1}}{\dfrac{X_2}{v_2}}$ where X_1 and X_2 are chi-square with v_1 and v_2 degrees of freedom respectively.

ing fact is that the F distribution has a fixed end point at 0 (no negative values are possible since it is made up of the ratio of squared numbers), a mean of 1, and a strong right skew (Figure 9A–7).

Other distributions

The distributions just listed are the most commonly used for statistical testing in marketing research. Other distributions are used in special circumstances, especially stochastic modeling, including the negative binomial, exponential, gamma (of which both the exponential and chi-square are special cases), and the beta.

ESTIMATES AND TRUTH

The distributions just described were given in terms of their true parameters. Unfortunately a researcher rarely knows the true parameters (μ, σ, etc.). We mortals then must estimate (guess) what the parameters are. The estimates are typically given by the following:

	True value	Estimate
Mean	μ	$\bar{X} = \dfrac{\Sigma X}{n}$
Variance	σ^2	$s^2 = s_X^2 = \dfrac{\Sigma(X - \bar{X})^2}{n - 1}$
Standard deviation (of population)	$\sigma = \sqrt{\sigma^2}$	$s = \sqrt{s^2}$
Standard deviation (of mean)	$\sigma_{\bar{X}} = \dfrac{\sigma}{\sqrt{n}}$	$s_{\bar{X}} = \dfrac{s}{\sqrt{n}}$
Proportion	θ	$p = \dfrac{\text{No. successes}}{n}$

Notice that by convention, Greek letters stand for true values and Arabic letters for approximations. (Everyone knows the ancient Greeks had truth, don't they?)

CONFIDENCE INTERVAL

A confidence interval is a range into which we expect a value to fall. There are actually the following two types of confidence intervals:

1. Given true parameters (e.g., μ and σ), where will a measured value (e.g., $\bar{X}$) fall?
2. Given a measured value (e.g., $\bar{X}$ and s), in what range are the true values (e.g., μ) likely to be?

A confidence interval of the first type can be expressed graphically (Figure 9A–8). The confidence level $(1 - \alpha)$ is the probability that an event will fall in the confidence level. The significance level (α) is the probability an event will occur outside the confidence level.

FIGURE 9A–8
Confidence interval

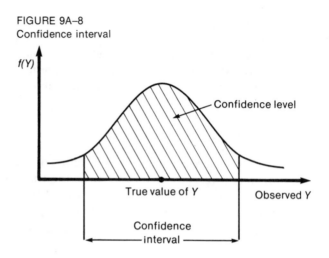

THE NOTION OF STATISTICAL INFERENCE

This section will briefly describe the concept of statistical inference. If you (a) already understand the concept, (b) are a purist, or (c) have a fetish for complete treatment of this subject, please skip the section and/or refer to a basic statistics book. The purpose of this section is to provide a brief intuitive feel for inference.

The basic motivation for statistical inference is to detect significant unusual behavior. The notion of statistical inference suggests that it is possible for two numbers to be different mathematically but not different significantly. For example, one person might weigh 180.23 pounds and another 180.12. While these weights are different, (a) for most decisions the difference is unimportant and (b) the difference is well within the range of accuracy of most measuring devices and hence insignificant statistically. Hence it is useful to distinguish between three kinds of differences:

1. *Mathematical.* If numbers are not exactly the same, they are different. (In marketing research, two results are almost always different.)
2. *Important.* If the numerical difference would matter in a managerial sense, then the difference is important.
3. *Statistical significance.* If the difference is big enough to be unlikely

to have occurred due to chance, then the difference is statistically significant.

In determining statistically significant differences, I must make a trade-off between two extremes:

Calling every difference, no matter how small, significant. For example, someone with a weight fetish might weigh themselves at 8 P.M. after a huge pasta dinner and again at 8 P.M. the next night immediately after a fish dinner. If the weights were 181 and 179 pounds respectively, they could think they had lost 2 pounds. Alternatively, however, they could think (*a*) that fish is lighter than pasta, (*b*) that they exercised differently, or (*c*) that the accuracy of the scale given changes in temperature, humidity, and position of the scale in the bathroom is insufficient to call a 2-pound difference statistically significant. Calling a difference significant when it is not is traditionally called Type I or α error.

Requiring absolute proof that a difference is significant. Carrying the weight example further, it is possible to argue that any change might have been due to a "fluke" measurement. Hence it is possible that a weight change from 181 to 170 is not important or significant. (However, anyone with the 24-hour flu would strongly disagree.) Calling a difference insignificant when it is significant is called a Type II or β error.

The problem of detecting significant results by trading off these two considerations arises in many contexts:

1. *Machine retooling.* A machine in the middle of an assembly line has to produce parts within a given tolerance. If the machine is to be retooled, the assembly line must be stopped. If the machine produces bad parts, considerable repair costs are required. Based on a sample of parts from the machine, do I retool or not?
2. *Evaluating a taste testing result.* In a blind test between two versions of the same product (one less costly), 37 prefer version A and 43 version B. Is the difference significant or can I use the cheaper version without sacrificing sales?
3. *Judicial decisions.* In rendering a decision, a judge or jury must implicitly decide between two risks: putting an innocent person in jail or letting a guilty person go free.

Interestingly most of the basic literature on statistics, the practices of marketing research, and the legal system in the United States focuses on the Type I (α) error. Hence we will limit further discussion of statistical significance to mean significantly different beyond "reasonable doubt."

SAMPLING DISTRIBUTIONS

The key concept to determining statistical significance is that of a sampling distribution. A sampling distribution is the representation of the likelihood that a given value (e.g., an individual's weight, the mean diameter of a part, or the percent of a consumer sample who prefer a certain color) will occur. This likelihood could be based on past experience or alternatively a set of standards or specifications. The uncertainty in the results may be due to the measurement process and/or random differences among respondents. We can see this graphically in Figure 9A–9. The

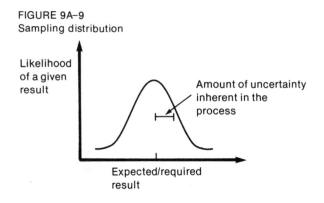

FIGURE 9A–9
Sampling distribution

question which must be answered, then, is whether a particular sample result is "different." In answering this question we are really addressing the question, "Is the population from which the sample result was drawn different from the original population?" Consider the three situations in Figure 9A–10. In case A, the sample result is well outside the typical range of values, and hence would be called significantly different. This implies that the population from which the sample was drawn is different from the original population in terms of this particular characteristic. In

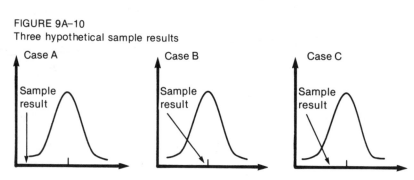

FIGURE 9A–10
Three hypothetical sample results

case B, the sample result is very close to the expected result and well within the range of typical values. Hence the result in case B is not significantly different. (Put differently, this result probably came from the same population of results as did the previous results.) In case C, the sample result is different from the expected result but not so different as to be completely beyond the range of typical results. Hence what will determine statistical significance is whether there is a reasonable likelihood that as "odd" a result would occur due to chance.

The reasonable chance cutoff (α level or Type I error) can be set at any level. In social science, however, the level is typically either .10, .05, or .01 and by far the most widely used cutoff is .05. In other words, if there is less than a 5 in 100 chance that the sample result or a more extreme result would come from the hypothesized process, then the sample result is declared significantly different.

The effect of sample size on statistical significance is very important. Consider again case C. If the sample result is based on a single observation, we would conclude it is not possible to label that person as significantly different from the original population. If it is the average of ten observations, we are more likely to feel the population from which the sample is drawn is different from the original population. If the sample size were 2,000, we would almost certainly feel the second population is different from the first. While it is possible to subjectively take sample size into account, a more methodical way is available in two important cases: averages and proportions.

Sampling distribution of an average ($\overline{X}$)

Assume the value of a particular result has mean $\overline{X}$ and standard deviation s_X (usually just written as plain s). Then the mean and standard deviation of the sampling distribution (likely results) of the average of a sample of size n would be as follows:

$$\text{Mean of sample size } n = \overline{X}$$
$$\begin{array}{l}\text{Standard deviation of} \\ \text{the mean of the} \\ \text{sample of size } n\end{array} = s_{\bar{x}} = \frac{s}{\sqrt{n}}$$

What this means is that the sampling distribution becomes tighter as sample size increases (Figure 9A–11). Hence the result which is not significant as an isolated instance may become significant if it occurs repeatedly.

A useful result is that the mean ($\overline{X}$) follows the normal distribution even if the underlying distribution of X is not normal (courtesy of the central

FIGURE 9A–11

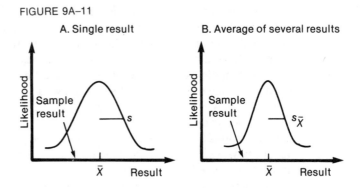

A. Single result   B. Average of several results

limit theorem). What this means is that we can use the normal distribution to check for statistical significance. It is also interesting to note that precision increases as the square root of sample size. In other words, in order to be twice as confident of what the results are (cut the range in half), you need four times the sample size. (This has some real implications for the diminishing marginal utility of increasing sample size.)

Sampling distribution of a proportion

The sampling distribution of the proportion of respondents exhibiting a particular behavior (i.e., owning a color TV) is given by

$$\text{Expected proportion} = p$$

$$\text{Standard deviation} = s_p = \sqrt{\frac{p(1-p)}{n}}$$

Notice that the closer p is to 50 percent, the greater the standard deviation. Since this distribution is also approximately normally distributed for n greater than 30, we can get the notion of how accurate proportions are. If we wish to get a range into which 95 percent of actual results are likely to fall (commonly known as the 95 percent confidence level), we get $P \pm 1.96 s_p$. If we think p is .50 and take a sample of 100, this becomes

$$.50 \pm 1.96 \sqrt{\frac{(.5)(.5)}{100}} = .50 \pm .10 = .40 \text{ to } .60$$

In other words, we are 95 percent sure that the results would be between 40 and 60 percent. This is a very broad range and brings forth an important point: proportions are very imprecise measures and apparently big differences are often not significant.

HYPOTHESIS TESTING

Hypothesis testing is the process of determining whether a result is or is not statistically significantly different from an expected result. As such, it is the applied use of the notion of statistical inference. Numerous hypotheses can be tested. For marketing research, however, a few basic tests cover the majority of the situations encountered. These commonly used tests are introduced in this book when the problems to which they apply are discussed.

10 _____

Coding and editing responses

When the results of a study come in, there is an understandable desire to get to the interpretation phase as quickly as possible. There are, however, two basic stages between data collection and interpretation. The most interesting of these is the analysis phase. However, before analysis can begin, the data must be converted into a form suitable for analysis. The conversion of the data from "raw" form—typically questionnaires—to a form which facilitates analysis is the subject of this chapter. The problem of converting secondary data to a form ready for analysis is a much simpler but still important task.

SIMPLE INSPECTION

When the number of observations is small, it is possible to do the analysis by hand (assuming no fancy analyses are desired and that there are a fairly small number of variables). Pilot studies of size 20 and industrial marketing studies of 25 purchasing agents may be analyzed without resorting to computers. Here a combination of scanning the results and a simple question-by-question tabulation is often sufficient.

COMPUTER ANALYSIS

Assuming (a) there are a reasonably large number of respondents, (b) there are a large number or responses, or (c) there is a desire to get more than simple tabulations of the responses, the practical way to proceed is to prepare the data for computer analysis. By far the most popular way to do this is to punch the data on computer cards. Recently it has become popular to put data directly into computer memories, but since the format is usually "card image" and the method the same, this procedure will not be further discussed here.

The basic unit of data storage, the computer card, is essentially a table of 12 rows and 80 columns. The rows from top to bottom are:

```
12(+)
11(−)
0
1
2
3
4
5
6
7
8
9
```

Information is recorded by punching a hole in the card. Each of the 80 columns can contain a separate piece of information. For example column 8 might be the response to a question about how well I like yogurt, column 9 a question about what type of car I own, and so forth. Groups of columns can also be used to store information (e.g., age might be in columns 19 and 20). Whenever more data exists for a respondent than can be fitted onto a single card, a second card is used (and so forth).

In order to keep track of individual respondents, it is desirable to keep a set of columns for identification purposes. For example, we could use columns 1–4 for an ID number. Assuming there is more than one card per respondent, column 5 might be used to indicate card number (actually any column will do, and many suppliers tend to use column 80 to indicate card number).

Data is stored in a person-by-person fashion. Hence assuming we had a sample of four people with three cards per person, the data cards might look like Figure 10–1.

FIGURE 10–1

	Column					
	ID				Card No.	Data
Card	1	2	3	4	5	6 · · · 80
1......	0	0	0	1	1	
2......	0	0	0	1	2	
3......	0	0	0	1	3	
4......	0	0	0	2	1	
5......	0	0	0	2	2	
6......	0	0	0	2	3	
7......	0	0	0	3	1	
8......	0	0	0	3	2	
9......	0	0	0	3	3	
10......	0	0	0	4	1	
11......	0	0	0	4	2	
12......	0	0	0	4	3	

In the "old" days, tabulation analysis was performed by mechanical card sorters which physically sorted the cards based on the code in one column. Currently most of the analysis is done by "canned" (already written) computer programs. (For the curious, the vast majority of these programs are written in Fortran IV.) This allows a variety of analysis to be performed with a few simple instructions.

EDITING QUESTIONNAIRES

Rough screening

The first thing that is typically done when a survey is completed is to do a rough screening job on the returned questionnaires. This essentially consists of looking for grossly "bad" respondents with illegible, incomplete, or inconsistent responses.

Illegible responses. This is a common problem for poorly supervised personal interviews and questionnaires with a large number of open-ended responses.

Incomplete responses. Many returned questionnaires will have a large percentage of nonresponses to individual questions.

Inconsistent responses. Sometimes a casual glance will indicate the respondent is not very believable (e.g., income > $50,000, age < 15, loves sports, never participates in sports, etc.). Alternatively the respondent may have given the same response to the large number of consecutive questions, indicating a certain lack of interest.

Corrections

Since there are inevitably some "bad" respondents, a question which immediately arises is what to do with them. The decision concerning what to do with bad respondents is heavily dependent on how many good respondents there are. When there are a large number of good respondents both in an absolute sense and relative to the number of bad respondents, it may be possible to ignore them. When, on the other hand, data points are expensive and more are needed for purposes of analysis and/or projectability, then some way must be found to "fix up" the bad responses. Three basic approaches are used in dealing with bad respondents: going back to get better information, using the data as they are, and throwing out bad respondents.

Going back to get better information. Assuming the individuals in question can be identified, it is possible to go back and try to get the respondent to "correct" his/her responses. This is obviously fairly expensive in the case of a large-scale national survey. If (a) the percentage of bad respondents is small (less than 20 percent), (b) the bad respondents are not different in obvious ways (e.g., income, product usage, etc.) from good respondents, and (c) there is a reasonably large sample size (e.g., greater than 500), then it is probably better to avoid going back for more data. In the case of either lab experiments or industrial marketing surveys of a small number of key accounts, on the other hand, it is often relatively easy to go back to collect key pieces of missing data. It is important to realize, however, that data collected the second time may be different from the data at the time of the original survey because of both changes over time and the different means of gathering the data (e.g., phone callbacks to mail survey respondents).

Using the data as they are.   It is possible to use the data exactly as it is received for basic analysis. This approach is commonly used by suppliers, not surprisingly so since they are typically committed to getting a certain number of respondents. Tabulations can keep track of the nonresponses as a separate category. Inconsistent responses might be assumed to average out over the sample. As long as only simple tabulations are performed, the results may not be too badly distorted. Whenever "fancy" analysis (e.g., regression) is to be performed, however, this approach leads to considerable problems.

Throwing out bad respondents.   The simplest thing to do is discard the "bad" respondents. This is the easiest thing to do and a widely followed approach given sufficient sample size to allow it. There are, however, three main drawbacks to this approach. First is that it is an extra step not typically performed by suppliers which requires time and effort. Secondly, the "bad" respondents may in fact be very meaningful in that they are in essence saying the topic of your survey is so uninteresting and irrelevant that they refuse to take the time to complete it. Finally, by deciding on what is a "bad" respondent, especially an inconsistent one, the potential for researchers bias influencing the final results is high. Put differently, the bad respondents may be different from good resondents in terms of the variables being measured and hence excluding them may bias the results. While these problems discourage many researchers from discarding bad respondents, the key point to remember is the purpose of information collection and analysis is to improve the odds of making a good decision. Hence if the researcher believes the results will be more useful if bad respondents are removed, s/he can make the managerial decision to remove them, and hopefully carefully record and report the procedure used.

CODING

The next step in preparing for analysis is to convert the responses into a coded form for punching on cards. Since open-ended questions require individual attention (theoretically by multiple coders to ensure good results), most questions should generally be closed-end multiple choice questions in a large-scale survey. It is essentially a two-step process to convert responses to computer cards: (*a*) converting the responses to code values on coding sheets (80-column-wide sheets in which the appropriate codes are placed in the appropriate columns) and (*b*) punching the cards. In order to save time and money, it is usually possible to eliminate the first step by precoding the questionnaire so that a keypunch operator can punch cards directly from the questionnaire. It is the desire to have precoded responses which pushes market researchers into the almost exclusive use of multiple choice questions.

Two standard approaches are used for coding. The first is to code possible responses from left to right beginning with "1." For example, if we asked the question

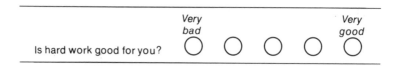

it would be coded 1 through 5, with a "1" representing a "very bad" response and so forth. The second standard approach is to treat all nonresponses the same way. Some suppliers leave nonresponses blank, others punch a "9" or a "12" (+). In many cases it may be useful to code a nonresponse to a question separately from don't know responses. One more point is extremely important: do not attempt to save space by "packing" data into a small number of columns. Let each piece of information have a separate column (in general, even if this requires extra cards per respondent).

To see how a questionnaire can be converted into a computer card, consider the example in Figure 10–2. In this case, the first five columns are devoted to an identification field—here the respondent number "12345."

Column 6 will be coded "1" since the first category was indicated on question 1.

Question 2 will occupy columns 7–14. Each separate piece of information gets its own column. In this case, the blanks checked indicate values 3, 2, 4, 3, 3, 5, 2, and 4.

Question 3 occupies columns 15–19 with the numbers 3, 5, 4, 2, 2.

Question 4 occupies columns 20–24 with numbers 4, 4, 4, 5, 5.

Question 5 occupies columns 25–28 with values 3, 5, 4, and 2.

Question 6 is coded into column 29 with a 4 since "daily" is the fourth category.

Question 7 takes up three separate columns (30–32) since it would be

FIGURE 10–2
Sample questionnaire

1. Do you use toothpaste?   ✓_____   _____   ID 1-5
                              Yes   No   6

2. Please indicate your degree of agreement with the following statements by
    circling a 6 if you strongly agree, a 1 if you strongly disagree, or some-
    where in between depending on your degree of agreement with the
    statement.

		Strongly disagree				Strongly agree		
Hard work is good for you.	1	2	③	4	5	6	7
I am very health conscious.	1	②	3	4	5	6	8
I tend to be conservative in my dress	1	2	3	④	5	6	9
I enjoy participating in vigorous exercise.	1	2	③	4	5	6	10
I am very family centered.	1	2	③	4	5	6	11
My appearance is very important to me.	1	2	3	4	⑤	6	12
I use mouthwash often.	1	②	3	4	5	6	13
I enjoy meeting people.	1	2	3	④	5	6	14

3. Please rate each of the following brands of toothpaste by marking a 6 if
    you feel the brand is very good, a 1 if you feel the brand is very poor, or
    somewhere in between depending on how good you feel the brand is.

	Very poor				Very good		
Aim	1	2	③	4	5	6	15
Colgate	1	2	3	4	⑤	6	16
Crest	1	2	3	④	5	6	17
Macleans	1	②	3	4	5	6	18
UltraBright	1	②	3	4	5	6	19

4. Please rate the following brands in terms of their *breath freshening ability*
    by marking a 6 if you feel the brand is very good, a 1 if you feel the brand
    is very poor, or somewhere in between depending on how good you feel
    the brand is.

	Very poor				Very good		
Aim	1	2	3	④	5	6	20
Colgate	1	2	3	④	5	6	21
Crest	1	2	3	④	5	6	22
Macleans	1	2	3	4	⑤	6	23
UltraBright	1	2	3	4	⑤	6	24

5. Please indicate how important each of the following features of toothpaste
    are to you by circling a 6 if the feature is very important, a 1 is the feature
    is very unimportant or somewhere in between depending on how important
    the feature is to you.

	Very unimportant				Very important		
Breath freshening	1	2	③	4	5	6	25
Decay prevention	1	2	3	4	⑤	6	26
Taste	1	2	3	④	5	6	27
Price	1	2	③	4	5	6	28

FIGURE 10–2 (*continued*)

6. How often do you brush your teeth?

| Never | Rarely | Few times a day | Daily ✓ | Two times a day | More than two times a day | 29 |

7. Who makes the purchase decision concerning which brand of toothpaste your household uses?

Male head of household	✓	30
Female head of household	✓	31
Children	_____	32

8. What brand of toothpaste did your household last purchase?

CREST 33

9. How old would you like to be?

| Under 20 | 21–35 ✓ | 36–50 | Over 50 | 34 |

10. What is the highest level of education you have completed?

| 6th grade | High school | College ✓ | Graduate school | 35 |

11. What is your total annual household income?

| Under $5,000 | $5,000– $9,999 | $10,000– $14,999 | $15,000– $19,999 | Over $20,000 ✓ | 36 |

12. What is your occupation?

| White collar | Blue collar | Homemaker | Student | Other | 37 |

13. How many people live in your household?   **4**   38

14. What is your sex?

| Male ✓ | Female | 39 |

15. What is your marital status?

| Single | Married ✓ | Divorced, widowed, or separated | Other | 40 |

16. Do you own a

House?

| _____ | ✓ | 41 |
| Yes | No | |

Car?

| ✓ | _____ | 42 |
| Yes | No | |

Snowmobile?

| ✓ | _____ | 43 |
| Yes | No | |

Color TV?

| _____ | ✓ | 44 |
| Yes | No | |

CB Radio?

| ✓ | _____ | 45 |
| Yes | No | |

17. How old are you? **27**   46–47

possible and logical to check more than one response (as this respondent did). While we could (and would if we were old-time coders) indicate this by punching both a 1 and a 2 in column 30 (called *multiple punching*), this would play havoc with many of the analysis routines to be used later. Hence we use three separate columns and indicate 1, 1, blank. (If we had asked which person has the most influence, then only one answer would have been appropriate and the data could have been coded in column 30 as a 1—male head of household, 2—female head of household, or 3—children.)

Question 8 is an open-ended question which must be manually coded. Actually it could have been precoded by including the major brands and an "all other—please specify" category. Assuming our code were 1 = Aim, 2 = Colgate, 3 = Crest, 4 = Macleans, 5 = UltraBright, and 6 = all others, we would place a 3 in column 33.

Question 9 will produce a 2 in column 34.

Question 10 will produce a 3 in column 35.

Question 11 will generate a 5 for column 36.

Column 37 will be a 1 to represent the "white-collar" response to Question 12.

Question 13 will place a 4 in column 38. Notice here that a response of 10 or more is unaccounted for. Hence either I must collapse 10 into another value such as 9 or save 2 columns (38–39) for the response.

Question 14 implies a 1 for column 39.

Question 15 implies a 2 for column 40.

Question 16 fills columns 41–45 with 2, 1, 1, 2, and 1. Notice again that rather than collapse the information into a single column, each durable ownership response occupies a separate column.

Question 17 fills columns 46–47 with 27. If someone is over 100, we would (*a*) punch a 99 and (*b*) congratulate them and ask for their secret of success. If someone is 8, we would place the 8 in column 47, a process known as right justifying. The reason for this is the computer will read a __8 as 8, and an 8__ as 80.

One other point worth mentioning is that it is highly desirable to use fixed field codes. This means that (*a*) the number of cards for each observation is the same, and (*b*) the same piece of data appears in the same column for all observations. Failure to do this is disastrous for most analytical procedures. The tendency to use uneven record lengths comes from questions where the respondent lists several items (e.g., family members, cars owned, credit cards carried). Since in order to use fixed record lengths the code will be determined by those with the largest number of responses, there will be a large amount of blank space on the cards of those respondents with few responses. Here the puritan ethic of not wasting space will lead to the wrong decision. The cost of the blank space is usually far smaller than the cost of uneven record length. For example, we might leave room for four cars which will cover over 99 percent of the responses. (While we could include the 1 person with 13 cars, this is such an unusual observation that it is not in general worth the trouble of keeping track of all 13.)

The conversion of secondary data into computer form is also fairly simple. Assume I collected data on annual dishwasher sales in units and GNP:

Year	Dishwasher sales (units)	GNP (billion $)
1960	555,321	503.7
1965	1,260,462	684.9
1970	2,116,119	977.1
1972	3,199,201	1,155.2
1973	3,701,982	1,289.1

The ID Field would be year, probably in columns 1–4. Since plenty of space is available, we could skip some space before beginning dishwasher sales in some column such as 11. Clearly we could punch in seven columns' worth of data for dishwasher sales. However, the accuracy of the last three columns as well as their value given only five data points is very questionable. Hence it seems more reasonable to only include the data in thousands of units. Since the maximum number of columns needed is 4 (for 3,702, the largest number), we assign columns 11–14 for dishwasher sales (remembering they are now measured in thousands of units sold).

In punching GNP, it is possible to punch the data as is. However, it is unnecessary to punch the decimal point as (a) we could interpret the results just as well in units of hundreds of millions as units of billions and (b) we can tell the computer where the decimal point belongs and have it replaced during analysis. (For Fortran fans, use F 5.1). Hence since 12891 is the largest number, we can use five columns (15–19) to represent GNP. The resulting data would then be punched as is shown in Figure 10–3.

FIGURE 10–3
Coded dishwasher sales data

Card	1	2	3	4	5	6	7	8	9	10	11	12	13	14	15	16	17	18	19
															Column				
1	1	9	6	0								5	5	5		5	0	3	7
2	1	9	6	5							1	2	6	0		6	8	4	9
3	1	9	7	0							2	1	1	6		9	7	7	1
4	1	9	7	2							3	1	9	9	1	1	5	5	2
5	1	9	7	3							3	7	0	2	1	2	8	9	1

PUNCHING

The task of punching data is straightforward and essentially the same as typing. An experienced keypunch operator can turn out 80–100 cards per hour at a cost of about 10 cents per card from a supplier. Because keypunch operators occasionally make errors, it is usually desirable to check their work. The standard way to do this is to "verify" the work. This is done by a second operator using a machine known as a verifier. The operator at the verifier essentially repunches the card from the original questionnaire. Instead of punching holes in the cards, however, the verifier shoots a beam of light at the card. If the light goes through (meaning there is a hole in the correct space), the card proceeds to the next column. If the light does not go through, the card remains in the same position. The verifier then tries again. If the light still fails to go through, the card is marked and returned to be repunched. This verification process essentially doubles both the time and cost of punching.

One final word of caution is in order. Never rely on a single data set. Data sets have a habit of becoming mutilated. Typically large data sets are stored on magnetic tape. The minimum safety margin is a card set and a tape record, stored in different places.

CODE BOOK

The punched cards delivered by a supplier are accompanied by a code book giving a column-by-column explanation of the relation between the codes on the cards and the responses to the questions. These can be quite extensive, as the code book from the nutrition study turned out to be. That 8-page questionnaire produced a 30-page code book, which is presented in abbreviated form in Appendix 10–A. Also typically included will be information as to how to access the data (where it is physically stored if it is in card form, what instructions access it if it is stored on tape or disc).

CLEANING THE DATA: MISSING RESPONSES

Cleaning the data for final analysis has several steps. First, a column-by-column count of the responses is made. Typical results are shown in Figure 10–4, taken from card 1 of the nutrition study. These results give indications of illegal punches and also an initial glympse at the results.

The other stage of cleaning the data consists of deciding what to do with isolated missing responses. These are questions which an otherwise "good" respondent left blank. There are four major choices:

Leave them blank.   This is fine for tabs and cross-tabs but is a problem for many programs such as regression which treats blanks as zeros.

Substitute a neutral value.   Typically this approach involves substitut-

FIGURE 10–4
Sample basic tab from nutrition study

							Card #1							
COLUMN	TOTAL	-12-	-11-	-0-	-1-	-2-	-3-	-4-	-5-	-6-	-7-	-8-	-9-
	CODED												
061	940				645	67	1	227					
062	940	3	234	135	39	109	59	41	135	113	50	3	19
063	940			407	362	171							
064	940			93	188	71	122	131	119	138	55	67	44
065	940				784	107	49						
066	940			8	758	168	6						
067	940		57	10	504	299	60	8	1	1			
068	940		478	206	226	20	8		1	1			
069	940			1	910	28	1						
070	940			367	109	59	49	77	123	102	31	23	
071	940			349	99	39	64	90	73	60	65	52	49
072	940			545	20	21	10	2	296	20	9	9	8
073	940				246	694							
074	940				53	156	186	88	142	67	96	41	111
075	940				178	107	179	219	257				
076	940				185	164	175	185	231				
077	940				309	159	202	131	139				
078	940					415	191	160	107	42	19	4	2
079	940			940									
080	940				940								

ing a value, usually the mean response to the question, for the missing response. This approach keeps the mean constant and also tends to have a relatively small effect on calculations such as correlations. Good as this may sound, putting a 3.5 (the mean for the missing question *across all respondents*) on the card of a respondent who mainly indicated 1's and 2's seems questionable.

Assign the value the individual "would have used" if s/he had answered the question. This approach suggests that by looking at the individual's pattern of responses to other questions, we can logically deduce an appropriate answer to the missing question. Since this method (*a*) requires considerable effort and (*b*) risks considerable researcher bias, it is not very popular. Still it is an approach which may be useful for some situations.

Assume they were "don't know" or "not applicable" responses.   A nonresponse may mean the question does not apply (NA). For example, a survey may branch so that only owners of trucks fill out certain questions, meaning that nontruck owners will leave several questions blank. Alternatively, it may be that the respondent genuinely doesn't know (DK) the answer. (Do you know who advertises "Brings the taste to light"?)

SUMMARY

Unless the data is converted accurately to a usable form, subsequent analysis will be both difficult and misleading. The secret is simply to be careful in establishing procedures for coding the data. This is fairly simple if appropriate care is taken. Several key points need reiterating:

Keep an identification field which indicates both person and card number (if more than one). The ID field allows you to go back to the questionnaire if the data is incorrectly punched, or to the respondent if further information is needed. Also keeping the card number allows you to re-sort the cards if for some reason they ever get out of order (a not infrequent occurrence given butterfingered analysts and hungry card readers).

Code the data in a disaggregated form.   Do not pack data in a few columns as this is a false economy.

Don't multiple punch.   Multiple punches are disastrous for most computer routines. In fact, some people strive valiantly to keep the number of possible responses to nine or fewer to reduce the tendency to multipunch. Also take care to force suppliers into not multipunching, since left to their own devices they invariably multipunch.

Keep fixed record lengths.   Saving space is a false economy.

Keep backup data sets.   Those who keep a single data set deserve the frustration of seeing it mangled.

Spend some time cleaning the data.   This means both throwing out hopelessly bad respondents and seeing if nonresponses can be converted to responses.

Be lucky.   Those who aren't careful almost always get burned, but it helps to be lucky to avoid trouble.

PROBLEMS

1. Assume you wished to build a model relating GNP, Housing Starts, the Dow-Jones average, the Consumer Price Index, and automotive

sales in the United States on a yearly basis from 1960–75. Set up the code sheets for your data set.

2. How would you interpret nonresponse to each of the following questions below?

Do you own an air conditioner?	————	————
	Yes	No

How many children do you have? ————

	Dislike very much				Like very much
How well do you like peas?	1 2	3		4	5 6

What is the largest selling brand of shampoo? _____

3. Set up a coding scheme for the questionnaire above.

BIBLIOGRAPHY

Pessemier, Edgar A. "Data Quality in Marketing Information Systems." *Control of Error in Market Research Data,* pp. 109–44. Edited by John U. Farley and John A. Howard. Lexington, Mass.: Lexington Books, 1975.

Siedl, Philip S. "Coding." In *Handbook of Marketing Research,* pp. 2–178 to 2–199. Edited by Robert Ferber. New York: McGraw-Hill, 1974.

———— APPENDIX 10-A ————
NUTRITION STUDY CODEBOOK

Column	CARD 1: NFO Standard Family Background Codes* Code
1–6	Application number (identification)
7–8	State Codes—NFO standard codes
9–11	County codes—NFO standard codes
12–14	City codes—NFO codes
15	Live within city limits: 1—Inside city limits 2—Outside city limits
16	NFO use
17	Marital status: 1—Now married 2—Never married 3—Divorced 4—Widowed 5—Separated 0—No answer

* Source: National Family Opinion, Inc., New York.

	CARD 1 (*continued*)
Column	*Code*

18–19 Year married:
Last two digits of year punched actual
00—No answer

20–22 Homemaker:
20 Month of birth
1—January
2—February
3—March
4—April
5—May
6—June
7—July
8—August
9—September
0—October
X—November
+—December
21–22 Year of birth (last two digits of year punched actual)

23–25 Husband:
23 Month of birth (see codes for column 20)
24–25 Year of birth (see codes for columns 21 & 22)
X—Living away from home (service)
Blank—No husband

26–53 Other family members:
26 Month of birth (see codes for column 20)
27–28 Year of birth (see codes for columns 21 and 22)
29 Sex
1—Male
2—Female

54–56 NFO use

57 Homemaker's education:
1—Attended grade school
2—Graduated from grade school
3—Attended high school
4—Graduated from high school
5—Attended college
6—Graduated from college
7—Masters
8—Doctors
0—No answer

58 Husband's education:
1—Attended grade school
2—Graduated from grade school
3—Attended high school
4—Graduated from high school
5—Attended college
6—Graduated from college
7—Masters
8—Doctors
0—No answer
X—No husband

CARD 1 (*continued*)

Column	Code
59	Homemaker's employment:

59 — Homemaker's employment:
1—Full time
2—Part time
3—Not employed
4—No answer

60 — Husband's employment:
1—Full time
2—Part time
3—Not employed
0—No answer
X—No husband

61 — Principal wage earner:
1—Husband
2—Homemaker
3—Other
4—No wage earner (income derived from source other than employment)

62 — Occupation:
0—Professional, technical, and kindred workers
1—Farmers and farm managers
2—Managers, officials, and proprietors (except farm)
3—Clerical and kindred workers
4—Sales workers
5—Craftsmen, foremen, and kindred workers
6—Operative and kindred workers
7—Service workers (including private household)
8—Farm laborers and foremen
9—Laborers (except farm and mine)
X—Retired, students, disabled, unemployed, and armed forces
+—No answer

63–64 — Annual family income:
03—Under $3,000
04—$3,000–$3,999
05—$4,000–$4,999
06—$5,000–$5,999
07—$6,000–$6,999
08—$7,000–$7,999
09—$8,000–$8,999
10—$9,999–$9,999
11—$10,000–$10,999
12—$11,000–$11,999
13—$12,000–$12,999
14—$13,000–$13,999
15—$14,000–$14,999
16—$15,000–$15,999
17—$16,000–$16,999
18—$17,000–$17,999
19—$18,000–$18,999
20—$19,000–$19,999
21—$20,000–$24,999
22—$25,000–$29,999
23—$30,000–$35,000
24—Over $35,000

CARD 1 (continued)

Column	Code
65	Type of residence: 1—House 2—Apartment 3—Other 0—No answer
66	Home ownership: 1—Own 2—Rent 3—Live with relatives (in their home) 4—Other 0—No answer
67	Car ownership: 1—1 car 2—2 cars 3—3 cars 4—4 cars 5—5 cars 6—6 cars 7—7 cars 8—8 cars 9—9 cars X—None 0—No answer
68	Truck ownership: (see codes for car ownership)
69	Homemaker's race: 1—White 2—Negro or black 3—Oriental 4—Other 0—No answer
70–72	Metropolitan area NFO code
73	NFO use
74	Geographic divisions: 1—New England 2—Middle Atlantic 3—East North Central 4—West North Central 5—South Atlantic 6—East South Central 7—West South Central 8—Mountain 9—Pacific
75	Population densities: 1—Rural 2—Cities, 2,500–49,999 Metropolitan areas: 3—50,000–499,999 4—500,000–1,999,999 5—2,000,000 and over

---

CARD 1 (concluded)

Column   Code

76   Homemaker's age coded:
1—Under 30 years
2—30 through 39 years
3—40 through 49 years
4—50 through 59 years
5—60 years and over

77   Income coded:
1—Under $6,000
2—$6,000–$9,999
3—$10,000–$14,999
4—$15,000–$19,999
5—$20,000 and over

78   Size of family
2—2 members
3—3 members
4—4 members
5—5 members
6—6 members
7—7 members
8—8 members
9—9 or more members

79   NFO panel number

80   Card No. 1

CARD 2

Column   Code

1–6   Application number
7–8   Coded income

Section I—Food and shopping habits

9   Q. 1   Portion of household food shopping done personally:
1. None of it.
2. Less than half of it.
3. About half of it.
4. Most of it.
5. All of it.
0. No answer.

CARD 2 (continued)

Column	Code

10   Q. 2   Number of times per week shop for food:
    1. Less than once a week.
    2. Once a week.
    3. 2–4 times a week.
    4. 5 or more times a week.
    0. No answer.

11   Q. 3a Shopping list prepared before going to the store:
    1. Yes.
    2. No.

12   Q. 3b What portion of items purchased at store are on shopping list:
    1. None of them.
    2. Some of them.
    3. About half of them.
    4. More than half.
    5. Almost all of them.
    0. No answer.

13   Q. 4   Approximately how much money is spent on food in average week:
    1. Under $15.
    2. $15–$29.
    3. $30–$44.
    4. $45–$60.
    5. Over $60.
    0. No answer.

14   Q. 5   Approximately how much different is the amount spent now on food each week compared to one year ago:
    1. Spend at least $10 less than last year.
    2. $5–$10 less than last year.
    3. About the same as last year.
    4. $5–$10 more than last year.
    0. No answer.

15   Q. 6   When buying staple products, how many brands and sizes do you usually consider?
    1. Only 1 or 2.
    2. Many brands, one size.
    3. Many sizes, one brand.
    4. Many brands and sizes.
    0. No answer.

16   Q. 7   Which best describes the way you shop for food?
    1. I actively seek information about food in terms of nutritional value, price, etc.
    2. I sometimes try new foods because of new information, but generally buy the same foods.
    3. The food I buy is almost always the same, and I spend very little time thinking about it.
    0. No answer.

17   Q. 8   You or any members of your immediate family ever used food stamps?
    1. Never.
    2. Use to, but do not use them now.
    3. We are presently using them.
    0. No answer.

316

Column	Code	
18–27	Q. 9	How important are the following considerations when deciding which foods to serve? 1. Very important 2. 3. Somewhat important. 4. 5. Not very important. 0. No answer.
28–38	Q. 10	When deciding which brand to buy, how much attention do you pay to the following? 1. Pay a great deal of attention. 2. Pay some attention. 3. Pay little or no attention. 0. No answer.
39–41	Q. 11	Number of times per week you, personally, eat the following meals. 1. Never. 2. 1–2. 3. 3–4. 4. 5–6. 5. Every day. 0. No answer.
42	Q. 12	Number of snacks you, personally, have in a typical day. 1. None. 2. One. 3. Two. 4. Three or more. 0. No answer.
43	Q. 13	How much food do you can yourself? 1. None. 2. A small amount. 3. A large amount. 0. No answer.
44–73	Q. 14	How often do you personally consume each of the following? 1. Never. 2. A few times a year. 3. One to two times a month. 4. Weekly. 5. Several times a week. 6. Once a day. 7. More than once a day. 0. No answer.
74–78	Q. 15	How has the amount your household consumed of each of the following changed in the past year? 1. Much less. 2. Somewhat less. 3. About the same. 4. Somewhat more. 5. Much more. 0. No answer.
79	BLANK	
80	Card No. 2.	

CARD 3

Column	Code
1–6	Application number

Section I—Food and shopping habits (continued)

7–31   Q. 15   How has the amount your household consumed of each of following changed in the past year?
1. Much less.
2. Somewhat less.
3. About the same.
4. Somewhat more.
5. Much more.
0. No answer.

Section II—Nutritional information

32–43   Q. 1   Degree of information gained from listed sources.
1. None.
2. Very little.
3. Some.
4. Quite a bit.
5. A tremendous amount.
0. No answer.

44–46   Q. 2   In past year, have you read any books about any of the following?

44   Dieting:
1. No.
2. Yes.
0. No answer.

45   Nutrition:
1. No.
2. Yes.
0. No answer.

46   Cooking:
1. No.
2. Yes.
0. No answer.

47–56   Q. 3   If government launched a major nutrition education campaign aimed at adults, which form would you prefer?

47   0. No answer.
     1. Column in newspaper.
48   1. TV special.
49   1. Special edition of a prominent magazine.
50   1. Government brochure.
51   1. Extension courses.
52   1. Workshops.
53   1. Public service TV announcements.
54   1. Information on packages.
55   1. Information in TV advertisements.
56   1. Don't care.

57   Q. 4   Amount willing to pay to subscribe to a service providing information about nutritional value of brands offered in local supermarkets:
1. Nothing.
2. 10¢–19¢.
3. 20¢–49¢.

CARD 3 (continued)

Column	Code	
		4. 50¢–99¢.
		5. $1–$2.
		6. Over $2.
		0. No answer.
58	Q. 5	Any formal nutrition course in any of the following?
		High school:
		1. No.
		2. Yes.
		0. No answer.
59		College:
		1. No.
		2. Yes.
		0. No answer.
60		Adult education/workshops:
		1. No.
		2. Yes.
		0. No answer.

Section III—Background information

Column	Code	
61–72	Q. 1	Any members of household on any special diet?
61–66		Self-imposed:
61		0. No answer.
		+. No members of household on a diet.
		1. Low cholesterol.
62		1. Low fat/calorie.
63		1. Diabetic.
64		1. Low salt.
65		1. Vegetarian.
66		1. Low triglyceride.
67–72		Doctor's orders:
67		0. No answer.
		1. Low cholesterol.
68		1. Low fat/calorie.
69		1. Diabetic.
70		1. Low salt.
71		1. Vegetarian.
72		1. Low triglyceride.
73	Q. 2	How often do you smoke?
		1. Never.
		2. Occasionally.
		3. Regularly, but light (less than one pack of cigarettes each day).
		4. Regularly (one pack of cigarettes a day).
		5. Heavily (more than one pack each day or equivalent).
		0. No answer.
74–79	Blank	
80	Card 3	

CARD 4

Column   *Code*

1–6   Application number

Section III—Background information (continued)

Section IV—General attitude information

Section V—Food opinions

7–13   Q. 3   Which of following vitamin pills do you personally take?
7   0.   No answer.
    1.   None.
8   1.   Multiple.
9   1.   Vitamin C.
10   1.   Vitamin G.
11   1.   Vitamin B-12 complex.
12   1.   Vitamin A.
13   1.   Iron.

14   Q. 4   Amount of time spent watching TV on average day—
    1.   None.
    2.   Less than 1 hour.
    3.   1–2 hours.
    4.   3–4 hours.
    5.   Over 4 hours.
    0.   No answer.

15   Q. 5   How has your family income changed in the last year?
    1.   Gone down a lot.
    2.   Gone down a little.
    3.   Stayed about the same.
    4.   Gone up a little.
    5.   Gone up a lot.
    0.   No answer.

16   Q. 6   How has your household size changed in the past year?
    1.   Decreased by two or more.
    2.   Decreased by one.
    3.   Stayed the same.
    4.   Increased by one.
    5.   Increased by two or more.
    0.   No answer.

17–39   Section IV—General attitude information

Indicate how much you agree or disagree with the following statements.
    1.   Strongly agree.
    2.   Somewhat agree.
    3.   Neither agree nor disagree.
    4.   Somewhat disagree.
    5.   Strongly disagree.
    0.   No answer.

40–77   Section V—Food opinions
40–49   Q. 1   Opinions about certain types of food:
    1.   True.
    2.   False.
    3.   Don't know.
    0.   No answer.

CARD 4 (continued)

Column	Code
50–77	Q. 2 Which foods contribute importantly to listed functions?
50–53	Eyes are aided by:
	1—Whole milk.
	0—No answer.
51	1—Beef.
52	1—Tomatoes.
53	1—Enriched bread.
54–57	Teeth and bones are aided by:
	Code same as columns 50–53
58–61	Muscle tissue is aided by:
	Code same as columns 50–53
62–65	Repair of body tissues is aided by:
	Code same as columns 50–53
66–69	Blood cells are aided by:
	Code same as columns 50–53
70–73	Fighting infection is aided by:
	Code same as columns 50–53
74–77	Nervous system is aided by:
	Code same as columns 50–53
78–79	BLANK
80	Card No. 4

CARD 5

Column	Code
1–6	Application number
	Section V—Food opinions (continued)
7–14	Q. 2 Which foods contribute importantly to listed functions?
7–10	Skin is aided by:
	1—Whole milk.
	0—No answer.
8	1—Beef.
9	1—Tomatoes.
10	1—Enriched bread.
11–14	Proper growth of children is aided by:
	Code same as columns 7–10
15–62	Q. 3 Nutrients contained in listed items:
15–26	Whole milk:
15	1—There is a lot of vitamin A in—
	0—No answer.
16	1—There is a lot of thiamin (vitamin B) in—
17	1—There is a lot of riboflavin (vitamin B2) in—
18	1—There is a lot of niacin in—
19	1—There is a lot of vitamin C in—
20	1—There is a lot of vitamin D in—
21	1—There is a lot of protein in—
22	1—There is a lot of carbohydrates in—
23	1—There is a lot of fat in—
24	1—There is a lot of calories in—
25	1—There is a lot of iron in—
26	1—There is a lot of calcium in—

CARD 5 (continued)

Column

27–38	Beef: Code same as columns 15–26
39–50	Tomatoes: Code same as columns 15–26
51–62	Enriched bread: Code same as columns 15–26
63–79	BLANK
80	Card No. 5

CARD 6

Column   *Code*

1–6	Application number

Section V—Food opinions (continued)

7–62   Q. 4   Listed foods that you think have a lot of the same benefits to the body:

	1st col.	1.	Whole milk
		0.	No answer
	2d col.	1.	Beef
		0.	No answer
	3d col.	1.	Tomatoes
		0.	No answer
	4th col.	1.	Enriched bread
		0.	No answer

7–10	Oatmeal provides a lot of the same benefits as—
11–14	Fish provides a lot of the same benefits as—
15–18	Rice provides a lot of the same benefits as—
19–22	Navy beans
23–26	Chicken
27–30	Potatoes
31–34	Eggs
35–38	Macaroni
39–42	Pork and lamb
43–46	String beans
47–50	Carrots
51–54	Bananas
55–58	Peanut butter
59–62	Cottage cheese
63–79	BLANK
80	Card No. 6

PART THREE

Analytical methods

11 _____

Basic analysis

Having carefully coded and punched the data, it is time to begin analysis. This chapter deals with the fundamental kinds of analysis which are standard practice in marketing research. The procedures disclosed in this chapter are the staples of present "real-world" marketing research.

SIMPLE TABULATION

The simplest way to analyze data is to tabulate the responses on a question-by-question basis. This form of tabulating the data (not so ingeniously called tabs) is the most common form of analysis. The only calculation involved is that after the number of respondents who chose each of the available answers is tabulated, the percentage of the time each response is given is calculated. For example, assume the following question was asked of 940 female heads of households:

What portion of the food spending for your household do you do personally?"

| _____ None of it.
| _____ Less than half of it.
| _____ About half of it.
| _____ Most of it.
| _____ All of it.

The tabulated results would be of the form of Table 11–1. It takes very little statistical analysis to see what this implies. Over half the sample are doing all the shopping, and almost another one third doing most of it. Hence the vast majority of the sample are experienced food shoppers.

TABLE 11–1
Portion of food shopping done

Response	Frequency	Percent
1 (none)	15	1.6
2 (less than half)	34	3.6
3 (about half)	52	5.5
4 (most)	295	31.4
5 (all)	538	57.2
0 (no answer)	6	.6
	940	99.9

In order to highlight such results, a common approach is to construct a bar chart to represent the results graphically (Figure 11–1). Since bar charts typically are not standard computer output but must be hand drawn, this refinement is often skipped.

FIGURE 11–1
Bar chart of Table 11–1 responses

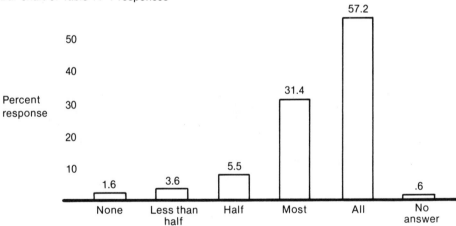

Amount of food shopping done personally

It is also often the case that a particular response is the key one (i.e., the proportion of people who buy our brand). Hence the percent who give a particular response is frequently more important than the entire distribution. This is especially true for questions such as intention, where often only the most positive (top box) response is considered to be a useful measure of intention.

SIMPLE CALCULATIONS

The other way to indicate the pattern of responses to a single question is to compute a statistic.

Mode

One common statistic is called the mode. This is the most typical response (in the case of Table 11–1, 5–all of it—is the most typical result).

Median

Another statistic commonly calculated is called the median. This is the score of the person who is exactly in the middle of the responses (in Table 11–1, this is also 5).

Mean

Another statistic which is often calculated is the mean (average) response. This is calculated by using the code value for each response and weighting by the frequency which the response is given.

Nonresponse problem. A problem exists in calculating the mean in that the no-response answers must be dealt with. Consider the response pattern of Table 11–2. A major problem in analyzing these results is the

TABLE 11–2
Sample response pattern

Response	Code	Frequency
None	1	425
1–2	2	61
3–4	3	11
5 or more	4	340
No answer	9	83

nonresponses. There are three major choices: do nothing with nonresponses, convert the no-answer response, and exclude no-answer responses.

Do nothing with nonresponses. If we do nothing, most computer programs will by default count nonresponses as whatever code they were given. In this case, that would mean the following:

Code	Frequency	Code × frequency
1	425	425
2	61	122
3	11	33
4	340	1,360
9	83	747
	920	2,687

Hence the mean $= \dfrac{2,687}{920} = 2.92$. Putting the 9's in implies that no answer means the person would have responded much more than 5. This is clearly ridiculous and the mean of 2.92 is biased. However, if the number of nonresponses to all the questions are small (less than 1–2 percent), their effect on the mean will be slight enough so as to be unlikely to change any significant conclusions. Still, striving to prevent nonresponses is very desirable in that it makes later gyrations to deal with them unnecessary.

Convert the no-answer response. Sometimes it is possible to logically assign no answers to a category. In this case, we might assume that nonresponses were some respondents' way of saying the question was irrelevant and hence really were responding "none." Thus we could add them into the "none" category (code = 1). The results would then be as follows:

Code	Frequency	Code × frequency
1	508 (425 + 83)	508
2	61	122
3	11	33
4	340	1360
	920	2,023

Here the mean $= \dfrac{2,023}{920} = 2.20$.

Exclude no-answer responses. It is possible to simply exclude no-answer respondents from each calculation. This is both easy given current computer algorithms and popular. One source of its popularity is that in excluding these respondents, it appears that we are getting a "good" answer. Actually the answer is good only if the nonresponses would, had we been able to convert them to responses, follow the same pattern as the responses. Since this is often not the case, converting no answers may be better than ignoring them. The results of ignoring the no responses for our example would be as follows:

Code	Frequency	Code × frequency
1	425	425
2	61	122
3	11	33
4	340	1,360
	837	1,940

$$\text{Mean} = \frac{1,940}{837} = 2.32$$

Usefulness of averages. Averages (means) are a popular measure. They are only useful, however, when the following conditions are met:

The data should be intervally scaled. If the codes (Table 11–2) had stood for favorite color (1 = blue, 2 = red, 3 = green, 4 = yellow), then the data says that blue and yellow are popular and red and green are not. Calculating an average of 2.3 could be misleading. (Both the mode—in this case 1 = blue—and the median—in this case 2 = red—would also be misleading.) When the data constitutes an ordinal scale, it is also theoretically incorrect to compute an average. Nonetheless, since most ordinal scales are fairly close to interval scales in their composition and since respondents may well respond to an ordinal scale as though it were an interval scale, calculation of averages on ordinal scales is a widely accepted practice in marketing research where the trade-off between simplification and theoretical correctness often leans toward simplification.

The data should have some central tendency. In other words, most responses should be clustered around the mean. In this example, a mean of 2.3 is misleading since almost the entire sample checked 1 or 4. The irrelevance of the mean can be seen by considering the temperature people prefer for tea. Most people either like tea hot or iced. Averaging the preferred temperatures produces room temperature, which represents no one's preference very well.

Sensitivity of the mean. It is also interesting to note how insensitive the mean is to fairly large changes in the response distribution. In the previous example, when we added the nonrespondents (10 percent of the original sample) to the extreme of the distribution (code = 1), the mean only changed from the 2.32 obtained by excluding them to 2.20 found by including them. Given the importance of top box responses (e.g., definitely will buy the product responses), the average is a fairly insensitive measuring device and small changes in it may be very important managerially.

The standard deviation

In order to keep track of the accuracy of the mean in representing responses, a measure of central tendency is needed. Consider the following three (hypothetical) response distributions:

Code	A	B	C
1	400	100	600
2	300	800	0
3	200	100	200
4	100	0	200

In each case, the mean response is 2. Yet obviously the distributions are very different. In fact, only in case B does the mean represent a typical response well, and in case C the mean response of 2 was given by none of the 1,000 respondents. By graphing the three distributions (Figure 11–2)

FIGURE 11–2
Three distributions with equal means

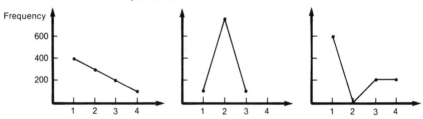

we see that the major difference is the spread (width) of the response patterns about the mean. The difference in spread is sometimes easier to see in a continuous case (Figure 11–3). Here both cases have means of 2, but in case A there is more spread about the mean than in case B.

In order to have an index which captures this spread, most people use the standard deviation. It is estimated as follows:

$$s_x = s = \sqrt{\frac{\sum\limits_{\substack{all \\ observations}} (X - \bar{X})^2}{\text{Number of observations} - 1}}$$

$$= \sqrt{\frac{\sum\limits_{i=1}^{n} (X_i - \bar{X})^2}{n - 1}}$$

FIGURE 11–3
Two response distributions

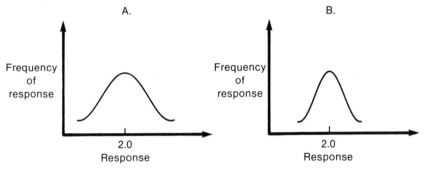

When data is grouped into categories (as it usually is in survey data), this formula reduces to

$$s = \sqrt{\frac{\sum_{j=1}^{c} f_i(X_i - \overline{X})^2}{n-1}}$$

where

f_i = frequency of the ith response
c = number of response codes

Using this formula on the three hypothetical sets of data, we find standard deviations of 1, .45, and 1.27 respectively. These values indicate the relative usefulness of the average in representing the responses. The smaller the standard deviation, the closer the actual responses are to the mean. Hence in this case, we again see that in case B the mean is a relatively good representation and in case C the mean is a particularly terrible representation of responses. In fact, only in case B is there a noticeable central tendency.

To give one example of the calculation of a standard deviation, we return to the example in Table 11–2. Assuming nonresponses were excluded (and hence the mean was 2.32), we get the following:

Code	Frequency (f_i)	$(X_i - \overline{X})^2$	$f_i(X_i - \overline{X})^2$
1	425	1.74	739.50
2	61	.10	6.10
3	11	.46	5.06
4	340	2.82	959.62
	837		1,710.28

Thus

$$s = \sqrt{\frac{1,710.28}{836}} = 1.43$$

COMPARING RESPONSES TO TWO OR MORE QUESTIONS

Until now, this chapter has been devoted to analyzing questions one at a time. This section, by contrast, discusses techniques for comparing the responses to several questions.

Consider, for example, rankings of a series of attributes in terms of their importance in decision making. Typically most of the attributes will be rated as important. The key issue, however, is to uncover which are the most important attributes. Hence looking at the responses must be done across questions to see which are the most important.

Plotting

The simplest way to do this is to plot the mean responses in a profile chart. Consider the example of Table 11–3, taken from question 9 in the

TABLE 11–3
Importance of attribute in choosing food

Attribute	Mean importance (1 = very important, 5 = very unimportant)
Variety	2.02
Taste	1.24
Other family members' preferences	1.71
Diet restrictions	2.98
Price	1.74
Availability	2.16
Ease of preparation	2.78
Habit	2.82
Advertised specials	2.26
Nutritional value	1.66

nutrition study which rated importance of attributes of food on a five-point scale from 1 (very important) to 5 (very unimportant). We can construct a plot of these results to highlight them (Figure 11–4). It is obvious from this plot that taste is the key attribute, with other family members' preferences, price, and nutritional value all closely bunched as

FIGURE 11-4
Food attribute importances

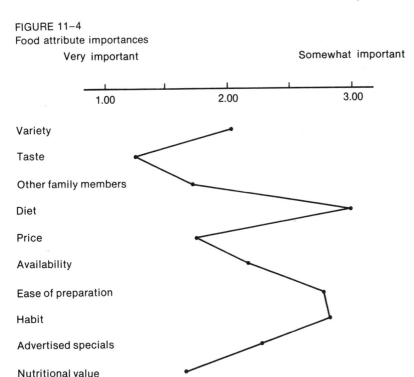

next most important. (Given the socially correct answer favors nutrition, my guess is that it is in fact the fourth most important attribute.)

Ranking

Another way to analyze the results is simply to rank the attributes by the mean response. In this case, we find the results are the following:

1. Taste.
2. Nutritional value.
3. Other family members' preferences.
4. Price.
5. Variety.
6. Availability.
7. Advertised specials.
8. Ease of preparation.
9. Habit.
10. Diet restrictions.

This ranking has several shortcomings. First, there is undoubtedly no statistical significance in some of the differences such as between 3 and 4, and 8 and 9. Presentation of rankings (and to a lesser extent, the profile chart) tends to downplay this point. Secondly, the attribute "diet restrictions" intuitively is not the tenth most important. This is because it is essentially a binary attribute; either you have a diet restriction or you do not. Hence for those who think it is very important (26.7 percent), it may well be the most important attribute. Since we are ranking average importance, however, it appears unimportant and we could falsely conclude that it can be ignored.

Indexing

A final approach for indicating relative scores is to recalibrate the scale. This approach is related to the issues of normalizing and standardizing discussed in Chapter 5. We can do this by first finding the typical average important score for an attribute by taking the average of the average importance scores:

$$
\begin{array}{r}
2.02 \\
1.24 \\
1.71 \\
2.98 \\
1.74 \\
2.16 \\
2.78 \\
2.82 \\
2.26 \\
1.66 \\
\hline
21.37 \\
\end{array}
$$

$$\text{Average} = \frac{21.37}{10} = 2.14$$

We then can recompute averages in terms of either differences from this average value or as an index of the ratio of the average on the particular attribute to the overall average (Table 11–4).

TABLE 11–4
Attribute importance indexes

Attribute	Difference index	Ratio index
Taste	−.12 (2.02 − 2.14)	.94 (2.02/2.14)
Nutritional value	−.90	.58
OFM preferences	−.43	.80
Price	.84	1.39
Variety	−.40	.81
Availability	.02	1.01
Advertised specials	.64	1.30
Ease of preparation	.68	1.32
Habit	.12	1.06
Diet restrictions	−.48	.78

The advantage of these indexes is that they highlight extreme cases and quickly indicate relatively important and unimportant attributes.

All of these procedures have advantages which may make them suitable to a particular situation. Blindly applying these procedures for no particular purpose is likely to create confusion. On the other hand, taking only the output of a computer routine as a basis for analysis may lead to overlooking important conclusions. In short, some logical number juggling will often be very beneficial in uncovering results in a set of data.

BASIC ANALYSIS EXAMPLES

Typically, analysis by a supplier is simply a series of tabulations. If a more elaborate form of presentation is desired, one would expect to see some interpretation interspersed with a question-by-question reporting of basic analyses. While there is no typical format, the report of the nutrition study in Appendix 11–A may provide, in addition to some interesting results, a basic format for preparation of such reports.

A more focused example of the use of basic analyses can be found in a study of purchasing agents. Lehmann and O'Shaughnessy (1974) have reported an attempt to assess which product attributes are most important for different types of products. Forty-five purchasing agents were asked to rate the importance of 17 product attributes for the following four situations:

Type I: Routine order product.

Type II: Procedural problem products (where the principal user must be taught to use the product).

Type III: Performance problem products (where there is some question about whether the product will perform adequately).

Type IV: Political problem products (where there is an extremely large capital outlay and/or several departments are involved in the decision).

Importances were rated on six-point bipolar adjective scales rated from 1 = very unimportant to 6 = very important. Ignoring the real question of representativeness given a sample size of 45 (26 in the United States and 19 in the United Kingdom), the average results were computed (Table 11–5).

Looking at the average leads to several interesting conclusions. First, all attributes are rated in the important half of the scale for all product types with the exception of training offered and required for Type I products. (This is a typical result for importance questions since individuals seem averse to indicating anything is unimportant.) Second, as expected, the more complex problems produced higher importance ratings on all the

TABLE 11–5

Average attribute importance for the four product types

| | Product type | | | | | | | |
| | I | | II | | III | | IV | |
Attribute	Mean	Rank	Mean	Rank	Mean	Rank	Mean	Ra
1. Reputation	4.84[a] (1.09)	4	5.33 (.80)	7	5.29 (.82)	5	5.53 (.69)	
2. Financing	4.51 (1.39)	9	4.07 (1.29)	16	3.91 (1.31)	16	4.91 (1.24)	1
3. Flexibility	5.07 (1.12)	3	5.40 (.62)	5	5.42 (.62)	2	5.51 (.59)	
4. Past experience	4.71 (.94)	6	4.93 (.86)	13	5.07 (.69)	9	5.04 (.93)	1
5. Technical service	4.36 (1.28)	12	5.53 (.66)	1	5.38 (.89)	3	5.40 (.62)	
6. Confidence in salespersons	3.96 (1.35)	14	4.73 (1.23)	15	4.42 (1.20)	15	4.58 (1.20)	1
7. Convenience in ordering	3.80 (1.32)	15	3.73 (1.29)	17	3.71 (1.34)	17	4.08 (1.24)	1
8. Reliability data	4.47 (1.24)	11	5.16 (1.07)	11	5.33 (.67)	4	5.53 (.59)	
9. Price	5.60 (.62)	2	5.29 (.70)	8	5.18 (.94)	8	5.56 (.69)	
10. Technical specifications	4.73 (1.25)	5	5.22 (.67)	9	5.27 (.69)	6	5.42 (.72)	
11. Ease of use	4.51 (1.29)	10	5.53 (.59)	2	5.24 (.80)	7	5.18 (.83)	
12. Preference of user	4.00 (1.19)	13	4.76 (1.11)	14	4.53 (1.14)	13	4.84 (.90)	1
13. Training offered	3.22 (1.18)	16	5.42 (.87)	3	4.73 (1.19)	12	5.00 (.83)	1
14. Training required	3.22 (1.22)	17	5.11 (1.23)	12	4.44 (1.22)	14	4.69 (1.02)	1
15. Reliability of delivery	5.64 (.53)	1	5.42 (.72)	4	5.44 (.66)	1	5.53 (.69)	
16. Maintenance	4.60 (1.05)	8	5.20 (.69)	10	4.82 (.96)	11	5.00 (.74)	1
17. Sales service	4.64 (1.25)	7	5.36 (.77)	6	5.07 (.84)	10	5.09 (.70)	
Product type mean	4.46		5.07		4.90		5.11	

[a] Mean (standard deviation).

Source: Donald R. Lehmann and John O'Shaughnessy, "Differences in Attribute Importance for Differe[] Industrial Products." Reprinted from *Journal of Marketing,* published by the American Marketing Associa[] vol. 38 (April 1974), p. 39.

attributes. In terms of seeing which were the most important attributes, however, the means alone are not easily interpretable. Hence the attributes were ranked in terms of average importance for each of the four product types. The results here are quite interesting if not surprising. Reliability of delivery is always one of the most important attributes, not surprising given the criticism a purchasing agent has to endure when deliveries are late. For the routine order product, price, flexibility, and reputation also rank high. For the procedural problem product, technical service, ease of use, and training offered rank highest. For the performance problem product, flexibility, technical service, and reliability data are the other most important attributes. The unexpected results were those dealing with the political problem product. Here the high importance attributed to price and reliability data was contrary to prior expectations. One explanation for this result is that purchasing agents aren't involved in such decisions and hence the results are not meaningful. Alternatively, it may be that political problems are so amorphous and difficult that decision makers search for something they can evaluate, and look to such concrete attributes as price and reliability data to make or at least justify (especially if something goes wrong) the appropriateness of their choice.

Another way to look at the data is to recalibrate the importance scale by subtracting the mean importance for the product type from the average importance for each attribute. (For example, the recalibrated score for the attribute reputation for Type I products is $4.84 - 4.46 = .38$.) This gives a quick partitioning of the attributes into relatively more important (positive values) and relatively less important attributes (Table 11–6).

It is possible to compare the average importance of each of the attributes across the four product types. When significance tests are performed (see Chapter 13 for an explanation of how the tests are done), the original attribute ratings were found to change significantly at the .05 significance level in 13 of the 17 attributes and in 10 of the 17 attributes at the .01 significance level. This establishes beyond reasonable doubt the fact that the ratings did change. However, we know that much of the change is due to the increasing importance attributed to all attributes as the product becomes more complex. Hence to see if relative importance changes, we need to test for significant changes in the adjusted scores. Six of the 17 attributes change significantly across the four product types. Two of these are price and reliability of delivery, which are by far the most important for Type I and about equally important for the other three product types. The other significant changes were for training offered and required (highest for Type II products), financing (highest for Type I products), and technical service (highest for Type II and III products). These significant results are all perfectly reasonable. (Notice that the seemingly counterintuitive result previously discussed for Type IV products is not significant when the results are viewed in this way.)

Two important points need to be made. First, it often takes some manipulation of data or results to get the results in a form best suited for interpretation. Second, it is very desirable to check for statistical significance before interpreting results. This avoids the difficult and often mis-

TABLE 11–6
Significance of differences in mean importance across product types

Attribute	Significance† raw	Adjusted average importance* I	II	III	IV	Adjusted significance‡ canc
Reputation	.01	.38	.26	.39	.42	—
Financing	.01	.05	−1.00	−.99	−.20	.01
Flexibility	—	.61	.33	.52	.40	—
Past experience	—	.25	−.13	.17	−.07	—
Technical service	.01	−.10	.46	.48	.29	.01
Confidence in salespersons	.05	−.50	−.34	−.48	−.53	—
Convenience in ordering	—	−.60	−1.34	−1.19	−1.03	—
Reliability data	.01	.01	.09	.43	.42	—
Price	.05	1.14	.22	.28	.45	.01
Technical specifications	.01	.27	.15	.37	.31	—
Ease of use	.01	.05	.46	.34	.07	—
Preference of user	.01	−.46	−.31	−.37	−.27	—
Training offered	.01	−1.24	.35	−.17	−.11	.01
Training required	.01	−1.24	.04	−.46	−.42	.01
Reliability of delivery	—	1.18	.35	.54	.42	.01
Maintenance	.05	.14	.13	−.18	−.11	—
Sales service	.01	.18	.29	.17	−.02	—

* For each product type, the mean product importance across the 17 attributes was subtracted from importance for each of the 17 attributes.
† Significance of difference among product types based on raw average importance.
‡ Significance of difference among product types based on adjusted average importance.
Source: Donald R. Lehmann and John O'Shaughnessy. "Differences in Attribute Importance for Differ Industrial Products." Reprinted from Journal of Marketing, published by the American Marketing Associati vol. 38 (April 1974), p. 40.

leading task of inventing explanations for what could well be chance results.

RELATIONS BETWEEN VARIABLES: CROSS-TABS

Two variables

The question of how the response to one question relates to that of another question is crucial to most research. For example, I might like to see how heaviness of usage of a product category, region of the country, and household income relate to each of the questions in a survey. This is commonly done by specifying usage, region, and income as what are known as banner points. As the survey results are tabulated question by question, each question is tabulated and percentaged both in total and by each banner point. Hence a typical page of the output might look like Table 11–7. From this table, one would probably conclude that most

TABLE 11–7
Tabulation by banner points (Question 17: Do you like Znarts?)

Response	Total	Usage			Region				Income		
		Low	Medium	High	East	Midwest	South	West	Under $10,000	$10,000–$20,000	Over $20,000
1 (yes)	10%	8%	11%	15%	12%	16%	4%	7%	6%	11%	14%
2	20	15	18	26	25	23	15	18	15	22	24
3	40	38	42	37	38	37	42	43	45	41	31
4	20	31	19	14	14	15	25	24	22	14	20
5 (no)	8	3	9	6	7	5	13	7	7	10	8
N.A.	2	4	1	2	4	4	1	1	5	2	3
Total ..	100%	100%	100%	100%	100%	100%	100%	100%	100%	100%	100%

N.A. = not available.

people are pretty neutral toward Znarts, that heavy users of the product category (which also includes such well-known brands as Whafles, Splibles, and Snuzzles) are somewhat more favorable toward it but not wildly so, that the brand is strongest in the Midwest and East, and that the brand appeals to high-income consumers.

In drawing conclusions from such pages, the key element of analysis is the cross-tabulation between two variables. For example, assume we had the tabulation of purchase level versus region for a sample of 1,000 people shown in Table 11–8. This raw tabulation is interesting but in general not

TABLE 11–8
Purchase level by region

	Purchase Level			
Region	0–1	2–3	4 or more	Total
A	200	140	60	400
B	60	80	60	200
C	140	180	80	400
Total	400	400	200	1,000

very telegraphic in conveying what is going on in the data. Hence we need two things: a better way of highlighting results and a way to tell whether the results are meaningful or just a chance occurrence.

Highlighting results

The most common way of highlighting results is to calculate conditional probabilities or as they are often called, contingencies. We can compute a table of the conditional probability of region given purchase level. The purpose of this would be to isolate where heavy and light users of the product are located. This is done here by calculating the percent each entry is of the column total (often ingeniously called the column percent). For example, the probability that a person is from region B given the person is a light (0–1) purchaser is 60/400 = 15 percent. The complete contingency table is shown as Table 11–9. Hence from this we can see that heavy users tend to be in region C and light users in region A.

We can also compute the row percents (the purchase level given region). This indicates which purchase levels are most prevalent in which regions. The percent of those people in region B who are light (0–1) purchasers is 60/200 = 30 percent. Similarly we get Table 11–10. Here we see that in region B, 30 percent are heavy purchasers, making region B the strongest market (at least in the past) for our product.

TABLE 11-9
Column percents (region given purchase level)

Region	Purchase level		
	0–1	2–3	4 or more
A	50%	35%	30%
B	15	20	30
C	35	45	40
	100%	100%	100%

TABLE 11-10
Row percents (purchase level given region)

Region	Purchase level		
	0–1	2–3	4 or more
A	50%	35%	15%
B	30	40	30
C	35	45	20

Checking for statistical significance

There are an incredible number of different ways to check a table for the presence of a significant relation between the variables (see, for example, Siegel, 1956). The most common, however, is a chi-square (χ^2) test. The χ^2 test has three basic steps:

1. It assumes as a basis of comparison that the two variables are not related (H_0: the two variables are independent).
2. It computes an index (χ^2 value) which measures how different the actual results are from what the results would have been if the variables had been independent.
3. The index is compared with a table value; and if the calculated index is bigger than the table value, then the assumption of independence is rejected (and therefore the two variables are related).

Computation of the standard of comparison. The standard of comparison assumes that the probability of being in each cell is independent of the two variables. Put differently, the probability of being in a particular cell is the product of the probability of being in that row and the probability of being in that column (these row and column probabilities are often called the marginals, presumably because they appear on the margin of the table).

Returning to the example in Table 11–8, we get the row and column probabilities as in Table 11–11. We can now calculate the expected number in each cell. For example, the probability of being from region B and having purchase level 0–1 is (Probability of being from region B) · (Prob-

TABLE 11–11
Relation of purchase level and region

| Region | Purchase level | | | | Row probability |
	0–1	2–3	4 or more	Total	
A	200	140	60	400	.4
B	60	80	60	200	.2
C	140	180	80	400	.4
Total	400	400	200	1,000	
Column probability	.4	.4	.2		1.0

ability of having purchase level 0–1) = (.4)(.2) = .08. The number of people expected in this cell is simply the probability of being in the cell times the total number of people in the table: $.08(n) = .08(1,000) = 80$. Hence we can derive an expected table from:[1]

Number expected in cell i, j = (Probability of being in row i) ·
(Probability of being in row j) ·
(Number of people in the table)   (11.1)

Here we get the expected numbers as in Table 11–12.

TABLE 11–12
Expected cell sizes

| Region | Purchase level | | |
	0–1	2–3	4 or more
A	160	160	80
B	80	80	40
C	160	160	80

---

[1] For hand computational purposes, it is possible to use a short form of either (Probability of being in row i) (Number of people in row j) or (Number of people in row i) (Probability of being in row j). While mathematically identical, these formulas do not convey as clearly the role of the independence assumption in generating the expected values and hence were not used in the main presentation.

Build an index.   The index used measures the difference between the expected and actual number of observations in each cell of the table. The index is the sum of the squared differences between expected and observed numbers as a percent of the expected number in each cell (to keep the numbers a manageable size) for all cells:

$$\text{Index} = \sum_{\text{all cells}} \frac{(\text{Observed number in cell } i,j - \text{Expected number in cell } i,j)^2}{\text{Expected number in cell } i,j}$$

$$= \sum_{i=1}^{r} \sum_{j=1}^{c} \frac{(f_{\text{obs}} - f_{\text{exp}})^2}{f_{\text{exp}}} \tag{11.2}$$

Obviously the larger the index, the more different the observed and expected values are. In this case by comparing Tables 11–8 and 11–12 we get

$$\text{Index} = \frac{(200 - 160)^2}{160} + \frac{(140 - 160)^2}{160} + \frac{(60 - 80)^2}{80} + \frac{(60 - 80)^2}{80}$$

$$+ \frac{(80 - 80)^2}{80} + \frac{(60 - 40)^2}{40} + \frac{(140 - 160)^2}{160}$$

$$+ \frac{(180 - 160)^2}{160} + \frac{(80 - 80)^2}{80}$$

$$= 10 + 2.5 + 5 + 5 + 0 + 10 + 2.5 + 2.5 + 0$$
$$= 37.5$$

Evaluating the index.   The standard of comparison for this index is the chi-square (χ^2) table. Specifically, the index is χ^2 with $(r - 1)(c - 1)$ degrees of freedom.[2] In this case, the χ^2 value has $(3 - 1)(3 - 1) = 4$ degrees of freedom.

---

[2] The degree of freedom notion is fairly subtle. The basic idea is that an observation is "free" if its value is unconstrained. Since in calculating the expected cell sizes we "rigged" the data so that the number in each row was equal to the actual number, there is one degree of freedom lost. (In other words, if you tell me all but one of the expected values, the other can be found.) Since this is true for each row and column, we are left with the following table without the bordering row and column in terms of free observations:

		x
		x
x	x	x

Hence there are $(r - 1)(c - 1)$ "free" observations left. (If this brief explanation is unappealing, either (a) see a statistics book or (b) memorize $(r - 1)(c - 1)$, an inelegant but effective approach.)

Remembering the way the index was constructed, we are only willing to reject the independence assumption if the index is large. (Hence it is almost universally accepted that a one-tail test is appropriate.) Therefore for this case and the .05 significance level, we get from a table $\chi^2_{4,.05} =$ 9.49. Since 37.5 is much larger than 9.49, we reject the independence hypothesis and therefore conclude that region and purchase level are related. What this means practically is that the contingency table percentages are in fact worth studying.

An example

Returning again to the nutrition data, an interesting issue is what is the relation between household income and weekly food expenditures. In order to investigate this, data was categorized according to the scheme in Table 11–13. A cross-tab between food expenditures and income was then

TABLE 11–13
Code values for food survey

Code	Meaning
Weekly food expenditures:	
13	Less than $15
23	$15–$29
38	$30–$44
53	$45–$59
70	$60 or more
Income:	
1	Under 10,000
2	10,000–20,000
3	Over 20,000

completed using the SPSS computer program (see Appendix 11–B). The results appear in Table 11–14. Each cell contains four numbers:

1. *Count:* The number of people in the cell (i.e., 33 people had incomes under $10,000 and spent less than $15 per week on food).
2. *Row pct:* The percent of the people in the row who are in the column (i.e., 33/464 = 7.1 percent of the people with incomes under $10,000 spent less than $15 per week on food).
3. *Col pct:* The percent of the people in the column who are in the row (i.e., 33/39 = 84.9 percent of the people who spent less than $15 per week on food had incomes under $10,000).
4. *Tot pct:* The percent of the total sample in the particular cell (i.e., 33/933 = 3.5 percent).

TABLE 11–14
Cross-tabulation of income versus food expenditures

COUNT ROW PCT COL PCT TOT PCT	Food Expenditures					ROW TOTAL
	13.0	23.0	38.0	53.0	70.0	
1.0	33 7.1 84.6 3.5	226 48.7 70.2 24.2	149 32.1 47.8 16.0	45 9.7 23.1 4.8	11 2.4 16.9 1.2	464 49.7
2.0	5 1.5 12.8 0.5	73 22.0 22.7 7.8	121 36.4 38.8 13.0	102 30.7 52.3 10.9	31 9.3 47.7 3.3	332 35.6
3.0	1 0.7 2.6 0.1	23 16.8 7.1 2.5	42 30.7 13.5 4.5	48 35.0 24.6 5.1	23 16.8 35.4 2.5	137 14.7
COLUMN TOTAL	39 4.2	322 34.5	312 33.4	195 20.9	65 7.0	933 100.0

(Income, vertical label on the left)

While somewhat overwhelming, the table indicates that income and food expenditures are positively related (high income tends to go with high food expenditures and low income with low food expenditures). This is confirmed by the χ^2 statistic of 167.2, a huge value for $(5 - 1)(3 - 1) = 8$ degrees of freedom.[3] Notice, however, that the relationship between income and food expenditure does not "leap out" of the table. Since income and food expenditure are both ordinally (and close to intervally) scaled variables, more efficient means for describing the relationship may be appropriate.

You may also notice in Appendix 11–B that a variety of other statistics are output besides chi-square. These statistics are sometimes useful in specific situations. Nonetheless, most researchers and all managers can get along just fine without ever using them.

Multiway tables

In many cases it is desirable to consider three or more variables simultaneously. In such instances it is customary to break the data into multiple

---

[3] A useful fact is that the mean of the chi-square is the number of degrees of freedom and, as the number of degrees of freedom increases, the test statistic becomes approximately normally distributed with a standard deviation equal to the square root of two times the number of degrees of freedom. This fact makes it possible to quickly tell when something is clearly significant as well as estimate significance if table values are not available.

tables. For example, assume I wished to simultaneously study the effect of income and education on food expenditures. Hence I might first "remove" the effect of income on expenditures by separating the sample into low- and high-income consumers and then doing a two-way cross-tab of education and expenditures for the two samples. The results would look something like the following:

	Low income		High income	
	Low ed.	High ed.	Low ed.	High ed.
Low expenditures				
High expenditures				

Often three-way and higher tabulations reveal interesting results. Consider for example the study by Dr. Edwin Salzman and associates concerning the effect of aspirin on reducing blood clotting following major surgery for 95 patients (Lublin, 1977). In this case, aspirin appeared to be useful when the total sample was used. Breaking the sample by sex, however, revealed that aspirin seemed to be very useful for men ($\chi^2 = 7.62$) and not at all useful for women ($\chi^2 = .01$) (Table 11–15). Here the simple two-way results were apparently misleading.

TABLE 11–15
Relation between aspirin therapy and blood clots after surgery

	Clot	No clot
Total sample:		
Aspirin	11	33
Placebo	23	28
Men:		
Aspirin	4	19
Placebo	14	11
Women:		
Aspirin	7	14
Placebo	9	17

Source: Joann S. Lublin. "Aspirin Found to Cut Blood-Clotting Risks in Men, Not Women," *The Wall Street Journal*, December 8, 1977. Adapted with permission.

Cross-tabs: Pros and cons

Cross-tabs are obviously a very useful tool. They have the following advantages:

1. They present results in a simple tabular form which is easy to communicate to management.

2. They work on nominal scale (categorical) data, something that most of the "fancy" analyses do not do.
3. They make no assumption about the form of the relationship. In the purchase level versus region example, the relationship between purchase level and region was not a "simple" monotonic one (i.e., as region gets "bigger," so does purchase level). While the χ^2 analysis uncovered this relation, analysis based on such measures as a correlation coefficient might not have. It is important to recognize, however, that 2×2 cross-tab tables will also hide nonlinear relationships. One classic example of this was a study by Donald Cox (Buzzell, Cox, and Brown, 1969, pp. 174–75) on the relation between the persuadability of 121 shoppers and their self-confidence. The original 2×2 table made the two variables appear unrelated. When self-confidence was broken into three categories, however, the results changed (Table 11–16). Now we see a nonlinear relationship between persuadability

TABLE 11–16
Persuadability versus self-confidence

	Persuadability	
Original results:		
Self-confidence	Percent persuaded	Percent unpersuaded
Low	47	53
High	45	55
Revised results:		
Very low	37	63
Moderately low	62	38
High	45	55

Source: Robert D. Buzzell, Donald F. Cox, and Rex V. Brown, *Marketing Research and Information Systems: Text and Cases* (New York: McGraw-Hill, 1969), pp. 174–75.

and self-confidence. (The relationship has an interesting implication for salespersons: Concentrate your efforts on those who have moderate self-confidence—those with high self-confidence can't be influenced and those with low self-confidence can't make up their minds.)

In spite of these advantages, there are some problems in using cross-tabs:

1. *There should be at least five expected observations in each cell.* When less than five appear in a cell, the χ^2 value becomes unreliable.[4] Hence it is often necessary to collapse categories together in order to get

---

[4] Assume one cell had two observations and an expected size of .3 observations. This one cell would contribute $\dfrac{(2 - .3)^2}{.3} = 9.6$ to the total χ^2 value which alone is enough to make it significant at the .05 level for 4 degrees of freedom.

sufficient *expected*[5] size in each cell. For example, we might have to combine the "fairly strongly" and "strongly" categories to get sufficient representation in those cells.

2. *Cross-tabs are not an efficient way to search for results.* If there are 100 variables, there are 4,950 possible two-way cross-tabs to perform. Looking at all these is a huge chore, and generating them mainly creates a big pile of scrap paper. (It also is interesting to notice that you would expect at the .05 level to get .05(4950) = 248 "significant" results due to chance alone.) The portrayal of the results is also fairly cumbersome in that a table of conditional probabilities is more clumsy than a correlation coefficient.

3. *Cross-tabs burn up sample size.* An obvious extension of two-way cross tabs is to sort the observations based on three or more variables at a time. Unfortunately we soon find cells with few people in them. Assuming there are six categories for the first variable, four for the second, and five for the third, there are (6)(4)(5) cells or 120 different cells. Even with big sample sizes (e.g., 1,000), this is likely to leave small cell sizes. (How many green-eyed midwesterners bought Bufferin last time?) Hence the procedure tends to break down when complex relations are being studied.

4. *The size of the chi-square value depends on the number of degrees of freedom, and hence is a poor index of association.* Put differently, the chi-square value does not indicate the strength of the relationship between the two variables.

In summary then, cross-tabs are an extremely useful tool. They are well suited to initial investigation of the relation between a few key variables and the other variables. They are not particularly well suited to searching for relations in many-variable data sets. If results are uncovered, however, they often serve as a convenient format for conveying the results to "normal" people.

CORRELATION COEFFICIENTS

Probably the most popular method for quickly summarizing the degree of relation between two variables is a correlation coefficient. The essence of a correlation coefficient is that it is an index which ranges from +1 (the two variables are perfectly positively related—they both get larger together) to −1 (the two variables are perfectly negatively related; as one gets larger the other gets smaller).[6]

---

[5] The reason the expected size is the key and not the observed is that the expected size is the denominator of the fraction.

[6] By contrast, the size of the chi-square value depends on the number of degrees of freedom and hence is a poor index of association. For example, a chi-square value of 42 would indicate no significant relationship if there were 48 degrees of freedom, and a value of 12 would show a significant relationship if there were only 2 degrees of freedom.

Pearson (product-moment) correlation coefficient

The most common correlation coefficient is the Pearson product-moment correlation (better known as r). This is the coefficient found in essentially all canned computer output. The computational formula for the correlation between two variables X_i and X_j is

$$r = \frac{\sum_{i=1}^{n}(X_i - \bar{X}_i)(X_j - \bar{X}_j)}{\sqrt{\sum_{i=1}^{n}(X_i - \bar{X}_i)^2}\sqrt{\sum_{i=1}^{n}(X_j - \bar{X}_j)^2}}$$

$$= \frac{\sum_{i=1}^{n}(X_i - \bar{X}_i)(X_j - \bar{X}_j)}{n(s_{X_i})(s_{X_j})}$$

For example, assume we had the following ten observations:

X_i (income)	X_j (food expenditures)
1	2
3	4
3	1
3	4
1	3
2	3
1	1
1	3
3	5
2	4

We could plot these as in Figure 11–5. Hence there appears to be a positive relation between income and food expenditure. The computations would proceed as follows:

Find the means:

$$\Sigma X_i = 20, \therefore \bar{X}_i = 2$$
$$\Sigma X_j = 30, \therefore \bar{X}_j = 3$$

Compute the correlations using equation (11.3) (see Table 11–17).

The correlation coefficient can be tested for statistical significance using the following statistic:

$$\frac{r}{\dfrac{\sqrt{(1 - r^2)}}{\sqrt{n - 2}}} = \frac{r\sqrt{n - 2}}{\sqrt{1 - r^2}}$$

FIGURE 11–5
Food expenditure versus income

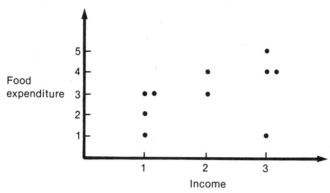

This statistic is approximately distributed according to the t distribution with $n - 2$ degrees of freedom. In the previous example, that means comparing a table value of $t_{.05,8} = 2.31$ with

$$\frac{(.44)\sqrt{8}}{\sqrt{1 - (.44)^2}} = \frac{.44(2.83)}{.90} = 1.38$$

Since 1.38 is less than 2.31, the correlation is not significant. (In other words, the apparent relation may be due to chance and hence misleading.) Obviously as the sample size gets bigger, the chance for a particular size correlation being significant increases. (In fact, a correlation of .001 is statistically significant given a large enough sample size.) Also the t dis-

TABLE 11–17
Calculations to obtain a correlation

X_i	X_j	$X_i - \bar{X}_i$	$X_j - \bar{X}_j$	$(X_1 - \bar{X}_i)^2$	$(X_j - \bar{X}_j)^2$	$(X_i - \bar{X}_i) \cdot (X_j - \bar{X}_j)$
1	2	−1	−1	1	1	+1
3	4	+1	+1	1	1	+1
3	1	+1	−2	1	4	−2
3	4	+1	+1	1	1	+1
1	3	−1	0	1	0	0
2	3	0	0	0	0	0
1	1	−1	−2	1	4	+2
1	3	−1	0	1	0	0
3	5	+1	+2	1	4	+2
2	4	0	+1	0	1	0
				8	16	5

Therefore $r = \dfrac{5}{\sqrt{8}\,\sqrt{16}} = \dfrac{5}{11.3} = .44$

tribution is approximately normal for large (greater than 30) sample sizes. Hence if we like to use the .05 significance level to quickly filter out important linear relations, for samples above 30 in size we can simply look for t values above 2 in absolute value.

Limitations

There are the following two major limitations on the value of a correlation coefficient:

Both variables are intervally scaled and continuous.   Actually for most purposes, this is an overly rigid assumption. Ordinally scaled data may be used if you recognize the resulting correlation will be biased downward slightly. Consider the following data:

X_1	X_2 (rank)
1	1
3	2
4	3
8	4
9	5

Obviously the ordinal (rank) measure of X_1 is not an accurate reflection of the true value. Still the correlation between the true and rank values of X_1 is high ($r = .98$), and hence the correlation between the ordinal measure of X_1 and anything that the true X_1 is correlated with will also tend to remain high. In short, the coefficient is very robust (stands up well) to modest violations of this assumption (Morrison, 1972).

The relationship between the variables is linear.   Consider the cases in Figure 11–6. In case A, there is a strong positive correlation (i.e., $r =$

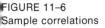

FIGURE 11–6
Sample correlations

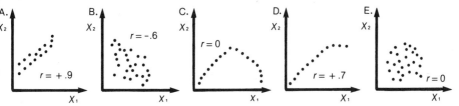

+.9). In case B, there is a negative relation, albeit weaker than case A ($r = -.6$). In case C, there is a clear relationship, but the simple correlation coefficient would be 0 ($r = 0$). This is because the correlation cannot detect severely curvilinear (nonmonotonic) relations. In case D we have a nonlinear relation, but since the relation is monotonic (as X_1 gets bigger so does X_2), the correlation will still be positive enough to indicate a substantial relationship ($r = +.7$). Case E gives an example where there is genuinely no relation between X_1 and X_2.

Correlation for ranked (ordinal) data

When data are ordinally rather than intervally scaled, the following two choices appear:

Use the product-moment correlation as an approximation. While this would make a purist cringe, it is often a good approximation. Similarly, binary scales (e.g., yes-no) can be used to compute correlations which do indicate whether the construct (e.g., the taking of aspirin) is related to another variable.

Use a special correlation which takes the ordinal nature of the data into account. There are many such coefficients including the coefficient of concordance, the coefficient of consistency, and Kendall's tau. As an example of this type of correlation, Spearman's rank correlation coefficient computes the correlation between two sets of rankings using the following formula:

$$R = 1 - \frac{6 \sum_{i=1}^{n} d^2}{n^3 - n} \tag{11.4}$$

where

d = number of places that an object differs in the two rankings
n = number of objects ranked

An example of the use of this formula appears in Table 11–18.

TABLE 11–18
Calculation of Spearman rank correlation
coefficient

1st person's ranking	2d person's ranking	Difference in rankings (d)	d^2
3	2	1	1
5	5	0	0
6	1	5	25
2	6	4	16
1	3	2	4
4	4	0	0
			46

$$R = 1 - \frac{6(46)}{6^3 - 6} = 1 - \frac{276}{210} = -.31$$

DATA ADJUSTMENT PROCEDURES

In analyzing a set of data, a variety of procedures are sometimes used. Two of the most common are recoding and weighting for unequal response rates.

Recoding

Data are often recoded. This is done for the following two major reasons:

To produce more simplified results. For example, frequently examining the initial tabs indicates several responses (e.g., brand used last) receive a very small percentage of mentions. In such cases, it is often desirable to combine infrequently given responses into an "all other" category in order to simplify the analysis.

To make the top end of the scale "up." Data can be collected in many different ways. For example, importances can be collected on five-point scales with "5" representing very important or alternatively "5" representing very unimportant. This means that it is impossible to interpret a result (e.g., a score of 4) without knowing which end of the scale is "up." The problem is compounded when two variables are combined, as in a correlation coefficient. A numerical correlation may be positive and the relation between the underlying constructs negative or vice versa. For example, assume importance placed on money were coded 1–5 with a low number indicating great importance and income was coded 1–6 with 6 being the highest category. If we assume that the importance of money would decrease as income increases, we would expect the basic concepts to be negatively related. Given this coding scheme, however, the correlation would be positive. Unless carefully interpreted, this positive number could lead to mistakenly concluding that the importance of money and income were positively related. In order to avoid such possible confusion, it is often desirable to recode all variables so that a bigger code value means more of the variable.

Weighting for unequal response rates

Given a sample which truly represents the frame, analysis can proceed directly. When the sample does not match the frame, however, the question of how to adjust the results arises. Consider again the nutrition example, which consciously oversampled lower income respondents:

Income	Sample	U.S.
Less than $10,000	49.7%	39.2%
$10,000–$19,999	35.6%	42.2%
$20,000 or more	14.7%	18.6%

In general, relationships among variables (e.g., correlations) are not affected by unequal sampling. The levels (means) of other variables, however, may be. In fact, for any variable which is related to income, a direct projection will be erroneous, although not necessarily greatly in error. The issue then becomes, "How can I weight responses to get a useful projection?" The procedure utilized is based on the stratified sampling formulas of Chapter 9. In this case, we can weight people in different income classes as follows:

Income	Weight
Less than $10,000	392/497 = .789
$10,000–$19,999	422/356 = 1.185
$20,000 or more	186/147 = 1.265

This weighting scheme will insure that people in the less than $10,000 income category account for 39.2 percent of the responses, and so forth. (Actually the weights should be calculated to more significant digits, but these are enough to demonstrate the process.) To show the effect of this weighting, assume that income were related to food expenditures as in Table 11–19. Assume we coded the expenses as $13, $23, $38, $53, and

TABLE 11–19
Raw cross-tabs

Income	Expense per week					
	Under $15	$15– $29	$30– $44	$45– $60	Over $60	Total
Under $10,000	33	226	149	45	11	464
$10,000–$19,999	5	73	121	102	31	332
$20,000 and over	1	23	42	48	23	137
Total	39	322	312	195	65	933
	4.2%	34.5%	33.4%	20.9%	7.0%	100%

$70, respectively for the five categories (essentially substituting the category median). The estimated unweighted mean expenditures would then be $13(.042) + $23(.345) + $38(.334) + $53(.209) + $70(.070) = $0.55 + $7.94 + $12.69 + $11.08 + $4.90 = $37.16.

Alternatively, we could reweight the data, producing Table 11–20. This implies a mean consumption of $13(.035) + $23(.315) + $38(.337) + $53(.233) + $70(.080) = $0.46 + $7.25 + $12.81 + $12.35 + $5.60 = $38.47. Hence failure to weight the data would produce a noticeable but

TABLE 11–20
Weighted cross tabs

| | Expense per week | | | | | |
Income	Under $15	$15–$29	$30–$44	$45–$60	Over $60	Total
Under $10,000	26.0	178.3	117.6	35.5	8.7	366.1
$10,000–$19,999	5.9	86.5	143.4	120.9	36.7	393.4
$20,000 and over	1.3	29.1	53.1	60.7	29.1	173.3
Total	33.2	293.9	314.1	217.1	74.5	932.8
	3.5%	31.5%	33.7%	23.3%	8.0%	100%

small (about 3.5 percent) error in the estimate of consumption expenditures. Obviously had the sample been closer to the actual U.S. income distribution, this error would have been reduced.

The weighting problem can be further complicated if the sample is off in terms of two or more variables. In this case, the weights must be developed in order to account for two or more characteristics (e.g., income and age) which are disproportionately represented simultaneously. In such a case, use (a) common sense and (b) a consultant.

Given the need to weight, a mundane question arises about how to do it. The dominant solution is to use a canned (prewritten) program which allows unequal weights. If such a program is unavailable, the alternatives are the following:

Write your own routine (a tedious solution).

Adjust your sample. This can be done by reducing the sample to match the cell which is the most underrepresented. Assume, for example, we have the following results:

Income group	Original sample size	Sample percent	"Correct" percent
A	500	50	50
B	400	40	30
C	100	10	20

We can now adjust the sample to match income group C, the most underrepresented. Since group C should represent 20 percent of the population, we will take all 100 respondents in group C for our new sample. The resulting reduced sample will thus be as follows:

Income group	Original sample size	Reduced sample size
A	500	250
B	400	150
C	100	100

The 250 people in group A will be chosen randomly from the original 500; similarly the 150 in group B will be chosen from the 400 originals in group B.

As can be seen from this example, this procedure is fairly inefficient in that 500 responses, half the original sample, are unused. Because of this (and a penchant for big sample sizes), many researchers will blowup rather than reduce a sample. This is done by increasing the results to match the overrepresented cell. In this case, we would match group B as the most overrepresented group. The resulting "sample" would then be as follows:

Income group	Original sample size	Blown-up sample size
A	500	667
B	400	400
C	100	267
	1,000	1,334

The new group A would consist of the original 500 plus 67 of the original 500 reproduced at random. The 267 of group C would consist of two duplicate sets of the original 100 plus 67 of the 100 chosen at random. While this method will produce an unbiased estimate of the means of variables, the increased sample size is deceiving. Hence while this method may "trick" computer programs into weighting responses, it may also trick researchers into thinking they have a better sample than they really do.

The weighting of unequal responses is thus a nontrivial problem. It also makes statistical interpretation of the results much more difficult. The dominant solution is to get a good sample. Failing that, the researcher must choose between somewhat biased results and the prospect of some gyrations to overcome the unfortunate sampling result.

SUMMARY

This chapter has presented a variety of ways for analyzing data. All these methods are standard procedures in the market research business, but the most standard is cross-tabs. As the book proceeds to more complicated analyses, remember that in most studies the majority of the results can be deduced from or at least reported in the form of such mundane but understandable procedures.

PROBLEMS

1. A judge admonishes the jury: "I want you to be absolutely certain before you return a guilty verdict." What will the outcome be?
2. Given:

x	8	1	4	2	3	6	5	7
y	7	2	3.5	1	3.5	8	5	6

What is—
a. The Pearson correlation.
b. The Spearman rank correlation.
3. How can I test to see if two nominally scaled variables are related?
4. I sample 800 people to determine their cereal preferences. The results of the study are as follows:

	Brand			
Preference	He-Man	Supa-Sweet	Little Crispies	Slush Puppies
Like	90	100	90	120
Dislike	110	100	110	80

Are preferences and brands related?
5. In order to ascertain preferences for three new package designs, prototypes of each of the packages were shown to some people who then classified them as superior, average, or inferior. Interpret these results:

Rating

Design	Inferior	Average	Superior	Total
1	60	80	60	200
2	160	140	100	400
3	80	80	40	200
Total	300	300	200	800

6. Interpret the following tabulation of 2,500 responses:

Number of contacts by school	Contributions to alumni fund			
	None	Small	Large	Total
1	150	150	200	500
2–3	350	200	450	1,000
4 or more	500	150	350	1,000

7. In estimating the demand for a new household appliance, the following table was compiled:

	Definitely would buy					
	Version A ($400)		Version B ($200)		Version C ($200)	
	No.	%	No.	%	No.	%
Under 25	211	23.8	964	17.2	240	13.3
25–34	253	28.5	1,916	34.2	606	33.5
35–44	34	3.8	906	16.2	166	9.2
45–54	279	31.1	1,324	23.6	615	34.0
55 and over	115	13.0	490	8.7	181	10.0

Interpret.

8. Are region and sales significantly related?

	Region		
Brand	A	B	C
1	40	50	60
2	20	40	90
3	30	60	150

9. In a blind taste test, 100 respondents tasted our brand of detergent cake mix (after baking) and rated its bleach content as follows:

16%	too little bleach
12	almost enough
36	just right
20	slightly too much
16	too much bleach
100%	

Another 200 respondents tasted our main competitor's mix and rated its bleach content as follows:

8%	too little bleach
12	almost enough
60	just right
12	slightly too much
8	too much bleach
100%	

Should we get concerned about the bleach level in our detergent since only 36 percent of the respondents rated ours "just right"?

10. The sale of beer to relatively few heavy users accounts for a large portion of the sales volume of Suds brand beer. The brand manager of Suds would like to expand the distribution but does not know which city should be selected to expand or "roll out" into. Three cities are being considered: Bluelaw, Wasdry, and Spilltown. The affluence of the citizens varies greatly between the towns. A survey of 200 Suds purchasers indicated that 70 percent of the purchasers were light users, and 50 percent had incomes above $8,000, as shown in the following table of percentages:

	High income	Low income
Heavy user	20%	10%
Light user	30%	40%

If the usage rate and income are not related, then the Suds brand manager will try to expand into Spilltown, but if they are related then the manager will select the town with a favorable income distribution. What advice would you give the Suds brand manager?

11. A sample of 200 persons revealed that 55.0 percent of the sampled people who shop regularly in our chain of supermarkets usually buy our private brand of coffee. However 63.3 percent of the sampled people who shop regularly in competing supermarkets usually buy the private label coffee in those stores. The sample included 80 persons who regularly shop in our stores and 120 persons who regularly shop in competing stores. We make more money on private brand coffee than on other coffee. The difference between 55.0 percent and 63.3 percent seems like a lot, especially when you consider all of our millions of customers. Does the sample indicate that our private brand coffee sales are significantly lower than competitors, or shouldn't we worry?

12. The sales of baby food to elderly people accounts for a significant portion of the sales volume. A canner has developed a line of "adult" mushy, easily digestible foods and tried selling the new products to older customers in a store in Retirement Village. Sampling 50 shoppers in the store the canner found that 20 percent had "no money worries," 20 percent "get along O.K.," and 60 percent are "financially insecure." Also, 30 percent of the shoppers indicated that they had tried the new brand, as shown in the following table of percentages:

	Tried	Did not try
"No money worries"	12%	8%
"Get along OK"	2%	18%
"Financially insecure"	16%	44%

If trial and income are not related, then the food canner feels the distribution of the product can be increased quickly. However, if they are related, then perhaps the effect of income should be studied before distribution is expanded. What advice would you give the food canner?

13. A prestigious East Coast research house conducted a national telephone survey. The firm had been hired partly because of its sophisticated sampling capability. The final report indicated the following number of interviews in each geographic areas, compared to the 1970 census breakdown for the same areas.

	Sample size	U.S. Percent of population
Northeast	125	24.4%
South	171	30.4
Northcentral	155	27.6
West	145	17.6
	597	100%

Is the geographic distribution of interviews consistent with the firm's contract to obtain a simple random sample of the U.S. population with telephones? What weighting of observations would you use in computing statistics from these interviews?

14. Four different BLUGOS price promotions have been advertised in successive Wednesday night newspapers. The sales (cases) of BLUGOS during the following three days were recorded each week:

Promotion	Sales
16¢ off, no coupon	105
18¢ off, no coupon	95
20¢ off, 5¢ coupon	113
25¢ off, 8¢ coupon	89

How much time should you spend understanding this data and determining "the implications" for our BLUGOS promotions?

15. Given the following situation where the population is divided into two strata:

Stratum	Stratum size (million)	Sample size	Average consumption
A	20	900	48
B	80	100	3

What is your best estimate for overall average consumption?

16. Consider again the nutrition study described in Table 9–3 (page 275). If income and family size were the two main determinants of weekly food expenditures, how would you weight the sample to produce an accurate representation of average food expenditures?

17. A distribution of the responses to a survey of 681 users of the product class is displayed below for the following measures:

Preferred brand (A–D)
Income level (under or over $18,000 for family)
City (E–H)
Marital status (M, S, O)

Respondents in city E or F

Low income—married:
  45 prefer A; 7, B; 8, C; 8, D
Low income—single:
  50 prefer A; 9, B; 8, C; 7, D
Low income—other:
  23 prefer A; 4, B; 4, C; 3, D
High income—married:
  16 prefer A; 13, B; 12, C; 16, D
High income—single:
  17 prefer A; 15, B; 13, C; 12, D
High income—other:
  9 prefer A; 7, B; 7, C; 8, D

Respondents in city G or H

Low income—married:
  40 prefer A; 11, B; 13, C; 11, D
Low income—single:
  35 prefer A; 13, B; 11, C; 11, D
Low income—other:
  28 prefer A; 5, B; 5, C; 7, D
High income—married:
  30 prefer A; 12, B; 13, C; 14, D
High income—single:
  28 prefer A; 15, B; 13, C; 11, D
High income—other:
  17 prefer A; 5, B; 6, C; 7, D

Use contingency tables to evaluate the difference in effect between advertising theme "value" (which has been played for years in cities E and F) and theme "style" (which has been played for years in cities G and H).

18. Over the past year a manufacturer has increased advertising by 50 percent in city B. In order to assess the effectiveness of this move, the manufacturer has surveyed 300 people in city B and 300 people in city A, where the advertising has remained at the lower level.

The respondents have been broken down by (1) income and (2) marital status:

Respondents in city A	*Respondents in city B*
Married—low income:	Married—low income:
39 preferred our brand	19 preferred our brand
20 preferred their brand	40 preferred their brand
Married—high income:	Married—high income:
48 preferred our brand	94 preferred our brand
92 preferred their brand	47 preferred their brand
Single—low income:	Single—low income:
21 preferred our brand	46 preferred our brand
10 preferred their brand	23 preferred their brand
Single—high income:	Single—high income:
22 preferred our brand	11 preferred our brand
48 preferred their brand	20 preferred their brand

Interpret.

BIBLIOGRAPHY

Buzzell, Robert D.; Cox, Donald F.; and Brown, Rex V. *Marketing Research and Information Systems; Text and Cases.* New York: McGraw-Hill, 1969.

Lehmann, Donald R., and O'Shaughnessy, John. "Difference in Attribute Importance for Different Industrial Products." *Journal of Marketing,* vol. 38 (April 1974), pp. 36–42. (Material reprinted from *Journal of Marketing* published by the American Marketing Association.)

Lublin, Joann S. "Aspirin Found to Cut Blood-Clotting Risks in Men, Not Women." *Wall Street Journal,* December 8, 1977.

Morrison, Donald G. "Regression with Discrete Random Variables: The Effect on R^2". *Journal of Marketing Research,* vol. 9 (August 1972), pp. 338–40.

Siegel, Sidney. *Nonparametric Statistics.* New York: McGraw-Hill, 1956.

_____ APPENDIX 11–A _____

BASIC ANALYSIS OF NUTRITIONAL HABITS SURVEY

Basic results

This section reports the simple question-by-question tabulations of the questionnaire on a percentage basis. The responses are unweighted, and hence the results are not directly projectable to the entire population of the United States. The decision to leave the data unweighted was based on the fact that a "national census" was impossible with this data since only households with two or more members which included a female (wife, etc.) were included. All averages are based on those respondents who answered the particular question being analyzed with nonresponses excluded.

SECTION I—SHOPPING HABITS

1. Portion of shopping done by the respondent:

	Percent
No answer	.6
None of it	1.6
Less than half	3.6
About half	5.5
Most of it	31.4
All of it	57.2

Interpretation: The respondents are, as expected, the principal food shoppers for their households.

2. Number of times they shop for food each week:

	Percent
No answer	.5
Less than once	12.8
Once a week	49.1
2–4 times a week	35.7
5 or more times a week	1.8

Interpretation: Most of this sample shop for food about once a week.

3. Portion of the items purchased which are on a shopping list:

	Percent
No answer	.7
None (no list)	19.0
Some	3.3
About half	5.1
More than half	14.0
Almost all	57.8

Interpretation: While most people prepare a fairly complete list before shopping, almost 20 percent go to the store with no list at all.

4. Amount of money spent on food per week:

	Percent
No answer	.7
Under $15	4.1
$15–$29	34.3
$30–$44	33.2
$45–$60	20.7
Over $60	6.9

Interpretation: A "typical" family spends $35–$40 per week on food.

SECTION I (continued)

5. Change in weekly spending from last year:

	Percent
No answer	.9
Spend at least $10 less than last year	2.6
$5–$10 less than last year	3.6
About the same as last year	13.2
$5–$10 more than last year	48.7
Over $10 more than last year	31.1

Interpretation: The typical household is spending $5–$10 more per week for food this year than last. This implies an increase of about 20 percent.

6. Number of brands and sizes considered in buying staple products (soup, ketchup, etc.):

	Percent
No answer	.3
Only 1 or 2	49.5
Many brands, one size	8.6
Many sizes, one brand	3.3
Many brands and sizes	38.3

Interpretation: This question was intended to find out the number of people who actively shop for a product versus the number who have previously decided which alternative to select. Interestingly, about half the people have predetermined choices and hence are presumably very insensitive to new offerings, point of purchase materials, and specials.

7. Approach to food shopping:

	Percent
No answer	1.0
I actively seek information about food in terms of nutritional value, price, etc.	29.0
I sometimes try new foods because of new information, but generally buy the same foods	53.1
The food I buy is almost always the same, and I spend very little time thinking about it	16.9

Interpretation: This question was intended to find out how many people actively seek information about food. The 29 percent who say they do is probably biased upward since it is in some sense the "right" answer. The fact that 70 percent are not very interested in new information suggests that attempts to change behavior through "rational" appeals will not be easy, as food manufacturers can no doubt attest.

8. Use of food stamps by the immediate family:

	Percent
No answer	.1
Never used	87.9
Used to, but do not use them now	6.9
We are presently using them	5.1

Interpretation: Food stamp usage has occurred among 12 percent of the sample with 5.1 percent currently using them.

9. Importance of attributes in the decision about which food to serve:

Attribute	No answer	Very important		Not very important	Average importance	Rank of average importance
Variety	4.5%	38.8%	21.0%	32.2%	2.0%	1.5%	2.02	5
Taste	3.9	79.1	11.7	4.7	.2	.3	1.24	1
Other family members' preferences	5.2	51.5	23.5	16.8	1.6	1.4	1.71	3
Diet restrictions	6.8	26.7	10.5	21.1	7.6	27.3	2.98	10
Price	3.6	54.6	16.8	22.2	1.2	1.6	1.74	4
Availability at stores where you normally shop	6.1	35.4	21.6	28.9	2.9	5.1	2.16	6
Ease of preparation	5.9	18.4	17.6	36.6	9.5	12.1	2.78	8
Habit (past eating patterns)	7.9	13.0	20.3	40.1	10.5	8.2	2.82	9
Advertised specials	4.0	38.2	18.9	23.8	6.2	8.8	2.26	7
Nutritional value	3.2	55.5	21.9	16.6	2.0	.7	1.66	2

Interpretation: The importance of diet restrictions divides the sample in thirds: 27 percent find them very important, 46 percent somewhat important, and 27 percent find them completely unimportant. In terms of relative importance, taste is by far the most important variable. Nutrition is maintained to edge out price and other family members' preferences as second most important, although this is an obvious "right" answer and hence the stated importance of nutrition is inflated. Overall, it appears that taste and price dominate food selection decisions.

10. Attention paid to different product features:

		Amount of attention paid				
	No answer	Great deal	Some	Little or none	Average	Rank
Brand name	2.8%	38.5%	51.2%	7.6%	1.68	7
Number of servings	4.5	43.2	40.2	12.1	1.68	6
Net weight or volume	3.8	48.1	36.0	12.1	1.63	5
Total price	2.0	80.6	15.2	2.1	1.20	1
Amount of ingredients ...	4.9	39.6	40.3	15.2	1.74	8
Unit price	4.8	51.5	32.7	11.1	1.58	4
List of ingredients	4.7	33.4	46.3	15.6	1.81	9
Nutritional value	3.7	50.0	39.1	7.1	1.56	3
Recipes	4.8	13.9	41.8	39.5	2.27	11
Food additives and preservatives	3.7	31.3	37.2	27.8	1.96	10
Date of manufacture or expiration	2.8	65.5	26.4	5.3	1.38	2

Interpretation: Total price is by far the most salient characteristic of the purchase event. Freshness comes second with nutritional value third and unit price a close fourth. Recipes seem to be largely overlooked as are food additives and preservatives, possibly because few people (experts included) know what they really do.

11. Number of times per week the respondent eats different meals:

	No answer	Never	1–2	3–4	5–6	Everyday
Breakfast	1.7%	10.1%	13.9%	8.9%	6.0%	59.4%
Lunch	2.4	1.6	7.3	12.4	11.3	64.9
Dinner	1.7	.3	1.3	1.6	6.1	89.0

Interpretation: One third of the population eats breakfast irregularly. Surprisingly, lunch is more often consumed than breakfast. Not surprisingly, dinner is almost universally eaten at least six days a week.

12. Number of snacks consumed per day:

	Percent
No answer	1.5
None	18.0
One	44.6
Two	27.9
Three or more	8.1

Interpretation: Less than 20 percent of the sample avoids snacks. On the other hand, only 8.1 percent and the author admit to three or more snacks per day.

13. Amount of food canned:

	Percent
No answer	2.0
None	39.7
Small amount	36.3
Large amount	22.0

Interpretation: About 60 percent of the sample indicated that they can food. This seems very high and suggests that this may have been a bad question.

14. Frequency of consumption of different foods:

	No answer	Never	A few times a year	1–2 times a month	Weekly	Several times a week	Once a day	More than once a day	Mean	Rank
Canned fruit	2.1%	1.2%	18.5%	34.1%	20.2%	20.3%	2.9%	.6%	3.52	16
Fresh fruit	2.0	.7	4.1	12.7	22.4	30.3	19.0	8.6	4.73	4
Bread	2.0	.5	.9	2.2	6.0	18.4	36.3	33.7	5.90	2
Rice	1.9	5.3	19.8	45.3	22.2	4.8	.1	.5	3.04	23
Butter	5.4	30.3	17.7	6.9	4.0	9.0	12.3	14.3	3.40	20
Margarine	4.0	4.8	3.0	2.7	8.6	19.1	23.1	34.7	5.53	3
Cheese	3.3	1.4	2.2	12.7	25.4	44.6	7.8	2.7	4.48	5
Ice cream	1.8	3.4	15.6	35.4	21.9	18.9	2.3	.5	3.47	17
Whole milk	4.3	27.0	9.5	8.4	5.7	10.4	17.1	17.6	3.88	11
Skim milk or low fat milk	6.2	34.3	10.5	6.1	4.8	10.6	13.2	14.4	3.47	18
Snack foods (potato chips, pretzels, etc.)	2.6	9.4	15.5	28.4	20.7	18.0	3.8	1.6	3.41	19
Desserts	2.9	1.5	6.0	18.3	21.9	28.9	16.0	4.6	4.41	7
Alcoholic beverages (beer, wine, liquor)	1.9	35.4	21.4	16.5	10.0	8.6	5.2	1.0	2.54	29
Soft drinks	2.4	9.8	13.3	21.6	16.6	19.4	8.4	8.5	3.84	13
Fish	1.9	4.4	17.7	41.9	28.7	5.1	.2	.1	3.14	22
Cold cereal	2.0	12.6	13.9	19.9	15.6	22.9	12.1	1.0	3.64	15
Frozen vegetables	1.9	4.5	10.0	20.1	21.8	32.8	8.2	.7	3.98	10
Fresh vegetables	2.1	1.5	5.7	14.5	22.9	38.7	11.3	3.3	4.42	6
Canned vegetables	2.3	2.7	5.3	13.6	23.4	41.2	10.1	1.4	4.34	9
Poultry	1.5	.5	3.7	32.3	52.3	8.5	.9	.2	3.69	14
Beef (hamburger or stew meat)	1.2	.5	.4	7.3	47.4	40.6	2.1	.3	4.37	8
Beef (steak or roast)	3.0	1.0	3.9	24.5	48.0	18.6	1.0	.1	3.85	12
Pork	3.2	6.8	21.1	39.6	23.2	5.0	1.2	.0	3.02	24
Tuna fish	2.1	8.1	21.0	40.3	20.4	7.8	.3	.0	3.00	25
Frozen dinners	1.7	35.2	39.3	18.1	4.4	1.4	.0	.0	1.96	30
Hot dogs	2.6	7.6	24.6	40.9	19.9	3.4	.3	.9	2.91	26
Coffee or tea	3.2	4.7	1.6	2.1	2.8	5.5	14.9	65.2	6.19	1
Pasta (pizza, spaghetti, etc.)	2.4	6.5	13.2	43.1	28.9	5.9	.0	.0	3.15	21
Food at "fast food" restaurant (i.e. McDonald's, etc.)	2.3	12.8	35.1	35.2	12.0	2.1	.3	.1	2.56	28
Food at regular restaurants	1.8	7.7	42.8	31.0	14.1	2.3	.3	.0	2.61	27

Interpretation: Coffee and tea are the most widely consumed food followed closely by bread. Frozen dinners are the least frequently consumed followed by alcoholic beverages and food eaten at restaurants. Overall, "junk" food is rated as relatively little consumed although here again this is obviously the socially accepted response. Interestingly, margarine is consumed more frequently than butter and skim milk almost as often as whole milk.

	No answer	Much less	Somewhat less	About the same	Somewhat more	Much more	Mean	Rank
Canned fruit	1.5%	8.9%	15.4%	64.8%	7.2%	2.1%	2.78	18
Fresh fruit	1.7	3.2	9.5	57.9	22.3	5.4	3.18	3
Bread	1.8	2.8	11.5	66.0	13.7	4.3	3.05	8
Rice	2.3	8.4	14.4	64.3	9.5	1.2	2.80	16
Butter	7.1	24.0	13.6	47.3	6.3	1.6	2.44	28
Margarine	2.4	3.9	7.3	66.2	15.7	4.4	3.10	7
Cheese	2.1	1.8	7.4	59.6	24.3	4.8	3.23	1
Ice cream	2.8	7.6	21.3	53.7	12.0	2.7	2.80	15
Whole milk	4.4	15.6	13.5	51.9	9.4	5.2	2.74	20
Skim milk or low fat milk	8.7	16.7	7.2	45.2	16.0	6.2	2.87	13
Snack foods (potato chips, pretzels, etc.)	3.1	16.5	24.6	46.6	7.4	1.8	2.52	26
Desserts	3.4	9.9	26.0	53.7	5.6	1.4	2.61	23
Alcoholic beverages (beer, wine, liquor)	9.5	21.1	11.5	53.0	4.7	.3	2.47	27
Soft drinks	3.2	13.6	18.8	50.3	11.6	2.4	2.70	22
Fish	2.9	5.9	14.8	63.6	11.4	1.5	2.88	12
Cold cereal	2.8	6.4	12.8	59.4	15.9	2.9	2.96	9
Frozen vegetables	1.9	5.5	11.8	68.5	10.6	1.6	2.91	11
Fresh vegetables	1.9	2.3	6.9	69.6	16.6	2.7	3.11	6
Canned vegetables	1.9	4.7	10.9	72.0	9.0	1.5	2.92	10
Poultry	1.8	2.3	8.1	67.2	17.6	3.0	3.11	5
Beef (hamburger or stew meat)	1.3	1.6	5.0	65.3	22.6	4.3	3.23	2
Beef (steak or roast)	2.4	7.2	19.7	59.5	9.3	1.9	2.78	17
Pork	3.6	20.6	26.8	44.4	3.2	1.4	2.36	29
Tuna fish	3.6	11.0	14.4	59.4	10.5	1.2	2.76	19
Frozen dinners	5.1	25.6	17.3	46.7	4.9	.3	2.34	30
Hot dogs	2.8	11.1	19.1	54.4	11.2	1.5	2.72	21
Coffee or tea	3.0	3.3	5.6	68.1	13.8	6.1	3.14	4
Pasta (pizza, spaghetti, etc.)	3.5	9.5	13.1	61.3	11.2	1.5	2.82	14
Food at "fast food" restaurants (i.e., McDonald's, etc)	3.6	18.0	17.6	49.9	9.5	1.5	2.57	24
Food at regular restaurants	2.7	19.9	17.9	47.4	10.1	2.0	2.55	25

Interpretation: Frozen dinner consumption decreased the most followed by pork, butter, and alcoholic beverages. Cheese consumption increased the most followed by beef, fresh fruit, and coffee or tea. On balance, people seem to have cut back on food consumption of most items with 22 of the 30 products showing decreased average consumption.

SECTION II—NUTRITIONAL INFORMATION SOURCES

1. Amount of information gained from various sources:

	No answer	None	Very little	Some	Quite a bit	A tremendous amount	Mean	Rank
Books	3.7%	20.6%	21.0%	35.3%	14.9%	4.5%	2.60	5
Magazines	3.2	8.7	12.6	44.9	26.3	4.4	3.05	3
Labels on the packages food comes in	3.7	5.7	16.5	43.6	26.4	4.0	3.07	2
Your mother	7.3	38.7	16.4	21.8	12.0	3.7	2.20	10
Other family members	6.0	34.7	23.8	26.7	7.2	1.6	2.12	11
Friends	5.5	22.4	26.5	36.8	8.1	.6	2.34	8
Doctors	5.0	29.6	22.4	28.8	11.2	3.0	2.32	9
TV programs	4.9	19.6	25.0	38.8	10.3	1.4	2.46	7
TV advertisements	4.8	17.8	27.1	39.1	10.1	1.1	2.47	6
Newspapers	5.2	12.9	20.7	44.1	15.5	1.5	2.71	4
Your own experience	4.1	4.3	6.2	35.4	39.3	10.7	3.48	1
Courses in school	5.4	50.9	9.1	16.1	11.1	7.4	2.10	12

Interpretation: Personal experience is by far the most important source of nutritional information with labels on packages and magazines next most important. The importance of school courses, other family members, doctors, and friends is rated very low. Whether this reflects unavailability or lack of expertise is not clear.

2. Books read in the past year:

	No answer	No	Yes
Dieting	5.5%	51.7%	42.8%
Nutrition	8.0	58.7	33.3
Cooking	4.1	35.2	60.6

Interpretation: People read more to make gourmet treats or to solve a specific problem than to learn about nutrition in general. Still one third of the sample claim to have read a book about nutrition this year.

3. Preferred sources of information from a federal government campaign:

	Percent	Rank
Column in the newspapers	39.1	2
TV special	36.1	3
Special edition of a prominent magazine	15.9	7
Government brochure	19.8	6
Extension courses	11.1	9

	Percent	Rank
Workshops	9.9	10
Public service TV announcements	25.0	4
Information on packages	39.8	1
Information in TV advertisements	22.1	5
Don't care	11.3	8

Interpretation: No source of information is favored by a majority. Information on packages edges out column in newspaper and TV special as most preferred. Workshops and extension courses inspire only about 10 percent of the sample's interest. The author's favorite, a government brochure, finished a dismal sixth.

4. Amount willing to pay per week for a service providing nutritional information about available brands:

	Percent
No answer	3.3
Nothing	48.2
10¢–19¢	25.3
20¢–49¢	17.1
40¢–99¢	5.3
$1–$2	.7
Over $2	.0

Interpretation: Half the sample is unwilling to pay anything to find out nutritional information about available brands, and only 6 percent is willing to pay over 40 cents per week. If this is not an artifact of the question, it suggests that consumers would not support such a service in the free market.

5. Formal courses in nutrition:

	No answer	No	Yes
High school	6.1%	62.2%	31.7%
College	17.3	71.9	10.7
Adult education/workshop	18.5	74.6	6.9

Interpretation: Very few of this sample have taken a formal nutrition course.

SECTION III—BACKGROUND

1. Diets any member of the household is on:

Diet	Self-imposed	Doctor's orders	Total
Low cholesterol	7.3%	13.1%	20.4%
Low fat/calorie	17.0	11.3	28.3
Diabetic	1.5	9.6	11.1
Low salt	5.0	13.0	18.0
Vegetarian	1.3	.3	1.6
Low triglyceride	1.0	1.7	2.7

Interpretation: A substantial fraction of the households sampled have a member on one diet or another with self-imposed low fat/calorie most prevalent followed by doctor-imposed low cholesterol, low salt, low fat/calorie, and diabetic. Very few low triglyceride and vegetarian diets were in evidence.

2. Smoking frequency:

	Percent
No answer	1.2
Never	70.2
Occasionally	5.0
Regularly, but light (less than one pack of cigarettes each day	8.6
Regularly (one pack of cigarettes a day)	9.1
Heavily (more than one pack each day or equivalent)	5.9

Interpretation: Over two thirds of this sample were nonsmokers with 15 percent heavy smokers.

3. Vitamin pills taken personally:

	Percent
No answer	1.9
None	48.9
Multiple	29.7
Vitamin C	17.3
Vitamin G	.0
Vitamin B-12 complex	8.9
Vitamin A	3.7
Iron	15.7

Interpretation: Half the sample take no vitamins at all. The most prominent vitamin is multiple followed by vitamin C and iron. Sur-

4. Time spent watching TV per day:

	Percent
No answer	.7
None	3.0
Less than 1 hour	10.0
1–2 hours	33.6
3–4 hours	35.4
Over 4 hours	17.2

Interpretation: The typical respondent watches 2–3 hours of TV daily and only 3 percent abstain entirely.

5. Change in family income:

	Percent
No answer	.9
Gone down a lot	11.4
Gone down a little	11.6
Stayed about the same	30.7
Gone up a little	41.4
Gone up a lot	4.1

Interpretation: Most people's incomes have stayed the same or increased slightly. On the other hand; 11.4 percent have experienced a large drop in income compared to only 4.1 percent who experienced a large increase.

6. Change in family size:

	Percent
No answer	1.4
Decreased by two or more	2.4
Decreased by one	9.7
Stayed the same	77.6
Increased by one	8.0
Increased by two or more	1.0

Interpretation: More of these families decreased in size than increased, a result of their age and tendency to enter the "empty nest" stage of the life cycle. Over three fourths however remained unchanged.

SECTION IV—GENERAL ATTITUDES

	No answer	Strongly agree	Somewhat agree	Neither agree nor disagree	Somewhat disagree	Strongly disagree	Average response	Rank
People need to eat meat to be healthy	1.0%	23.8%	38.2%	17.6%	13.7%	5.7%	2.39	8
A high level of consumption is necessary to maintain a high standard of living	2.6	3.0	11.0	17.9	29.1	36.5	3.87	23
I am personally more conscientious in conserving energy than I was 3 years ago	1.8	55.0	33.6	6.3	2.2	1.1	1.58	2
The government should be more active in giving information about nutrition to consumers	1.6	32.6	36.4	22.9	4.3	2.3	2.06	4
I expect things to get better for my family next year	1.5	16.6	34.5	34.4	10.4	2.7	2.47	9
I feel the need for more information about nutrition	1.6	20.1	37.0	32.1	6.3	2.9	2.34	7
All people would have better diets if there were fewer mouths to feed	2.3	7.9	14.8	25.5	23.6	25.9	3.46	20
All cold cereals are about the same nutritionally	2.3	7.7	24.5	19.9	26.5	19.0	3.25	18
Health is more important than money	1.3	83.6	11.1	2.6	.4	1.1	1.22	1
I get more exercise than the average person	1.7	12.2	25.4	33.0	20.6	7.0	2.85	13
We entertain at home more than the average family	2.8	2.7	9.9	23.6	29.5	31.6	3.80	22
I am healthier than the average American	2.8	7.3	23.6	43.0	15.6	7.7	2.93	15
I consider myself better informed about nutrition than the average American	1.5	5.6	21.4	43.6	18.4	9.5	3.05	17

National brands of food are a better buy than local brands	1.6	3.7	12.2	27.1	37.0	18.3	3.55	21
Life is going well for me	2.2	31.5	37.2	19.3	6.9	2.9	2.10	6
Prices of food are so high that my nutrition is suffering	1.8	7.2	21.1	26.2	24.1	19.6	3.28	19
Television advertising has an adverse effect on diets because it encourages people to eat "junk" foods	1.3	35.9	33.3	16.8	10.1	2.7	2.09	5
I am heavier than I should be	1.3	30.6	25.7	11.0	12.0	19.4	2.63	11
I would be willing to eat less if the food were sent to the poor in the United States	1.0	21.2	26.3	33.9	8.6	9.0	2.58	10
America has a responsibility to share our agricultural abundance with hungry people in poor countries as well as home in the United States	1.5	13.5	40.0	16.9	17.9	10.2	2.71	12
The U.S. government should pass laws which would encourage and reward the farmer for full-scale production	1.4	38.5	32.8	18.6	6.1	2.7	2.00	3
The children in our household have a large influence on what we eat	8.6	10.2	26.8	26.7	15.0	12.7	2.92	14
Filling out this questionnaire has made me think about things which will change the types of foods I buy	1.2	6.1	25.7	43.5	12.7	10.9	2.96	16

Interpretation: The respondents believe health is more important than money, that they are more conscientious in conserving energy, and that government should encourage full-scale farm production. They *do not believe* a high level of consumption is necessary to maintain a high standard of living, that they entertain at home more than the average family, that national brands are a better buy than local brands, that people would be better off if there were fewer mouths to feed, or that high food prices are hurting them nutritionally. The most surprising result is the lack of enthusiasm for the potential benefits of population control. The moderate support for more information was expected.

1. Knowledge questions:

	No answer	True	False	Don't know
Hamburger contains substantially more protein per ounce than do soy beans	1.4%	13.8%	[54.7]%	30.1%
Pasta is high in cholesterol	1.7	31.8	[31.0]	35.5
Poultry are more efficient than cattle as producers of protein	1.8	[37.4]	35.4	25.3
A large amount of one vitamin is sufficient to overcome deficiencies of other vitamins	1.4	2.2	[85.2]	11.2
Beans and rice together are a low-protein meal	1.7	17.7	[59.6]	21.1
Eating a variety of foods from the supermarket will ensure a balanced diet	1.5	32.1	58.0	8.4
The cost of the vitamins needed to meet 100 percent of the minimum daily requirements is less than 10 cents per day	1.4	[38.1]	16.7	43.8
Food coloring additives create hyperactivity in children	1.9	[25.1]	33.3	39.7
Sugar causes cavities in children	1.6	[73.8]	15.5	9.0
Whole wheat bread is healthier than enriched white bread	.9	[69.6]	17.0	12.6

Interpretation: Many respondents have a reasonable knowledge of nutrition but a disconcertingly large fraction are unsure or even worse, incorrect in their opinions. For four of the questions, less than half the sample knew the correct answer ("correct" answers are in brackets).

2. Which foods aid which functions:

	Whole milk	Beef	Tomatoes	Enriched bread
Eyes	49.4%	31.3%	37.0%	22.6%
Teeth and bones	[96.3]	33.3	13.4	27.4
Muscle tissue	46.1	[80.2]	14.5	32.4
Repair of body tissues	[57.9]	[65.6]	25.5	31.9
Blood cells	37.4	[76.8]	26.1	21.3
Fighting infection	47.7	41.1	45.9	25.7
Nervous system	[56.7]	44.3	26.4	36.3
Skin	[70.3]	36.6	37.0	27.7
Proper growth of children	[93.3]	[69.1]	49.8	[67.3]

Interpretation: As expected, whole milk is thought to be a "super" food. Beef is also very highly regarded by the sample; especially for muscle and blood. Interestingly, enriched bread is perceived to be more related to proper growth of children than tomatoes

3. Which foods contain a lot of different nutrients?

	Whole milk	Beef	Tomatoes	Enriched bread
Vitamin A	58.8%	16.9%	31.5%	25.3%
Thiamin (vitamin B_1)	28.4	31.6	13.0	48.8
Riboflavin (vitamin B_2)	31.3	32.3	10.5	44.5
Niacin	22.7	23.4	15.5	45.2
Vitamin C	19.8	4.6	[76.0]	9.6
Vitamin D	[63.4]	11.8	11.2	13.7
Protein	41.7	[81.9]	3.4	22.0
Carbohydrates	28.4	14.0	9.9	[72.7]
Fat	[71.4]	49.1	.7	27.9
Calories	[56.9]	38.6	3.7	[73.9]
Iron	26.3	[64.0]	21.4	23.6
Calcium	[91.0]	6.1	4.9	18.7

Interpretation: More than half the sample felt whole milk had a lot of vitamin D, fat, calories, and calcium and over 40 percent listed protein. For beef, protein and iron were the main characteristics followed by fat. Tomatoes are perceived to mainly have vitamin C, while enriched bread is associated with carbohydrates and calories followed by vitamins A, B_1 and B_2 (answers above 50 percent are in brackets).

4. Foods similar in benefits to the body:

	Whole milk	Beef	Tomatoes	Enriched bread
Oatmeal	22.6%	14.6%	2.2%	[75.6]%
Fish	21.3	[76.1]	6.3	7.6
Rice	11.1	12.1	3.4	[78.8]
Navy beans	10.9	[59.1]	8.3	37.8
Chicken	14.6	[82.4]	3.0	11.2
Potatoes	11.0	6.6	14.4	[77.1]
Eggs	44.4	[61.0]	2.9	11.4

SECTION V (continued)

Macaroni	9.6	6.9	1.3	[83.3]
Pork and lamb	11.4	[82.9]	2.8	6.7
String beans	7.3	9.2	[73.5]	6.3
Carrots	17.9	5.9	[72.4]	6.3
Bananas	24.8	11.1	43.2	24.5
Peanut butter	26.0	[73.8]	4.0	19.9
Cottage cheese	[76.7]	36.3	4.8	10.7

Interpretation: People seem to group foods based on the four basic food groups (answers above 50 percent are in brackets).

ACCURACY OF NUTRITIONAL KNOWLEDGE

In order to get some overall indication of the accuracy of people's nutritional knowledge, a summed score was developed based on some of the answers to Section V, question 1 (the true-false questions). Specifically, a summed score was developed as follows:

	Answer		
	True	False	Don't know
Hamburger contains substantially more protein per ounce than do soy beans	-.25	+1	0
Pasta is high in cholesterol	-.25	+1	0
Poultry are more efficient than cattles as producers of protein	+1	-.25	0
A large amount of one vitamin is sufficient to overcome deficiencies of other vitamins	-.25	+1	0
Beans and rice together are a low protein meal	-.25	+1	0
The cost of the vitamins needed to meet 100% of the minimum daily requirements is less than 10¢ per day	+1	-.25	0
Sugar causes cavities in children	+1	-.25	0

The distribution of this "Nutritional Knowledge Score" was as follows.

Score	Absolute frequency	Adjusted frequency	Cumulative frequency
-1.25	1	.1%	.1%
-1.00	1	.1	.2
-.75	2	.2	.4
-.50	4	.4	.9
-.25	10	1.1	1.9
.0	17	1.8	3.7
.25	6	.6	4.4
.50	10	1.1	5.4
.75	17	1.8	7.2
1.00	27	2.9	10.1
1.25	25	2.7	12.8
1.50	32	3.4	16.2
1.75	36	3.8	20.0
2.00	33	3.5	23.5
2.25	37	3.9	27.4
2.50	57	6.1	33.5
2.75	51	5.4	38.9
3.00	22	2.3	41.3
3.25	29	3.1	44.4
3.50	81	8.6	53.0
3.75	83	8.8	61.8
4.00	34	3.6	65.4
4.50	49	5.2	70.6
4.75	88	9.4	80.0
5.00	41	4.4	84.4
5.75	55	5.9	90.2
6.00	50	5.3	95.5
7.00	42	5.4	100.0
Total	940	100.0	

Interpretation: The average score was 3.465, and the standard deviation, 1.786. Nutritional knowledge varies widely across the sample with very few people extremely knowledgeable in an objective sense. Put differently, a substantial fraction of the sample is misinformed about nutrition.

APPENDIX 11-B: SAMPLE CROSS-TAB OUTPUT

STATISTICAL PACKAGE FOR THE SOCIAL SCIENCES SPSSH - VERSION 6.00

SPACE ALLOCATION FOR THIS RUN..

    TOTAL AMOUNT REQUESTED   80000 BYTES

    DEFAULT TRANSPACE ALLOCATION   10000 BYTES

      MAX NO OF TRANSFORMATIONS PERMITTED   100
      MAX NO OF RECODE VALUES   400
      MAX NO OF ARITH..OR LOG.OPERATIONS   300

RESULTING WORKSPACE ALLOCATION   70000 BYTES

    FILE NAME   LEHNLTRI
    VARIABLE LIST   INCOME,FAMSIZE,EXPENSE
    INPUT MEDIUM   DISK
    N OF CASES   UNKNOWN
    INPUT FORMAT   FIXED(76X,2F1.0/12X,F1.0////)

ACCORDING TO YOUR INPUT FORMAT, VARIABLES ARE TO BE READ AS FOLLOWS

VARIABLE	FORMAT	RECORD	COLUMNS
INCOME	F 1. 0	1	77- 77
FAMSIZE	F 1. 0	1	78- 78
EXPENSE	F 1. 0	2	13- 13

THE INPUT FORMAT PROVIDES FOR   3 VARIABLES.   3 WILL BE READ
IT PROVIDES FOR 6 RECORDS ('CARDS') PER CASE.   A MAXIMUM OF   78 'COLUMNS' ARE USED ON A RECORD.

    RECODE   FAMSIZE (2=1)(3,4=2)(5 THRU 9=3)/
                  INCOME (1,2=1)(3,4=2)(5=3)/
                  EXPENSE (1=12.5)(2=22.5)(3=37.5)
                  (4=52.5)(5=70)

    MISSING VALUES EXPENSE (0)
    READ INPUT DATA

DATA TRANSFORMATICN DONE UP TC THIS POINT..

NO OF TRANSFORMATIONS   0
NO OF RECODE VALUES   0
NO OF ARITHM. OR LOG. OPERATICNS   0
THE AMOUNT OF TRANSPACE REQUIRED IS   0 BYTES

CROSSTABS   TABLES= INCOME BY EXPENSE
STATISTICS   ALL

***** GIVEN WORKSPACE ALLOWS FOR   4374 CELLS AND   2 DIMENSIONS FOR CROSSTAB PROBLEM *****

* * * * * * * * * * * * * * * *   C R O S S T A B U L A T I O N   O F   *
INCOME
* * * * * * * * * * * * * * * *   BY EXPENSE   *   PAGE 1 OF 1

	EXPENSE					
COUNT						ROW
ROW PCT						TOTAL
COL PCT						
TOT PCT	13.	23.	38.	53.	70.	
INCOME						
1.	33	226	149	45	11	464
	7.1	48.7	32.1	9.7	2.4	49.7
	84.6	70.2	47.8	23.1	16.9	
	3.5	24.2	16.0	4.8	1.2	
2.	5	73	121	102	31	332
	1.5	22.0	36.4	30.7	9.3	35.6
	12.8	22.7	38.8	52.3	47.7	
	0.5	7.8	13.0	10.9	3.3	
3.	1	23	42	48	23	137
	0.7	16.8	30.7	35.0	16.8	14.7
	2.6	7.1	13.5	24.6	35.4	
	0.1	2.5	4.5	5.1	2.5	
COLUMN	39	322	312	195	65	933
TOTAL	4.2	34.5	33.4	20.9	7.0	100.0

CHI SQUARE = 167.23013 WITH   8 DEGREES OF FREEDOM   SIGNIFICANCE = 0.0
CRAMER'S V = 0.29937
CONTINGENCY COEFFICIENT = 0.38987
LAMBDA (ASYMMETRIC) = 0.16418 WITH INCOME DEPENDENT.   = 0.11948 WITH EXPENSE DEPENDENT.
LAMBDA (SYMMETRIC) = 0.13889
UNCERTAINTY COEFFICIENT (ASYMMETRIC) = 0.09231 WITH INCOME DEPENDENT.   = 0.06745 WITH EXPENSE DEPENDENT.
UNCERTAINTY COEFFICIENT (SYMMETRIC) = 0.07820
KENDALL'S TAU B = 0.36468 SIGNIFICANCE = 0.0
KENDALL'S TAU C = 0.36058 SIGNIFICANCE = 0.0
GAMMA = 0.53056
SOMERS'S D (ASYMMETRIC) = 0.33443 WITH INCOME DEPENDENT.   = 0.39767 WITH EXPENSE DEPENDENT.
SOMERS'S D (SYMMETRIC) = 0.36332
ETA = 0.40195 WITH INCOME DEPENDENT.   = 0.41076 WITH EXPENSE DEPENDENT.

12

An overview of multivariate analytical procedures

Most research issues can be addressed by using the analytical procedures of the past chapter (plus possibly those of the first three sections of Chapter 13). The purpose of this chapter is to briefly describe the various more complicated/fancy/sophisticated techniques which occupy the next five chapters of this book. The procedures mentioned here are becoming increasingly widely used (and unfortunately misused). Knowledge of them is important to users of research, since they are likely to have to decide whether to accept the results of such analysis. While it is possible to reject such analyses out of hand as new fangled nonsense or to blindly accept the results since they are computerized and sophisticated, an approach somewhere in between these two extremes is probably warranted. By understanding what these techniques do, a user of research can more intelligently respond to various suggestions for or results of complex analyses.

This chapter will hopefully provide a useful road map of the next five chapters. It will also provide a good after-the-fact summary. For those of you who decide to skip those chapters, at least you'll have some idea what you're missing.

WHY USE MULTIVARIATE PROCEDURES?

The use of multivariate procedures has become increasingly widespread in marketing research. The reasons for this increased use are also numerous, including the following:

1. Multivariate procedures can assess complex interrelationships among variables more efficiently than simpler procedures such as cross-tabs. This is especially important when a key variable (e.g., sales) is assumed to depend on several other variables simultaneously.

2. Given the large data sets available, multivariate procedures are useful for simplifying them. This simplification often leads to the development of a model which captures much of the information contained in the full data set in a more parsimonious way (e.g., a data set containing a key variable such as sales and 107 possible influences on sales can often be reduced to a model which has sales related to five to ten variables).

3. Multivariate procedures often uncover relations which simpler procedures such as two-way cross-tabs overlook. Conversely, multivariate procedures sometimes indicate that apparently important correlations or cross-tabs are illusory.

4. Multivariate procedures are easy and relatively cheap to use given canned computer programs. (This has led to considerable misuse as well as use.) Also more researchers and managers are appearing who have at least been exposed to such methods.

5. Some people attribute users of multivariate procedures special technical competence (which may or may not be true) as well as greater general competence in making decisions (rarely true). This leads some researchers to use multiviarate procedures to increase their perceived credibility.

There are, then, at least five reasons for the increased use of multivariate procedures. While the fourth (increased availability) may be the most important reason, the first three reasons (advantages vis-a-vis simpler procedures) are good enough to outweight the fifth (false scientification) so that multivariate procedures are a net positive addition to the researcher's tool kit.

SOME KEY MULTIVARIATE METHODS

This section is intended to give a brief/terse overview of some of the most widely used multivariate methods. It is not intended to be either all encompassing or self-sufficient. Rather it provides a brief mention of the techniques which can serve to help decide which to study further. This section also may serve as a useful integrating/review device for those readers who actively study these multivariate methods.

Analysis of variance

Motivation. The basic motivation of analysis of variance (ANOVA) is to discover whether certain variables (factors) influence a key (criterion) variable.

Model. The general form of the model is

Value of criterion variable = Overall mean + Effect of the factors
+ Random component

The specific model depends on the number of factors involved and how they are assumed to effect the criterion variables.

Significance.   The results are tested for statistical significace by a test statistic of the following general form:

$$\text{Test statistic } (F) = \cfrac{\cfrac{\text{Variation in criterion variable attributable to the factors}}{\text{Degrees of freedom of the factors}}}{\cfrac{\text{Unexplained variation}}{\text{Remaining degrees of freedom}}}$$

The larger the test statistic, the larger the effect of the factors is in relation to the residual variation (assumed to be due to chance). Hence big F values imply the factors significantly affect the criterion variables.

Interpretation.   The estimates of the amount of effect each factor has on the criterion variable are the basis for managerial interpretation.

Uses.   The most common use of ANOVA is to analyze the results of an experiment where a few factors are systematically varied to assess their effect on the dependent (criterion) variable. Hence both lab and field experiments often lend themselves to ANOVA. So do various "natural" (unplanned) experiments where, in collecting data, a collection of categorical variables seem likely to have influenced a criterion variable.

Example.   Assume we had a data set which measured the following:

1. Average weekly food expenditures.
2. Number of weekly shopping trips.
3. The importance of nutrition.
4. Age.
5. Income.
6. Family size.

TABLE 12–1
Average weekly food expenditures

Income	Family size			
	2	3 or 4	5 or more	
Under $10,000	$26.00	$35.40	$44.50	$30.60
$10–$20,000	$32.50	$40.90	$52.10	$41.50
Over $20,000	$34.10	$46.20	$56.50	$45.50
	$28.20	$39.70	$50.90	$36.70

If we assumed that Average weekly food expenditures $= f$ (income, family size), we could build a table such as Table 12–1. To see what the influence of income and family size was on food expenditures, we would look at the pattern of average food expenditure in each of the cells of the table. Here we see that both family size and income influence food expenditure, with family size a somewhat stronger influence. To see if the results were statistically significant, we would run an ANOVA and evaluate the resulting F statistic.

AID

AID is a special type of ANOVA which searches a set of possible influences on a criterion variable for the most significant factors in a sequential manner. Its special feature is that it also detects interactions between factors (e.g., it may suggest that education affects food expenditures only in combination with income).

Regression analysis

Motivation. The basic motivation of regression analysis is to predict a criterion (dependent) variable as a function of one or more independent (predictor) variables. It differs from ANOVA in that it assumes the independent variables are intervally scaled.

Model. The basic model of regression is that the dependent variable (Y) is a weighted index of a set of k independent variables:

$$Y = B_0 + B_1 X_1 + B_2 X_2 + \cdots + B_k X_k + \mu$$

where

μ = random component

For example,

Food expenditures $= B_0 + B_1$(income) $+ B_2$(age) $+ \cdots$

Statistical method. The B's ($B_0, B_1, \ldots$) are selected so that the predicted values of the dependent variable, $\hat{Y} = B_0 + B_1 X_1 + B_2 X_2 + \cdots$, are as close to the actual values (Y) as possible. Specifically, the sum of the squared differences between actual and predicted Y values is minimized.

Interpretation. The predictive power of the results is summarized by R, the correlation between the predicted and actual values of the dependent variable. Typically R^2 is analyzed, since it is interpretable as the percent of variation in the dependent variable that is explained by the independent variables. Its range is from 0 (the independent variables are worthless as predictors) to 1 (the independent variables are perfect predictors of the dependent variable). The effects of each of the independent variables are summarized by the B's, which in regression play a role analogous to the effects of the factors in ANOVA and are called, not surprisingly, regression coefficients. B_i is interpreted as the amount the dependent variable (Y) would change if X_i increased by one (in whatever units in which it was measured, for example, dollars, pounds, etc.)

Uses.   Regression analysis is used for a tremendous variety of purposes. Some of the most common are derivation of segments, forecasting, and model building.

Example.   Assume you wanted to use GNP as a predictor of sales of men's clothing. If you plotted the data, you might get Figure 12-1. Re-

FIGURE 12-1
Men's clothing sales versus GNP

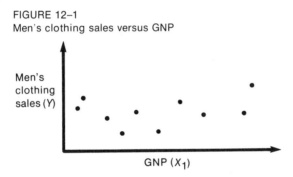

gression analysis would fit a line through these points as in Figure 12-2. The results would be summarized by B_0 (the constant) and B_1 (the amount Y would increase if X_1 went up one). Also R^2 would be available for assessing how well the line fits the points.

FIGURE 12-2
Regression line of men's clothing sales versus GNP

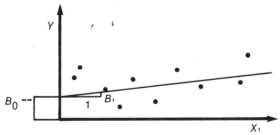

Discriminant analysis

Motivation.   Discriminant analysis is very similar to regression. As in regression analysis, discriminant analysis tries to predict a dependent variable as a function of a set of independent variables. The difference between discriminant analysis and regression analysis is that in discriminant analysis, the dependent variable is assumed to be categorical (e.g., brand last purchased). Hence the thrust of discriminant analysis is to predict group membership.

Model/method. Discriminant analysis constructs indexes of the independent variables which best discriminate between groups. These indexes (known as discriminant functions) are of the following form:

$$\text{Index} = B_1 X_1 + B_2 X_2 + \cdots + B_k X_k$$

Interpretation. The interpretation of discriminant analysis is essentially the same as regression. The B's (discriminant coefficients) are interpreted as the effect of variables on the index. Hence the larger the B associated with a particular variable is, the more important that variable is as a discriminator. The percent of people who can be correctly classified into the correct group by using the discriminant function is interpreted (analogous to R^2) as the measure of the overall accuracy of the results.

Uses. There are two main uses of discriminant analysis. The first use is to search a set of variables to find out which variables best discriminate between the groups. Second, one can utilize the index as a shortcut means of optimally classifying people. This is done by building the weighted index score for a particular case and comparing the score with a cutoff value. (This is the essence of all credit application forms—to collect data which will discriminate good risks from bad risks based on the characteristics of the individual case.)

Example. Assume we were trying to find out who skis based on age and income. If we plotted the data for skiers (S) and nonskiers (N), we might get the results in Figure 12–3. The obvious interpretation of this is that skiers tend to be younger and richer than nonskiers. Here the resulting discriminant function might be

$$\text{Index} = -1.2 \ (\text{age}) + .9 \ (\text{income})$$

FIGURE 12–3
Skiers' (S) and nonskiers' (N) ages and incomes

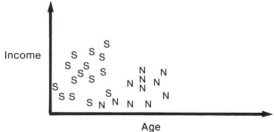

Income

Age

Cluster analysis

Motivation.   The basic purpose of cluster analysis is to group together similar "things" in order to simplify analysis of a situation. For example, I may wish to cluster together consumers with similar characteristics (demographics, psychographics, usage patterns, etc.) in order to create segments.

Method.   Cluster analysis is a loose term for a collection of algorithms which group similar cases together. There are two basic steps involved. First, a measure of similarity between cases must be developed. Second, a procedure for forming groups (clusters, segments) must be selected. Practically, these choices are almost always dictated by available computer algorithms.

Interpretation.   The groups which result are typically profiled in terms of a set of characteristics. If the groups are segments of consumers, the segments are often used to predict the likely results of different marketing strategies.

Example.   Assume I wish to use cluster analysis to form segments of my present and potential customers. Also assume I have a sample of 1,000 respondents who answered a questionnaire about product use, demographics, and psychographics. One approach would be to cluster people based on present product use and look at their characteristics. Alternatively, I might group people based on their demographic and psychographic characteristics and then see if different types of people had different product usage patterns.

Factor analysis

Motivation.   Factor analysis is a special type of cluster analysis. Its essential motivation is to group together variables which are highly correlated.

Model.   The model assumes that the observed variables (X's) are a weighted combination of a set of p underlying factors (f's):

$$X_i = \lambda_{i1}f_1 + \lambda_{i2}f_2 + \cdots + \lambda_{ip}f_p + e_i$$

The procedure most commonly used finds the λ's which best separate the variables into groups.

Interpretation.   The groups are determined by examining the λ's. These values (often called loadings) are the correlations between the variable and the factor. When several variables "load" on a factor, they are assumed to be a group. The overall redundancy of variables can be assessed by examining how well a small number of factors account for the information in the original variables.

Uses. There are several uses of factor analysis, including the following:

1. To find out which variables are most highly correlated.
2. To provide a way to eliminate redundant variables for either subsequent analysis or future data collection.
3. To find a "true" underlying structure.

Example. Assume I had four variables and I wished to reduce them to two. Also assume the correlations were those in Table 12–2. Simply look-

TABLE 12–2
Correlations

Variable	Variable			
	1	2	3	4
1	1	.8	.9	.1
2		1	.7	.05
3			1	.1
4				1

ing at the date would indicate that it would be logical to group variables 1, 2, and 3 together since they all are fairly highly correlated with each other, and to keep variable four separate since it is almost perfectly uncorrelated with the other three variables. That is essentially what factor analysis would do. My reduced set of two variables could then be variable 4 plus any one of variables 1, 2, or 3.

Multidimensional scaling (MDS)

Motivation. The basic assumption underlying multidimensional scaling is that individuals view stimuli in terms of their position on a set of attributes. The purpose of multidimensional scaling is to deduce the geometric (graphical) model they use.

Method. The basic input required is a measure of the similarity between pairs of objects. Given this input, multidimensional scaling algorithms try to construct geometric models where the more similar pairs of objects appear close together and the less similar pairs appear far apart. These procedures typically begin with an initial solution and then attempt to improve it in an iterative manner.

Interpretation. The major element of interpretation is to deduce what dimensions the individual(s) used. This is largely done subjectively. Essentially "naming" the dimensions is done by finding out what characteristics of the objects best explain their relative positions on the dimensions.

Use. The major use of multidimensional scaling is to find the space in which consumers evaluate alternative brands. Having done this, alternative strategies (most notably new product concepts) may be suggested by the results, and a first-cut estimate of their likely success derived.

Example. Assume I asked a sample of consumers to rate the similarity between seven soft drinks. After running a multidimensional scaling program, the output might be that of Figure 12–4. Here we would probably

FIGURE 12–4
Soft drink multidimensional scaling configuration

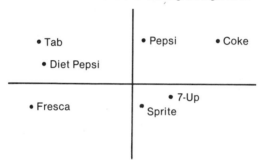

conclude that the horizontal dimension is calories (diet-nondiet) and the vertical dimension flavor (cola–lemon-lime).

Conjoint measurement

Motivation. Conjoint measurement is a special type of ANOVA. It is based on the assumption that an individual's overall evaluation of a product can be explained by the sum (or product) of the utility attributed to its level on each of several attributes. Hence in spirit conjoint measurement is related to multidimensional scaling in that both assume evaluations of alternatives are based on the position of the alternatives on a set of attributes.

Method. Conjoint measurement begins by getting overall evaluations of various combinations of levels on the attributes. These overall evaluations are then decomposed into the utilities attributable to each of the levels of each attribute.

Interpretation. The derived utilities are the basis for interpretation. Attributes on which the utilities differ the most are interpreted as the most important.

Uses. The major use of conjoint measurement is to evaluate the likely consumer attitude toward alternative product designs.

Example. Assume I asked an individual to rank preference for combinations of gas mileage and acceleration. The results might be those of
Table 12–3. Looking at the data, we see that this person is much more
interested in acceleration than gas mileage. Conjoint analysis would quan-

TABLE 12–3
Preference ranking of combinations of mileage and
acceleration

Gas mileage	Acceleration (0–60 mph)		
	7 sec.	10 sec.	18 sec.
15 mpg	3	6	9
20 mpg	2	5	8
25 mpg	1	4	7

tify this by attaching utilities to the three levels of gas mileage and the
three levels of acceleration. For example, these utilities might be as
follows:

Gas mileage			Acceleration (0–60)		
15 mpg	20 mpg	25 mpg	7 sec.	12 sec.	18 sec.
.8	1.0	1.2	1.6	.9	.5

Canonical correlation

Canonical correlation is a mathematical procedure which attempts to
find the relation between a set of independent and a set of dependent
variables. In other words, it is regression with multiple dependent variables. It proceeds by finding linear combinations of the independent variables which are maximally correlated with linear combinations of dependent variables. The approach is mathematically elegant. However, interpretation (and communication) is sufficiently difficult that in general
this is not a very useful technique for most marketing research, and hence
it will not be further discussed.

A TYPOLOGY

There are innumerable ways to distinguish between types of analyses.
Two of the best known appear in Sheth (1971) and Kinnear and Taylor
(1971). Most such typologies place considerable importance on the form

of the data in terms of its scale properties (nominal, ordinal, interval, or ratio). While the type of data available has an important role to play in determining what technique to use, its role is secondary to first deciding what the technique does. (It is also important to point out that the type of data available can be chosen during the design phase of a study and hence overconcern on the scale issue may be unwarranted.) By contrast, this typology focuses on the strength of preconception held by the researcher. As such, it is related to the type of study typology (exploratory, descriptive, causal) previously discussed.

The typology discussed here assumes that analysis ranges from simple perusal of the data to careful model testing and refinement. For the sake of simplicity, most analytical methods can be classified into four categories: descriptive, relationship discovery, structure, derivation, and effect assessment.

Descriptive

Descriptive procedures make no assumptions about the data; they merely describe data. The major example of this type is tabulation which simply reports the percentage of the time each answer was recorded. Other examples include medians and percentiles (if the data is ordinal) and means (if the data is intervally scaled). Hence most of the univariate procedures used in exploratory studies fit this category.

Relationship discovery

These procedures examine variables (usually one pair at a time) to see if they are related. No prior notion about the nature of the relationship is required. The major example of this type of analysis is cross-tabs. If the general nature of the relationship is known, more "powerful" procedures such as Spearmen's rank correlation coefficient (if the relationship is monotonic) or the product-moment correlation (if the relationship is linear) become useful. Such procedures are often used in descriptive studies, especially to uncover which variables are related to two or three key variables.

Structure derivation

These procedures assume that data was generated according to some underlying but unknown structure; they attempt to deduce the structure from the data. For example, cluster analysis assumes that the observations came from groups and attempts to rediscover the groups. Factor analysis is a special case of cluster analysis which attempts to group either variables (based on the correlations between variables across people) or

394

people (based on the correlation of people in terms of their values on the variables across variables). Multidimensional scaling assumes that similarity or preference data was generated by a geometric model of the stimuli and tries to deduce the underlying geometric model.

Effect assessment

These procedures assume that there is a particular kind of relationship in the data. They assume that one variable (called the dependent or criterion) depends on a number of other variables (called independent or predictor variables) in a particular mathematical way. They then proceed to assess/estimate the strength of the dependence of the criterion variables on the predictor variable. The appropriate method of this type to use depends on the scale-type of the independent and dependent variables. Examples of this type of analysis include ANOVA, regression analysis, and discriminant analysis. The advantage of these techniques is that when the researcher correctly identifies (*a*) the critical variables and (*b*) the way they relate to each other, these techniques produce far more information

FIGURE 12–5
Typology of analytical procedures

General category	09 Specific type	Data scale requirements
Descriptive	Tabulations	Categorical (nominal)
	Medians, per- centiles	Ordinal
	Mean	Interval
Relationship discovery	Cross-tabulation	Categorical
	Rank correlation	Ordinal
	Product moment correlation	Interval
Structure derivation	Cluster analysis	Different procedures for each type
	Factor analysis	Interval
	Multidimensional scaling	Ordinal
Effect assessment	ANOVA	Dependent-interval Independent-categorical
	AID	Dependent-interval Independent-categorical
	Regression analysis	Dependent-interval Independent-interval
	Discriminant analysis	Dependent-categorical Independent-interval
	Conjoint	Dependent-ordinal Independent-categorical

than simpler techniques. Their disadvantage is that if the researcher incorrectly identifies the variables or the form of the relationship, the results may be misleading.

A summary of the major types of analytical procedures appears in Figure 12–5. Generally all the techniques in a given category are substitutes for each other and complements to the techniques in the other categories. Put differently, an analysis plan which includes tabulations, factor analysis, and regression may be reasonable while one which attempts to study the relationship of sales to a collection of other variables by means of ANOVA, AID, regression analysis, and discriminant analysis is relatively inefficient.

SUMMARY

On balance, multivariate procedures provide a useful competitive advantage for the researcher who knows how to use them. Three caveats are in order. First, proper use of them requires a reasonable amount of understanding and experience. Second, because many of the techniques are related, there is a diminishing marginal utility of multivariate techniques. Put differently, there is no reason to try every conceivable analytical procedure on a given study—pick the most appropriate one or two. Finally, communication of the results often causes considerable problems. The "uninitiated" may respond with either unabashed (and unjustified) approval or open distrust (often motivated by insecurity). To make the results really useful, every attempt should be made to convert them to a simple form so that the implications can be seen and understood by nontechnicians.

A final point is that it is not necessary to have a deep understanding of the intricacies of all of the procedures. Regression analysis has been in the past and will be for the foreseeable future the most widely used "fancy" marketing research technique. In fact its versatility allows a researcher who understands it plus the basic analytical procedures to handle almost any situation. The moral of this is if you have to pick one of these techniques to learn, pick regression. It is also true that understanding regression makes learning of other multivariate procedures much easier.

BIBLIOGRAPHY

Kinnear, Thomas C., and Taylor, James R. "Multivariate Methods in Marketing Research: A Further Attempt at Classification." *Journal of Marketing,* vol. 35 (October 1971), pp. 56–58.

Sheth, Jagdish N. "The Multivariate Revolution in Marketing Research." *Journal of Marketing,* vol. 34 (January 1971), pp. 13–19.

13 _____

Comparing differences in key variables

In most marketing research studies, there are usually a small number of variables which are the keys to interpretation. For example, in a pricing experiment the key variable is typically sales. When the key variable is measured on an interval or ratio scale, more powerful (parametric) analytical techniques than cross-tabulations are applicable. This chapter will detail some of these analytical procedures.

TESTS CONCERNING ONE SAMPLE, ONE VARIABLE

Concept

Assume that the average consumption of beer in bottles per month were collected from a sample of 289 consumers. Since these consumers were rugby players, it seemed interesting to examine the theory that rugby players are heavy consumers of beer. Assume the data were as follows:

"Typical" beer consumption = 59.8

Sample result: Average beer consumption = 76.2

Given this result, it seems pretty obvious that rugby players are indeed heavy beer consumers. This managerial result/conclusion requires nothing more than the eyeball comparison of the sample mean with the standard. Unfortunately, results are not always this clear-cut. For example, if the average beer consumption in the sample of 289 rugby players had been 61.1, it is unclear whether the "extra" 1.3 bottles are the result of a "true" difference between rugby players and the general population or merely the result of having chosen a particularly heavy drinking sample of rugby players. Similarly if the sample size had been 9 instead of 289, we again become unsure as to the meaningfulness of the difference. In both cases, obviously the *sample* of rugby players differ from the typical consumer. The issue, however, is whether rugby players *in general* differ.

Approach

Whether a difference in a mean is significant or not depends on three things:

1. The standard of comparison (μ).
2. The sample mean ($\bar{x}$).
3. The degree of uncertainty concerning how well the sample mean represents the mean of the population of interest (in the previous example, all rugby players).

We can build an index of significance as follows:

$$\text{Index} = \frac{\text{Sample mean} - \text{Standard}}{\text{Uncertainty}}$$

This index increases as the difference between the sample mean and the standard increases, and decreases as the uncertainty increases.

Drawing on our statistics training (or asking someone who knows what to do), we recall that the uncertainty of our estimate of the sample mean is quantified by its standard deviation:

$$s_{\bar{x}} = \frac{s}{\sqrt{n}}$$

Hence the index becomes

$$t_{n-1} = \frac{\bar{x} - \mu}{s/\sqrt{n}} \tag{13.1}$$

This is the well-known (if you've recently taken a statistics course) t statistic. It tests the null hypothesis:

$H_0 =$ The mean of the population represented by
the sample is equal to the standard ($\bar{x} = \mu$)

Hence a large value for the index would reject the null hypothesis and consequently imply that the population represented by the sample differs from the standard in terms of average behavior. The values can be checked for significance against the values in a t table with $n - 1$ degrees of freedom. Whenever the index is larger than the appropriate table value, the null hypothesis is rejected. For large sample sizes, t is approximately normally distributed. Combining these two points, we can see that (using the .05 significance level as a crude screen) in general t values above 2 will be significant, and those less than 2 are usually not significant.

Examples

Example A. Applying this test to the beer consumption example, we get the following results:

Given:

$$\mu = 59.8$$
$$\bar{x} = 76.2$$
$$n = 289$$
$$s = 34$$

Thus the index becomes

$$t = \frac{76.2 - 59.8}{\frac{34}{\sqrt{289}}} = \frac{16.4}{2} = 8.2 > 2$$

and hence the difference is, as we thought, significant. This means that rugby players consume more beer than typical consumers.

Example B. Now assume the sample mean had been 61.1 instead of 76.2.

Given:

$$\mu = 59.8$$
$$\bar{x} = 61.1$$
$$n = 289$$
$$s = 34$$

The index would now be

$$t = \frac{61.1 - 59.8}{\frac{34}{\sqrt{289}}} = \frac{1.3}{2} = .65 < 2$$

This is not significant. Hence in this case, there is a reasonable chance that the difference between the sample mean and the standard is not representative of a "true" difference in average consumption between rugby players and the typical person.

Example C. Finally, assume we had a sample mean of 76.2, but only a sample size of 9. The results would now be as follows:

Given:

$$\mu = 59.8$$
$$\bar{x} = 76.2$$
$$n = 9$$
$$s = 34$$

Therefore

$$t = \frac{76.2 - 59.8}{\dfrac{34}{\sqrt{9}}} = \frac{16.4}{11.33} = 1.45 < 1.64$$

Hence in this case the difference is not significant. While this may seem surprising given the large difference in mean values, what it says is there is a nontrivial chance that the difference is a fluke due to the small sample size. (A general corollary to this result is that given a large enough sample size, even the smallest numerical difference becomes significant.)

TESTS CONCERNING ONE SAMPLE, ONE PROPORTION

Approach

When the key variable is a binary variable such as a yes-no question, the test just discussed is inappropriate. However, if the proportion of respondents (p) who answer yes is calculated, this can often be compared to a standard (θ) as follows:

$$\text{Index} = \frac{\text{Sample proportion} - \text{Standard}}{\text{Uncertainty}}$$

$$= \frac{p - \theta}{\sqrt{\dfrac{\theta(1 - \theta)}{n}}} \tag{13.2}$$

As n increases, this index[1] becomes approximately normally distributed. The bigger the n and the closer to .5 the p, the better the approximation. Nonetheless, in order to have an arbitrary cutoff, we will say when n is above 30 and p between .1 and .9, this index is approximately normally distributed.

Here the null hypothesis is that the proportion answering yes in the population represented by the sample is the same as the standard: $H_0 : p = \theta$. A big index value (>2 for the .05 significance level) indicates the difference is significant.

Since in many cases we are only concerned about values that exceed (or fall short of) the standard, the test may be set up as a one-tail test as follows: $H_0 : p \geq \theta$ or $H_0 : p \leq \theta$ and hence an index value of greater than 1.64 (or less than -1.64) will be necessary to statistically significantly reject the null hypothesis at the .05 significance level.

---

[1] Some people use $\dfrac{p - \theta}{\sqrt{\dfrac{p(1 - p)}{n}}}$

For practical purposes, the two formulas are usually equivalent because of the insensitivity of $p(1 - p)$ to p.

Examples

Example A. Given:

$$\theta = .2$$
$$p = .3$$
$$n = 100$$

Question: Does the sample group differ from the standard? This indicates we should test $H_0 : p = \theta$. The index (test statistic) becomes

$$\frac{.3 - .2}{\sqrt{\dfrac{(.2)(.8)}{100}}} = \frac{.1}{\dfrac{.4}{10}} = 2.5$$

Hence since $2.5 > 2$, the results in the sample group differ significantly from the standard.

Example B. Given:

$$\theta = .2$$
$$p = .28$$
$$n = 100$$

Question: Are the results significantly greater in the sample group? $(H_0 : p \leq \theta)$

Test statistic:

$$\frac{.28 - .2}{\sqrt{\dfrac{(.2)(.8)}{100}}} = \frac{.08}{\dfrac{.4}{10}} = 2$$

Since $2 > 1.64$ (this is a one-tail test), H_0 is rejected and therefore we conclude that the proportion in the sample group is greater than .2.

TESTS CONCERNING TWO MEANS

Concept

In many circumstances, measurements may be taken on a key variable in samples of two different populations (e.g., experimental and control groups, users and nonusers, etc.). The obvious question which can be asked therefore is whether the two populations represented by the samples are significantly different in terms of some key variable.

Approach

We can again build an index of the significance as follows:

$$\text{Index} = \frac{\text{Difference in means}}{\text{Uncertainty about difference in means}}$$

Let

$\bar{x}_1$ = mean in first sample
n_1 = size of first sample
s_1 = standard deviation of first sample

Then we get

$$\text{Index} = \frac{\bar{x}_1 - \bar{x}_2}{s_{\bar{x}_1 - \bar{x}_2}} \tag{13.3}$$

which is t distributed with $n_1 + n_2 - 2$ degrees of freedom. The null hypothesis is $H_0 : \mu_1 = \mu_2$ (or alternatively $\mu_1 \geq \mu_2$ or $\mu_1 \leq \mu_2$ if we are doing a one-tail test).

The formula for $s_{\bar{x}_1 - \bar{x}_2}$ comes in two forms:

1. If we do not assume $s_1 = s_2$, we have

$$s_{\bar{x} - \bar{x}_2} = \sqrt{\frac{s_1^2}{n_1} + \frac{s_2^2}{n_2}} \tag{13.4}$$

2. If we make the assumption that $s_1 = s_2$, we get

$$s_{\bar{x}_1 - \bar{x}_2} = \hat{s} \sqrt{\frac{1}{n_1} + \frac{1}{n_2}} \tag{13.5}$$

where

$$\hat{s}^2 = \frac{(n_1 - 1)s_1^2 + (n_2 - 1)s_2^2}{n_1 + n_2 - 2}$$

The advantage of assuming $s_1 = s_2$ is that the test is slightly more powerful in that we become more likely to reject the null hypothesis that the means are equal. Practically, however, the results are almost always identical when in fact s_1 and s_2 are close in size.

Example

Given:

$$\bar{x}_1 = 20 \qquad \bar{x}_2 = 22$$
$$s_1^2 = 3.78 \qquad s_2^2 = 10.44$$
$$n_1 = 10 \qquad n_2 = 10$$

Question: Is the mean of the first group significantly less than that of the second?

$$(H_0 : \mu_1 \geq \mu_2)$$

Test statistic:

$$\frac{20 - 22}{\sqrt{\dfrac{3.78}{10} + \dfrac{10.44}{10}}} = \frac{-2}{\sqrt{.378 + 1.044}}$$

$$= \frac{-2}{\sqrt{1.422}} = \frac{-2}{1.19}$$

$$= -1.68 > -1.73(t_{18})$$

Hence we cannot reject H_0 at the .05 significance level, which indicates that the mean of the first group is not significantly less than the mean of the second group.

MATCHED SAMPLE TESTS

The test presented in the previous section assumed the two samples were independent. Yet in many cases, a measure will be taken twice on the same sample. For example, attitudes may be measured before and after exposure to an advertisement. Consider the data in Table 13–1. (As

TABLE 13–1

| Person | Attitude | | Change |
	Before	After	
1	21	24	+3
2	19	23	+4
3	18	19	+1
4	22	18	−4
5	21	25	+4
6	16	17	+1
7	21	24	+3
8	22	22	—
9	21	26	+5
10	19	22	+3
$\bar{x} =$	20	22	20

you may recognize, this is the data which generated the example in the previous section.) Also recall that treating the data as two independent samples led to the conclusion that their means are not different. The real question is whether the average change differed from zero. There are two basic approaches for examining the changes for statistical significance.

Sign test

First, we can simply observe the number of positive changes and see if this is different from 50 percent. If there were no change, we would expect that half would increase and half decrease. This can be set up as a sign test:

$$(13.6)$$

$$\text{Test statistic} = \frac{\text{Proportion of positive changes} - 50 \text{ percent}}{\sqrt{\dfrac{(50)(50)}{n}}}$$

$$H_0 : \text{proportion of positive changes} = 50 \text{ percent}$$

If n is greater than 30, this statistic is approximately normally distributed. Since n is only 10 in Table 13–1, however, we would have to make use of a set of binomial tables. Since these tables indicate that there is a .057 chance of 8, 9, or 10 positive changes given a $p = .5$, we would (just barely) fail to reject the hypothesis of 50 percent at the .05 significance level and hence conclude the changes may be random.

Paired difference test

The second approach to testing for a significant change is to see if the average change is different from zero. The test statistic is

$$t = \frac{\text{Average change}}{\dfrac{s_{change}}{\sqrt{n}}} \tag{13.7}$$

In the example of Table 13–1, we get

$$\text{Average change} = +2.0$$
$$\text{Standard deviation of change} = +2.62$$

Here $(s^2_{change} = \Sigma(\Delta - \bar{\Delta})^2 = \Sigma(\Delta - 2)^2 = (3 - 2)^2 + (4 - 2)^2 + \cdots + (3 - 2)^2 = 62$. Thus $s_{change} = \sqrt{62/9} = 2.62$.)

Thus

$$t = \frac{2}{\dfrac{2.62}{\sqrt{10}}} = \frac{2}{\dfrac{2.62}{3.17}} = 2.41$$

Hence at the .05 level, we can reject the null hypothesis since the table value of t is $1.83 < 2.41$. (Note this is not a very dramatic change from the results of the t test assuming independence of the two samples.) The point, however, is that it is incorrect to treat matched samples as independent, and some significant changes may be lost if the incorrect procedure is applied.

TESTS CONCERNING TWO PROPORTIONS

Approach

Just as it is possible to test two means to see if they differ significantly, so is it possible to compare two proportions. The formula for this is

$$\text{Index} = \frac{p_1 - p_2}{s_{p_1-p_2}}$$

where

p_1, p_2 = proportions having the characteristic in the first and second samples respectively

n_1, n_2 = sizes of the first and second samples respectively

$s_{p_1-p_2}$ = standard deviation of the difference in proportions

This index is approximately normally distributed for large sample sizes. A pooled estimate of the overall proportion is derived by assuming the proportions are equal in the two groups.

$$\pi = \frac{n_1 p_1 + n_2 p_2}{n_1 + n_2} \tag{13.8}$$

Thus

$$s_{p_1-p_2} = \sqrt{\frac{\pi(1 - \pi)}{n_1} + \frac{\pi(1 - \pi)}{n_2}} = \sqrt{\frac{n_1 + n_2}{n_1 n_2}} \sqrt{\pi(1 - \pi)} \tag{13.9}$$

Example

Given:

1st sample	2d sample
$n_1 = 100$	$n_2 = 150$
$p_1 = .2$	$p_2 = .3$

$$H_0 : \theta_1 = \theta_2 \quad \text{(no significant difference)}$$

Test statistic:

$$\frac{.2 - .3}{s_{p_1-p_2}}$$

Hence

$$\pi = \frac{20 + 45}{250} = .26$$

$$s_{p_1-p_2} = \sqrt{(.26)(.74)} \sqrt{\frac{250}{15,000}}$$
$$= (.439)(.129)$$
$$= .0566$$

Therefore the test statistic $= \dfrac{.1}{.0566} = 1.77 < 1.96.$

In this case, the difference is not significant at the .05 level. Notice here that an apparently large difference in proportions is not significant. The reason for this is the remarkable unreliability of proportions based on samples as large as 100 in size. Hence one moral of this example is beware of being overly zealous in interpreting differences in proportions; they may not be significant.

An alternative (and equivalent) test is available based on the χ^2 for a 2×2 contingency table. For the previous example, we can derive Table 13–2. The frequency expected table becomes that of Table 13–3. Hence

TABLE 13–2
Actual data

	Response		
Sample	Yes	No	Total
1	20	80	100
2	45	105	150
Total	65	185	250

TABLE 13–3
Expected data

	Response		
Sample	Yes	No	Total
1	26	74	100
2	39	111	150
Total	65	185	250

we get

$$\chi^2 = \frac{(20 - 26)^2}{26} + \frac{(80 - 74)^2}{74} + \frac{(45 - 39)^2}{39} + \frac{(105 - 111)^2}{111}$$
$$= \frac{36}{26} + \frac{36}{74} + \frac{36}{39} + \frac{36}{111}$$
$$= 1.38 + .49 + .92 + .32$$
$$= 3.11$$

Since the .05 "cutoff" for a significant χ^2 with one degree of freedom is 3.84, we again conclude that the difference is not significant. (This test can be easily expanded to many samples.)

TESTS CONCERNING SEVERAL MEANS

In some situations, multiple samples are available. For example, different respondents may be exposed to four separate ads. To see if the four groups differ, two basic approaches are possible. First, all pairs (in this case six) of samples can be compared with the two-sample t tests. This is fairly cumbersome. (Also, given enough t tests, some are likely to appear significant due to chance; for example, 1 of 20 at the .05 significance level.) Hence many people prefer to examine the four samples simultaneously. The methodology for such examination is essentially an extension of the two-sample t test known as ANOVA—analysis of variance.

Motivation

The simplest form of ANOVA deals with the case where there are multiple samples with each sample corresponding to a different level of a single control variable. For example, assume I measured the sales response to three different color packages in an experiment with four different stores using each color (Table 13–4). Ignoring for the moment the

TABLE 13–4
Sales as a function of package color

	Package color		
	A	B	C
	14	8	8
	10	14	6
	11	3	5
	9	7	1
Average sales	11	8	5

crucial issue of whether the stores were comparable, we address the issue of whether the sales differed under the three colors. This can best be seen managerially by plotting the average sales versus color curve of Figure 13–1. Apparently color A is the best. The question which might be asked, however, is whether these differences are statistically significant.

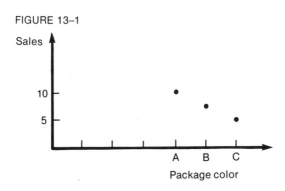

FIGURE 13–1

Procedure

Analysis of variance is logically quite simple. It consists of seeing whether the means of the several samples are far apart relative to our uncertainty as to what the means really are. Again we can construct an index:

$$\text{Index} = \frac{\text{Difference among means}}{\text{Uncertainty}}$$

For simple one-way ANOVA with only two groups (only one variable changes across the samples), the problem can be seen graphically (Figure 13–2). In case 1, the two samples clearly differ in that all the x values for sample A are less than the x values for sample B. The same is true in case 2. Even though the means are close together, the results are sufficiently consistent to indicate a significant difference in means between the two samples. Case 3 shows a weak relationship, but in spite of the largest mean difference, substantial overlap exists due to the variability of results within samples A and B. Case 4 shows so much overlap that we might well argue the difference in means is not significant. In order to capture the essence of this logic, the index could well be

$$\text{Index} = \frac{\bar{x}_A - \bar{x}_B}{s_{\bar{x}_A - \bar{x}_B}}$$

which was the two-sample t statistic discussed previously. In order to extend this to more than two samples, two changes are required. First, instead of measuring the difference between pairs of sample means, we

408

FIGURE 13–2

Case 1 $f(x)$

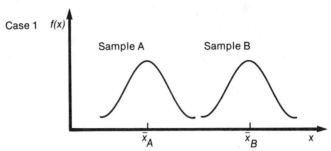

Sample A   Sample B

$\bar{x}_A$ $\bar{x}_B$ x

Case 2 $f(x)$

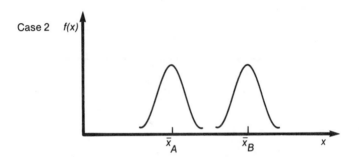

$\bar{x}_A$ $\bar{x}_B$ x

Case 3 $f(x)$

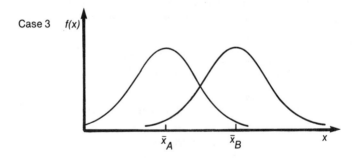

$\bar{x}_A$ $\bar{x}_B$ x

Case 4 $f(x)$

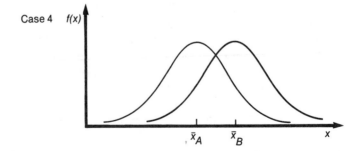

$\bar{x}_A$ $\bar{x}_B$ x

FIGURE 13–3

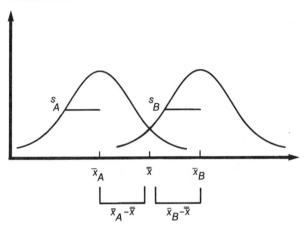

measure the difference between each sample mean and the overall mean ($\bar{\bar{x}}$) (see Figure 13–3). Secondly, we use as a measure of uncertainty the pooled estimate of s_A and s_B. By squaring these differences and also the measure of uncertainty, we get

$$\text{Index} = \frac{(\bar{x}_A - \bar{\bar{x}})^2 + (\bar{x}_B - \bar{\bar{x}})^2}{\hat{s}^2}$$

where $\bar{\bar{x}}$ is the overall mean across both samples. Since both numerator and denominator are variances (hence the term analysis of variance), this index follows the F distribution and can be checked for statistical significance.

ONE-WAY ANOVA

Formulas

Mathematics often are so formidable that they inhibit understanding. Also since practical applications of ANOVA generally are done on "canned" computer programs, knowledge of the algebra used is unnecessary to use the procedure for detecting significant influences. Nonetheless, in this case some derivations are very useful for explaining the "magic" formulas used. Hence this section attempts to briefly delineate the formulas used for one-way ANOVA.

Each observation differs in value from the overall mean by some amount ($x - \bar{\bar{x}}$). Some of this difference may be attributable to the influence of another variable (i.e., color A or B). The rest is essentially random/unexplained. The procedure followed in ANOVA attempts to partition the variance ($x - \bar{\bar{x}}$) into two subsets: that attributable to the influence of another variable (commonly called the treatment effect) and the rest. The model which underlies this analysis is, in words:

Value of dependent variable = f(levels of independent variables) + random element

The dependent variable is assumed to be intervally scaled and the independent variables treated as though they were categorical (nominally scaled). For one-way ANOVA, the model becomes

$$x_{jk} = \bar{\bar{x}} + C_j + e_{jk} \tag{13.8}$$

where

x_{jk} = value of the dependent variable for the kth person in the jth sample (exposed to the jth level of the independent variable)
$\bar{\bar{x}}$ = overall mean
C_j = treatment effect of the jth level of the independent variable
$\quad = \bar{x}_j - \bar{x}$
e_{jk} = random part of the kth observation in the jth sample.

Consider again our original example for one-way ANOVA with three colored packages (Table 13–4). In this case, the overall mean ($\bar{\bar{x}}$) is 8. The treatment effect of the first level (C_1) is $\bar{x}_1 - \bar{\bar{x}} = 11 - 8 = +3$. Similarly C_2 and C_3 are 0 and -3 respectively. To see how the model works, consider the second observation in the color A sample:

$$x_{12} = \bar{\bar{x}} + C_1 + e_{12}$$

or

$$10 = 8 + 3 + e_{12}$$

Hence

$$e_{12} = -1 \text{ to "balance" the books}$$

(Equivalently, $e_{12} = x_{12} - \bar{x}_1 = 10 - 11 = -1$.)

The statistical test for significant differences will thus be based on the relative size of the C_j's and the e_{jk}'s. The test is developed by taking the total variance in the x values and partitioning it into two parts: that due to the differences between group means and the overall mean (C_j's) and that due to the "residual" error (e_{jk}'s):

$$\text{Total variation} = \sum_{j=1}^{c} \sum_{k=1}^{n_j} (x_{jk} - \bar{\bar{x}})^2 \tag{13.9}$$

where

c = number of categories of the independent variable (for example, three colors)
n_j = number of observations of the key variable when exposed to level j of the independent variable

x_{jk} = value of the key variable in the kth observation in the jth sample
$\bar{\bar{x}}$ = overall mean

This can be rewritten as the sum of two parts:

"Between" sum of squares (treatment):

$$\sum_{j=1}^{c} \sum_{k=1}^{n_j} (\bar{x}_j - \bar{\bar{x}})^2 = \sum_{j=1}^{c} n_j(\bar{x}_j - \bar{\bar{x}})^2 \tag{13.10}$$

"Within" sum of squares (unexplained):

$$\sum_{j=1}^{c} \sum_{k=1}^{n_j} (x_{jk} - \bar{x}_j)^2 \tag{13.11}$$

Two assumptions are necessary:
1. The variances in the separate samples are equal ($s_1^2 = s_2^2 = \cdots = s_c^2$).
2. The key variable (x) is normally distributed.

Statistical test

The key issue in ANOVA is whether the differences in means between the groups is large in relation to the uncertainty/variability within the groups on the key variable. Hence we develop an index as follows:

$$\text{Index} = \frac{\sum_{j=1}^{c} n_j(\bar{x}_j - \bar{\bar{x}})^2 \Big/ (c-1)}{\sum_{j=1}^{c} \sum_{k=1}^{n_j} (x_{jk} - \bar{x}_j)^2 \Big/ (n-c)} \tag{13.12}$$

This index can be compared with the F table with $(c-1)$ and $(n-c)$ degrees of freedom. The calculation steps for obtaining this statistic are often summarized in a table (Table 13-5). The null hypothesis is that all

TABLE 13–5
One-way ANOVA

Source	Sum of squares	Degrees of freedom	Mean square (SS/d.f.)	F
Treatment (influencing variable)	$\sum_{j=1}^{c} n_j(\bar{x}_j - \bar{\bar{x}})^2$	$c-1$	$\dfrac{\sum_{j=1}^{c} n_j(\bar{x}_j - \bar{\bar{x}})^2}{c-1} = A$	$\dfrac{A}{B}$
Unexplained	$\sum_{j=1}^{c} \sum_{k=1}^{n_j} (x_{jk} - \bar{x}_j)^2$	$n-c$	$\dfrac{\sum_{j=1}^{c} \sum_{k=1}^{n_j} (x_{jk} - \bar{x}_j)^2}{n-c} = B$	
Total	$\sum_{j=1}^{c} \sum_{k=1}^{n_j} (x_{jk} - \bar{\bar{x}})^2$	$n-1$		

the treatment groups have equal means $(H_0 : \bar{x}_1 = \bar{x}_2 = \cdots = \bar{x}_c)$. The test statistic is $F_{c-1,n-c,\alpha}$.

Numerical example

Returning again to the packaging color example (Table 13–4), we have

$$\text{Total sum of squares} = \sum_{j=1}^{3} \sum_{k=1}^{4} (x_{jk} - \bar{\bar{x}})^2$$
$$= (14 - 8)^2 + (10 - 8)^2 + (11 - 8)^2 + (9 - 8)^2$$
$$+ (8 - 8)^2 + (14 - 8)^2 + (3 - 8)^2 + (7 - 8)^2$$
$$+ (8 - 8)^2 + (6 - 8)^2 + (5 - 8)^2 + (1 - 8)^2$$
$$= 174$$

$$\text{Treatment sum of squares} = \sum_{j=1}^{3} \sum_{k=1}^{4} (\bar{x}_j - \bar{\bar{x}})^2$$
$$= \sum_{j=1}^{3} 4(\bar{x}_j - \bar{\bar{x}})^2$$
$$= 4(11 - 8)^2 + 4(8 - 8)^2 + 4(5 - 8)^2$$
$$= 72$$

$$\text{Unexplained sum of squares} = \sum_{j=1}^{3} \sum_{k=1}^{4} (x_{jk} - \bar{x}_j)^2$$
$$= (14 - 11)^2 + (10 - 11)^2 + (11 - 11)^2$$
$$+ (9 - 11)^2 + (8 - 8)^2 + (10 - 8)^2$$
$$+ (3 - 8)^2 + (7 - 8)^2 + (8 - 5)^2$$
$$+ (6 - 5)^2 + (5 - 5)^2 + (1 - 5)^2$$
$$= 102$$

(Alternatively, Unexplained sum of squares = Total sum of squares − Treatment sum of squares = 174 − 72 = 102.)

Interpretation

By using either the formulas just discussed or a canned computer program, we can construct an ANOVA table (Table 13–6). The key to in-

TABLE 13–6
ANOVA table

Source	Sum of squares	Degrees of freedom	Mean square	F
Treatment (colors)	72	2	36	3.18
Unexplained	102	9	11.33	
Total	174	11		

terpretation is the test statistic F of 3.18. This statistic follows the F distribution with 2, 9 degrees of freedom. Going to the F table, we see that at the .05 significance level, $F_{2,9} = 4.26$. Since $3.29 < 4.26$, we fail to reject the null hypothesis of equal mean response to the three package colors. In other words, the differences are not significant. The reason for this is that the variation within the three samples "swamps" the differences in means among the three samples.

TWO-WAY ANOVA

The next logical extension of the ANOVA method is to the case where there are two influencing variables. For example, assume that in addition to varying package color, we also changed advertising strategy, as in Table 13–7. This is a factorial design: all possible combinations

TABLE 13–7
Sales results as a function of package color and advertising strategy

	Package color			Average sales for each advertising strategy	Effect of advertising strategy (R_i)
	A	B	C		
Advertising strategy I:	14	8	8	10	+2
	10	14	6		
Advertising strategy II:	11	3	5	6	−2
	9	7	1		
Average sales for each color	11	8	5		
Effect of color (C_j)	+3	0	−3		

$(2 \times 3 = 6)$ of package color and advertising strategy are tested. There are also samples of size 2 in each of the six possible treatments. The possible treatments are often called cells. The condition of equal cell sizes is common to many experiments.

Model

This section describes the model used. As such it is culturally interesting but for many readers, its costs may outweigh the benefits. In short, if it's confusing, skip it. The section is useful but not essential to the use of ANOVA.

Examining the relative effects of the two variables is done by extending the one-variable procedure. We redefine the model as follows:

$$x_{ijk} = \bar{\bar{x}} + R_i + C_j + I_{ij} + e_{ijk} \qquad (13.13)$$

where

x_{ijk} = kth observations in the sample with the ith level of the row variable and the jth level of the column variable.

R_i = average effect of the ith level of the row variable = $\bar{x}_i - \bar{\bar{x}}$

C_j = average effect of the jth level of the column variable = $\bar{x}_j - \bar{\bar{x}}$

I_{ij} = interaction effect of the ith level of the row variable interacting with the jth level of the column variable = $\bar{x}_{ij} - \bar{x}_i - \bar{x}_j + \bar{\bar{x}}$

$\bar{x}_{ij}$ = mean of the dependent variable in the ith level of the row variable and the jth level of the column variable.

Conceptually, an interaction is the special effect due to putting two or more features in combination which cannot be predicted by knowing the effects of the two features separately. Hence it is related to the notion of synergy and the discovery of particularly felicitous (or disastrous) combinations of factors in terms of their effect on the key (dependent) variable. Besides such obvious examples as nitro and glycerin, a variety of examples can be cited, but aesthetic items (music, paintings, etc.) are obvious examples of cases in which the whole is not the sum of the parts. For example, a blue color package combined with an advertising strategy using mood images and jazz music might be more effective than we would expect from the addition of a blue color and mood advertising effects. Put differently, red might be the best color and factual the best advertising strategy when studied separately but the combination of blue and mood advertising might be better than the combination of red and factual advertising, as in Table 13–8. The importance of the interaction term is that its significance indicates that there is a synergistic/nonadditive combination of the two variables which is particularly effective. If an interaction term is not significant, it means that optimum overall strategy

TABLE 13–8
Average responses ($\bar{x}_{ij}$)

Ad type	Color			$\bar{x}_i$	R_i
	Red	Blue	Yellow		
Mood	7	11	3	7	.33
Factual	10	4	10	8	1.33
Score	7	3	5	5	-1.67
$\bar{x}_j$	8	6	6	6.67	
C_j	1.33	-.67	-.67		

may be obtained by separately choosing the best level of the two variables and then using them in combination. In order to estimate interactions, there must be at least two observations per cell.

Statistical formulas

The partitioning of the variance done in the two-variable case with equal cell sizes can be viewed as a sequential process of continually pulling apart (decomposing) the "unexplained" variance into that part attributable to some variable and that part which is not. By first removing the variance attributable to the column variables as in one-way ANOVA, one can proceed to pull out the variance attributable to the row variables and then the variance attributable to the interactions as follows:

$$\text{Total variance:} \quad \sum_{i=1}^{r} \sum_{j=1}^{c} \sum_{k=1}^{n_{ij}} (x_{ijk} - \bar{\bar{x}})^2 \tag{13.14}$$

$$\text{Column variance:} \quad \sum_{i=1}^{r} \sum_{j=1}^{c} \sum_{k=1}^{n_{ij}} (\bar{x}_j - \bar{\bar{x}})^2 = \sum_{j=1}^{c} n_j(\bar{x}_j - \bar{\bar{x}})^2 \tag{13.15}$$

$$\text{Row variance:} \quad \sum_{i=1}^{r} \sum_{j=1}^{c} \sum_{k=1}^{n_{ij}} (\bar{x}_i - \bar{\bar{x}})^2 = \sum_{i=1}^{r} n_i(\bar{x}_i - \bar{\bar{x}})^2 \tag{13.16}$$

$$\text{Residual variance:} \quad \sum_{i=1}^{r} \sum_{j=1}^{c} \sum_{k=1}^{n_{ij}} (x_{ijk} - \bar{x}_i - \bar{x}_j + \bar{\bar{x}})^2 \tag{13.17}$$

$$\text{Interactions:} \quad \sum_{i=1}^{r} \sum_{j=1}^{c} \sum_{k=1}^{n_{ij}} (\bar{x}_{ij} - \bar{x}_i - \bar{x}_j + \bar{\bar{x}})^2$$

$$= \sum_{i=1}^{r} \sum_{j=1}^{c} n_{ij}(\bar{x}_{ij} - \bar{x}_i - \bar{x}_j + \bar{\bar{x}})^2 \tag{13.18}$$

$$\text{Within variance:} \quad \sum_{i=1}^{r} \sum_{j=1}^{c} \sum_{k=1}^{n_{ij}} (x_{ijk} - \bar{x}_{ij})^2 \tag{13.19}$$

where

c = number of categories in the column variable
r = number of categories in the row variable
n_{ij} = number of observations exposed to the ith level of the row variable and the jth level of the column variable

This process can be viewed graphically in Figure 13–4. Notice that the within variance is the difference between the cell mean and the individual values in the cell. This is in essence the irreducible variance which is unexplained and unexplainable given the two variables. (You may also notice that unless there is more than one observation per cell, there is no way to calculate the within variance and hence no way to separate the

FIGURE 13–4
Variance decomposition in two-way ANOVA

Level of partitioning

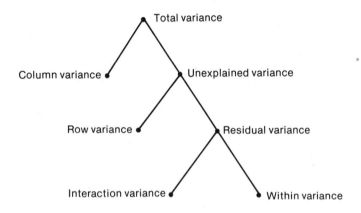

interaction effect from within variance.) The other three variances (column, row, and interaction) divide up the explainable variance by assigning it to its "cause."

Example

Two-way ANOVA with no interactions. The simplest form of two-way ANOVA assumes no interactions. Hence the variance is partitioned into three parts (see Table 13–9):

TABLE 13–9
Two-way ANOVA without interactions

Source	Sum of squares	Degrees of freedom	Mean square
Column	$\sum_{j=1}^{c} n_j(\bar{x}_j - \bar{\bar{x}})^2 = ①$	$c - 1$	$\dfrac{①}{c - 1} = A$
Row	$\sum_{i=1}^{r} n_i(\bar{x}_i - \bar{\bar{x}})^2 = ②$	$r - 1$	$\dfrac{②}{r - 1} = B$
Residual ...	$\sum_{i=1}^{r}\sum_{j=1}^{c}\sum_{k=1}^{n_{ij}} (x_{ijk} - \bar{x}_i - \bar{x}_j + \bar{\bar{x}})^2 = ③$	$n - r - c + 1$	$\dfrac{③}{n - r - c + 1} = C$
Total .	$\sum_{i=1}^{r}\sum_{j=1}^{c}\sum_{k=1}^{n_{ij}} (x_{ijk} - \bar{\bar{x}})^2$	$n - 1$	

Column variance: Equation (13.15).
Row variance: Equation (13.16).
Residual variance:[2] Equation (13.17).

The test for column effects (H_0: all $\bar{x}_j$'s are equal) is F with $c - 1$ and $n - r - c + 1$ degrees of freedom, and compares the column and residual variances. Similarly the test for row effects (H_0: all $\bar{x}_i$'s are equal) is F with $r - 1$ and $n - r - c + 1$ degrees of freedom, and compares the row and residual variances. To see how to apply these formulas, again return to the package color and advertising strategy example (Table 13–7). First calculate the sums of squares:

$$\text{Column sum of squares} = 4(11 - 8)^2 + 4(8 - 8)^2 + 4(5 - 8)^2$$
$$= 72$$

$$\text{Row sum of squares} = 6(10 - 8)^2 + 6(6 - 8)^2$$
$$= 48$$

$$\text{Residual}^3 \text{ sum of squares} = 174 - 72 - 48 = 54$$

The resulting ANOVA table then becomes Table 13–10.

TABLE 13–10

Source	Sum of squares	Degrees of freedom	Mean square (SS/d.f.)	F
Columns (colors)	72	2	36	5.33
Rows (advertising)	48	1	48	7.11
Residual	54	8	6.75	
Total	174	11		

---

[2] It is easier to compute the residual variance as Total variance – Column variance – row variance.

[3] To calculate the residuals directly, we first generate a table for $\bar{x}_i + \bar{x}_j - \bar{\bar{x}} = \bar{\bar{x}} + R_i + C_j$:

13	10	7
9	6	3

We then get the residual sum of squares as $= (14 - 13)^2 + (10 - 13)^2 + (8 - 10)^2 + (14 - 10)^2 + (8 - 7)^2 + (6 - 7)^2 + (11 - 9)^2 + (9 - 9)^2 + (3 - 6)^2 + (7 - 6)^2 + (5 - 3)^2 + (1 - 3)^2 = 54$.

The test for the significance of the column effect at the .05 significance level is to compare 5.33 with $F_{2,8} = 4.46$. Since $5.33 > 4.46$, we reject the null hypothesis that the column means are equal. In other words, the package colors produce significantly different sales. Similarly we can test the rows by comparing 7.11 with $F_{.05,1,8} = 5.32$. Since $7.11 > 5.32$, we conclude that advertising also significantly influence sales. (Put differently, we can predict sales significantly more accurately from $\bar{x} + C_j + R_i$ than we can from $\bar{x}$ alone.)

It is interesting to note that the column effects now appear to be significant whereas in the simple one-way analysis they were not. The explanation for this is that the row effects, which were not accounted for in the one-way ANOVA, inflated the unexplained variance sufficiently to mask the effect of package color.

Two-way ANOVA with interactions. The same data just analyzed can be examined for the presence of interactions (Table 13–11). The column,

TABLE 13–11
ANOVA table

Source	Sum of squares	Degrees of freedom	Mean square
Column	$\sum_{j=1}^{c} n_j(\bar{x}_j - \bar{\bar{x}})^2 = \boxed{1}$	$c - 1$	$\dfrac{\boxed{1}}{c - 1} = A$
Row	$\sum_{i=1}^{r} n_i(\bar{x}_i - \bar{\bar{x}})^2 = \boxed{2}$	$r - 1$	$\dfrac{\boxed{2}}{r - 1} = B$
Interaction	$\sum_{i=1}^{r}\sum_{j=1}^{c} n_{ij}(\bar{x}_{ij} - \bar{x}_i - \bar{x}_j + \bar{\bar{x}})^2 = \boxed{3}$	$rc - c - r + 1$	$\dfrac{\boxed{3}}{rc - c - r + 1} = C$
Within	$\sum_{i=1}^{r}\sum_{j=1}^{c}\sum_{k=1}^{n_{ij}} (x_{ijk} - \bar{x}_{ij})^2 = \boxed{4}$	$n - rc$	$\dfrac{\boxed{4}}{n - rc} = D$
Total		$n - 1$	

row, and total variance formulas are identical to those of the two-way without interaction formulas. The interaction and within formulas are those of (13.18) and (13.19):

$$\text{Interaction variance: } \sum_{i=1}^{r} \sum_{j=1}^{c} n_{ij}(\bar{x}_{ij} - \bar{x}_i - \bar{x}_j + \bar{\bar{x}})^2$$

$$\text{Within variance: } \sum_{i=1}^{r} \sum_{j=1}^{c} \sum_{k=1}^{n_{ij}} (x_{ijk} - \bar{x}_{ij})^2$$

Returning to our example, we calculate the interaction variance as follows:

TABLE 13–12
Cell means

	Color		
Ad strategy	A	B	C
I	12	11	7
II	10	5	3

First, produce a table of cell means ($\bar{x}_{ij}$'s) as in Table 13–12. Second, produce the following $\bar{\bar{x}} + R_i + C_j = \bar{x}_i + \bar{x}_j - \bar{\bar{x}}$ table:

13	10	7
9	6	3

The difference between the values in the two tables are the interactions (I_{ij}'s):

−1	1	0
1	−1	0

Hence the interaction variance is given by

$$2(-1)^2 + 2(1)^2 + 2(0)^2 + 2(1)^2 + 2(-1)^2 + 2(0)^2 = 8$$

To calculate the within variance, we compare the values of each observation with the cell means $\bar{x}_{ij}$:

$$
\begin{aligned}
\text{Within variance} = {}& (14 - 12)^2 + (10 - 12)^2 + (8 - 11)^2 \\
& + (14 - 11)^2 + (8 - 7)^2 + (6 - 7)^2 \\
& + (11 - 9)^2 + (9 - 9)^2 + (3 - 5)^2 \\
& + (7 - 5)^2 + (5 - 3)^2 + (1 - 3)^2 \\
= {}& 46
\end{aligned}
$$

The resulting ANOVA table is shown as Table 13–13. The table values with which we compare the computed F are $F_{.05, 2, 6} = 5.14$ for both the

TABLE 13–13
Two-way ANOVA with interactions

Source	Sum of squares	Degrees of freedom	Mean square	F
Column	72	2	36	4.69
Row....................	48	1	48	6.26
Interaction	8	2	4	.52
Within	46	6	7.67	
Total	174	11		

column and interaction effects and $F_{.05, 1, 6} = 5.99$ for the row effects. This implies that only the row effects are significant. The column effects now appear to be insignificant (at the .05 significance level). While the "right" way to interpret this depends on the purpose of the analysis, it would be appropriate to return to the simple two-way without interaction analysis and conclude that both color and advertising influence sales and that they can be considered independently of each other.

ANOVA—A PICTORIAL/MANAGERIAL INTERPRETATION

The awkward formulas and terminology of ANOVA often obscure what is going on. Remembering that the objective of any type of analysis is to make data clearer, it is useful to look at the example just completed in managerial terms. We can best do that by the inelegant but effective method of plotting the results. The mean sales for the different package

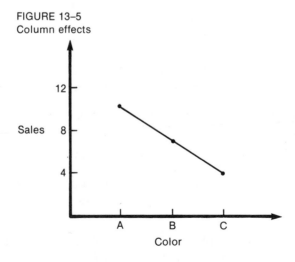

FIGURE 13–5
Column effects

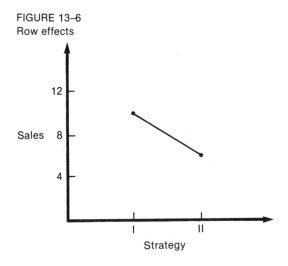

FIGURE 13–6
Row effects

Sales

Strategy

designs and ads are shown in Figures 13–5 and 13–6. Let us first make two rather broad assumptions that (*a*) all the colors are equally costly, as are the advertising strategies, and (*b*) the short-run experiment will be projectable both to the total market and over time. Faced with these results, any manager (or person with an IQ above that of a kumquat) would decide to use color A and advertising strategy I—exactly the correct decision. One need only compute conditional means to draw this conclusion, and it is in fact the correct decision regardless of whether the differences are statistically significant or not. What checking for statistical significance does is provide a flag to indicate whether the best guess (e.g., color A) is really so much better than the other choices that it is worth arguing for.

The interaction concept is only slightly more involved. We recall that the average sales for each of the cells were those in Table 13–12. Faced with this, the manager would again select the combination of color A and advertising strategy I. Conceivably, however, a slight change could have made color B and advertising strategy I best, even though on average color A and advertising strategy I were best when color and advertising strategy were considered separately. The "flag" for this situation would be a significant interaction term in the analysis. In fact, all possible combinations of significant interactions and row or column variables are possible. These possible combinations can be displayed graphically (Figure 13–7). The managerial value of ANOVA, then, is obtained by observing the average response to different combinations of the influencing variables. The statistical tests indicate whether the differences are real or illusory.

FIGURE 13–7
Sales as a function of color and advertising

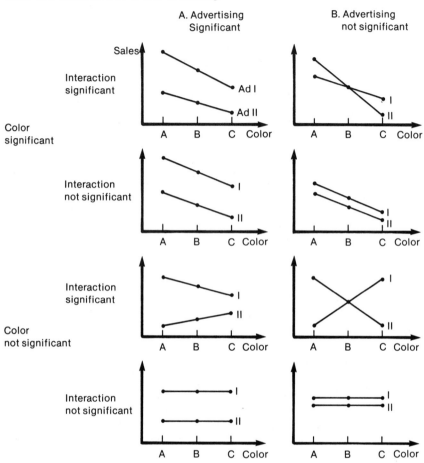

A NUTRITION EXAMPLE

In order to see how ANOVA can be applied to nonexperimental data, consider again the nutritional study which has been mentioned throughout this book. In this case, assume we want to examine the effect of family size and household income on weekly food expenditures. The original data on 933 respondents (7 failed to answer all three questions) was coded as in Table 13–14. As you may notice, this categorization is somewhat unusual since both family size and income are variables which could be considered intervally scaled. Similarly the use of median category values to represent food expenditure on an interval scale is not without error.

TABLE 13–14
Coding method

Family size	
Actual number	*Category*
2	1
3 or 4	2
5 or more	3
Income	
Actual answer	*Category*
Under $10,000	1
$10,000–$20,000	2
Over $20,000	3
Food expenditure	
Answer	*Value*
Under $15	$12.50
$15–$29	22.50
$30–$44	37.50
$45–$60	52.50
Over $60	70.00

Suffice it to say that such recoding is both pedigogically and practically useful, in this case mostly the former.

It is possible to look at the variables separately. Studying the effect of family size, we find that average expenditures vary by family size (Table 13–15). Obviously this difference is very substantial. One-way ANOVA

TABLE 13–15
Family size versus expenditure

Family size category	Number in category	Average expenditures	Effect
1 (2)	411	$28.17	−$ 8.51
2 (3 or 4)	350	39.70	3.02
3 (5 or more)	172	50.86	14.18

(Table 13–16) clearly confirms this. The F of 222.4 is very significant at any reasonable significance level. Food expenditures also vary by income category (Table 13–17). This difference, though not quite as massive as that due to family size, is still clearly significant (Table 13–18).

Since both of these variables are significant, an obvious extension of the analysis is to perform a two-way ANOVA with interactions. In this

TABLE 13–16
One-way ANOVA for family size

Source	d.f.	Sum of squares	Mean square	F
Between (family size)	2	67,535	33,767.5	222.4
Within (unexplained)	930	141,190	151.8	
Total	932	208,725		

TABLE 13–17
Income versus expenditure

Income category	Number in category	Average expenditure	Effect
1	464	$30.64	−$6.04
2	332	41.47	4.79
3	137	45.51	8.83

TABLE 13–18
One-way ANOVA for income

Source	d.f.	Sum of squares	Mean square	F
Between (income)	4	35,217	8,804.3	47.1
Within (unexplained)	928	173,507	187.0	
Total	932	208,724		

case, however, we no longer have an equal number of observations per cell. Put differently, family size and income are related. Hence unlike the previous example, the sequential partitioning formulas for the variance no longer apply. Fortunately someone programmed the computer with the correct formulas (we hope). The average expenditure pattern shows substantial variation between cells (Table 13–19). Again it is obvious that both income and family size affect food expenditures. The ANOVA results (Table 13–20) confirm this. Even without resorting to the F table we can see that family size and income have significant effects on expenditures. Also clearly the interactions are not significant.

Notice that the sum of squares attributed to family size and income separately is less than that attributed to both row and column effects. This is due to the unequal cell sizes which make part of the explained variance common to both variables. To understand where the 44,696.1 comes from, recall that income alone accounted for 35,217.0 in the one-way ANOVA. Hence the marginal contribution of family size is 79,913.4 − 35,217.3 =

TABLE 13–19
Average food expenditures

	Income		
Family size	1	2	3
1	26.03	32.47	34.11
2	35.39	40.85	46.23
3	44.51	52.07	56.50

TABLE 13–20
Two-way ANOVA with interactions

Source	Sum of squares	d.f.	Mean square	F
Main effects (row and column)	79,913.4	4	19,978.3	143.7
Family size	44,696.1	2	22,348.1	160.8
Income	12,377.6	2	6,188.8	44.5
Interactions	355.5	4	88.9	0.6
Residual (within)	128,435.4	924	139.0	
Total	208,704.3	932		

FIGURE 13–8
Variance partitioning: Food expenditures

Total variance: 208,704.3		
Within: 128,435.4	Joint family size and income effect: 22,839.7	Family size effect: 44,696.14
		Income effect: 12,377.6
		Interaction effect: 355.5

44,696.1. Similarly the marginal contribution of income is 79,913.4 − 67,535.0 = 12,377.6. The variance partitioning[4] can best be seen in Figure 13–8.

---

[4] It is interesting to note that a large fraction of the variance in food expenditure is explained by the model. This fraction is:

$$\frac{79,913.4 + 355.5}{208,704.3} = 38.3 \text{ percent}$$

and is what will be subsequently called R squared (R^2) in the regression chapter.

MORE GENERAL ANOVA

The more general case occurs when there are more than two influencing (independent) variables, which all may affect the key (dependent) variable. Depending on how many variables there are and how many interactions are to be considered, the algebra may get extremely difficult. The concept, fortunately remains the same: assessing which variables are significantly related to the key dependent variable. Practically, more general ANOVA is performed by using canned computer programs.

MULTIPLE DEPENDENT VARIABLES

In some instances, more than one variable may be the key. For example, I might be concerned about the effect of different advertisements on the ratings of a product on several attributes. One way to handle this situation is to perform a separate ANOVA for each attribute. Alternatively, it is possible to simultaneously test the notion that all the attribute ratings remained constant. This second approach is beyond the scope of this book. Practically, it is carried out by using a canned computer program such as MANOVA—multivariate analysis of variance.

SUMMARY

Analysis of variance, therefore, can be a fairly messy technique. While the basic idea of looking at conditional means is very straightforward, assessing statistical significance using formulas based on interminable squaring of numbers is fairly foreboding. Fortunately use of canned programs has made the algebraic manipulations a nonissue.

ANOVA's major strengths are the ability to uncover a lot of information from relatively few observations and the fact that the influencing variables need only be categorical. Useful as analysis of variance can be, it is possible for a manager and even a market researcher to survive and prosper knowing very little about it. There are two major reasons for this. The first is that the conditional means, the basis for managerial interpretation, can be calculated without knowing anything about ANOVA. The second is that the technique we will take up in the next chapter—regression analysis—can do essentially everything ANOVA does plus some.

PROBLEMS

1. MESS, a manufacturer of specialty steel products, traditionally held a 20 percent share of a market. After introductions of new products by both the company and a major competitor, the company called 100 potential customers and found 28 had purchased from MESS.

a. Has anything significant happened?

b. What could explain the change?

2. Using a random digit phone survey, a company surveyed potential customers in two regions. In region A, 46 of 100 were aware of the company, while in region B, 104 of 200 were aware of the company.

a. Is the difference significant?

b. What could explain the difference?

3. A large packaged goods manufacturer tried out a new package design in several stores. The results were as follows:

Store	Sales with old design	Sales with new design
1	137	152
2	573	581
3	490	480
4	102	95
5	87	120
6	237	252
7	81	98
8	123	140

a. How should I interpret the change?

b. What besides package design might have caused a change?

4. In region A, managed by M. B. Alright, average sales were $11,200 per account with a standard deviation of 3,400 based on a sample of 100 accounts. In region B, managed by I. M. Dropout, average sales were $12,100 with a standard deviation of 2,800 based on a sample of 64 accounts.

a. Is there a difference?

b. What could explain the difference?

5. A company claims to produce a product with an average weight of at least 2,100 kilograms. Having bought five products recently, a client finds they weigh 2,060, 2,090, 2,050, 2,060, and 2,040 respectively.

a. Is there a reason to complain?

b. Assume the client publicly claims the company is short weighting its products and sues. The company counter sues for libel. Who should win? Does the matter depend on who has the burden of proof?

6. Given the following test-market results for two stores in each cell (i.e., the two stores in Peoria exposed to strategy A sold 110 and 90 units respectively).

	Display strategy	
	A	B
Peoria, Ill.	110, 90	40, 80
Springfield, Mass.	140, 100	60, 100
Gainesville, Fla.	60, 80	40, 60

What can I conclude about the display strategies?

7. Interpret the following results of a two-way ANOVA:

	d.f.	F
Advertising	1	1.31
Price	4	5.68
Interactions	4	7.26
Residual	10	

8. The All-Thumbs Hardware Stores advertised outdoor grills, using three different advertising copy versions. The sales of their downtown store and suburban store following each ad are shown below.

Ads	Downtown	Suburban
"Smokey"	1	5
"Hot Dogs"	2	2
"Summer Evening"	3	5

Is the "Summer Evening" copy significantly better than the other advertising copy?

9. Smith's Department Store ran two advertisements, one featuring men's suits, the other featuring sports clothes. The two salespersons Al and Bob sold the following number of suits during each of the two weekends while each ad version ran:

Ads	Al	Bob
Men's suits	3, 5	5, 7
Sports clothes	2, 2	4, 4

(For example, during the two weekends when the men's suits version was playing, Al sold three suits one weekend and five on the other weekend.) Is there any real difference between the salespersons? Between the ad versions?

10. The DSNOB clothing store ran two different advertising campaigns: one an on-price promotion and the other an off-price promotion. Salespersons Jones and Smith both worked during the test period for both campaigns. During the two weekends when the off-price commercials were playing, Jones sold one men's suit each weekend. However, Smith sold four suits one of these weekends and six the other. Similarly during the two weekends when the on-price ads were playing, Jones sold 0 and 2 suits, while Smith sold one and one. What can you conclude about the campaigns? Does Smith really do unusually well with the off-price campaign, or could it have been just luck that Smith sold ten suits on those two weekends?

11. Three different detergent brands were tested for "whitening" effectiveness at three different water temperatures using a full-factorial design. The measured "whiteness" of each of the three replications for each combination of detergent and temperature was as follows:

Detergent Brand

Water temperature	Jiff-0	All-Temp	Hill Fresh
45°F	47, 48, 52	50, 50, 53	54, 56, 58
95°F	48, 49, 47	45, 46, 44	49, 46, 49
145°F	56, 51, 52	49, 53, 51	47, 48, 52

a. What do you conclude about the "whitening" effectiveness of these detergents?

b. The present All-Temp advertising claim is "All-Temp washes equally well in hot or cold water." Could the claim be changed to "All-Temp washes equally well in any temperature water"?

12. The distributor of a perishable good ran an experiment to explore the differences between three advertising executions: Grabber, Holder, and Interest, and between three promotional deals, denoted simply A, B, and C. The experiment was run in three test cities: Denver, Elmira, and Fort Wayne using a Latin square design. The test weeks were spaced about four weeks apart to lessen the order effects of previous promotions and deals. No other advertising or promotion was conducted in these cities during the three-month test. The number of cases sold during the week of the advertising and promotion plus the number sold in the following two weeks are shown below:

	City		
Advertising copy	Denver	Elmira	Fort Wayne
"Grabber"	A 16	B 21	C 23
"Holder"	B 16	C 24	A 20
"Interest"	C 16	A 21	B 23

a. If you had to select one advertising copy and one promotional deal for national use, which would you select?

b. How confident are you that you have selected the correct choices?

13. An experiment was performed by a local retailer in which the price of an item was varied between 30 cents and 40 cents during eight

weekly periods. During some of these periods an advertisement was also run. The sales of the product in each period are tabulated below:

	Week							
	1	2	3	4	5	6	7	8
Price	30	40	30	40	30	40	30	40
Ad run	Yes	No	Yes	No	No	Yes	No	Yes
Sales	7	7	4	5	1	13	8	11

What can you conclude about the sales response to the different prices?

14. The Hardsell Company tried two different sales pitches for its door-to-door salespersons. The old pitch was basically a demonstration. The new pitch is basically a verbal sales pitch. One of the salespersons, Smith, used the new pitch and the old pitch in two suburbs of Denver, Colorado, which is a popular city for test marketing. Smith makes 200 calls each week. During the eight weeks Smith was selling in Denver, the following number of units in the two suburban areas known locally as Rockview and Plainview were sold:

	Rockview	Plainview
Demonstration	90,100	70,60
Verbal	80, 90	80,70

For example: Using the demonstration pitch in Rockview, Smith sold 90 units one week and 100 units another week. What advice would you give Smith?

15.

  a. Assume you have just taken a job as assistant brand manager for General Products, Inc. Your first assignment is to help your boss decide which of three package designs and four advertising campaigns should be used next year for one of the company's major products. Your boss wants to do this by getting the opinions of a sample of 200 individuals from the panel which G.P.I. maintains. What alternatives (and their pros and cons) to the approach your boss has suggested should s/he be made aware of before s/he makes a decision?

  b. Assume your boss decided to use the following test and got the following sales reports:

San Antonio, Tex.	Albany, N.Y.	Muncie, Ind.	Portland, Oreg.
Package design 1	Package design 2	Package design 3	Package design 3
Ad campaign 1	Ad campaign 2	Ad campaign 3	Ad campaign 4
Sales:	Sales:	Sales:	Sales:
A&P 4	A&P 6	K-Mart 7	A&P 10
X-Mart 5	Grand	A&P 5	Fred's 11
	Union.... 8		

(1) Is there any difference?

(2) Assume there is a statistical difference. How should I interpret it?

BIBLIOGRAPHY

Banks, Seymour. *Experimentation in Marketing.* New York: McGraw Hill, 1965.

Cochran, W., and Cox, G. *Experimental Designs.* 2d ed. New York: Wiley, 1957.

Green, Paul E. "On the Design of Choice Experiments Involving Multifactor Alternatives." *Journal of Consumer* Research, vol. 1 (September 1974), pp. 61–68.

Hicks, Charles R. *Fundamental Concepts in the Design of Experiments.* New York: Holt, Rinehart and Winston, 1964.

Holland, Charles W., and Cravens, David W. "Fractional Factorial Experimental Designs in Marketing Research." *Journal of Marketing Research,* vol. 10 (August 1973), pp. 270–76.

Winer, B. J. *Statistical Principles in Experimental Design.* New York: McGraw-Hill, 1971.

STATISTICAL PACKAGE FOR THE SOCIAL SCIENCES SPSSH - VERSION 6.00   1C/04/76

SPACE ALLOCATION FOR THIS RUN..

    TOTAL AMOUNT REQUESTED   80000 BYTES

    DEFAULT TRANSPACE ALLOCATION   10000 BYTES

    MAX NO OF TRANSFORMATIONS PERMITTED   100
    MAX NO OF RECODE VALUES   400
    MAX NO OF ARITHM.OR LOG.OPERATIONS   800

    RESULTING WORKSPACE ALLOCATION   70000 BYTES

        FILE NAME   LEHNUTRI
        VARIABLE LIST   INCCME,FAMSIZE,EXPENSE
        INPUT MEDIUM   DISK
        N OF CASES   UNKNOWN
        INPUT FORMAT   FIXED(76X,2F1.0/12X,F1.0///)

ACCORDING TO YOUR INPUT FORMAT, VARIABLES ARE TO BE READ AS FOLLOWS

VARIABLE	FORMAT	RECORD	COLUMNS
INCCME	F 1. 0	1	77- 77
FAMSIZE	F 1. 0	1	78- 78
EXPENSE	F 1. 0	2	13- 13

THE INPUT FORMAT PROVIDES FOR 3 VARIABLES. 3 WILL BE READ
IT PROVIDES FOR 6 RECORDS ('CARDS') PER CASE. A MAXIMUM OF 78 'COLUMNS' ARE USED ON A RECORD.

        RECODE   FAMSIZE (2=1)(3,*=2)(5 THRU 9=3)/
                 INCCME (1,2=1)(3,4=2)(5=3)/
                 EXPENSE (1=12.5)(2=22.5)(3=37.5)
                 (4=52.5)(5=70)

        MISSING VALUES EXPENSE (0)
        READ INPUT DATA

AFTER READING   940 CASES FROM SUBFILE LEHNUTRI, END OF FILE WAS ENCOUNTERED ON LOGICAL UNIT # 8

BREAKDOWN   TABLES=EXPENSE BY FAMSIZE BY INCOME/
EXPENSE BY FAMSIZ=/EXPENSE BY INCOME

***** GIVEN WORKSPACE ALLOWS FOR 2915 CELLS AND   2 DIMENSIONS FOR SUBPRCGRAM BREAKDOWN *****

STATISTICAL PACKAGE FOR THE SOCIAL SCIENCES SPSSH - VERSION 6.00   10/04/76   PAGE   3

FILE   LEHNUTRI (CREATICN DATE = 10/04/76)

- - - - - - - - - - - - D E S C R I P T I O N   O F   S U B P O P U L A T I O N S - - - - - - - - - - - -

CRITERION VARIABLE   EXPENSE
BROKEN DOWN BY   FAMSIZE
BY   INCOME

VARIABLE	CODE	VALUE LABEL	SUM	MEAN	STD DEV	VARIANCE	N
FOR ENTIRE POPULATION			34220.000	36.6774	14.9651	223.9528	(933)
FAMSIZE	1.		11577.500	28.169	10.274	105.557	(411)
INCOME	1.		7417.500	26.026	8.747	76.518	(285)
INCOME	2.		2727.500	32.470	11.774	138.630	(84)
INCOME	3.		1432.500	34.107	11.789	138.97C	(42)
FAMSIZE	2.		13895.000	35.700	13.572	184.186	(350)
INCOME	1.		4530.000	35.351	13.174	173.567	(128)
INCOME	2.		6822.500	40.853	12.923	167.001	(167)
INCOME	3.		2542.500	46.227	13.315	177.286	(55)
FAMSIZE	3.		8747.500	50.858	14.024	196.666	(172)
INCOME	1.		2270.000	44.510	13.304	177.006	(51)
INCOME	2.		4217.500	52.068	13.612	185.281	(81)
INCOME	3.		2260.000	56.500	12.920	166.923	(40)

TOTAL CASES =   940
MISSING CASES =   7 OR   0.7 PCT.

FILE   LEHNUTRI (CREATION DATE = 10/04/76)

- - - - - - - - - - - - - -   D E S C R I P T I O N   O F   S U B P O P U L A T I O N S   - - - - - - - - - - - - - - - - -

CRITERION VARIABLE   EXPENSE
BROKEN DOWN BY   FAMSIZE
- - - - - - - - - - -

VARIABLE	CODE	VALUE LABEL	SUM	MEAN	STD DEV	VARIANCE	N
FOR ENTIRE POPULATION			34220.0000	36.6774	14.9651	223.9539	(933)
FAMSIZE	1.		11577.500	28.169	10.274	105.557	(411)
FAMSIZE	2.		13895.000	39.700	13.572	184.186	(350)
FAMSIZE	3.		8747.500	50.858	14.024	196.666	(172)

TOTAL CASES =   940
MISSING CASES =   7 OR   0.7 PCT.

FILE   LEHNUTRI (CREATION DATE = 10/04/76)

- - - - - - - - - - - - - -   D E S C R I P T I O N   O F   S U B P O P U L A T I O N S   - - - - - - - - - - - - - - - - -

CRITERION VARIABLE   EXPENSE
BROKEN DOWN BY   INCOME
- - - - - - - - - - -

VARIABLE	CODE	VALUE LABEL	SUM	MEAN	STD DEV	VARIANCE	N
FOR ENTIRE POPULATION			34220.0000	36.6774	14.9651	223.9528	(933)
INCOME	1.		14217.500	30.641	12.417	154.191	(464)
INCOME	2.		13767.500	41.468	14.544	211.527	(342)
INCOME	3.		6235.000	45.511	15.364	236.043	(137)

TOTAL CASES =   940
MISSING CASES =   7 OR   0.7 PCT.

CATA TRANSFORMATION DONE UP TC THIS PCINT..

```
NO OF TRANSFORMATIONS              0
NO OF RECODE VALUES                0
NO OF ARITHM. OR LOG. OPERATICNS   0
THE AMOUNT OF TRANSPACE REQUIRED IS      0 BYTES
```

ONEWAY   EXPENSE BY FAMSIZE(1,31/
                RANGES=SCHEFFE(.101/

***** ONEWAY PROBLEM REQUIRES   128 BYTES WORKSPACE *****

- - - - - - - - - - - - - - - - O N E W A Y - - - - - - - - - - - - - - - - - - -

VARIABLE EXPENSE

ANALYSIS OF VARIANCE

SOURCE	D.F.	SUM OF SQUARES	MEAN SQUARES	F RATIO	F PROB.
BETWEEN GROUPS	2	67535.0000	33767.5000	222.422	0.000
WITHIN GROUPS	930	141190.000	151.8172		
TOTAL	932	208725.000			

- O N E W A Y -

VARIABLE   EXPENSE

MULTIPLE RANGE TEST

SCHEFFE PROCEDURE
RANGES FOR THE 0.100 LEVEL -

3.02   3.02

3.02   3.02

HOMOGENEOLS SUBSETS   (SUBSETS OF GROUPS, NO PAIR OF WHICH HAVE MEANS THAT DIFFER BY MORE THAN THE SHORTEST
                            SIGNIFICANT RANGE FOR A SUBSET OF THAT SIZE)

SUBSET   1

GROUP   GRP01
MEAN   28.1691
- - - - - - - -

SUBSET   2

GROUP   GRP02
MEAN   39.7000
- - - - - - - -

SUBSET   3

GROUP   GRP03
MEAN   50.8575
- - - - - - - -

ONEWAY

EXPENSE BY INCOME(1,5)/
RANCES=SCHEFFE(.10)/

***** ONEWAY PROBLEM REQUIRES   192 BYTES WORKSPACE *****

FILE   LEHNUTRI (CREATICN CATE = 10/04/76)

- - - - - - - - - - - - - - O N E W A Y - - - - - - - - - - - - - - - - - - -

VARIABLE EXPENSE

ANALYSIS OF VARIANCE

SOURCE	D.F.	SUM OF SQUARES	MEAN SQUARES	F RATIO	F PROB.
BETWEEN GROUPS	4	35217.0000	8804.2500	47.089	0.000
WITHIN GROUPS	928	173507.000	186.9687		
TOTAL	932	208724.000			

- - - - - - - - - - - - - - - - - O N E W A Y -

VARIABLE   EXPENSE

MULTIPLE RANGE TEST

SCHEFFE PROCEDURE
RANGES FOR THE 0.100 LEVEL -

     3.94   3.94   3.94   3.94

HOMOGENEOUS SUBSETS   (SUBSETS OF GROUPS, NO PAIR OF WHICH HAVE MEANS THAT DIFFER BY MORE THAN THE SHORTEST
                         SIGNIFICANT RANGE FOR A SUBSET OF THAT SIZE)

SUBSET   1

GROUP   GRP01
MEAN   30.6412
- - - - -

SUBSET   2

GROUP   GRP02
MEAN   41.4684
- - - - - -

SUBSET   3

GROUP   GRP03
MEAN   45.5109
- - - - - -

ANOVA   EXPENSE BY FAMSIZE (1,3) INCOME (1,5)

'ANOVA' PROBLEM REQUIRES   1995 BYTES OF SPACE.

FILE   LEHNUTRI (CREATION DATE = 10/04/76)

* * * * * * * A N A L Y S I S   O F   V A R I A N C E * * * * * * * * * * * * * * * *

      EXPENSE
    BY FAMSIZE
      INCOME

* *

SOURCE OF VARIATION	SUM OF SQUARES	DF	MEAN SQUARE	F	SIGNIF OF F
MAIN EFFECTS	79913.375	4	19978.344	143.730	0.001
FAMSIZE	44696.141	2	22348.070	160.778	0.001
INCOME	12377.625	2	6188.812	44.524	0.001
2-WAY INTERACTIONS	355.500	4	88.875	0.639	0.999
FAMSIZE INCOME	355.470	4	88.867	0.639	0.999
RESIDUAL	128435.375	924	138.999		
TOTAL	208704.250	932	223.932		

540 CASES WERE PROCESSED.
7 CASES (0.7 PCT) WERE MISSING.

14 _____

Regression analysis

Of all the "fancy" multivariate procedures, regression analysis is by far the most widely used in marketing research. The basic purpose of regression analysis is to estimate the relationship between variables. While many people find it useful for forecasting, regression is not restricted to forecasting, and its applicability extends to problems such as market segmentation and model building.

To use regression, a researcher must specify which variable (e.g., sales) depends on which other variable(s) (e.g., GNP, price, etc.). The procedure then calculates estimates of the relationship between the independent variables (GNP, price, etc.) and the dependent variable (sales).

This chapter will proceed by first discussing the simple case of regression analysis where there is only one independent variable as a means of introducing and explaining the procedure. The more realistic case of more than one independent variable will be discussed next. After describing some of the problems which affect interpretation, applications of regression analysis to several situations will be described. Finally. the important distinction between correlation and causation will be addressed.

Before proceeding, one comment about the name "regression analysis" is appropriate. Like so many terms in our language, the term regression analysis bears no useful relationship to the technique. While the story of "how the technique got its name" is culturally interesting, suffice it to say that the title is a historical anachronism (Galton, 1889). Having saved you innumerable hours of frustration in attempting to understand the name of the technique, this chapter now turns to the real business of understanding regression analysis.

SIMPLE (TWO-VARIABLE) LINEAR REGRESSION ANALYSIS

Basic concept

The simplest case of regression analysis is the situation where one variable is presumed to depend on only one other variable. (For example, we may assume that sales depends on GNP.) In such a case, the researcher would gather data on sales and GNP for several different occasions. As a first means of analyzing the relationship, the data should be plotted (Figure 14–1). Simple observation of the data indicates that as

FIGURE 14–1

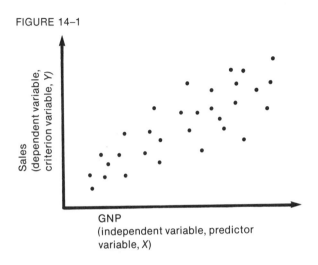

GNP increases, so do sales. In order to summarize the relationship, one would tend to draw a straight line through the data points (Figure 14–2). The line summarizes, in some average sense, the relationship between GNP and sales. Hence we could express the relationship between GNP and sales mathematically as follows:

$$\text{Estimated sales} = B_0 + B_1\text{GNP}$$

FIGURE 14–2

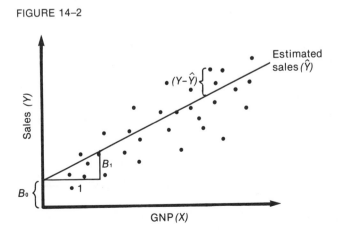

The term B_0 is the constant or intercept. This might be interpreted literally as the predicted level of sales if GNP dropped to zero. However, since such a level of GNP has never been experienced, extrapolating to this level is foolish. (Also, if GNP goes to zero we'll all be dead, so who cares what sales would be?) The term B_1 is the slope of the line (soon to be called the regression coefficient) and is interpreted as the amount sales would increase if GNP increased one (in whatever units, e.g., billions of dollars, the original data was measured). The error in prediction, calculated as $Y - \hat{Y}$, is simply the difference between estimated and actual sales.

Estimation

A variety of other straight lines could also be drawn through the data (Figure 14–3), some (A and B) which obviously do not represent the data

FIGURE 14–3

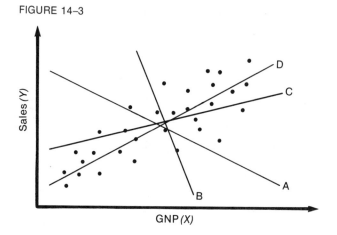

and others (C and D) which also seem to represent the data fairly well. A problem, therefore, is to decide which line best fits the data. The following procedures exist for deciding on the best line:

1. *Graphical eyeball: Pick the line that looks best.* This procedure is often useful. Unfortunately, it breaks down when there are either numerous data points or more than one independent variable.
2. *Find the line that optimizes some criterion measure of a good fit.* Two of these criteria include the following:
    a. The sum of the absolute differences between the predicted sales and actual sales ($\Sigma|Y - \hat{Y}|$)
    b. The sum of the squared differences between the predicted and actual sales values ($\Sigma(Y - \hat{Y})^2$).

The absolute differences, unfortunately, turn out to be relatively cumbersome mathematically. Hence, the generally accepted method is to minimize the sum of the squared errors (often called least squares estimation). One property of the squared differences is that they give slightly more weight to "far out" data points than does the absolute difference criterion. (In other words, the least squares criterion would favor a line which produced four differences of size two as opposed to a line which produced three of size one and one of size four.) Simple linear regression analysis calculates the coefficients of the line (B_0 and B_1) which minimize the sum of the squared differences between the actual value of the dependent variable and the value predicted by the line $\hat{Y} = B_0 + B_1 X$.

Regression coefficients. In order to find the B_0 and B_1 which thus generate the "best" line, one need only plug into the two formulas (see Appendix 14–B for their derivation):

$$B_1 = \frac{\Sigma(X - \bar{X})(Y - \bar{Y})}{\Sigma(X - \bar{X})^2} = \frac{\Sigma XY - n\bar{X}\bar{Y}}{\Sigma X^2 - n\bar{X}^2} \tag{14.1}$$

and

$$B_0 = \bar{Y} - B\bar{X} \tag{14.2}$$

These formulas can be used manually. Much more desirable, however, is to utilize either a "canned" regression program on a computer or a "fancy" calculator. Suffice it to say that hand calculations are rarely used for any problem with more than eight to ten data points. The following two other measures are often also calculated:

The standard error of estimate ($S_{Y.X}$). This is a measure of the "typical" deviation of the predictions from the actual values of the dependent variable (Y). It is analogous to the standard deviation (hence the term "standard error") and is calculated as

$$S_{Y.X} = \sqrt{\frac{\Sigma(Y - \hat{Y})^2}{n - 2}} = \sqrt{\frac{\Sigma(Y - \bar{Y})^2 - B_1\Sigma(X - \bar{X})(Y - \bar{Y})}{n - 2}} \tag{14.3}$$

The coefficient of determination (r^2). While the standard error of estimate provides one measure of the accuracy of prediction, it is not particularly easy to interpret, much less compare across different analyses because it depends on the units in which Y is measured. (Is a fit with a standard error of two cartons better or worse than one with a standard error of three dollars?) The correlation coefficient measures the closeness of the relation between the predicted and actual values of the dependent variable. In regression, r^2, known as the coefficient of determination, is used

$$r = \frac{\Sigma(X - \bar{X})(Y - \bar{Y})}{\sqrt{\Sigma(X - \bar{X})^2}\sqrt{\Sigma(Y - \bar{Y})^2}} = \frac{\Sigma XY - n\bar{X}\bar{Y}}{n s_X s_Y} \tag{14.4}$$

We can compute r^2 directly from

$$r^2 = 1 - \frac{\Sigma(Y - \hat{Y})^2}{\Sigma(Y - \bar{Y})^2}$$

$$= 1 - \frac{\text{Unexplained variance in } Y}{\text{Total variance in } Y}$$

$$= \text{percent of the variance in } Y \text{ explained by } X$$

Applications of these formulas are shown in Appendix 14–A.

Interpretation

The previous section dealt with a description of the mechanics of how the regression coefficients are derived. The key issue for a user, however, is how to interpret the results. There are three major elements which are especially important outputs of a regression analysis: the regression coefficients, the standard error of estimate/prediction ($S_{Y.X}$), and the coefficient of determination.

The regression coefficients

The constant or intercept, B_0, is interpreted as the value Y would take on if X were zero. Since many situations exist where the X values are unlikely to approach zero (for example, a sales versus GNP equation), this interpretation is often either unnecessary or inappropriate.

The regression coefficient or slope, B_1, is interpreted as the amount Y would increase if X increased one unit. (A negative regression coefficient means that as X goes up, Y decreases in value as would be the expected result from an equation: Sales $= B_0 + B_1$ (price) where we expect B_1 to be negative.) Hence, the slope is a measure of the marginal sensitivity of Y to changes in X. Consider, for example, the equation: Sales in cartons $= 2.5 + 2$ (advertising in \$). Assuming for a moment that the relationship is causal, this implies that increasing advertising one dollar would increase sales by two cartons. The use of this would then suggest if the marginal profit of two cartons of sales were greater than a dollar, then increasing advertising would increase profits in the short run. Conversely, if two cartons of sales produced less than one dollar of profit, then reducing advertising might improve profits.

The standard error of estimate/prediction ($S_{Y.X}$). One of the uses of regression is as a predictive tool. Continuing the sales versus advertising example, a manager might ask the question "what if" advertising were set at ten dollars? Using the equation, the forecast would be

$$\text{Sales in cartons} = 2.5 + 2(10) = 22.5$$

This is the best guess available. In planning, however, it is necessary to know the range of likely outcomes as well as the most likely result to make production scheduling, and so forth, more efficient. Consider the

FIGURE 14–4

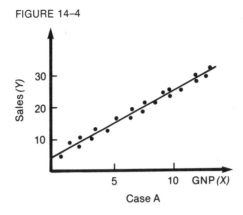

Case A

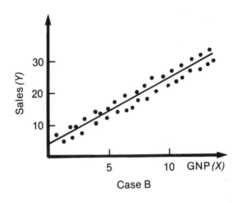

Case B

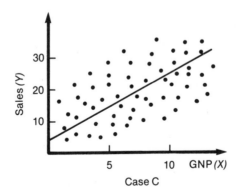

Case C

three cases in Figure 14–4. In case A, the past data seems to fall exactly on the line. Hence, if the rather heroic assumption that nothing is changing in the market can be made, we would be fairly confident in the prediction of 22.5. Put differently, we would tend to hedge the prediction very little, using as the forecast 22.5 ± .5. In case B, the data fall less closely to the line and the prediction would be hedged to a greater extent, leading to a forecast of 22.5 ± 2. Case C shows a situation where the spread of data points about the line is much greater; hence the forecast might be 22.5 ± 14. Since deciding on the range by graphing the data is both tedious and inexact, an efficient procedure is to use the standard error of estimate as a measure of the likely accuracy of the prediction. In order to be 95 percent sure that actual sales fall within the range, this suggests predicting sales will be approximately $22.5 \pm 2S_{Y.X}$. This could be represented graphically as Figure 14–5. As long as a reasonably large sample

FIGURE 14–5

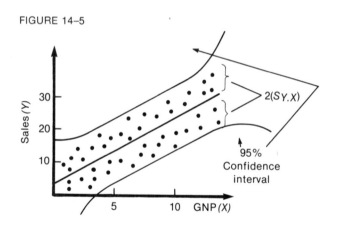

size were used and the advertising figure used were within the range of past experience, this would be a reasonable prediction. Should either the sample size (n) get small or the value of the dependent variable be well outside the range of past data (sometimes called the relevant range) however, then a forecaster would correctly feel more squeamish about his/her estimates and consequently want to give a larger range of possible outcomes. The formula which quantifies this squeamishness is

$$\text{Forecast of } Y = \hat{Y} \pm t_{n-2}S_{Y.X} \sqrt{1 + \frac{1}{n} + \frac{(X' - \bar{X})^2}{\Sigma(X - \bar{X})^2}} \qquad (14.5)$$

where X' is the value of X for which the forecast is being generated. Since t_{n-2} is the number from the t distribution with $n - 2$ degrees of freedom, this reduces to approximately $\hat{Y} \pm 2S_{Y.X}$ (at the famous 95 percent confidence level) for large sample sizes or predictions well within the relevant range.

The coefficient of determination.   The correlation coefficient is an index of the fit between the predicted and actual values of the dependent variable. A value of ± 1 indicates "perfect" correlation, meaning that X is a perfect predictor of Y. A value of 0 indicates no correlation between X and Y. (What this means practically is that X is useless as a predictor of Y.) A value between 0 and ± 1 indicates somewhere between no and perfect correlation.

The value of r^2, the coefficient of determination, is the percent of the variance in the values of Y accounted for (predictable by, explained by, associated with) the variance in X. Hence, an r of .7 means an r^2 of .49 which in turn indicates that about half the variance in Y is accounted for by variance in X.

FIGURE 14–6

Plot of points	Regression coefficient	Standard error of estimate	Correlation
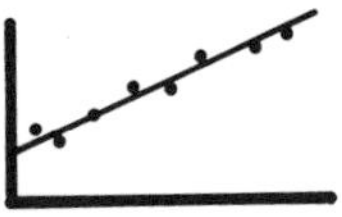	Positive	0	+ 1.0
	Positive	Small	.95
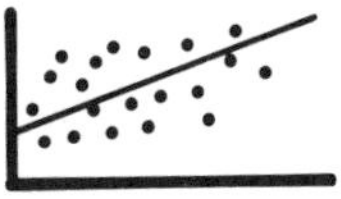	Positive	Large	.20
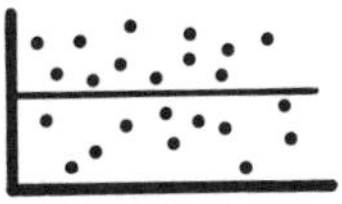	0	"Very" large (equal to the standard deviation of Y, s_Y)	0
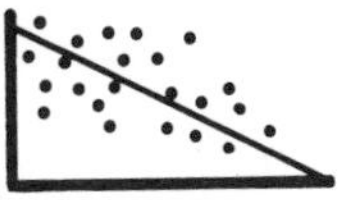	Negative	Large	−.20
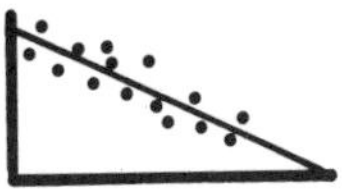	Negative	Small	−.95
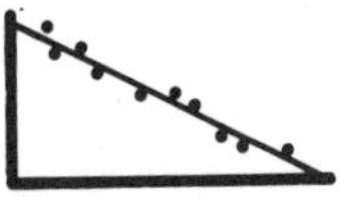	Negative	0	−1.0

The size of the correlation is related to both the regression coefficient B_1 and the standard error. This relationship is summarized in Figure 14–6.

Two examples of simple linear regression

Motor vehicle registrations. In the first example, we will consider the relationship between motor vehicle registrations and time between 1961 and 1968. The raw data, used as input, are as follows:

Year (X)	U.S. motor vehicle registrations (Y) (million)
1	63.2
2	65.8
3	68.8
4	71.7
5	74.9
6	77.8
7	80.0
8	83.2

Plotting this data shows a very strong linear relation between time and motor vehicle registrations. Obviously registrations are increasing at about 3 million a year and in year 0 (in this case, equal to 1960), a shade

TABLE 14–1

Variable	Mean	Standard deviation
X	4.5	2.29
Y	73.2	6.58

Constant (B_0) = 60.3
Slope (B_1) = 2.87
Standard error $(S_{Y.X})$ = .21
Coefficient of determination (r^2) = .999

X	Y	Estimated Y($\hat{Y}$)	Y − $\hat{Y}$
1	63.2	63.1	.1
2	65.8	66.0	−.2
3	68.8	68.9	−.1
4	71.7	71.7	0
5	74.9	74.6	.3
6	77.8	77.4	.4
7	80.0	80.4	−.4
8	83.2	83.2	0

over 60 million cars must have been registered. Performing the appropriate calculations leads to the results in Table 14–1. Hence we conclude the following:

1. Motor vehicle registrations = 60.3 + 2.87 (number of years since 1960).
2. The relationship between time and motor vehicle registrations is very close (r^2 = .999, $S_{Y.X}$ is 200,000 compared to values of Y of about 70,000,000). Predicted 1969 sales based on this model would then be

$$60.3 + 2.87(9) \pm t_6(.21) \sqrt{1 + \frac{1}{8} + \frac{(4.5)^2}{\Sigma(X - \bar{X})^2}} = 86.1 \pm .75$$

Since actual 1969 registrations turned out to be 86.4 million, this was a "good" prediction.

MBA salaries. Now consider the relation between the salary an MBA received in 1972 and the number of years which had elapsed since s/he graduated. Using a sample of over 4,000 graduates of the "big name" schools (and obviously a computer), the following results were obtained:

$$\text{Intercept} = \$19,650$$
$$\text{Slope} = \$630$$
$$r^2 = .184$$
$$S_{Y.X} = \$10,440$$

We therefore conclude a typical MBA's salary would be $19,650 + $630 (number of years since graduation). However, the relationship between years since graduation and salary, though significant, is subject to wide variation as indicated by the r^2 of .184 and the standard error of estimate of $10,440. This means that the forecast of the 1972 salary of an MBA ten years after graduation would be

$$19,650 + 630(10) \pm 2(10,440) = 25,950 \pm 20,880$$

In order to be 95 percent confident of including an individual's actual salary, a prediction would have to be between $5,000 (Peace Corps, unemployment) and $47,000 (corporate stardom).

Three factors contribute to this large uncertainty. The first is that the relation between salary and years since graduation is likely to be somewhat nonlinear. For example, the true relation might be that of Figure 14–7. Since most of the individuals in the sample had between 5 and 15 years experience, this is really the only relevant range for the regression results. A nonlinear model would presumably improve the fit. It also would change the intercept to a lower figure than the implausible $19,650 (starting salaries for MBA's in 1972 were lower). The $630 a year is more believable since the "standard" $1,000–$1,500-a-year raise would be partially offset by annual increases in the starting salary.

FIGURE 14-7

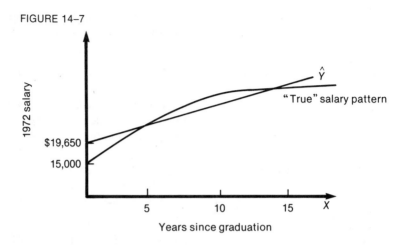

A second contributor to the low predictive value is the omission of other key variables. One would presume other variables such as school attended, major, and industry employed in would all affect salary. Inclusion of multiple variables will be discussed in another section.

The final explanation of the large variation of the predicted results is the possibility that salaries are uncertain. This uncertainty may stem from two sources. The first source is essentially noise in the data, consisting of such problems as the inaccuracy of the reported salary (how honest would you be in disclosing your salary?), the exclusion of bonuses and commissions from the salary measure of compensation, and any of a variety of coding and processing errors. The second source of uncertainty is essentially pure randomness which stems from the fact that, at least given present technology, a large component of salary is unpredictable "luck."

MULTIPLE REGRESSION

Basic concept

The basic concept of multiple regression is the same as that of simple regression: to find the relation between independent and dependent variables. In multiple regression however, there are several independent variables. In other words, we might assume that sales depend not just on GNP but also on price, advertising, and distribution. The model is, assuming there are k independent variables:

$$Y = B_0 + B_1X_1 + B_2X_2 + \cdots + B_kX_k + \mu$$

Estimation

The estimation procedure developed for multiple regression is analogous to that for simple regression. The objective is to minimize the sum of the squared deviations between the actual and predicted values of the dependent variable. The regression coefficients are obtained from a math-estimates all the coefficients (see Appendix 14–B). In practice the results are always found by using canned computer programs. In addition to the regression coefficients, the other two measures which are most useful are, as in the case of simple regression, the standard error of estimate and the coefficient of determination (R^2), which are direct extensions of the simple regression counterparts. The standard error of estimate is

$$S_{Y.X} = \sqrt{\frac{\Sigma(Y - \hat{Y})^2}{n - k}}$$

and

$$R^2 = 1 - \frac{S_{Y.X}^2}{s_Y^2} = 1 - \frac{\text{Unexplained variance}}{\text{Total variance}} = \frac{\text{Percent total variance in } Y \text{ explained by } X}{}$$

At this point one might ask, "Why not run a series of simple regressions and use the coefficients from each of the separate regressions?" In addition to being considered bad modeling, there are three other reasons for not doing this:

1. It is difficult to decide what the intercept B_0 should be since each separate regression would produce a different intercept.
2. If some of the independent variables are strongly interrelated, then the estimates obtained from the simple regressions may be "bad." That is, the coefficients from the simple regressions may either over- or understate the effect of these independent variables on the dependent variable. This is due to what is called omitted variable bias, which will be discussed later.
3. It is inefficient. For example, 20 independent variables will require 20 separate regressions.

General interpretation

Interpretation of the results of multiple regression is similar to interpretation of simple regression. The three major elements to consider are the regression coefficients, the standard error of estimate, and the coefficient of multiple determination (R^2).

The regression coefficients

The constant, B_0, is the "baseline" value of Y which is interpreted as the value Y would take on if all the independent variables were zero. As in the case of simple regression, this is rarely a meaningful interpretation since in most marketing models the only way for all the independent variables to go to zero is for the world to end (which also tends to make the interpretation meaningless).

The regression coefficients $(B_1$ through $B_k)$. A particular regression coefficient, B_i is interpreted as the amount by which the dependent variable would change if the ith independent variable increased by one unit and all the other variables remained unchanged. In other words, a regression coefficient is the marginal influence of a single independent variable on the dependent variable. For example, if we obtained

Sales in cartons $= 1.2 + 1.3$(advertising \$) $- .2$(price in \$)
$+ .1$(GNP in billions of dollars)

then the effect of increasing advertising one dollar while holding price and GNP constant would be to increase sales by 1.3 cartons. In general, both the sign (indicating the direction of the effect) and the absolute size (indicating the magnitude of the effect) of a coefficient should be examined.

The standard error of estimate. As in the case of simple regression, the standard error of estimate is used as a quantification of the amount a prediction must be hedged. Assuming that $S_{Y.X}$ were 15 in the previous example, the best estimate of sales given advertising of \$20, price of \$60, and GNP of 1,000 billion dollars would be

Sales $= 1.2 + 1.3(20) - .2(60) + .1(1,000)$
$= 115.2$

The 95 percent confidence interval, assuming a large sample size ($n > 100$ in this case) and that the values of the independent variables were typical of past data, would be approximately

$$115.2 \pm 2(15) = 115 \pm 30$$

The coefficient of multiple determination (R^2). The coefficient of multiple correlation (R) is an index of the closeness of the relation between the dependent variable and the independent variables. It is calculated as the square root of the coefficient of determination, R^2. The coefficient of determination is interpreted as the percent of the variance in the dependent variable predicted by variation in all the independent variables. For the special case of only one independent variable, the multiple correlation coefficient is equal to the simple correlation coefficient.

Statistical interpretation

Interpretation of the results of regression are often aided by the following two types of statistical tests:

Tests on the individual coefficients (B_i's). The individual coefficient estimates, the B_i's, are obviously subject to error. Since the estimates are usually assumed to be normally distributed, we can estimate the true value of a particular coefficient as

$$\text{``True'' value of } B_i = \text{Estimated value of } B_i \pm t_\alpha \begin{pmatrix} \text{standard} \\ \text{deviation} \\ \text{of } B_i \end{pmatrix}$$

One interesting question is whether the true B_i is really different from zero. (In other words, does the ith variable really influence the dependent variable?) This can be tested by either a t or F test (some computer outputs use each of these equivalent tests) as follows:

Hypothesis	t test statistic	F test statistic
The true value of the ith regression coefficient is zero ($B_i = 0$)	$\dfrac{B_i - 0}{S_{B_i}}$	$\left(\dfrac{B_i}{S_{B_i}}\right)^2$

Ignoring degrees of freedom and using the 95 percent confidence level, this means that to be significant, the t ratio must be greater than about 2 and the F ratio greater than 4. (Actually the t test statistic is t with $n - k - 1$ degrees of freedom and the F test statistic is F with 1 and $n - k - 1$ degrees of freedom.) Failure to be significant indicates that although the variable may be related to the dependent variable, the variable fails to marginally affect the dependent variable (and hence aid predictions) when the effects of the other independent variables are removed. What this means practically is that variables with nonsignificant coefficients may be eliminated from the equation without greatly harming predictions. Interpretation, on the other hand, may be more difficult as the variables are removed.

Test on the coefficient of determination (R^2). The tests on the individual coefficients address the question of whether a particular variable improves prediction. A test of R^2, on the other hand, addresses the question of whether the independent variables as a group are significantly related to the dependent variable. The test is based on an analysis of variance table (Table 14–2). The F test is

$$\frac{\dfrac{\text{Explained sum of squares}}{k}}{\dfrac{\text{Unexplained sum of squares}}{n - k - 1}} = \frac{\dfrac{\Sigma(Y - \bar{Y})^2 - \Sigma(Y - \hat{Y})^2}{k}}{\dfrac{\Sigma(Y - \hat{Y})^2}{n - k - 1}}$$

TABLE 14-2

	SS	d.f.	MSS
Explained variation	$\Sigma(Y - \bar{Y})^2 - \Sigma(Y - \hat{Y})^2 = ESS$	k	$\dfrac{ESS}{k}$
Unexplained variation	$\Sigma(Y - \hat{Y})^2 = USS$	$n - k - 1$	$\dfrac{USS}{n - k - 1}$
Total variation in Y ...	$\Sigma(Y - \bar{Y})^2 = TSS$	$n - 1$	

where k is the number of independent variables. This can be shown to be equivalent to

$$\frac{\dfrac{R^2}{k}}{\dfrac{1 - R^2}{n - k - 1}} \quad \text{which is } F_{k,n-k-1}$$

When the F test on R is insignificant, it means that the entire regression is essentially worthless (unless, of course, a negative finding is what the researcher wanted in the first place).[1]

NUTRITION SURVEY EXAMPLE

In analyzing the data from the nutrition study, one objective was to build a model which explained different levels of expenditures on food based on other variables. Food expenditures were regressed against 15 other variables:

1. Income (coded 1–6).
2. Age of respondent (in years).
3. Family size.
4. Number of brands and sizes shopped for (coded 1–4).
5. Habitual buying versus information seeking (coded 1–3).
6. Importance of variety (coded from 1 = very important to 5 = very unimportant).
7. Importance of taste.
8. Importance of other family members' preferences.
9. Importance of diet restrictions.
10. Importance of price.

---

[1] The more independent variables you have, the higher R^2 will be. Consequently many researchers prefer to use a criterion which takes the number of independent variables into account. Hence an adjusted R^2 is often used as follows:

$$\text{Adjusted } R^2 = 1 - (1 - \text{unadjusted } R^2) \left(\frac{n - 1}{n - k} \right)$$

11.   Importance of availability.
12.   Importance of ease of preparation.
13.   Importance of habit.
14.   Importance of specials.
15.   Importance of nutritional value.

The weekly expenditure variable was recoded into dollar terms in the following manner:

Response	Recode
Under $15	$12.50
$15–$29	22.50
$30–$44	37.50
$45–$60	52.50
Over $60	70.00

The 762 (of 940) individuals who provided usable responses to all 16 variables were then chosen for analysis. The means of all the variables are shown in Table 14–3. While looking at the means may seem trivial, it is a very good way to make certain that the data was input accurately. For example, had the mean of the diet importance variable been less than 1 or

TABLE 14–3

Variable	Mean	Standard deviation
Food expenditures	37.52	15.12
Income (coded 1–6)	2.75	1.42
Age of respondent (in years)	43.70	16.54
Family size	3.29	1.38
Number of brands and sizes shopped for (coded 1–4)	2.34	1.42
Habitual buying versus Information seeking (coded 1–3)	1.87	.65
Importance of variety (coded from 1 = very important to 5 = very unimportant)	2.04	.96
Importance of taste	1.24	.57
Importance of other family members' preferences ...	1.70	.90
Importance of diet restrictions	3.04	1.57
Importance of price	1.75	.96
Importance of availability	2.17	1.13
Importance of ease of preparation	2.75	1.22
Importance of habit	2.79	1.14
Importance of specials	2.26	1.25
Importance of nutritional value	1.67	.88

more than 5, the data would obviously have been input incorrectly. This check for "reasonable" means (or actual ones, if they are known) should always be made.

FIGURE 14–8

Regression results for predicting food expenditures

Variable	Regression coefficient	Beta	F
Importance of nutrition	.47	.03	.76
Income	2.89	.27	80.11
Age	.08	.09	8.85
Family size	5.86	.53	313.61
Brands shopped	.01	.00	.00
Information sought	−1.09	−.05	2.43
Importance of variety	.02	.00	.00
Importance of taste	−1.40	−.05	2.82
Importance of others' preferences	−.28	−.02	.32
Importance of diet	−.46	−.05	2.65
Importance of price	.29	.02	.33
Importance of availability	−.24	−.02	.35
Importance of ease of preparation	.28	.02	.59
Importance of habit	−1.07	−.08	7.18
Importance of specials	.49	.04	1.82
Constant	12.76		
R squared	.43		
Adjusted R^2	.42		
Standard error	11.53		

Analysis of variance

	d.f.	Sum of squares	Mean square	F
Regression	15	74,667.73	4,977.85	37.43
Residual	746	99,200.62	132.98	

The first 15, all independent variables were regressed against food expenditures. The results (Figure 14–8) were obtained from the SPSS program. These results can be interpreted as explained in this section.

Overall predictive power

The R^2 is .43, a "moderate" value indicating that the independent variables help predictively but are not overly accurate in predicting individual food consumption expenditures. The test for the null hypothesis that all the regression coefficients are zero (and that the independent variables are worthless as predictors) is

$$F = \frac{\dfrac{R^2}{\text{No. independent variables}}}{\dfrac{1 - R^2}{n - \text{No. independent variables} - 1}}$$

$$= \frac{4,978}{133} = 37.4$$

This compares with a "Table" $F_{15,746}$ of about 2.1 at the 1 percent significance level and indicates that the null hypothesis is convincingly rejected and hence that the independent variables definitely help in predicting food consumption expenditures.

The overall predictive power can also be seen in terms of the size of the standard error of estimate, $11.53. This is obviously fairly large but noticeably smaller than the $15.12 standard deviation of food consumption expenses. This also suggests that 95 percent of household weekly food consumption expenditures can be predicted within ± (1.96)(11.53) or about $23.

Key determinants

An obvious question is which of the independent variables are the most useful predictors of the dependent variable. The following three basic approaches are used.

The absolute size of the regression coefficients. The size of the regression coefficient indicates how much an increase of one unit of the independent variable would increase the dependent variable assuming all the other independent variables remained unchanged. The results indicate that an increase of one in family size would increase weekly consumption expenditures by $5.86, whereas movement to the next income category would increase expenditures by $2.89 per week.

The beta coefficients. One problem with looking at the regression coefficients is that they depend on the scale of the variables. Hence if income had been measured in dollars, the regression coefficient would have been much smaller. For this reason, many researchers (and especially those in psychology) prefer to use something called beta coefficients. These coefficients are the regression coefficients which would have been obtained if the regression had been performed on standardized (standard deviation equal to one) variables. Hence a beta of .27 between income and expense indicates that if an individual's income increased by one standard deviation (1.42 scale points), then food expenses would increase by .27 standard deviations. In general:

$$\text{Beta} = B \, \frac{\text{Standard deviation of independent variable}}{\text{Standard deviation of dependent variable}}$$

$$\left(\text{In this example, } .27 = 2.89 \, \frac{1.42}{15.12}.\right)$$

The marginal significance of the variable. Each independent variable can be separately examined for the marginal contribution it makes to predicting the dependent variable. To do that we estimate how much variation in Y can be explained by each variable which is unexplained when the other independent variables are used alone. This is tested by an F statistic (here the statistic is $F_{1,746}$). The bigger the F, the greater the significance. In this case, family size is the most significant ($F = 314$) with income also very significant and both age and habit significant at the 5 percent significance level.

ISSUES IN USING REGRESSION ANALYSIS

Users of multiple regression often encounter a variety of problems. While market researchers are rarely experts on these problems, because of their effect on interpretation it is important to be able to recognize when the problems occur, understand their effect on interpretation, and have a general idea of what to do next. (Calling in a statistician without a specific assignment often creates more problems than it solves.) This section is devoted to highlighting these problems.

Multicollinearity

One of the most common problems encountered in regression is the result of strong interrelations among the independent variables. This does not violate any assumptions (the independent variables do not have to be independent of each other) nor affect predictions. It does, however, make the estimates of the regression coefficients unreliable.

Detection. The most obvious way to detect collinearity is to check the simple correlations among the independent variables. When collinearity is the result of complex relations among several variables, this simple approach may fail to uncover the collinearity. Alternatively, in examining the results of a regression, large standard errors of the coefficients (leading to insignificant coefficents) are often a sign that serious collinearity may be present. Similarly implausible coefficients may be a sign of collinearity.

Cure. One cure for collinearity is to reduce the variables to a set which are not collinear. This is best done on the basis of judgment but many researchers employ factor analysis or stepwise regression as a means of deciding which variables to retain. Unfortunately, reducing the number of variables may lead to another problem, omitted variable bias.

Autocorrelation

Autocorrelation occurs when the errors are correlated in a serial manner. Positive autocorrelation means if you encounter one positive error (the predicted value of the dependent variable is smaller than the actual value), you are likely to find the next error is also positive and vice versa. This is a typical problem in time series data when a cycle has been ignored. It occurs occasionally in cross-sectional data when nonlinear relations exist.

Detection.   Autocorrelation may be detected by plotting the data or by means of the serial correlation coefficient or the Durbin-Watson statistic. These means of detection are related as can be seen by examining the three cases in Figure 14–9.

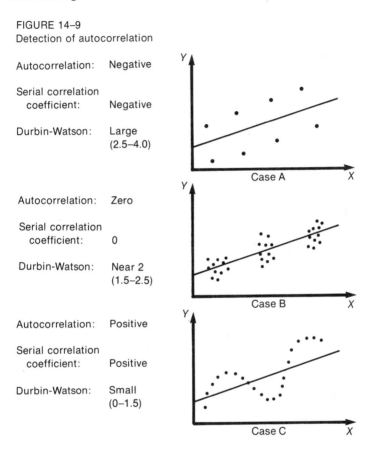

FIGURE 14–9
Detection of autocorrelation

Autocorrelation:	Negative
Serial correlation coefficient:	Negative
Durbin-Watson:	Large (2.5–4.0)

Case A

Autocorrelation:	Zero
Serial correlation coefficient:	0
Durbin-Watson:	Near 2 (1.5–2.5)

Case B

Autocorrelation:	Positive
Serial correlation coefficient:	Positive
Durbin-Watson:	Small (0–1.5)

Case C

Cure.   The cure for autocorrelation is to add some variable to remove the cycle (or nonlinearity) from the data. In time series data, this often involves either deseasonalizing data or using dummy variables to estimate the seasonal effect.

Heteroscedasticity

Heteroscedasticity, in addition to being the opposite of homoscedasticity and a terrific cocktail party shocker, is the situation where the error is related to the size of an independent variable (Figure 14–10). In this case, the larger the value of X, the larger the typical error in prediction. This problem usually occurs when there are orders of magnitude differences on

FIGURE 14–10
Heteroscedasticity

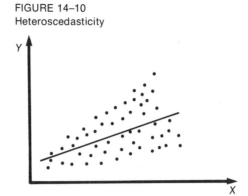

the values of each of a few variables. (Individuals studying output of companies or countries of vastly different sizes are especially likely to encounter this.)

Detection. The easiest way to detect heteroscedasticity is to calculate the correlation between the residuals and each of the independent variables.

Cure. The usual cure is to divide through by a variable which reduces the disparity in the values of the variables. (For example, use income per capita instead of GNP.)

Omitted variables (specification)

One of the most serious problems occurs when variables which are related to both the dependent and at least one of the independent variables are omitted. While not always disastrous predictively, this will distort the coefficients and hence may lead to some inappropriate interpretations of the results. Consider, for example, the following equation:

$$\text{Sales in units} = 2.1 + 3.2(\text{price})$$

An obvious implication of this is that increasing price would increase sales. While it is possible this is so, this is counterintuitive, and the result can be explained as the effect of an omitted variable. Assume sales really depends on quality and is slightly negatively price elastic. Also assume that the higher priced products used in the study were higher in quality. In such a case, the positive price coefficient is really some weighted average of the positive quality effect and the negative price effect where the quality effect happened to be stronger.

Detection. Detection of this problem is often very difficult. The major tip-off is implausible coefficients which cannot be explained on the basis of multicollinearity.

Cure.   The cure is to find the omitted variable and include it in the equation. Unfortunately this is not always easy and requires considerable judgment and knowledge of the situation being modeled. Even when the omitted variable can be identified, it may be difficult to find adequate measurements of it. While it is true that the inclusion of omitted variables tends to increase the problems of multicollinearity, this is usually not a good reason for leaving the variables out.

The use of categorical variables

A lot of data available to marketing researchers is categorical in nature (e.g., sex, occupation, region of the country). Since such variables are often presumed to be related to the dependent variables, it is obvious that it would be advantageous if such nominally scaled variables could be used in regressions. Four basic approaches are possible:

1. *Ignore the fact that the variables are categorical and run the analysis anyway:* Sales = $B_0 + B_1$ (advertising) + B_2 (region). This strategy is foolish (but may be used inadvertantly by anyone who simply "throws the data in and lets the computer decide what's important"). Consider the variable region, where New England is coded 1, the West 2, Midwest 3, and South 4. It seems unlikely that the region variable would be related to anything and even if it were, how would we interpret a significant coefficient?
2. *Ignore the variable.*   This is the easy way out but is not much better than the first approach.
3. *Use the variable as a means of segmenting the sample.*   This would mean running a separate analysis for each region: Sales = $B_0 + B_1$ (advertising). Both the constant and the slope could vary across regions (Figure 14–11). This is the "best" method in terms of prediction and understanding. Unfortunately, it is also the most expensive in terms of sample requirements. If there are four regions, five occupations, and three marital statuses under consideration, the original sample must be divided into 4(5)(3) = 60 subsamples. Even given an

FIGURE 14–11

| New England | Midwest | South | West |

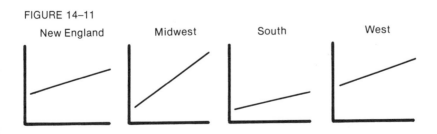

original sample size of 1,000, this is likely to lead to inadequate sample sizes in many of the 60 categories.

4. *Generate a set of dummy variables.* This procedure is somewhat of a compromise between strategies 2 and 3. The basic assumption is that the effect of the other variables (e.g., advertising) is the same in all the regions but the constant differs for each of the regions.

Consider the following data on quarterly fuel oil shipments to the United Kingdom in 1964–66 (Table 14–4). In plotting this data, we see that

TABLE 14–4
Fuel oil shipments to the United Kingdom

Quarter	Year	Sales
1	1964	210
2		120
3		140
4		260
1	1965	220
2		125
3		145
4		270
1	1966	225
2		128
3		149
4		275

there is, as expected a very strong seasonal trend (Figure 14–12). Clearly ignoring the seasonal component would be a major error. (It would also produce significant autocorrelation.) Running four separate regressions is impractical because there would only be three observations per regression. It would be possible to deseasonalize the data before performing the regression, using an adjustment factor for each quarter such as

$$\frac{\text{Average sales for the particular quarter}}{\text{Average sales for all quarters}}$$

Possibly the most appealing approach, however, is to employ dummy variables. This would consist of first creating ("dummying up") a variable for each of the four quarters (Table 14–5). The following equation would then be estimated by regression:

$$\text{Shipments} = B_0 + B_1 \text{ (time)} + B_2 \text{ (winter)} + B_3 \text{ (spring)} + B_4 \text{ (summer)}$$

FIGURE 14–12

Fuel oil
shipments

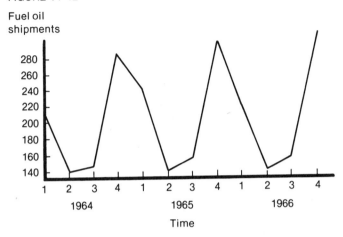

Time

TABLE 14–5

Shipments	Time	Dummy variables			
		Winter	Spring	Summer	Fall
210	1	1	0	0	0
120	2	0	1	0	0
140	3	0	0	1	0
260	4	0	0	0	1
220	5	1	0	0	0
125	6	0	1	0	0
145	7	0	0	1	0
270	8	0	0	0	1
225	9	1	0	0	0
128	10	0	1	0	0
149	11	0	0	1	0
275	12	0	0	0	1

Note that one of the possible dummy variables must be left out so the computer program will run. If all the independent variables are included, the independent variables are perfectly multicollinear. In this case it is impossible to invert a key matrix and the program will bomb. (Alternatively, we could drop the constant B_0 and retain all four dummy variables if that were an option of the computer program being used.) In general, if a categorical variable has c categories, $c - 1$ dummy variables must be employed. Here fall was excluded. This does not affect the final interpretation of the results, which are independent of the variable deleted. The results were

$$B_0 = 256.5$$
$$B_1 = 1.468$$
$$B_2 = -45.6$$
$$B_3 = -141.1$$
$$B_4 = -122.2$$

Predictions for each of the quarters are thus:

Winter:

$$\begin{aligned}
\text{Shipments} &= B_0 + B_1(\text{time}) + B_2(1) \\
&\quad + B_3(0) + B_4(0) \\
&= (B_0 + B_2) + B_1(\text{time}) \\
&= 210 + 1.468(\text{time})
\end{aligned}$$

Spring:

$$\begin{aligned}
\text{Shipments} &= (B_0 + B_3) + B_1(\text{time}) \\
&= 115.5 + 1.468(\text{time})
\end{aligned}$$

Summer:

$$\begin{aligned}
\text{Shipments} &= (B_0 + B_4) + B_1(\text{time}) \\
&= 134.4 + 1.468(\text{time})
\end{aligned}$$

Fall:

$$\begin{aligned}
\text{Shipments} &= B_0 + B_1(\text{time}) \\
&= 256.6 + 1.468(\text{time})
\end{aligned}$$

The results are shown graphically as Figure 14–13. The coefficients of the dummy variables are interpreted as the difference in the average value of

FIGURE 14–13

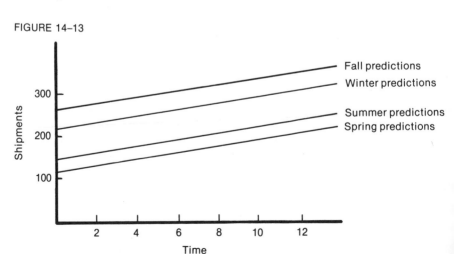

the dependent variable between the category of the dummy variable and the category of the variable which has no dummy variable.

Here the coefficients of the dummy variables indicate the difference in average sales between each quarter and the fall quarter. For example, average shipments in the spring are 45.6 less than shipments in the fall. In essence, dummy variables perform analysis of variance. In fact if all the variables are dummied, analysis of variance and regression are essentially equivalent. (Cultural digression: When some of the independent variables are dummies and some are "real," regression analysis is called analysis of covariance.)

If this model were used to predict shipments in the second quarter of 1968, the "best guess" prediction would then be

$$\text{Predicted shipments} = 115.5 + 1.468(18) = 142$$

Stepwise regression

When faced with a large number of potential independent variables, a researcher often wishes to let the computer select those variables which are in some sense best. The most popular approach is stepwise regression. This procedure begins by selecting the independent variable which is most correlated with the dependent variable, and then a regression is performed. Next the variable which makes the greatest marginal improvement in prediction is added and a second regression run.

The basic criterion used by most of these programs is the correlation between each independent variable not in the equation and the portion of the variance in the dependent variable unexplained by variables in the equation, known as the partial correlation. Whichever independent variable has the largest partial correlation with the dependent variable is entered next. The procedure continues checking partial correlations, adding variables, and performing regressions until it (a) reaches a specified number of variables or (b) ceases to add variables which achieve a specified level of improvement in prediction.

Consider the following example based on a sample of 513 housewives taken in 1968. In order to attempt to profile Gleem toothpaste preferers, Gleem preference was regressed against seven other variables. The simple correlations among the variables are typical of the correlations among demographics, preferences, and importances (Table 14–6). Steps 1, 2, and 7 are summarized in Table 14–7. Examining these steps indicates that in step 1, the procedure selected the variable which had the greatest (absolute) simple correlation with Gleem, importance of price. In the second step, however, it found that the importance of taste was most helpful marginally even though Cepacol preference had a larger simple correlation (.13 versus .10). The final step, which includes all the independent

TABLE 14–6
Correlation matrix

	Prefer-ence for Gleem	Impor-tance of nutritional value (orange juice)	Impor-tance of taste/ flavor (tooth-paste)	Impor-tance of price (tooth-paste)	Cepacol preference	Lavoris preference	Like Hawaii 5-0	Own residence
Preference for Gleem	1.0	.12	.10	-.15	.13	.09	.09	-.08
Importance of nutritional value (orange juice)		1.0	.22	-.03	.02	.04	-.13	.10
Importance of taste/flavor (toothpaste)			1.0	.13	-.05	.02	-.09	.07
Importance of price (toothpaste)				1.0	-.08	-.05	-.03	-.03
Cepacol preference					1.0	-.28	-.04	.01
Lavoris preference						1.0	.04	.11
Like Hawaii 5-0							1.0	-.09
Own residence								1.0

TABLE 14-7

Variable	Coefficient	F ratio
Step 1:		
Constant	3.52	
Importance of price (toothpaste)	−.11	5.9
R = .15		
Step 2:		
Constant	3.31	
Importance of taste/flavor (toothpaste)	.11	4.0
Importance of price (toothpaste)	−.13	7.2
R = .19		
Step 7:		
Constant	2.20	
Importance of nutritional value (orange juice)	.14	3.2
Importance of taste/flavor (toothpaste)	.11	3.7
Importance of price (toothpaste)	−.11	5.7
Cepacol preference	.14	7.2
Lavoris preference	.11	4.4
Like Hawaii 5-0	.08	2.8
Own residence	−.21	3.5
R = .3190		

variables, indicates that in spite of the model's relatively small overall predictive power ($R^2 = .1$), many of the variables are significantly related to Gleem preference (F ratios > 4). This is typical of segmentation type regression results which often uncover key correlates and tendencies but rarely predict individual consumer behavior well.

The advantages of stepwise regression are essentially twofold:

1. It produces a parsimonious model.
2. The resulting model tends to have relatively little multicollinearity among the independent variables.

Unfortunately, there are some important disadvantages to stepwise regression:

1. The results are notoriously unstable in split-half checks where each half of the data is analyzed separately. (The variables often enter differently in the two halves of the sample, thus making interpretation hazardous.)
2. The technique tends to increase the odds of omitting a key variable. For example, assume that the correlations between education and income with the dependent variable were .71 and .70 respectively. A stepwise procedure would then enter education first. If education and income were fairly highly correlated however, income might never be

brought in. Hence an apparent interpretation of the results would be that education influenced the dependent variable but income did not, while in fact income could be at least as important a determinant.

3. Stepwise regression is inferior methodology if any prior model or theory exists. Most studies are more useful if a logical model is first constructed (how else do I know what variables to measure?) and then examined rather than if the results depend on some search algorithm.

Hence stepwise regression must be used with great care. While it may be an easy way to select variables, it is not clear that is a good one.

Nonlinear relations

In some situations, the relation between the independent and dependent variables will be nonlinear. In such situations, the researcher has a choice between two alternatives: building a separate procedure for estimating the relationship or somehow utilizing the linear regression procedure to estimate the parameters of a nonlinear model. Practicality and laziness usually dictate the latter approach.

Using canned linear regression programs to generate nonlinear parameters basically involves "tricking" the computer. Consider the following data concerning registered small aircraft versus time (Figure 14–14). The decline appears to be of the logarithmic/exponential variety. By plotting the logarithms of the number of registered aircraft versus time, the plot appears to be much closer to linear (Figure 14–15). Mathematically, we are saying:

$$\log(\text{registered aircraft}) = a + b(\text{time})$$

By simply inputting the log of registered aircraft as the dependent variable and time as the independent variable, estimates of a and b are obtained.

This procedure can be extended to many other situations. For example, consider the situation where you believe

$$Y = B_0 X_1^{B_1} X_2^{B_2}$$

By taking logarithms of both sides, the model becomes

$$\log Y = \log B_0 + B_1 \log X_1 + B_2 \log X_2$$

By setting:

$$Y^* = \log Y$$
$$X_1^* = \log X_1$$
$$X_2^* = \log X_2$$

and running the linear regression:

$$Y^* = A_0 + A_1X_1^* + A_2X_2^*$$

we can deduce the original parameters as

$$B_0 = \log^{-1}A_0$$
$$B_1 = A_1$$
$$B_2 = A_2$$

Nonlinear forms involving a single variable are equally easy to handle. Consider $Y = B_0 + B_1X_1 + B_2X_1^2$. By submitting X_1 and X_1^2 as the two independent variables to a standard linear regression program, estimates of B_0, B_1, and B_2 can be directly obtained. There are two problems with the process of using linear regression programs to estimate nonlinear models. The first problem is that the estimates obtained are not exactly those which would have been obtained by a specially designed procedure, and are in some sense inferior. Given the precision in most marketing data, however, this is unlikely to be a major problem. The second problem is

FIGURE 14–14
Registered small aircraft (three seats and less) per hundred thousand residents plotted against time

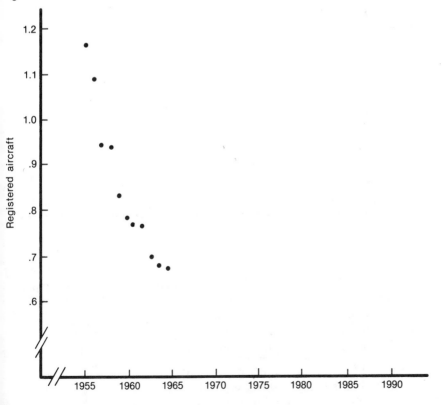

470

FIGURE 14–15
Registered small aircraft (three seats and less) per hundred thousand residents
plotted against time—logarithmic scale

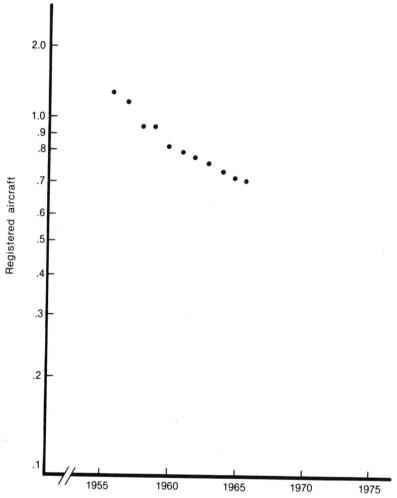

that the procedure may be difficult to use under certain circumstances. For example, an equation involving X, X^2, and X^3 terms will be tremendously unstable due to high collinearity.

One final point worth making concerns why linear models are so widely used. The following three major reasons exist:

1. Canned programs do linear regression. This may be a bad normative reason but is a key descriptive explanation.

2. Linear models are usually good approximations of nonlinear models, especially over a small range. This is especially true when there is noise in the data, as in the case of survey research.
3. There is one linear model for a set of variables but an infinite number of nonlinear ones. This makes trying to find an appropriate nonlinear model hazardous and time consuming.
    Some good advice, therefore, is to always try a linear model unless.
    a. The predictive power of the linear model is inadequate, or
    b. Some theory exists which suggests nonlinearity.

SOME USES OF REGRESSION ANALYSIS

Given the aggravation associated with understanding regression analysis, a reasonable question is whether the benefits outweigh the costs. Regression is an extremely useful tool for a variety of purposes. This section will delineate three major areas of applicability which highlight some of the benefits of regression.

Forecasting

Regression analysis is a widely used forecasting tool which is applied in two basic ways:

1. Using time as the key independent variable.
2. Using other variables (such as price and competitive advertising) as the independent variables.

In both cases the objective is a good prediction which means a big R^2 and a small standard error of estimate. The coefficients themselves are used for generating predictions but are not important in their own right. Many times series regressions and regressions involving aggregate economic data often produce R^2's over .99.

Segmentation

Regression is often used to define segments of customers in terms of demographics, life-styles, or general attitudes (Massy, Frank, and Lodahl, 1968; Frank, Massy, and Wind, 1972). This typically produces R^2 of .10 or smaller. If the goal were prediction of individual behavior, this would be poor. The goal of segmentation, however, is to find general tendencies, not to predict individual behavior. Since marketing strategy for frequently purchased products is directed at groups (e.g., high income), the basic goal is to find groups of consumers where concentrating effort would bring a greater average response. Consider the results from a study of 513 housewives. Obviously knowing a person's income would not make possible an accurate prediction of the amount of time that particular individual spends watching TV. In fact, the R^2 was .048. On the other hand, it is obvious that average behavior is related to income (Figure 14–16). In fact, a regression between income level and average TV

FIGURE 14–16

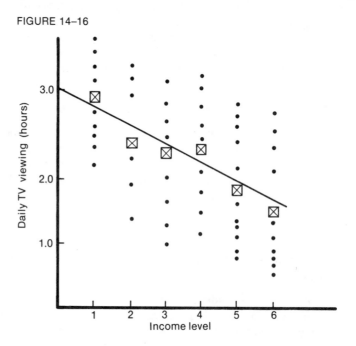

- Individual data point

☒ AverageTV viewing for all individuals in a particular income level

Source: Donald R. Lehmann, "Validity and Goodness of Fit in Data Analysis," *Advances in Consumer Research*, ed. Schlinger (Ann Arbor, Mich.: Association for Consumer Research, 1975), p. 746.

viewing behavior produced an R^2 of .878 (Lehmann, 1975). Practically, this shows that very low-income people watch, on average, twice as much TV as high-income people.

A variety of examples concerning the use of regression as a tool for identifying market segments appear in Bass, Tigert, and Lonsdale (1968). Using *Milwaukee Journal* panel data, the authors found the typical low R^2's using demographic variables (age, income, occupation, number of children, education, and TV viewing) as predictors of various frequently purchased products. The differences in average consumption, however, were very noticeable (Figure 14–17). The point, then, is the low R^2's

FIGURE 14–17
Light and heavy buyers by mean purchase rates for different socioeconomic cells

R^2	Product	Description		Mean consumption rate ranges		Ratio of highest to lowest rate
		Light buyers	Heavy buyers	Light buyers	Heavy buyers	
.08	Catsup	Unmarried or married over age 50 without children	Under 50, three or more children	.74–1.82	2.73–5.79	7.8
.07	Frozen orange juice	Under 35 or over 65, income less than $10,000, not college grads, two or less children	College grads, income over $10,000, between 35 and 65	1.12–2.24	3.53–9.00	8.0
.04	Pancake mix	Some college, two or less children	Three or more children, high school or less education	.48–.52	1.10–1.51	3.3
.08	Candy bars	Under 35, no children	35 or over, three or more children	1.01–4.31	6.56–22.29	21.9
	Cake mix	Not married or under 35, no children, income under $10,000, TV less than 3½ hours	35 or over, three or more children, income over $10,000	.55–1.10	2.22–3.80	6.9
.09	Beer	Under 25 or over 50, college education, nonprofessional, TV less than 2 hours	Between 25 and 50, not college graduate, TV more than 3½ hours	0–12.33	17.26–40.30	∞
.02	Cream shampoo	Income less than $8,000, at least some college, less than five children	Income $10,000 or over with high school or less education	.16–.35	.44–.87	5.5
.06	Hair spray	Over 65, under $8,000 income	Under 65, over $10,000 income, not college graduate	0–.41	.52–1.68	∞
.09	Toothpaste	Over 50, less than three children, income less than $8,000	Under 50, three or more children, over $10,000 income	1.41–2.01	2.22–4.39	3.1
.03	Mouthwash	Under 35 or over 65, less than $8,000 income, some college	Between 35 and 65, income over $8,000, high school or less education	.46–.85	.98–1.17	2.5

Source: Frank Bass, Douglas Tigert, and Ronald Lonsdale, "Market Segmentation—Group versus Individual Behavior." Reprinted from *Journal of Marketing Research*, published by the American Marketing Association, vol. 5 (August 1968), p. 267.

mean that individual predictions cannot be made accurately, not that the results are worthless. In fact, when using survey data, R^2's above .6 usually mean that either the equation is essentially a tautology or that the data was incorrectly analyzed.

Model parameter estimation and testing

In certain circumstances a model is relatively well established and regression is employed to estimate its parameters. In such a case, the R^2 is of only limited interest. The major concern is with the sign and size of the coefficients. If a prior theory gives a range of acceptable values for the coefficients, then the estimated coefficients may be used as a basis for accepting or rejecting the model.

For example, one might assume (based on some theory or analysis) that the effect of raising price one dollar would be to decrease sales by between one and three units. Hence in a multiple regression, with sales as the dependent variable and price as one of the independent variables, we would expect the regression coefficient relating price to sales to be between -1 and -3. If the estimated coefficient fell outside the range, then the model would be rejected.

In deciding what model to use to represent a situation, one less "pure" approach is to try several alternatives and see which produces the "best" regression result (high R^2's, plausible and significant coefficients, etc.). While this application of regression is theoretically inferior, in practice it is widely used.

CAUSATION VERSUS CORRELATION

Regression analysis is a correlational procedure which does not directly address the issue of causality. Low R^2's or insignificant regression coefficients may indicate either weak causality, bad data, or a poor mathematical representation of the relation between variables. Similarly, high R^2's or significant regression coefficients may indicate bad data or tautologies. Even with good data, a high R^2 can mislead a researcher into imputing causality where none exists. For example, assume a researcher ran the following regression:

$$\text{Fertilizer applied} = B_0 + B_1 \text{ (yield)}$$

Presumably both R^2 and B_1 would be significant. If the data were based on an experiment using equally productive fields, however, the conclusion that yield caused fertilizer application could be exactly wrong.

Numerous examples of strong correlation not necessarily indicating causation can be found. Consider football. NFL football statistics for 1973 indicate that the winning team gained more yards rushing than the losing team. The apparent implication is to stress rushing in the game plan in order to win. On further reflection, however, this may not be so wise. A team with a lead tends to run to use up the clock and avoid turnovers. Hence being ahead (which is quite conducive to winning) may lead to rushing yards just as much as rushing yards leads to winning. Another example is the correlation between the stork population and the human birth rate. While the most popular explanation is that more people mean more houses, more houses more chimneys, and more chimneys more storks, the alternatives are quite interesting.

Probably the classic example of correlation is the result attributed to Jevons who found that sun spot activity was strongly related to business cycles. Obviously this is purely coincidental say the pundits. On the other hand, it is conceivable that the relationship is causal. Sun spots change the gravitational pull of the sun, which in turn affects the orbit of the earth and its rotation. Changing the rotation of the earth then affects its electromagnetic field. Since individuals' nervous systems function by a type of electricity, this would affect the way people think and behave and hence business. While this may seem like a far out explanation (or possibly a false one if you know much about physics), the point is that it is difficult to differentiate causality and correlation. It would not be surprising if astrology turned out to be related to changing gravitational pulls "when Jupiter aligns with Mars," and so forth.

The point of this section, therefore, is that causality is essentially impossible to determine from regressions. Any causal implications must be the result of prior knowledge and judgment. What regression can do for someone interested in causality is to estimate the strength of causality which has been correctly prespecified by the researcher.

Simultaneous equation regression

In many circumstances, one would posit that two variables are interrelated. For example, consider the relation between advertising and sales. Sales is generally thought to depend on advertising. On the other hand, advertising budgets are often set as a percent of sales, and hence sales affect advertising. This means that a single regression of sales versus advertising would produce an aggregate summary of the advertising to sales and the sales to advertising relations and hence be relatively useless. In order to get around this problem of joint effects, one alternative is to construct two equations:

$$\text{Sales} = f(\text{advertising, other variables})$$

$$\text{Advertising} = f(\text{sales, other variables})$$

By estimating the two equations simultaneously, it is sometimes possible to estimate the separate effects of advertising on sales and sales on advertising. While simultaneous procedures are fairly technical and are beyond the scope of this book (see Appendix 14–D), the recognition of the problem of joint causation and the realization that procedures exist for dealing with the problem is very useful. If you think you have encountered such a problem, call an expert.

MAKING REGRESSION USEFUL

A key question is: "How can a researcher use regression without 'putting off' potential users?" This question raises two issues. The first issue concerns how to go about building a useful model. In deciding what variables to include, a variety of considerations/criteria must be considered:

1. *Parsimony.* The boss is a busy person; don't overtax his/her brain with complicated models.
2. *Data availability.* Use what is readily available, as data collection is both expensive and tedious.
3. *Plausibility.* Try to use variables which are logically related to the dependent variables (sun spots are a no-no).
4. *Goodness of fit.* Try to get a big R^2. Low R^2's may be significant but are hard to sell.
5. *Good coefficients.* Use only variables whose coefficients are significant with plausible signs and coefficients.
6. *Technical limitations.* The entire range of technical issues (multicollinearity, autocorrelation, heteroscedasticity, omitted variables, etc.) should be considered.

Since many of these criteria conflict (e.g., parsimony versus goodness of fit), the researcher must exercise judgment. Building a regression model is thus as much a craft as a science.

The other major issue in making regression useful is in communicating the results. In this regard, remember that F tests and Durbin-Watson statistics may be important aids to interpretation but usually become barriers to communication. With rare exception the users of regressions are, quite properly, not statisticians. Hence they do not understand or care about statistical jargon and tend to be irritated by it (sometimes as a defense against feeling inadequate). The wise researcher, therefore, attempts to simplify the results. One especially effective trick is the "what if" approach. Rather than simply presenting the resulting equation, calculate estimates for different levels of the key variables by plugging the values into the equation and discuss them (i.e., if we spend $100,000 on advertising, then sales will be X while if we spend $200,000, sales will be Y). In short, never forget that for marketing research, regression is only a means to the end of providing more useful information on which to base real decisions.

SUMMARY

Motivation

Regression analysis is an attempt to predict one dependent variable (Y) as a linear combination of a set of k independent variables (X's). Example:

$$\text{Sales} = f(\text{income, education, age, . . .})$$

Model

$$Y = B_0 + B_1X_1 + B_2X_2 + \cdots + B_kX_k + \mu$$

(i.e., Sales $= B_0 + B_1(\text{income}) + B_2(\text{education}) + \cdots.$)

Solution

B's are chosen so as to minimize $\Sigma(Y - \hat{Y})^2$ (the differences between the actual and predicted values of Y).

Input

The raw data on the X's and Y for a number (n) of observations.

Output

1. The regression coefficients (B's).
2. Index of fit (R^2).
3. Standard error of prediction ($S_{Y.X}$).

Interpretation

1. The B's are interpreted as the amount of change in Y which would be caused by a change of one unit in each of the X's. B_0 is the constant (intercept) which is the prediction for Y if all the X's were zero.
2. $R^2 =$ the percent of the variance in Y explained ($1 =$ all, $0 =$ none).
3. $S_{Y.X}$: A measure of how uncertain (inaccurate) predictions made using the results will be.

The interpretation is complicated if—

1. Multicollinearity exists (the X's are highly correlated).
2. Autocorrelation exists (the μ's are correlated, a typical problem in time series data where cycles exist).
3. Certain important variables are omitted.

4. The measurements are biased.
5. Heteroscedasticity exists (the expected error term, μ, is not constant).

Uses

There are many uses, including the following:

1. Forecasting: Prediction $= \hat{Y} + 2S_{Y.X}$.
2. Segmentation.
3. Model building and parameter estimation.

Glossary of equivalent terms and symbols

1. Dependent variable, criterion variable, Y.
2. Independent variable, predictor variable, X_i.
3. Intercept, constant, B_0.
4. Slope, regression coefficient, B_i.
5. e, $Y - \hat{Y}$, error, residual, deviation.

PROBLEMS

1. The frequency of purchase of a luxury nondurable may be a function of a person's income. The following sample has been obtained:

Income	Purchases per year
10	1
15	2
20	2
15	1
20	3
20	4
25	5
5	0
5	1
20	3
15	3
15	2
5	2
10	2
25	3
10	3
10	2
5	2
15	4
15	3

a. Estimate the regression line graphically.
b. Examine the plot of purchase rate versus income to determine if the assumption of homoseodasticity seems granted. That is, does the variance of the disturbance term appear to be independent of income?
c. Examine the plot of mean purchases for each income level. Does the linear model appear to be adequate or should a nonlinear model be used?

2. In a study, 155 full-page magazine ads were studied. The percent of the people who read the ads (as measured by Starch scores) was regressed against a variety of mechanical layout variables, copy/message variables, and product class. The sixth step of a stepwise regression was as follows:

Variable	B	S_B
Bleed	4.05	1.00
Product category 11	−.48	.13
Product category 12	.51	.22
Size....................	−.40	.22
Product category 5	−1.44	.84
Product category 17	−.24	.16
Constant	10.19	

$$R^2 = .24.$$
Standard error $= 5.87.$

a. Interpret the results statistically.
b. What managerial conclusions can you draw?

3. Let $X_1, X_2, \ldots, X_{20}$ represent the number of Ph.D. degrees awarded by U.S. universities in the years 1951, 1952, . . . , 1970. Let $Y_1, Y_2, \ldots, Y_{20}$ represent the GNP for the United States in those same years. Assume that we have performed a simple correlation analysis on the time series X verses the time series Y.
a. What do you feel the approximate value of r will be (both magnitude and sign)? Justify your answer.
b. What can be said about the causal effect of Ph.D.'s on GNP?

4. In using multiple regression when is collinearity (high correlation among the independent variables) a problem and when is it not a problem?

5. Assume I am interested in the relationship of income to age and height for a sample of ten males. The data are as follows:

Income	Age	Height (inches)
$13,000	29	69
20,000	35	76
40,000	37	70
15,000	21	73
8,000	18	64
19,000	29	71
31,000	42	67
5,000	17	72
29,000	45	75
32,000	31	68

Interpret—

a. By tabular analysis.

b. By graphical analysis of the two independent variables separately.

c. By using multiple regression.

6. How might I use regression analysis to estimate b and c if I think $Y = kX^b Z^c$, given a set of measurements on Y, X, Z?

7. Is it possible for all the individual regression coefficients to be non-significant and the R^2 to be significant? Why not *or* what would it mean?

8. When will omitted variable bias occur in regression analysis?

9. The following regression model was estimated to explain the annual sales of a mail-order house.

$$S_t = 105 + 3.0A_t + 12.0M_t + .5C_t; R^2 = .95$$
$$(4.2) \quad (1.0) \quad (1.1)$$

where

$S_t = \$$ sales in year t

$A_t = \$$ advertising expenditures in year t

$M_t = \$$ merchandise mailing expenditures in year t

$C_t = $ number of catalogs distributed in year t

The estimated standard errors are in parenthesis below the coefficient estimates. The customer service manager suggests that we should increase our mailing expenditures next year by sending more shipments first class rather than parcel post since the mailing expenditures coefficient is "significant" in the regression. What would you advise?

10. Joe Planner is in charge of sales forecasting for Trinket Company. He collected 20 monthly variables which he thought might be related to Trinket Company sales. The first was U.S. automobile sales (sea-

sonally adjusted). The 20th was monthly rainfall in Morningside Heights. Joe ran a regression using the 20 monthly variables to explain the monthly sales (dollars) of Trinket Company for the last 96 months. The regression had an R^2 of .95. Joe is predicting sales for this month of $100, based upon this regression model.

a. Interpret his work. Joe thinks that the R^2 is a good measure of his model's performance. Is it?

b. You now find that the third variable in Joe's regression was the monthly expenditure (dollars) for salespersons entertaining customers. The coefficient of this variable was 5.2, with an estimated standard error of .2. Joe figures that since we make 40 percent gross margin on sales, that it would be profitable to increase the entertaining budget:

Spend	$ 1	more on entertaining
×	5.0	(minimum sales increase/$) from regression
	$ 5	sales increase
×	40%	gross margin
	$ 2	increase in contribution to profits
−	1	recover added entertaining cost
	$ 1	leaves $1 profit improvement

Is Joe's conclusion correct? Why?

c. Joe's rival suggests that the monthly entertaining budget should be changed monthly, and should be set randomly, based upon the last digit of the winning number in the New Jersey State Lottery each month. Interpret the recommendation of Joe's rival. What would this recommendation gain us?

11. If my independent variables in a regression are highly correlated,

a. Are the regression assumptions violated?

b. What will happen to my coefficient estimates?

c. What will happen to R?

12. What is a way to detect if the disturbances (errors) in regression are correlated?

13. What is the difference between predictive, causal, and correlational relationships?

BIBLIOGRAPHY

Bass, Frank M.: Tigert, Douglas J.; and Lonsdale, Ronald T. "Market Segmentation—Group versus Individual Behavior." *Journal of Marketing Research,* vol. 5 (August 1968), pp. 264–70.

———, and Wittink, Dick R. "Pooling Issues and Methods in Regression Analysis with Examples in Marketing Research." *Journal of Marketing Research,* vol. 12 (November 1975), pp. 414–25.

Draper, N., and Smith, H. *Applied Regression Analysis.* New York: Wiley, 1966.

Frank, Ronald E.; Massy, William F.; and Wind, Yoram. *Market Segmentation.* Englewood Cliffs, N.J.: Prentice-Hall, 1972.

Galton, F. *Natural Inheritance.* London: MacMillan, 1889.

Johnston, J. *Econometric Methods.* 2d ed. New York: McGraw-Hill, 1972.

Lehmann, Donald R. "Validity and Goodness of Fit in Data Analysis." In *Advances in Consumer Research,* edited by Schlinger. Ann Arbor, Mich.: Association for Consumer Research, 1975, pp. 741–49.

Massy, William F.; Frank, Ronald E.; and Lodahl, Thomas M. *Purchasing Behavior and Personal Attributes.* Philadelphia: University of Pennsylvania Press, 1968.

--------- APPENDIX 14–A ---------

HAND CALCULATION

Hand calculations of regression coefficients are rarely made. Nonetheless, to see how these estimation formulas can be applied is useful. Consider the following data:

X	Y
1	8
3	16
5	19
7	25
9	36
11	34

Assuming we were forced to solve this problem by hand, we could set up Table 14A–1. Hence we get

$$B_1 = \frac{196}{70} = 2.8$$

$$B_0 = 23 - \frac{196}{70}(6) = 23 - 16.8 = 6.2$$

$$r = \frac{196}{\sqrt{70}\ \sqrt{584}} = .969$$

Alternatively we could use the raw data in Table 14A–2. Here the results would be

$$B_1 = \frac{1,024 - 6(6)(23)}{286 - 6(6)^2} = \frac{196}{70} = 2.8$$

$$B_0 = 23 - 2.8(6) = 6.2$$

$$r = \frac{1,024 - 6(6)(23)}{\sqrt{286 - 6(6)^2} \ \sqrt{3,758 - 6(23)^2}} = \frac{196}{\sqrt{70} \ \sqrt{584}} = .969$$

To calculate the standard error of estimate, we can calculate the values of $\hat{Y} = 6.2 + 2.8X$ (Table 14A–3). Thus

$$S_{Y.X} = \sqrt{\frac{35.20}{4}} = 2.97$$

TABLE 14A–1

	X	Y	$(X - \bar{X})$	$(Y - \bar{Y})$	$(X - \bar{X})$ $(Y - \bar{Y})$	$(X - \bar{X})^2$	$(Y - \bar{Y})^2$
	1	8	−5	−15	75	25	225
	3	16	−3	−7	21	9	49
	5	19	−1	−4	4	1	16
	7	25	1	2	2	1	4
	9	36	3	13	39	9	169
	11	34	5	11	55	25	121
Sum	36	138	0	0	196	70	584
Average ...	6	23					

TABLE 14A–2

	X	Y	XY	X^2	Y^2
	1	8	8	1	64
	3	16	48	9	256
	5	19	95	25	361
	7	25	175	49	625
	9	36	324	81	1,296
	11	34	374	121	1,156
Sum	36	138	1,024	286	3,758
Average	6	23			

TABLE 14A–3

X	Y	$\hat{Y}$	$Y - \hat{Y}$	$(Y - \hat{Y})_2$
1	8	9	−1	1.00
3	16	14.6	1.4	1.96
5	19	20.2	−1.2	1.44
7	25	25.8	−.8	.64
9	36	31.4	4.6	21.16
11	34	37.0	−3.0	9.00
				35.20

APPENDIX 14-B

FORMULA DERIVATION

This Appendix presents a brief outline of the derivation of the formulas used in regression analysis. For a complete treatment, see Johnston (1972).

Two-variable case

Model: $Y = \alpha + \beta X + \mu$

Procedure: Select $\hat{\alpha}$, $\hat{\beta}$ in order to Min $\sum_{i=1}^{n} (Y_i - \hat{Y}_i)^2 = \Sigma e_i^2$

Method: $\sum_{i=1}^{n} (Y - \hat{Y})^2 = \sum_{i=1}^{n} (Y_i - \hat{\alpha} - \hat{\beta}X_i)^2$

Taking partial derivatives with respect to $\hat{\alpha}$ and $\hat{\beta}$, we get

$$\frac{\partial \Sigma e_i^2}{\partial \hat{\alpha}} = \sum_{i=1}^{n} 2(Y_i - \hat{\alpha} - \hat{\beta}X_i)(-1)$$

$$\frac{\partial \Sigma e_i^2}{\partial \hat{\beta}} = \sum_{i=1}^{n} 2(Y_i - \hat{\alpha} - \hat{\beta}X_i)(-X_i)$$

(N.B.: The second-order conditions for a minimum are met.) Setting the partial derivatives equal to 0,

$$\sum_{i=1}^{n} 2(Y_i - \alpha - \beta X_i) = 0$$

$$\sum_{i=1}^{n} 2X_i(Y_i - \hat{\alpha} - \hat{\beta}X_i) = 0$$

These two equations (sometimes called the normal equations for some obscure reason) can be solved for $\hat{\alpha}$ and $\hat{\beta}$:

$$\hat{\alpha} = \bar{Y} - \hat{\beta}\bar{X}$$

$$\hat{\beta} = \frac{\sum_{i=1}^{n} X_i Y_i - n\bar{X}\bar{Y}}{\sum_{i=1}^{n} X_i^2 - n\bar{X}^2} = \frac{\sum_{i=1}^{n} (X - \bar{X})(Y - \bar{Y})}{\sum_{i=1}^{n} (X_i - \bar{X})^2}$$

General linear model

Model:

$$Y_i = B_0 + B_1X_{1i} + B_2X_{2i} + \cdots + B_kX_{ki} + \mu_i$$

Matrix notation:

$$Y = XB + \mu$$

where

$$Y = \begin{bmatrix} Y \\ Y_2 \\ \cdot \\ \cdot \\ \cdot \\ Y_n \end{bmatrix} \qquad X = \begin{bmatrix} 1 & X_{11} & X_{k1} \\ 1 & X_{12} & X_{k2} \\ & \cdot & \\ & \cdot & \\ & \cdot & \\ 1 & X_{1n} & X_{kn} \end{bmatrix}$$

$$B = \begin{bmatrix} B_0 \\ B_1 \\ B_2 \\ \cdot \\ \cdot \\ B_k \end{bmatrix} \qquad \text{and} \qquad \mu = \begin{bmatrix} \mu_1 \\ \mu_2 \\ \cdot \\ \cdot \\ \cdot \\ \mu_n \end{bmatrix}$$

Procedure: Select $\hat{\beta}$ in order to minimize

$$\sum_{i=1}^{n} (Y_i - \hat{Y}_i)^2$$

In matrix form, this becomes

$$(Y - X\hat{\beta})'(Y - X\hat{\beta}) = e'e$$

In order to

$$\text{Min} \sum_{i=1}^{n} (Y_i - \hat{Y}_i)^2 = \text{Min}[Y'Y - 2\hat{\beta}X'Y + \hat{\beta}X'X\hat{\beta}]$$

we take the first derivative with respect to the vector $\hat{\beta}$.

Therefore

$$\frac{\partial e'e}{\partial \hat{\beta}} = -2X'Y + 2X'X\hat{\beta}$$

Setting this equal to 0 and solving, we get

$$\hat{\beta} = [X'X]^{-1}X'Y$$

APPENDIX 14-C
SAMPLE REGRESSION OUTPUT

STATISTICAL PACKAGE FOR THE SOCIAL SCIENCES SPSSH - VERSION 6.00   06/27/77

SPACE ALLOCATION FOR THIS RUN..

TOTAL AMOUNT REQUESTED   80000 BYTES

DEFAULT TRANSPACE ALLOCATICN   13000 BYTES

MAX NO OF TRANSFORMATIONS PERMITTED   100
MAX NO OF RECODE VALUES   400
MAX NO OF ARITHM.OR LOG.OPERATIONS   800

RESULTING WORKSPACE ALLOCATION   70000 BYTES

VARIABLE LIST   YRBORN,INCCME,FAMSIZE,EXPENSE,
                   BRAND,INFO,VARIETY,TASTE,OTHERS,DIET,PRICE,
                   AVAIL,EASE,HABIT,SPECIAL,NUTRI

INPUT MEDIUM   DISK
N OF CASES   UNKNOWN
INPUT FORMAT   FIXED(20X,F2.0,54X,2F1.0/12X,F1.0,1X,
                   2F1.0,1X,10F1.0////)

ACCORDING TO YOUR INPUT FORMAT, VARIABLES ARE TO BE READ AS FOLLOWS

VARIABLE	FORMAT	RECORD	COLUMNS
YRBORN	F 2.0	1	21- 22
INCCME	F 1.0	1	77- 77
FAMSIZE	F 1.0	1	78- 78
EXPENSE	F 1.0	2	13- 13
BRAND	F 1.0	2	15- 15
INFO	F 1.0	2	16- 16
VARIETY	F 1.0	2	19- 19
TASTE	F 1.0	2	20- 20
OTHERS	F 1.0	2	21- 21
DIET	F 1.0	2	22- 22
PRICE	F 1.0	2	23- 23
AVAIL	F 1.0	2	24- 24
EASE	F 1.0	2	25- 25
HABIT	F 1.0	2	26- 26
SPECIAL	F 1.0	2	27- 27
NUTRI	F 1.0	2		

THE INPUT FORMAT PROVIDES FOR 16 VARIABLES.   16 WILL BE READ
IT PROVIDES FOR   6 RECORDS ('CARDS') PER CASE.   A MAXIMUM OF 78 'COLUMNS' ARE USED ON A RECORD.

RECODE   EXPENSE(1=12.5)(2=22.5)(3=37.5)
               (4=52.5)(5=70)

CCMPUTE   AGE=75-YRBORN
MISSING VALUES EXPENSE(0),YRBORN(00),FAMSIZE(0),INCOME(0)/
               BRAND,INFO,VARIETY,TASTE,OTHERS,DIET,PRICE,
               AVAIL,EASE,HABIT,SPECIAL,NUTRI(0)

```
                    BRAND,INFO,VARIETY,TASTE,OTHERS,DIET,PRICE,
                    AVAIL,EASE,HABIT,SPECIAL,NUTRI/
                    REGRESSION=EXPENSE WITH INCOME TO NUTRI(2)/
                    REGRESSION=EXPENSE WITH INCOME TO NUTRI(1)/
        STATISTICS  ALL
```

***** REGRESSION PROBLEM REQUIRES   5120 BYTES WORKSPACE, NOT INCLUDING RESIDUALS *****

READ INPUT DATA

AFTER READING   940 CASES FROM SUBFILE NONAME , END OF FILE WAS ENCOUNTERED ON LOGICAL UNIT # 8

FILE   NONAME   (CREATION DATE = 06/27/77)

VARIABLE	MEAN	STANDARD DEV	CASES
EXPENSE	37.5230	15.1153	762
INCOME	2.7520	1.4208	762
AGE	43.7008	16.5416	762
FAMSIZE	3.2874	1.3756	762
BRAND	2.3425	1.4150	762
INFO	1.8740	0.6504	762
VARIETY	2.0407	0.9603	762
TASTE	1.2362	0.5656	762
OTHERS	1.6955	0.8578	762
DIET	3.0433	1.5749	762
PRICE	1.7520	0.9619	762
AVAIL	2.1654	1.1285	762
EASE	2.7546	1.2245	762
HABIT	2.7927	1.1390	762
SPECIAL	4.2559	1.2511	762
NUTRI	1.6745	0.8800	762

FILE NONAME (CREATION DATE = 06/27/77)

CORRELATION COEFFICIENTS

A VALUE OF 59.00000 IS PRINTED
IF A COEFFICIENT CANNOT BE COMPUTED.

	EXPENSE	INCOME	AGE	FAMSIZE	BRAND	INFO	VARIETY	TASTE	OTHERS	DIET	PRICE	AVAIL
EXPENSE	1.00000	0.41605	-0.08544	0.57810	0.03772	-0.01307	0.00627	-0.02907	-0.01740	0.01790	0.08422	-0.04510
INCOME	0.41605	1.00000	-0.12226	0.27252	-0.00606	-0.03244	0.02474	-0.04357	0.01180	0.06882	0.25973	-0.01045
AGE	-0.08544	-0.12226	1.00000	-0.27220	-0.10066	0.06135	-0.02248	-0.01154	-0.02234	-0.15224	0.02787	-0.04620
FAMSIZE	0.57810	0.27252	-0.27220	1.00000	0.09850	0.03316	-0.01897	0.03592	0.04967	0.11919	-0.01359	-0.02050
BRAND	0.03772	-0.00606	-0.10066	0.09850	1.00000	-0.14867	-0.01897	0.02325	-0.04269	-0.05148	-0.14218	0.00563
INFO	-0.01307	-0.03244	0.06135	0.03316	-0.14867	1.00000	0.11131	0.00956	0.03999	0.10925	0.12432	-0.01097
VARIETY	0.00627	0.02474	-0.02248	-0.01897	-0.01897	0.11131	1.00000	0.32582	0.20949	0.14394	0.05362	0.12194
TASTE	-0.02907	-0.04357	-0.01154	0.03592	0.02325	0.00956	0.32582	1.00000	0.33071	0.04455	0.04020	0.07829
OTHERS	-0.01740	0.01180	-0.02234	0.04967	-0.04269	0.03999	0.20949	0.33071	1.00000	0.13573	0.02808	0.07803
DIET	0.01790	0.06882	-0.15224	0.11919	-0.05148	0.10925	0.14394	0.04455	0.13573	1.00000	0.10772	0.20125
PRICE	0.08422	0.25973	0.02787	-0.01359	-0.14218	0.12432	0.05362	0.04020	0.02808	0.10772	1.00000	0.20125
AVAIL	-0.04510	-0.01045	-0.04620	-0.02050	0.00563	-0.01097	0.12194	0.07829	0.07803	0.20125	0.20125	1.00000
EASE	-0.01904	-0.01162	-0.00577	-0.02516	0.04099	-0.11477	0.05097	0.08001	0.05865	0.02868	0.12452	0.30326
HABIT	-0.12929	-0.08542	-0.00964	-0.04753	0.04413	-0.16303	0.08822	0.11692	0.12709	0.03578	0.05854	0.23015
SPECIAL	0.02835	0.03206	-0.04843	-0.00843	0.13495	0.13456	0.08648	0.09273	0.07531	0.02238	0.32362	0.17289
NUTRI	0.03267	0.05937	0.00070	0.03938	-0.02916	0.26807	0.25361	0.22594	0.14054	0.27946	0.22741	0.08470

	EASE	HABIT	SPECIAL	NUTRI
EXPENSE	-0.01904	-0.12929	0.02835	0.03267
INCOME	-0.01162	-0.08542	0.03206	0.05937
AGE	-0.00577	-0.00964	-0.04843	0.00070
FAMSIZE	-0.02516	-0.04753	-0.00843	0.03938
BRAND	0.04099	0.04413	0.13495	-0.02916
INFO	-0.11477	-0.16303	0.13456	0.26807
VARIETY	0.05097	0.08822	0.08648	0.25361
TASTE	0.08001	0.11692	0.09273	0.22594
OTHERS	0.05865	0.12709	0.07531	0.14054
DIET	0.02868	0.03578	0.02238	0.27946
PRICE	0.12452	0.05854	0.32362	0.22741
AVAIL	0.30326	0.23015	0.17289	0.08470
EASE	1.00000	0.28569	0.06163	-0.00837
HABIT	0.28569	1.00000	0.09907	0.02305
SPECIAL	0.06163	0.09907	1.00000	0.18079
NUTRI	-0.00837	0.02305	0.18079	1.00000

STATISTICAL PACKAGE FOR THE SOCIAL SCIENCES SPSSH - VERSION 6.00   06/27/77   PAGE   5

FILE   NGNAME   (CREATION DATE = 06/27/77)

*   M U L T I P L E   R E G R E S S I O N   * * * * * * * * * * * * * * * * * * *   VARIABLE LIST   1
                                                                                                                            REGRESSION LIST 1

DEPENDENT VARIABLE..   EXPENSE

VARIABLE(S) ENTERED ON STEP NUMBER 1..   NUTRI
                                            INCOME
                                            AGE
                                            FAMSIZE
                                            BRAND
                                            INFO
                                            VARIETY
                                            TASTE
                                            OTHERS
                                            DIET
                                            PRICE
                                            AVAIL
                                            EASE
                                            HABIT
                                            SPECIAL

MULTIPLE R   0.65532
R SQUARE   0.42945
ADJUSTED R SQUARE 0.41870
STANDARD ERROR   11.53155

ANALYSIS OF VARIANCE   DF   SUM OF SQUARES   MEAN SQUARE   F
REGRESSION   15.   74667.73002   4977.84867   37.43399
RESIDUAL   746.   99200.61808   132.97670

------------- VARIABLES IN THE EQUATION -------------   -------------- VARIABLES NOT IN THE EQUATION --------------

VARIABLE	B	BETA	STD ERROR B	F	VARIABLE	BETA IN	PARTIAL	TOLERANCE	F
NUTRI	0.47245	0.02750	0.54198	0.760					
INCOME	2.88617	0.27128	0.32247	80.108					
AGE	0.07983	0.08737	0.02683	8.851					
FAMSIZE	5.85584	0.53293	0.33067	313.636					
BRAND	0.00635	0.00059	0.30616	0.000					
INFO	-1.08607	-0.04673	0.69705	2.428					
VARIETY	0.02149	0.00137	0.47587	0.002					
TASTE	-1.39632	-0.05225	0.83180	2.818					
OTHERS	-0.28381	-0.01686	0.50323	0.318					
DIET	-0.46426	-0.04837	0.28538	2.647					
PRICE	0.28637	0.01822	0.49990	0.329					
AVAIL	-0.24058	-0.01796	0.40468	0.353					
EASE	0.28449	0.02305	0.37152	0.586					
HABIT	-1.06932	-0.08058	0.39900	7.182					
SPECIAL	0.49106	0.04064	0.36442	1.616					
(CONSTANT)	12.76075								

ALL VARIABLES ARE IN THE EQUATION

FILE   NONAME   (CREATION DATE = 06/27/77)

* * * * * * * * * * * * * * * * * * *   M U L T I P L E   R E G R E S S I O N   * * * * * * * * * * * * * * * * * * *   VARIABLE LIST   1
                                                                                                                        REGRESSION LIST   1

DEPENDENT VARIABLE..   EXPENSE

SUMMARY TABLE

VARIABLE	MULTIPLE R	R SQUARE	RSQ CHANGE	SIMPLE R	B	BETA
NUTRI	0.03267	0.00107	0.00107	0.03267	0.47245	0.02750
INCOME	0.41612	0.17316	0.17209	0.41605	2.88617	0.27128
AGE	0.41759	0.17438	0.00122	-0.08544	0.07983	0.08737
FAMSIZE	0.64366	0.41429	0.23992	0.57810	5.85584	0.53293
BRAND	0.64367	0.41431	0.00001	0.03772	0.00635	0.00059
INFO	0.64425	0.41506	0.00075	-0.01307	-1.08607	-0.04673
VARIETY	0.64473	0.41574	0.00067	0.00627	0.02149	0.00137
TASTE	0.64720	0.41887	0.00313	-0.02907	-1.39632	-0.05225
OTHERS	0.64772	0.41954	0.00067	-0.01740	-0.28381	-0.01686
DIET	0.64959	0.42197	0.00243	0.01790	-0.46426	-0.04837
PRICE	0.64991	0.42239	0.00042	0.08422	0.28637	0.01822
AVAIL	0.65029	0.42288	0.00049	-0.04510	-0.24058	-0.01796
EASE	0.65032	0.42292	0.00004	-0.01904	0.28449	0.02305
HABIT	0.65426	0.42806	0.00514	-0.12929	-1.06932	-0.08058
SPECIAL	0.65532	0.42945	0.00139	0.02835	0.49106	0.04064
(CONSTANT)					12.76075	

STATISTICAL PACKAGE FOR THE SOCIAL SCIENCES SPSSH - VERSION 6.00   06/27/77   PAGE   7

FILE   NONAME   (CREATION DATE = 06/27/77)

* M U L T I P L E   R E G R E S S I O N *   VARIABLE LIST   1
                                                                                                                            REGRESSION LIST 2

DEPENDENT VARIABLE..   EXPENSE

VARIABLE(S) ENTERED ON STEP NUMBER 1..   FAMSIZE

MULTIPLE R   0.57810   ANALYSIS OF VARIANCE   DF   SUM OF SQUARES   MEAN SQUARE   F
R SQUARE   0.33420   REGRESSION   1.   58106.10040   58106.10040   381.47701
ADJUSTED R SQUARE 0.33420   RESIDUAL   760.   115762.24769   152.31875
STANDARD ERROR   12.34175

------------ VARIABLES IN THE EQUATION ------------   ------------ VARIABLES NOT IN THE EQUATION ------------

VARIABLE   B   BETA   STD ERROR B   F   VARIABLE   BETA IN   PARTIAL   TOLERANCE   F

FAMSIZE   6.35215   0.57810   0.32525   381.477   INCOME   0.27925   0.32927   0.92573   92.298
(CONSTANT) 16.64090   AGE   0.07767   0.09159   0.92591   6.421
                                                                  BRAND   -0.01944   -0.02371   0.99029   0.427
                                                                  INFO   -0.03229   -0.03955   0.99890   1.189
                                                                  VARIETY   -0.02548   -0.03119   0.99700   0.739
                                                                  TASTE   -0.04990   -0.06111   0.99871   2.845
                                                                  OTHERS   -0.04622   -0.05658   0.99753   2.438
                                                                  DIET   -0.05174   -0.06296   0.98579   3.021
                                                                  PRICE   0.09209   0.11285   0.99982   9.790
                                                                  AVAIL   -0.03326   -0.04076   0.99958   1.263
                                                                  EASE   -0.00450   -0.00551   0.99937   0.023
                                                                  HABIT   -0.09635   -0.11789   0.99669   10.697
                                                                  SPECIAL   0.03323   0.04072   0.99993   1.261
                                                                  NUTRI   0.00992   0.01215   0.99845   0.112

STATISTICAL PACKAGE FOR THE SOCIAL SCIENCES SPSSH - VERSION 6.00   06/27/77   PAGE   8

FILE   NONAME   (CREATION DATE = 06/27/77)

* * * * * * * * * * * * * * * * * * *   M U L T I P L E   R E G R E S S I O N   * * * * * * * * * * * * * * * * * * *   VARIABLE LIST   1
                                                                                                                          REGRESSION LIST 2

DEPENDENT VARIABLE..   EXPENSE

VARIABLE(S) ENTERED ON STEP NUMBER 2..   INCOME

MULTIPLE R   0.63748   ANALYSIS OF VARIANCE   DF   SUM OF SQUARES   MEAN SQUARE   F
R SQUARE   0.40638   REGRESSION   2.   70657.10393   35328.55197   259.80087
ADJUSTED R SQUARE   0.40560   RESIDUAL   759.   103211.24416   135.98319
STANDARD ERROR   11.66118

---------- VARIABLES IN THE EQUATION ----------   ----------- VARIABLES NOT IN THE EQUATION -----------

VARIABLE   B   BETA   STD ERROR B   F   VARIABLE   BETA IN   PARTIAL   TOLERANCE   F

FAMSIZE   5.51597   0.50200   0.21938   298.281   AGE   0.09242   0.11527   0.92341   10.207
INCOME   2.97087   0.27925   0.30923   92.298   BRAND   -0.01017   -0.01313   0.98912   0.131
(CONSTANT) 11.21403   INFO   -0.02073   -0.02687   0.99704   0.548
                                                                    VARIETY   -0.02823   -0.03659   0.99689   1.016
                                                                    TASTE   -0.05942   -0.07702   0.99748   4.523
                                                                    OTHERS   -0.04574   -0.05929   0.99753   2.674
                                                                    DIFT   -0.06213   -0.08000   0.98437   4.883
                                                                    PRICE   0.02001   0.02498   0.92485   0.473
                                                                    AVAIL   -0.03190   -0.04140   0.99955   1.301
                                                                    EASE   -0.00317   -0.00411   0.99934   0.013
                                                                    HABIT   -0.07722   -0.09979   0.99144   7.625
                                                                    SPECIAL   0.02367   0.03069   0.99865   0.715
                                                                    NUTRI   -0.00369   -0.00478   0.99589   0.017

STATISTICAL PACKAGE FOR THE SOCIAL SCIENCES SPSSH - VERSION 6.00   06/27/77   PAGE   9

FILE   NONAME   (CREATION DATE = 06/27/77)

*   M U L T I P L E   R E G R E S S I O N   *

DEPENDENT VARIABLE..   EXPENSE   VARIABLE LIST   1
                                                                                             REGRESSION LIST 2

VARIABLE(S) ENTERED ON STEP NUMBER   3..   AGE

MULTIPLE R   0.64364   ANALYSIS OF VARIANCE   DF   SUM OF SQUARES   MEAN SQUARE   F
R SQUARE   0.41427   REGRESSION   3.   72028.40852   24009.46951   178.70374
ADJUSTED R SQUARE   0.41273   RESIDUAL   758.   101839.93958   134.35348
STANDARD ERROR   11.59109

------------- VARIABLES IN THE EQUATION -------------   ------------ VARIABLES NOT IN THE EQUATION ------------

VARIABLE   B   BETA   STD ERROR B   F   VARIABLE   BETA IN   PARTIAL   TOLERANCE   F

FAMSIZE   5.77801   0.52585   0.32789   310.535   BRAND   -0.00313   -0.00406   0.98294   0.012
INCOME   3.02193   0.28405   0.30779   96.396   INFO   -0.02719   -0.03539   0.99200   0.949
AGE   0.08445   0.09242   0.02643   10.207   VARIETY   -0.02758   -0.03598   0.99684   0.981
(CONSTANT)   6.52153   TASTE   -0.05941   -0.07754   0.99748   4.578
                                                                     OTHERS   -0.04492   -0.05862   0.99744   2.610
                                                                     DIET   -0.05185   -0.06670   0.96931   3.383
                                                                     PRICE   0.01626   0.02041   0.92330   0.316
                                                                     AVAIL   -0.02717   -0.03545   0.99662   0.952
                                                                     EASE   -0.00198   -0.00258   0.99916   0.005
                                                                     HABIT   -0.07459   -0.09700   0.99053   7.190
                                                                     SPECIAL   0.02827   0.03686   0.99606   1.030
                                                                     NUTRI   -0.00499   -0.00650   0.99568   0.032

FILE NONAME (CREATION DATE = 06/27/77)

* * * * * * * * * * * * * * * * * * * M U L T I P L E   R E G R E S S I O N * * * * * * * * * * * * * * * * * * *   VARIABLE LIST 1
REGRESSION LIST 2

DEPENDENT VARIABLE..   EXPENSE

VARIABLE(S) ENTERED ON STEP NUMBER 4..   HABIT

MULTIPLE R	0.64791	
R SQUARE	0.41978	
ADJUSTED R SQUARE	0.41748	
STANDARD ERROR	11.54405	

ANALYSIS OF VARIANCE	DF	SUM OF SQUARES	MEAN SQUARE	F
REGRESSION	4.	72986.62405	18246.65601	136.91993
RESIDUAL	757.	100881.72405	133.26516	

------------ VARIABLES IN THE EQUATION ------------

VARIABLE	B	BETA	STD ERROR B	F
FAMSIZE	5.74106	0.52248	0.22685	538.531
INCOME	2.96086	0.27830	0.30739	92.783
AGE	0.08232	0.09008	0.02634	9.761
HABIT	-0.98989	-0.07459	0.36916	7.190
(CONSTANT)	9.66876			

------------ VARIABLES NOT IN THE EQUATION ------------

VARIABLE	BETA IN	PARTIAL	TOLERANCE	F
BRAND	0.00028	0.00036	0.98090	0.000
INFO	-0.04046	-0.05220	0.96547	2.065
VARIETY	-0.02089	-0.02726	0.98831	0.562
TASTE	-0.05109	-0.06649	0.98257	3.357
OTHERS	-0.03584	-0.04659	0.98050	1.645
DIET	-0.04873	-0.06293	0.96756	3.006
PRICE	0.02278	0.02864	0.91703	0.621
AVAIL	-0.01075	-0.01371	0.94461	0.142
EASE	0.02088	0.02626	0.91803	0.522
SPECIAL	0.03609	0.04705	0.98604	1.677
NUTRI	-0.00279	-0.00365	0.99481	0.010

STATISTICAL PACKAGE FOR THE SOCIAL SCIENCES SPSSH - VERSION 6.00   06/27/77   PAGE 11

FILE   NONAME   (CREATION DATE = 06/27/77)

*   M U L T I P L E   R E G R E S S I O N   *   VARIABLE LIST 1
                                                                                                                           REGRESSION LIST 2

DEPENDENT VARIABLE..   EXPFNSE

VARIABLE(S) ENTERED ON STEP NUMBER 5..   TASTE

		ANALYSIS OF VARIANCE	DF	SUM OF SQUARES	MEAN SQUARE	F
MULTIPLE R	0.64988	REGRESSION	5.	73432.55368	14686.51074	110.54826
R SQUARE	0.42235	RESIDUAL	756.	100435.79442	132.85158	
ADJUSTED R SQUARE	0.41929					
STANDARD ERROR	11.52613					

------------ VARIABLES IN THE EQUATION ------------   -------- VARIABLES NOT IN THE EQUATION ------------

VARIABLE	B	BETA	STD ERROR B	F		VARIABLE	BETA IN	PARTIAL	TOLERANCE	F
FAMSIZE	5.75875	0.52409	0.32646	311.129		BRAND	0.00110	0.00143	0.98065	0.002
INCOME	2.98583	0.28065	0.30721	94.462		INFO	-0.03893	-0.05030	0.96457	1.915
AGE	0.08249	0.09028	0.02630	9.840		VARIETY	-0.00527	-0.00654	0.88911	0.032
HABIT	-0.90670	-0.06632	0.37137	5.961		OTHERS	-0.02174	-0.02684	0.88073	0.544
TASTE	-1.36528	-0.05109	0.74520	3.357		DIET	-0.04700	-0.06079	0.96639	2.800
(CONSTANT)	10.98957					PRICE	0.02398	0.03021	0.91657	0.690
						AVAIL	-0.00566	-0.00721	0.93542	0.039
						EASE	0.02351	0.02961	0.91585	0.662
						SPECIAL	0.04048	0.05271	0.97960	2.104
						NUTRI	0.00891	0.01140	0.94593	0.098

STATISTICAL PACKAGE FOR THE SOCIAL SCIENCES SPSSH - VERSION 6.00

FILE   NCNAME   (CREATICN DATE = 06/27/77)   06/27/77   PAGE   19

* * * * * * * * * * * * * * * * * * * M U L T I P L E   R E G R E S S I O N * * * * * * * * * * * * * * * *

DEPENDENT VARIABLE..   EXPENSE

VARIABLE(S) ENTERED ON STEP NUMBER 13..   PRICE

MULTIPLE R	0.65532	ANALYSIS OF VARIANCE	DF
R SQUARE	0.42945	REGRESSION	13.
ADJUSTED R SQUARE	0.42031	RESIDUAL	748.
STANDARD ERROR	11.51614		

ANALYSIS OF VARIANCE

	DF	SUM OF SQUARES	MEAN SQUARE	F
REGRESSION	13.	74667.40535	5743.64657	43.30854
RESIDUAL	748.	99200.94275	132.62158	

------- VARIABLES IN THE EQUATION -------

VARIABLE	B	BETA	STD ERROR B	F
FAMSIZE	5.85684	0.53302	0.32893	317.038
INCOME	2.88617	0.27128	0.32202	80.331
AGE	C.C7979	0.08732	0.02672	8.920
HABIT	-1.C6634	-0.08050	0.39797	7.206
TASTE	-1.33708	-0.05191	0.80594	2.962
DIET	-C.46314	-0.04832	0.28381	2.670
SPECIAL	C.49058	0.04060	0.36205	1.836
INFO	-1.08545	-0.04671	0.69050	2.471
NUTRI	0.47603	0.02771	0.53588	0.789
EASE	0.28493	0.02308	0.37081	0.590
OTHERS	-0.28140	-0.01671	0.50019	0.317
AVAIL	-0.23969	-0.01790	0.40374	0.352
PRICE	0.28491	0.01813	0.49667	0.329
(CONSTANT)	12.79161			

------- VARIABLES NOT IN THE EQUATION -------

VARIABLE	BETA IN	PARTIAL	TOLERANCE	F
BRAND	0.C0058	0.00073	0.93130	0.000
VARIETY	0.00136	0.00164	0.83697	0.002

F-LEVEL OR TOLERANCE-LEVEL INSUFFICIENT FOR FURTHER COMPUTATION

STATISTICAL PACKAGE FOR THE SOCIAL SCIENCES SPSSH - VERSION 6.00   06/27/77   PAGE   20

FILE   NCNAME   (CREATION DATE = 06/27/77)

* M U L T I P L E   R E G R E S S I O N *   VARIABLE LIST   1
                                                                                                                                REGRESSION LIST 2

DEPENDENT VARIABLE..   EXPENSE

SUMMARY TABLE

VARIABLE	MULTIPLE R	R SQUARE	RSQ CHANGE	SIMPLE R	B	BETA
FAMSIZE	0.57810	0.33420	0.33420	0.57810	5.85684	0.53302
INCOME	0.63748	0.40638	0.07219	0.41605	2.88617	0.27128
AGE	0.64364	0.41427	0.00789	-0.08544	0.07979	0.08732
HABIT	0.64791	0.41978	0.00551	-0.12929	-1.06834	-0.08050
TASTE	0.64966	0.42235	0.00256	-0.02907	-1.38708	-0.05191
DIET	0.65152	0.42448	0.00213	0.01790	-0.46374	-0.04832
SPECIAL	0.65278	0.42612	0.00164	0.02835	0.49058	0.04060
INFO	0.65398	0.42769	0.00157	-0.01307	-1.08545	-0.04671
NUTRI	0.65449	0.42835	0.00066	-0.03267	0.47603	0.02771
EASE	0.65475	0.42873	0.00038	-0.01904	0.28493	0.02308
OTHERS	0.65497	0.42899	0.00025	-0.01740	-0.28140	-0.01671
AVAIL	0.65513	0.42920	0.00021	-0.04510	-0.23969	-0.01790
PRICE	0.65532	0.42945	0.00025	0.08422	0.28491	0.01813
(CONSTANT)					12.79161	

_____ APPENDIX 14–D _____

SIMULTANEOUS EQUATION REGRESSION

Problem

The basic regression model assumes there is one dependent variable which is affected by a set of independent variables. This is a useful model but often not an accurate assumption about the way the world operates. Consider the issue of the influence of advertising on sales. If we plotted sales versus advertising, we might get Figure 14D–1. It is easy to assume

FIGURE 14D–1

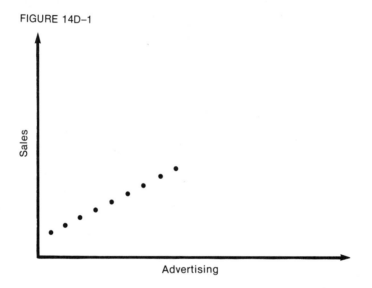

Sales

Advertising

that this data can be approximated by a line which indicates the effect of advertising on sales. Presumably advertising does indeed affect sales. On the other hand, advertising budgets are traditionally set as a percentage of anticipated sales. Hence the observed points could well be a set of inter-sections of lines which indicate how advertising affects sales and how sales affects advertising (Figure 14D–2). In this case, the simple plot of sales versus advertising produces some weighted average of the advertising-to-sales and sales-to-advertising effects.

Method

A basic method for disentangling two-way effects among variables is simultaneous equation regression. The trick is to specify one equation for

FIGURE 14D–2

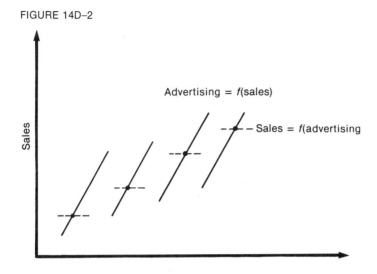

each direction of causation. In the sales-advertising example, that means two equations:

$$\text{Sales} = f(\text{advertising})$$
$$\text{Advertising} = f(\text{sales})$$

The method is then to simultaneously estimate coefficients of both equations.

The key to the success of simultaneous equations estimation is the presence of other (exogenous) variables which act only as independent variables. If these other independent variables are fortuitous, then their influences can be used to disentangle the two-way relations among the basic (endogenous) variables. The ability of a system of equations to separate two-way relations is tied to the concept of identification. There are three types of identification: under, exact, and over.

Underidentification

Underidentification is the situation where the "other" variables are insufficient to separate the two-way effects. For example, Sales = B_1(advertising), and Advertising = B_2(sales). In this case, which comes first (sales or advertising) becomes a chicken-egg argument with no solution. Unless the model can be logically altered, no estimates can be obtained.

Exact identification

The "neatest" situation is so-called exact identification. In this case, the estimates of the two-way relations are derived in a straightforward two-step process. Assume:

$$\text{Sales} = B_1(\text{advertising}) + \gamma_1(\text{GNP})$$
$$\text{Advertising} = B_2(\text{advertising}) + \gamma_2(\text{Competitive advertising})$$

Call   GNP $= X_1$
  Competitive advertising $= X_2$ }Exogenous variables
  Sales $= Y_1$
  Advertising $= Y_2$ }Endogenous variables

We can now write the two equations in matrix form as

$$\begin{bmatrix} -1 & B_1 \\ -B_2 & -1 \end{bmatrix}\begin{bmatrix} Y_1 \\ Y_2 \end{bmatrix} + \begin{bmatrix} \gamma_1 & 0 \\ 0 & \gamma_2 \end{bmatrix}\begin{bmatrix} X_1 \\ X_2 \end{bmatrix} = \begin{bmatrix} \mu_1 \\ \mu_2 \end{bmatrix}$$

or

$$BY + \Gamma X = \mu$$

To solve for Y, we multiply both sides by B^{-1}:

$$B^{-1}BY + B^{-1}\Gamma X = B^{-1}\mu$$

or

$$Y = -B^{-1}\Gamma X + B^{-1}\mu$$

Since we assume $B^{-1}\mu = 0$,

$$Y = -B^{-1}\Gamma X$$

Hence we have now set the endogenous variables as a function of the exogenous variables, often called the reduced form equations. The two-step process first requires one to run regular regression (ordinary least squares—OLS) on the reduced form equations:

$$Y_1 = a_1X_1 + a_2X_2$$
$$Y = a_3X_3 + a_4X_4$$

The next step is to deduce the B_i's and γ_i's from the a_i's:

$$\begin{bmatrix} a_1 & a_2 \\ a_3 & a_4 \end{bmatrix} = -\beta^{-1}\Gamma$$

$$= \frac{-1}{1 - \beta_1\beta_2}\begin{bmatrix} -1 & -\beta_1 \\ -\beta_2 & -1 \end{bmatrix}\begin{bmatrix} \gamma_1 & 0 \\ 0 & \gamma_2 \end{bmatrix}$$

$$= \frac{-1}{1 - \beta_1\beta_2}\begin{bmatrix} -\gamma_1 & -\beta\gamma_2 \\ -\beta_2\gamma_1 & -\gamma_2 \end{bmatrix}$$

Hence

$$a_1 = \gamma_1$$
$$a_2 = \beta_1\gamma_2$$
$$a_3 = \beta_2\gamma_2$$
$$a_4 = \gamma_2$$

Hence $\beta_1 = \dfrac{a_2}{a_4}$, and so forth. This process is called indirect least squares (ILS).

Overidentification

Overidentification is the situation where the exogenous variables are more than sufficient to identify the two-way causations. For example:

$$\text{Sales} = \beta_1(\text{advertising}) + \gamma_1(\text{GNP}) + \gamma_3(\text{CPI})$$
$$\text{Advertising} = \beta_2(\text{sales}) + \gamma_2(\text{competitive advertising})$$
$$+ \gamma_4(\text{share}) + \gamma_5(\text{media rates})$$

Here no simple solution can be traced from the reduced form back to the original coefficients.

The most common estimation procedure in this case is two-stage least squares (TSLS). Here the steps are as follows:

1. Find A from $Y = AX$ (run the reduced form equations by OLS)
2. Set $Y^* = AX$ (replace the actual values of Y with their predicted values from AX) and then run $BY^* + \Gamma X = \mu$ by OLS.

Identification checking

In checking for identification, there are the following two common approaches:

Order condition.   The order condition is a necessary but not sufficient condition for identification. It is a counting rule which says for each equation,

number of endogenous variables included $-$ 1
$$\leq \text{number of exogenous variables excluded}$$

Rank condition.   The rank condition is a sufficient condition for identification. It requires one to form the augmented β, Γ matrix: $\beta\Gamma$. Now for each equation (e.g., the second), remove the row of that equation (e.g., second row) and any column where the equation removed had a nonzero element. If the rank of the reduced matrix is equal to the number of original equations minus 1, then the equation is identified. If the rank is less than that, then the equation is not identified.

Consider the example in the exact identification case. Here the $B\Gamma$ matrix is

$$\begin{bmatrix} -1 & B_1 & \gamma_1 & 0 \\ -B_2 & 1 & 0 & \gamma_2 \end{bmatrix}$$

To check on the second equation, remove the second row and all columns with a non-zero value in the second row. This leaves

$$[\gamma_1]$$

Since the reduced matrix is of order $2 - 1 = 1$, then the equation is identified.

Estimation

Estimation problems in simultaneous equation models get very complex. The problem is all the nice assumptions about the error terms are often false, and hence OLS may not be the best approach. On the other hand, for recursive[2] models, OLS is the best and it does quite well in many other situations as well. In short, simultaneous equation estimation is a technical problem which calls for technical help.

----

[2] A recursive model is one in which the direction of causation is in one direction (no feedback exists) such as awareness → attitude → intention → choice. If choice were assumed to also influence attitude, the model would then be nonrecursive.

15

Additional predictive procedures

The last chapter spent a considerable amount of time detailing what regression analysis is and how it can be used. Regression analysis is a very flexible tool which can be used in a wide variety of situations. Nonetheless, there are other predictive procedures which also are used in marketing research. This chapter therefore is devoted to describing two such "other" predictive procedures: discriminant analysis and AID.

TWO-GROUP LINEAR DISCRIMINANT ANALYSIS

Basic notion

Many marketing situations revolve around two distinct groups of consumers. For example, we often are concerned with the differences between users and nonusers of a particular product or brand. In such situations, we are often interested in identifying the characteristics (e.g., age, income, education) of users versus nonusers of the product. One technique for analyzing which characteristics "discriminate" members of the two groups is imaginatively called discriminant analysis.

In order to understand how discriminant analysis works, consider the following graph representing the incomes and ages of purchasers (P) and nonpurchasers (N) of a particular product (Figure 15–1). Purchasers of this product appear to be younger and richer than nonpurchasers. Hence if a 30-year-old drove up to my store in a Mercedes, he (assuming he hadn't stolen it) would be a good prospect for my product whereas a 65-year-old pensioner would not be. In this case, both age and income discriminate between purchasers and nonpurchasers.

Now consider Figure 15–2. In this situation, height is apparently a perfect discriminator between purchasers and nonpurchasers while liking of yogurt is essentially worthless as a discriminator.

504

FIGURE 15–1
Purchasers (P) versus nonpurchasers (N) by age
and income

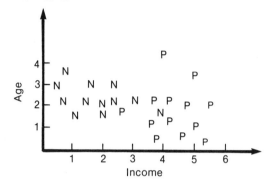

FIGURE 15–2
Purchasers (P) versus nonpurchasers (N) by
height and liking of yogurt

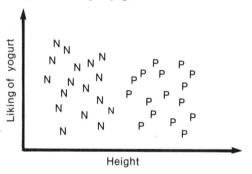

The process of plotting members of the two groups on axes to find out which variables discriminate has some severe limitations. First, it allows for considering only two independent variables at once. Second, it is tedious. And third, it does not give concise results which indicate quantitatively the effect of each of the characteristics on group membership. Hence a more formal approach is usually employed.

The index approach

An effective way to analyze which variables discriminate between members of two groups is to build an index which separates the two groups on the basis of their values on the measured characteristics. When the procedure called discriminant analysis is used, the index is called (again ingeniously) the discriminant function, and the characteristics become the independent variables:

$$f = w_1x_1 + w_2x_2 + \cdots + w_kx_k \tag{15.1}$$

where

$x_1, x_2, \ldots, x_k$ = the measured characteristics (variables)
f = the index (discriminant function)
w_i = the weight (discriminant coefficient) of the ith characteristic in discriminating between the two groups

Discriminant analysis finds the set of weights which spreads the values of index for the two groups apart as far as possible. Returning to the example involving purchasers (group 2) and nonpurchasers (group 1) (see Figure 15–1), we see that the best index involving income and age might be as follows:

$$f = 3(\text{income}) - 2(\text{age})$$

We can represent this graphically as in Figure 15–3. Consider the person with both age and income equal to 2. The value of the index for this person

FIGURE 15–3
Purchasers (P) versus nonpurchasers (N): Discriminant function

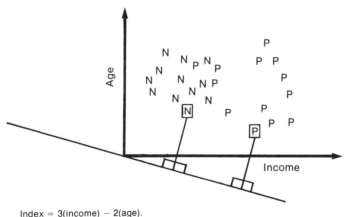

Index = 3(income) − 2(age).

would be $3(2) - 2(2) = 2$. Similarly the person with age of 1 and income of 5 would have an index of $3(5) - 2(1) = 13$. In fact all the people in the sample can now be represented by a position on the new index (Figure 15–4). Hence we can predict group membership based on a person's score on the discriminant function. If the score is closer to the mean of the purchasers, the person would be classified as a purchaser and vice versa. This is equivalent to drawing a "cutoff" line through the space such that,

FIGURE 15–4
Positions on the discriminant function

f = 3(income) − 2(age).

as much as possible, the purchasers lie on one side of the line and the nonpurchasers on the other side. (For a more complete discussion of the weights and the use of discriminant analysis for classification, see Appendix 15–B.)

Equivalence to regression. The basic approach of linear discriminant analysis is identical to that of linear regression analysis: using weighted linear combination of independent variables to predict a dependent variable. The only difference is that the dependent variable in regression is a "real" variable (at least intervally scaled) whereas in discriminant analysis the dependent variable is group membership (and hence only nominally scaled). For two groups, however, it is easy to generate a dummy variable to represent group membership (i.e., code 1 for group one membership and 0 for group two membership). By using such a dummy variable as the dependent variable, a regression can be run. The resulting regression coefficients will be proportional to the weights which would have been obtained from discriminant analysis. Hence two-group discriminant analysis is essentially equivalent to regression analysis using a dummy dependent variable.

Computer input and output interpretation

The basic purpose of discriminant analysis is to identify which variables are the best predictors of group membership. Since this usually requires a computer program, the key questions are what to input and what to look at in the output.

Input. The input consists of a set of observations for both groups. Values of the predictor variables for both groups are the actual input. Group membership is identified a priori. (Discriminant analysis describes existing groups; it does not find groups.) Some programs (BMDO4M, BMDO5M) require that data be sorted into groups before being input while others (e.g., SPSS) allow a variable to be used to define the groups.

Output. Like most computer output, there is more information given than can be profitably used (see Appendix 15–A). This overload is the result of two causes: (a) in order to "debug" a program, a lot of intermediate calculations are output to make it easy to see if the program is working correctly; and (b) the desire to output enough so that specialized uses can be made of the results. While much of this output has some purpose, the general user will find the information that follows sufficient in most applications.

Means of the variables for the two groups.   The profiles of the groups in terms of means on the variables serve two basic purposes. First, they are useful to check whether the data was input correctly (a mean of 5.4 on a variable scaled 1 to 5 indicates the input is "messed up"). More importantly, they give the first indication of which variables distinguish between members of the two groups. Large differences in means on a particular variable suggest that the variable is an important discriminator between the groups. If all the variables have approximately the same standard deviation and there is relatively little correlation among the independent variables, the size of the differences between the means will provide the same ranking of the importances of the variables in discriminating as the size of the discriminant coefficients.

In order to summarize the results, a profile chart is often very effective. Returning to our hypothetical example, we could plot the purchaser and nonpurchaser groups as in Figure 15–5. Such a plot is very useful in understanding how the two groups differ.

FIGURE 15–5
Profile of purchasers versus nonpurchasers

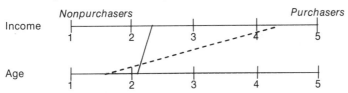

The discriminant coefficients (w_i's).   The discriminant coefficients indicate the relative contribution of a unit on each of the independent variables to the discriminant function. A large discriminant coefficient means that a one-unit change in that particular variable produces a large change in the discriminant function and vice versa. In short, discriminant coefficients are interpreted exactly the same way as regression coefficients.

Discriminant coefficients (like regression coefficients) are affected by the scale of the independent variable. In order to remove this scale effect, many researchers either standardize the variables before inputting or divide each discriminant coefficient (w_i) by the standard deviation of the variable (s_i). The resulting coefficients indicate how much a change of one standard deviation in each of the independent variables would affect the discriminant function. Whether this is a more useful importance measure depends on the circumstances. Whenever the scales of the independent variables vary widely (causing large differences in the size of the standard deviations), however, the unstandardized discriminant coefficients and the standardized discriminant coefficients may give very different importance ratings to the variables.

Returning to the example in Figure 15–1, we see that income is measured on a larger scale than age. Assuming these scales produce standard deviations of income and age equal to 1 and 2 respectively, we can compute the standardized discriminant coefficients by dividing the "regular" discriminant coefficients by the appropriate standard deviations, obtaining 1.5 and −2. The resulting measure of importance compared with three simpler measures is shown in Table 15–1. In this hypothetical case, the

TABLE 15–1
Alternative measures of the importance of a variable in discriminating

Variable	Raw difference in mean	Standard deviation	Raw difference in mean / Standard deviation	"Regular" discriminant coefficient	Standardized discriminant coefficient
Income	2.0	2	1	3	1.5
Age..........	−.5	1	−.5	−2	−2.0

relative importance of the variables in discriminating depends on your definition of importance.

The hit-miss table. Most discriminant analysis programs produce a "hit-miss" table (also known as a classification table or confusion matrix). This table indicates how successful the discriminant function would have been in classifying the same observations used to form the function back into their respective groups. (Usually these tables are constructed under the assumption of equal prior probabilities of group membership). Such a table might look like the following:

	Predicted group	
Actual group	1	2
1	21	12
2	56	111

The percent correctly classified is often used as a summary measure of the value of the independent variables in predicting group membership. Hence the percent correctly classified in discriminant analysis is somewhat analogous to R^2 in regression. In this case, the number of correct predictions is 21 + 111 = 133. Since there were 200 observations in all,

$\frac{133}{200} = 66.5$ percent is a measure of how effective the independent variables were in predicting group membership.

Statistical aspects of interpretation

Differences in means. The differences in means between the groups for each variable can be tested by the "old fashioned" t test or the equivalent one-way ANOVA F test:

$$\frac{\bar{x}_{1j} - \bar{x}_{2j}}{s_{1j-2j}} \quad \text{is} \quad t_{\alpha, n_1 + n_2 - 2}$$

or

$$\frac{(\bar{x}_{1j} - \bar{x}_{2j})^2}{s^2_{1j-2j}} \quad \text{is} \quad F_{\alpha, 1, n_1 + n_2 - 2}$$

Such a test can be applied to each of the independent variables.[1]

Rather than test the variables separately, it is possible to test all the variables simultaneously. This test examines whether the means on all the variables (e.g., income, age, etc.) are the same for the two groups. This multivariable analysis of variance test produces a variety of equivalent test statistics, the most common of which are an F statistic and the Mahalanobis D^2 (which turns out to be approximately chi-square distributed). A "large" (significant) F or D^2 indicates the means of the two groups are different on the variables and hence that the variables are helpful in separating the groups. A small F (or D^2) indicates that the independent variables are essentially worthless as predictors of group membership.

The percent correctly classified. By examining this hit-miss table, the number of correct classifications can be calculated. The percent correctly classified can be compared statistically against the following four main criteria:

Random. The easiest test to beat is to compare the percent correctly classified (p) with the result of random classification. In the two-group case, that means 50 percent. The one-tail test statistic is

$$z = \frac{p - 50}{\sqrt{(50)(50)}} \sqrt{n_1 + n_2}$$

---

[1] Since most computer programs do not automatically produce these tests (a definite oversight in my opinion), they require some effort to perform. The difference in means on the jth variable $\bar{x}_{1j} - \bar{x}_{2j}$ is easily computed from the means of the variables. The standard deviation is not directly available and must be obtained from the square root of the jth diagonal element in the pooled variance-covariance matrix.

where z is standard normally distributed. Hence when z is big (greater than 2), the independent variables have made a significant contribution to prediction. Returning to our previous example, we had the following:

	Predicted group	
Actual group	1	2
1	21	12
2	56	111

Hence we can compare 66.5 percent with 50 percent as follows:

$$z = \frac{66.5 - 50}{\sqrt{(50)(50)}} \sqrt{200} = \frac{16.5}{50} \sqrt{200} = 4.7 > 2$$

Thus we have done significantly better than random at the 95 percent level.

The largest group criterion. The "toughest" criterion is to compare the percent correctly classified with the percent that would be correctly classified by assuming everyone was a member of the largest group. This criterion becomes extremely hard to beat as one group becomes dominant. In the previous example, $\frac{167}{200} = 83.5$ percent of the people are in the largest group (nonpurchasers). Hence simply saying everyone is a nonpurchaser will give the fewest misclassifications since 83.5 is greater than 66.5. This criterion is somewhat inappropriate in a practical sense, however, since we are much more concerned with finding purchasers than with avoiding contacting nonpurchasers. Beating the largest group criterion is thus sufficient to demonstrate the worth of the independent variables but is not necessary for the variables to be useful.

Proportional chance criterion. A compromise between random and largest group criteria is the proportional chance criterion (Morrison, 1969). This criterion is

$$C_{\text{pro}} = P_1^2 + P_2^2 \tag{15.8}$$

In the previous example, this becomes

$$C_{\text{pro}} = \left(\frac{33}{200}\right)^2 + \left(\frac{167}{200}\right)^2 = 72.7 \text{ percent}$$

Comparison of the actual percent with this percent gives a "fairer" measure of the power of variables than comparison with the largest group. (This should also be tested for statistical significance.)

The "fairest" criterion. In some sense the fairest criterion is to assume that likelihood of correct classification is dependent on both the probability of group membership (P_i) and the fraction assigned to each group (f_i) (Mostellar and Bush, 1954). The criterion is

$$C_{\text{fair}} = f_1(P_1) + f_2(P_2) \tag{15.9}$$

In the previous example, that would be

$$C_{\text{fair}} = \frac{77}{200}\left(\frac{33}{200}\right) + \frac{123}{200}\left(\frac{167}{200}\right) \doteq 58 \text{ percent}$$

Therefore we would compare the 66.5 percent correctly classified with 58 percent.

The bias problem. Using the same observations to examine the ability of the discriminant function to correctly classify observations as were used to create the discriminant function produces an upward bias in the percent correctly classified. The obvious way to remove the bias is to split the sample into an analysis sample which is used to construct the discriminant function and a holdout sample. The holdout sample is then classified into groups based on the discriminant function derived from the analysis sample, eliminating the bias. The problem with this approach is that for a large sample ($n > 300$), the bias is relatively small. For a small sample ($n < 50$) on the other hand, there are probably not enough observations to split the data into two groups. Hence the "split-half" approach is useful mainly for "moderate" sample sizes.

An extreme but effective way to remove the bias in classifying is to run $n_1 + n_2$ separate discriminant analyses. In each of these analyses, one observation is the holdout observation. Hence we use the discriminant function based on the $n_1 + n_2 - 1$ observations to classify the holdout observation. By rotating the holdout observation, one can estimate the percent correctly classified. Fortunately, for most problems such an extreme remedy is unnecessary.

Issues in applications

Where. Two-group discriminant analysis can be applied anywhere the criterion variable can be divided into two groups. This means situations including purchasers versus nonpurchasers, buyers of brand A versus buyers of all other brands, good risks versus bad risks, and so forth, are candidates for two-group discriminant analysis.

In everyday life, one need only apply for a credit card or a loan to be subjected to the results of discriminant analysis. Your income, age, length of residence, and so forth, are all considered (and appropriately weighted) in deciding whether to give you a loan. The weights are often rounded to even numbers so a clerk can easily calculate your "score." If your score is above a certain level, you get the credit card or loan. If not, you have literally been discriminated against.

How.   Building a discriminant model is equivalent to building a regression model. Hence all the caveats and suggestions about model building made in the past chapter apply here as well. Two other issues often are raised by users of discriminant analysis. One question is whether the two groups must be of equal size. As long as the objective is to find the best discriminant function possible given a sample has already been drawn, the best approach is to use all the data points available. In short, the groups do not have to be of equal size. In designing a sample, on the other hand, guaranteeing relatively equal sample sizes in the two groups for a fixed total sample size will somewhat improve the reliability of the results.

Another issue is what will happen when the two basic assumptions of normality and equal covariances in the two groups are violated? Violation of the basic assumptions makes statistical interpretation of the results very difficult. If the covariances in the two groups are sufficiently unequal, the optimal discriminant function becomes nonlinear. Nonetheless, for the purpose of finding interesting relations, discriminant analysis is remarkably robust. Hence such relaxations as using binary (dummy) variables as independent variables can be done in practice if not in theory.

Two examples

Innovators versus noninnovators.   The first example concerns the difference between personalities of innovators and noninnovators in the purchase of a new home appliance (Robertson and Kennedy, 1968). In this study, 60 innovators were compared with 40 noninnovators on seven personality variables (Table 15–2). The two groups are profiled in Figure 15–6. The discriminant coefficients indicate that venturesomeness is the best discriminator (among the seven personality measures studied) and that interest range is the worst. You may notice that the size of the

TABLE 15–2
Differences between innovators and noninnovators

	Innovator mean	Noninnovator mean	Discriminant coefficient
Venturesomeness	4.88	4.12	3.59
Social mobility	3.93	3.20	3.08
Privilegedness	3.68	3.25	2.04
Social integration	4.13	3.78	2.44
Status concern	2.00	1.73	.95
Interest range	5.27	5.00	.59
Cosmopolitanism	2.77	3.03	−2.86

Source: Thomas Robertson and James Kennedy, "Prediction of Consumer Innovators: Application of Multiple Discriminant Analysis." Adapted from *Journal of Marketing Research,* published by the American Marketing Association, vol. 5 (*February* 1968), *pp.* 66–67.

FIGURE 15–6
Profile of innovators and noninnovators

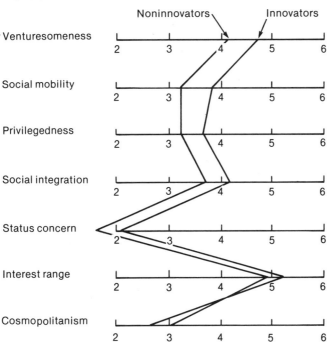

discriminant coefficients produces a ranking different from that which would be generated by looking at the differences in the means on the variables. The reasons for this are (*a*) unequal variances of the variables and/or (*b*) multicollinearity among the predictor variables.

U.S. versus U.K. purchasing agents.   This example deals with industrial purchasing agents (Lehmann and O'Shaughnessy, 1974). In order to compare purchasing agents in the United Kingdom with those in the United States, the importances they attributed to 17 attributes for four product types were analyzed. One part of the analysis involved discriminant analysis between U.S. and U.K. purchasing agents. Four two-group discriminant analyses were performed, one for each of the four product types. The resulting discriminant functions are shown in Table 15–3. Notice here that unstandardized discriminant coefficients are reported. Since the 17 attributes were all rated on the same scale and had approximately the same standard deviations, the standardized coefficients would be expected to be very similar to the unstandardized coefficients.

In interpreting these results, it is important to recognize that the function arbitrarily placed U.K. purchasing agents at the top of the scale.

TABLE 15-3
Discriminant functions: U.K. versus U.S. purchasing agents

Attribute	Product type			
	I	*II*	*III*	*IV*
Reputation	−1.10	−.16	−.95	−1.02
Financing	−.01	.50	.85	1.64
Flexibility	−.19	.53	1.07	−1.73
Past experience	−1.16	−.11	−.27	−1.05
Technical service	.19	2.38	1.57	−.96
Confidence in salespersons	.81	.42	−.55	.48
Convenience in ordering	1.13	1.11	−.01	.18
Reliability data	−.58	−.67	−.24	.44
Price	−.81	−2.10	−.21	.27
Technical specifications	1.33	−.66	−.69	−.30
Ease of use	−.09	.18	.87	−1.17
Preference of user	−.45	−2.02	−.09	.88
Training offered	.15	−2.63	−.96	−1.16
Training required	−1.55	.39	−.45	−.12
Reliability of delivery	2.41	2.60	.64	1.36
Maintenance	.87	1.04	.42	1.50
Sales service	−.39	1.03	1.30	1.96

(This can be ascertained by either looking at the group means on the discriminant functions, or by simply examining the group means on the separate variables and then deducing which way the function goes.) With this in mind it is possible to interpret the results by looking for big (relatively) discriminant coefficients. In this example, any coefficient greater than 1 in absolute size was identified as "big" in interpreting the results.

U.K. purchasing agents place greater emphasis on reliability of delivery and maintenance for all four product types, on convenience in ordering for Type I and II products, and on sales service and financing for products which give rise to procedural (Type III) or political (Type IV) products. U.S. purchasing agents, on the other hand, tend to stress reputation for Type I, III, and IV products, past experience for Type I and IV, training offered for Type II, III, and IV products, and price for Type I and II products. Hence one might conclude that U.K. purchasing agents are relatively more service oriented and U.S. agents somewhat more experience/reputation oriented. Interestingly these results largely reinforce the results of simple *t* tests for differences in mean importance on the 17 attributes.

The reason that discriminant coefficients are not proportional to the simple *t* values is multicollinearity among the independent variables (the attribute importance ratings in this case). In multiple regression, an independent variable may have a high simple correlation with the dependent variable but the regression coefficient may be small and/or insignificant if the independent variable is also highly correlated with other independent variables. In discriminant analysis, a variable may be significantly different between two groups, but the discriminant coefficient insignificant due to collinearity with other independent variables. In other words, collinearity among the independent variables makes interpreting discriminant coefficients difficult exactly the way collinearity makes regression coefficients unreliable and hard to interpret.

In order to get a measure of how well the 17 attributes predict group membership, there are two common approaches. The first is to test whether the independent variables taken as a whole differ significantly across the groups. Most canned programs calculate an F statistic to test this significance. In the current example, the test statistic used was a Mahalonobis D^2. This formidable sounding statistic is approximately chi-square distributed with (Number of groups $-$ 1) (Number of variables) degrees of freedom. Here there were $(2 - 1)(17) = 17$ degrees of freedom. The Mahalonobis D^2's were 41.0, 50.8, 29.2, and 45.6 respectively for the four product types. Since at the .05 significance level the cutoff for a significant chi-square with 17 degrees of freedom is 27.6, the independent variables contribute significantly (if not spectacularly) to predicting group membership. In other words, U.S. and U.K. purchasing agents attribute significantly different importances to product attributes.

The other way to see how well the discriminant function performs is to use it to classify some observations and see how well it does in terms of correct classifications. Ideally a fresh sample of observations should be classified. Since the purchasing agent project budget was exhausted, a fresh sample was not feasible. The next best approach is to use a holdout sample for classifications which was not used to compute the discriminant functions. Given the small sample size here (26 in one group, 19 in the other), this was not feasible. The least desirable approach is to see how well the discriminant function performs in classifying the observations used in constructing the functions. In spite of the inflated value this can give in terms of the percent correctly classified, the fact that canned programs do this automatically makes this a common way to look at the results. In this case, the percent correctly reclassified was 84.4 percent, 86.7 percent, 77.8 percent, and 84.4 percent respectively for the four product types. These are "pretty good" results and again support the notion that product attribute importances differ between U.S. and U.K. purchasing agents.

MORE THAN TWO-GROUP DISCRIMINANT ANALYSIS

When there are more than two groups, there are two different approaches to discriminant analysis: the classical (pairwise) and the simultaneous approaches.

Classical approach

The classical approach to more than two-group discriminant analysis is a direct extension of the two-group procedure. Assuming there are g groups, the classical approach is to produce a single classification function (CF_i) for each group. These functions can be used to calculate a value for a particular observation on each function. The group whose classification function produces the largest value turns out to be the group to which the observation is most likely to belong. Assume for a moment I had three groups with the following classification functions:

Variable	CF_1	CF_2	CF_3
1	7	5	4
2	5	3	1
Constant.........	2	5	9

If I were to try and classify an observation with values 2 and 3 on the two variables into one of the three groups, I could directly use the multivariate normal distribution and a computer algorithm to find the likelihood that an observation with values 2 and 3 came from each of the three groups. A shortcut is available, however, by using the three classification functions:

$$\text{Value of } CF_1 = 7(2) + 5(3) + 2 = 31$$
$$\text{Value of } CF_2 = 5(2) + 3(3) + 5 = 24$$
$$\text{Value of } CF_3 = 4(2) + 1(3) + 9 = 20$$

Since the value of CF_1 is largest, it turns out that this particular observation is most likely to belong to the first group.

Classification functions are occasionally interpreted directly, with a big value attributed to a variable which is a major contributor to group membership. To see which variables discriminate, however, the actual discriminant functions are needed. For g groups, there are $\binom{g}{2} = \dfrac{g(g-1)}{2}$ discriminant functions, one for each pair of groups. Graphically, these functions can be displayed as in Figure 15–7. Mathematically, the discriminant functions turn out to be the differences between pairs of classification functions (e.g., $f_{12} = CF_1 - CF_2$, etc.).

Returning to our previous example, we would derive the classical discriminant function between groups 1 and 3 (f_{13}) as follows:

$$f_{13} = (7 - 4)X_1 + (5 - 1)X_2 = 3X_1 + 4X_2$$

FIGURE 15–7
Classical approach to more than two-group discriminant analysis

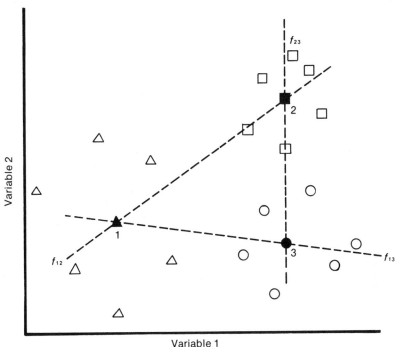

The constant is usually ignored.[2] This classical approach to more than two-group discriminant analysis is used less frequently than the next approach to be discussed.

The simultaneous approach

The second approach to more than two-group discriminant analysis is to first attempt to find a single function which simultaneously spreads all groups apart as far as possible. Next a second function (independent of the first) is found which best further explains differences in group membership and so forth. For g groups, there will be g-1 such functions. This can be viewed graphically as Figure 15–8. The functions are mathematically derived by canonical correlation.

---

[2] It turns out, however, that the difference in the constant terms produces the cutoff point for maximum likelihood classification. Hence in this case the cutoff point would be $2 - 9 = -7$. Alternatively retaining the constant term makes the cutoff point equal to zero.

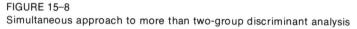

FIGURE 15–8
Simultaneous approach to more than two-group discriminant analysis

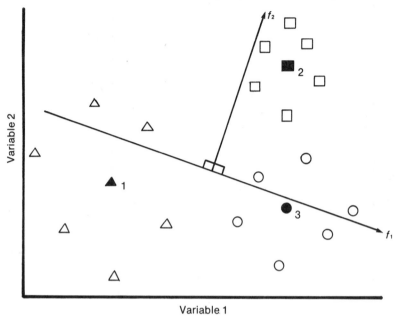

Variable 1

Difference between the two approaches

The two major approaches to multiple group discriminant analysis thus differ noticeably, although they turn out to be identical for the two-group case. The first, or "classical" approach, develops functions which best discriminate among each pair of groups and can be interpreted accordingly. This approach is closely tied to the likelihood function and can thus be used rather easily for maximum likelihood, Bayesian, or minimum opportunity cost classification. The second, or canonical correlate, approach to discriminant analysis attempts, on the other hand, to find functions which discriminate among all the groups at once. These functions can be used to form a reduced basis in which to consider the groups. This parsimonious representation has substantial appeal. In addition, the classical approach is practically limited by computational constraints to a very small number of groups (such as 5 in BMDO5M), while the canonical correlate approach can handle many more groups. On the other hand, the canonical correlate approach does not directly aid in optimal classification (it can provide very good classification, however) nor does it make possible determination of which variables discriminate between a particular pair of groups. Thus choice between the two approaches must depend on the goals involved (and the computer program available).

A nutritional example

Returning to the nutrition study, assume we are again interested in explaining weekly food consumption expenditures in terms of other characteristics. Since there were five response categories to the food expenditure question, we have five groups of respondents ranging from those who spend less than $15 per week to those who spend over $60 per week. (This data is really at least as well suited to regression—the alert reader will notice that food expenditure was the dependent variable in the regression example in the previous chapter—since food expenditure is at least ordinally and probably intervally scaled. This example is used, therefore, mainly for pedagogical purposes.)

The SPSS input and output appear in Appendix 15–A. 853 respondents provided complete data in terms of education of both husband and wife, age, income, family size, how often they shopped, the number of alternatives considered (section I of the questionnaire, question 6), and information receptivity (section II, question 6), as well as food expenditures. Examination of the mean values shows "reasonable numbers" and relatively equal standard deviations. The group means are shown in Table 15–4. These means indicate that larger spenders tend to be more edu-

TABLE 15–4
Variable averages for five food expenditure level groups

	Group				
	1 < $15	2 $15–$29	3 $30–$44	4 $45–$59	5 > $60
Education of homemaker	3.32	4.11	4.29	4.47	4.49
Education of husband	2.79	3.75	4.08	4.57	4.69
Age	4.09	3.46	3.06	2.50	2.72
Income	1.62	2.06	2.75	3.47	3.75
Family size	2.09	2.52	3.13	4.14	5.11
How often they shop	1.91	2.18	2.27	2.29	2.62
Number of brands shopped for	1.82	2.25	2.34	2.25	2.72
Information sought	1.91	1.91	1.81	1.84	1.87
Sample size	34	284	293	181	61

cated, younger, have higher incomes and larger family size, and to shop more extensively.

The significance of the differences among the five groups on a variable-by-variable basis are given by the F tests which appear next in the output. The 106.0 for family size is the largest with the 49.1 for income next biggest, indicating that these variables are the most important in separating the five groups. Interestingly, education, age, and how often they shop are all also significantly ($F > 4$) related to food expenditures.

(Alas, my favorite variables, number of brands shopped and information sought are not significantly related to food expenditures.)

The program then (after giving some gratuitous information) proceeds to enter variables stepwise into a discriminant analysis in the following order:

1. Family size.
2. Income.
3. How often they shop.
4. Age.
5. Education of the homemaker.
6. Number of brands shopped for.

This order differs substantially from that which the size of simple F's indicates due to multicollinearity.

Next the classification function coefficients are output (Table 15–5). These functions can be used for (a) classification and (b) finding the two-

TABLE 15–5
Classification functions

	Group				
	1	2	3	4	5
Education of homemaker	2.92	3.35	3.28	3.21	3.22
Age	3.61	3.41	3.36	3.32	3.70
Income........................	.42	.44	.83	1.21	1.38
Family size	3.13	3.38	3.82	4.55	5.48
How often they shop	2.83	3.56	3.83	4.00	4.69
Number of brands shopped for ...	1.18	1.33	1.34	1.24	1.44
Constant	−19.61	−22.89	−25.23	−28.80	−37.02

group discriminant function (unstandardized) between a particular pair of groups. Here, for example, the function which best discriminates between groups 1 and 2 is

−.43	Education of homemaker
+.20	Age
−.02	Income
−.25	Family size
−.73	How often they shop
−.17	Number of brands shopped for

while that between 2 and 3 is

+.07	Education of homemaker
+.05	Age
−.39	Income
−.44	Family size
−.27	How often they shop
−.01	Number of brands shopped for

Hence it appears that the variable which most discriminates between those who spend under $15 and those who spend $15–$29 is how often they shopped while what separates the $15–$29 from the $30–$44 spenders is income and family size.

The simultaneous functions are also output in both standardized and unstandardized forms. The first function is the most useful, the second next most useful, and so forth. The output indicated (by means of a chi-square test of Wilks Lamda) that three functions are significant at the .05 (or .01, for that matter) level. The most important variables in the first function are family size, income, and how often they shop. The results can be portrayed graphically as Figure 15–9. Hence these results largely rein-

FIGURE 15–9
Group means on first two discriminant functions

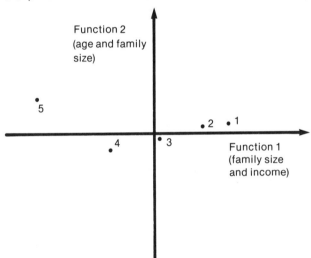

force the analysis of the means and simple F tests as well as the ANOVA and regression results of previous chapters.

Conclusion

Three basic points are worth reiterating:

1. Discriminant analysis, unlike classification procedures, focuses on explaining differences in groups rather than on correctly classifying observations.
2. Dummy dependent variable regression is a substitute for two-group discriminant analysis.

3. There are two major approaches to multiple group discriminant analysis. The "classical" approach is closely tied to the likelihood function and essentially produces the functions which best discriminate among each pair of groups. The simultaneous approach, on the other hand, attempts to find functions which discriminate among all the groups simultaneously.

AUTOMATIC INTERACTION DETECTOR (AID)

Another predictive technique which has often been used in marketing is AID. This technique assumes that the dependent variables are intervally scaled but that all the independent variables are only nominally scaled (as opposed to regression which assumes they are intervally scaled). The technique proceeds by a stepwise procedure to "explain" the dependent variable.

Method

A hypothetical example is the best way to explain AID. Assume I were interested in explaining beer consumption among business school professors in terms of their weight, age, number of articles published, outside income, and degree of sports-mindedness. If I collected data on these variables and consumption from 439 professors, AID would proceed as follows:

1. First it computes average beer consumption (assume here it is 3.4 liters/class).
2. Next it looks at each variable separately to see which "best" explains beer consumption, by using each possible combination of categories to break the total sample into two groups. For example, if age is distributed

$$
\begin{aligned}
1 &= \text{under } 30 & (n &= 112) \\
2 &= 30 - 45 & (n &= 201) \\
3 &= \text{over } 45 & (n &= 126)
\end{aligned}
$$

we can compare average beer consumption of those under 30 (1's) with those over 30 (2's and 3's):

Under 30	Over 30
4.0	3.2

Alternatively, we could compare those under 45 (1's and 2's) with those over 45 (3's). These are the only two possible monotonic (ordered) splits. If we are willing to accept any combination (such as 1's and 3's—under 30 and over 45's versus 2's), more splits are possible. The program computes the amount explained by each possible age split based on a between sum of squares calculation:

$$\text{BSS} = n_1 \bar{Y}_1^2 + n_2 \bar{Y}_2^2 - (n_1 + n_2) \bar{\bar{Y}}^2$$

where

$$\bar{\bar{Y}} = \text{mean beer consumption of the overall group}$$
$$\bar{Y}_1 \text{ and } \bar{Y}_2 = \text{means of the two groups}$$
$$n_1 \text{ and } n_2 = \text{sizes of the two groups}$$

(In essence, AID performs ANOVA on each possible way to split the sample.) The "best" split is then retained for this variable.

FIGURE 15–10
Hypothetical AID analysis of professors' beer consumption

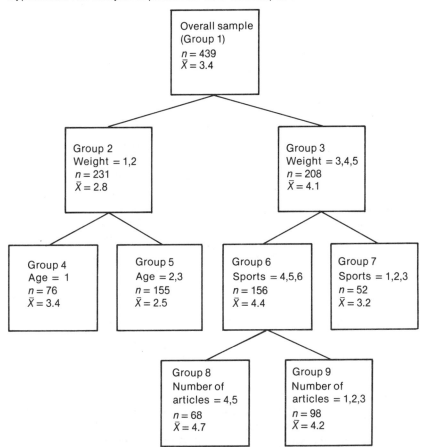

3. The program proceeds to get the best split for each independent variable separately. Next it selects that variable which best spreads out beer consumption and splits the sample accordingly. For example, we might split on weight as follows:

Group 2: (weight = 1, 2) $n = 231$
Average consumption = 2.3
Group 3: (weight = 3, 4, 5) $n = 208$
Average consumption = 4.1

4. The program takes each resulting group (here groups 2 and 3) and goes back to step 2 to see if each group can be further subdivided and still explain a minimum amount of the variance and/or retain a minimum group size. Every time a subsample is formed, an attempt is made to see if the group can be further separated.

5. The results are output. Typically they are summarized in a chart such as Figure 15–10. Here the heaviest consumers of beer (4.7 liters/class) are heavy, sports-minded, and publish a lot (possibly under the influence of their consumption).

Summary

The AID procedure thus has several properties:

It is a segmenting process which begins with the entire sample and then subdivides it into segments which differ in terms of the dependent variable.

The splitting process is binary: Each group is split into exactly two subgroups.

After the first split, variables may enter in different orders down the various branches of the "tree." In this example, the lightweights (group 2) split on age while the heavier professors were split on the basis of sports-mindedness. This feature is where the "interaction" in AID comes from: A variable may be important only in conjunction with another, something a standard stepwise regression program would not uncover.

The process may split on the same variable more than once. For example, the procedure might next split group 7 on the basis of weight into weight category 3 versus weight categories 4 and 5.

At some point, the program stops splitting. There are two basic stopping rules:

1. The sample size in a cell (either the original or one of the resulting segments) is too small to be split.
2. Not enough variance is accounted for by the split.

The program is then really an elaborate tabular approach. AID is used mainly to search for identifiable segments who respond differently with respect to some criterion (dependent) variable such as consumption, attitude, and so forth. Like most procedures, however, it has some shortcomings:

Because it requires "physically" splitting the sample, the procedure needs a massive sample if more than two or three splits are sought.

The technique, like all stepwise procedures, is very sensitive to collinearity and hence unstable. Running two halves of a sample through AID programs separately often creates quite different looking results and consequently different interpretations.

The computer program itself tends to be among the most difficult to decipher.

Unless discipline is exercised, it is possible to allow the program to continue to split into groups of size 2 or 3 which are more likely to be misleading than informative.

In short, then, AID is a very useful tool for generating hypotheses about segments and is very useful in exploratory studies. To use it for other purposes, however, is to invite trouble.

SUMMARY

This chapter has discussed two other predictive procedures: discriminant analysis and AID. These procedures complement previously discussed predictive procedures: tabular analysis, ANOVA, and regression. They do not complete the list of predictive procedures. In addition to these there are canonical correlation, multiple classification analysis (MCA) which is very much like a dummy variable regression program, and probit analysis which treats both the dependent and the independent variables as nonintervally scaled. In fact, one could fill several volumes with such procedures. Such an all-inclusive approach is not useful for marketing research. Given time constraints and computer limitations, it is unrealistic to expect researchers to know all the possible techniques well. It is much more profitable to understand one well (I vote for regression) and to know enough about the others (especially ANOVA and discriminant analysis) to know when their special properties make their use advantageous.

Put differently, predictive procedures have severely diminishing marginal utility. Running multiple predictive procedures on the same set of data is more likely to increase the computer bill than understanding. Also very few people really understand these procedures. To really understand them requires a start-up cost in terms of time and trial-and-error learning.

Finally, don't be afraid to ask the "professional" a question; good ones can provide answers which are at least partially intelligible.

PROBLEMS

1. Assume I run a discriminant analysis on business school majors using aptitude scores as independent variables and get the following classification matrix:

	Predicted group				
Actual group	International business	Marketing	Finance	Production	Others
International business	70	40	30	20	40
Marketing	50	90	30	10	20
Finance	20	20	80	60	20
Production	20	30	40	80	30
Others	20	20	40	20	100

       a. How well have I done (statistically)?

       b. What do the results indicate?

2. Explain the difference between discriminant analysis and classification.

3. In two-group discriminant analysis, could the *sign* of a discriminant coefficient and the *sign* of the difference between means on the variable differ? What would it mean?

4. Explain the difference between discriminant analysis and cluster analysis. Give an example of the type of marketing problems for which each is useful.

5. Your researcher wants to use a discriminant analysis to see if s/he can "predict the people who try a new brand" compared to those who do not try the new brand. You know that the market share of the new brand is only 5 percent and observe that you can predict 95 percent of the population correctly by simply assuming "Each person did not try the new brand." Yet you are bothered by this assumption because it suggests that the market share of the new brand should be zero. You do not think your researcher will be able to predict 95 percent correctly with his/her discriminant analysis model, so you are reluctant to pay for such an investigation. Can anything possibly come out of the discriminant analysis research which might justify the cost of the investigation? What?

6. The following are the income (in $1,000) and age of a sample of 20 purchasers of an expensive automobile brand. A particular accessory was purchased by 12 of the sample but was not purchased by 8 of the sample. The age and income of the sample were as follows:

Twelve purchasers		Eight nonpurchasers	
Age	Income ($000)	Age	Income ($000)
30	20	30	50
40	50	40	30
40	60	40	40
50	40	40	40
50	70	50	20
60	30	50	30
60	40	60	20
60	40	60	50
60	50		
60	60		
60	70		
70	20		

  a. Graphically determine a linear discriminant function which will well predict the purchase of the accessory.
  b. Determine the values of the discriminant function which correspond to nonpurchase, and the values which correspond to purchase of the accessory.
  c. How well does the function discriminate?
7. Of what use are the following outputs of a discriminant analysis?
  a. Mahalonobis D^2 test statistic.
  b. The discriminant function in a two-group analysis.
  c. The first discriminant function in a three-group analysis.
  d. The second discriminant function in a three-group analysis.
  e. The hit-miss classification table for the estimation sample.
  f. The hit-miss classification table for a holdout sample.

BIBLIOGRAPHY

Assael, Henry. "Segmenting Markets by Group Purchasing Behavior: An Application of the AID Technique." *Journal of Marketing Research,* vol. 7 (May 1970), pp. 153–58.

Cooley, William, W., and Lohnes, Paul R. *Multivariate Data Analysis.* New York: Wiley, 1971.

Lehmann, Donald R., and O'Shaughnessy, John. "Difference in Attribute Importance for Different Industrial Products." *Journal of Marketing,* vol. 38 (April 1974), pp. 36–42.

Morgan, J. N., and Sonquist, J. A. *The Determination of Interaction Effects.* Monograph No. 35. Ann Arbor: Survey Research Center, Institute for Social Research, University of Michigan, 1964.

Morrison, Donald F. *Multivariate Statistical Methods.* 2d ed. New York: McGraw-Hill, 1976.

528

Morrison, Donald G. "On the Interpretation of Discriminant Analysis." *Journal of Marketing Research,* vol. 6 (May 1969), pp. 156–63.

Mostellar, Frederich, and Bush, Robert R. "Selective Quantitative Techniques." In *Handbook of Social Psychology,* vol. 1, edited by Gardner Lindzey. Reading, Mass.: Addison-Wesley, 1954.

Robertson, Thomas S., and Kennedy, James N. "Prediction of Consumer Innovators: Application of Multiple Discriminant Analysis." *Journal of Marketing Research,* vol. 5 (February 1968), pp. 64–69.

APPENDIX 15–A: SAMPLE DISCRIMINANT ANALYSIS OUTPUT

```
STATISTICAL PACKAGE FOR THE SOCIAL SCIENCES SPSSH - VERSION 6.00                    10/19/76      PAGE

     SPACE ALLOCATION FOR THIS RUN..

        TOTAL AMOUNT REQUESTED                              80000 BYTES

        DEFAULT TRANSPACE ALLOCATION                        10000 BYTES

             MAX NO OF TRANSFORMATIONS PERMITTED      100
             MAX NO OF RECODE VALUES                  400
             MAX NC OF ARITHM.OR LOG.OPERATIONS       800
        RESULTING WORKSPACE ALLOCATION                      70000 BYTES

             FILE NAME       LEHNUTRI
             VARIABLE LIST   EDUC1,EDUC2,AGE,INCOME,FAMSIZE,HOWOFTEN,EXPENSE,
                             BRAND,INFO
             INPUT MEDIUM    DISK
             N OF CASES      UNKNOWN
             INPUT FORMAT    FIXED(56X,2F1.0,17X,3F1.0/9X,F1.0,2X,F1.0,X,2F1.0////)

        ACCORDING TO YOUR INPUT FORMAT, VARIABLES ARE TO BE READ AS FOLLOWS

             VARIABLE   FORMAT   RECORD    COLUMNS

             EDUC1      F 1. 0      1       57-  57
             EDUC2      F 1. 0      1       58-  58
             AGE        F 1. 0      1       76-  76
             INCOME     F 1. 0      1       77-  77
             FAMSIZE    F 1. 0      1       78-  78
             HOWOFTEN   F 1. 0      2       10-  10
             EXPENSE    F 1. 0      2       13-  13
             BRAND      F 1. 0      2       15-  15
             INFO       F 1. 0      2       16-  16
THE INPUT FORMAT PROVIDES FOR    9 VARIABLES.     9 WILL BE READ
IT PROVIDES FOR   6 RECORDS ('CARDS') PER CASE.   A MAXIMUM OF   78 'COLUMNS' ARE USED ON A RECORD.

                 MISSING VALUES EDUC1 TO EXPENSE (C)
                 READ INPUT DATA
AFTER READING    940 CASES FROM SUBFILE LEHNUTRI,   END OF FILE WAS ENCOUNTERED ON LOGICAL UNIT # 8


STATISTICAL PACKAGE FOR THE SOCIAL SCIENCES SPSSH - VERSION 6.00                    10/19/76      PAGE
             DISCRIMINANT   GROUPS=EXPENSE(1,5)/VARIABLES=EDUC1 TO HOWOFTEN,BRAND,
                            INFO/METHOD=WILKS/
             OPTIONS        5,7,11,12,13,14
             STATISTICS     ALL
FIRST ANALYSIS LIST IS MISSING. ALL VARIABLES WILL BE   USED WITH INCLUSION LEVELS OF ONE.

***** WARNING *****    OPTIONS 13 THRU 19  AND STATISTICS 7, 8  ARE NOT YET IMPLEMENTED AND WILL BE IGNOR

   ***** THIS DISCRIMINANT ANALYSIS REQUIRES   5624 BYTES OF WORKSPACE *****
```

FILE   LEHNUTRI (CREATICN CATE = 10/19/76)

GROUP COUNTS

	GROUP 1	GROUP 2	GROUP 3	GROUP 4	GROUP 5	TCTAL
COUNT	34.CCCC	284.0000	293.COCC	181.OCCC	61.OOCC	853.0000

MEANS

	GROUP 1	GROUP 2	GROUP 3	GROUP 4	GROUP 5	TOTAL
EDUC1	3.3235	4.1092	4.29C1	4.4656	4.4918	4.2438
EDUC2	2.7941	3.7465	4.C751	4.5651	4.6885	4.0633
AGE	4.C882	3.4648	3.C648	2.4572	2.7213	3.0938
INCOME	1.6176	2.0634	2.7543	3.4696	3.7541	2.7022
FAMSIZE	2.C882	2.5211	3.1331	4.1281	5.1148	3.2427
HOWOFTEN	1.9118	2.1831	2.2730	2.2873	2.6230	2.2567
BRAND	1.8225	2.2465	2.3379	2.2541	2.7213	2.2966
INFO	1.9118	1.9120	1.80£9	1.8398	1.8689	1.8581

STANDARD DEVIATICNS

	GROUP 1	GROUP 2	GROUP 3	GROUP 4	GROUP 5	TOTAL
EDUC1	1.3645	1.2854	1.1912	1.2044	1.1453	1.2500
EDUC2	1.6838	1.6769	1.5321	1.4495	1.4668	1.6202
AGE	1.5249	1.6156	1.43C8	1.C586	0.8969	1.4634
INCOME	C.9539	1.3008	1.3451	1.2847	1.2471	1.4366
FAMSIZE	C.2879	0.8834	1.3083	1.2054	1.45C3	1.3987
HOWOFTEN	0.6682	0.6685	0.6829	0.7C34	0.7564	0.6977
BRAND	1.2666	1.3797	1.4185	1.4C69	1.4734	1.4067
INFO	0.7535	C.7251	0.68C7	0.6558	0.6449	0.6919

WILKS' LAMBDA (U-STATISTIC) AND UNIVARIATE F-RATIO WITH   4   AND   848   DEGREES OF FREEDOM

VARIABLE	WILKS' LAMBDA	F
EDUC1	0.9643	7.8525
EDUC2	0.9314	15.6173
AGE	0.9201	18.4185
INCOME	0.8119	49.1218
FAMSIZE	0.6667	106.0062
HOWOFTEN	0.9662	7.4155
BRAND	0.9880	2.5646
INFO	0.9558	0.8873

WITHIN GROUPS COVARIANCE MATRIX

	EDUC1	EDUC2	AGE	INCOME	FAMSIZE	HOWOFTEN	BRAND	INFO
EDUC1	1.5138							
EDUC2	1.1412	2.4565						
AGE	-0.4561	-0.8300	1.9795					
INCOME	0.6210	0.9189	-0.3880	1.6835				
FAMSIZE	0.0554	0.1346	-0.5922	0.1254	1.3103			
HOWOFTEN	-0.0036	-0.0498	0.2460	0.0426	-0.0979	0.4726		
BRAND	0.0959	0.2142	-0.3385	-0.0120	0.1527	-0.0106	1.9644	
INFO	-0.0890	-0.0890	0.0798	-0.0126	0.0043	0.0188	-0.1537	0.4789

WITHIN GROUPS CORRELATION MATRIX

	EDUC1	EDUC2	AGE	INCOME	FAMSIZE	HOWOFTEN	BRAND	INFO
EDUC1	1.0000							
EDUC2	0.5918	1.0000						
AGE	-0.2635	-0.3764	1.0000					
INCOME	0.3890	0.4519	-0.2125	1.0000				
FAMSIZE	0.0422	0.0750	-0.3683	0.0844	1.0000			
HOWOFTEN	-0.0042	-0.0462	0.2544	0.0478	-0.1244	1.0000		
BRAND	0.0556	0.0975	-0.1717	-0.0066	0.0952	-0.0110	1.0000	
INFO	-0.1046	-0.0910	0.0820	-0.0140	0.0055	0.0395	-0.1584	1.0000

TOTAL COVARIANCE MATRIX

	EDUC1	EDUC2	AGE	INCOME	FAMSIZE	HOWOFTEN	BRAND	INFO
EDUC1	1.5625							
EDUC2	1.2322	2.6251						
AGE	-0.5428	-0.5966	2.1414					
INCOME	0.7429	1.1668	-0.6340	2.0638				
FAMSIZE	0.2064	0.4482	-0.8878	0.6134	1.9563			
HOWOFTEN	0.0207	-0.0045	0.2063	0.1056	-0.0056	0.4868		
BRAND	0.1213	0.2570	-0.3662	0.0450	0.2331	0.0083	1.9788	
INFO	-0.0945	-0.1084	0.0968	-0.0254	-0.0113	0.0165	-0.1551	0.4787

VARIABLE ENTERED ON STEP NUMBER 1..   FAMSIZE

			DEGREES OF FREEDOM		SIGNIFICANCE
WILKS' LAMBDA	0.66665	APPROXIMATE F	106.00616	3 848.00	0.000
RAO'S V	424.01978	CHANGE IN V	424.01978	4	0.0

F MATRIX - DEGREES OF FREEDOM: 1, 848

	GROUP 1	GROUP 2	GROUP 3	GROUP 4
GROUP 2	4.34259			
GROUP 3	25.38301	41.21944		
GROUP 4	91.79056	220.58722	86.24487	
GROUP 5	152.61307	257.78857	151.30698	33.21054

------- VARIABLES IN THE ANALYSIS -------

VARIABLE	ENTRY CRITERION	F TO REMOVE
FAMSIZE	106.00616	106.00616

------- VARIABLES NOT IN THE ANALYSIS -------

VARIABLE	TOLERANCE	F TO ENTER	ENTRY CRITERION
EDUC1	0.99822	5.11005	7.85246
EDUC2	0.99437	7.94118	15.61726
AGE	0.86432	4.42566	18.41850
INCOME	0.99287	26.45332	49.12177
HOWOFTEN	0.98452	10.83165	7.41548
BRAND	0.99094	1.48431	2.56460
INFO	0.99997	0.86361	0.88735

VARIABLE ENTERED ON STEP NUMBER 6..   BRAND

			DEGREES OF FREEDOM		SIGNIFICANCE
WILKS' LAMBDA	0.55066	APPROXIMATE F	22.86526	24 2942.09	0.000
RAO'S V	65E.016E5	CHANGE IN V	6.45825	4	0.167

F MATRIX - DEGREES OF FREEDOM: 6, 843

	GROUP 1	GROUP 2	GROUP 3	GROUP 4
GROUP 2	4.25634			
GROUP 3	11.24604	13.42533		
GROUP 4	26.76587	55.89760	19.24010	
GROUP 5	39.71443	60.87253	34.04955	10.43001

------ VARIABLES IN THE ANALYSIS ------

VARIABLE	ENTRY CRITERION	F TO REMOVE
EDUC1	2.08656	2.02444
AGE	3.39772	2.95604
INCOME	26.44332	21.00511
FAMSIZE	106.00616	71.84845
HOWOFTEN	8.69083	7.48475
BRAND	1.55753	1.55752

------ VARIABLES NOT IN THE ANALYSIS ------

VARIABLE	TOLERANCE	F TO ENTER	ENTRY CRITERION
EDUC2	0.54819	0.84227	0.89131
INFO	0.96163	0.84561	0.81323

F LEVEL INSUFFICIENT FOR FURTHER COMPUTATION

FILE LEHNUTFI (CREATION DATE = 10/19/76)

- - - - - - - - - - - - - - D I S C R I M I N A N T   A N A L Y S I S - - - - - - - - - - - - - - -

SUMMARY TABLE

STEP NUMBER	VARIABLE ENTERED REMOVED	NUMBER INCLUDED	F TO ENTER OR REMOVE	WILKS' LAMBDA	SIG.	RAO'S V	CHANGE IN RAO'S V	SIG. OF CHANGE
1	FAMSIZE	1	106.00616	0.66665	0.000	424.01978	424.01978	0.0
2	INCOME	2	26.45332	0.59262	0.000	577.29126	153.27148	0.0
3	HOWOFTEN	3	8.69083	0.56923	0.000	628.94336	51.65210	0.000
4	AGE	4	3.39772	0.56022	0.000	642.81152	13.86816	0.008
5	EDUC1	5	2.08856	0.55473	0.000	651.55859	8.74707	0.068
6	BRAND	6	1.55753	0.55066	0.000	658.01685	6.45825	0.167

CLASSIFICATION FUNCTION COEFFICIENTS

	GROUP 1	GROUP 2	GROUP 3	GROUP 4	GROUP 5
EDUC1	2.91570	2.35136	3.28176	3.20768	3.21836
AGE	3.60670	3.40733	3.36344	3.31698	3.69674
INCOME	0.41949	0.44196	0.82507	1.21068	1.37844
FAMSIZE	3.12835	3.38411	3.61591	4.55318	5.47836
HOWOFTEN	2.82546	2.56189	3.62936	3.59922	4.69368
BRAND	1.18224	1.32601	1.93864	1.23757	1.47313
CONSTANT	-19.61284	-22.88771	-25.23024	-28.75979	-37.01587

DISCRIMINANT FUNCTION	EIGENVALUE	RELATIVE PERCENTAGE	CANONICAL CORRELATION
1	0.72246	93.10	0.648
2	0.02870	3.70	0.167
3	0.02188	2.82	0.146
4	0.00296	0.38	0.054

FUNCTIONS (DERIVED)	WILKS' LAMBDA	CHI-SQUARE	DF	SIGNIFICANCE
0	0.5507	505.055	24	0.0
1	0.9485	44.769	15	0.000
2	0.9757	20.820	8	0.008
3	0.9971	2.499	3	0.475

REMAINING COMPUTATIONS WILL BE BASED ON 4 DISCRIMINANT FUNCTION(S)

STANDARDIZED DISCRIMINANT FUNCTION COEFFICIENTS

	FUNC 1	FUNC 2	FUNC 3	FUNC 4
EDUCI	C.02931	C.01147	-0.7C139	C.52128
AGE	-0.01743	C.80563	0.29404	-C.20102
INCOME	-0.41692	-C.42982	0.30218	-C.69749
FAMSIZE	-C.77391	C.56026	0.29381	0.53745
HOWOFTEN	-C.20329	C.24330	-0.54126	-C.17733
BRAND	-C.01463	C.37179	-0.37260	-C.42580

UNSTANDARDIZED DISCRIMINANT FUNCTION COEFFICIENTS

	FUNC 1	FUNC 2	FUNC 3	FUNC 4
EDUCI	0.02345	C.00918	-0.56111	C.417C2
AGE	-0.01191	C.55054	C.2CC93	-C.13737
INCOME	-C.29021	-C.29919	0.21C35	-C.62473
FAMSIZE	-0.55321	C.40056	0.21C06	C.38425
HOWOFTEN	-C.29136	C.34870	-C.8C440	-C.25415
BRAND	-C.01040	C.26430	-0.26467	-C.3C270
CONSTANT	3.19721	-3.62650	2.93368	0.36612

CENTROIDS OF GROUPS IN REDUCED SPACE

	FUNC 1	FUNC 2	FUNC 3	FUNC 4
GROUP 1	1.02553	C.15579	0.64837	-C.05555
GROUP 2	C.59904	C.06620	-0.06331	C.C4861
GROUP 3	C.C4177	-C.05837	-0.06789	-C.C6758
GROUP 4	-C.71423	-C.19783	0.C6564	C.C45E5
GROUP 5	-1.44158	C.47234	-0.0C654	-C.CC484

PREDICTION RESULTS -

ACTUAL GROUP	NO. OF CASES	PREDICTED GROUP MEMBERSHIP				
		GP. 1	GP. 2	GP. 3	GP. 4	GP. 5
GROUP 1	34.	20. 58.8%	13. 38.2%	1. 2.9%	0. 0.0%	0. 0.0%
GROUP 2	284.	86. 30.3%	106. 37.3%	59. 20.8%	24. 8.5%	9. 3.2%
GROUP 3	292.	50. 17.1%	65. 22.2%	90. 30.7%	57. 19.5%	31. 10.6%
GROUP 4	181.	7. 3.9%	7. 3.9%	33. 18.2%	84. 46.4%	50. 27.6%
GROUP 5	61.	2. 3.3%	1. 1.6%	6. 9.8%	12. 19.7%	40. 65.6%

PERCENT OF "GROUPED" CASES CORRECTLY CLASSIFIED: 39.66%

_____ APPENDIX 15–B _____
TECHNICAL ASPECTS OF DISCRIMINANT ANALYSIS

The discriminant function

The discriminant coefficients can be expressed as a matrix product as follows:

$$d = W^{-1}(\bar{x}_1 - \bar{x}_2) \tag{15B.1}$$

where

W = the pooled within group covariance matrix
$\bar{x}_1$ = vector of means of the first group on all k variables
$\bar{x}_2$ = vector of means of the second group on all k variables

This formulation can be better understood by considering the special case where the predictor variables are perfectly independent of each other. In this case, the discriminant function becomes

$$d = \left[\frac{\bar{x}_{11} - \bar{x}_{21}}{s_1^2}\right] x_1 + \left[\frac{\bar{x}_{12} - \bar{x}_{22}}{s_2^2}\right] x_2 + \cdots + \left[\frac{\bar{x}_{1k} - \bar{x}_{2k}}{s_k^2}\right] x_k$$

Hence the weight assigned a particular variable depends on (*a*) the difference in means between the two groups on that variable and (*b*) the variance of that variable. Practically this means that variables on which the two groups differ significantly will be weighted heavily by the discriminant function. The relation between the differences in mean between groups and standard deviation on a particular variable and the discriminant coefficient is summarized in Table 15B–1.

TABLE 15B–1
The effect of difference in mean and variance
on discriminant coefficients

Difference in means	Variance	Discriminant coefficient
Small	Small	Moderate
Small	Large	Close to zero
Large	Small	Large
Large	Large	Moderate

Optimal classification

The basic motivation of discriminant analysis is to determine which of a set of characteristics are most important as discriminators between members of the two groups. Discriminant analysis, therefore, is not primarily addressed to the objective of classifying an individual into one of two groups based on the values the individual has on the predictor variables. The resulting discriminant function can, however, be used to optimally classify observations.

The basic approach in most classification procedures is to assign an individual to the group where the expected opportunity cost of misclassification is the smallest. This requires taking the following three pieces of information into account:

1. *The cost of misclassifying a member of one group as a member of another:*

   $C(1|2)$ = cost of classifying a person as a member of group 1 given s/he is really a member of group 2 (e.g., classifying a customer as a noncustomer)

   $C(2|1)$ = cost of classifying a person as a member of group 2 given the person is really a member of group 1.

2. *The relative likelihoods that a person in the two groups would exhibit the values on the variables of the individual who is to be classified:*

   $L(Z|1)$ = likelihood that a person in group 1 would exhibit a set of characteristics equal to Z

   $L(Z|2)$ = likelihood that a person in group 2 would exhibit a set of characteristics equal to Z

3. *The overall (prior) probability that any individual will be a member of each of the two groups:*

   $P(1)$ = probability that an individual is a member of group 1

   $P(2)$ = probability that an individual is a member of group 2

In order to classify a person as a member of group 1, the following inequality must hold:

$$\text{Expected cost of classifying as a 1} < \text{Expected cost of classifying as a 2} \qquad (15B.2)$$

or

$$[P(1)]\,[C(2\,|\,1)]\,[L(Z\,|\,1)] > [P(2)]\,[C(1\,|\,2)]\,[L(Z\,|\,2)]$$

This can be rewritten as

$$\frac{[P(2)][C(1|2)]}{[P(1)][C(2|1)]} < \frac{L(Z|1)}{L(Z|2)}$$

For the case with equal priors and costs of misclassification, the formula reduces to classify an observation as a member of group 1 if $L(Z|1) > L(Z|2)$.

To this point nothing has depended on performing discriminant analysis. The likelihoods can be evaluated directly. Direct evaluation, however, is not very easy without a computer given the messy formulas involved. Fortunately the discriminant function can be used to get optimal classification if the following two assumptions are met:

1. The predictor variables are normally distributed.
2. The variances are equal in the two groups.

In this case, the linear discriminant function will provide optimal classification if the following rule is followed:

$$\text{Let } K = \frac{[P(2)][C(1|2)]}{[P(1)][C(2|1)]} \tag{15B.3}$$

$\bar{f}_1, \bar{f}_2$ = mean value of the groups on discriminant function which are calculated by multiplying the discriminant weights (w_i's) times the means of the variables for each group

$$\bar{f}_1 = w_1\bar{x}_{11} + w_2\bar{x}_{12} + \cdots + w_k\bar{x}_{1k} \tag{15B.4}$$
$$\bar{f}_2 = w_1\bar{x}_{21} + w_2\bar{x}_{22} + \cdots + w_k\bar{x}_{2k}$$

n = total number of observations ($n_1 + n_2$)

$$f = w_1Z_1 + w_2Z_2 + \cdots + w_kZ_k \tag{15B.5}$$

= value of the person to be classified on the discriminant function

Then (assuming $\bar{f}_1 < \bar{f}_2$) we would classify an observation as a member of group 1 if

$$f < \frac{\bar{f}_1 + \bar{f}_2}{2} - \log_e k \tag{15B.6}$$

For equal priors and costs of misclassifying, this reduces to

$$f < \frac{\bar{f}_1 + \bar{f}_2}{2} \tag{15B.7}$$

Using the discriminant function for classification

Recalling the earlier example involving nonpurchasers and purchasers measured in terms of age and income, we had

$$f = 3(\text{income}) - 2(\text{age})$$

If the group means on income and age were 2.5 and 2 respectively for nonpurchasers and the group means for purchasers were 4.5 and 1.5, the mean values for the two groups on the discriminant function are as follows:

$$\bar{f_1} = 3(2.5) - 2(2) = 3.5$$

and

$$\bar{f_2} = 3(4.5) - 2(1.5) = 10.5$$

Thus the "cutoff" can be derived from formula (15B.7) as:

$$\frac{\bar{f_1} + \bar{f_2}}{2} = \frac{3.5 + 10.5}{2} = 7$$

Now assume we wished to classify a person as a member of group one or two based on the person's income of 3 and age of 2. In this case $f = 3(3) - 2(2) = 5$. Since $5 < 7$, we would classify this person as a nonpurchaser.

16

Grouping data

In the past few chapters, various procedures for predicting a criterion variable have been discussed. In this chapter, the focus turns to grouping things—variables, customers, and so forth—together. The purpose of grouping procedures is not prediction but simplification.

The desire to categorize large numbers of data points into a more manageable classification scheme is a basic human trait. It also is a practical necessity for many marketing and marketing research problems. It is simply not feasible to consider each user of toothpaste separately or to use 317 variables in most studies. Large amounts of data need to be reduced into more manageable forms. This chapter will discuss some of the methods used in marketing research for grouping data.

FACTOR ANALYSIS

Two basic purposes

There are two basic reasons for using factor analysis. First, there is the desire for simplification. While it is possible to analyze 67 variables in detail, it would be much easier both to analyze and communicate the study if only 15 variables were used. One use of factor analysis is to reduce the 67 variables to 15 with the minimum possible loss of information. The second reason for using factor analysis is to uncover an underlying structure in the data. This use of factor analysis assumes that the 67 variables are manifestations of a small number (e.g., 10) of key but unmeasured constructs. It then attempts to deduce what the underlying constructs are from examining the relations among the 67 measured variables. These two reasons for using factor analysis are, though closely related, sufficiently different that they place different emphasis on how the results are interpreted and used.

540

Basic notion: Factor analysis for simplification

In marketing research, the major use of factor analysis is to group together redundant variables. The purpose of this grouping is to help the researcher select a smaller number of variables for further analysis (without excluding variables which contain a substantial amount of information not available from the reduced set of variables). The reduced set of variables are then used (*a*) to more efficiently analyze the results of a given study or (*b*) to reduce the amount of data needed in subsequent studies.

Consider the correlation matrix of Table 16–1. Here we have four variables which were questions on a pilot study. Assume we need to reduce

TABLE 16–1
Hypothetical correlations among four variables

Variable	Variable			
	1	2	3	4
1	1	.9	.7	.2
2		1	.8	.05
3			1	.1
4				1

these four variables to two variables (e.g., there is only room for two questions on the next wave of the study, the computer algorithm we want to use can only handle two variables). The best way to simplify is to have a theory dictating which variables to retain. Absent theory, common sense suggests that I discard those variables which give me the least additional information value if retained. To do this, I might find out which variables are most correlated with each other. In this example, variables 1, 2, and 3 all seem fairly highly correlated with each other, and 4 seems to be different. Hence I might classify 1, 2, and 3 as type A variables and 4 as a type B variable, and then pick a representative of each type. What factor analysis essentially does (when all the theory is stripped aside) is to group together those variables which are highly correlated.

The key output of a factor analysis is what might be called an assignment matrix. This matrix indicates which variables belong to each group. In the previous example, the suggested assignment pattern is given in Table 16–2, where a "1" indicates that the variable belongs in the factor and a "0" indicates it does not. Actually the world is never quite as simple as this example indicates. The previous assignment matrix implies the assignment was perfectly clear-cut and would result from a correlation

TABLE 16–2
Hypothetical two-factor
assignment table

	Factor	
Variable	1	2
1	1	0
2	1	0
3	1	0
4	0	1

TABLE 16–3
Sample correlation matrix

	Variable			
Variable	1	2	3	4
1	1	1	1	0
2	1	1	1	0
3	1	1	1	0
4	0	0	0	1

matrix like that in Table 16–3. The actual correlation matrix showed variable 4 to be somewhat correlated with variables 1, 2, and 3 and variables 1, 2, and 3 less than perfectly correlated with each other. Hence a more tentative assignment scheme is likely to result, such as that in Table 16–4.

As we proceed to discuss factor analysis in a more formal manner, it is important to recall that its major output will be an assignment matrix of the type just discussed.

TABLE 16–4
Two-factor assignment matrix

	Factor	
Variable	1	2
1	.9	.02
2	.92	.05
3	.81	.09
4	.11	.93

Basic model: Factor analysis for construct derivation

The model underlying factor analysis for construct derivation is that observed data (X's) are really "produced" by some underlying and unobserved factors (f's). The model presented here is essentially an adaptation from psychology. The objective is often to understand the structure of the data (e.g., individual scores on various aptitude tests), and the method deduces the structure indirectly. Believing this model is not necessary for using factor analysis for some purposes such as removing redundant variables. Nonetheless much of the "flavor" of the interpretation of factor analysis for both construct derivation and variable reduction purposes comes from this model. The basic form of the model is

$$\begin{array}{ccc} \text{Observed value of} & & f(k\text{th person's scores on the} \\ \text{the } k\text{th person on the} & = & \text{underlying factors and a} \\ j\text{th variable} & & \text{random element)} \end{array}$$

Put mathematically, this becomes

$$X_{ik} = \lambda_{i1}f_{1k} + \lambda_{i2}f_{2k} + \cdots + \lambda_{im}f_{mk} + e_i \qquad (16.1)$$

where

X_{ik} = value of variable i for the kth observation

f_{jk} = value of the jth factor for the kth observation (commonly called factor scores)

λ_{ij} = relation of the ith variable with the jth common factor

and there are m factors and p variables, $m \leq p$.

The λ_{ij}'s (often called loadings) indicate how the underlying constructs (factors) are related to the measured variables. The loadings also play the role of the assignment matrix for purposes of variable reduction (Table 16–5).

TABLE 16–5
Assignment (loading) matrix

Variable	Factor			
	1	2	$\cdots$	m
1	λ_{11}	λ_{12}	$\cdots$	λ_{1m}
2	λ_{21}	λ_{22}	$\cdots$	λ_{2m}
.	.	.		.
.	.	.		.
.	.	.		.
p	λ_{p1}	λ_{p2}	$\cdots$	λ_{pm}

General method

The purpose of factor analysis, therefore, is to derive a "good" set of λ's. A good set of λ's has two basic properties. First, the λ's must produce X's which closely match the observed X's. Second, the λ's must clearly indicate which variables belong with which factors. The problem is that both the factor values and the loadings are unknown. A variety of approaches to deriving the λ's can be imagined including the inelegant (and inefficient) method of trial-and-error guessing. The most common approach, however, requires two basic steps.

1. The principal components are calculated. Principal components (*PC*'s) are derived from the original X's by the following model:

$$PC_j = a_{j1}X_1 + a_{j2}X_2 + \cdots + a_{jp}X_p \qquad (16.2)$$

where

$PC_j = j$th principal component

a_{ji} = the coefficient relating the ith variable to the jth component

These components are uniquely derived mathematically (see Appendix 16–A) so that the first contains as much of the total information in all the p original variables as possible, the second (which is independent of the first) contains as much as possible of the remaining information, and so forth. (In this context, the information in a variable is operationalized as its variance.) Graphically, the first principal component can be viewed as finding a line (plane) which passes through the data so as to most spread out the observations (Figure 16–1). What principal components really do

FIGURE 16–1
Principal components of two variables

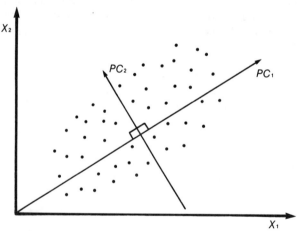

is to change the p original variables into p components which are perfectly independent of each other. The greater the collinearity among the original variables, the more of the original variance is accounted for by the first principal component.

It is possible to use the a_{ji} values as a basis for assigning variables to groups. Unfortunately these results tend to be fairly muddled, with no clear-cut pattern of which variable belongs in which groups. For example, it is common to have most of the variables appear to be related to the first component. For this reason, a second step is used.

    2.   The original configuration is rotated.   Recall that the original goal was to achieve an assignment matrix which is clear in indicating which variables belong in which grouping (factor). Since the a_{ji}'s in principal components are not very useful in this regard, the obvious solution is to "improve" them. The method for improving the results is to "massage" the original a_{ji}'s so that the new values (λ_{ij}'s) are numbers which are closer to 1 or 0. The method for this massaging is to rotate the original components in order to make the λ_{ij}'s close to 1's or 0's. A variety of formal objective functions exist for this process of which the most commonly used is called varimax. Consider again Figure 16–1. By rotating the original components, we can achieve a picture like Figure 16–2. In both

FIGURE 16–2
Rotated factors

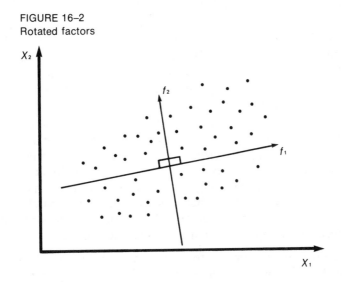

cases, the factors are orthogonal (independent) and "explain" (represent) the original data equally well. Hence if the rotated factors better delineate which variable belongs in which group, they are a "better" result.

Interpretation and use of factor analysis

    Having outlined the basic steps in factor analysis as it is commonly applied, it is now important to delineate what decisions the user makes and how the results are interpreted. The basic decisions are which variables to include, number of factors to retain, which final solution to use, and naming the factors.

Which variables to include. A very important (but often overlooked) step is the selection of variables to be analyzed. Factor analysis can only reduce data present in the original variables; it cannot help indicate what important factors or variables have been omitted. Factor analysis also will reproduce "obvious" results. For example, if someone factor analyzed participation in two sports, consumption of two wines, and reading of two magazines such as *Harper's* and *Atlantic Monthly,* they might get an interesting cross-fertilization (e.g., *Harper's* readers consume a certain kind of wine, etc.). More likely, however, they would obtain three factors: sports, wine consumption, and magazine readership.

Number of factors to retain. Principal components produces one component for each variable. Hence rotating p components will reproduce the original p variables—hardly a simplified result. To be parsimonious, a smaller number of factors ($m < p$) must be retained. The question of how many factors exist in the data is settled in the following variety of ways:

Prior theory. By far the best way to determine how many factors exist in the data is to employ prior theory (e.g., a theory that people think about colors on three dimensions).

Available space. Sometimes the available space on a questionnaire or the limitations of a computer program or analytical procedure will dictate the maximum number of variables to retain.

Examining the results. When prior theory is unavailable (or questionable) as a guide, a researcher must resort to examining the data for a clue as to how many factors exist. One approach is to use trial and error, finding the best solution for two factors, three factors, and so forth, and then choosing the solution which is most useful/ felicitous/pleasing. Aside from the potential for researcher bias influencing the choice adversely, this method is not very efficient. Hence a more mechanical approach is often desired.

The most common approach for determining the number of factors is to examine the eigenvalues (characteristic values) of the principal components solution. Recall that the principal components solution produced p components for p variables. As a bonus, they indicate what percent of the total variance is accounted for by each of the factors. The percent of the variance accounted for by the jth component is given by

$$\frac{\text{Percent total variation in original } p \text{ variables accounted for by } j\text{th principal component}}{} = \frac{\text{Eigenvalue}_j}{\sum\limits_{i=1}^{p} (\text{eigenvalue}_i)} \quad (16.3)$$

When (as is typically done) the correlation matrix is used as the basis for factoring, this becomes

$$\frac{\text{Eigenvalue}_j}{\text{Number of variables}} \quad (16.4)$$

This formula allows the percent of total variance accounted for to be used as a criterion for determining the number of factors in several ways:

1. By requiring inclusion of enough factors to reach a certain level of total variance explained.
2. By requiring any factor to explain at least the amount of variance which a truly independent variable would explain. If all the original variables were independent, then each component (which would equal one variable) would explain 1/n percent of the total variance and have an eigenvalue equal to 1. This criterion is often known as the eigenvalue-greater-than-one rule and tends to produce good (interpretable) results.[1]
3. By requiring each subsequent factor to explain a substantial and/or significant amount of the residual variance. This sequential testing approach can be done in many ways (Morrison, 1976; Lehmann and Morrison, 1977), but is not widely used in marketing research.

To see how these schemes work, consider the example involving eight variables of Table 16–6. Notice that if I require 70 percent of the variance

TABLE 16–6
Eight-variable eigenvalue analysis

Eigen-value	Percent of total variance explained	Cumulative percent explained
4.0	4/8 = 50%	50
1.2	1.2/8 = 15%	65
.8	.8/8 = 10%	75
.7	.7/8 = 8.75%	83.75
.6	.6/8 = 7.5%	91.25
.4	.4/8 = 5%	96.25
.2	.2/8 = 2.5%	98.75
.1	.1/8 = 1.25%	100
8	100%	

to be explained, I would use three factors. On the other hand, if I use the eigenvalue-greater-than-one rule, I would use two factors. If I expect the variance explained by a factor to be substantially bigger than that ex-

---

[1] An interesting empirical phenomenon which occurs in survey research data is that one third of the components will have eigenvalues greater than one, and this one third of the components will account for two thirds of the variance in the original variables. For example, if there are 39 original variables, one would typically get about 13 eigenvalues greater than one. This "rule" also provides a tip-off to the amount of collinearity in the data since one third of the components accounting for 85 percent of the variance means unusually high collinearity, and one third accounting for 50 percent indicates atypically low intercorrelations among the original variables.

plained by the subsequent factor(s), I might use only one factor. Hence the correct number of factors is not always easy to deduce.

Which final solution to use. As was discussed earlier, the principal components rarely are used directly to identify either redundant variables or unmeasured constructs. Hence the initial components which are selected (e.g., those with eigenvalues greater than one) are revised to produce a more clear-cut partitioning of the variables while still retaining all the information of the original components. The method of revising the components is known as rotation (and involves some matrix algebra beyond the scope of this book).

A variety of rotation schemes exist for transforming the original solution into a more clear-cut assignment matrix (commonly called simple structure). The major decision is whether the factors can be correlated (in which case they can be rotated obliquely), or are independent (in which case they must be rotated orthogonally). For the occasional/typical user, orthogonal rotation is probably the best choice. Several orthogonal rotation schemes exist, including quartimax, varimax, and so forth. These schemes provide a criterion for rotation which places a premium on having the loadings (λ_{ij}'s) close to one or zero. Varimax is the most commonly used, mainly because orthogonal varimax rotation is the default option in most canned computer programs.

Naming the factors. It is common practice to try to name factors. This is done by seeing what the variables which load heavily on the factor have in common. Exactly what "load heavily" means is somewhat vague and really depends on the study. However many people choose an arbitrary cutoff level such as .5 for the loadings so that each variable tends to load on exactly one factor. For example, a factor which includes income, education, and occupational status might be called "well-offness." The naming of factors is quite subjective but also "fun" and occasionally produces an interesting insight.

Nutritional example

One of the questions on the now infamous food survey dealt with actual consumption of 30 foods. Specifically, frequency of consumption was asked for these foods (section I, question 14). An obvious question which arises is whether there are patterns of consumption which occur across people. In order to examine this notion, a factor analysis of the 30 variables was performed. The basic input data was the reported consumption of the 30 foods for the 940 respondents. The actual output appears in Appendix 16–B.

There were seven eigenvalues greater than one, and the first seven factors accounted for 49.2 percent of the variance in the original 30 variables. This indicated a generally low level of collinearity among the vari-

TABLE 16–7
Food consumption factor loadings

Food	Factor							Communality
	1	2	3	4	5	6	7	
Canned fruit	−.12	.46	.04	.06	.00	.30	−.02	.32
Fresh fruit	−.10	.41	.22	.15	.23	.30	−.15	.41
Bread	.07	.52	−.10	.09	.13	.15	.15	.36
Rice	.05	.17	−.00	.16	.34	.10	.03	.18
Butter	.10	.13	.18	.00	.12	.04	−.49	.32
Margarine	.11	.31	.02	.00	.23	.13	.65	.60
Cheese	.13	.18	−.00	.11	.35	.21	.08	.23
Ice cream	.21	.51	−.05	.01	.08	.05	−.06	.32
Whole milk	.07	.21	−.67	.09	−.02	.05	−.06	.52
Skim milk	.07	.15	.70	.18	.03	.08	.13	.58
Snack foods (potato chips, pretzels)	.62	.11	−.07	.11	.04	.02	.04	.41
Desserts	.22	.58	−.06	.06	.09	−.08	−.01	.40
Alcholic beverages	.14	−.12	−.04	.07	.52	−.01	−.04	.31
Soft drinks	.56	−.06	−.03	.06	.01	.16	−.04	.35
Fish	.00	.16	.14	.41	.34	.22	−.13	.40
Cold cereal	−.03	.43	.03	.14	.02	.07	.05	.22
Frozen vegetables	.05	.18	.13	.05	.31	.27	−.01	.22
Fresh vegetables	−.09	.30	.10	.11	.32	.45	−.04	.43
Canned vegetables	.18	.18	.02	.28	−.04	.39	−.11	.30
Poultry	.10	.15	.00	.41	.26	.30	−.01	.36
Beef (hamburger)	.25	.25	.00	.25	.14	.46	−.12	.43
Steak or roast beef	.24	.09	−.03	.00	.21	.48	−.01	.34
Pork	.32	.12	−.09	.01	.15	.36	−.05	.28
Tuna fish	.20	.01	.08	.49	.25	.09	−.04	.36
Frozen dinners	.30	.06	.03	.22	.07	−.03	.06	.15
Hot dogs	.33	.07	−.07	.38	−.04	.03	.06	.27
Coffee or tea	.04	.18	−.01	.09	.30	.21	.11	.19
Pasta	.43	.14	−.01	.21	.25	.14	.08	.33
Food of fast food restaurants	.66	.02	.10	.04	−.17	.10	−.10	.50
Food at regular restaurants	.30	.12	.14	−.11	.34	.15	−.15	.30

ables. These seven variables were then rotated to produce a more interpretable grouping pattern. The results are shown in Table 16–7. The factors thus appear to be:

1. Junk/convenience foods.
2. Calories/desserts.
3. Skim versus whole milk.
4. Meat substitutes.
5. Alcohol.
6. Beef.
7. Margarine versus butter.

Exactly what this means is unclear. The skim versus whole milk and margarine versus butter factors represent obvious conscious choices. The junk/convenience food, meat substitute, and beef factors are also obvious groupings, as are the desserts. The fact that alcoholic beverages seem to have their own factor is only mildly interesting. The communalities indicate the position of the variation in each variable accounted for by the six factors. Notice that some of the communalities (portion of variance in each of the variables accounted for by the factors) are extremely low, indicating for example that only 15 percent of the variance in consumption of frozen dinners is accounted for by the seven factors. This suggests that either (a) the data is very noisy/unreliable or (b) consumption of one food is relatively independent of consumption of other foods.

Uses of factor analysis

Factor analysis is a very flexible tool. Nonetheless, there are two major uses: discovering constructs/variable groups and reducing variables to a more manageable number.

Discovering constructs/variable groups. A major use of factor analysis is to uncover a set of factors which are interpretable and contribute to understanding. Put differently, a researcher can try to name the factors and then see if these names give any insight into a problem. This is a search for an "ah-ha" phenomenon where a result leads to fairly immediate enlightenment. Recognizing that the factors are bound by the original variables and hence in no sense guaranteed to include all important constructs, this "soft" use of factor analysis still is both cheap and potentially rewarding.

Reducing variables to a more manageable number. Early in the study of a problem, a large number of variables (e.g., 70) may appear as candidates for study. Yet such a large number will encumber both survey and model alike. There is a strong desire, therefore, to reduce the 70 variables to a more manageable number. The obvious place to start is to require the variables to be theoretically/logically useful and measurable. Beyond that, it is generally agreed that reducing redundancy is an efficient way to improve the variable set. Since factor analysis groups variables into factors such that all the variables in a factor are correlated with each other, it is obviously a useful technique for this problem. The problem comes in deciding how to eliminate variables. There are at least three major approaches:

> *Pick one variable to represent each factor.* The representative should be both a good variable (well measured and understood) and have a high loading on the factor. It is also important to include variables which do not load highly on any factor, since they are unique/

unrelated to the other variables. This is the easiest approach and by no means clearly inferior to the more complicated methods.

Build an index based on the major variables on each factor. This index could be a simple sum or some weighted combination of the "big loading" variables.

Use the factor scores. The scores of each observation on the underlying factors can be estimated and used to represent each factor (see Appendix 16–A). This result can guarantee truly independent variables. Unfortunately it does not reduce variables to be measured for future studies since it requires all of them to be included in the score. It also is harder to interpret a factor score than a single variable or a simple sum of two or three variables.

TABLE 16–8
Factor loadings

Variable	Factor 1	2
Education of wife	.71	.08
Education of husband	.86	.16
Age	−.39	−.40
Income.	.53	.37
Family size	.07	.88
Weekly food expenditure	.19	.64

To see how these three methods are used, consider the six-variable example in Appendix 16–A, summarized in Table 16–8. Here the three approaches might be applied as follows:

1. Representative method: Choose husband's education to represent factor 1 and family size to represent factor 2.
2. Index method: Use total education (wife's education plus husband's education) to represent factor 1 and an index equal to family size plus one half of weekly food expenditure to represent factor 2.
3. Factor score method: Use the factor score coefficients to get—

Factor 1 score = .26(education 1) + .64(education 2) − .05(age)
   + .13(income) − .16(family size)
   + .01(food expenditures)

Factor 2 score = −.06(education 1) − .07(education 2) − .04(age)
   + .10(income) + .73(family size)
   + .20(food expenditure)

It is common to use these factor scores as independent variables in a regression to predict some other variable. Using the six original variables we would have

$$Y = B_0 + B_1X_1 + B_2X_2 + \cdots + B_6X_6$$

Now we get $Y = C_0 + C_1f_1 + C_2f_2$. Using the factor scores reduces collinearity and thus we are more certain about the regression coefficients. Unfortunately we are also now unsure what the variables are. Given the choice between known variables and uncertain coefficients and unknown variables and certain coefficients, many people prefer known variables.

It is also worth pointing out that using the representative method of variable selection is likely to create an omitted variable/specification problem. Assume that I use only husband's education in a regression, but that the homemaker's education is really the key variable. In this case the coefficient of husband's education could well lead me to falsely conclude that it is the key variable. Hence all three methods reduce redundancy but not without cost. While none is universally the best, the index method often proves the most useful.

In using factor analysis to reduce a data set, two other points are crucial. First, if there is a key variable, it is often desirable to retain several variables which are closely related to it. In the six-variable case just mentioned, assume we were interested in explaining food expenditures. In that case we would keep all variables which loaded heavily on the same factor with it: family size, income, and age. (Actually a more efficient procedure would be to include all variables which had a simple correlation with food expenditure above some cutoff level.) Second, there is nothing inherently important about the first few factors. They are first because they represent a large number of redundant variables, not because those variables are important or useful per se.

A product attribute rating example

This example involves the ratings given to a particular new small car on ten product attributes. The data was collected as part of the monitoring of the introduction of a new car. The purpose of this analysis was to see what was the underlying structure of these ratings so that the consumers' basic choice criteria could be understood. Put differently, the question was whether there were really ten separate attributes of the car. The first three eigenvalues were 5.15, 1.14, and .86; and the first three factors accounted for 71.4 percent of the variance. The rotated loadings matrix is shown in Table 16–9. These three factors tend to delineate "style and

TABLE 16–9
Car attribute loading matrix

	Factor			
Attribute	1	2	3	Communality
Resale value	.13	.12	.91	.850
Gas economy	.29	.73	.26	.688
Value for money	.42	.58	.50	.756
Exterior appearance	.74	.04	.44	.736
Easy and fun to drive	.65	.38	.15	.586
Easy maintenance	.43	.52	.41	.618
Reliability and construction	.67	.21	.51	.752
Pickup	.77	.18	.15	.652
Inexpensive	.07	.89	−.03	.793
Features	.81	.21	.02	.706
				7.144

drivability," "price," and "resale value" as the three major categories of these car attributes. (When only two factors were rotated, the "price" and "resale value" factors were combined. In this case the use of three factors was the result of the default option on the DATATEXT computer program.) Interestingly, the same basic split between style and driving attributes and economy/price attributes occurred for eight different small cars and four samples of consumers over four waves of data collection. (In all, the factor analyses produced a 4-inch pile of computer output and as a side benefit a lifetime supply of scrap paper.) Hence these two factors appear to be enduring rather than transitory. Incidentally, the same two factors could have been derived by examination of the simple correlations among pairs of attributes.

A life-style example

Another example of a use of factor analysis involved a study of life-style measures (Villani and Lehmann, 1975). A set of 504 housewives had been asked to indicate their degree of agreement with a series of 153 statements both in 1971 and 1973. One issue in the study was whether the structure/pattern of responses remained constant. In order to measure structure, factor analyses were employed.

Comparing the 1971 and 1973 factor analyses showed a high degree of stability in the structure. Using the eigenvalue-greater-than-one rule, both 1971 and 1973 data sets produced 51 factors accounting for 67 percent of the variance in the original 153 variables. The factors themselves also seemed to be quite stable. The first four factors (subjectively named creative cook, attitude toward television, home cleanliness, and religious practices and attitudes) were essentially identical (Table 16–10).[2] In all, 34 of the 51 factors appear to be unchanged in content (but did not necessar-

TABLE 16–10
Life-style factors

	Factor loadings	
	1971	1973
1. Creative cook		
I look for ways to prepare fancy meals	.62	.74
I like to try new recipes	.66	.62
I think of myself as a creative cook	.70	.69
I am more interested in new food products than most people	.56	.56
I like to make gourmet dishes	.70	.73
2. Attitude toward television		
Television has added a great deal of enjoyment to my life	.70	.69
I don't like watching television and so I rarely do	−.73	−.64
Television is a friendly companion when I am alone	.75	.62
I watch television to be entertained	.56	.66
I watch television more than I should	.53	.40
I like having television on while I do other things around the house	.57	.27
I watch television in order to quietly relax	.39	.67
I watch television to get away from the ordinary cares of the day	.28	.56
3. Home cleanliness		
I try to wash the dishes promptly after each meal	.55	.62
I usually keep my house very neat and clean	.58	.68
I am uncomfortable when my house is not completely clean	.73	.66
My idea of housekeeping is "once over lightly"	−.55	−.66
A house should be dusted and polished at least three times a week	.51	.46
I usually have regular days for cleaning, cooking, and shopping	.51	.33
4. Religious practices and attitudes		
I pray several times a week	.73	−.75
I go to church regularly	.78	−.80
Women should be allowed to have an abortion they feel necessary	−.56	.50

Source: Kathryn Villani and Donald Lehmann, "An Examination of the Stability of AIO Measures." Reprinted from *1975 Combined Proceedings*, Fall Conference, published by the American Marketing Association, 1975, p. 486.

ily appear in the same order). The 17 factors which do not match consisted of factors with only one or two variables in them and hence are inherently less stable. The conclusion one can draw from this is that there are underlying life-style patterns which do endure over a reasonable length of time.

---

[2] Notice that all the signs in the fourth factor change between 1971 and 1973. Since the sign is arbitrary (the 1971 factor might be called proreligious and the 1973 factor antireligious), this is unimportant.

CLUSTER ANALYSIS

Introduction

Cluster analysis (also known as classification or numerical taxonomy) is a broad field spanning many disciplines. Much of the literature involves examples from such diverse fields as biology, auditory and visual perception, and linguistics. There is even a professional society, the Classification Society, devoted to the problems of clustering. An excellent historical perspective and introduction is provided by Sokal (1974) and a very complete treatment of the subject is provided by Sneath and Sokal (1973). Its use has, like that of most other multivariate procedures, been greatly facilitated by computers, without which applications become extremely tedious. The common element to these problems is that a large number of objects have been measured on a number of variables, and the objects need to be grouped. In marketing, cluster analysis has been largely used for two basic purposes (Frank and Green, 1968):

1. Clustering (grouping) customers into segments.
2. Clustering/matching potential subjects or study areas (e.g., cities for test markets) in order to assure a "balanced" sample or data collection process.

The steps involved in both these cases are as follows:

1. Identification of clusters.
2. Description of clusters.
3. Use of the clusters to simplify the world and make it more understandable.

This chapter will proceed by first describing the major alternative approaches to clustering in terms of these three steps.

Cluster definition: Basic notion

If we decided to classify a number of observations based on their values on two variables (X_1 and X_2), the observations could be plotted (Figure 16–3). In this case, three obvious clusters emerge. The reason these clusters are appealing is that the members of each cluster are quite similar to each other and quite different from members of other clusters in terms of the two variables. What cluster analysis algorithms attempt to do is to uncover such distinct clusters.

Unfortunately, the world is rarely as cooperative as the previous example suggests. A more likely situation would be that of Figure 16–4. Here the "best" clusters are much harder to identify.

FIGURE 16–3
Three "obvious" clusters in two dimensions

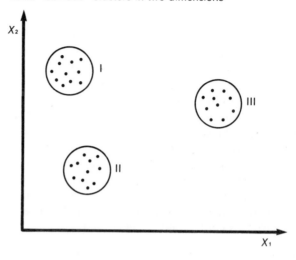

FIGURE 16–4
"Typical" observations on two variables

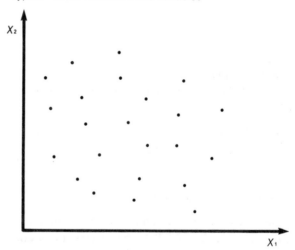

In order to derive clusters other than graphically, first a measure which indicates the closeness of each pair of points (and therefore observations) is needed. Then some algorithm for grouping observations together based on the measure is required. The next two sections cover the alternative measures and algorithms available for use.

Similarity/distance measures

The basic notion that cluster analysis is built upon is to group together variables which are "similar" in terms of their values on the variables. Here we define similarity as a construct where a big number indicates that two objects are close together and a small number that two objects are far apart. Thus similarity is the logical inverse of the concept of distance, where a large number indicates that objects are far apart and a small number that objects are close together. For purposes of clustering, either similarity or distance measures can serve as the basis. (The only problem is that it is not uncommon to confuse which type of measure is being used, leading to some interesting but useless results.) Similarity/distance measures come in three basic types: matching coefficients, distance measures, and pattern measures.

Matching coefficients. The simplest way to determine if two observations are similar is to compute the number of characteristics on which they match. Such a measure is most appropriate when the variables are categorical. For example, we might use such a measure for classifying furniture buyers based on their favorite style (early American or modern), pattern (plain, plaid, or floral), and color (blue, yellow, red, or green). Here the data might be as follows:

Customer	Style	Favorite Pattern	Color
1	1	3	1
2	1	2	2
3	2	3	3
4	2	2	3

Unweighted. The simplest matching coefficient simply counts the number of matches between two objects:

$$S_{ij} = \sum_{i=1}^{p} Z_c \qquad (16.5)$$

where

S_{ij} = similarity between objects i and j
p = number of characteristics (variables) measured
Z_c = 1 if $X_{ic} = X_{jc}$
  = 0 otherwise

In the furniture example,

$$S_{12} = 1 + 0 + 0 = 1$$
$$S_{13} = 0 + 1 + 0 = 1$$
$$S_{14} = 0 + 0 + 0 = 0$$
$$S_{23} = 0 + 0 + 0 = 0$$
$$S_{24} = 0 + 1 + 0 = 1$$
$$S_{34} = 1 + 0 + 1 = 2$$

Weighted. Simple matching coefficients tend to be dominated by the variables with few categories. (It is much easier to get a match if there are only 2 categories than if there are 20.) For that reason, many researchers choose to weight the matches by their "difficulty." A common way to do this is to weight a match on a characteristic by the number of categories of the characteristic:

$$S_{ij} = \sum_{c=1}^{p} V_c Z_c \tag{16.6}$$

where

V_c = number of values of characteristic c

In the previous example, this suggests:

$$S_{12} = 2(1) + 3(0) + 4(0) = 2$$
$$S_{13} = 2(0) + 3(1) + 4(0) = 3$$
$$S_{14} = 2(0) + 3(0) + 4(0) = 0$$
$$S_{23} = 2(0) + 3(0) + 4(0) = 0$$
$$S_{24} = 2(0) + 3(1) + 4(0) = 3$$
$$S_{34} = 2(1) + 3(0) + 4(1) = 6$$

Distance measures. Matching coefficients are necessary when data is purely categorical. Whenever data is intervally scaled, however, they tend to produce unappealing results. Consider the data in Table 16–11. Variables 1–3 are attitudes measured on a 7-point scale, and variable 4 is an interest scale which ranges between 11 and 40. The matching coefficients, using equations (16.5) and (16.6) are as follows:

	Unweighted	Weighted
S_{12} =	0	0
S_{13} =	0	0
S_{14} =	0	0
S_{15} =	0	0
S_{23} =	0	0
S_{24} =	1	7
S_{25} =	0	0
S_{34} =	0	0
S_{35} =	2	37
S_{45} =	0	0

TABLE 16–11
Sample data

Object/ observation/ person	Variable/characteristic			
	1	2	3	4
1 2		4	6	32
2 5		2	5	36
3 3		3	7	30
4 1		2	3	16
5 4		3	2	30

These results suggest that objects 3 and 5 are very similar, objects 2 and 4 somewhat similar, and all other pairs completely different. Yet this result is unappealing since objects 2 and 4 seem to be very different except for the match on variable 2, and objects 1 and 3 very similar on all four variables. The reason for this is that being close is given no credit by a matching coefficient; either two objects match exactly or not at all. For this reason, many people prefer distance measures which explicitly incorporate closeness. Some of the most popular include the following:

Sum of absolute deviations

$$D_{ij} = \sum_{c=1}^{p} |X_{ic} - X_{jc}| \qquad (16.7)$$

In this case,

$$D_{12} = |2 - 5| + |4 - 2| + |6 - 5| + |32 - 38|$$
$$= 12$$
$$D_{13} = 5, \text{ and so forth}$$

Sum of squared differences

$$D_{ij} = \sum_{c=1}^{p} (X_{ic} - X_{jc})^2 \qquad (16.8)$$

Here

$$D_{12} = (2 - 5)^2 + (4 - 2)^2 + (6 - 5)^2 + (32 - 38)^2$$
$$= 9 + 4 + 1 + 36 = 50$$
$$D_{13} = 7, \text{ and so forth.}$$

Minkowski metric. The most general form of the distance measures such as (16.7) and (16.8) is given by

$$D_{ij} = \left[\sum_{c=1}^{p} W_c (X_{ic} - X_{jc})^k \right]^{1/k} \qquad (16.9)$$

This fairly overwhelming formula reduces to (16.7) if we assume that $W_c = 1$ for all characteristics and let $k = 1$, and to the square root of (16.8) if we let $k = 2$. As you can see (Figure 16–5), $k = 2$ produces "as the crow flies" or Euclidean distance. For $k = 1$, this distance measure is

FIGURE 16–5
City block and euclidean distance

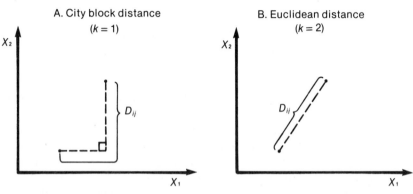

sometimes called "city block," since in New York City to go from 43rd and 5th Avenue to 44th and 7th Avenue, you must walk one block north (43rd to 44th) and two blocks west (5th to 7th Avenue) for a total of three blocks (unless, of course, you can find a way through buildings, leap buildings in a single bound, etc.).

Properties. All these distance measures are affected by the scale of the variables used. In the example presented in Table 16–11 variable 4 tends to dominate the distance measures because it has a bigger range of numbers. To reduce this effect, the variables can be standardized before being input to the clustering program. Alternatively, the distances on each characteristic can be weighted by either using the inverse of the standard deviation $\left(W_c = \dfrac{1}{S_c}\right)$ or the simpler inverse of the range of the variable $\left(W_c = \dfrac{1}{\text{range}}\right)$. While this will reduce the scale effect, it does not remove the effect of collinearity. If several of the variables are related to each other, whatever construct/factor they represent will dominate the distance measure. A researcher may desire to have it do so. If such dominance is undesirable, however, the redundancy must be reduced. This can be done by simply omitting redundant variables. Alternatively, Mahalanobis D^2 distance measure can be used. This measure removes both scale and collinearity effects from the distance calculations and is often promoted as "the" measure (Morrison, 1967).

Pattern measures. Distance measures assume that the absolute values of variables contain useful information. If only the relative values have meaning, then another form of distance measure is needed. Consider again the five-object example of Table 16–11 in terms of S_{14}:

	Variable			
Object	1	2	3	4
1	2	4	6	32
2	1	2	3	16

So far all the matching and distance measures have indicated 1 and 4 as very dissimilar objects. Yet the values for object 1 are all exactly twice the values for object 4. Hence in terms of the pattern of responses, 1 and 4 are identical. Two major alternative procedures produce measures which reflect the pattern in the data:

1. The first approach is to standardize each object[3] ahead of time and then use the previously discussed measures.
2. Alternatively, we could calculate a correlation coefficient between objects 1 and 4 over the four variables.[4]

Summary. In summary, then, there are a variety of similarity and distance measures available. Choice of the best one depends somewhat on technical issues (Green and Rao, 1969) but much more heavily on logical questions. Put differently, the researcher must decide whether exact matches, absolute differences, or patterns of responses are a more meaningful basis for grouping objects. Fortunately a very strong pattern will tend to be recovered over a broad range of similarity measures and a weak one may be pretty useless anyway.

Grouping approaches

Assuming a satisfactory similarity measure is developed, a grouping algorithm must be chosen. Fortunately this is usually a less difficult (and important) choice than the choice of a similarity measure. The choice is typically dictated by available computer algorithms. It is still useful, however, to understand how some of these approaches operate.

In order to facilitate description of the grouping algorithms, the example of Table 16–12 will be used. The example is portrayed graphically in Figure 16–6. Using the sum of squared distances, we can derive a distance matrix (Table 16–13).

---

[3] That means convert 2, 4, 6, and 32 by subtracting the mean of 11 and dividing by the standard deviation.

[4] That means correlating X_1 (2, 4, 6, and 32) with X_2 (1, 2, 3, and 16).

TABLE 16–12
Two-variable example

	Variable	
Object	1	2
1	2	4
2	5	2
3	3	3
4	1	2
5	4	3

FIGURE 16–6
Plot of two-variable example

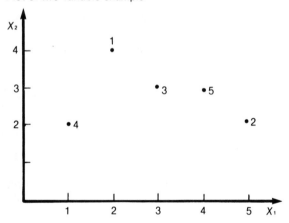

TABLE 16–13
Distance matrix: Sum of
squared differences

Object	Object				
	1	2	3	4	5
1		13	2	5	5
2			5	16	2
3				5	1
4					10
5					

The basic approaches to clustering can be described in terms of the following two basic dimensions:

Hierarchical versus "other."   In deciding which objects belong together, the most direct way to begin is to take the two most similar objects and group them together. Next the similarities between objects (or objects and the newly formed group) are recomputed and again the most similar object pairs are combined. This procedure continues, until all the objects are clustered. This approach bears the impressive description "hierarchical agglomerative" and is the most widely used procedure. (For culture fans, its opposite is called "hierarchical divisive" and begins with all objects in one cluser and sequentially removes dissimilar objects from groups.) It is also possible to devise schemes for clustering which are nonhierarchical. The simplest of these would be to define "typical" members of each cluster and then group objects into the cluster whose typical member they were most similar to.

Calculation of similarity between an object and a cluster.   Once a cluster is formed, a means must be used for determining how similar an object is to the cluster. The following three basic approaches exist:

As similar as the most similar object.   This approach says that an object is as similar to a cluster as it is to the nearest object in the cluster. This method is efficient computationally but tends to produce snaketype clusters (Figure 16–7).

FIGURE 16–7
Snake-type clusters

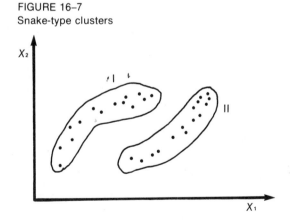

As similar as the least similar object.   The polar extreme of the first approach is to assume that an object is as similar to a cluster as it is to the object in the cluster with which it is least similar. This tends to produce "nicer" results in most marketing applications. An example of a procedure which uses both of these cluster forming approaches is found in Johnson's Hierarchical Clustering System (Johnson, 1967).

Centroid (average) method. The most widely used approach is the so-called centroid method. Here once two objects are grouped together, their values on the variables are averaged and the two objects replaced by a new "object" (centroid) which is the average of objects included in the cluster.

Examples. To show how these approaches operate, let's return to the example of Table 16–13.

A "most similar" hierarchical procedure would proceed as follows:

Step 1: Objects 3 and 5 (the most similar pair) are combined.

Step 2: "New" distance matrix is formed:[5]

	Object			
Object	1	2	3, 5	4
1		13	2	5
2			2	16
3, 5				5
4				

Step 3: Add either object 1 or object 2 (or both) to cluster 3, 5.

Step 4: Assuming we add object 1 to cluster 3, 5, we get a new distance matrix:

	Object		
Object	2	1, 3, 5	4
2		2	16
1, 3, 5			5
4			

Step 5: Add object 2 to cluster 1, 3, 5.

Step 6: Form distance matrix:

	Object	
Object	1, 2, 3, 5	4
1, 2, 3, 5		5
4		

---

[5] Since object 1 is 2 from object 3 and 5 from object 5, its distance from the closest object in the cluster is 2.

Step 7:   Form "final" cluster: 1, 2, 3, 4, 5.

Output: The output would then be as follows:

Distance level	Groups
0	1; 2; 3; 4; 5
1	1; 2; 3, 5; 4
2	1, 3, 5; 2; 4
2	1, 2, 3, 5; 4
5	1, 2, 3, 4, 5

Notice if you plot the cluster on the graph at distance level 2, you get the classic snake-type cluster (Figure 16–8).

FIGURE 16–8
Most similar method result

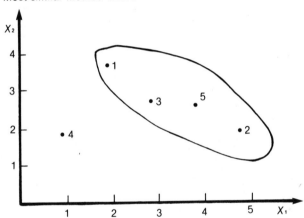

The "least similar" hierarchical procedure would proceed as follows:

Step 1:   Objects 3 and 5 are combined.

Step 2:   New distance matrix is formed.[6]

	Object			
Object	1	2	3, 5	4
1		13	5	5
2			5	16
3, 5				10
4				

---

[6] Now the distance from object 1 to the cluster of objects 3 and 5 becomes 5, since object 5 is the farthest object from object 1 in the cluster.

Step 3: We now have a tie which could be broken in several ways. Assume we group 1 and 4 together (it makes the example work out better).

Step 4: Distance matrix:

	Object		
Object	1, 4	2	3, 5
1, 4		16	10
2			5
3, 5			

Step 5: Group 2, 3, and 5 together.

Step 6: Distance matrix:

	Object	
Object	1, 4	2, 3, 5
1, 4		16
2, 3, 5		

Step 7: Group 1, 2, 3, 4, and 5 together.

Output:

Distance level	Groups
0	1; 2; 3; 4; 5
1	1; 2; 3, 5; 4
5	1, 4; 2; 3, 5
5	1, 4; 2, 3, 5
16	1, 2, 3, 4, 5

Notice here that at the distance level of 5, the clusters become in some sense more appealing graphically (Figure 16–9).

The centroid (average) method would proceed as follows:

Step 1: Group 3 and 5 together (as before).

FIGURE 16-9
Least similar method results

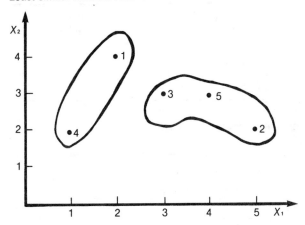

Step 2: In order to calculate distance, we must first replace objects 3 and 5 with their average:

	Variable	
Object	1	2
1	2	4
2	5	2
3.5	3.5	3
4	1	2

The distances thus become

	Object			
Object	1	2	3.5	4
1		13	3.25	5
2			3.25	16
3.5				7.25
4				

Step 3: Group together either 1 or 2 with 3, 5. Assume we choose 2. (If we choose 1, the "answer" changes markedly.)

Step 4: The object positions become

		Variable
Object	1	2
2, 3, 5	4	2.67
1	2	4
4	1	2

Thus the distances become

	Object		
Object	1	2, 3, 5	4
1		5.76	5
2, 3, 5			9.45
4			

Step 5: Group 1 and 4 together.
Step 6: The positions are

		Variable
Object	1	2
1, 4	1.5	3
2, 3, 5	4	2.67

Now the distances are

	Object	
Object	1, 4	2, 3, 5
1, 4		6.36
2, 3, 5		

Step 7: Form group 1, 2, 3, 4, 5.

These examples have been provided to show how the computations operate. Obviously the typical user will be concerned mainly with interpreting and using resulting clusters rather than actually forming them.

Cluster definition

The definition of clusters is a very straightforward task. The usual first step is to define clusters in terms of the cluster members' values of the variables used in the clustering algorithm. As a second step, the cluster members are often compared in terms of other available variables. The two analytical procedures commonly used are as follows:

1. Examination of differences in mean values on each variable separately.
2. Discriminant analysis as a tool to "validate" the clusters. Here discriminant analysis can be used both to see if the clusters differ significantly and also to indicate (by means of the percent correctly classified) how different the clusters really are.

Cluster usage

Usage of cluster analysis falls into two broad categories. The first category is the use of the resulting clusters as input to another problem. One example of this type is using clusters as sampling strata in consumer or industrial data collection. Another example of this use of clusters is as a means to simulate the results of possible marketing programs. Assume the clusters which had been derived were segments of customers who had different demographic and product usage characteristics. By estimating the effect of various possible programs on the type of customer in each segment and then aggregating the estimates, estimates of results of such programs can be obtained.

The other major use of cluster analysis is much less mechanical. Like any other analytical procedure, cluster analysis can be used as a generator of ideas. If the results of a cluster analysis give additional insight into a problem, the analysis must be deemed a success. It is very hard to define exactly what insight is (a light bulb going on, an "ah-ha" response), but it is at least easy to know when it occurs.

Issues in applying cluster analysis

Whenever a researcher decides to use cluster analysis, there are several questions s/he should address:

Is a fancy approach needed? Assuming there is a real need to group objects (customers, competing products, etc.), a question which arises is whether a simple grouping procedure will not suffice. Assume I wish to develop segments of customers. An obvious way to approach the problem is to base the grouping on either brand preference or level of usage, or a combination of both:

Brand used most often	Product usage level		
	Low	Medium	High
A	1	2	3
B	4	5	6
C	7	8	9
Others	10	11	12

I have thus defined 12 segments which differ in a known, important way. While use of a cluster analysis routine may seem more "unbiased," it really just has hidden the biases (in the choice of variables used, similarity/distance measure employed, etc.) and is certainly not as "natural" a way of developing groups (unless Minkowski metrics and computer altorithms are your concept of nature) as some proponents claim. Some use of cluster analysis can best be described as pseudo-scientification. In short, before you roll out a cluster analysis cannon, make sure the problem isn't a mouse.

What variables to include? This is the key to the results, so more time should be spent here than typically is. Ideally, relevant, nonredundant variables should be used. In practice, care should be taken to include variables which represent the constructs which are assumed to be impor-tant without overrepresenting any of the constructs.

What weights to use? The issue of how to weight each of the variables in forming the similarity or distance measure really encompasses the vari-able inclusion problem, since exclusion of a variable means a weight of zero has been assigned to that particular variable. In any event, the choice of weights is a logical rather than a mathematical problem. Commonly, the simple option of equal weights is employed.

What computer program to use? The answer depends on a combina-tion of program constraints (number of variables, number of objects, etc.) and availability.

What do I do with a big sample? Even the largest programs rarely handle more than 1,000 objects. Hence if you have a sample of 3,000, a problem exists. One solution is to cluster a random or representative subsample of 1,000. These results can be used directly or the remaining 2,000 can be brought into the groups by assigning them to the closest group. (A good mechanical way to do this is by calculating discriminant functions on the original sample and then using them to classify the "holdout" sample.)

How many clusters are needed? The issue of how many clusters a researcher uses depends on the problem, taste, and sample size. There is generally no way to get reliable clusters of size less than 30–50 from survey data. Hence $\frac{n}{50}$ gives a tentative boundary on the maximum number of clusters. Also, the problem may be one in which many clear segments can be expected to exist or one where everything is "mush" (put more properly, the objects are homogeneous). Finally, if the goal is insight, some researchers prefer a small number of big segments, while others like to see as many segments as can reasonably be generated.

Reliability checking.   Given the number of choices involved in cluster analysis, one should feel uncomfortable looking at the results of a single approach. For an important problem, sensitivity analysis is called for, and separate results should be generated for alternative similarity measures, numbers of clusters, samples, and so forth. Only when the clusters consistently point the same way can a researcher safely conclude that a "real" set of segments have been uncovered.

Relation to factor analysis

Factor analysis can be viewed as a special type of cluster analysis. As it was presented earlier in the chapter, factor analysis attempted to find groups of variables where the similarity measure was the correlation coefficient between pairs of variables. Actually factor analysis computer programs can be used to group observations as well as variables.

The use of factor analysis to group observations is known as Q-type factor analysis. This technique involves "tricking" the factor analysis computer program. The trick goes like this: The computer program expects the data in the form of the left half of Table 16–14. By transposing the data, we can input the data in the right half of Table 16–14. The computer now proceeds thinking the columns are the variables to be factored/grouped. Since the columns are in fact observations, the program actually groups observations based on their correlations across the p variables.

This approach has some severe problems. For one thing, the number of observations to be grouped is severely limited, often to less than 100 (as, incidentally, are the number of variables in "regular" factor analysis). Second, unless the variables are standardized, the variable with the largest numerical value will tend to dominate the correlations and hence dictate the groups. Still Q-type factor analysis is occasionally useful.

An example

In this example, 940 housewives were clustered on the basis of 12 food shopping variables. The variables were as follows:

Importance of variety
Importance of taste
Importance of diet restrictions
Importance of price

TABLE 16–14

| Typical factor analysis input data format | Q-type factor analysis input data format |

Typical factor analysis input data format

	Variable			
Observation	1	2	...	p
1				
2				
.				
.				
.				
n				

Q-type factor analysis input data format

	New variable (really the observation)			
New observation (old variable)	1	2	...	n
1				
2				
.				
.				
.				
P				

Importance of availability
Importance of ease of preparation
Importance of habit
Importance of advertised specials
Importance of nutritional value
Agreement with:
"People need meat to be healthy"
"I feel the need for more nutritional information"
"We entertain more at home than the average family"

In all cases, a "1" is a high value (very important, strongly agree), and a "5" a low value. The Howard-Harris program (currently probably the most widely used in marketing) was used for clustering. Solutions were generated for 2, 3, 4, 5, 6, and 7 clusters. For the sake of simplicity, only the four-cluster solution is discussed. Part of the actual output appears as Appendix 16–C.

The output has two basic parts. The first is the cluster deliniations. Specifically, the identification of the members of each of the four clusters is made. Hence Group 1 has persons 9, 11, 16, and so forth, in it. The clusters had 246, 258, 208, and 228 people in them respectively.

The other major part of the output contains the means of clusters on the 12 variables. This is the cluster definition stage of the output. The results are shown in Table 16–15. Naming clusters requires as much creative writing as research skill. Nonetheless, the following descriptors were generated:

Cluster 1: This cluster seemed to attach great importance to all the attributes. Hence they were called the "all important" cluster.

Cluster 2: This cluster is fairly neutral on all the attributes except diet restrictions (which were unimportant) and advertised specials (which were very important). The lack of importance attributed to other

TABLE 16–15
Food shopping segments means

| | Cluster | | | |
Variable	1	2	3	4
Importance of variety	1.80	2.18	2.42	1.89
Importance of taste	1.15	1.26	1.62	1.25
Importance of diet restrictions	1.72	4.67	3.49	1.97
Importance of price	1.38	1.63	2.62	1.63
Importance of availability	1.51	1.96	2.80	2.69
Importance of ease of preparation	1.88	2.64	2.91	3.85
Importance of habit	2.38	2.65	3.00	3.37
Importance of advertised specials	1.85	1.72	3.78	2.03
Importance of nutritional value	1.33	1.89	2.28	1.39
Agreement with: "People need meat to be healthy"	2.31	2.43	2.33	2.50
"I feel the need for more nutritional information"	2.00	2.62	2.67	2.12
"We entertain more at home than the average family"	3.86	3.84	3.72	3.67

family members' preferences could be due to their not having children at home. This was called the "specials shopper" cluster.

Cluster 3: This cluster is almost the opposite of cluster one, indicating that all the attributes are relatively unimportant. This may be a sign of caution or lack of interest. In any event, they were called the "unexcited" cluster.

Cluster 4: This cluster is fairly neutral except that it rates both ease of preparation and habit as particularly unimportant. Apparently this group enjoys thinking about and working on food preparation and may contain all the gourmets. This cluster was called the "nonsimplifiers" or "food preparers."

The results of this study were interesting but failed to produce a great intuitive revelation about food shopping. In fact, the most interesting result was the existence of clusters 1 and 3 who consistently rated all attributes either important or unimportant. This has led to some interesting research on survey response patterns but not much additional knowledge about food consumption decisions.

CONCLUSION

This chapter has presented some procedures aimed at reducing data by grouping similar objects/variables/people together. It is possible to become either turned off by or enamored with the mathematical properties and technical niceties of these techniques. Still their use is much more of an art form than most people care to admit. Hence users should concern themselves with ensuring that these (or any other) procedures are (*a*) being used to solve a real problem and (b) being used in a way which makes logical/common sense.

PROBLEMS

1. Interpret the following factor analysis of the importance of 17 attributes used by purchasing agents in making decisions about suppliers:

Rotated factor matrix

Attribute	Factor				
	1	2	3	4	5
Supplier reputation	.16	.04	.89	.09	−.10
Financing	.15	.79	.08	−.10	−.12
Flexibility	.11	.72	.02	.12	.43
Past experience	.17	.15	.03	.07	.85
Technical service	.47	.42	.22	−.27	.39
Confidence in salespersons ...	.60	.27	.27	.14	.40
Convenience in ordering	.33	.67	−.20	.03	.14
Reliability data	.57	.02	.29	.21	.46
Price	.08	.06	.03	.84	−.01
Technical specifications	.49	−.03	.07	.43	.59
Ease of use	.52	.19	−.13	−.30	.52
Preference of user	.13	.33	.57	−.43	.38
Training offered	.87	.18	.24	−.12	.06
Reliability of delivery	−.16	.61	.29	.05	.13
Maintenance	.25	.12	−.07	−.18	.77
Sales service	.75	.09	−.28	.29	.13
Training required	.78	.02	.12	−.01	.34
Unrotated eigenvalues	6.30	2.02	1.44	1.37	1.08

2. What is the difference between Q and R type factor analysis?
3. How would you go about reducing a set of 150 candidate variables for a model of consumer satisfaction to a more manageable number?
4. You have designed a new product and want to advertise its introduction. You want to place advertisements in several different magazines. Your job is to select the particular set of magazines in which the ads should run. Your researcher wants to help you by running a factor analysis of your data. You know which of the 100 largest circulation magazines was read by each person in a sample of 1,000 people during the last month. That is, you have a data matrix which is 100 magazines by 1,000 people in size. Each cell has either zero (person did not read last issue of this magazine) or one (person did read the last issue of this magazine).
   a. If you believe your ad "must be seen many times" in order to have any effect, then how can your researcher help you select the magazines? Please be specific about the factor analysis you want the researcher to run and how you will use the results.

b. If you instead believe that your ad is so great that people who see it will "instantly recognize" the benefits of your new product, then how can your researcher use factor analysis to help you select the magazines? Again, please be specific.

c. For your analyses in parts (a) and (b) above, would you prefer that your researcher provide you the principle components unrotated factor loadings or the rotated factor loadings? Why?

d. If your researcher found that three factors explained 98 percent of variance in the readership data for the 100 magazines, what would you conclude? If only 5 percent?

5. Suppose that you have been collecting opinions about many various items of a new product. You notice that people seem to respond similarly to many of the questions.

a. How would you determine which questions are related to each other?

b. How would you select the questions which are redundant, so that they could be eliminated from future studies without loss of most of the information in the original set of questions?

6. You have a set of 38 time series variables, which you wish to use to explain the sales of heavy-duty machine tools. Describe two ways you might use factor analysis before running your regression. What are the advantages and disadvantages of these approaches?

7. Indicate on a quantitative one to ten scale how similar are the following pairs:

a. The words "pretty" and "happy."
   The words "ugly" and "homely."
   The words "big" and "important."

b. The following people:
   Jimmy Carter, Gerald Ford.
   wife, mother-in-law.

8. Using Table 16–13 as a starting point, produce a graphical summary of the steps in clustering the five objects using the "least similar" method.

9. How would you go about clustering counties in the United States?

10. Assume you were national sales manager for Xerox. How would you proceed to cluster present and potential accounts?

11. Assume a large security dealer asked you to help segment their accounts by means of cluster analysis. What would you do?

BIBLIOGRAPHY

Frank, Ronald E., and Green, Paul E. "Numerical Taxonomy in Marketing Analysis: A Review Article." *Journal of Marketing Research*, vol. 5 (February 1968), pp. 83–94.

Green, Paul E., and Rao, Vithala R. "A Note on Proximity Measures and Cluster Analysis." *Journal of Marketing Research,* vol. 6 (August 1969), pp. 359–64.

Harman, Harry H. *Modern Factor Analysis.* Chicago: University of Chicago Press, 1967.

Howard, N., and Harris, B. "A Hierarchical Grouping Routine, IBM 360/65 FORTRAN IV Program." University of Pennsylvania Computer Center, October 1966.

Johnson, S. C. "Hierarchical Clustering Schemes." *Psychometrika,* vol. 32 (September 1967), pp. 241–54.

Lehmann, Donald R. "Some Alternatives to Linear Factor Analysis for Variable Grouping Applied to Buyer Behavior Variables." *Journal of Marketing Research,* vol. 11 (May 1974), pp. 206–13. (Material reprinted from the *Journal of Marketing Research,* published by the American Marketing Association.)

————, and Morrison, Donald G. "A Random Splitting Criterion for Selecting the Number of Factors." Working paper. New York: Columbia University Graduate School of Business, 1977.

Morrison, Donald F. *Multivariate Statistical Methods.* 2d ed. New York: McGraw-Hill, 1976.

Morrison, Donald G. "Measurement Problems in Cluster Analysis." *Management Science,* vol. 13 (August 1967), pp. B775–B780.

Sneath, P. H. A., and Sokal, R. R. *Numerical Taxonomy.* San Francisco: Freeman, 1973.

Sokal, R. R. "Numerical Taxonomy." *Science,* vol. 185 (September 1974), pp. 1115–23.

Villani, Kathryn E. A., and Lehmann, Donald R. "An Examination of the Stability of AIO Measures." *Proceedings,* Fall Conference, American Marketing Association, 1975, pp. 484–88.

———— APPENDIX 16–A ————

FOUNDATIONS OF FACTOR ANALYSIS

This Appendix provides a simple (six-variable) factor analysis example so that facility in interpreting results may be improved by careful study of a manageable problem. The basic data and outputs were as follows:

Variables

1. Education of homemaker.
2. Education of husband.
3. Age.
4. Income.
5. Family size.
6. Weekly food expenditures.

Correlations

	Variable					
Variable	1	2	3	4	5	6
1		−61	−.30	.42	.12	.17
2			−.42	.50	.20	.25
3				−.30	−.44	−.27
4					.31	.43
5						.57

Eigenvalues

Eigenvalues	Percent variance	Cumulative percent
2.78	46.4	46.4
1.23	20.5	66.9
.76	12.8	79.7
.50	8.3	88.0
.38	6.3	94.3
.34	5.7	100.0

Principal components

	Component					
Variable	1	2	3	4	5	6
1	.65	.57	.04	.39	.23	−.21
2	.75	.46	−.03	.03	−.32	.34
3	−.66	.08	.67	.22	.06	.21
4	.74	.10	.41	−.48	.21	−.01
5	.63	−.63	−.14	.19	.28	.28
6	.65	−.53	.35	.16	−.31	−.23

Two-factor (unrotated) solution
with communality ≠ 1

	Factor	
Variable	1	2
1	.58	.41
2	.75	.45
3	−.55	.05
4	.64	.07
5	.63	−.61
6	.57	−.36

Notice here that interpretation is very difficult due to the fact that all six variables appear to load on factor 1.

Squared loadings

Variable	Factor 1	Factor 2	Communalities
1	.34	.17	.51
2	.56	.20	.76
3	.30	.00	.30
4	.41	.00	.41
5	.40	.37	.77
6	.32	.13	.45
Eigenvalues	2.33	.87	3.20
Percent explained	233/6 = 38.8%	.87/6 = 14.5%	53.3%

Notice that the 38.8 percent is really the average squared correlation between factor 1 and each of the six original variables. You can also note that the reason the percent of variance explained in the first variable (51 percent) is the sum of the percent explained by the first factor (34 percent) plus the percent explained by the second factor (17 percent) is that the two factors are orthogonal.

Two-factor (orthogonally rotated)
solution ("loadings")

Variable	Factor 1	Factor 2
1	.71	.08
2	.86	.16
3	−.38	−.40
4	.53	.37
5	.07	.88
6	.19	.64

Notice that the interpretation is now much easier. Factor 1 is apparently largely education while factor 2 is mainly family size. Income tends to go with education and age really doesn't fit either category well.

Squared loadings

Variable	Factor 1	2	Communality
1	.50	.01	.51
2	.74	.03	.77
3	.14	.16	.30
4	.28	.14	.42
5	.00	.77	.77
6	.04	.41	.45
Eigenvalue	1.70	1.52	3.22
Average percent variance explained	28.3%	25.3%	53.6%

Notice here that the effect of the rotation is to redistribute much of the variance from the first to the second factor. The total variance explained and the communalities, however, are unaffected.

Factor score coefficients

Variable	Factor	
	1	2
1	.27	−.06
2	.64	−.07
3	−.06	−.04
4	.13	.10
5	−.15	.73
6	.01	.20

Notice that these coefficients mean that the first factor score will be largely determined by the value of variable 2 while the second factor is dominated by variable 5, which turn out to be the variables with the biggest loadings on each factor.

Factor scores are estimates of the position of each observation on each unmeasured factor. Several methods of estimation are available (e.g., Harman, 1967). The most widely used form is

$$f = XS^{-1}\Lambda$$

where

f = matrix of factor scores (an $n \times m$ matrix)
X = raw data (an $n \times p$ matrix)
S^{-1} = inverse of covariance matrix of the original p variables (a $p \times p$ matrix)
Λ = estimated loadings (a $p \times m$ matrix)

APPENDIX 16–B: SAMPLE FACTOR ANALYSIS OUTPUT

SPACE ALLOCATION FOR THIS RUN..

TOTAL AMOUNT REQUESTED   80000 BYTES

DEFAULT TRANSPACE ALLOCATION   10000 BYTES

MAX NO OF TRANSFORMATIONS PERMITTED   100
MAX NO OF RECODE VALUES   400
MAX NO OF ARITHM.OR LOG.OPERATIONS   800

RESULTING WORKSPACE ALLOCATION   70000 BYTES

```
RUN NAME         FOOC-Q14
VARIABLE LIST    V244 TO V273
INPUT MEDIUM     DISK
N OF CASES       940
INPUT FORMAT     FIXED(/43X,30F1.0////)
```

ACCORDING TO YOUR INPUT FORMAT, VARIABLES ARE TO BE READ AS FOLLOWS

VARIABLE	FORMAT	RECORD	COLUMNS
V244	F 1. 0	2	44- 44
V245	F 1. 0	2	45- 45
V246	F 1. 0	2	46- 46
V247	F 1. 0	2	47- 47
V248	F 1. 0	2	48- 48
V249	F 1. 0	2	49- 49
V250	F 1. 0	2	50- 50
V251	F 1. 0	2	51- 51
V252	F 1. 0	2	52- 52
V253	F 1. 0	2	53- 53
V254	F 1. 0	2	54- 54
V255	F 1. 0	2	55- 55
V256	F 1. 0	2	56- 56
V257	F 1. 0	2	57- 57
V258	F 1. 0	2	58- 58
V259	F 1. 0	2	59- 59
V260	F 1. 0	2	60- 60
V261	F 1. 0	2	61- 61
V262	F 1. 0	2	62- 62
V263	F 1. 0	2	63- 63
V264	F 1. 0	2	64- 64
V265	F 1. 0	2	65- 65

ACCORDING TO YOUR INPUT FORMAT, VARIABLES ARE TO BE READ AS FOLLOWS

VARIABLE	FORMAT	RECORD	COLUMNS
V267	F 1. 0	2	67— 67
V268	F 1. 0	2	68— 68
V269	F 1. 0	2	69— 69
V270	F 1. 0	2	70— 70
V271	F 1. 0	2	71— 71
V272	F 1. 0	2	72— 72
V273	F 1. 0	2	73— 73

THE INPUT FORMAT PROVIDES FOR 30 VARIABLES.   30 WILL BE READ
IT PROVIDES FOR 6 RECORDS ('CARDS') PER CASE. A MAXIMUM OF 73 'COLUMNS' ARE USED ON A RECORD.

        FACTOR   VARIABLES=V244 TO V273/
        STATISTICS   2,4,5,6,8

***** FACTOR PROBLEM REQUIRES 16272 BYTES WORKSPACE *****

CORRELATION COEFFICIENTS..

	V244	V245	V246	V247	V248	V249	V250	V251	V252	V253
V244	1.00000	0.29938	0.26993	0.12491	0.05573	0.15649	0.14975	0.24135	0.08034	0.10216
V245	0.29938	1.00000	0.27027	0.19368	0.11570	0.12112	0.22934	0.23013	-0.05233	0.22743
V246	0.26993	0.27027	1.00000	0.18648	0.11149	0.34905	0.20291	0.25943	0.18468	0.09629
V247	0.12491	0.19368	0.18648	1.00000	0.08283	0.17819	0.21786	0.15937	0.01512	0.06385
V248	0.05573	0.11570	0.11149	0.08283	1.00000	-0.27590	0.04162	0.10585	0.17725	-0.13395
V249	0.15649	0.12112	0.34905	0.17819	-0.27590	1.00000	0.20701	0.13060	0.03662	0.18192
V250	0.14975	0.22934	0.20291	0.21786	0.04162	0.20701	1.00000	0.18882	0.04174	0.07872
V251	0.24135	0.23013	0.25943	0.15937	0.10585	0.13060	0.18882	1.00000	0.14016	0.04881
V252	0.08034	-0.05233	0.18468	0.01512	0.17725	0.03662	0.04174	0.14016	1.00000	-0.44514
V253	0.10216	0.22743	0.09629	0.06385	-0.13395	0.18192	0.07872	0.04881	-0.44514	1.00000
V254	-0.01356	0.00625	0.10267	0.05924	0.07344	0.14978	0.13223	0.21811	0.12205	0.04400
V255	0.24020	0.21957	0.33804	0.13516	0.13189	0.22486	0.17129	0.39235	0.15206	0.05242
V256	-0.07354	0.05492	0.00973	0.17457	0.09420	0.05625	0.20665	0.05339	0.00208	-0.00810
V257	-0.09618	0.01043	0.05259	0.04880	0.09182	0.05561	0.12934	0.10803	0.07829	0.03625
V258	0.20815	0.32000	0.14672	0.19072	0.10401	0.10710	0.19673	0.19429	-0.00783	0.20187
V259	0.22808	0.23525	0.24611	0.08258	-0.00151	0.18434	0.06295	0.13228	0.18312	0.18151
V260	0.18119	0.22567	0.10889	0.20213	0.05989	0.16110	0.19953	0.14452	0.00499	0.19962
V261	0.27204	0.44751	0.25317	0.18466	0.09800	0.19814	0.26042	0.12957	0.03335	0.16277
V262	0.25284	0.18862	0.20750	0.09468	-0.02925	0.15297	0.20911	0.15585	0.05308	0.12532
V263	0.13637	0.25879	0.19311	0.26622	0.05650	0.15350	0.23673	0.25120	0.09886	0.12033
V264	0.22182	0.24068	0.26118	0.20930	0.03544	0.25112	0.28538	0.14222	0.07462	0.15557
V265	0.17307	0.18156	0.15954	0.16602	0.08876	0.16437	0.18231	0.18979	0.11142	0.08638
V266	0.13482	0.14368	0.17451	0.09787	0.15739	0.13959	0.15987	0.07008	0.11860	0.02303
V267	0.03052	0.16615	0.09219	0.18465	0.05482	0.07401	0.19299	0.12035	0.02993	0.18773
V268	0.07675	0.30490	0.04438	0.09114	0.02303	0.09960	0.12006	0.11565	0.02034	0.09956
V269	0.00265	0.04393	0.12942	0.06016	0.03451	0.10992	0.05782	0.11996	0.11821	0.05786
V270	0.11909	0.20111	0.23886	0.14299	0.03279	0.21038	0.21350	0.17592	0.02690	0.07061
V271	0.03958	0.10143	0.23193	0.22053	0.06352	0.19021	0.23482	0.16162	0.07224	0.12125
V272	-0.01503	0.05140	0.08467	0.14253	0.10802	0.07780	0.14046	0.14556	0.01229	0.10631
V273	0.09322	0.17695	0.08650	0.07461	0.11242	0.08809	0.18305	0.16162	-0.03365	0.09097

	V254	V255	V256	V257	V258	V259	V260	V261	V262	V263
V244	-0.01356	0.24020	-0.07354	-0.09618	0.20815	0.22808	0.18119	0.27204	0.25284	0.13637
V245	0.00625	0.21957	0.05492	0.01043	0.32000	0.23525	0.22567	0.44751	0.18862	0.25879
V246	0.10267	0.33804	0.00973	0.05259	0.24611	0.24611	0.10889	0.25317	0.20750	0.19311
V247	0.05924	0.13516	0.17457	0.04880	0.19072	0.08258	0.20213	0.18406	0.09468	0.26622
V248	0.07344	0.13189	0.09420	0.09182	0.10401	-0.00151	0.05989	0.09800	-0.02925	0.05650
V249	0.14678	0.22486	0.05625	0.05501	0.10710	0.18434	0.16110	0.19814	0.15297	0.15350
V250	0.13223	0.17129	0.02476	0.12934	0.19673	0.06295	0.19953	0.26042	0.20911	0.23673
V251	0.21811	0.39235	0.00208	0.05319	0.10803	0.19429	0.13228	0.14452	0.12957	0.15585
V252	0.12205	0.15206	-0.CC810	0.07829	-0.00783	0.18312	0.00499	0.03335	0.05308	0.09886
V253	0.04400	0.05242	0.14567	0.03625	0.20187	0.18151	0.19962	0.16277	0.12532	0.12033
V254	1.00000	0.20540	0.14567	0.41038	0.04923	0.07234	0.07350	0.00633	0.16682	0.16082
V255	0.20540	1.00000	-0.00135	0.10662	0.12975	0.22106	0.20115	0.13195	0.15220	0.16082
V256	0.14567	-0.00135	1.00000	0.03301	0.17915	-0.03298	0.12454	0.14144	-0.00176	0.13195
V257	0.41038	0.10662	0.03301	1.00000	0.07388	-0.03298	0.07071	0.01966	0.16664	0.12525
V258	0.04923	0.12975	0.17915	0.07388	1.00000	0.16373	0.22046	0.31358	0.17794	0.16750
V259	0.07234	0.22106	-0.03298	-0.03298	0.16373	1.00000	0.13541	0.20135	0.11512	0.24843
V260	0.07350	0.20115	0.12454	0.07071	0.22046	0.13541	1.00000	0.31897	0.25724	0.29881
V261	0.00633	0.13195	0.14144	0.01966	0.31358	0.20135	0.31897	1.00000	0.06664	0.23485
V262	0.16682	0.15220	-0.00176	0.16664	0.17794	0.11512	0.25724	0.06664	1.00000	0.23485
V263	0.16082	0.16082	0.13195	0.12525	0.16750	0.24843	0.29881	0.23485	0.23485	1.00000
V264	0.25146	0.19242	0.09624	0.17860	0.24413	0.07660	0.24999	0.24716	0.34909	0.38255
V265	0.16248	0.04746	0.14649	0.17691	0.18786	0.20060	0.23142	0.20393	0.19677	0.24952
V266	0.20917	0.06824	0.12507	0.25694	0.07660	0.08510	0.18624	0.14216	0.21618	0.15268
V267	0.18157	0.07472	0.18474	0.12603	0.02060	0.03864	0.04427	0.01494	0.22626	0.29388
V268	0.21834	0.14375	0.15772	0.14574	0.16382	0.05631	0.02476	0.02589	0.15670	0.12711
V269	0.24157	0.21900	0.06040	0.18610	0.34243	0.12455	0.18490	0.21743	0.18944	0.16453
V270	0.06189		0.15882	0.03154	0.08989	0.07518	0.18336	0.19882	0.21783	0.18005
V271	0.28208	0.13245	0.17376	0.25378	0.13868	0.04249	0.11553	0.06552	0.22905	0.19520
V272	0.39123	0.17967	0.13418	0.38530	0.21904	0.08568	0.18217	0.18871	0.14473	0.18389
V273	0.167C4		0.21563	0.17717	0.13762				0.09255	0.12862

	V264	V265	V266	V267	V268	V269	V270	V271	V272	V273
V244	0.22182	0.17307	0.13482	0.03052	0.07675	0.00265	0.11909	0.03958	-0.01503	0.09322
V245	0.24068	0.18156	0.14368	0.16615	0.00490	0.04393	0.20111	0.10143	0.05140	0.17695
V246	0.26118	0.15994	0.17451	0.09219	0.04438	0.12942	0.23886	0.23193	0.08467	0.08650
V247	0.20930	0.16602	0.09787	0.16465	0.09114	0.06016	0.14299	0.20530	0.14253	0.07461
V248	0.03544	0.08876	0.15739	0.05462	0.02303	0.03451	0.03279	0.06352	0.10802	0.11242
V249	0.25112	0.16437	0.13959	0.07491	0.09960	0.10992	0.21038	0.19021	0.07780	0.08809
V250	0.28538	0.18231	0.15987	0.19239	0.12006	0.05782	0.21350	0.23482	0.14046	0.18305
V251	0.25120	0.14222	0.18979	0.07008	0.12035	0.11565	0.11996	0.17592	0.14556	0.16162
V252	0.07462	0.11142	0.11860	0.02993	0.02034	0.11821	0.02690	0.07224	0.01229	-0.03365
V253	0.15557	0.08638	0.22303	0.14773	0.09956	0.05786	0.07061	0.12125	0.10631	0.39097

FILE   NONAME   (CREATION DATE = 03/31/77)

	V264	V265	V266	V267	V268	V269	V270	V271	V272	V273
V254	0.25146	0.16248	0.20917	0.18157	0.21834	0.24157	0.06189	0.28208	0.39123	0.16704
V255	0.24502	0.15409	0.19242	0.04766	0.06824	0.07472	0.14875	0.21900	0.13245	0.17967
V256	0.09624	0.14649	0.12507	0.18474	0.11572	0.06040	0.15882	0.17376	0.13418	0.21563
V257	0.17860	0.17691	0.25694	0.14603	0.14574	0.18610	0.03154	0.25378	0.38530	0.17717
V258	0.24413	0.18744	0.16382	0.34243	0.08989	0.13868	0.19948	0.21904	0.13762	0.20332
V259	0.18786	0.07660	0.02060	0.08510	0.03864	0.05631	0.12455	0.07518	0.04249	0.08568
V260	0.24999	0.23142	0.18624	0.14636	0.04427	0.02476	0.18490	0.18336	0.11553	0.18217
V261	0.31405	0.24716	0.20393	0.14216	0.01494	0.02589	0.21743	0.19882	0.06552	0.18871
V262	0.34939	0.19677	0.21616	0.22646	0.15670	0.18944	0.21783	0.22905	0.14473	0.09255
V263	0.38255	0.24952	0.15268	0.29388	0.12711	0.16453	0.18005	0.19520	0.18389	0.12862
V264	1.00000	0.39771	0.23869	0.22821	0.14915	0.22337	0.23693	0.27550	0.23222	0.14872
V265	0.39771	1.00000	0.32837	0.14931	0.06571	0.09287	0.16500	0.22841	0.25067	0.23887
V266	0.23869	0.32837	1.00000	0.16864	0.05873	0.14875	0.17001	0.28600	0.24074	0.17705
V267	0.22821	0.14931	0.16864	1.00000	0.17039	0.24443	0.14160	0.27634	0.21556	0.14022
V268	0.14915	0.06571	0.05873	0.17039	1.00000	0.21050	0.09934	0.19170	0.23130	0.08858
V269	0.22337	0.09287	0.14875	0.24443	0.21050	1.00000	0.02774	0.24238	0.21251	0.01942
V270	0.23693	0.16500	0.17001	0.14160	0.09934	0.02774	1.00000	0.22244	0.04800	0.17133
V271	0.27550	0.22841	0.28600	0.27634	0.19170	0.24238	0.22244	1.00000	0.39265	0.13650
V272	0.23222	0.25067	0.24074	0.21556	0.23130	0.21251	0.04800	0.39265	1.00000	0.40098
V273	0.14872	0.23887	0.17705	0.14022	0.08858	0.01942	0.17133	0.13650	0.40098	1.00000

DETERMINANT OF CORRELATION MATRIX = 0.0019456EI   0.19456137D-02

FILE NCNAME (CREATION CATE = 03/31/77)

VARIABLE	EST COMMUNALITY
V244	0.26620
V245	0.33675
V246	0.32008
V247	0.17657
V248	0.22846
V249	0.32054
V250	0.21425
V251	0.25511
V252	0.36164
V253	0.37134
V254	0.32592
V255	0.28416
V256	0.18223
V257	0.28941
V258	0.32629
V259	0.21585
V260	0.21455
V261	0.35700
V262	0.26112
V263	0.32566
V264	0.37924
V265	0.27448
V266	0.24483
V267	0.25774
V268	0.14004
V269	0.16575
V270	0.19048
V271	0.32384
V272	0.40546
V273	0.27926

FACTOR	EIGENVALUE	PCT OF VAR	CUM PCT
1	5.55247	18.5	18.5
2	2.23002	7.4	25.9
3	1.78448	5.9	31.9
4	1.53661	5.1	37.0
5	1.30329	4.3	41.4
6	1.22577	4.1	45.4
7	1.12953	3.8	49.2
8	0.99539	3.3	52.5
9	0.94962	3.2	55.7
10	0.93334	3.1	58.8
11	0.86933	2.9	61.7
12	0.81081	2.7	64.4
13	0.80714	2.7	67.1
14	0.77290	2.6	69.7
15	0.75752	2.5	72.2
16	0.73587	2.5	74.6
17	0.70721	2.4	77.0
18	0.68020	2.3	79.3
19	0.66865	2.2	81.5
20	0.64558	2.2	83.7
21	0.61143	2.0	85.7
22	0.58673	2.0	87.6
23	0.57111	1.9	89.6
24	0.52931	1.8	91.3
25	0.48426	1.6	92.9
26	0.47818	1.6	94.5
27	0.45340	1.5	96.0
28	0.41991	1.4	97.4
29	0.39989	1.3	98.8
30	0.36986	1.2	100.0

CONVERGENCE REQUIRED 22 ITERATIONS

FOOD-C14

FILE   NCNAME   (CREATICN CATE = 03/31/77)

FACTOR MATRIX USING PRINCIPAL FACTCR WITH ITERATIONS

	FACTOR 1	FACTOR 2	FACTCR 3	FAITOR 4	FACTOR 5	FACTOR 6	FACTOR 7
V244	0.34956	-0.36230	0.17554	-0.02341	0.09853	0.11869	-0.09118
V245	0.46621	-0.37331	-0.03570	0.18805	0.13041	0.09560	0.01234
V246	0.45587	-0.20029	0.25715	-0.17707	0.09909	-0.00728	0.09363
V247	0.36384	-0.06457	-0.02734	0.08538	-0.09601	-0.09687	0.14170
V248	0.14812	0.12926	0.24052	0.40604	0.18587	0.11559	0.07449
V249	0.40237	-0.18267	-0.01039	-0.51269	-0.17473	-0.33360	0.05353
V250	0.44503	-0.03990	-0.02270	0.05283	-0.06871	-0.15412	0.04292
V251	0.40736	-0.06942	0.25289	-0.09449	0.21850	0.07225	0.14876
V252	0.14069	0.15447	0.64432	0.06355	-0.23397	0.03231	0.02150
V253	0.27216	-0.24084	-0.57357	-0.22069	0.20639	0.16976	0.03545
V254	0.38576	0.46040	0.03925	-0.19230	0.08848	0.04879	0.04475
V255	0.43931	-0.08840	0.30211	-0.14871	0.26343	0.00548	0.13139
V256	0.24834	0.16129	-0.13754	0.25421	-0.11634	0.02622	0.20243
V257	0.31258	0.46975	-0.04034	-0.06279	0.08505	0.13263	-0.13796
V258	0.48538	-0.13740	-0.17867	0.25640	0.13773	0.13931	0.10123
V259	0.30270	-0.24083	0.13433	-0.12125	0.04407	0.11452	0.11452
V260	0.40310	-0.13995	-0.08991	0.11858	0.04857	-0.12461	-0.02944
V261	0.51389	-0.32726	-0.01462	0.19087	-0.00111	-0.06772	-0.11731
V262	0.44054	-0.01923	-0.00504	-0.11244	-0.12608	0.17276	-0.22818
V263	0.52107	-0.03756	-0.07318	0.14016	-0.22647	0.11172	-0.01000
V264	0.61051	-0.01432	0.00921	-0.07188	-0.09823	-0.04706	-0.20002
V265	0.47646	0.06459	0.02064	0.09296	0.02202	-0.13904	-0.28784
V266	0.43499	0.16383	0.09003	0.06216	0.06489	-0.07828	-0.19485
V267	0.41832	0.13040	-0.22059	0.11691	-0.23671	0.17905	0.13770
V268	0.25573	0.20439	-0.08116	-0.10818	-0.05634	0.09737	0.11832
V269	0.29533	0.25747	-0.00511	-0.13505	-0.17896	0.24406	0.05444
V270	0.38016	-0.11722	-0.00216	0.02389	-0.08663	-0.15397	0.02233
V271	0.50972	0.24415	-0.05088	-0.06604	-0.04749	-0.03510	0.06187
V272	0.44055	0.48931	-0.13678	-0.02193	0.22140	-0.01706	0.01141
V273	0.37733	0.12543	-0.05454	0.15045	0.27604	-0.18530	0.03750

FILE   NCNAME   (CREATION DATE = 03/31/77)

FACTOR	EIGENVALUE	PCT OF VAR	CUM PCT
1	4.90524	47.1	47.1
2	1.60750	15.4	62.6
3	1.23732	11.9	74.5
4	0.94044	9.0	83.5
5	0.67992	6.5	90.0
6	0.59448	5.7	95.7
7	0.44347	4.3	100.0

VARIABLE	COMMUNALITY
V244	0.31721
V245	0.41253
V246	0.35798
V247	0.18327
V248	0.31531
V249	0.60291
V250	0.23327
V251	0.31636
V252	0.51909
V253	0.58289
V254	0.41151
V255	0.40088
V256	0.31329
V257	0.35050
V258	0.39854
V259	0.21684
V260	0.22300
V261	0.42618
V262	0.30492
V263	0.36179
V264	0.43005
V265	0.34483
V266	0.27633
V267	0.36137
V268	0.15212
V269	0.26633
V270	0.19055
V271	0.33377
V272	0.50214
V273	0.30170

FOOD-Q14

FILE   NONAME   (CREATION DATE = 03/31/77)

VARIMAX ROTATED FACTOR MATRIX

	FACTOR 1	FACTOR 2	FACTOR 3	FACTOR 4	FACTOR 5	FACTOR 6	FACTOR 7
V244	-0.11549	0.45781	0.04241	0.06169	0.00379	0.29704	-0.02071
V245	-0.10678	0.44952	0.21542	0.14782	0.23114	0.30065	-0.14609
V246	0.07299	0.52001	-0.09987	0.09105	0.13121	0.15439	0.15104
V247	0.05499	0.16730	-0.00184	0.16312	0.33859	0.09857	0.03582
V248	0.39986	0.12840	-0.17567	0.00354	0.12068	0.04140	-0.49163
V249	0.11125	0.31042	0.02373	0.00804	0.22518	0.12589	0.65345
V250	0.12622	0.17709	-0.00130	0.11410	0.34993	0.21134	0.07639
V251	0.20936	0.50701	-0.04679	0.01600	0.08175	0.05083	-0.06131
V252	0.37156	0.21354	-0.67320	0.08901	-0.02101	0.05408	-0.06228
V253	0.07114	0.15483	0.70382	0.17869	0.02877	0.07881	0.13972
V254	0.61600	0.11152	-0.06651	0.10820	0.03631	0.02342	0.04049
V255	0.21516	0.57625	-0.05771	-0.06261	0.09384	0.07973	-0.01058
V256	0.13960	-0.11658	-0.04034	0.06750	0.52211	-0.00811	-0.03688
V257	0.56116	-0.06237	-0.03217	0.05912	0.01237	0.16135	-0.03718
V258	0.00264	0.16139	0.14440	0.40880	0.34305	0.22304	-0.13221
V259	-0.02513	0.43327	0.03352	0.14215	0.02284	0.06566	0.04816
V260	0.04590	0.17722	0.12687	0.04574	0.31283	0.27066	-0.01325
V261	-0.09372	0.29973	0.10044	0.11458	0.32195	0.44575	-0.04465
V262	0.17558	0.17839	0.01728	0.28122	-0.03632	0.38628	0.11113
V263	0.10100	0.14595	0.00173	0.41154	0.26324	0.30216	-0.01533
V264	0.24735	0.25209	0.00401	0.24859	0.14016	0.45753	0.12052
V265	0.24025	0.09124	-0.03211	0.00453	-0.20989	0.48339	-0.00378
V266	0.31872	0.11995	-0.08668	0.00677	0.15421	0.35550	-0.05132
V267	0.20382	0.00989	0.08009	0.49230	0.24834	0.08969	-0.03515
V268	0.29540	0.06274	0.03017	0.22482	0.06886	-0.03306	0.06022
V269	0.32774	0.05660	-0.07558	0.37685	-0.04400	0.02536	0.06658
V270	0.03717	0.18407	-0.05514	0.09005	0.30230	0.20739	0.11293
V271	0.42612	0.13675	-0.01178	0.20809	0.25005	0.14496	0.08065
V272	0.66259	0.02262	0.10144	0.04634	0.17492	0.09554	-0.10218
V273	0.30343	0.12282	0.14384	-0.11760	0.33854	0.14713	-0.15418

APPENDIX 16-C: SAMPLE CLUSTER ANALYSIS OUTPUT

LARGE HOWARD HARRIS CLUSTERING PROGRAM
THIS VERSION BY C.P.P.C.
JULY 9, 1973

HOWARD-TYPE CLUSTERING ...PROGRAMMED BY WORDLEY AND MODIFIED BY CARMONE

FOOD CLUSTER

OF OBSERVATIONS OR CASES   940
OF VRIABLES PER CASE   12
   NO OF CLUSTERS   4
RMAT (12F2.0)

UT TAPE NC.   8

RE WEIGHTS 1.00 1.00 1.CC 1.00 1.00 1.00 1.00 1.00 1.00 1.00 1.00 1.00

RAW DATA--MEANS--VARIANCES

	1	2	3	4	5	6	7	8	9	10	11	12
1	1.000	1.000	3.000	3.0CC	3.000	4.000	2.000	1.000	1.000	2.00C	2.000	2.000
2	2.000	1.000	1.00C	1.000	3.000	3.000	4.000	1.000	1.000	3.000	2.000	4.000
3	2.000	1.000	3.000	1.0CC	1.000	4.00C	3.000	1.000	1.000	2.000	2.00C	4.000
4	3.000	1.000	5.00C	3.0CC	2.000	3.000	3.00C	2.000	1.000	2.00C	3.000	5.000
5	2.000	1.000	1.000	3.0CC	3.000	3.000	3.000	1.000	1.000	2.00C	2.000	3.000
6	2.000	1.000	1.00C	1.0CC	2.000	5.00C	5.C00	1.000	1.000	1.000	2.000	3.000
7	3.000	3.000	3.000	3.0CC	3.000	3.000	3.000	3.000	3.000	2.000	3.000	2.000
8	1.000	1.000	1.00C	1.0CC	3.C00	5.00C	5.000	5.000	1.000	1.000	2.000	5.000
9	1.000	1.000	1.00C	1.0CC	3.000	1.000	5.000	3.000	3.000	1.000	3.000	5.000
10	3.000	1.000	5.00C	1.0CC	1.000	3.000	5.000	1.000	3.000	2.00C	3.000	4.000
11	1.000	1.000	3.00C	1.0CC	1.000	1.00C	5.C00	1.000	1.000	5.000	3.000	5.000
12	3.000	3.000	3.000	1.000	3.000	3.000	3.000	3.000	3.000	2.000	2.000	3.000
13	2.000	1.000	5.00C	3.000	3.000	5.00C	3.000	1.000	1.000	3.00C	3.000	2.000
14	3.C00	1.000	5.00C	1.0CC	3.000	3.000	3.000	1.000	1.000	3.00C	2.000	4.000
15	1.000	1.000	3.00C	3.000	1.000	3.000	3.000	1.000	1.000	3.000	3.000	5.000
16	1.000	1.000	3.00C	1.000	3.000	1.00C	1.000	1.000	1.000	1.000	1.000	4.000
17	1.000	1.000	1.000	1.0CC	1.C00	3.000	1.000	3.000	1.000	2.00C	1.00C	3.000
18	1.000	1.000	3.00C	1.0CC	3.000	5.00C	5.C00	1.000	1.000	5.000	2.000	4.000
19	5.000	3.000	5.000	4.000	3.000	4.00M	4.000	3.000	3.000	1.000	2.000	4.000
20	1.000	1.000	2.00C	1.0CC	3.000	3.000	4.000	1.000	2.000	2.000	2.000	3.000
21	3.000	1.000	3.00C	2.0CC	1.000	3.000	2.C0C	1.000	1.000	5.00C	1.000	3.000
22	1.000	1.000	3.000	3.000	3.000	3.000	3.000	3.000	1.000	5.00C	4.000	3.000
23	3.000	1.000	1.000	1.0CC	1.000	3.000	3.000	3.000	1.000	4.000	2.000	2.000
24	3.000	1.000	4.00C	3.000	2.000	2.000	2.000	1.000	3.000	2.00C	4.000	5.000
25	3.000	1.000	2.00C	3.0CC	2.000	2.000	3.000	1.000	1.000	3.000	2.000	5.000
26	1.000,	1.000	3.00C	3.0CC	3.000	5.000	1.000	3.000	1.000	1.000	3.000	3.000
27	1.000	1.000	1.00C	1.0CC	1.000	1.000	1.000	1.000	1.000	1.000	3.000	3.000
28	3.000	1.000	1.00C	1.0CC	1.000	1.000	3.000	5.000	1.000	1.000	1.000	4.000
29	4.000	3.000	5.000	3.0CC	3.000	3.00C	4.000	4.000	3.000	2.000	3.000	5.000
30	1.000	1.000	1.00C	2.0CC	2.000	2.000	2.C00	1.000	1.000	1.000	2.000	4.000
31	2.000	1.000	3.000	2.0CC	3.000	2.000	2.000	3.000	2.000	4.000	3.000	5.000
32	1.000	1.000	1.00C	2.0CC	3.000	2.00C	5.000	1.000	1.000	5.00C	1.000	3.000
33	2.000	2.000	5.00C	3.0CC	3.000	3.000	3.000	2.000	2.000	5.00C	4.000	5.000
34	2.C00	1.000	4.00C	1.0CC	2.000	2.000	3.000	1.000	1.000	3.000	3.000	3.000
35	1.000	1.000	1.00C	1.0CC	3.000	3.000	5.000	3.000	1.000	4.000	1.00C	3.000
36	2.000	1.000	2.00C	1.0CC	1.000	2.000	3.000	1.000	1.000	1.000	3.000	5.000
37	3.000	3.000	3.00C	3.000	1.000	3.00C	3.000	3.000	1.000	2.000	3.000	3.000
38	1.000	1.000	3.00C	3.000	1.000	3.00C	5.000	3.000	1.000	2.000	1.000	3.000
39	1.000	1.000	1.00C	3.000	5.00C	3.000	3.000	1.000	2.000	1.000	3.000	4.000
40	3.000	3.000	1.00C	1.0CC	4.000	4.000	5.000	1.000	1.000	2.000	2.000	4.000
41	2.000	1.000	3.00C	1.000	1.000	1.00C	4.C00	2.000	1.000	1.00C	3.C0C	2.000
42	3.000	3.000	3.000	3.0CC	3.000	3.000	3.000	3.000	3.000	2.000	1.000	4.000
43	4.000	1.000	2.00C	2.0CC	3.000	1.000	3.000	3.000	3.000	1.000	2.000	4.000
44	3.000	1.000	3.00C	1.0CC	3.000	3.000	3.000	3.000	1.000	1.000	2.000	3.000
45	3.C00	1.000	4.000	3.000	1.000	2.000	1.C0C	2.000	3.000	1.000	3.000	4.000
46	2.000	1.000	5.00C	1.0CC	1.000	3.000	2.000	1.000	1.000	1.000	2.000	5.000
47	3.000	3.000	1.000	3.0CC	3.000	1.000	3.000	1.000	1.000	1.000	1.00C	3.000
48	3.000	2.000	2.00C	2.0CC	2.000	2.00C	2.000	1.000	1.000	3.000	1.000	4.000
49	1.000	1.000	1.00C	1.0CC	1.C00	1.000	1.000	1.000	1.000	1.000	1.000	4.000
50	1.000	1.000	3.000	3.000	3.000	3.000	3.C00	3.000	3.000	4.000	3.000	5.000
51	1.000	1.000	3.00C	2.000	3.000	4.00C	4.000	2.000	1.000	2.000	3.000	5.000
52	3.000	1.000	2.00C	3.0CC	2.000	4.00C	3.000	1.000	1.000	4.000	2.000	4.000
53	3.000	1.000	2.00C	3.0CC	1.000	3.000	1.000	3.000	2.000	2.000	3.000	4.000
54	1.000	1.000	5.00C	1.0CC	2.000	2.00D	1.000	1.000	1.000	2.000	1.000	5.000
55	3.C00	1.000	3.00C	1.000	2.000	3.000	3.000	2.000	2.000	3.00C	3.C00	3.000
56	1.000	3.000	1.00C	1.000	3.000	3.000	5.000	3.000	1.000	1.000	2.000	3.000
57	3.000	1.000	3.00C	1.000	5.000	5.00C	3.000	3.000	1.00C	4.000	2.000	4.000
58	3.000	2.000	3.00C	3.000	3.000	3.000	3.000	4.000	1.000	3.00C	3.000	5.000

GROUP NO. 1

1	2	3	5	6	9	11	16	17	18	20	21	23	25	27	28	30	32	35	36	39	40	41	43	47
48	49	51	56	60	61	62	63	66	67	69	72	73	76	78	80	81	85	87	90	91	93	94	95	96
97	98	101	113	115	118	119	120	122	123	124	134	135	138	141	142	143	146	148	149	158	159	163	164	166
168	169	170	172	174	175	176	179	183	185	186	190	192	194	195	197	200	205	208	216	221	224	226	227	228
229	231	232	233	234	237	289	291	292	298	299	300	307	311	312	319	323	324	325	327	329	330	331	332	334
271	274	275	780	282	285	353	358	359	360	361	363	367	368	369	371	372	375	377	384	385	391	395	398	402
335	337	340	341	345	351	421	423	424	425	426	427	432	433	438	440	442	447	448	450	452	459	463	464	465
404	410	413	414	417	419	488	490	493	497	503	504	506	507	511	516	517	519	520	521	522	523	524	526	534
468	469	471	479	480	485	554	561	562	564	569	571	573	577	579	585	587	588	597	598	600	601	604	610	611
535	537	543	544	547	552	632	634	635	636	638	640	646	647	651	652	654	654	658	660	669	670	674	676	677
612	615	622	625	628	630	695	696	704	708	713	716	719	721	722	723	724	726	730	731	733	737	738	742	743
678	681	685	687	688	693	756	758	760	762	769	763	766	768	771	784	786	794	783	785	787	790	791	792	795
746	748	749	750	751	752	802	809	811	813	816	817	820	821	822	823	825	828	834	835	836	850	851	853	859
796	797	798	799	800	801	872	876	880	881	884	885	887	890	891	894	897	900	907	908	911	912	916	921	923
860	862	863	867	868	871																			
925	928	931	934	935	940																			

GROUP NO. 2

4	10	13	14	15	24	33	34	45	46	54	55	59	64	65	68	70	74	75	82	83	84	86	92	99
100	106	108	110	111	114	121	126	128	129	130	131	132	144	145	155	161	162	165	177	178	182	189	196	99
198	201	207	209	213	218	220	222	225	236	243	244	244	246	253	254	255	264	266	272	276	277	283	284	288
290	293	295	296	302	304	308	308	310	315	316	315	316	317	320	326	328	338	342	346	347	350	352	357	367
364	366	376	378	379	381	383	387	388	389	390	392	354	396	397	399	401	403	406	407	411	412	415	420	472
430	434	437	439	445	446	451	453	454	461	470	475	556	481	482	484	487	491	492	496	498	499	502	505	508
509	518	528	529	530	532	541	542	545	548	549	555	607	558	560	563	563	565	567	570	572	574	575	576	578
580	583	583	590	593	595	595	596	602	605	606	606	660	608	614	619	623	626	627	629	631	637	642	645	648
649	650	655	656	659	661	662	663	664	666	668	675	775	689	694	694	697	700	701	706	700	711	712	715	725
734	739	740	741	747	753	754	755	765	767	769	774	846	777	778	784	786	794	803	804	812	815	818	819	824
826	827	829	830	831	833	838	840	841	842	844	846	922	847	852	852	854	855	857	864	865	870	873	874	877
882	888	888	889	895	901	903	905	909	910	913	920		929	930	933	937	938	939						

GROUP NO. 3

7	8	12	19	22	26	29	31	37	38	42	44	50	52	53	57	58	71	77	79	83	86	88	102	103	104
105	107	109	112	116	117	125	127	133	136	137	139	140	147	150	151	152	153	154	156	157	160	182	167	171	173
180	181	184	187	191	193	199	203	204	206	207	210	211	212	214	215	218	219	223	230	235	247	189	249	251	259
263	270	278	279	281	286	287	294	297	301	305	306	314	318	321	322	328	333	336	343	344	348	277	348	354	355
356	365	370	373	374	380	382	386	474	400	405	408	409	416	418	428	429	431	435	436	441	443	350	444	449	455
456	457	458	460	462	466	472	473	550	476	477	478	483	486	489	494	495	500	501	510	512	513	499	514	515	525
527	531	533	536	538	539	540	546	644	551	553	557	566	568	581	584	586	589	591	592	603	609	574	613	616	617
618	620	621	674	633	641	642	643	727	653	665	667	671	672	673	679	682	683	684	686	691	692	637	698	699	702
703	705	709	710	714	717	718	720	832	728	729	732	735	736	744	745	757	761	764	770	772	773	711	780	781	788
789	793	805	806	807	808	810	814	917	837	839	843	848	856	858	861	866	869	875	878	879	886	815	892	893	896
898	899	902	904	906	914	915	917		919	924	926	927	932	936								870			

NO. IN EACH GROUP

381	294	265

GROUP MEANS BY VARIABLE

VAR 1	1.7507	2.1939	2.3698
VAR 2	1.1549	1.2517	1.5925
VAR 3	1.7060	4.5714	3.0566
VAR 4	1.4488	1.6463	2.4189
VAR 5	1.9265	2.0578	2.7736
VAR 6	2.6194	2.6973	3.1509
VAR 7	2.7664	2.6735	3.0943
VAR 8	1.7008	1.7585	3.7094
VAR 9	1.2808	1.9048	2.0943
VAR 10	2.3753	2.4490	2.3585
VAR 11	1.9895	2.6769	2.4981
VAR 12	3.7979	3.8605	3.6453

GROUP VARIANCES BY VARIABLE

VAR 1	C.7508	0.8978	1.0406
VAR 2	0.2044	0.3244	C.7773
VAR 3	0.7167	0.5034	1.5704
VAR 4	0.5518	0.7388	1.1642
VAR 5	0.8975	1.1701	1.3374
VAR 6	1.5C08	1.5308	1.1017
VAR 7	1.1449	1.2199	1.1420
VAR 8	0.8396	0.707C	0.9307
VAR 9	0.3437	0.8957	0.9458
VAR 10	1.4156	1.3494	1.1960
VAR 11	0.7138	1.0282	0.7934
VAR 12	1.1534	1.1812	1.1346

GROUP NO.   1

```
 9  11  16  17  21  23  25  27  28  30  36  41  43  47  48  49  53  61  62  67  69  72  73  74  76
78  80  81  87  89  93  94  96  97  98  98 113 114 118 118 119 198 134 143 145 158 164 166 168 170
172 174 183 185 186 195 199 205 206 216 216 224 227 228 229 231 233 240 241 245 247 243 252 256 258
269 270 271 274 275 277 282 291 292 298 299 300 312 315 319 323 324 329 330 334 335 337 341 351 359
359 360 361 363 367 368 371 375 375 377 377 385 391 395 398 402 404 410 413 414 423 425 427 432 433
438 440 452 463 465 468 469 479 480 493 494 516 520 523 524 526 534 535 536 544 552 554 562 564 566
569 573 577 579 600 601 610 612 622 626 628 630 632 634 635 638 640 646 658 660 663 669 676 677 678
681 688 693 696 698 704 708 713 721 722 724 726 730 731 733 735 737 743 746 750 756 758 759 760 762
763 768 771 776 780 785 785 791 791 792 796 797 758 799 800 807 811 813 816 826 834 836 850 853 862
863 867 868 869 871 881 887 890 891 894 897 900 907 911 912 923 925 927 931 934 935
```

GROUP NO.   2

```
 4  10  13  14  15  19  22  24  33  34  45  46  54  55  58  64  65  68  70  75  82  84  92
126 128 129 130 131 125 127 131 141 144 148 155 161 165 152 177 178 189 196 198 201 202 209
236 243 244 246 253 219 219 219 255 266 272 276 283 284 263 288 290 293 295 296 302 303 304
320 326 338 339 342 230 230 230 347 352 357 362 362 366 376 378 379 381 383 387 388 389 390
401 403 406 407 412 354 407 407 420 422 430 434 437 439 380 445 446 451 454 461 467 470 470
492 458 502 505 508 457 508 508 518 528 529 529 530 532 476 541 542 545 548 549 555 559 560
575 576 578 582 583 553 582 582 590 594 596 599 599 602 589 605 606 607 608 614 619 623 629
649 656 659 656 661 675 659 659 664 668 679 679 680 689 705 690 694 700 701 707 711 712 715
747 753 754 755 765 682 755 755 767 775 777 778 784 784 778 786 804 812 815 818 819 824 826
838 840 841 842 844 805 842 842 847 855 857 865 870 870 843 873 877 882 883 888 889 895 901
920 922 929 930 933 918 930 930 938 935 936 939       857
```

GROUP NO.   3

```
 7  12  19  22  26  20  32  35  38  39  40  51  52  56  77  71  59  58  44  42  37  31  37  18  85
116 117 217 223 142 139 146 149 150 154 159 160 162 163 157 156 153 152 147 140 137 136 135 138 179
215 217 219 223 212 210 226 232 234 237 343 239 250 257 281 278 273 263 251 249 242 235 208 207 265
336 344 349 354 325 327 331 333 340 340 345 348 348 353 281 386 382 376 374 370 365 362 311 311 408
456 457 553 556 450 448 453 459 464 471 485 488 490 496 483 478 477 476 473 472 466 462 447 444 506
550 551 553 556 538 527 539 547 558 558 563 561 571 585 609 542 591 589 584 581 580 568 557 525 603
672 675 675 682 647 643 652 654 653 657 670 674 685 687 717 714 609 705 699 691 686 684 636 627 703
789 793 794 805 749 744 751 752 761 766 782 783 783 770 718 710 591 702 699 691 814 808 806 736 703
904 915 917 918 851 849 852 856 859 860 872 876 880 884 864 858 845 843 837 836 932 526 835 825 908
924 928 940                                           861
```

GROUP NO.   4

```
 1   2   3   5   6 122 123 197 429 424 426 517 620 627   91  90  86  85  63  66  92 104 105 107 108 109 110 111
101 106 152 123 124 194 197 294 442 425 521 675 736 832 188 187 184 179 176 175 175 191 193 203 204 211 222 211
190 152 285 197 297 285 294 429 448 525 627 620 738 825 279 268 267 265 262 264 369 308 314 318 321 316 316 322
280 424 289 429 297 426 429       450 527 636 620   940 419 417 409 408 405 504 503 436 510 531 533 507 540 443
421 514 426 517 442 515 521       453 538 643 627       512 511 507 506 503 499 497 488 495 497 588 533 540 546
514 616 517 620 444 620 675       539 647 751 636       615 611 604 603 598 504 598 563 644 692 695 585 667 671
616 719 620 627 525 627 736       652 751 852 751       716 709 706 703 702 695 697 670 745 732 695 697 773 781
719 821 627 736 636 736           651 749 848 852       716 817 706 803 702 788 802 782 814 803 706 776 773 781
821 924 823 825 738 825           647 849                809 817 802 885 795 788 802 880 849 803 809 817 916 820
924 928 940                                            921 188 279 419 512 615 716 781 902 908 914 899 910 921
```

GROUP MEANS BY VARIABLE

VAR 1	1.8049	2.1783	2.4231	1.8860
VAR 2	1.1504	1.2597	1.6154	1.2544
VAR 3	1.7154	4.6744	3.4904	1.9737
VAR 4	1.3821	1.6279	2.6202	1.6316
VAR 5	1.5122	1.9612	2.7981	2.6930
VAR 6	1.8780	2.6434	2.9087	2.8465
VAR 7	2.3821	2.6473	2.9952	3.3684
VAR 8	1.8537	1.7171	3.7788	2.0307
VAR 9	1.3252	1.8876	2.2788	1.3860
VAR 10	2.3130	2.4302	2.3317	2.4956
VAR 11	2.0000	2.6202	2.6683	2.1228
VAR 12	3.8577	3.8372	3.7163	3.6667

GROUP VARIANCES BY VARIABLE

VAR 1	0.8156	0.8907	1.0037	0.9431
VAR 2	0.2172	0.3395	C.7559	0.3739
VAR 3	0.7158	0.3669	1.3557	1.0081
VAR 4	0.4881	0.7298	1.1009	0.6888
VAR 5	0.5425	1.0528	1.2092	1.0724
VAR 6	0.6599	1.3767	0.9388	0.7966
VAR 7	0.9759	1.1973	0.9856	1.0573
VAR 8	1.1981	0.6525	0.8646	1.1964
VAR 9	0.4227	0.8982	0.9222	0.4475
VAR 10	1.4915	1.3769	1.1255	1.2851
VAR 11	0.7642	1.0108	0.8178	0.7481
VAR 12	1.1789	1.1906	1.0494	1.1959

17

Multiattribute modeling

BASIC CONCEPT

A basic tenet of much of the research in marketing is that consumers evaluate alternative products on a series of relevant attributes. These attributes (which are also called characteristics or dimensions—the terms are used interchangeably) vary from product category to product category. Hence for toothpaste one would expect attributes such as decay prevention and tooth whitening to be relevant, while for a machine tool attributes such as accuracy, downtime, and initial price would be expected to be important. Preference and subsequently choice is presumed to be determined by each customer selecting the brand which has the best combination of the relevant attributes.

Such models have great intuitive appeal as the logical/"right" way to behave. These models are essentially rational economic man models and have been developed in most branches of social science. Models in the same spirit include those of Fishbein (1967) and Rosenberg (1956) in social psychology, Lancaster (1966) in microeconomics, and the expectancy theory models in organizational behavior. It is important to note that such models are designed to help explain/understand preferences or attitudes. In order to predict choice, a single preference or attitude measure will often do as well as a more complex measure. The advantage of these models is that they attempt to explain why preferences exist and hence suggest what can be done to change them.

In order to use such a multiattribute model, the following three basic pieces of information are needed:

1. The identity of the relevant attributes.
2. The positions of the alternatives (brands) on the attributes.
3. The desired (ideal) levels of each attribute.

From these three pieces of information, an overall value (utility, attitude, preference) for each of the alternatives is derived. Usually value is assumed to be a function of the position of the alternatives on the relevant attributes. Often value is obtained by simply multiplying the positions on the attributes by the importances (weights) of the attributes.

Multiattribute models can be viewed graphically. (This helps explain why they are often called spatial models, geometric models, or perceptual maps.) Consider Figure 17–1 with two attributes (brilliantly labeled 1 and

FIGURE 17–1
Brand locations in two dimensions

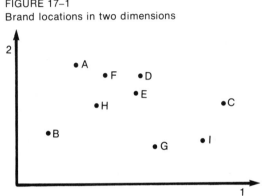

2) and nine alternatives (labeled A–I). In this example, alternative C has the most of attribute 1 and alternative A has the most of attribute 2. If you assume alternative I represents the ideal (desired) level on the attributes, then the most preferred brand(s) should be the ones closest to I. In this case, that means alternatives C and G. Whether C or G is most preferred depends on whether attribute 1 or 2 is more important.

Attribute models are conceptually models of individual consumers. Yet the practicality of their use in marketing usually depends on some form of aggregation. Hence most users of such techniques assume some things are constant across customers (at least those in a given segment) such as the attributes and the positions of the alternatives on the attributes.

Attribute models can be developed in a number of ways. One inelegant but interesting approach is seat-of-the-pants executive judgment. In other words a knowledgeable person may be able to directly draw such a model.

Assuming such a savant is unavailable (or at least needs to be checked up on), a researcher must resort to an analytical procedure to generate attribute models. The remainder of this chapter is devoted to describing some of the major analytical techniques for developing and utilizing such models.

DIRECT QUESTIONING

An inelegant but potentially useful way to generate such models is to ask consumers directly. This approach has been used for decades in commercial research, often under the name of brand scoring or brand rating methods. The approach is explained in this section.

Attribute identification

Identification of the relevant attributes can be done in many ways. The most commonly used commercial approach is to begin with focus groups. The focus groups are used to generate a list of potential attributes. This list of attributes is then submitted to a sample of customers who each indicate (check off) the important attributes. The commonly checked attributes are then identified as the relevant attributes. An alternative approach is the so-called protocol procedure. In a protocol procedure, customers are asked to describe in detail the steps they went through in buying a particular product. Attributes mentioned are then recorded and compiled as the relevant attributes. It is also common to have subjects list attributes in response to an open-ended question (often called free elicitation). A less elegant but useful alternative is to have the researcher and/or manager specify the attributes based on experience. This method is (a) inexpensive and (b) full of researcher bias.

Deriving positions of alternatives on the attributes

The positions of the alternatives on the attributes are obtained by direct ratings. These ratings are typically done on six- to ten-point bipolar adjective scales, although more elaborate graphical scales are occasionally used. Ratings can be obtained in two basic ways:

Rating a single alternative on all the dimensions at one time:

	Very low					Very high
Crest:						
Decay prevention	1	2	3	4	5	6
Tooth whitening	1	2	3	4	5	6
. . .						
Colgate:						
Decay prevention	1	2	3	4	5	6
Tooth whitening	1	2	3	4	5	6
. . .						

Rating all the alternatives on a single dimension:

	Very low					Very high
Decay prevention:						
Crest	1	2	3	4	5	6
Colgate	1	2	3	4	5	6
UltraBright	1	2	3	4	5	6
. . .						
Tooth whitening:						
Crest	1	2	3	4	5	6
Colgate	1	2	3	4	5	6
UltraBright	1	2	3	4	5	6
. . .						

There is strong evidence that respondents tend to "halo" their responses toward brands by rating the brands they like high on all attributes and vice versa. Hence the first approach is not very desirable because it makes it very easy for the respondent to think only of the alternative and not about the attribute, and thus all the ratings may be repeated measures of how well the respondent likes the alternative. The second approach makes the attribute the focus of attention. This causes (hopefully) a respondent to place his or her rating of an alternative in the context of the rating of other alternatives on the attribute. Hence it makes it less likely that alternative A will be rated higher on the attribute than alternative B unless it really is higher (at least in the view of the respondent).

Determination of desired (ideal) levels

The determination of ideal levels can be obtained by direct questioning. Unfortunately, the results have often been discouraging (Lehmann, 1971; Neidell, 1972). For one thing, many of the attributes used tend to be of the "more is better" type (e.g., decay prevention) and hence the ideal logically belongs at the end of the scale. Moreover, respondents seem to have difficulty with the ideal concept on nonobjective attributes and tend to confuse the ideal position on an attribute with, among other things, the importance they attribute to the attribute. Consequently, many researchers use attributes where one end of the scale is clearly preferred or alternatively try to deduce the ideal points indirectly (see the section on multidimensional scaling).

Determination of value of positions on the attribute

The determination of the value of different positions on the attributes has typically centered on finding the importances (weights) consumers attach to the relevant attributes. A common model indicating the overall evaluation of an alternative is

$$\begin{array}{c} \text{Overall} \\ \text{evaluation} \\ \text{of an} \\ \text{alternative} \end{array} \quad \sum_{\substack{\text{all} \\ \text{relevant} \\ \text{attributes}}} \left(\begin{array}{c} \text{Weight of} \\ \text{attribute} \end{array}\right) \left|\begin{array}{cc} \text{Position} & \text{Ideal level} \\ \text{on the} & - & \text{on the} \\ \text{attribute} & \text{attribute} \end{array}\right|$$

or

$$A_j = \sum_{i=1}^{n} W_j |P_{ji} - I_i| \qquad (17.1)$$

The weights are usually obtained by using six- to eight-point bipolar adjective scales scaled from very important to very unimportant. This approach has two major problems. First, respondents have a strong tendency to rate all attributes as at least somewhat important, leading to difficulty in separating the attributes in terms of importance because many end up with the same rating. Second, the weights obtained are at best intervally scaled, whereas the model requires ratio scaled data.[1] Although this usually does not change the predictive power significantly, ratio scaled importances (and position ratings) should be sought, probably by means of constant sum scales. Perhaps fortunately, the weights seem to make very little difference in the predictive power of the models (Beckwith and Lehmann, 1973). This suggests that equal weighting of the attributes is often sufficient.

Summary

The direct approach to obtaining attribute models is easy to use and communicate. Further, the results are often "good" in terms of both predictive power and insight. Nonetheless, several problems do exist with these procedures. First, it is very hard to be sure if all the relevant dimensions for respondents have been obtained. Second, there is a tendency for respondents to give socially acceptable answers in terms of both the identity of the relevant dimensions and their importance (i.e., obviously for a food product, it is "right" to say that nutrition is important). Third, respondents have a strong tendency to "halo" their responses about the alternatives. This means that they respond mainly in terms of whether they like the alternative regardless of the attribute in question, and hence the value of the direct ratings is substantially decreased (Beckwith and Lehmann, 1975). For these and other reasons, many researchers use alternative methods to obtain attribute models.

---

[1] If I multiply together two intervally scaled variables, the result depends on the arbitrary zero value and on the size of the interval involved. This means that not only are the attitude scores not unique but also that the order of predicted preference may be incorrect.

MULTIDIMENSIONAL SCALING (MDS)

Multidimensional scaling is in many ways the opposite of direct questioning as a means of obtaining multiattribute models. The identity of the relevant attributes and the positions of alternatives on the attributes are an output of analysis rather than input to a questionnaire. This technique was developed by psychometricians, notably Shepard (1962) and Kruskal (1964), and has received great attention in marketing (Green and Carmone, 1970; Green and Rao, 1972). Its purpose is to deduce indirectly the dimensions a respondent uses to evaluate alternatives. The reason for using the indirect approach (aside from the cultural explanation that it came to marketing by way of psychologists) is that in many cases, the attributes may be unknown and respondents unable (what attributes do you use to evaluate paintings?) or unwilling (why do you yell at your kids?) to accurately represent their reasons. The term multidimensional scaling has come to refer to a variety of procedures for deducing attribute models from simple (and seemingly innocent) input data. This section will proceed to examine these procedures.

Simple space

The basic type of multidimensional scaling involves deducing graphical models of alternatives from similarity judgments. Here we ask a respondent to rate pairs of objects in terms of their overall similarity. For three objects, this would require as input the following:

Pair	Similarity rating
A, B	3 (most similar)
A, C	1
B, C	2

The procedure then deduces as output the positions of the alternatives on a prespecified number of attributes. The purpose of the next two sections is to give an indication of how this "magic" (translation: big computer program) works.

Initial solution. Simple space analysis proceeds in two basic stages. The first is to develop an initial solution. One alternative is to randomly place points on the desired number of dimensions. This, however, is so horribly inefficient that other procedures are used.

An intuitively appealing starting rule is a variation on the old navigation by triangulation trick. Consider Figure 17–2. If distance data were generated from this figure, we might have the input data (note we are using metric input merely for illustrative purposes) of Table 17–1. The question addressed by multidimensional scaling is how to go from data such as that in Table 17–1 to a picture such as Figure 17–2.

600

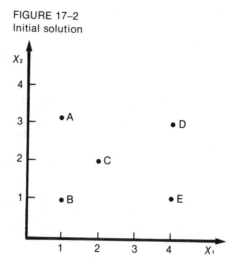

FIGURE 17–2
Initial solution

TABLE 17–1
Input data

Pair	Approximate distance
A, B	2
A, C	1.4
A, D	3.0
A, E	3.6
B, C	1.4
B, D	3.5
B, E	3.2
C, D	2.4
C, E	2.3
D, E	2

To get an initial solution, we can arbitrarily pick any two points, preferably two which are fairly far apart. Here we use A and D and plot them (Figure 17–3). Now choose one more point (C) and draw circles around A and D of length 1.4 and 2.4 respectively (Figure 17–4). You will notice that these circles meet in two places. Arbitrarily choose one point and label it C. Now add the next point (B) by drawing arcs around A, C, and D of appropriate lengths and see where they intersect (Figure 17–5). If the input measures were perfect, they will meet in one point. If the input data contains some error, then the three arcs will almost meet in a small area. Choose the center of the area for the point's location and continue.[2]

------

[2] This method depends on the three original points being "good" ones in terms of the accuracy with which the input data represents their distances.

FIGURE 17-3
Initial points

A •

D •

FIGURE 17-4
Third point added

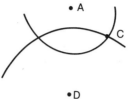

• A

C

•D

FIGURE 17-5
Four-point solution

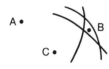

A •

B

C •

D •

FIGURE 17-6
Five-point solution

• A   • B

•C

•D   E

Finally, adding E we have Figure 17–6. Notice that this configuration is approximately the original one, the difference being due to the error in the input data, although the picture has been rotated 90 degrees and reflected (the mirror image to Figure 17–2 appears in Figure 17–6). Hence we see that what is preserved is the original orientation among the points and not their exact positions.

Second stage. Stage two consists of taking the initial solution and trying to improve it. This is accomplished by a procedure known as the gradient (for math fans) or hill-climbing (for poets) approach. To see how this works, return to the original three-alternative example:

Input:

Pair	Similarity rating
A, B	3 (most similar)
A, C	1
B, C	2

Assume the initial solution were that of Figure 17–7. At this point, one might wish to evaluate how good a solution this is. One way to do this is to

FIGURE 17–7
Three-brand model

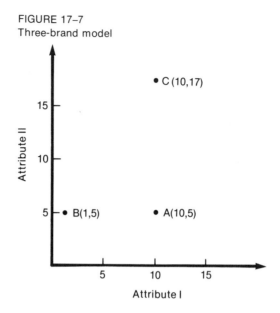

calculate the distances between points and see if they match the original input data in that the most similar pair of alternatives should have the smallest distance between them and so forth. Here we obtain the following:

Pair	Similarity	Distance	"Error"
A, B	3	9	—
A, C	1	12	−1.5
B, C	2	15	+1.5

As hoped, the most similar pair (A, B) is closest together. The other two pairs, unfortunately, are "messed up" since B, C should be closer together than A, C. One way to see how bad the solution is is to try to "fudge" the distance data so that the similarity data and the derived distances are consistent. The easiest way to do this would be to move both the A, C and B, C distances to 13.5, and hence the error terms are 0, −1.5, and +1.5 respectively. To see how much fudging was required, we can construct an error index:

$$\frac{\Sigma \text{ errors squared}}{\Sigma \text{ distances squared}}$$

$$= \frac{(0)^2 + (1.5)^2 + (1.5)^2}{81 + 225 + 144} \approx .01$$

This index can then be used as a criterion for when a new solution is better or worse than the old solution (the smaller the index, the better the solution).

One way to improve the original solution in this example is to move alternative C a little to the left, thus making it simultaneously closer to alternative B and farther from alternative A. The second stage of an MDS program would do this. Next the program recomputes the index and again moves points to improve the index. Hence stage two consists of moving the points around until the distances match the original similarity data well enough or the maximum number of iterations is reached.

Output

The results which are output and interpreted are the positions of the alternatives on the attributes. Assuming the initial picture (Figure 17–7) represented the final output, we would get as the output Table 17–2.

TABLE 17–2
Output of multidimensional scaling

	Dimension	
Alternative	I	II
A	10	5
B	1	5
C	10	17

These results are missing one very important facet: the names of the dimensions. Developing the names of the dimensions is an art form akin to labeling factors in factor analysis. Here we look for a common characteristic of alternatives which fall on the extremes of a dimension. In this example, whatever dimension I is, A and C have a lot of it and B has very little of it. Similarly C has a lot of whatever is represented by dimension II and A and B not much of it. While it is possible to search for names for a dimension by seeing what other variables correlate with the positions on the dimensions,[3] the typical naming procedure is much more subjective.

Some semitechnical issues

In using simple space MDS procedures, several points are important to keep in mind.

---

[3] One popular "trick" for aiding in naming the dimensions is to also collect similarities between the alternatives and various key words which are thought to be related to the major dimensions. By scaling both alternatives and words simultaneously, the words then appear in the picture and may facilitate the task of naming the dimensions.

The results are tentative, not conclusive. Some early applications of MDS accepted the apparent dimensions as "truth" without question or validation, which often proved to be disastrous. Hence a major point in using MDS is to use it more as a generator of hypotheses rather than as a final model of a market. Any important result should be confirmed on a separate sample with a separate method such as direct questioning before the results are given too much credence.

The dimensions are not unique. MDS generates a configuration in which the relative positions of the brands are unique. The dimensions themselves, however, are not. The "picture" can be changed by several operations without changing the relationship among the interpoint distances (assuming Euclidean distance is used, which it almost always is). These operations are portrayed in Figure 17–8. Hence the dimensions that appear in the output are not unique. (Still it is fortunate how often the dimensions which are output from the analysis turn out to be useful/interpretable ones.)

Determining the number of dimensions is sometimes difficult. A prior theory about the number of dimensions is the best place to start. Absent a good theory, the most common approach is to examine the results of

FIGURE 17–8
Equivalent multidimensional scaling results

Original configuration

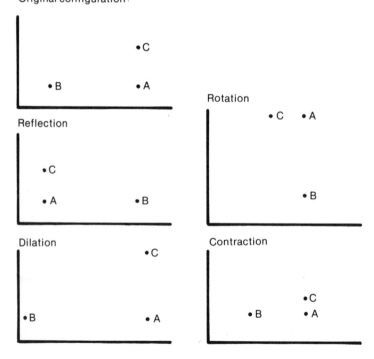

solutions in 2, 3, 4, and so forth, dimensions and choose the "best" one. There are two basic criteria for best. The first involves getting the index used as a criterion for fit to some predetermined level. (When Kruskal's stress is used, many researchers attempt to get stress below .05, with anything above .10 being unacceptable.) The second approach involves plotting the stress values and seeing where the addition of a dimension stops significantly (in a visual sense) improving the index (see Figure 17–9). In this case, the index seems to improve substantially going from a

FIGURE 17–9
Badness of fit index versus number of dimensions

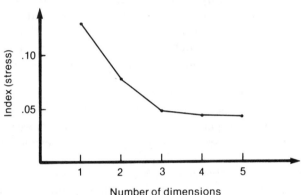

one- to two-dimensional solution. Similarly the index improves going from a two- to three-dimensional solution. The addition of a fourth dimension, on the other hand, seems to aid the solution very little. Hence most researchers would say there are three dimensions for this set of alternatives. Finding the point where the plot of the index turns flat is often called looking for the "elbow" in the plot.

Collection of similarity/distance data can be done in many ways. A variety of means have been used for collecting similarity data (McIntyre and Ryans, 1977). The following are among the most useful:

Card sorting. A common approach used in personal interviewing is to physically produce a separate card for each possible pair of alternatives (e.g., for ten alternatives, there will be 45 cards). Subjects are then asked to go through a two-step process. First they are asked to sort the cards into a small number of piles based on the similarity between the pair of alternatives (e.g., very similar, somewhat similar, somewhat dissimilar, very dissimilar). Next, they are asked to rank pairs within each pile in terms of similarity. By picking up the cards in order (and not dropping them), the researcher obtains a ranking of all pairs of alternatives in terms of similarity.

Ratings. For situations where card sorting is impractical (e.g., mail surveys), respondents are asked to rate pairs of brands on a scale (e.g., an eight-point scale from very similar to very dissimilar). Alternatively some researchers prefer to get similarity ratings with respect to a reference brand. By rotating the reference brand, all pairs can be obtained.

Derived similarity data. In many studies similarity measures are derived from other data. For example, ratings of a series of brands on a set of attributes (e.g., rating G.E., Zenith, and other TV's on quality of picture, service, style, etc.) can form the basis of a similarity measure. The basic method of deriving similarity is to compute a distance measure which assesses the similarity of the different brand profiles on the attributes. Any of the similarity or distance measures discussed in the cluster analysis section of the previous chapter can be used, although the two most commonly used are a matching coefficient (when the attributes are categorical) or Euclidean distance (when the attribute ratings are intervally scaled).

Burden on respondents. A major problem in data collection is the burden on respondents as the number of alternatives increases (e.g., 20 alternatives requires 190 pairs). Hence many researchers assume homogeneity for a number of respondents and give different respondents different sets of alternative pairs to evaluate.

The results depend on the alternatives. The dimensions which appear are a direct function of the alternatives used in the study. Leaving out an important set of alternatives (e.g., unsweetened cereal from a study of breakfast foods) means that a key dimension (e.g., sweetness) may not appear in the results. Similarly, defining the competition too broadly will result in trivial solutions. For example, studying cereals, dinner entrees, and drinks together will generally produce three clusters of alternatives: cereals, dinner entrees, and drinks. Hence care must be taken to include (or represent) all "real" competitive alternatives if the results are to be useful.

The number of alternatives needed is substantial. The number of alternatives needed to produce a certain dimensional solution is much greater than the number of dimensions. While a variety of rules exist, a useful requirement[4] is:

$$\text{Number of alternatives} > 3(\text{number of dimensions})$$

---

[4] The reason for this requirement is that there are $\binom{n}{2} = \frac{n(n-1)}{2}$ pairs of alternatives and hence $\frac{n(n-1)}{2} - 1$ constraints on the solutions. The solution has $n(d)$ degrees of freedom. Therefore to get a constrained solution, $\frac{n(n-1)}{2} - 1 > n(d)$. Hence $n \geq 3d$ allows a safety margin to get a well-constrained solution.

This suggests (as one may have suspected) that there are an infinite number of "perfect" solutions for the three-alternative, two-dimensional example used here for pedagogical purposes.

Variety seeking is not considered.   As it is used in marketing, MDS attempts to model how a consumer chooses the best alternative at a given point in time. In doing so, it does not explicitly take into account immediate past behavior. Assuming my favorite drink were Coke, it seems likely that after 103 straight Cokes I might at least temporarily prefer something (anything) else. The notion of variety seeking is not easily incorporated into MDS models.

Some examples

The best way to get a grasp of how MDS works is to examine several examples. In doing so, this section will draw on examples both from the author's work and that of others, most notably Paul Green at Wharton who as much as anyone in the academic community is responsible for introducing MDS into marketing research. The solutions shown tend to be two-dimensional since (a) many of them actually appear to be two-dimensional and (b) it is hard to draw three-dimensional solutions on a piece of paper. Figure 17–10 comes from one of Green's earliest published examples and is based on housewives' ratings of breakfast foods. In playing the

FIGURE 17–10

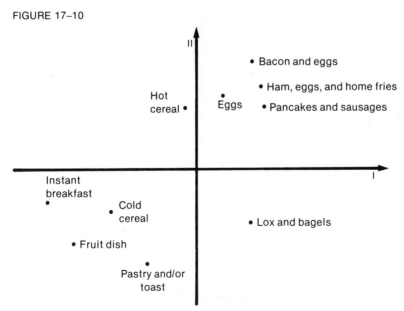

Source: Reprinted with permission of Professor Paul E. Green, Wharton School, University of Pennsylvania.

name-the-dimensions game, we might call the horizontal dimension preparation time. The vertical dimension could well be called nutritional value. On the other hand, it could also be called hot-cold. This brings up a crucial point; many names may fit the same dimension. Hence it is important to use other methods to check which name is really appropriate. Otherwise, we might spend our entire advertising budget stressing how nutritional our brand was when all consumers care about is its temperature. Assuming advertising copy matters, this is a good way to get burned.

Figure 17–11 was based on similarity judgments of 264 subjects collected in the summer of 1969. The purpose of the analysis was to confirm

FIGURE 17–11
Soft drinks: Judged similarity based MDS output

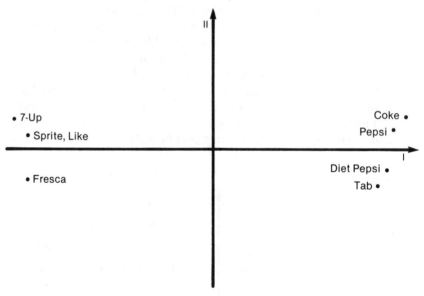

Source: Donald Lehmann, "Judged Similarity and Brand-Switching Data as Similarity Measures." Reprinted from *Journal of Marketing Research,* published by the American Marketing Association, vol. 9 (August 1972), p. 332.

the design of an experiment which included two each of the four possible combinations of lemon-lime versus cola and diet versus nondiet (Bass, Pessemier, and Lehmann, 1972). The results clearly indicate cola versus lemon-lime as the horizontal and dominant dimension. The vertical dimension is calories (diet versus nondiet) with one key exception. Like, a diet soft drink was positioned with the nondiet lemon-limes. Given this mispositioning, it is not surprising that the product failed. It is also not surprising that the product was reintroduced as Sugar Free 7-Up, making such a misperception highly unlikely.

In the same set of data, respondents were also asked to rate how similar the eight brands were to their ideal brand. Using this data, nine alternatives (the eight brands plus the ideal) were scaled. The results are shown in Figure 17–12. This figure indicates several interesting things. First, in

FIGURE 17–12
Soft drinks with ideal brand

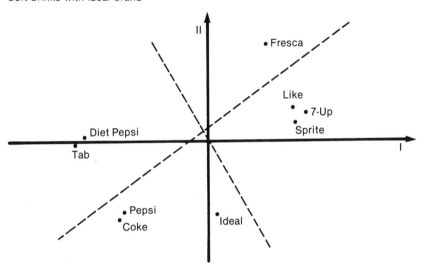

order to get a "proper" interpretation, the dimensions must be rotated to reproduce the lemon-lime versus cola and diet versus nondiet dimensions. Second, the position of the ideal brand suggests that the ideal soft drink would be cola with some lemon-lime added. This may well be the result of an averaging fallacy. Compute the average temperature that tea should be served from those who drink hot tea and those who drink iced tea and you will find that room temperature tea is "best"—not a very appealing result. On the other hand, given products like Dr. Pepper (cherry coke taste with prunes as content) and cream soda (basically vanilla soda), it is conceivable that such a product could succeed. The 1976 introduction of Pepsi-Lite was consistent with this interpretation (except that Pepsi-Lite is partly diet).

There is nothing sacred about using judged similarities as an input to MDS programs. One would expect more brand switching among similar brands. Hence by using brand-switching probabilities as similarity measures, a behavior-based map can be derived. The results in the case of the soft drink study are shown in Figure 17–13 (Lehmann, 1972). The major (horizontal) axis appears to be diet-nondiet, and the cola–lemon-lime dimension is somewhat muddled. This suggests (as in fact happened) that

FIGURE 17–13
Soft drinks based on brand switching

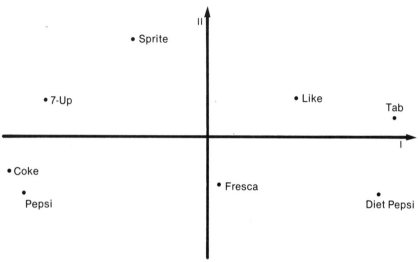

Source: Donald Lehmann, "Judged Similarity and Brand-Switching Data as Similarity Measures."
Reprinted from *Journal of Marketing Research,* published by the American Marketing Association,
vol. 9 (August 1972), p. 333.

consumers would be more likely to give up flavor than to switch from a
nondiet to a diet drink or vice versa. It also indicates that preference
dimensions may be different from the dimensions on which consumers
make similarity judgments.

For a final example, we will consider again some data from the food
consumption survey discussed frequently in this book. Specifically, the
final question dealt with how similar different pairs of foods are perceived
to be. The percent of the sample who checked each pair as similar appear
in Table 17–3. Simple inspection of the results indicates that the foods
were rated according to the four basic food groups. (Actually this result
could have been at least partially influenced by the design, where the
four-column-heading foods represent the four basic food groups.)

In order to use multidimensional scaling on the data, it was necessary
to build an index of similarity between all pairs of food. As a first pass, the
4 reference brands were ignored and the 14 other foods used as alternatives. Distances between pairs of brands were defined based on the difference in the percent who rated the brands similar to each of the four
reference brands. Hence, for example, the distance between oatmeal and
fish was derived based on the difference in the percent who rated each
similar to whole milk, beef, tomatoes, and enriched bread.[5] The resulting

---

[5] The distance from oatmeal to fish was given by $(|226 - 213| + |146 - 761| + |22 - 63| + |756 - 76|)/4$.

TABLE 17–3
Foods similar in benefits to the body

		Whole Milk	Beef	Tomatoes	Enriched bread
A.	Oatmeal	22.6%	14.6%	2.2%	75.6%
B.	Fish	21.3	76.1	6.3	7.6
C.	Rice	11.1	12.1	3.4	78.8
D.	Navy beans	10.9	59.1	8.3	37.8
E.	Chicken	14.6	82.4	3.0	11.2
F.	Potatoes	11.0	6.6	14.4	77.1
G.	Eggs	44.4	61.0	2.9	11.4
H.	Macaroni	9.6	6.9	1.3	83.3
I.	Pork and lamb	11.4	82.9	2.8	6.7
J.	String beans	7.3	9.2	73.5	6.3
K.	Carrots	17.9	5.9	72.4	6.3
L.	Bananas	24.8	11.1	43.2	24.5
M.	Peanut butter	26.0	73.8	4.0	19.9
N.	Cottage cheese	76.7	36.3	4.8	10.7

distance measures were then input to the KYST program and the output (Appendix 17–A) indicated the following:

No. dimensions	Stress
4	.010
3	.018
2	.071

This seems to suggest a three-dimensional solution, since the fourth dimension does not improve stress noticeably. Since the third dimension was not easily interpretable, the two-dimensional solution is shown as Figure 17–14.

The exact names of these dimensions are unclear, but the horizontal attribute appears to be a protein content dimension. The vertical dimension seems to separate dairy products and fruits and vegetables from meat and starch. Hence the four basic food groups do seem to be the basis of this sample's food similarity judgments.

Joint space (direct)

The approach for jointly positioning subjects and alternatives in the same map is known as joint space analysis. The direct method of getting such a space is known as unfolding and requires that respondents rank the alternatives in terms of preference. The procedure then attempts to simultaneously place both alternatives and subjects in a given dimensional space so that people are close to their preferred alternatives and far from

FIGURE 17–14

FIGURE 17–15
Hypothetical joint space result (letters = brands;
numbers = subjects)

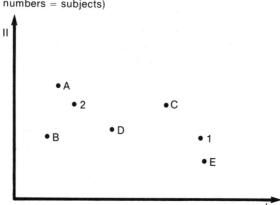

their nonpreferred alternatives. Consider the hypothetical example of Figure 17–15 where brands are represented by letters and subjects by numbers. This picture suggests that person 1 would rank E most preferred, C second, D third, and so forth. On the other hand, subject 2's preference order is presumably A, then B, then D, and so forth.

This unfolding type of procedure is very appealing. Unfortunately the results tend to be disappointing or confusing as well as very unstable. For these reasons many researchers do not employ this approach. In short, don't use unfolding unless you are (a) well versed in scaling and (b) use a second method to check the results.

Joint space (indirect)

The indirect approach to joint space analysis requires that the positions of alternatives on the attributes be established as a first step. As the second step, preference data is gathered and then subjects are overlayed on the picture based on their preference ranking. The most commonly used procedure of this type is PREFMAP, which places subjects on the map in four ways. The two commonly used ways are to represent subjects as vectors (Phase III) where the further along the vector a brand appears, the more preferred it is or as an actual ideal point (Phase IV).

Other approaches

There are a large number of alternative scaling procedures (Table 17–4). One of the most appealing is INSCALE, which assumes all sub-

TABLE 17–4
Approaches to multidimensional scaling

Type	Input data	Output data	Major available computer programs
Simple space	Similarity judgments	Positions of alternatives on attributes	TORSCA KYST
Joint space: Direct	Preference rankings	1. Positions of alternatives on attributes 2. Location of respondents in terms of their ideal alternative	MDPREF
Joint space: Indirect	1. Positions of the alternatives on attributes 2. Preference ranking	1. Positions of alternatives on attributes 2. Location of respondents in terms of their ideal alternative	PREFMAP

jects have the same perceptions but weight the dimensions differently. The derived weights can then be used to cluster subjects. Numerous other approaches (e.g., ALLSCALE) also exist. The key point for a typical user is to find out (*a*) if what is available will do, and (*b*) if not, to find someone who knows enough to help.

THE DISCRIMINANT ANALYSIS APPROACH

An alternative way to generate a perceptual map is to use discriminant analysis. The basic input data is direct ratings of the alternatives on a set of prespecified attributes. Rather than plotting the results directly, however, multiple group discriminant analysis (the canonical correlate type) is used to generate compound dimensions which explain the ratings. The trick is to generate input data by using the brands as groups (Table 17–5). The brands thus appear as the groups in the output. The location of the

TABLE 17–5
Input format for discriminant analysis approach to deriving attribute models

		Rating on the prespecified attribute			
		1	2	...	c
Group 1:					
Subject	Ratings of alternative 1				
1					
2					
.					
.					
.					
n					
Group 2:					
Subject	Ratings of alternative 2				
1					
2					
.					
.					
.					
n					
Group g:					
Subject	Ratings of alternative g				
1					
2					
.					
.					
.					
n					

brands on the attributes is given by the group centroids (means on the discriminant functions). The discriminant functions themselves are combinations of the original dimensions. These compound dimensions are relatively easy to name, since how closely related each of the original attributes is to each of the derived dimensions is part of the output. Since they are totally dependent on the prespecified attributes, however, discriminant analysis only simplifies the direct rating approach and does not deduce unknown dimensions.

Some of the best examples of this approach appear in the work of Richard Johnson (Johnson, 1971). One of his classic examples involved brands of beer. The two-dimensional solution consisted of a premium-local dimension and a heavy (Budweiser) versus light (Miller) dimension. Interestingly, in terms of some ingredients, Miller is heavier than Budweiser. The message here is that "there is naught but thinking makes it so." If you advertise with the Clydesdales, Ed McMahon, and a squat brown bottle you can convince people you're heavier than a "champaign of bottle beer" which is sold in a tall, clear bottle. Another classic example of Johnson's (1970) involved the 1968 presidential campaign. The two-dimensional picture which included both cadidates and voter segments provides an interesting vantage point for studying the strategies of the major candidates.

A soft drink example

Another major user of this approach is Edgar Pessemier, who has developed a way that discriminant analysis can be used to map a single respondent (Pessemier, 1973). One of his applications was to the soft drink experiment previously discussed in this chapter (Lehmann and Pessemier, 1973). The results can be viewed in three parts: the basic map, the relation of the original attributes to the derived dimensions, and (by means of PREFMAP) the location of ten major segments in the derived space.

Basic map.   The basic map appears as Figure 17–16. This basic map confirms the results obtained by using multidimensional scaling on the switching data (Figure 17–13).

Relation of the original attributes to the derived dimensions.   In order to represent the relation of the original attributes to derived dimensions, the correlations between the attributes and dimensions can be used to plot the attributes in the space[6] (Figure 17–17). These attributes clearly indicate the vertical axis is flavor (lemon-lime versus cola). The horizontal axis is highly correlated with two attributes: calories (diet versus nondiet) and

---

[6] This is done by using a vector to represent the original attributes. The length of the vector is proportional to the ability of the two derived dimensions to explain the original attributes. The correlation between the attribute and the discriminant functions is used to determine the direction of the vector by using a form of $r = \cos(\text{angle})$.

FIGURE 17–16
Basic map

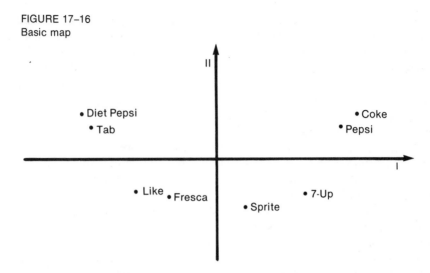

popularity with others. It is the appearance of the popularity with others attribute which is most surprising. This suggests that subjects may have been at least as concerned about the general acceptability of their choice (or its availability) as they were about its caloric content.

Joint space map. Subjects were grouped into ten major segments based on their frequency of purchase of the eight brands. The segments

FIGURE 17–17
Relation of the original attributes to the discriminant functions

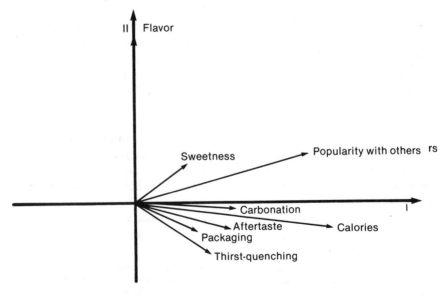

were then overlayed on the basic map by means of PREFMAP (Phase III). The segments (indicated by the letters) and their sizes are shown in Figure 17–18. For example, the biggest segment (9) appears to prefer Coke and then Pepsi. These results clearly indicate that Coke and Pepsi

FIGURE 17–18
PREFMAP results

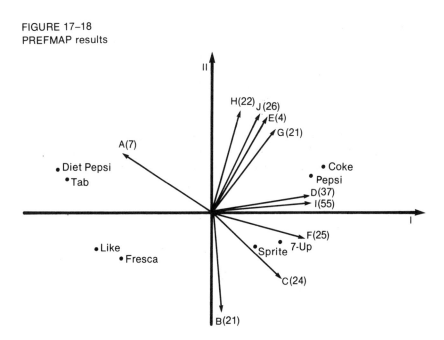

will do well (they are the two biggest sellers) and that Like is left out in the cold.

APPLICATIONS

Attribute-based market maps can be used for a variety of purposes. Among the uses are new product idea generation, potential estimation, and advertising/promotional strategy selection. To see how attribute models might be used in these ways, consider the hypothetical example of Figure 17–19 where the numbers represent segments and the letters represent existing alternatives. Quick perusal of this graph suggests that alternative B is in excellent shape, having segment 1 representing 30 percent of the total market essentially to itself. By contrast, alternative A seems to appeal mainly to segment 6 with 10 percent of the market. To see how this picture could be used to simulate the results of marketing decisions, consider the following two problems:

New product identification

Assume you were assigned to develop a new product for this market. Technical/production problems aside, the following two major alternatives exist:

Target on segment 2 by making a product which is a "2" on attribute I and a "2.7" on attribute II. Since E, C, and D are all somewhat removed from segment 2, it appears there is a reasonable chance of capturing the bulk of this segment and hence close to 20 percent of the market. (Also, since the product lies between E and C, it is probably a feasible product to produce.)

Target on segment 1 by making a product which is "3" on attribute I and "4.5" on attribute II. The advantage of this is that this segment has 30 percent of the market. The disadvantage is that B already is there, and if they are a strong competitor, you are going to be in a big war if you target here.

FIGURE 17–19
Hypothetical joint space configuration

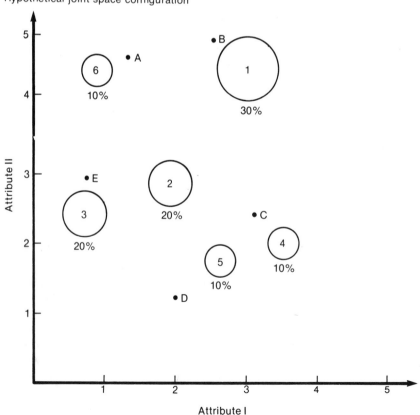

Now complicate the problem somewhat by assuming your company already makes C, D, and E. If we still go for segment 2, we will largely canibalize sales of our own products. Hence segment 1 looks more appealing. Actually, however, the decision about which (if any) to produce depends heavily on likely competitors' actions and reactions. If we "attack" alternative B, the makers of alternative B may well attack us by going for segment 2. On the other hand, if we fail to attack, there is no guarantee that competitors will do likewise. What the map does is provide a good focus for highlighting some implications of these strategic decisions.

Repositioning

Assume you were put in charge of alternative D. After updating your resume in anticipation of possible termination, you might consider trying to reposition the product. While many repositionings are theoretically possible, moving D up on attribute II to appeal to segment 2 seems most promising. This could be done by changing the actual product. Alternatively or additionally, advertising could stress that "product D is full of attribute II." If product D is an old brand, "new" product D with attribute II added might be introduced.

Limitations

The point of the two previous examples is to suggest that attribute-based maps can serve as market simulators for the purpose of considering various product policy and promotional strategy decisions. In such use, however, it is important to recognize some of the major limitations of these maps:

Their reliability is not perfect.   In order to use such maps, it is important to have the basic dimensions, and so forth, constant over time. Yet changes in the market often make assumptions of constant maps over time untenable.

The dimensions must be usable.   Often dimensions appear which are either uninterpretable or so compound/abstract that it is unclear exactly what they are, much less how we give a product more of them (e.g., what gives a toothpaste more sex appeal?).

Many products are infeasible.   The general state of technology as well as company strengths and weaknesses often preclude many "obvious" strategies. (While a segment usually exists which wants a low-cost, high-quality product, producing one may prove an elusive goal.)

The rational model may be wrong.   Choice may not be determined by this mapping/trade-off type of decision making. Hence predictions of behavior based on this type of model can be quite deceptive.

The major uses of mapping models are hence twofold. First, they are very useful for generating hypotheses/ideas (which then should be further investigated). Even small samples (i.e., 15 office workers) occasionally produce interesting results. Second, these maps are extremely useful communication devices. They often serve to get a room full of people to agree on a general plan of attack and this agreement, sometimes more than the plan, can lead to improved performance.

CONJOINT ANALYSIS

An approach similar in spirit but very different in application to attribute mapping is conjoint analysis. This procedure assumes that both the attributes and the positions of the alternatives on the attributes are known. The procedure then attempts to attach values (utilities) to the levels of each of the various attributes. Input data is typically rankings of various combinations of attribute levels, and the output is the utility of the different levels on the various attributes. This can be best seen in terms of an example.

Assume we are interested in cars and believe two attributes—fuel economy and trunk space—are the key attributes. If there are four levels of fuel economy and three of trunk space, there are 12 combinations of attribute levels. Assume the respondent has a value (utility) for each of the possible 12 combinations. Unfortunately, we suspect the respondent cannot/will not accurately give us those utilities in response to a direct question. However, we feel that the respondent would be willing to rank the combinations from most to least preferred. Hence as input data, I could collect the data by asking respondents to rank order the 12 combinations of attributes (Table 17–6). By observing how they trade off the

TABLE 17–6
Assumed underlying (unmeasured) utility for various combinations

Usable trunk space (cu. ft.)	Fuel economy (mpg)			
	11–15	16–20	21–25	26–30
7–10	1.4	1.8	2.1	2.6
11–14	1.5	1.9	2.2	2.7
15–18	1.6	2.0	2.3	2.8

attributes (Table 17–7) I attempt to deduce their underlying utilities for the attribute levels.

Computationally, utilities are derived by means of a computer algorithm. The most commonly used algorithm is MONANOVA (Kruskal,

TABLE 17–7
Preference ranking input data for conjoint analysis

Usable trunk space (cu. ft.)	Fuel economy (mpg)			
	11–15	16–20	21–25	26–30
7–10	12	10	6	3
11–14	11	9	5	2
15–18	8	7	4	1

1965) which assumes that overall utility for an alternative is an additive function (with no interactions) of the attribute level utilities:

$$\text{Utility for an alternative} = \sum_{\substack{\text{all} \\ \text{attributes}}} \left(\begin{array}{c} \text{Utility for level of the} \\ \text{alternative on an attribute} \end{array} \right)$$

In this algorithm utility values are chosen to produce overall utilities which match the original preference ranking. Logically, this is done by seeing which attribute the subject is most unwilling to give up and assigning it an accordingly higher utility. It is also possible and in some ways preferable to use dummy variable regression analysis to get estimates of the utilities of the various characteristics (see Appendix 17–B).

In the car example, a subject whose first three ranked preferences are 26–30 mpg for 15–18, 10–14, and 7–10 cubic feet of trunk space respectively is indicating a considerably higher value for fuel economy than for trunk space. The subject's utility levels for each of the attributes might be those of Table 17–8.

TABLE 17–8
Output of conjoint
analysis

Fuel economy level (mpg)	Utility
11–15	.5
16–20	.9
21–25	1.2
26–30	1.7

Trunk space level	Utility
7–10	.9
11–14	1.0
15–18	1.1

The resulting output of Table 17–8 can be used directly to reconstruct the utilities of Table 17–6. (For example, the utility of a car with fuel economy 11–15 mpg and trunk space of 7–10 cubic feet would be .5 + .9 = 1.4.) In this hypothetical example the reconstruction is without error, something which almost never occurs in practice. In addition to using the derived utilities of the levels to estimate the overall utility of existing and potential new products, the derived utilities on the levels are also used to indicate the relative importance of the attributes. Most commonly, the range of utility levels on an attribute is used as a measure of attribute importance. In the car example, the importance of fuel economy would be estimated as 1.2 = 1.7 − .5 while that of trunk space as .2 = 1.1 − .9. Hence this hypothetical respondent is apparently more concerned about economy than carrying capacity.

Pros and cons

The advantages of conjoint measurement include the following:

The results are easy to interpret, and the key attributes readily established. (The range of the utilities on an attribute is typically taken as a measure of attribute importance.)

The attributes can be categorical (e.g., colors, styles, etc.) *as well as intervally scaled constructs.*

The major disadvantages are as follows:

The relevant attributes and key levels must be known in advance. This means not just the physical attributes which are important to engineers but also the attributes consumers actually use to make decisions need to be specified. Choosing the correct levels may seem trivial but the author encountered one study involving prices of 5, 7, and 9 when the actual price tended to be less than 2. This cast serious doubt on the interpretation of the whole study. Also the attributes should probably be objective (e.g., horsepower) rather than subjective (e.g., power) whenever possible.[7]

The additive utility function may not be appropriate. At least for objects of art, one could question whether the "whole is the sum of its parts."

The approach gets messy with many attributes and levels. Since the alternatives are essentially factorial combinations of the attributes, the number of possible alternatives quickly gets out of hand. This has led researchers like Green to resort to suing orthogonal subsets of the

---

[7] It may well be that some innovative results can be generated by using soft attributes but to date this has not widely been tried.

possible alternatives (Green, 1974). As long as there is no complex interaction effect, this approach works quite well. Another approach is the pairwise trade-off matrix approach of Johnson (1974). This approach consists of getting respondents to make trade-offs in terms of two attributes at a time. In the case of the car example, this means ranking the 12 combinations of fuel economy and trunk space in the matrix, then ranking the possible combinations of fuel economy and price, and so forth, until each pair of attributes has been presented. The results can produce both utilities on individual attributes (in Johnson's model, utilities are multiplicative rather than additive) and simple one-way interactions.

Uses for conjoint analysis are still being explored. At present its major use is for estimating potential for various new product possibilities.

An example

The example presented here is due to Green who has also applied the technique to air carrier selection, tire replacement decisions, and bar

TABLE 17–9
Data collected

		Product			Respondent's evaluation (rank number)
Package design	Brand name	Price	Good Housekeeping seal?	Money-back guarantee?	
A	K2R	1.19	No	No	13
A	Glory	1.39	No	Yes	11
A	Bissell	1.59	Yes	No	17
B	K2R	1.39	Yes	Yes	2
B	Glory	1.59	No	No	14
B	Bissell	1.19	No	No	3
C	K2R	1.59	No	Yes	12
C	Glory	1.19	Yes	No	7
C	Bissell	1.39	No	No	9
A	K2R	1.59	Yes	No	18
A	Glory	1.19	No	Yes	8
A	Bissell	1.39	No	No	15
B	K2R	1.19	No	No	4
B	Glory	1.39	Yes	No	6
B	Bissell	1.59	No	Yes	5
C	K2R	1.39	No	No	10
C	Glory	1.59	No	No	16
C	Bissell	1.19	Yes	Yes	1

soaps (Green and Wind, 1975). It involves preference for spot removers for upholstery and carpets. The following attributes were analyzed:

Package design (A, B, C)
Brand names (K2R, Glory, Bissell)
Price ($1.19, $1.39, $1.59)
Good Housekeeping seal (yes or no)
Money-back guarantee (yes or no)

Since there are $3 \times 3 \times 3 \times 2 \times 2 = 108$ possible combinations, it seemed infeasible to test all possible products. Hence an orthogonal array of 18 combinations was used (translation: a representative subset of the original 108 products was selected). The data from one subject appears in Table 17–9. The resulting utilities appear as Table 17–10.

TABLE 17–10
Utilities for spot remover attributes

Feature	Utility
Package design:	
A	.1
B	1.0
C	.6
Brand name:	
K2R	.3
Glory	.2
Bissell	.5
Price:	
1.19	1.0
1.39	.7
1.59	.1
Good Housekeeping seal:	
Yes	.3
No	.2
Money-back guarantee:	
Yes	.7
No	.2

Source: Paul Green and Yoram Wind, "New Ways to Measure Consumers' Judgments," *Harvard Business Review*, vol. 53 (July–August, 1975), p. 110, Copyright © 1975 by the President and Fellows of Harvard College; all rights reserved.

The results indicate a strong preference for package design B and (surprise) a low price. A money-back guarantee also seems to help, while the brand name and Good Housekeeping seal seem to be relatively unimportant. The results are useful for comparing the relative utility of various existing and new products.

SUMMARY

This chapter has introduced a collection of techniques aimed at aiding understanding of consumers' thinking. These models suggest that individuals process information in choosing among a set of alternatives. For many frequently purchased products, however, it is unlikely that consumers actively process information about many brands on many attributes before making a choice. Rather their behavior is likely to be relatively routinized. Hence these models are useful for explaining preference formation and indicating likely long-run equilibrium positions but are not necessarily good models of repetitive decision making.

In-depth knowledge requires considerable additional investigation. A good starting point is provided by Green and Wind (1975). A serious student of these procedures, however, will want to consult an informal trilogy: Green and Carmone (1970), Green and Rao (1972), and Green and Wind (1973), as well as some of the works of Carroll (e.g., Carroll and Chang, 1970) and others at Bell Labs. It is difficult to gauge the practical utility of these techniques. There is no question that the techniques (a) have been used in the real world and (b) have been involved in decisions which turned out both well and badly. Suffice it to say that these techniques (a) have generated a lot of computer output, (b) have not revolutionized marketing, and (c) have the potential to be useful in some situations.

PROBLEMS

1. Assume you were brand manager for Lay's potato chips. Also assume people make choices based on multiattribute models. What data would you collect and how would you analyze it if you had—
   a. A budget of $10,000 and two months?
   b. A budget of $100,000 and four months?
   c. A budget of $250,000 and eight months?
2. Assume you had the following distance data:

Object	Object					
	1	2	3	4	5	6
1		4	6	5	6.5	3.5
2			4.5	6	9	8
3				3.5	7	8
4					4	6
5						4.5
6						

What is the underlying configuration? (Hint: Try graphing by hand.)

3. Your boss indicates an interest in conjoint analysis, which the boss says is "better than MDS." Outline a 15-minute talk you would give to explain the two techniques and their relations.

4. A series of subjects rated soft drinks on the following:
   1. Carbonation.
   2. Calories.
   3. Sweetness.
   4. Thirst quenching.
   5. Popularity with others.

   These ratings were on 1–6 scales where 6 represented a rating of very high and 1 a rating of very low. They also rated importances of the attributes on a scale of 1–6 where 6 represents very important. Given the following data for two individuals:

Respondent	Attribute	Importance	Coke	7 Up	Tab	Like	Pepsi	Sprite	Diet Pepsi	Fresca	"Ideal"
A	1	3	5	3	2	2	6	5	3	4	3
	2	2	3	5	2	4	6	2	6	5	3
	3	2	6	5	6	5	6	5	5	5	4
	4	1	3	6	5	5	1	4	5	3	6
	5	6	5	5	2	4	4	6	2	1	6
	Preference ranking		2	5	7	6	1	4	3	8	
B	1	3	5	4	2	2	4	4	3	3	3
	2	2	4	4	4	4	4	3	3	5	2
	3	2	3	4	5	4	3	4	5	3	4
	4	2	4	5	5	4	4	4	4	3	6
	5	3	5	5	2	5	3	4	3	3	4
	Preference ranking		6	3	8	4	2	1	7	5	

   a. Using the attitude model, $\sum_1^5$ (importance) · |Brand rating − Ideal|, calculate the predicted ranking of the 8 brands and compare it with the actual ranking.

   b. If you drop the ideal point and importances from the model, what are the results?

5. Professional launderers prefer different detergents for different types of clothing. The preferred level of "harshness" and "color fastness" and also the fraction of each type of business are as follows:

Clothing	Share of Total	Preferred level	
		Harshness	Color fastness
Heavy whites	50	1	5
Fine whites	10	5	5
Heavy colors	20	2	1
Fine colors	20	5	1

The four present brands have the following properties:

Brand	Harshness	Color fastness
A	2	4
B	4	5
C	2	2
D	4	2

a. Estimate the share of sales of each brand by assuming—
   (1) Distance to brand = $\sum |\text{actual} - \text{preferred level}|$
   (2) $\text{Share}_j = (1/\text{distance to } j) \Big/ \sum_{i=1}^{4} (1/\text{distance to } i)$

b. Estimate the share of sales which a new "general-purpose" detergent might achieve if it had a harshness level of 3 and a color-fastness level of 3.

c. What does your model assume? What does your model ignore? Can you think of a new model which you "like better" for addressing question (b)?

6. Assume you had to design the data collection instrument to do conjoint analysis in a situation where there were two attributes, both with three levels. What would the instrument be?

7. Assume you were to analyze the results of a conjoint analysis on a single subject (the chief executive officer) for type of desk preferred. Two attributes were employed: size (regular, massive) and material (plastic, metal, wood). The six combinations were as follows:

	Size	Material
A	Regular	Plastic
B	Regular	Metal
C	Regular	Wood
D	Massive	Plastic
E	Massive	Metal
F	Massive	Wood

The data were ranked from most to least preferred, as F, E, C, B, D, A. Try to deduce the boss's utility function.

8. Assume you were to design a conjoint study on home stereo systems. How would you proceed?

BIBLIOGRAPHY

Bass, Frank M.; Pessemier, Edgar A.; and Lehmann, Donald R. "An Experimental Study of Relationships between Attitudes, Brand Preference, and Choice." *Behavioral Science,* vol. 17 (November 1972), pp. 532–41.

Beckwith, Neil E., and Lehmann, Donald R. "The Importance of Halo Effects in Multi-Attribute Attitude Models." *Journal of Marketing Research,* vol. 12 (August 1975), pp. 265–75.

―――― and ――――. "The Importance of Differential Weights in Multiple Attribute Models of Consumer Attitude." *Journal of Marketing Research,* vol. 10 (May 1973), pp. 141–45.

Carroll, J. Douglas, and Chang, Jih-Jie. "Analysis of Individual Differences in Multidimensional Scaling Via an N-Way Generalization of 'Eckart-Young' Decomposition." *Psychometrika,* vol. 35 (September 1970), pp. 283–19.

Fishbein, Martin. "Attitude and the Prediction of Behavior." *Readings in Attitude Theory and Measurement,* pp. 477–92. Edited by Martin Fishbein. New York: Wiley, 1967.

Green, Paul E. "On the Analysis of Interactions in Marketing Research Data." *Journal of Marketing Research,* vol. 10 (November 1973), pp. 410–20.

――――. "On the Design of Choice Experiments Involving Multifactor Alternatives." *Journal of Consumer Research,* vol. 1 (September 1974), pp. 61–68.

――――, and Carmone, Frank J. *Multidimensional Scaling and Related Techniques in Marketing Analysis.* Boston: Allyn & Bacon, 1970.

――――, and Rao, Vithala R. *Applied Multidimensional Scaling: A Comparison of Approaches and Algorithms.* New York: Holt, Rinehart and Winston, 1972.

――――, and Wind, Yoram. "New Way to Measure Consumers' Judgments." *Harvard Business Review,* vol. 53 (July–August 1975), pp. 107–17.

――――, and ――――. *Multiattribute Decisions in Marketing, a Measurement Approach.* Hinsdale, Ill.: Dryden, 1973.

Johnson, Richard M. "Trade-Off Analysis of Consumer Durables." *Journal of Marketing Research,* vol. 11 (May 1974), pp. 121–27.

――――. "Market Segmentation: A Strategic Management Tool." *Journal of Marketing Research,* vol. 8 (February 1971), pp. 13–18.

――――."Political Segmentation." *Marketing Review,* vol. 25 (February 1970), pp. 20–24.

Kruskal, J. B. "Analysis of Factorial Experiments by Estimating Monotone Transformations of the Data." *Journal of the Royal Statistical Society,* series B, vol. 27 (1965), pp. 251–63.

————. "Multidimensional Scaling by Optimizing Goodness of Fit to a Non-metric Hypothesis." *Psychometrika*, vol. 29 (March 1964), pp. 1–27.

————. "Nonmetric Multidimensional Scaling: A Numerical Method." *Psychometrika*, vol. 29 (June 1964), pp. 115–29.

Lancaster, Kelvin J. "A New Approach to Consumer Theory." *Journal of Political Economy*, vol. 74 (April 1966), pp. 132–57.

Lehmann, Donald R. "Judged Similarity and Brand-Switching Data as Similarity Measures." *Journal of Marketing Research*, vol. 9 (August 1972), pp. 331–34.

————. "Television Show Preference: Application of a Choice Model." *Journal of Marketing Research*, vol. 8 (February 1971), pp. 47–55.

————, and Pessemier, Edgar A. "Predicted Probability of Brand Choice Market Segments and Discriminant Attribute Configurations in Joint Space Market Analyses." Presented at Annual Meeting, Operations Research Society of America, Milwaukee, May 1973.

McIntyre, Shelby H., and Ryans, Adrian B. "Time and Accuracy Measures for Alternative Multidimensional Scaling Data Collection Methods: Some Additional Results." *Journal of Marketing Research*, vol. 14 (November 1977), pp. 607–10.

Neidell, Lester A. "Procedures for Obtaining Similarities Data." *Journal of Marketing Research*, vol. 9 (August 1972), pp. 335–37.

Pessemier, Edgar A. "Single Subject Discriminant Configurations." Institute Paper #406, Institute for Research in the Behavioral, Economic, and Management Sciences, Krannert Graduate School of Industrial Administration, Purdue University, 1973.

Rosenberg, M. J. "Cognitive Structure and Attitudinal Affect." *Journal of Abnormal and Social Psychology*, vol. 53 (November 1956), pp. 367–72.

Shepard, Roger N. "The Analysis of Proximities: Multidimensional Scaling with an Unknown Distance Function I." *Psychometrika*, vol. 27 (June 1962), pp. 125–39.

————. "The Analysis of Proximities: Multidimensional Scaling with an Unknown Distance Function II." *Psychometrika*, vol. 27 (September 1962), pp. 219–46.

Steffler, Volney. "Market Structure Studies: New Products for Old Markets and New Markets (Foreign) for Old Products." In *Applications of the Sciences in Marketing Management*, pp. 251–68. Edited by Frank M. Bass, Charles W. King, and Edgar A. Pessemier. New York: Wiley, 1968.

Winer, B. J. *Statistical Principles in Experimental Design.* New York: McGraw-Hill, 1971.

APPENDIX 17–A: SAMPLE KYST OUTPUT

```
DIMMAX=2,DIMMIN=2,DIMDIF=1

SFORM1,R=2.0

REGRESSION=ASCENDING

NOCARDS,PRINT=DATA,PRINT=HISTORY,PRINT=NODISTANCES

PLOT=SCATTER=SOME,PLOT=CONFIGURATION=ALL

COORDINATES=ROTATE

ITERATIONS=50,STRMIN=.01

SRATST=.999

TORSCA,PRE-ITERATIONS=1

LOWERHALFMATRIX,DIAGONAL=ABSENT

DATA

DERIVED PROXIMITIES,14 FOOD ITEMS
 14  1  1

(13F4.3)

COMPUTE
```

I	J	DATA	WGHT	GP	NO		I	J	DATA	WGHT	GP	NO		I	J	DATA	WGHT	GP	NO
2	1	0.337	1.00	1	1.		11	6	0.341	1.00	1	51.							
3	1	0.046	1.00	1	2.		11	7	0.391	1.00	1	52.							
3	2	0.371	1.00	1	3.		11	8	0.394	1.00	1	53.							
4	1	0.251	1.00	1	4.		11	9	0.384	1.00	1	54.							
4	2	0.149	1.00	1	5.		12	1	0.039	1.00	1	55.							
4	3	0.233	1.00	1	6.		12	2	0.245	1.00	1	56.							
5	1	0.352	1.00	1	7.		12	3	0.306	1.00	1	57.							
5	2	0.050	1.00	1	8.		12	4	0.272	1.00	1	58.							
5	3	0.355	1.00	1	9.		12	5	0.275	1.00	1	59.							
5	4	0.147	1.00	1	10.		12	6	0.338	1.00	1	60.							
6	1	0.083	1.00	1	11.		12	7	0.249	1.00	1	61.							
6	2	0.394	1.00	1	12.		12	8	0.307	1.00	1	62.							
6	3	0.245	1.00	1	13.		12	9	0.300	1.00	1	63.							
6	4	0.046	1.00	1	14.		12	10	0.359	1.00	1	64.							
6	5	0.392	1.00	1	15.		13	1	0.168	1.00	1	65.							
7	1	0.332	1.00	1	16.		13	2	0.149	1.00	1	66.							
7	2	0.114	1.00	1	17.		13	3	0.300	1.00	1	67.							
7	3	0.375	1.00	1	18.		13	3	0.054	1.00	1	68.							
7	4	0.168	1.00	1	19.		13	4	0.130	1.00	1	69.							
7	5	0.129	1.00	1	20.		13	5	0.374	1.00	1	70.							
8	1	0.413	1.00	1	21.		13	6	0.074	1.00	1	71.							
8	2	0.073	1.00	1	22.		13	7	0.102	1.00	1	72.							
8	3	0.404	1.00	1	23.		13	8	0.374	1.00	1	73.							
8	4	0.033	1.00	1	24.		13	9	0.095	1.00	1	74.							
8	5	0.265	1.00	1	25.		13	10	0.414	1.00	1	75.							
8	6	0.386	1.00	1	26.		13	11	0.395	1.00	1	76.							
8	7	0.052	1.00	1	27.		13	11	0.269	1.00	1	77.							
8	9	0.406	1.00	1	28.		13	12	0.358	1.00	1	78.							
9	1	0.372	1.00	1	29.		14	1	0.250	1.00	1	79.							
9	2	0.053	1.00	1	30.		14	2	0.398	1.00	1	80.							
9	3	0.360	1.00	1	31.		14	3	0.298	1.00	1	81.							
9	4	0.152	1.00	1	32.		14	4	0.277	1.00	1	82.							
9	5	0.021	1.00	1	33.		14	5	0.428	1.00	1	83.							
9	6	0.397	1.00	1	34.		14	6	0.149	1.00	1	84.							
9	7	0.149	1.00	1	35.		14	7	0.431	1.00	1	85.							
9	8	0.390	1.00	1	36.		14	8	0.295	1.00	1	86.							
9	9	0.401	1.00	1	37.		14	9	0.422	1.00	1	87.							
10	2	0.371	1.00	1	38.		14	10	0.403	1.00	1	88.							
10	3	0.371	1.00	1	39.		14	11	0.323	1.00	1	89.							
10	4	0.373	1.00	1	40.		14	12	0.245	1.00	1	90.							
10	5	0.388	1.00	1	41.		14	13				91.							
10	6	0.409	1.00	1	42.														
10	7	0.383	1.00	1	43.														
10	8	0.372	1.00	1	44.														
10	9	0.383	1.00	1	45.														
11	1	0.388	1.00	1	46.														
11	2	0.409	1.00	1	47.														
11	3	0.383	1.00	1	48.														
11	4	0.387	1.00	1	49.														
11	5	0.386	1.00	1	50.														

DERIVED PROXIMITIES,14 FOOD ITEMS

INITIAL CONFIGURATION COMPUTATION   NO. PTS.= 14   DIM= 2

PRE-ITERATION   STRESS

    0   0.1462
    1   0.1437

MAXIMUM NUMBER OF PRE-ITERATIONS 1, REACHED.

THE BEST INITIAL CONFIGURATION OF 14 POINTS IN 2 DIMENSIONS HAS STRESS 0.144 FORMULA 1

HISTORY OF COMPUTATION. N= 14.   THERE ARE 91 DATA VALUES, SPLIT INTO 1 LISTS.   DIMENSION = 2

ITERATION	STRESS	SRAT	SRATAV	CAGRGL	COSAV	ACSAV	SFGR	STEP
0	0.141	0.800	0.800	0.000	0.000	0.000	0.0037	0.0130
1	0.136	0.967	0.852	0.987	0.651	0.651	0.0034	0.0349
2	0.125	0.917	0.873	0.943	0.844	0.844	0.0027	0.1143
3	0.110	0.876	0.874	-0.278	0.103	0.471	0.0023	0.0955
4	0.092	0.840	0.863	0.284	0.223	0.348	0.0019	0.1147
5	0.089	0.967	0.896	-0.624	-0.336	0.530	0.0027	0.0601
6	0.076	0.851	0.881	0.017	-0.103	0.192	0.0008	0.0462
7	0.072	0.955	0.905	-0.038	-0.060	0.090	0.0006	0.0401
8	0.073	1.011	0.939	-0.785	-0.539	0.549	0.0009	0.0174
9	0.071	0.773	0.950	0.856	0.382	0.752	0.0003	0.0192
10	0.071	1.004	0.968	-0.870	-0.444	0.830	0.0005	0.0065
11	0.071	0.994	0.977	0.981	0.496	0.930	0.0002	0.0076
12	0.071	0.999	0.984	-0.755	-0.330	0.815	0.0001	0.0027
13	0.071	1.000	0.989	0.281	0.073	0.462	0.0000	0.0018
14	0.071	1.000	0.993	0.830	0.573	0.705	0.0000	0.0028
15	0.071	1.000	0.995	0.294	0.388	0.433	0.0000	0.0037
16	0.071	1.000	0.997	-0.719	-0.342	0.622	0.0001	0.0015
17	0.071	1.000	0.998	0.978	0.529	0.857	0.0000	0.0018
18	0.071	1.000	0.998	-0.781	-0.335	0.807	0.0000	0.0006
19	0.071	1.000	0.999	0.856	0.451	0.839	0.0000	0.0007
20	0.071	1.000	0.999	0.108	0.224	0.356	0.0000	0.0007

MINIMUM WAS ACHIEVED

THE FINAL CONFIGURATION HAS BEEN ROTATED TO PRINCIPAL COMPONENTS.

THE FINAL CONFIGURATION OF 14 POINTS IN 2 DIMENSIONS HAS STRESS 0.071 FORMULA 1

ABEL FCR CONFIGURATION PLOTS

FINAL CONFIGURATION

		1	2
A	1	0.808	-0.491
B	2	-0.812	-0.222
C	3	0.911	-0.512
D	4	-0.148	-0.462
E	5	-0.805	-0.372
F	6	1.037	-0.362
G	7	-0.855	-0.004
H	8	1.040	-0.576
I	9	-0.863	-0.403
J	10	0.476	1.226
K	11	0.451	1.255

DERIVED PROXIMITIES,14 FOOD ITEMS

_____ APPENDIX 17–B _____

DERIVATION OF ATTRIBUTE UTILITIES IN CONJOINT ANALYSIS

Conjoint analysis really consists of two stages. The first stage is data collection which attempts to efficiently uncover utilities for attribute levels using as few alternatives as possible. The "trick" to doing this is to understand experimental design well, and to have a copy of a book such as Winer (1973) readily available.

The second stage of conjoint analysis involves estimating the utilities for each level of each attribute. This is often done by use of MONANOVA. What MONANOVA does is to proceed in two basic steps. First, an initial solution is produced which assumes the ranking or rating data for the combinations can be treated as intervally scaled. Second, the intervally scaled assumption is relaxed and the initial solution is iteratively adjusted to make the stated ranking and predicted ranking match as closely as possible.

While the MONANOVA approach is preferable, it is possible to quickly estimate utilities by less specialized procedures. For example, it is possible to estimate utilities by means of dummy variable regression. In order to do this, the attribute levels are converted into a series of dummy variables. The stated ranking is then inverted so that a big number indicates high utility. For example, the cleaning product example of Green and Wind (1975) can be converted to a regression problem with 18 observations (one for each alternative) and 8 dummy variables (Table 17B–1). By running a regression on this data, utilities can be estimated which are essentially the first step in MONANOVA. (Notice also that if the data is sufficient, dummy variables representing interactions can also be created and estimated.)

In the special case when the alternatives are derived according to a full factorial design or an orthogonal array, it is possible to estimate the utilities by hand calculation. The steps to be followed are as follows:

1. Estimate the average value of the dependent variable for each level of each attribute. For example, package design A appears in 6 combinations and the average score is given by $(6 + 8 + 2 + 1 + 11 + 4)/6 = 5.33$ (Table 17B–2).
2. If you wish to scale utilities on a particular scale, convert the average scores to a utility scale. In this case, the averages were rescaled from their range of 5.3–13.33 to a range of .1–1.0.[8] The results appear in Table 17B–3, along with the results presented by Green and Wind (1975). Notice the close but imperfect correspondence between the two results, especially in terms of the range of utilities on each attribute.

_____
[8] This was by linear interpolation so that $5.33 = .1$, $6.22 = .2$, $7.11 = .3$, and so forth.

TABLE 17B-1
Dummy coding scheme

| Dependent variable (19-ranking) | Package design | | | | Price | | Good Housekeeping seal | Money-back guarantee |
	A	B	K2R	Glory	1.19	1.39		
6	1	0	1	0	1	0	0	0
8	1	0	0	1	0	1	0	1
2	1	0	0	0	0	0	1	0
17	0	1	1	0	0	1	1	1
5	0	1	0	1	0	0	0	0
16	0	1	0	0	1	0	0	0
7	0	0	1	0	0	0	0	1
12	0	0	0	1	1	0	1	0
10	0	0	0	0	0	1	0	0
1	1	0	1	0	0	0	1	0
11	1	0	0	1	1	0	0	1
4	1	0	0	0	0	1	0	0
15	0	1	1	0	1	0	0	0
13	0	1	0	1	0	1	1	0
14	0	1	0	0	0	0	0	1
9	0	0	1	0	0	1	0	0
3	0	0	0	1	0	0	0	0
18	0	0	0	0	1	0	1	1

TABLE 17B-2
Average score for attribute levels

	Score
Package design:	
A	5.33
B	13.33
C	9.83
Brand name:	
K2R	9.17
Glory	8.67
Bissell	10.67
Price:	
1.19	13.00
1.39	10.17
1.59	5.33
Good Housekeeping seal:	
Yes	10.50
No	9.00
Money-back guarantee:	
Yes	12.50
No	8.00

TABLE 17B–3
Attribute utilities

	Simple sums	MONANOVA
Package design:		
A	.1	.1
B	1.0	1.0
C	.6	.6
Brand name:		
K2R	.5	.3
Glory	.5	.2
Bissell	.7	.5
Price:		
1.19	1.0	1.0
1.39	.6	.7
1.59	.1	.1
Good House-keeping seal:		
Yes	.7	.3
No	.5	.2
Money-back guarantee:		
Yes	.9	.7
No	.4	.2

TABLE 17B–4
Predicted utilities from conjoint results

Predicted utility: MONANOVA	Predicted utility: Simple sum	Predicted rank: MONANOVA	Predicted rank: Simple sum	Stated rank
1.8	2.5	13	13.5	13
1.9	2.6	11.5	11	11
1.2	2.0	17	17	17
3.0	3.7	2	2	2
1.7	2.5	14.5	13.5	14
2.9	3.6	3	3	3
1.9	2.6	11.5	11	12
2.4	3.2	6.5	6	7
2.2	2.8	8.5	9	9
1.0	1.8	18	18	18
2.2	3.0	8.5	8	8
1.7	2.3	14.5	15	15
2.7	3.4	4	4	4
2.4	3.2	6.5	6	6
2.5	3.2	5	6	5
2.0	2.6	10	11	10
1.3	2.1	16	16	16
3.1	3.9	1	1	1

In order to check on the consistency of these results with the data, the predicted utilities were calculated for both the simple sums and MONANOVA utilities and compared with the stated rankings (Table 17B–4). The results indicate (*a*) that the MONANOVA results are consistent with the rankings and (*b*) that the simple sums results are also consistent and very similar to the MONANOVA. The point, therefore, is that dummy variable regression (or in certain circumstances even average scores) can be used to get quite good approximations of attribute utilities.

_____ PART FOUR

Applications

18 _____

Marketing forecasting

Mention of the term forecasting brings forth a myriad of images, including complex computerized models, planning, and bad guesses. To some people forecasting and marketing research are nearly synonymous. The diversity of associations that the term forecasting brings forth immediately suggests that forecasting encompasses many different problems and approaches. The purpose of this chapter is to briefly suggest what marketing forecasting is and how one might go about producing forecasts.

There is one general point about forecasting which is very important. When asking for a forecast, most people want a single number. Providing a best guess number is important. However, it is also important to provide a range of likely outcomes. In many cases, the range may be at least as important as the best guess. The range gives the user of the forecast a notion of how tightly s/he can plan. For example, if a sales forecast range is provided, the user can count on needing production capacity for meeting the low end of the range and can develop contingency plans for meeting demand up to the higher end of the range. Hence artificially tightening the range of a forecast may increase its credibility but damages its usefulness. One final point is worth making: Avoid silly precision in the forecasts. A result of 11,172.13 cases may sound better than 11,000 but is usually misleadingly precise. In short, there may be more initial selling required to gain acceptance for a forecast with a range (e.g., 11,000 ± 3,000 cases) but in the long run such forecasts are usually better.

PURPOSES

Probably the best place to begin a discussion of forecasting is by considering the various purposes of forecasting. Four of the most salient are evaluation of a market (market potential estimation), planning and budgeting, developing standards for evaluating performance, and answering "what if" questions.

Evaluation of a market (market potential estimation)

One of the most common forecasting problems involves assessing the potential sales of a product or service in a particular market. The market in question may be defined in terms of a set of competing products or a geographical area. The purposes of such estimates are usually (*a*) to determine whether a product or service has sufficient promise to warrant further effort or (*b*) to decide which region is more attractive and hence should receive more attention.

Planning and budgeting

In conjunction with a company's planning cycle, key inputs into the plan are forecasts of sales broken by product type, region, time period, and so forth. These forecasts are needed to schedule production, purchasing, and financial arrangements as well as to aid in allocating marketing effort.

Developing standards for evaluating performance

Given the popularity of bonus/incentive compensation systems, an obvious question which arises is what performance level serves as a base figure. Forecasts of the likely results under "typical" conditions provide a bench mark against which actual results can be compared.

Answering "what if" questions

Many times a forecast is requested to estimate the effect of various marketing policies (i.e., if advertising is cut 30 percent, what will happen to sales?). Such forecasts are especially prevalent in the areas of pricing policy and advertising/promotional strategy. This type of forecasting requires a model in which the independent/predictor variables are under the control of management. As such, it is qualitatively different from most forecasting, which tends to be concerned with extrapolating past trends.

WHAT TO FORECAST

The subject of forecasts can be grouped into two main categories. The first category of items includes short-run effects of marketing strategy such as coupon redemption rates or responses to temporary price changes. The second category includes the broader concerns which ultimately determine the success or failure of the entire business. These include sales, resources needed, costs, technology, and government actions.

Sales

This includes total revenue, units sold, product mix, and timing of sales, all of which depend heavily on competitive activity. Typically sales forecasts are the product of two separate forecasts: market size and market share.

Resources needed

Resource forecasts include cash (financial), raw materials, plant capacity, and people.

Costs

Costs estimates, especially for raw materials (e.g., sugar for candy manufacturers, steel for automobile makers), are vital numbers in planning.

Technology

Changing technologies can dramatically change an industry (e.g., Xerox, Polaroid), and hence anticipation of technological breakthroughs/ improvements is crucial for both consumer and industrial companies.

Government actions

Aside from the obvious impact of foreign governments on businesses, new regulations and tax policies of federal, state, and local governments can substantially alter the profitability of a business and hence these regulations need to be monitored/forecast (e.g., bans on saccharin and fluorocarbon propellents).

QUALITY/ACCURACY NEEDED IN THE FORECAST

The effort needed to generate a forecast depends on the benefits and costs of a good or bad forecast. In Chapter 2, a mathematical method for assessing the value of information was presented. Some of the major determinants of that value are:

Benefit determinants

Magnitude of the item forecast. If the item is large either in absolute terms or relative to the size of the business ($10,000 may not be much to General Foods, but it surely is to a corner grocery store), a "good" forecast becomes more important.

Variability/uncertainty in the item. In order for forecasting effort to pay off, there must be variability in the item's values.

Cost of an error. The greater the opportunity cost of a bad forecast, the greater the need for a good forecast. Reorder cost and time, cost of out-of-stock (which may simply delay the sale, create a lost sale, or even lead to a permanently lost customer), and inventory carrying costs all influence the cost of an error in forecasting.

Cost determinants

Number of items forecast. A model/method which is practical for a major product may be economically unfeasible to apply to 20,000 or more individual items.

Cost of forecast. Both the time and the monetary costs of a forecast must be considered.

Ease of communication and use. Forecasts which are hard to interpret or communicate have an important hidden cost associated with them.

MARKET POTENTIAL ESTIMATES (QUICK AND DIRTY)

The term market potential is fairly vague. Potential can be defined in terms of the most optimistic notion (maximum potential), some reasonable potential estimate (a best guess potential), or the minimum potential ("guaranteed" potential). Before undertaking any potential study, it is important to first decide which kind of potential measure is needed.

To obtain a good market potential estimate may require some fairly sophisticated analysis. Given the time and budget pressures under which many decisions are made, however, most complicated methods are not used. This section outlines three approaches which can be used for getting an answer quickly and by hand.

Successive ratio

The successive ratio method consists of beginning with the universe as all potential customers and then reducing this by conditional probabilities to get an estimate of "real" potential customers. The process works equally well for consumer or industrial goods. For the sake of illustration, the potential for a consumer good—diet scotch (if light beer, why not light scotch?)—and an industrial good—a new copying system—might be estimated as follows:

Diet scotch potential = (population)(percent diet conscious)(percent scotch drinkers)(per capita consumption of liquor)(expected share of diet scotch)

New copying system potential = (number of businesses)(percent have copiers)(percent "need" fancy features)(share attainable)

Segment buildup

A second procedure for estimating market potential is the so-called segment buildup approach. Using this approach requires that the market be split into segments which are readily identifiable. Sales to each segment are estimated separately and then totaled to get overall sales. This method is often used in industrial marketing with SIC codes as the basis for segments. Examples of this approach are shown in Table 18–1. Notice that in estimating sales in each segment, a successive ratio type approach

TABLE 18–1
Segment buildup approach to market potential estimation

Segment	(A) Size	(B) Amount consumed per capita	(C) Share attainable	(AxBxC) Segment potential
Diet scotch:				
Single males <30				
Single females <30				
Married males <30				
Married females <30				
Single males >30				
Single females >30				
Married males >30				
Married females >30				

	(A) Number	(B) Percent "need" this type	(C) Share attainable	(AxBxC) Segment potential
New copying system:				
Schools				
Retail businesses				
Banks				
Offices				
Warehouses				
Manufacturing facilities				
Other businesses				

was used. This brings up the important point that these methods may be used as complements as well as substitutes for each other.

Weighted index

The third approach is quite different from the other two. First, it is designed to measure relative rather than absolute potential. Second, it assumes that several factors contribute to potential. It derives an index which is a weighted combination of the factors which are thought to contribute to potential. The weights may be derived subjectively or by formal analysis of past data (e.g., by regression analysis). Typically the weights are chosen so that they sum to one. For example, the relative potential for a region could be estimated as

Diet scotch: Percent total population in region (P)
Percent retail sales in region (R)
Percent disposable income in region (DI)

$$\text{Index} = W_1P + W_2R + W_3DI$$

New copying system: Percent population in region (P)
Percent schools in region (S)
Percent retail businesses in region (RB)
Percent banks in region (B)
Percent offices in region (O)
Percent warehouses in region (WH)
Percent manufacturing facilities in region (MF)
Percent other businesses in region (OB)
Percent Xerox sales in region (XS)
Percent other copier sales in region (CS)

$$\text{Index} = W_1P + W_2S + W_3RB + W_4B + W_5O + W_6WH + W_7MF + W_8OB + W_9SX + W_{10}CS$$

The diet scotch index is a general one which could be applied to a variety of products. In fact, if the weights are .2 for population, .3 for retail sales, and .5 for disposable income, this becomes the *Sales Management* buying power index. By contrast, the index for the new copying system has many more factors included. This is done to allow the main target of the product (e.g., offices) to be given a major weight and other secondary targets (e.g., schools) to be included but at a lower weight. Also this index attempts to include sales of analogous products, in this case Xerox and other copier sales. Sales of analogous products often give the best indication of market potential.

Uses

The most common use of market potential estimates is for evaluating product potential. Put differently, having adequate market potential is a requirement before proceeding with new product development or testing.

Market potential can also be used as a control device for evaluating performance. For example, assume I had market potential estimates and sales data for several regions (Figure 18–1). In this case, the relation

FIGURE 18–1
Hypothetical sales versus market potential data

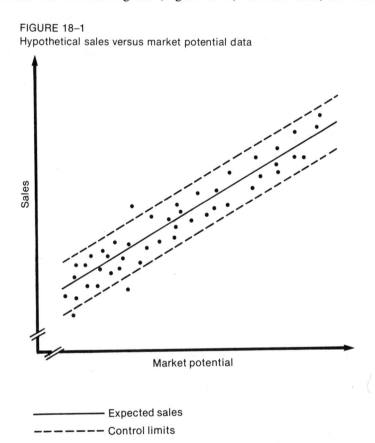

_____ Expected sales
- - - - - - - Control limits

between potential and actual sales is quite close. Hence I could use the sales versus potential curve for evaluating performance. Those regions whose sales fall above the upper control limit would be classified as "good," while those whose sales fall below the lower control limit would be "bad." While these results could then be tied directly to compensation for regional managers, this might not be appropriate. For example, a region which did very well could have done so because an important competitor folded or a major promotion was staged. Similarly a region which did badly could have done so because of increased competitive pressure. Hence the best use of market potential estimates for control is as a warning device to indicate when a region is doing especially well or poorly. One should then attempt to determine why (good management, competition, luck, etc.) the region had an exceptional performance and learn something from it.

One final word of caution is in order regarding using market potential estimates. For relatively un-new new products (e.g., an unsweetened cereal or a new tractor) the measures of market potential just described will do fairly well. For genuinely new products, however, it is possible for market potential forecasts, and especially those based on sales of other products, to be grossly in error. Some classic cases of underestimation of potential have occurred, notable in the case of IBM computers (would you believe a worldwide potential of 20–30 machines was forecast in the early 1950s?) and Xerox copiers. The point, therefore, is that while market potential estimates based on these approaches are likely to outperform blue-sky guessing, they are hardly foolproof.

FORECASTING METHODS

There are three basic types of forecasting: qualitative, extrapolative, and model building. This section will outline some of the major alternatives of these three types.

Qualitative

Judgment. The least complicated forecasting method is the use of expert judgment (guessing might be a more appropriate description). Here we simply ask someone what the future will be and record the answer. If the expert chosen happens to know the Delphic Oracle or be a mystic, the forecast may be excellent. Unfortunately, it is hard to know whether someone can predict the future a priori. The key to the value of expert judgment is the ability of the expert to recall from memory relevant data and assimilate the data in making a guess. While judgment is often unsystematic, it can be a very useful tool and can overcome some of the limitations of quantitative techniques. Probably the best use of judgment, however, is to adjust the results of quantitative procedures rather than as the sole forecasting tool. Alternatively, judgment based decision trees of the type described in Chapter 2 can be used in developing forecasts.

Polling of experts. The polling of experts method is really an extension of expert judgment under a safety-in-numbers assumption. Rather than trust a single expert, this approach collects forecasts from a number of experts. The forecasts are then combined in some manner such as a simple or weighted average (since some experts are presumably more expert than others, their forecasts are weighted more heavily). This method thus produces a forecast which is "neutral" and will (like most methods) avoid the unusual/radically different result. In fact, the most useful information from polling experts may be the range of the forecasts and the reasons given to support the forecasts rather than their average.

Panel consensus.   The panel consensus method of forecasting consists of putting a group of experts in a room and waiting for them to agree on a forecast. Aside from problems with dominant group members, this method will generally produce (assuming the panel members eventually agree) the conventional wisdom. Since experts have a nasty habit of being wrong (e.g., remember the new math, stock market forecasts, and the impossibility of an international oil cartel?), the experts' opinions can be deceptively impressive.

A variety of "fancy" techniques are available for gaining panel consensus. One of the best known of these is the Delphi procedure, which is often used as a budget-setting method. The process begins by asking a number of individuals to allocate funds to a set of projects. An outside person then collects the allocations and calculates average allocations. Next the outside person gives each participant back both the original allocation and the average allocations. At this point, each participant is asked to reconsider initial allocations. Typically (and hopefully) the participants then change their allocations to more nearly conform to the average. Hence if the process is repeated several times, consensus is achieved (see Appendix 5–B).

Extrapolation: Qualitative

As a starting point for or an alternative to expert judgment, a variety of extrapolation procedures exist. Two of these are essentially qualitative/judgmental in nature—last period $+ X$ percent and graphical eyeball.

Last period $+ X$ percent.   One of the most common approaches to forecasting is to estimate the percent change expected in the variable to be forecast. This is especially common in deriving annual sales forecasts for major product breakdowns. For example, we may forecast dishwasher sales in dollars as last year's plus 6 percent.

Graphical eyeball.   Similar to the last period $+ X$ percent method, the graphical eyeball approach requires that past data be plotted. Then the next value is "eyeballed" to match the past pattern (Figure 18–2). As should be obvious, this method does by graph what many quantitative techniques do by number crunching.

FIGURE 18–2
Graphical eyeball forecasting

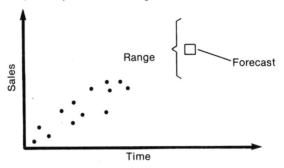

Extrapolation: Quantitative

A variety of quantitative extrapolation procedures are also available. Some of the most commonly used are given below.

Moving average. Moving averages, an old forecasting standby, are widely used as a means of reducing the noise in data to uncover the underlying pattern. In doing so, it is important to recognize that past data has at least four major components:

1. Base value. 3. Cycle(s) (seasonality).
2. Trend.   4. Random.

What moving averages essentially do is to smooth out random variation to make the patterns (trends and cycles) more obvious.

Complex moving-average models are available for estimating trends and cycles. For purposes of introduction however, we will consider only the simple moving-average approach. A three-period moving average of sales at time t is given by

$$\hat{S}_t = \frac{S_{t-1} + S_t + S_{t+1}}{3} \tag{18.1}$$

Note this implies that (*a*) each data point used is weighted equally and (*b*) no trend or cycle is accounted for. To see how this method works, consider the three-month moving average for the eight periods of data in Table 18–2. As can be seen readily, the fluctuation in values is much less in the moving averages than in the raw data and a consistent trend of increase of about ten units per period becomes quite apparent. Forecasts would now be based on the pattern of the moving averages rather than the raw data.

Moving-average methods can be extended to track trends and seasonal patterns as well. Recently, however, regression analysis (to be discussed later) has begun to replace moving averages as a forecasting tool for all but the simplest situations.

TABLE 18–2
Hypothetical data

Period	Sales	Three-month moving average
1	100	
2	110	105
3	105	115
4	130	125
5	140	130
6	120	140
7	160	152
8	175	

Exponential smoothing. A second major approach to extrapolation is exponential smoothing. As in the case of moving averages, this approach literally smooths out the random variation in period-to-period values. Also like moving averages, trends and cycles must be estimated (smoothed) separately. The simplest form of exponential smoothing produces a forecast which is a weighted combination of last period's results and last period's forecast. The formula for this is

$$\hat{S}_{t+1} = \alpha S_t + (1 - \alpha)\hat{S}_t \qquad (18.2)$$

where the smoothing constant α = weight of last period sales and $(1 - \alpha)$ = weight of the last forecast. Notice that when α equals 1, we are simply using last period results as a forecast. When $\alpha = 0$, on the other hand, we are completely ignoring last period sales and keeping the forecast constant. Typically, the "right" value of α is somewhere in between.[1]

---

[1] The term exponential smoothing comes from the property of this method which weights the most recent period most heavily, the next most recent next most heavily, and so forth in an exponential manner. This property can be seen by examining the simple model:

$$\hat{S}_{t+1} = \alpha S_t + (1 - \alpha)\hat{S}_t$$

But
$$\hat{S}_t = \alpha S_{t-1} + (1 - \alpha)\hat{S}_{t-1}$$

Therefore
$$\hat{S}_{t+1} = \alpha S_t + (1 - \alpha)[\alpha S_{t-1} + (1 - \alpha)\hat{S}_{t-1}]$$
$$= \alpha S_t + \alpha(1 - \alpha)S_{t-1} + (1 - \alpha)^2\hat{S}_{t-1}$$

Similarly we can substitute for $\hat{S}_{t-1}$ and get

$$\hat{S}_{t+1} = \alpha S_t + \alpha(1 - \alpha)S_{t-1} + \alpha(1 - \alpha)^2 S_{t-2} + (1 - \alpha)^3\hat{S}_{t-2}$$

By extension this becomes

$$\hat{S}_{t+1} = \alpha S_t + \alpha(1 - \alpha)S_{t-1} + \alpha(1 - \alpha)^2 S_{t-2} + \alpha(1 - \alpha)^3 S_{t-3} + \cdots + \alpha(1 - \alpha)^n S_{t-n} + \cdots$$

Hence the data points are weighted exponentially where the exponent indicates how old the data is.

Searching for the right α is really a trial-and-error process. Using the eight-period example of Table 18–2, we can see how a small α (.2) produces a slowly changing forecast while a large α (.8) tracks last period sales much more closely (Table 18–3). In both cases, a value of 100 was

TABLE 18–3
Exponential smoothing example

Sales	$\alpha = .2$			$\alpha = .8$		
	$\hat{S}_t$	$.2S_t$	$.8\hat{S}_t$	$\hat{S}_t$	$.8S_t$	$.2\hat{S}_{t-1}$
100	100	20	80	100	80	20
110	100	22	80	100	88	20
105	102	21	81.6	108	84	21.6
130	102.6	26	82.1	105.6	104	21.1
140	108.1	28	86.5	125.1	112	25.0
120	114.5	24	91.6	137.0	96	27.4
160	115.6	32	92.5	123.4	128	25.7
175	124.6	35	99.6	153.7	140	30.7
	134.6			170.7		

arbitrarily used for the first forecast. (The effect of this value on the forecast gradually decreases as more periods are included.) For $\alpha = .2$, the forecast for the second period becomes

$$\hat{S}_2 = .2(S_1) + .8(\hat{S}_1)$$
$$= .2(100) + .8(100) = 100$$

Similarly the third period forecast becomes

$$\hat{S}_3 = .2(S_2) + .8(\hat{S}_2)$$
$$= .2(110) + .8(100) = 102$$

Notice that both sets of forecasts lag behind actual sales. The reason for this is that the trend was ignored. To account for both trend and seasonality by means of exponential smoothing requires a more complex model:

$$\hat{S}_{t+1} = \frac{\alpha S_t}{F_{t-L}} + (1 - \alpha)(\hat{S}_t + R_{t-1}) \tag{18.3}$$

where the seasonality is given by

$$F_t = \beta \frac{S_t}{\hat{S}_{t+1}} + (1 - \beta)F_{t-L} \tag{18.4}$$

where L is the periodicity (length) of the seasonal pattern and the trend is obtained from

$$R_{t+1} = \gamma(S_{t+1} - S_t) + (1 - \gamma)R_t \tag{18.5}$$

and α, β, and γ are three separately estimated smoothing constants. Generally data involving cycles and trends is handled by means of regression analysis rather than exponential smoothing.

Time series regression. A third way to extrapolate data is by using regression analysis with time (period) as the independent variable. Time series regression produces estimates of the base level (intercept) and trend (slope). Seasonal patterns can be handled outside the regression (i.e., by removing the estimated seasonal component from the values of the dependent variable before performing the regression) or by various "tricks" within the regression (e.g., using dummy variables, see Wildt, 1977). Ignoring seasonality, the model is simply

$$Sales = a + b(time)$$

Addressing the same eight-period example in this manner produces the result of Table 18–4. The forecast for period 10 based on this model would thus be

$$\hat{S}_{10} = 85.4 + 9.88(10) = 184.2$$

In addition to the basic forecast, regression produces several bonuses:

Measure of goodness of fit: R^2 (percent of variance in sales which was explained).

Standard error of estimate: $S_{Y.X}$, which serves to quantify the range of likely outcomes. Typically a prediction is given by $\hat{S} \pm KS_{Y.X}$. (For most situations, $K = 2$ will prove adequate.)

Durbin-Watson: A statistic which indicates the presence of significant cycles or nonlinearities in the pattern. A Durbin-Watson less than 1 indicates a significant cycle (see Chapter 14).

Actually all three methods (moving average, exponential smoothing, and time series regressions) are very similar. They do weight data differently: moving average weights some of the data points equally, exponen-

TABLE 18–4
Time series regression example

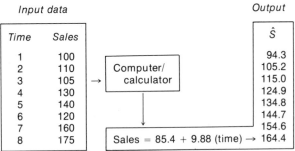

Input data		Output

Time	Sales		$\hat{S}$
1	100		94.3
2	110	Computer/	105.2
3	105	calculator	115.0
4	130		124.9
5	140		134.8
6	120		144.7
7	160		154.6
8	175	Sales = 85.4 + 9.88 (time) →	164.4

tial smoothing weights all the data points unequally, and regression typically weights all the points equally, although unequal weights can be used. Choice among the three is hence a matter of taste, availability, and experience. Since the reader is presumably already familiar with regression at this point, s/he might be well advised to use time series regression when the choice arises.

Spectral analysis.   Spectral analysis is a "fancy" technique for removing cycles from data. Based on some fairly advanced mathematics (Fourier Series), significant cycles are identified and removed from a series of values. For example, data may include an annual cycle, a seven-year cycle, and a weekly cycle. Spectral analysis will extract these three cycles. A detailed discussion of this method is beyond the scope of this book.

Box-Jenkins.   Another "fancy" technique is the so-called Box-Jenkins (guess who popularized it?) methodology. This method is essentially a regression approach which combines both moving average and time series components and has been widely used. For a description of this technique, as well as spectral analysis and other forecasting procedures, see Wheelwright and Makridakis (1973).

Additive versus multiplicative models.   One final point is important in considering extrapolation procedures. In building a model of sales as a function of base values, trends, and cycles, these components may be combined in more than one way. The best way to decide how to combine

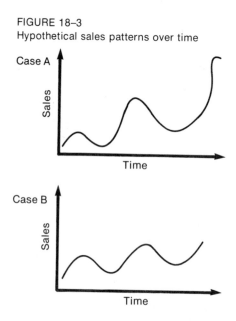

FIGURE 18–3
Hypothetical sales patterns over time

them is to look at a graph of the data such as Figure 18–3. In case A, the cycle "explodes" and hence a multiplicative model is appropriate:

$$\text{Sales} = (\text{base})(\text{trend})(\text{seasonality})$$

In case B, on the other hand, the spread of the cycle is constant, indicating a linear model:

$$\text{Sales} = \text{Base} + \text{Trend} + \text{Seasonality}$$

Generally, an additive type model will suffice.

Model based

Model based forecasting approaches are distinguished from extrapolatic procedures in that in addition to using past data for the item being forecast, they assume that future results will occur based on either a particular pattern or set of influences. Some of the most common model forms include experience models, epidemic models, input-output models, single equation regression models, and simultaneous equation models.

Experience models.   A basic pattern which occurs in many areas is that the cost of an operation (e.g., producing a product) decreases as cumulative experience increases. The shape of the cost versus experience curve, often called a learning curve, is typically exponential (Figure 18–4).

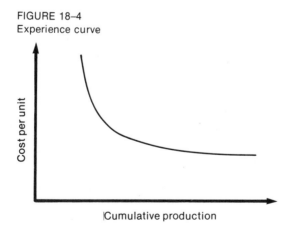

FIGURE 18–4
Experience curve

Cost per unit

Cumulative production

Hence by measuring cost during initial production and estimating the rate of decline in cost from either limited data or subjective estimation, costs can be forecast for various times and production levels in the future.

Epidemic models.   An approach to forecasting sales of a new product is to assume that initial sales of the product will follow the same shape

FIGURE 18–5
Trial over time for a new product

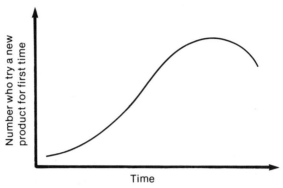

curve (Figure 18–5) as an epidemic (which given some new products may be an apt analogy). This curve implies that there will be a slow start during which the innovators become "infected" followed by a growth period in which sales of the product (or the disease) spread rapidly through the population. Sales then slow down as the number of eventual buyers (people susceptible to the disease) is approached (Figure 18–6). Such a

FIGURE 18–6
Cumulative trial over time

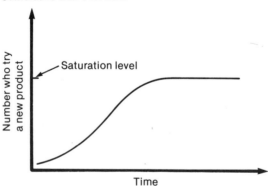

model has been presented by Bass (1969) and used in companies such as Eastman Kodak to forecast sales of new consumer durables in terms of when they would peak and how big the peak would be. While such models may be imperfect predictors, the basic notions of a pattern of sales growth over time and the existence of a saturation level are useful in considering any type of forecast.

Input-output models. An input-output model is essentially a model which balances production resources used with final products produced. These models typically are generally used to model an entire economy with different sectors of the economy (steel, etc.) used as the elements of the analysis. In general these models are not used in marketing research.

Single equation regression models. Single equation regression models are the most widely used form of models in marketing research. These models are developed in three stages.

First the variables which are assumed to affect the dependent variable are specified:

Sales $= f$(our price, competitors' prices, our advertising,
competitors' advertising, disposable income)

Next a model which indicates the form of the relation between the independent variables and sales is specified. These models are generally linear, such as

Sales in cartons $(S) =$ constant
$+ B_1$ (our price)
$+ B_2$ (our advertising)
$+ B_3$ (disposable income)

The model is then estimated by means of regression analysis:

$S = 1.2 - .2$(price in \$) $+ 1.3$(advertising in \$)
$+ .1$(disposable income in billions of \$)

These models serve two basic uses:

Straight forecasting. $\tilde{S} \pm 2S_{Y \cdot X}$. Notice that to use regression models to forecast one must first forecast the values of the independent variables. If this is difficult, then regression becomes less useful as a straight forecasting device. Put differently, in building a multiple regression model for purposes of forecasting, make sure that the independent variables are easily forecast.

Answering "what if" questions. In our example,

$B_1 =$ marginal effect of changing our price
$B_2 =$ marginal effect of changing our advertising share.

If you make the rather large assumption that the relation between price and sales is causal rather than just correlational, you can answer questions like, "What if I increase advertising by \$10?" In this case, a \$10 increase in advertising would lead to a $(1.3)(10) = 13$ carton change in sales.

Selection of variables. The criteria for which variables to include in a regression model are numerous, including the following:

1. Parsimony (bosses like simple models).
2. Data availability (available data typically dictates variable selection).
3. Plausibility (do the independent variables logically affect the dependent variable?).
4. Goodness of fit (does the independent variable help predict the dependent variable? Bosses hate low R^2's).
5. "Good" coefficients (are the signs of magnitudes of the coefficients reasonable?).

Given these multiple criteria, it is not surprising that building regression models is a trial and error process.

Simultaneous equation models. In order to improve the accuracy of a forecast for a particularly important variable (e.g., oil prices) it is often necessary to take into account the interactions between this variable and other variables. For example, the price of oil influences the price of food and the price of food influences the price of oil. In order to model such interdependency, systems of equations are specified. The parameters of these models are then estimated by simultaneous equation regression. Using these models requires considerable development cost and technical know-how, and hence they are used only in limited circumstances.

CHOICE OF FORECASTING METHOD

Time horizon

The time horizon has a major effect on the forecasting method which is appropriate and the accuracy. Put bluntly, anything will do to predict next week (with exceptions—e.g., umbrellas), and nothing can predict 30 years ahead. The relation between the time horizon of the forecast and the method to be used can be summarized as follows:

Term of forecast	*"Best" method*
1. Super short (less than 6 months)	Any method: The die is cast already
2. Short (6 months)	Simple extrapolation
3. Medium (1–5 years)	Quantitative (regression)
4. Long (5–30 years)	Model building
5. Super long (30 years and up)	FAC*

* Flip a coin; no one knows.

Use of quantitative procedures

Using quantitative procedures may at times seem tedious. Still there are several reasons why quantitative methods are beneficial:

1. They simplify routine, repetitive situations.
2. They force explicit statements of assumptions.

3. They provide a bench mark for qualitative thinking.
4. They are a way to start when the situation seems hopelessly complex.

When using quantitative procedures, remember:

If possible, graph the data. (A picture may be worth a thousand analyses.) As an example of how important a picture can be, consider again the eight-period example of Table 18–2. Graphed, the data looks like Figure 18–7. An interesting pattern thus emerges: two up

FIGURE 18–7
Plot of sales data example

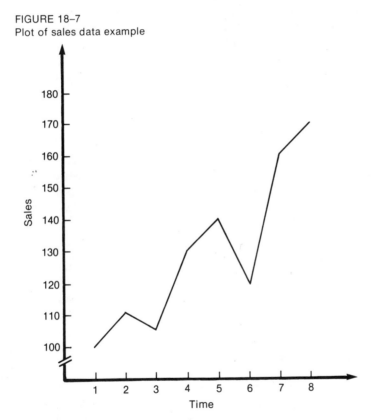

periods followed by a down period. While this pattern is only three cycles old, it does suggest that a forecast in the 130–40 area for period 9 would be supportable. This pattern can be overlooked by simple number crunching.

Do sensitivity analysis. Only when a result seems to be stable over method and data points (drop one or two points and rerun the analysis), can the forecast be advanced with much conviction.

Examine big "residuals."   By examining the characteristics of those periods (data points) when the forecast was bad, omitted variables can often be uncovered.

Avoid silly precision.   This means rounding off the forecast and giving an honest plus or minus range.

Be tolerant of errors.   Expect the methods to improve your odds of making a good forecast, not to guarantee them.

Remember you will generally miss all the turning points.   Quantitative (as well as qualitative) forecasting methods work well as long as the patterns which occurred in the past extend into the future. Whenever a major change occurs, however, most forecasts will be way off. Put differently most forecasting methods are generally useless for predicting major changes in the way the world operates (oil embargoes, changes in social values, etc.) and hence the effects of these are not included in most forecasts.

EXAMPLE: THE YEAR 2000

In 1970, a problem was posed which was, in essence, "What will the effect of different U.S. populations be on U.S. industries in the year 2000?" Given this rather nebulous topic, the decision was made to build a model of unit sales for 19 industries based on, among other things, population. A variety of approaches were considered and rejected:

1. Input-output analysis. (The researcher didn't know enough about it.)
2. Simultaneous equation regression models. (Insufficient time and budget.)
3. Index numbers. (Not enough experience with, too subjective.)

That left two good standbys:

1. Single equation regression.
2. Polling of experts.

The major thrust was to use a single equation model for each of the 19 industries. Also 35 experts were asked to indicate what they felt would happen to sales in the 19 industries under different population assumptions (Howard and Lehmann, 1971). These judgments were used mainly to backstop the quantitative methods and served to help eliminate predictions which would not be believable. (Having believable predictions tends to increase the speed with which a consultant gets paid.)

A wide variety of potential regression models are available. There being no particular reason for choosing one, a number were investigated[2]

---

[2] Actually many more could have been used if either more variables were used or if population were broken down by age groups.

TABLE 18–5
Alternative models of sales as a function of population

	1. $S_t = B_0 + B_1(\text{POP}_t)$
	2. $S_t = B_0 + B_1(\text{POP}_t) + B_2 \left(\dfrac{\text{DI}_t}{\text{CPI}_t}\right)$
	3. $S_t = B_0 + B_1(\text{POP}_t) + B_2 \left(\dfrac{\text{DI}_t}{\text{CPI}_t}\Big/ \text{POP}_t\right)$
	4. $S_t = B_0 + B_1(t) + B_2(\text{POP}_t) + B_3(\text{DI}_t/\text{CPI}_t)$
	5. $S_t = B_0 + B_1(t) + B_2(\text{POP}_t) + B_3 \left(\dfrac{\text{DI}_t}{\text{CPI}_t}\Big/ \text{POP}_t\right)$
	6. $S_t = B_0 + B_1(t) + B_2(\text{POP}_t)$
One-year lags	7. $S_t = B_0 + B_1(\text{POP}_{t-1})$
	8. $S_t = B_0 + B_1(\text{POP}_{t-1}) + B_2(\text{DI}_{t-1}/\text{CPI}_{t-1})$
	9. $S_t = B_0 + B_1(\text{POP}_{t-1}) + B_2 \left(\dfrac{\text{DI}_{t-1}}{\text{CPI}_{t-1}}\Big/ \text{POP}_{t-1}\right)$
	10. $S_t = B_0 + B_1(t-1) + B_2(\text{POP}_{t-1}) + B_3(\text{DI}_{t-1}/\text{CPI}_{t-1})$
	11. $S_t = B_0 + B_1(t-1) + B_2(\text{POP}_{t-1}) + B_3 \left(\dfrac{\text{DI}_{t-1}}{\text{CPI}_{t-1}}\Big/ \text{POP}_{t-1}\right)$
	12. $S_t = B_0 + B_1(t-1) + B_2(\text{POP}_{t-1})$
Five-year lags	13. $S_t = B_0 + B_1(\text{POP}_{t-5})$
	14. $S_t = B_0 + B_1(\text{POP}_{t-5}) + B_2(\text{DI}_{t-5}/\text{CPI}_{t-5})$
	15. $S_t = B_0 + B_1(\text{POP}_{t-5}) + B_2 \left(\dfrac{\text{DI}_{t-5}}{\text{CPI}_{t-5}}\Big/ \text{POP}_{t-5}\right)$
	16. $S_t = B_0 + B_1(t-5) + B_2(\text{POP}_{t-5}) + B_3(\text{DI}_{t-5}/\text{CPI}_{t-5})$
	17. $S_t = B_0 + B_1(t-5) + B_2(\text{POP}_{t-5}) + B_3 \left(\dfrac{\text{DI}_{t-5}}{\text{CPI}_{t-5}}\Big/ \text{POP}_{t-5}\right)$
	18. $S_t = B_0 + B_1(t-5) + B_2(\text{POP}_{t-5})$
First differ- ences	19. $(S_t - S_{t-1}) = B_0 + B_1(\text{POP}_t - \text{POP}_{t-1})$
	20. $(S_t - S_{t-1}) = B_0 + B_1(\text{POP}_t - \text{POP}_{t-1}) + B_2 \left(\dfrac{\text{DI}_t}{\text{CPI}_t} - \dfrac{\text{DI}_{t-1}}{\text{CPI}_{t-1}}\right)$
	21. $(S_t - S_{t-1}) = B_0 + B_1(\text{POP}_t - \text{POP}_{t-1})$ $+ B_2 \left(\dfrac{\text{DI}_t}{\text{CPI}_t}\Big/ \text{POP}_t - \dfrac{\text{DI}_{t-1}}{\text{CPI}_{t-1}}\Big/ \text{POP}_{t-1}\right)$
Logs*	22. $\log S_t = B_0 + B_1 \log(\text{POP}_t) + B_2 \log(\text{DI}_t/\text{CPI}_t)$
	23. $\log S_t = B_0 + B_1 \log(\text{POP}_t) + B_2 \log \left(\dfrac{\text{DI}_t}{\text{CPI}_t}\Big/ \text{POP}_t\right)$
Logs, one-year lags	24. $\log S_t = B_0 + B_1 \log(\text{POP}_{t-1}) + B_2 \log(\text{DI}_{t-1}/\text{CPI}_{t-1})$
	25. $\log S_t = B_0 + B_1 \log(\text{POP}_{t-1}) + B_2 \log \left(\dfrac{\text{DI}_{t-1}}{\text{CPI}_{t-1}}\Big/ \text{POP}_{t-1}\right)$
Logs, five-year lags	26. $\log S_t = B_0 + B_1 \log(\text{POP}_{t-5}) + B_2 \log(\text{DI}_{t-5}/\text{CPI}_{t-5})$
	27. $\log S_t = B_0 + B_1 \log \left(\dfrac{\text{DI}_{t-5}}{\text{CPI}_{t-5}}\Big/ \text{POP}_{t-5}\right)$

S = sales
POP = population
DI = disposable income
CPI = total consumer price index
t = time (year)
This implies $S_t = B_0(\text{POP}_t)^{B_1}(\text{DI}_t/\text{CPI}_t)^{B_2}$

(Table 18–5). The results were then examined and the best model chosen. Almost without exception, the lagged models and first difference models produced "funny" results when extrapolated 30 years into the future based on the data used (1948–69 and 1959–69). In fact, the "best" results seemed to come from using the 1959–69 data on model (2):

$$\text{Sales} = B_0 + B_1 (\text{POP}_t) + B_2 \frac{\text{DI}_t}{\text{CPI}_t}$$

The resulting equations were then used for forecasting unit sales in the year 2000 under two population estimates and two disposable income estimates. The results clearly illustrate the frustration of forecasting 30 years into the future based on 11 years' worth of data. First, the supposedly "low" population estimate at the time was 266,281,000, a number which currently appears, if anything, high. Second, it is hard to believe that some of the projections will come true. The best example of this is automobiles, where the forecasts for the year 2000 based on the lower population and disposable income estimates were as follows:

Domestic	1.2 million
Imported	19 million

This result is hard to believe on two counts. First, given oil shortages, it is difficult to project sales of 20 million cars in the year 2000 (at least cars as we know them today). Secondly, it seems unlikely that imported cars will be allowed (either by GM, etc., or the U.S. government) to so totally dominate the market. (It may be, however, that small cars will have such a dominant share.) This prediction is the result of the linear extrapolation of the past trend over a long time period. While linear extrapolations work well in the short run, they tend to be off in the long run. The point, therefore, is that these estimates cannot be maintained with much certainty (would you believe a confidence interval of zero to infinity?). That doesn't mean that long-range forecasts aren't important; airports, utilities, and so forth, all need to plan many years in the future. What it does mean is that anyone doing long-range forecasting deserves credit for courage and some sympathy.

SUMMARY

Forecasting is a trying undertaking. Besides a sense of security and humor, the following are useful tools:

1. Understanding of—
    a. The problem.
    b. The situation.
2. Common sense.
3. Willingness to live with uncertainty. (False precision costs money since it doesn't encourage proper contingency planning.)
4. A number cruncher (the ability to use quantitative methods).
5. A coin. At some point in the forecasting process, a guess will need to be made. By using a coin, you can blame the result on someone or

something else. If that won't do, hire a consultant. At least then when the forecast is bad you can have the satisfaction of firing him/her.

PROBLEMS

1. Prepare an estimate of dishwasher sales for—
   a. Next year.
   b. Five years from now.
   c. 2010.
   Use whatever sources of information and data are available (with appropriate citations) as well as any quantitative techniques you feel are relevant. Limit the "report" (exclusive of exhibits) to five pages.
2. A company plans to introduce a new small appliance aimed at homeowners which costs about $80. The product is essentially a decorative version of the basic equipment used by 90 percent of the homes and businesses.
   a. Using the information given, indicate the absolute and relative potential of the product in the two sales districts.
   b. What other information would you find useful?

	A (Center City)	B (Suburban County)
Number residential customers	61,200	48,200
Number businesses	16,000	6,600
Amount spent by residential customers on the service	1,400,000	1,240,000
Amount spent by business customers on the service	6,990,000	1,180,000
Income per capita	6,700	6,000
Population	146,000	141,000
Retail sales	60,000,000	47,000,000
Furniture/appliance sales	3,360,000	2,220,000

3. Given the following data:

Year	Sales
1970	28.2
1971	31.4
1972	30.3
1973	34.5
1974	37.8
1975	33.9
1976	38.6
1977	40.1
1978	37.8
1979	41.2

Forecast next year's sales by

a. Graphical eyeball.

b. Regression.

c. Extrapolating three period moving averages.

d. Using exponential smoothing to estimate the trend for $\alpha = .2$ and $\alpha = .8$.

4. Assume you were responsible for forecasting sales of Alcort Sunfish (a small sailboat). How would you proceed?

5. Assume you were assigned to model annual sales of beer for Schlitz.

a. What would your model look like and how would you proceed?

b. What would you do differently to forecast monthly beer sales?

BIBLIOGRAPHY

Bass, Frank M. "A New Product Growth for Model Consumer Durables," *Management Science*, vol. 15 (January 1969), pp. 215–27.

Chambers, John C.; Mullick, Satinder K.; and Smith, Donald D. *An Executive's Guide to Forecasting*. New York, Wiley, 1974.

———; ———; and ———. "How to Choose the Right Forecasting Technique." *Harvard Business Review*, vol. 49 (July–August 1971), pp. 45–74.

Draper, N., and Smith, H. *Applied Regression Analysis*. New York: Wiley, 1966.

Howard, John A., and Lehmann, Donald R. "The Effect of Different Populations on Selected Industries in the Year 2000." Commission on Population Growth and the American Future, Research Reports, vol. II. *Economic Aspects of Population Change*, edited by Elliot R. Morss and Ritchie H. Reed, 1972, pp. 145–58.

McLaughlin, Robert L. "The Breakthrough in Sales Forecasting." *Journal of Marketing*, vol. 27 (April 1963), pp. 46–54.

———; and Boyle, J. J. *Short Term Forecasting*. Chicago: American Marketing Association, 1968.

Wheelwright, S. C.; and Makridakis, S. *Forecasting Methods for Management*. New York: Wiley, 1973.

Wildt, Albert R. "Estimating Models of Seasonal Market Response Using Dummy Variables." *Journal of Marketing Research*, vol. 14 (February 1977), pp. 34–41.

19 _____

Product research

The purpose of this chapter is to give a brief overview of the types of research which are commonly carried out for a product. Aside from tradition, there are two basic reasons for performing research. The first is to aid in the development of a plan (typically an annual plan) which specifies marketing objectives, strategies, and tactics for the coming period. The purpose of such research is to help allocate effort efficiently for the coming year. The other major type of research is essentially fire fighting. This research is necessitated by sudden changes in the market, such as competitive product introductions or new government regulations (e.g., no aerosol sprays allowed). This chapter will begin by covering the major types of research done in conjunction with an existing brand and then describe the typical stages of new product research.

EXISTING PRODUCTS

Monitoring the overall market

The most common type of research is designed to simply monitor a market. This serves as a control mechanism for the annual plan so that unexpected changes are detected early. The most general type of monitoring concerns the state of the total market. Total market monitoring concerns four major categories: size, growth, competition, and segmentation.

Size. Size is usually studied with secondary data (trade association, government data). Analysis is typically restricted to simple description (sales were X, etc.). Seasonality/cycles are also monitored.

Growth. Market growth projections are sometimes available from secondary data, especially for basic industries. For more narrowly defined categories, however (e.g., scented antidandruff shampoos), secondary projections are likely to be nonexistent or unreliable. In such cases, both secondary and internal data are used to build forecasting schemes/ models ranging from graphical eyeball to complex regression models.

Competition. Very little information on competition is available from secondary data. A major source of information on competition is audits (such as Nielsen), where shares are reported by area, and so forth. Probably the best early warning system for competitive moves is a good competitive intelligence system. When this intelligence system fails, field salespersons are usually the first to encounter the effects of the competitive maneuver. Panel data is useful for analyzing switching patterns and by implication defining competition. Similarly survey data can be used both for analyzing switching (i.e., by comparing brand bought last time with brand bought the time before that) or for direct questioning of which brands compete and how. In addition to corporate competition, patterns in the elements of the marketing mix are also monitored.

Segmentation. One of the most widely acclaimed "principles" of marketing is market segmentation. Books have been devoted to the subject (Massy, Frank, and Wind, 1972). The basic notion of market segmentation is that a market is made up of groups of customers who are different in their manner of consumption. The key to a useful segmentation is to find groups of customers which—

Are definable. This means identifiable in terms of either obvious characteristics (such as age, income, etc.) or more subtle characteristics (e.g., life-styles).

Are reachable. Since most promotional schemes involve either advertising or personal selling, it is important to know how to reach different segments efficiently. This can be fairly obvious (e.g., reach sports-minded individuals by advertising in *Sports Illustrated*) or almost impossible (where do I advertise to find Heinz ketchup buyers, except on the labels of Heinz ketchup?).

Are different. Segments are most useful when they differ in their consumption patterns in terms of brands chosen and/or amount consumed.

Respond differently. Defining a target segments loses some of its value if the segment responds to elements of the marketing mix exactly the same way as the total market. The hope is to find one or more key segments which respond differently so that specialized marketing programs can be directed toward these segments.

Ideally, a segment should have all of these four properties. However, segments with any of these properties can be useful for gaining insight into the market and hence potentially ideas about how better to attack it.

Developing segments can be done in two basic ways. The first is logical definition, often based on physical characteristics. Examples of this would be dividing toothpaste into decay prevention and social segments or the "spread" market into premium stick margarine, low-priced tub margarine, and so forth. The second way is data based. At least four bases (corresponding to the four keys to segmentation) are used:

1. General characteristics, such as socioeconomic or psychographic variables.
2. Media/information sources.
3. Consumption patterns.
4. Response patterns.

Since response patterns are almost impossible to define and measure economically, the first three are most commonly used.

In deriving a segmentation scheme, two basic strategies are available. The first is to select the basis a priori (e.g., take usage level broken into none, light, medium, and heavy) and then use existing or special-purpose data (typically either consumer panel or survey data) to build the clusters. The clusters are then defined in terms of other variables such as demographics and media patterns.

The second strategy is to attempt to develop segments on the basis of several characteristics simultaneously. This is typically done by use of our old friend, cluster analysis. Cluster analysis can and has produced interesting groupings which have been used to select marketing strategy. However, to believe that cluster analysis is the only (or even best) way to segment suggests a lack of knowledge about what cluster analysis does. In fact, it is not unusual for a cluster analysis result to suggest a simplified basis for segmenting based on two to three variables.

Developing the annual plan

The basic tool of coordination for many products is the annual plan. This plan reviews past results and then gives a blueprint for marketing programs for the upcoming years. Development of these plans typically takes from five to six months (e.g., July–January). The major steps are as follows:

Updating the fact book.   The fact book is a compilation of statistical data on such items as sales by company profits, marketing programs, and so forth. Much of the monitoring data collected during the year ends up in the fact book.

Doing a situation analysis.   The situation analysis is the major research step in the plan development process. This step of marketing planning attempts to translate the fact book into a concise summary of the status of the market in terms of its current and future size, customer segments and preferences, present and future market shares, and present and projected elements of the marketing mix of the company and its major competitors. In addition, the analysis attempts to pinpoint opportunities for the company to improve performance by changing various elements of the marketing mix (e.g., advertising copy).

Reviewing long-run objectives.   The long-run objectives for a product are typically set in advance. Nonetheless, past and projected performance provide inputs which can be used to modify objectives (e.g., if the objective is to be a dominant member of a given market and the company's share is 2 percent after five years, the objective is probably in need of alteration).

Setting strategy and operational objectives.   First the key market segments are defined and basic appeals to be used to reach those segments are designed. This is usually called an annual strategy, and includes the general notion of product positioning. In this context, positioning includes defining strategy in terms of—

1.   Characteristics (attributes) of the product to stress.
2.   Target customers.
3.   Which competitors to challenge.

Next, specific operational objectives are set. These include the following:

1.   Overall sales/share/profit.
2.   Product positioning on key attributes.
3.   Pricing.
4.   Advertising (awareness, recall, etc.).
5.   Promotion.
6.   Sales (by segment, product, district, salespersons).
7.   Distribution (percent distribution coverage, etc.).
8.   Product development.
9.   Research (information needed to produce next year's plan).

Specifying market programs.   This stage in the planning cycle involves specifying the programs (tactics) which will lead to meeting the operational objectives. These programs include the various elements of the marketing mix:

1.   Pricing policy.
2.   Advertising.
     a.   Copy strategy.
     b.   Media schedule.
     c.   Timing.
3.   Promotions.
4.   Sales.
5.   Distribution.
6.   R&D.
7.   Market research.

Preparing a budget and proforma profit and loss and cash flow statements

Devising control procedures and contingency plans.   The control procedures usually require collecting data to monitor the market. If the results begin to differ substantially from the objectives, then alternative (contingency) plans are implemented.

Role of research

The major role of marketing research in the planning process (besides fighting for a bigger budget for next year) is in the situation analysis phase. The purpose here is to analyze the market so that the marketing programs next year will be more effective than they are this year. (The obvious hope is to achieve an optimal program, but attainment of this for any sustained period is the impossible dream.) The role of marketing programs can be seen in terms of an analogy. Assume you sat in front of a control panel on which were dials for the various elements of the marketing mix (Figure 19–1). Further, assume each dial had a number of fine-tuning features (e.g., advertising has fine-tuning for copy strategy, media mix, timing, etc.). The game is to set the dials in the correct positions. In doing so, however, there are several problems:

Competitive reaction.   All the competitors also have control boards. These boards are similar but not identical due to patents, channels of distribution used, and so forth. When competitors change their settings, your results change.

Trends.   There are trends in the market which make it impossible for a constant setting to be optimal.

Exogenous events.   Exogenous events, such as economic trends, shortages, and government regulations can produce such a strong effect that they swamp the effect of the settings on the control panel. (Ever tried to watch TV in a lightning storm?)

Execution.   The dials set the desired levels of the elements of the marketing mix. Unfortunately, the execution of this plan is usually less than perfect. In fact, many marketers feel good execution is at least as important as a good plan.

One way to go about setting the marketing mix panel is to initially set all the dials to zero (analogous to zero-based budgeting). Assuming things are going fairly well, however, this seems inefficient since the dials may well be somewhere near their optimal settings already. Hence the more common approach is to develop a plan which involves only slight changes from last year's. (Such a plan is also easier to sell, since your boss may be the person who wrote last year's plan.)

As mentioned before, the role of research in this process is to provide the analysis upon which marketing program selection is based. It does this in several ways: testing elements of the marketing mix, fire fighting, and forecasting.

FIGURE 19–1
Marketing program control board

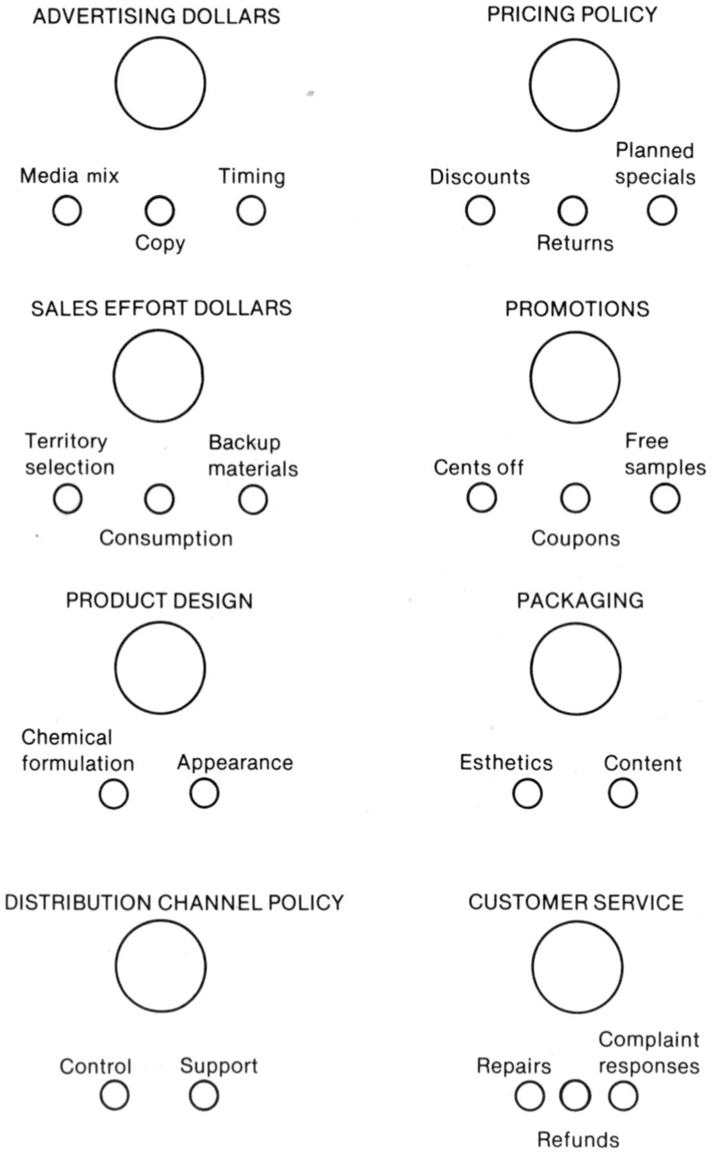

ADVERTISING DOLLARS

Media mix   Timing

Copy

PRICING POLICY

Planned
Discounts   specials

Returns

SALES EFFORT DOLLARS

Territory   Backup
selection   materials

Consumption

PROMOTIONS

Free
Cents off   samples

Coupons

PRODUCT DESIGN

Chemical
formulation   Appearance

PACKAGING

Esthetics   Content

DISTRIBUTION CHANNEL POLICY

Control   Support

CUSTOMER SERVICE

Complaint
Repairs   responses

Refunds

Testing elements of the marketing mix. A major question in budget setting is how much should be allocated to each of the general elements of the mix. Attempts to compare different elements of the mix appear in both academic publications and company practices (Prasad and Ring, 1976). Typically, however, each element of the mix is studied separately:

Advertising budgeting. Partly because of its size in relation to the total budget for many consumer products, the size of the advertising budget often has a large impact on profits. Investigation of the effectiveness of different advertising budgets has generally been done either by field experiment (these are hard to implement, partly because of the obvious resistance of a regional manager to cutting the ad budget in his/her region) or by means of simultaneous equation regression analysis (Bass, 1969; Beckwith, 1972). In addition, operations research models of the type first proposed by Vidale and Wolfe (1957) have been used to estimate advertising effects over time. More recently, effort has centered on estimating the length of time that advertising affects sales (Palda, 1964; Bass and Clarke, 1972; Parsons, 1975; Clarke, 1976; Dhalla, 1978). Decisions concerning choice of media are often made in conjunction with a model such as ADBUDG (Little and Lodish, 1969).

Pricing. Pricing studies fall into three major categories. The first category are experiments. Here in either field or controlled settings, consumers are exposed to prices in a "real" setting and the results are used to estimate price elasticity. The second basic type of study employs regression models. Here sales versus price data in different regions, time periods, and so forth, is used to estimate price elasticity. The problem in this type of study is in controlling for the other variables (e.g., advertising, competitive prices, etc.) which also varied. The third basic type of price study involves survey data. In its simplest form, this involves a "would you buy X at price Y?" type question. One problem with this approach is that the resulting data is unreliable as a predictor of actual behavior. Moreover, the practice when a demand curve is being sought is to ask the respondent "would you buy" at several prices (e.g., "Would you by at $10, $15, $20, . . .?"). The problem with this is that respondents quickly perceive the "game" and tend to "hold out" for the low price. A more subtle way to get at price sensitivity is through conjoint measurement. In conjoint measurement, the data collected provides an indication of consumers' utility for various product characteristics including price and hence by deduction a measure of price elasticity.

Promotions. The response to promotions could be estimated by using past results as bench marks and predicting accordingly. Alternatively, consumers could be asked to indicate their likely response to a promotion. While the absolute response may not be meaningful, by comparing the indicated response with the actual results of cases with similar responses, the actual results may be estimated. It is also important to consider the effects of a promotion both on the trade (wholesalers stocking up on the product) and on ultimate consumers (who may stockpile the product or increase consumption). Finally the effect of promotions can be estimated by experiments. In fact, promotional response is generally very well suited to experiments, especially of the controlled store variety.

Advertising copy. The likely response to advertising copy is an often-studied topic. The typical procedure is laboratory based, where a group of consumers view a commercial (usually embedded in a larger context, such as a TV show) and then indicate their reaction (*a*) to the brand itself and (*b*) to the ad. By comparing before-after values, the impact of the ad can be gauged. (Again remember that it is not absolute values but the values in comparison to the values of known "good" ads that is important.) Some of the typical measurements include awareness of copy points, overall attitude, and intention to buy. One interesting trick is to measure attitude on a constant sum scale compared to the major competitive brands. Ads are also sometimes judged by consumer juries directly in terms of their appeal. Here the jury views the ad and, like a focus group, proceeds to describe its reactions. Consumer juries are especially useful in evaluating strategies in mock-up/unfinalized form. It is also possible to evaluate ads by actual field experiments. This tends to be prohibitively expensive. However, special facilities exist (such as AdTel which has consumers on a split-cable TV setup so half the panel can see one ad and half another) which make such tests feasible. The actual conducting of advertising studies is typically done by the advertising agency which handles the product.

Fire fighting. Fire fighting research is called for when something goes wrong. The something that went wrong is usually failure of a program to reach its objective (e.g., sales are off 30 percent in the West). The other major thing that inspires emergency research is a major competitive move (e.g., a new product introduction, a major promotional campaign, etc.). Here much primary data collection is often impossible due to time and budget constraints. Besides looking at standard monitoring tools (Nielsen audit data, etc.) which are typically slow in responding (four to eight weeks lagged) to changes in the market, the best recourse tends to be a combination of interrogation of salespersons and people in the channels and consumer contact through phone interviews.

Forecasting. The plan which is adopted has a series of operational goals (Sales = X, etc.). These goals are really forecasts of what will happen given the particular set of marketing programs which are employed. Development of the forecasts is clearly a marketing research task. The general approach to obtaining the forecast is iterative. The first step is often to get forecasts at a very disaggregated level by, for example, asking salespersons or district managers how much they think that they will sell of the product. One of the major benefits of this is that it involves more people in the planning process and hence should increase commitment to the plan which is finally adopted. Also, being close to the market, sales-persons or district managers may have information about the current state of the market which is not yet known at corporate headquarters. These forecasts are then aggregated. At the same time, forecasts are prepared independently by staff personnel using quantitative techniques. Since the two forecasts typically differ noticeably (some salespersons sandbag, etc.) not only from each other but from long-range objectives, a series of ad-justments and negotiations are then carried out for the purpose of gaining broad agreement for the final forecast.

NEW PRODUCTS

The distinction between new and existing products is not as obvious as it appears to be. Part of the confusion has to do with perspective: If Bernie C. formed a detergent company, detergent would be a new product for him, hardly the case for Proctor and Gamble. There are also degrees of newness: Is another toothpaste with fluoride really a new product? In fact, it is safe to say that the vast majority of so-called new products are really new brands and not new in a technological sense at all. Nonethe-less, tradition dictates defining new brands as new and hence this section will focus on new brands at least as much as really new products.

Idea generation

The first stage in the development of a new product is idea generation. Many ideas appear as intuitive leaps. Some ideas are the result of techno-logical or R&D breakthroughs (e.g., Teflon). Others are brought by out-siders. When a company is under a deadline to come up with a new idea, however, serendipity cannot be relied on. Four major approaches are available for generating ideas:

1. Focus groups.
2. Brainstorming.
3. Examining customer complaints.
4. Attribute-based analysis.

Of these approaches, only the last requires much analytical skill. The notion of designing products which satisfy particular consumer wants has been called benefit segmentation (Kuehn and Day, 1962; Haley, 1968). Sometimes this involves geometric mapping procedures such as mul-tidimensional scaling.

Concept tests

Concept tests are initial screens of consumer reactions to new product concepts. The purposes of a concept test are to (a) choose the most promising from a set of alternatives, (b) get an initial notion of the commercial prospects of a concept, (c) find out who is most interested in the concept, and (d) indicate what direction further development work should take. Samples are often convenience oriented. Common sample sources include community groups, employees, and central locations (shopping centers).

The basic approach is to present consumers with a verbal/written statement of the product idea and then record their reactions. Recently many researchers have chosen to also include physical mock-ups and advertising statements in the concept test. (These are really prototype or prototype/concept tests.) The data gathered in both diagnostic (why do you like/not like the product?) and predictive (would you buy it if it cost $_____?). Including a concrete "would you by" question is crucial if the results are to be at all useful predictively. The data collection procedures fall into the following three major categories:

Surveys. Surveys are useful for getting large samples for projection purposes. On the other hand, it is often difficult to properly convey a concept in a survey, especially an impersonal one. Some different mail concept tests taken from an NFO brochure are shown in Appendix 19–A.

Focus groups. Focus groups' strength is their diagnostic power in that they can be used to get detailed discussions of various aspects of the concept. As predictors of actual sales, they are fairly inaccurate due to their small sample sizes.

Demonstrations. A popular way to present a concept is to gather a group of consumers, present them with a "story" about the new product, and record their reaction. Questions asked are typically related to—

1. Do they understand the concept?
2. Do they believe the concept?
3. Is the concept different from other products in an important way?
4. Is the difference beneficial?
5. Do they like or dislike the concept and why?
6. What could be done to make the product more acceptable?
7. How would they like to see the product (color, size, etc.)?
8. Would they buy it?
9. What price would they expect for it?
10. What would their usage be in terms of volume, purpose, source of purchase, and so forth?

Product use tests

This type of research consists of physically producing the product[1] and then getting consumers to use it. The purpose of a product test is to (a)

---

[1] Note that the product used in this phase is typically specially produced and hence may not match the quality of the product under mass production. For example, Knorr soup product test samples were produced in Europe while the actual mass produced product was made in a new computerized plant in Argo, Illinois. Hence success or failure of the test product does not necessarily imply success or failure of the actual product.

uncover product shortcomings, (b) evaluate commercial prospects, (c) evaluate alternative formulations, (d) uncover the appeal of the product to various market segments, and (e) if lucky, to gain ideas for other elements of the marketing program. Such tests may be either branded (best for estimating sales) or unbranded/blind (best for focusing directly on physical formulation).

There are three major types of product use tests. Initially such tests are usually conducted with small samples (often using convenience samples such as employees). These initial tests are diagnostic and are directed toward eliminating serious problems with the product (e.g., the jar won't fit in the door of a refrigerator), as well as getting a rough idea of how good it is vis-a-vis competitive products. This phase also allows the company to find out how the product is actually used and potentially to change the target appeal. Such employee testing is commonly used in connection with food products (e.g., Best Foods' new "Big H" sauce for hamburgers).

The second type of use test includes a limited time horizon forced trial situation where customers are given the product to use and at the end asked for their reactions to it. At the end a simulated purchase occasion is also used. This may consist of a hypothetical "would you buy" type question or better an actual choice situation where the customer either chooses one of a set of products including the new product (usually at a reduced price) or simply chooses to "buy" or not buy the new product. In order to get a result which is meaningful, many researchers tend to use a stratified sample. The strata are usually either product category usage rate (heavy, medium, light, none) or brand usually used. This stratification ensures adequate sample size to predict the effect of the product on the key market segments.

The most elaborate form of product use test requires placement of the product in homes for an extended period. For package goods, this is usually a period of about two months. The advantage of this extended period is that the results allow for both the wear-out of initial expectations and the development of problems which only manifest themselves over time (e.g., food which goes stale). Subjects are required to complete before and after questionnaires as well as maintain a diary of actual use of the new and competitive products over the period of the test. Here again, the inclusion at the end of the test of an actual choice situation helps to give the results a bottom-line orientation.

In addition to these product use tests, there are some specialized tests. The best known of these are the taste tests conducted for food products. Here the purpose is to experiment with alternative formulations which are supposed to (a) taste better or (b) cut costs. The problem is greatly complicated by carry-over effects (does the second beer ever taste as good as the first?) and the lack of discriminatory power for most consumers (try to tell Schlitz from Bud in a blind test). Taste tests fall in several categories:

Monadic. The respondent uses one product once and then evaluates it.

Successive monadic. The respondent uses several products sequentially and rates each one.

Paired comparison. Respondents use two products at the same occasion and then indicate which they prefer.

Replicated comparisons. In order to get a better fix on consumers' ability to discriminate and their preference, it is common to replicate the paired test. It is also possible to use groups of three products—called triangles or triads where two of the products are identical—to better estimate the ability of consumers to discriminate. To see why a replicated test is useful, consider the following situation (Johnson).

A set of subjects is presented with a pair of products (A and B) on two different occasions. We will assume there are three kinds of consumers:

1. Those who can tell the difference and prefer A.
2. Those who can tell the difference and prefer B.
3. Those who cannot distinguish among A and B and who randomly indicate preference.

The key is to estimate these three fractions. First we must observe the actual reported preference table:

Second preference	First preference	
	A	B
A	48%	15%
B	13	24

The naive interpretation is that 48 percent prefer A (since they consistently choose it) and 24 percent prefer B. As we will see, however, this is a bad estimate. Returning to the three kinds of consumers, we have the conditional probabilities of test result given true consumer preference shown in Table 19–1. Hence the expressed percent is a function of true preference as follows:

$$\%AA_e = \%A_t + \tfrac{1}{4}(\% \text{ Neither}_t)$$
$$\%BB_e = \%B_t + \tfrac{1}{4}(\% \text{ Neither}_t)$$

$$\% \text{ Neither}_e = \tfrac{1}{2}(\% \text{ Neither}_t)$$

where

$\%AA_e$ = the expressed percent who choose A both times
$\%A_t$ = true percent who prefer A

TABLE 19–1
Probability of expressed preference given true preference

"True" consumer preference	Expressed preference		
	AA	BB	AB, BA (Neither)
A	1	0	0
B	0	1	0
Neither	¼	¼	½

Solving this for the true fractions gives

$$\% \text{ Neither}_t = 2(\% \text{ Neither}_e)$$
$$\%A_t = \%AA_e - \tfrac{1}{4}(\% \text{ Neither}_t)$$
$$\%B_t = \%BB_e - \tfrac{1}{4}(\% \text{ Neither}_t)$$

Hence for our example, we get

$$\% \text{ Neither}_t = 2(13\% + 15\%) = 56\%$$
$$\%A_t = 48\% - \tfrac{1}{4}(56\%) = 34\%$$
$$\%B_t = 24\% - \tfrac{1}{4}(56\%) = 10\%$$

The correct interpretation of the results is thus (a) most people don't perceive a difference and (b) B is in trouble.

Factor tests. Factor tests involve separately testing for the effect of varying elements of the marketing program such as price, advertising copy, and so forth. These tests are conducted in essentially the same way for new products as they are for existing products. Most such tests are conducted in central locations or labs and involve exposing consumers to different "treatments" and seeing how they respond.

One of the most interesting ways to do this is through a controlled store test (Hardin, 1966). This entails testing a product in an actual store in which complete control over price, facings, point-of-purchase displays, and so forth, is maintained (several suppliers offer such services). As such, this procedure falls somewhere between a lab and field experiment in both realism and cost. This method is especially useful in testing packaging, pricing, facings, and point-of-purchase displays.

Market tests. The ultimate in realism is a market test. The purpose of such a test is (a) to predict sales and profits from a major product launch and (b) to "practice up" so that marketing, distribution, and production skills are developed before entering full-scale operations. Projections are typically made for both share and actual sales, appropriately adjusted to national levels. The major sources of concern are as follows:

1. Trial rate.
2. Repeat rate (for frequently purchased goods).
3. Usage rate/Number bought per customer.

In addition awareness, attitudes, and distribution are usually monitored. Given these measures, a projected sales estimate can be made.

In designing a market test, it is important to clearly delineate what information is to be gathered and why before proceeding. Several decisions must be made.

Action standards. Standards for evaluating the results should be set up in advance. These standards should specify when the various possible decisions (e.g., stop the test, continue the test, revamp the product, go national) will be implemented.

Where. The choice of where to test market is a serious problem. Most market tests are done in two to three cities. (This further emphasizes that the "test" is not designed to try out numerous strategies—at most two to three alternatives can be used.) Cities are chosen on the basis of representativeness of the population, the ability of the firm to gain distribution and media exposure in the area, and availability of good research suppliers in the area. Also areas which are self-contained in terms of media (especially TV) are preferred. The result is that certain medium-sized cities are often chosen, such as Syracuse, New York; Fresno, California; and Fort Wayne, Indiana.

What to do? The best test market designers are careful to make the effort in the area proportional to that which would reasonably be expected in a national launch. Notice here we mean effort and not budget. If a city has particularly expensive (the usual case when buying spot TV ads) or inexpensive media costs, allocating budget on a population basis would result in a media schedule which had either too few or too many exposures. The goal is to make distribution, price to consumers (price breaks to retailers and wholesalers are needed to gain distribution), and so forth, as representative as possible. What typically happens, however, is that the effort afforded the product (including the people talent) is typically greater than the comparable national effort.

How long? The question of how long to run a test is not easily answered. Obviously a longer run gives more information, but it also costs more and gives competitors more time to formulate a counterattack. Consumer package goods typically stay in test market between 6 and 12 months. The reason for the length of the test market is to include several purchase cycles so that repeat usage as well as trial can be accurately assessed. (It is not uncommon for a product to gain a big initial share due to trial and then lose share as repeat business fails to live up to trial.)

How much? The question of cost is a serious one. For consumer packaged goods, nonproduct costs tend to run between $100,000 and

$300,000 per test area, meaning a two- to three-city test often requires a budget of $500,000. Advertising and promotion typically account for 65–70 percent of the budget, with the rest of the budget divided between information gathering and analysis and miscellaneous administrative and other expenses.

Information gathering. During a test market, a variety of information is gathered, most of it related to actual sales. In monitoring sales, it is important to recognize that a large percentage of first-year factory sales (e.g., 30 percent) represent a one-time stocking up by the channels of distribution, and not sales to final consumers. The three major data sources are (a) actual sales audits (typically at least 40 stores per area) which monitor sales as well as distribution, promotion, and so forth; (b) surveys which measure awareness, attitude, and so forth; and (c) panels which report actual purchase and allow monitoring of trial and repeat rates.

Models for forecasting sales. Forecasting sales from a test market is always difficult. (If it weren't, all products which went national after test marketing would succeed.) However, at least for frequently purchased consumer products, some fairly widely used procedures have been developed. It is possible to simply wait and see at what level sales stabilize. Unfortunately this takes a fairly long period of time (up to two years) and hence a lot of money. Therefore what is really desired is an early warning system which forecasts the eventual sales level of a new product before it is attained. Assuming such a new product is really a new brand which fits into an existing product category, three basic factors are the keys to eventual sales:

1. The eventual proportion of consumers who will try the product.
2. The proportion of triers who remain with the brand.
3. The usage rate of the product category among the eventual users.

A large number of models exist which attempt to project these three factors early in the introduction.

Fourt-Woodlock. The earliest of the new product models which attained widespread interest was that of Fourt and Woodlock (1960). This model was intended to predict the market success of grocery products.

The first stage in the model attempts to predict penetration (eventual level of trial). It assumes that (a) there is an eventual penetration level (P) and that (b) each period some percentage of the nonbuyers who eventually will buy the product will buy it. The second stage in this model focuses on repeat purchase. Specifically, it focuses on the repeat ratios, the portion of initial buyers who repeat purchase once (N_1/N_F), the portion of first repeat purchasers who repeat purchase a second time (N_2/N_1), and so forth. This stage is used for forecasting sales in the next period as the sum of new buyers plus first repeaters plus second repeaters, and so forth.

This model has proved to be somewhat cumbersome in application. It also assumes that the market is constant in terms of advertising, distribution, pricing, and so forth, a very troublesome albeit useful assumption.

Parfitt and Collins. Parfitt and Collins (1968) produced a simpler model than Fourt and Woodlock. Their approach focuses on predicting market share rather than actual sales. The three key elements in using their model are (1) to estimate eventual penetration (*P*), (2) to estimate the ultimate share of their purchases that buyers of the new brand will make of the new brand (*M*), and (3) to estimate the relative product category usage rate of buyers of the new brand (*U*). The estimated eventual share is thus simply the product $P \cdot M \cdot U$.

Eventual penetration is usually estimated by simply plotting the fraction who have bought the product over time and graphically eyeballing the eventual result (Figure 19–2). Similarly eventual repeat rate can be de-

FIGURE 19–2
Typical penetration for new brand over time

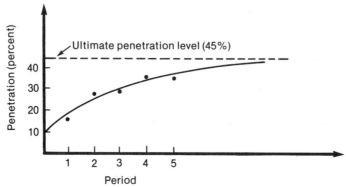

duced graphically (Figure 19–3). Finally, the relative product category usage rate of buyers of the new brand is obtained by either using purchase panel data to estimate it (the usual way) or judgmentally. Assuming this were .80 (eventual users of the product buy 80 percent as much as an average product category user), we would estimate the ultimate share to be $P \cdot M \cdot U$ = (45 percent)(15 percent)(.8) = 5.4 percent.

This model shares the shortcoming of Fourt-Woodlock in terms of basically assuming away changes in the competitive market place. Given the fact that test markets are rarely representative of national marketing programs, this is a big shortcoming. Nonetheless, the model is both simple and plausible and has been widely used.

N. W. Ayer. Both the Fourt-Woodlock and Parfitt-Collins approaches are based on observing repeat purchasing from panel data. The Ayer

FIGURE 19–3
Typical repeat rate for new brand over time

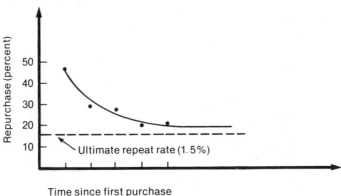

Time since first purchase

model, on the other hand, is based on the notion that the adoption of a product follows a series of stages. More specifically, three main stages are used: awareness, initial/trial purchase, and repeat purchase/loyalty. Using data from several product introductions, this model estimated the relationship between marketing variables and these three variables. This was done by means of three regressions:

Awareness $= a_1 + b_{11}$ (product positioning)
$\qquad + b_{12} \sqrt{\text{(media impressions) (copy execution)}}$
$\qquad + b_{13}$ (ad message containing consumer promotions)
$\qquad + b_{14}$ (category interest) $+ e_1$
Initial purchase $= a_2 + b_{21}$ (estimated awareness)
$\qquad + b_{22}$ {(distribution) (packaging)}
$\qquad + b_{23}$ (if a family brand)
$\qquad + b_{24}$ (consumer promotion)
$\qquad + b_{25}$ (satisfaction with product samples)
$\qquad + b_{26}$ (category usage) $+ e_2$
Repeat purchase $= f$(initial purchase, relative price, product satisfaction,
purchase frequency)

Source: Henry Claycamp and Lucien Liddy, "Prediction of New Product Performance: An Analytical Approach." Adapted from *Journal of Marketing Research,* published by the American Marketing Association, vol. 4 (November 1969), p. 416.

By inputing data to the estimated model, sales projections can be derived. Notice that many of the variables are marketing variables which is in some sense an improvement over the previous models. Notice also, however, that many of these variables (e.g., copy execution) must be subjectively estimated, hence making the results potentially more subject to researcher bias (Claycamp and Liddy, 1969).

Other models. A variety of other models exist for forecasting new product sales. One of the most widely used is Sprinter (Urban, 1970). This model is essentially a substitute for N. W. Ayer's model in that it also allows marketing variables as inputs and assumes a sequential adoption pattern (awareness, trial, etc.). Actually it involves a series of models, each more complete and expensive than the previous one ranging from around $10,000 to $100,000 in cost. (Most of the cost involved is for data collection.) Other well-known models include those of Massy (1967), Ehrenberg (1972), and Eskin (1973). A summary of many of these models is available in Kotler (1971).

In summary, test marketing is a major undertaking which entails both time and money expenses as well as a loss of surprise. Given notice of a test market, a competitor will often react by (*a*) trying to protect sales in the test-market area by advertising or promotional programs which also serve to confuse the interpretation of the test market, (*b*) doing whatever possible to mess up the results of the test, and (*c*) planning a counteroffensive for a possible national launch. Also there are many cases where test marketing is not practical. For example, any major durable where extensive tooling is required is not suitable for test marketing. For these and other reasons, many researchers and companies look for less costly and more controlled alternatives to test marketing (Klompmaker, Hughes, and Haley, 1976).

SUMMARY

This chapter has attempted to briefly outline some of the major forms of research which apply to old and new products. The only way to really grasp these approaches is to encounter them in a corporate situation. Unfortunately, different companies proceed differently so examination of just one company may give a biased picture in terms of approach followed, degree of regimentation, suppliers used, and so forth. This reinforces the point that there is no universally right way to proceed.

Figure 19–4 depicts a chronology for research through the development of a new product. The out-of-pocket costs increase as the stages unfold, with major out-of-pocket costs involved in product development for a product test (especially for high technology products), test marketing, and national launching. In some companies, these or similar steps must be followed in a lock-step manner, with research required at each step before going ahead to the next. In other companies the steps are much more likely to be reordered, combined, or eliminated. What is most important, therefore, is to follow a procedure which (*a*) makes sense and (*b*) is tied to some bench mark so that comparative judgments can be made.

FIGURE 19–4
Sequential new product evaluation

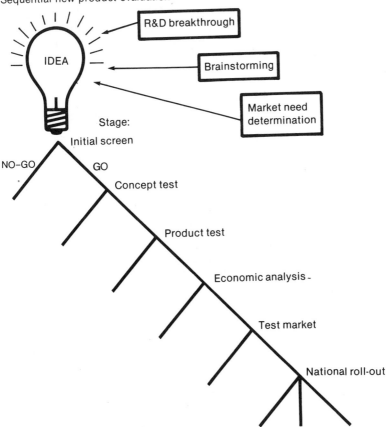

PROBLEMS

1. A large manufacturer Ajax, Inc., is considering the average price levels ($1.00, $1.10, and $1.20) for a product which presently sells for $1.10. Particularly troublesome is the response of the single large competitor, Acme Corporation. It is not known whether they will follow the price change or not. The problem is made more troublesome by the presence of a single large customer, who now buys over half of both Ajax and Acme production of this particular product. Discuss a *methodology* for selecting the best price level for Ajax. Be specific about how you would use this methodology at Ajax. Exactly what would you *do* if you were at Ajax?

2. What are the major decisions which face the product manager of a well-established brand and what research might help him/her make each of the decisions?

3. Assume I ran a repeat pair test on two different formulations of Zonko, an alcoholic beverage where formula A was 70 proof and formula B was 100 proof (the old formula). The results were as follows:

Preferred second time	Preferred first time	
	A	B
A	22%	14%
B	12	52

Interpret statistically and managerially.

4. How would you go about selecting a magazine in which to advertise—
   a. A specialty fashion item.
   b. Ketsup.
   c. A new car.
   d. A machine tool.
   e. A copying machine.

5. Assume sales of a new product followed the following pattern:

	Monthly period						
	1	2	3	4	5	6	7
Percent who have tried (panel data)	18	19	23	24	27	33	34
Share among past triers (panel data)	75	59	44	36	37	35	30
Share (audit data)	1.2	1.9	3.7	3.6	3.9	4.1	3.8

What is your projection for eventual share and what are the assumptions of this projection?

6. Assume you were in charge of monitoring the progress of a new convenience food.
   a. What would you monitor?
   b. How would you combine the measures in a coherent systems framework?

7. Consider the screening of new product ideas. Two product ideas, A and B, were evaluated using six criteria:

Decision criterion	Relative weight	Committee's average rating 5 = very good 1 = very poor		Minimum rating acceptable
		A	B	
Sales volume................	.3	4.2	3.2	3.5
Profit objective	.2	3.5	4.0	3
Insulation from competition	.15	2.3	2.6	3
Availability of capital	.15	5	4	4
Availability of raw materials	.10	4.3	2.8	4
Effect on present products	.10	3	3.5	2
	1.0			

For each product idea compute the quantity:

$$S = \Sigma \text{ relative weight} \times \text{Average rating}$$

Which product ideas are accepted under the decision rules?

a. Accept if S is greater than 3.

b. Accept if the product idea achieves the minimum acceptable rating on *all* criteria.

c. Accept if the product idea achieves the minimum acceptable rating on four or more criteria.

d. What other decision rules can you think of?

e. Which decision method is better?

f. What other factors are ignored in trying to put numbers in the decision process?

8. HPG, Inc., is planning to market test a new frozen toaster product: Baconeggs. Baconeggs is an all-synthetic textured vegetable protein (largely soybeans) which is sold frozen, in a sealed aluminum foil package. The homemaker places the frozen package in the toaster to warm, then removes the product from the aluminum foil package to serve. The product then looks and tastes like scrambled eggs with two strips of (fake) bacon on top. The product has succeeded (more or less) in a long succession of concept, product, and advertising tests, and now HPG will market test the item in Fort Wayne, Indiana. Describe the market test methodology. Exactly what data will you collect? How will you collect it? How (specifically) will you analyze it? What decisions are you trying to make for next year's annual marketing plan which will be facilitated by these analyses?

9. In market research home tests of new products, two waves of trials are often done on the same sample of households. For example, each household may be given two plain, numbered boxes of different detergents and asked to choose its favorite after using both boxes.

These same households are then given two more boxes, numbered differently but containing the same products as on the first trial. You have been asked to interpret results from two such tests, each with a sample of 1,000 people.

Trial 2	Trial 1		
	No. households choosing brand A	No. households choosing brand B	Total
No. households choosing brand A	280	220	500
No. households choosing brand B	260	240	500
Total	540	460	1,000

(The table is read as follows: 280 people chose brand A on both trials, 240 chose B both times, 260 chose A first, then B; and 220 chose B first and then A.)

a. Your supervisor wants to know "whether or not consumers can discriminate clearly between A and B"? What do you conclude and why? Warning—think carefully about what you want to test!

b. Suppose a pound of B costs twice as much to manufacture as a pound of A. What should management do? Why?

BIBLIOGRAPHY

Bass, Frank M. "A Simultaneous Regression Study of Advertising and Sales of Cigarettes." *Journal of Marketing Research,* vol. 6 (August 1969), pp. 291–300.

———, and Clarke, Darral G. "Testing Distributed Lag Models of Advertising Effect." *Journal of Marketing Research,* vol. 9 (August 1972), pp. 298–308.

Beckwith, Neil E. "Multivariate Analysis of Sales Response of Competing Brands to Advertising." *Journal of Marketing Research,* vol. 9 (May 1972), pp. 168–76.

Clarke, Darral G. "Econometric Measurement of the Duration of Advertising Effect on Sales." *Journal of Marketing Research,* vol. 13 (November 1976), pp. 345–57.

Claycamp, Henry J., and Liddy, Lucien E. "Prediction of New Product Performance: An Analytical Approach." *Journal of Marketing Research,* vol. 4 (November 1969), pp. 414–20.

Dhalla, Nairman K. "Assessing the Long-Term Value of Advertising." *Harvard Business Review,* vol. 56 (January–February, 1978), pp. 87–95.

Ehrenberg, A. S. C. *Repeat-Buying: Theory and Application.* London: North-Holland, 1972.

Eskin, Gerald J. "Dynamic Forecasts of New Product Demand Using a Depth of Repeat Model." *Journal of Marketing Research,* vol. 10 (May 1973), pp. 115–19.

Fourt, Louis A., and Woodlock, Joseph W. "Early Prediction of Market Success for New Grocery Products." *Journal of Marketing,* vol. 25 (October 1960), pp. 31–38.

Haley, R. I. "Benefit Segmentation: A Decision-Oriented Research Tool." *Journal of Marketing,* vol. 32 (July 1968), pp. 30–35.

Hardin, David K. "A New Approach to Test Marketing." *Journal of Marketing,* vol. 31 (October 1966), pp. 28–31.

Johnson, Richard M. "Simultaneous Measurement of Discrimination and Preference." Chicago: Market Facts.

Klompmaker, Jay E.; Hughes, G. David; and Haley, Russell I. "Test Marketing in New Product Development." *Harvard Business Review,* vol. 54 (May–June 1976), pp. 128–38.

Kotler, Philip. *Marketing Decision Making: A Model Building Approach.* New York: Holt, Rinehart and Winston, 1971.

Kuehn, Alfred A., and Day, Ralph, "Strategy of Product Quality." *Harvard Business Review,* vol. 40 (November–December 1962), pp. 100–110.

Little, John D. C., and Lodish, Leonard M. "A Media Planning Calculus." *Operations Research,* vol. 17 (January–February 1969), pp. 1–35.

Massy, William F. "Forecasting the Demand for New Convenience Products." *Journal of Marketing Research,* vol. 6 (November 1969), pp. 405–12.

————; Frank, Ronald E.; and Wind, Yoram. *Market Segmentation.* Englewood Cliffs, N.J.: Prentice-Hall, 1972.

Palda, Kristian S. *The Measurement of Cumulative Advertising Effects.* Englewood Cliffs, N.J.: Prentice-Hall, 1964.

Parfitt, J. H., and Collins, B. J. K. "Use of Consumer Panels for Brand-Share Prediction." *Journal of Marketing Research,* vol. 5 (May 1968), pp. 131–45.

Parsons, Leonard J. "The Product Life Cycle and Time-Varying Advertising Elasticities." *Journal of Marketing Research,* vol. 12 (November 1975), pp. 476–80.

Prasad, V. Kanti, and Ring, L. Winston. "Measuring Sales Effects of Some Marketing Mix Variables and Their Interactions." *Journal of Marketing Research,* vol. 13 (November 1976), pp. 391–96.

Urban, Glen L. "Sprinter Mod. III: A Model for the Analysis of New Frequently Purchased Consumer Products." *Operations Research,* vol. 18 (September–October 1970), pp. 805–54.

Vidale, M. L., and Wolfe, H. B. "An Operations-Research Study of Sales Response to Advertising." *Operations Research,* vol. 5 (June 1957), pp. 370–81.

APPENDIX 19–A SAMPLE CONCEPT TEST FORMATS*

PLAIN VERBAL DESCRIPTION OF THE PRODUCT OR

SERVICE AND ITS MAJOR BENEFITS

A major soft drink manufacturer would like to get your reaction to an idea for a new diet soft drink. Please read the description below before answering the questions.

NEW DIET SOFT DRINK

Here is a tasty, sparkling beverage that quenches thirst, refreshes and makes the mouth tingle with a delightful flavor blend of orange, mint and lime.

It helps adults (and kids too) control weight by reducing the craving for sweets and between-meal snacks. And best of all, it contains absolutely no calories.

Comes in 12-ounce cans or bottles and costs 16¢ each.

1. How different, if at all, do you think this diet soft drink would be from other available products now on the market that might be compared with it?

☐ Very Different
☐ Somewhat Different
☐ Slightly Different
☐ Not At All Different

2. Assuming you tried the product described above and liked it, about how often do you think you would buy it?

CHECK ONE

More than once a week.............☐
About once a week.................☐
About twice a month...............☐
About once a month................☐
Less often........................☐
Would never buy it................☐

* Source: National Family Opinion, Inc., *Concept Testing,* New York, 1975.

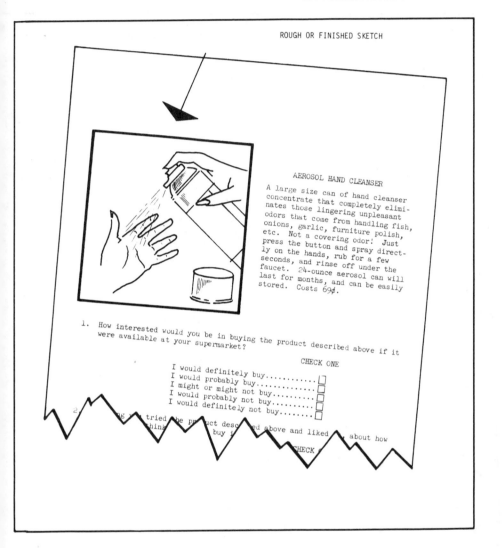

ROUGH OR FINISHED SKETCH

AEROSOL HAND CLEANSER

A large size can of hand cleanser concentrate that completely eliminates those lingering unpleasant odors that come from handling fish, onions, garlic, furniture polish, etc. Not a covering odor! Just press the button and spray directly on the hands, rub for a few seconds, and rinse off under the faucet. 24-ounce aerosol can will last for months, and can be easily stored. Costs 69¢.

1. How interested would you be in buying the product described above if it were available at your supermarket?

CHECK ONE

I would definitely buy............☐
I would probably buy..............☐
I might or might not buy..........☐
I would probably not buy..........☐
I would definitely not buy........☐

2. If I tried the product described above and liked it, about how think buy i CHECK

COLOR SKETCH OR PHOTOGRAPH

COLOR HALFTONE

THE NEW TWO-SUITER

For college vacations. For pleasure trips. For business trips. It's made of a new expandable vinyl that actually breathes and stretches to accomodate the load. Room for two suits inside, incidentals in two outside pockets. Combination lock you set for yourself. $49\frac{1}{2}$" x 13" x 8".

1. Based on what you have read above about this product, how would you compare the New Two-Suiter to conventional luggage in terms of:

	FAR SUPERIOR	MUCH BETTER	ABOUT THE SAME	NOT AS GOOD
Durability....................	☐	☐	☐	☐
Weather proof................	☐	☐	☐	☐
Easy to carry...............	☐	☐	☐	☐
Appearance...................	☐	☐	☐	☐
Size........................	☐	☐	☐	☐

2. What are some of the things you like about the New Two-Suiter?

_____

_____

3. What are some of the things you do not like about the New Two-Suiter?

20

Industrial marketing research

The area of industrial marketing is often overlooked in discussions of research. Yet industrial products constitute a far larger part of the economy than consumer goods. Here industrial marketing is defined as marketing of a product or service to an intermediate customer. This broad definition means that industrial marketing includes not only such obvious examples as machine tools but computers, textbooks, and ethical drugs as well. Hence the first point to be made is that there is no such thing as "typical" industrial marketing.

TYPES OF INDUSTRIAL MARKETING

Industrial marketing can be broken into categories in several ways. One method of categorizing industrial products is based on the complexity of the result of buying the product from the buyer's point of view. Four categories have been identified (Lehmann and O'Shaughnessy, 1974):

1. Routine products, where both the technical performance features of the product and application procedures are known.
2. Procedural problem products, where the technical performance is known but application procedures need to be developed.
3. Performance problem products, where the technical performance of the product is unknown.
4. Political problem products, where the product is a major buy affecting many organization units and costing a lot of money and both technical performance and application procedures are unclear.

Numerous other bases exist for categorizing industrial products. Among these are the following:

1. Price.
2. Criticalness of the product to the overall (a) operation and (b) appearance of the system as a whole.

3. Distribution method (direct sales versus wholesaler).
4. Amount of custom engineering involved (standard versus special order products).
5. Number of key customers.
6. Expertise of purchasing agents (high, e.g., doctor, versus low, e.g., clerk).

Given certain combinations of these characteristics, an industrial good can be quite similar to a consumer good and hence the marketing and marketing research problems and methods become very similar (Figure 20–1). The point is that many consumer goods have characteristics similar to industrial goods. By considering the family as the customer, the analogy is even closer. The purchasing agent role is even repeated in that whoever does the food shopping is really a purchasing agent for the household. Similarly big decisions (houses, cars, etc.) tend to involve many family members (organizational units) in the decision process. The result of this similarity is that industrial marketing research can use many of the techniques and procedures of consumer marketing research.

Industrial marketing researchers can learn from consumer product marketing research, partly because consumer product marketing has had the benefit (albeit often a dubious one) of fancy techniques being routinely applied. There is a great reluctance on the part of many industrial marketers to believe that they have anything to learn from either consumer product marketers or academics. In fact, there is an amazing amount of defensiveness and resentment toward marketing researchers on the part of industrial marketers. Perhaps this defensiveness has something to do with the sales orientation of industrial marketing. Still the defensiveness seems unfounded. In the first place, industrial marketing is in many ways superior to consumer marketing. It accounts for a larger share of GNP and pays at least as well as consumer marketing. Moreover, the products are, at least on an engineering level, more interesting than consumer products (somehow I find design of a computer or machine tool more interesting than design of a bar of soap). Still there tends to be a fairly provincial attitude that suggests consumer and industrial marketing are completely different. While there are differences, there are at least as many similarities as differences.

KEY FEATURES

Having argued that industrial marketing (and therefore industrial marketing research) is not that different from consumer marketing, we now turn to some of the features of industrial marketing which affect the research done. The major problems remain the same: preparing annual plans, assessing market potential, allocating effort to different elements of

FIGURE 20–1
Similarity of consumer and industrial products

Sample product			Characteristics of the industrial product					
Consumer	Industrial	Type	Price	Criticalness	Distribution	Custom engineering	Number of customers	Expertise of decision maker
Frequently purchased good (canned soup)	Bolt	I	Low	Low (unless fails)	Wholesale	None	Many	Low
Durable (dishwasher)	Machine tool	II	Moderate	Moderate	Direct	None	Many	Moderate
Electric car	New copying system	III	High	Moderate (unless fails)	Direct	Little	Moderate	Varies
House	Computer system	IV	Very high	High	Direct	Some	Few	Committee decision

the marketing program, and so forth. What changes are the environmental conditions which affect (a) the amount of different types of research done, and (b) the form of the research. Some of the most important features are purchasing agents and the buying process, direct (personal) sales, custom engineering, few key customers, hard-to-obtain interviews, and no test market.

Purchasing agents and the buying process

The formal institution of a purchasing agent separates industrial marketing from consumer marketing. Here someone is charged as their major reason for existence with making good buys (i.e., low price, reliable performance, delivered on time). Hence the purchasing agent becomes the principal contact point for sellers of routine order products (bolts, paper, etc.). The agents also have influence in more complex product selection. Moreover, they tend to serve a gate keeper role in which they screen sellers from the person or persons who make the actual buying decision. Hence an important research problem is (a) to find out who the purchasing agents are, (b) to find out what their preferences are, and (c) to find out for whom, if anyone, they are "fronting."

Direct (personal) sales

Personal selling is used for many consumer goods (insurance, encyclopedias, Avon products, etc.). In industrial marketing, however, the salesperson is typically accorded more prestige, power, and pay. Also the salesperson tends to serve something of a technical consulting role to the client. In fact, to many people industrial marketing is synonymous with sales and sales management. Hence research related to sales management is a big part of industrial marketing research. Some of the most common types of research which relate to salespersons are as follows:

1. Overall sales forecasting.
2. Potential estimation (by territory).
3. Sales effectiveness estimation.
4. Selection of salespersons.
5. Territory boundaries and salesperson's assignments
6. Salespersons' time allocation scheduling.
7. Salespersons' compensation schedules.

Interestingly, much of the research on these topics takes on an operations research orientation, especially territory, boundary, and assignment problems, time allocation scheduling, and compensation schedules (e.g., Farley, 1964) which are amenable to mathematical programming approaches. An excellent overview of the sales management area is available in Wotruba (1971). An example of a model which has been developed to aid in managing salespersons is CALLPLAN (Lodish, 1971).

Custom engineering

Many large-ticket industrial products such as power generators require custom engineering for each sale. Thus the technical expertise of the sales (or technical back-up) staff plays a large role in the sales effort. For this reason, research centering on (a) determining the importance of custom engineering, (b) determining the types of custom engineering needed, and (c) assessing the perceived competence of the sales staff is common. Similarly the importance of after-sales service becomes more crucial, and perceived competence in this area is also a key area of interest.

Few key customers

For many consumer products, the potential customers number in the millions. For specialized industrial goods, the number of key customers may be more in the range of 10–30 and can be as small as 1 or 2. Hence many of the statistical procedures which depend on large samples are not useful. The result of this is that analytical techniques which are used to study customers tend to be small-sample oriented, including mainly tabular procedures such as cross tabs.

Hard-to-obtain interviews

For consumer products it is relatively easy to find consumers who are willing to provide information about their preferences and usage patterns as well as to try out products. For many industrial products, it is sometimes hard to decide who to interview. Once the key individual is uncovered, getting an appointment and uninterrupted responses from busy executives is extremely difficult. Reliable data is also hard to obtain. For example, most executives or purchasing agents correctly perceive it is to their advantage to have many products available. Hence respondents tend to indicate more interest in new products than they really may have.

No test market

Possibly the most obvious distinguishing characteristic of much of industrial marketing research is the absence of test marketing. This is explainable by the fact that unlike most frequently purchased products, the costs of developing and making prototypes is usually very high. This makes potential estimates the crucial numbers in go-no-go decisions and hence places particular emphasis on market potential estimation.

DATA SOURCES

The sources of data used by industrial marketing research tend to lean heavily toward published data contained in either government reports or syndicated services. Besides reliance on secondary data, most research relies on interviews of key prospects. In getting such interviews, a common approach is to use salespersons as interviewers. This section will proceed to discuss some of the pros and cons of this approach.

Salespersons as interviewers

The appropriateness of using salespersons as interviewers depends on a variety of conditions.

Type of research and salespersons. If the research is fairly mundane (e.g., penetration studies designed to find out if a particular product is being used or questions about product line extensions) and the interview is very structured, ordinary salespersons are adequate. When the problem becomes more complex (new product concept tests, etc.), however, the salesperson needs to have some special skills in order to fruitfully complete the task.

Time available. Salespersons will push research to the back of their agenda (commissions are paid on the basis of sales, not completed questionnaires). Hence super busy (and good) salespersons generally are poor interviewers.

Type of customers. Some customers may resent interviews. When this is the case, the potential lost sales are probably not worth the information obtained, which will be of dubious value at best.

Access to right people. The thought of using salespersons as interviewers is appealing in that it is apparently a cost-saving approach. However, if the people to be interviewed are not regularly contacted by the salespersons, the apparent economies vanish.

Control of sample and interviewer cheating. Assuming a salesperson is given a quota of interviews to collect, s/he will typically (*a*) talk to best friends among the clients and (*b*) be tempted to cheat by personally filling out the questionnaires.

With these points in mind, the following are keys to successful salesperson interviewing:

1. Having a good questionnaire (pretested).
2. Training the sales force.
3. Having only a few surveys per year and limited time per survey.

In summary, then, the pros of salespersons' interviewing include speed, ease of implementation, and spin-off knowledge which the salespersons may acquire by being involved in the research. The cons include time diverted from sales calls, potential annoyance to salespersons and/or customers, and lack of training.

SUMMARY

This chapter has argued that many of the approaches used in consumer product marketing research are equally applicable to industrial marketing research. Still there are some unique features which make industrial marketing research a special field. This chapter is short because the differences are more environmental than analytical. Nonetheless someone interested in industrial marketing research will want to consult some other sources (e.g., Rawnsley, 1978).

BIBLIOGRAPHY

Beswick, Charles A., and Cravens, David W. "A Multistage Decision Model for Salesforce Management." *Journal of Marketing Research,* vol. 14 (May 1977), pp. 135–44.

Cardozo, Richard N., and Cagley, James W. "Experimental Study of Industrial Buyer Behavior." *Journal of Marketing Research,* vol. 8 (August 1971), pp. 329–34.

Cox, William E., Jr., and Havens, George N. "Determination of Sales Potentials and Performance for an Industrial Goods Manufacturer." *Journal of Marketing Research,* vol. 14 (November 1977), pp. 574–78.

Farley, John U. "An Optimal Plan for Salesmen's Compensation." *Journal of Marketing Research,* vol. 1 (May 1964), pp. 39–43.

Lamont, Lawrence M., and Lundstrom, William J. "Identifying Successful Industrial Salesmen by Personality and Personal Characteristics." *Journal of Marketing Research,* vol. 14 (November 1977), pp. 517–29.

Lehmann, Donald R., and O'Shaughnessy, John. "Difference in Attribute Importance for Different Industrial Products." *Journal of Marketing,* vol. 38 (April 1974), pp. 36–42.

Lodish, Leonard M. "CALLPLAN: An Interactive Salesman's Call Planning System." *Management Science,* vol. 18 (December 1971), pp. P25–P40.

O'Shaughnessy, John. "Industrial Buying Behavior: Implications for Individual Account Planning." Working paper, Columbia University Graduate School of Business, 1977.

Ozanne, Urban B., and Churchill, Gilbert A., Jr. "Five Dimensions of the Industrial Adoption Process." *Journal of Marketing Research,* vol. 8 (August 1971), pp. 322–28.

Rawnsley, Allan, ed. *Manual of Industrial Marketing Research.* New York: Wiley, 1978.

Sheth, J. A. "A Model of Industrial Buyer Behavior." *Journal of Marketing,* vol. 37 (October 1973), pp. 50–56.

698

Walker, Orville C., Jr.; Churchill, Gilbert A., Jr.; and Ford, Neil M. "Motivation and Performance in Industrial Selling: Present Knowledge and Needed Research." *Journal of Marketing Research,* vol. 14 (May 1977), pp. 156–68.

Webster, Frederick E., Jr., and Wind, Yoram. "A General Model for Understanding Organizational Buying Behavior." *Journal of Marketing,* vol. 36 (April 1972), pp. 12–19.

Weingard, Robert E. "Why Studying the Purchasing Agent is Not Enough." *Journal of Marketing,* vol. 32 (January 1968), pp. 41–45.

Wotruba, Thomas R. *Sales Management.* New York: Holt, Rinehart and Winston, 1971.

21 _____

Final comments

Having reached the end of this book, the reader may wonder if there is anything else worth saying about marketing research. Actually there is a lot more to be covered. Nonetheless for a variety of reasons (including a blister on the author's finger) this book has come to its end. The purpose of this chapter is to delineate a variety of topics which have not been covered: research proposals and resulting presentations, research in the international market and politics, legal issues, and some forecasts about the future of marketing research.

RESEARCH PRODUCTION IN THE ORGANIZATION

Request for research

In most large companies, a standard "request for research" form is required as the first step in the research process. The format varies from company to company, with some using a very brief one-page form and others a much more extensive format. The essential ingredients are as follows:

1. Problem definition.
2. Anticipated value of the research.
3. Methodology (general).
4. Time frame.
5. Budget.

In addition, predetermined action standards are often required (e.g., if we sell over ten in the test, introduce the new package).

The proposal writing stage should include informal discussions between research and management people. While it may look impressive to require huge documents à la proposals to outside agencies (e.g., National

Science Foundation), this is usually a waste of time and money inside a company. All proposals, however, must be well thought out and carefully prepared.

Doing the work

Getting the work done requires finding a supplier to do the job. This can be done either by keeping a standard supplier available, informally checking with two or three, or using a formal bid system. Once the supplier is chosen, the main task is to keep up sufficient contact to insure that the job is carried out and that any problems which arise are dealt with correctly.

Written report

Reporting the results of a study is typically done in a modular manner. At least five separate "reports" are frequently used:

1. A "cover letter" summary which describes in very general terms the research and its conclusion.
2. A short summary of three to six pages summarizing the basic methodology (e.g., a mail questionnaire survey of 1,500 with a 68 percent response rate . . .) and key findings.
3. An extensive report of all the findings.
4. A technical backup document describing sampling methodology, analytical procedures, and so forth.
5. A pile of computer output.

Generally, only the first two reports go beyond the research department. In fact, it is not unusual for reports three through five to be prepared by the supplier (naturally at extra cost). Preparation of items 3–5 is useful (a) to force attention to detail, (b) to make reinterpretation feasible if it seems required, and (c) to increase source credibility.

Oral report

Like most projects in business, a research project typically concludes with an in person presentation (often known as a "dog and pony" show) complete with flip charts, slides, and so forth. Actually two such "shows" may occur: one when the supplier presents the findings to the research department and a second when the research department presents the findings to the appropriate manager(s). Here, as in the written report, tabular or graphical presentations are superior to technical ones for all but the most specialized audiences.

THE EXPANDING WORLD OF MARKET RESEARCH

International

The marketing research portrayed in this book has been that of the United States. Exporting the methodology becomes increasingly difficult as differences become more apparent.

In other developed countries, the major differences are twofold. First, the existing suppliers differ although many U.S. suppliers such as Nielsen and I.M.S. also offer services abroad. Second, cultural differences are very important. In addition to social and legal taboos on certain behavior, subtle nuances of tradition and language make transfer of methodologies, especially survey based, very difficult. Simultaneous back and forth translation is a minimum for a U.S. researcher trying to gather data in a foreign culture. So is employment of a natural citizen to avoid some of the classic blunders which have occurred in the past. Even with safeguards, time pressures and communication breakdowns can lead to some serious shortcomings. This author well remembers a survey monitoring a test market done in Argentina in which a fairly key question—intention to buy the product—was inadvertently/sloppily omitted.

In developing countries, the problems become even more basic. Often accurate basic data on population, industry, and so forth, is unavailable. That, combined with the low literacy rates and the rural nature of many populations, makes many of the standard techniques useless. (Random digit dialing doesn't work too well when only 2 percent of the population have phones.)

Legal

Another arena which has recently experienced a boom in marketing research is the legal area. Led by the Federal Trade Commission, regulatory agencies have increasingly required "proof" of various types. For example, the FTC requires claim substantiation for ads which in turn requires marketing research. Research results have become crucial to various agency rulings. For example, the FTC has the power to order corrective advertising when deceptive advertising practices have created lasting false impressions. The role for research in such a case is to find out (a) whether the ads deceived people and (b) whether the deception persists. In point of fact, the hearings often feature expert witness testimony on both sides with FTC witnesses arguing both that the ads were deceptive and that the deception will persist, and the company witnesses arguing that the ads aren't all that deceptive and anyway, their effects are short-lived. (Not infrequently, this conflicting testimony is based on the same studies.)

Another problem is that during legal proceedings presumably confidential studies may be forced to be disclosed. This typically occurs during the discovery phase of a legal action, where the two parties to the action can request from the opposite side the data and analysis on which they based their claims. Hence all research reports are potentially subject to scrutiny in a legal setting.

The standards-of-evidence questions raised by legal cases are nontrivial. For example, clearly the natural level of confusion/deception is not zero. (Try to understand federal tax laws or the Bible, for example.) What, then, is the level of deception required to be called deception? Moreover, sampling procedures which managers accept as useful are criticizable as unrepresentative. Hence marketing research (like most of the rest of us) is still struggling to find its way in legal proceedings.

Political

Study any recent national political campaign and all the elements of marketing and marketing research are in evidence. Strategists worry about "positioning" candidates on attributes. Voters' (consumers') views on issues are monitored carefully. Target segments are identified which are vulnerable and programs are designed to reach them. Many of the top people in campaign organizations are marketing researchers. In short, political campaigns are run like businesses, with marketing and marketing research their key elements.

THE FUTURE

Projecting the future, as the chapter on forecasting hopefully conveyed, is a hazardous and uncertain business. Nonetheless, the author (partially on the assumption that most readers have given up by now and therefore bad forecasts cannot cause too much damage) feels the following trends will be evident.

Research will be more quantitative

This seems to be the general trend of all disciplines, and marketing is no more likely to be an exception than were physics or sociology.

Legal considerations will increase

On one hand, more research will be required for various regulatory purposes. On the other hand, new constraints in areas such as privacy protection will affect the type of research which can be done.

Technological changes will affect research methods

For example, innovations such as two-way cable TV will make a new type of in-home personal interview (without an interviewer physically present) possible. Similarly automated checkout systems will provide an extremely useful source of information.

Research and management functions will become more integrated

The first three predictions can be made confidently. This last one is at least as much hopeful as certain. Nonetheless, an increasingly complex world makes increased technical sophistication a likely requirement of managers. Similarly researchers have been found to occasionally have an idea as well as a number. Hence more of a team relationship is likely to evolve. Similarly, more rotational assignments between management and research are likely to occur.

CONCLUSION

The conclusion to a research book really is more of a commencement than a conclusion. This book has merely introduced the subject; it is up to the reader to pursue it in detail. There are some who claim research (and especially quantitative research) is worthless, others who believe it is the end itself. Both are foolish. Research can be a valuable tool, the kind of tool which an adept person uses as a competitive advantage. The way to learn about it is to think, ask questions, and observe. Hopefully this book (or at least its references) will help. As we say at the close of the course, "May you have good samples, big R^2's, and low collinearity." Chou.

APPENDIXES

APPENDIX A: RANDOM NUMBERS

56970	10799	52098	04184	54967	72938	50834	23777	08392
83125	85077	60490	44369	66130	72936	69848	59973	08144
55503	21383	02464	26141	68779	66388	75242	82690	74099
47019	06683	33203	29603	54553	25971	69573	83854	24715
84828	61152	79526	29554	84580	37859	28504	61980	34997
08021	31331	79227	05748	51276	57143	31926	00915	45821
36458	28285	30424	98420	72925	40729	22337	48293	86847
05752	96065	36847	87729	81679	59126	59437	33225	31280
26768	02513	58454	56958	20575	76746	40878	06846	32828
42613	72456	43030	58085	06766	60227	96414	32671	45587
95457	12176	65482	25596	02678	54592	63607	82096	21913
95276	67524	63564	95958	39750	64379	46059	51666	10433
66954	53574	64776	92345	95110	59448	77249	54044	67942
17457	44151	14113	02462	02798	54977	48340	66738	60184
03704	23322	83214	59337	01695	60666	97410	55064	17427
21538	16997	33210	60337	27976	70661	08250	69509	60264
57178	16730	08310	70348	11317	71623	55510	64750	87759
31048	40058	94953	55866	96283	40620	52087	80817	74533
69799	83300	16498	80733	96422	58078	99643	39847	96884
90595	65017	59231	17772	67831	33317	00520	90401	41700
33570	34761	08039	78784	09977	29398	93896	78227	90110
15340	82760	57477	13898	48431	72936	78160	87240	52710
64079	07733	36512	56186	99098	48850	72527	08486	10951
63491	84886	67118	62063	74958	20946	28147	39338	32109
92003	76568	41034	28260	79708	00770	88643	21188	01850
52360	46658	66511	04172	73085	11795	52594	13287	82531
74622	12142	68355	65635	21828	39539	18988	53609	04001
04157	50070	61343	64315	70836	82857	35335	87900	36194
86003	60070	66241	32836	27573	11479	94114	81641	00496
41208	80187	20351	09630	84668	42486	71303	19512	50277
06433	80674	24520	18222	10610	05794	37515	48619	62866
39298	47829	72648	37414	75755	04717	29899	78817	03509
89884	59651	67533	68123	17730	95862	08034	19473	63971
61512	32155	51906	61662	64430	16688	37275	51262	11569
99653	47635	12506	88535	36553	23757	34209	55803	96275
95913	11085	13772	76638	48423	25018	99041	77529	81360
55804	44004	13122	44115	01601	50541	00147	77685	58788
35334	82410	91601	40617	72876	33967	73830	15405	96554
57729	88646	76487	11622	96297	24160	09903	14047	22917
86648	89317	63677	70119	94739	25875	38829	68377	43918
30574	06039	07967	32422	76791	30725	53711	93385	13421
81307	13114	83580	79974	45929	85113	72268	09858	52104
02410	96385	79067	54939	21410	86980	91772	93307	34116
18969	87444	52233	62319	08598	09066	95288	04794	01534
87863	80514	66860	62297	80198	19347	73234	86265	49096
08397	10538	15438	62311	72844	60203	46412	65943	79232
28520	45247	58729	10854	99058	18260	38765	90038	94209
44285	09452	15867	70418	57012	72122	36634	97283	95943
86299	22510	33571	23309	57040	29285	67870	21913	72958
84842	05748	90894	61658	15001	94005	36308	41161	37341

APPENDIX B: STANDARD NORMAL DISTRIBUTION AREAS

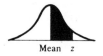

Mean z

z	.00	.01	.02	.03	.04	.05	.06	.07	.08	.09
0.0	.0000	.0040	.0080	.0120	.0160	.0199	.0239	.0279	.0319	.0359
0.1	.0398	.0438	.0478	.0517	.0557	.0596	.0636	.0675	.0714	.0753
0.2	.0793	.0832	.0871	.0910	.0948	.0987	.1026	.1064	.1103	.1141
0.3	.1179	.1217	.1255	.1293	.1331	.1368	.1406	.1443	.1480	.1517
0.4	.1554	.1591	.1628	.1664	.1700	.1736	.1772	.1808	.1844	.1879
0.5	.1915	.1950	.1985	.2019	.2054	.2088	.2123	.2157	.2190	.2224
0.6	.2257	.2291	.2324	.2357	.2389	.2422	.2454	.2486	.2518	.2549
0.7	.2580	.2612	.2642	.2673	.2704	.2734	.2764	.2794	.2823	.2852
0.8	.2881	.2910	.2939	.2967	.2995	.3023	.3051	.3078	.3106	.3133
0.9	.3159	.3186	.3212	.3238	.3264	.3289	.3315	.3340	.3365	.3389
1.0	.3413	.3438	.3461	.3485	.3508	.3531	.3554	.3577	.3599	.3621
1.1	.3643	.3665	.3686	.3708	.3729	.3749	.3770	.3790	.3810	.3830
1.2	.3849	.3869	.3888	.3907	.3925	.3944	.3962	.3980	.3997	.4015
1.3	.4032	.4049	.4066	.4082	.4099	.4115	.4131	.4147	.4162	.4177
1.4	.4192	.4207	.4222	.4236	.4251	.4265	.4279	.4292	.4306	.4319
1.5	.4332	.4345	.4357	.4370	.4382	.4394	.4406	.4418	.4429	.4441
1.6	.4452	.4463	.4474	.4484	.4495	.4505	.4515	.4525	.4535	.4545
1.7	.4554	.4564	.4573	.4582	.4591	.4599	.4608	.4616	.4625	.4633
1.8	.4641	.4649	.4656	.4664	.4671	.4678	.4686	.4693	.4699	.4706
1.9	.4713	.4719	.4726	.4732	.4738	.4744	.4750	.4756	.4761	.4767
2.0	.4772	.4778	.4783	.4788	.4793	.4798	.4803	.4808	.4812	.4817
2.1	.4821	.4826	.4830	.4834	.4838	.4842	.4846	.4850	.4854	.4857
2.2	.4861	.4864	.4868	.4871	.4875	.4878	.4881	.4884	.4887	.4890
2.3	.4893	.4896	.4898	.4901	.4904	.4906	.4909	.4911	.4913	.4916
2.4	.4918	.4920	.4922	.4925	.4927	.4929	.4931	.4932	.4934	.4936
2.5	.4938	.4940	.4941	.4943	.4945	.4946	.4948	.4949	.4951	.4952
2.6	.4953	.4955	.4956	.4957	.4959	.4960	.4961	.4962	.4963	.4964
2.7	.4965	.4966	.4967	.4968	.4969	.4970	.4971	.4972	.4973	.4974
2.8	.4974	.4975	.4976	.4977	.4977	.4978	.4979	.4979	.4980	.4981
2.9	.4981	.4982	.4982	.4983	.4984	.4984	.4985	.4985	.4986	.4986
3.0	.49865	.4987	.4987	.4988	.4988	.4989	.4989	.4989	.4990	.4990
4.0	.4999683									

Source: *Fundamental Statistics for Business and Economics,* Fourth Edition, by John Neter, William Wasserman, and G. A. Whitmore. Copyright © 1973 by Allyn and Bacon, Inc. Reprinted with permission.

APPENDIX C: THE *t* DISTRIBUTION

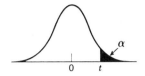

d.f. \ α	.10	.05	.025	.01	.005
1	3.078	6.314	12.706	31.821	63.657
2	1.886	2.920	4.303	6.965	9.925
3	1.638	2.353	3.182	4.541	5.841
4	1.533	2.132	2.776	3.747	4.604
5	1.476	2.015	2.571	3.365	4.032
6	1.440	1.943	2.447	3.143	3.707
7	1.415	1.895	2.365	2.998	3.499
8	1.397	1.860	2.306	2.896	3.355
9	1.383	1.833	2.262	2.821	3.250
10	1.372	1.812	2.228	2.764	3.169
11	1.363	1.796	2.201	2.718	3.106
12	1.356	1.782	2.179	2.681	3.055
13	1.350	1.771	2.160	2.650	3.012
14	1.345	1.761	2.145	2.624	2.977
15	1.341	1.753	2.131	2.602	2.947
16	1.337	1.746	2.120	2.583	2.921
17	1.333	1.740	2.110	2.567	2.898
18	1.330	1.734	2.101	2.552	2.878
19	1.328	1.729	2.093	2.539	2.861
20	1.325	1.725	2.086	2.528	2.845
21	1.323	1.721	2.080	2.518	2.831
22	1.321	1.717	2.074	2.508	2.819
23	1.319	1.714	2.069	2.500	2.807
24	1.318	1.711	2.064	2.492	2.797
25	1.316	1.708	2.060	2.485	2.787
26	1.315	1.706	2.056	2.479	2.779
27	1.314	1.703	2.052	2.473	2.771
28	1.313	1.701	2.048	2.467	2.763
29	1.311	1.699	2.045	2.462	2.756
30	1.310	1.697	2.042	2.457	2.750
40	1.303	1.684	2.021	2.423	2.704
60	1.296	1.671	2.000	2.390	2.660
120	1.289	1.658	1.980	2.358	2.617
∞	1.282	1.645	1.960	2.326	2.576

Source: Hoel, *Elementary Statistics*, 3d ed. (New York: John Wiley & Sons, Inc., 1971 c.).

APPENDIX D: THE χ^2-DISTRIBUTION

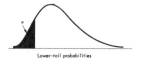

Lower-tail probabilities

df \ α	.001	.005	.010	.025	.050	.100
1	.000	.000	.000	.001	.004	.016
2	.002	.010	.020	.051	.103	.211
3	.024	.072	.115	.216	.352	.584
4	.091	.207	.297	.484	.711	1.06
5	.210	.412	.554	.831	1.15	1.61
6	.381	.676	.872	1.24	1.64	2.20
7	.598	.989	1.24	1.69	2.17	2.83
8	.857	1.34	1.65	2.18	2.73	3.49
9	1.15	1.73	2.09	2.70	3.33	4.17
10	1.48	2.16	2.56	3.25	3.94	4.87
11	1.83	2.60	3.05	3.82	4.57	5.58
12	2.21	3.07	3.57	4.40	5.23	6.30
13	2.62	3.57	4.11	5.01	5.89	7.04
14	3.04	4.07	4.66	5.63	6.57	7.79
15	3.48	4.60	5.23	6.26	7.26	8.55
16	3.94	5.14	5.81	6.91	7.96	9.31
17	4.42	5.70	6.41	7.56	8.67	10.1
18	4.90	6.26	7.01	8.23	9.39	10.9
19	5.41	6.84	7.63	8.91	10.1	11.7
20	5.92	7.43	8.26	9.59	10.9	12.4
21	6.45	8.03	8.90	10.3	11.6	13.2
22	6.98	8.64	9.54	11.0	12.3	14.0
23	7.53	9.26	10.2	11.7	13.1	14.8
24	8.08	9.89	10.9	12.4	13.8	15.7
25	8.65	10.5	11.5	13.1	14.6	16.5
26	9.22	11.2	12.2	13.8	15.4	17.3
27	9.80	11.8	12.9	14.6	16.2	18.1
28	10.4	12.5	13.6	15.3	16.9	18.9
29	11.0	13.1	14.3	16.0	17.7	19.8
30	11.6	13.8	15.0	16.8	18.5	20.6
35	14.7	17.2	18.5	20.6	22.5	24.8
40	17.9	20.7	22.2	24.4	26.5	29.1
45	21.3	24.3	25.9	28.4	30.6	33.4
50	24.7	28.0	29.7	32.4	34.8	37.7
55	28.2	31.7	33.6	36.4	39.0	42.1
60	31.7	35.5	37.5	40.5	43.2	46.5
65	35.4	39.4	41.4	44.6	47.4	50.9
70	39.0	43.3	45.4	48.8	51.7	55.3
75	42.8	47.2	49.5	52.9	56.1	59.8
80	46.5	51.2	53.5	57.2	60.4	64.3
85	50.3	55.2	57.6	61.4	64.7	68.8
90	54.2	59.2	61.8	65.6	69.1	73.3
95	58.0	63.2	65.9	69.9	73.5	77.8
100	61.9	67.3	70.1	74.2	77.9	82.4

APPENDIX D *(continued)*

Upper-tail probabilities

df \ α	.100	.050	.025	.010	.005	.001
1	2.71	3.84	5.02	6.63	7.88	10.8
2	4.61	5.99	7.38	9.21	10.6	13.8
3	6.25	7.81	9.35	11.3	12.8	16.3
4	7.78	9.49	11.1	13.3	14.9	18.5
5	9.24	11.1	12.8	15.1	16.7	20.5
6	10.6	12.6	14.4	16.8	18.5	22.5
7	12.0	14.1	16.0	18.5	20.3	24.3
8	13.4	15.5	17.5	20.1	22.0	26.1
9	14.7	16.9	19.0	21.7	23.6	27.9
10	16.0	18.3	20.5	23.2	25.2	29.6
11	17.3	19.7	21.9	24.7	26.8	31.3
12	18.5	21.0	23.3	26.2	28.3	32.9
13	19.8	22.4	24.7	27.7	29.8	34.5
14	21.1	23.7	26.1	29.1	31.3	36.1
15	22.3	25.0	27.5	30.6	32.8	37.7
16	23.5	26.3	28.8	32.0	34.3	39.3
17	24.8	27.6	30.2	33.4	35.7	40.8
18	26.0	28.9	31.5	34.8	37.2	42.3
19	27.2	30.1	32.9	36.2	38.6	43.8
20	28.4	31.4	34.2	37.6	40.0	45.3
21	29.6	32.7	35.5	38.9	41.4	46.8
22	30.8	33.9	36.8	40.3	42.8	48.3
23	32.0	35.2	38.1	41.6	44.2	49.7
24	33.2	36.4	39.4	43.0	45.6	51.2
25	34.4	37.7	40.6	44.3	46.9	52.6
26	35.6	38.9	41.9	45.6	48.3	54.1
27	36.7	40.1	43.2	47.0	49.6	55.5
28	37.9	41.3	44.5	48.3	51.0	56.9
29	39.1	42.6	45.7	49.6	52.3	58.3
30	40.3	43.8	47.0	50.9	53.7	59.7
35	46.1	49.8	53.2	57.3	60.3	66.6
40	51.8	55.8	59.3	63.7	66.8	73.4
45	57.5	61.7	65.4	70.0	73.2	80.1
50	63.2	67.5	71.4	76.2	79.5	86.7
55	68.8	73.3	77.4	82.3	85.7	93.2
60	74.4	79.1	83.3	88.4	92.0	99.6
65	80.0	84.8	89.2	94.4	98.1	106.0
70	85.5	90.5	95.0	100.4	104.2	112.3
75	91.1	96.2	100.8	106.4	110.3	118.6
80	96.6	101.9	106.6	112.3	116.3	124.8
85	102.1	107.5	112.4	118.2	122.3	131.0
90	107.6	113.1	118.1	124.1	128.3	137.2
95	113.0	118.8	123.9	130.0	134.2	143.3
100	118.5	124.3	129.6	135.8	140.2	149.4

APPENDIX E: CRITICAL VALUES OF THE *F* DISTRIBUTION AT A 5 PERCENT LEVEL AND A 1 PERCENT LEVEL OF SIGNIFICANCE

Degrees of freedom for numerator

Den.	1	2	3	4	5	6	7	8	9	10	12	15	20	24	30	40	60	120	∞
1	161	200	216	225	230	234	237	239	241	242	244	246	248	249	250	251	252	253	254
2	18.5	19.0	19.2	19.2	19.3	19.3	19.4	19.4	19.4	19.4	19.4	19.4	19.4	19.5	19.5	19.5	19.5	19.5	19.5
3	10.1	9.55	9.28	9.12	9.01	8.94	8.89	8.85	8.81	8.79	8.74	8.70	8.66	8.64	8.62	8.59	8.57	8.55	8.53
4	7.71	6.94	6.59	6.39	6.26	6.16	6.09	6.04	6.00	5.96	5.91	5.86	5.80	5.77	5.75	5.72	5.69	5.66	5.63
5	6.61	5.79	5.41	5.19	5.05	4.95	4.88	4.82	4.77	4.74	4.68	4.62	4.56	4.53	4.50	4.46	4.43	4.40	4.37
6	5.99	5.14	4.76	4.53	4.39	4.28	4.21	4.15	4.10	4.06	4.00	3.94	3.87	3.84	3.81	3.77	3.74	3.70	3.67
7	5.59	4.74	4.35	4.12	3.97	3.87	3.79	3.73	3.68	3.64	3.57	3.51	3.44	3.41	3.38	3.34	3.30	3.27	3.23
8	5.32	4.46	4.07	3.84	3.69	3.58	3.50	3.44	3.39	3.35	3.28	3.22	3.15	3.12	3.08	3.04	3.01	2.97	2.93
9	5.12	4.26	3.86	3.63	3.48	3.37	3.29	3.23	3.18	3.14	3.07	3.01	2.94	2.90	2.86	2.83	2.79	2.75	2.71
10	4.96	4.10	3.71	3.48	3.33	3.22	3.14	3.07	3.02	2.98	2.91	2.85	2.77	2.74	2.70	2.66	2.62	2.58	2.54
11	4.84	3.98	3.59	3.36	3.20	3.09	3.01	2.95	2.90	2.85	2.79	2.72	2.65	2.61	2.57	2.53	2.49	2.45	2.40
12	4.75	3.89	3.49	3.26	3.11	3.00	2.91	2.85	2.80	2.75	2.69	2.62	2.54	2.51	2.47	2.43	2.38	2.34	2.30
13	4.67	3.81	3.41	3.18	3.03	2.92	2.83	2.77	2.71	2.67	2.60	2.53	2.46	2.42	2.38	2.34	2.30	2.25	2.21
14	4.60	3.74	3.34	3.11	2.96	2.85	2.76	2.70	2.65	2.60	2.53	2.46	2.39	2.35	2.31	2.27	2.22	2.18	2.13
15	4.54	3.68	3.29	3.06	2.90	2.79	2.71	2.64	2.59	2.54	2.48	2.40	2.33	2.29	2.25	2.20	2.16	2.11	2.07
16	4.49	3.63	3.24	3.01	2.85	2.74	2.66	2.59	2.54	2.49	2.42	2.35	2.28	2.24	2.19	2.15	2.11	2.06	2.01
17	4.45	3.59	3.20	2.96	2.81	2.70	2.61	2.55	2.49	2.45	2.38	2.31	2.23	2.19	2.15	2.10	2.06	2.01	1.96
18	4.41	3.55	3.16	2.93	2.77	2.66	2.58	2.51	2.46	2.41	2.34	2.27	2.19	2.15	2.11	2.06	2.02	1.97	1.92
19	4.38	3.52	3.13	2.90	2.74	2.63	2.54	2.48	2.42	2.38	2.31	2.23	2.16	2.11	2.07	2.03	1.98	1.93	1.88
20	4.35	3.49	3.10	2.87	2.71	2.60	2.51	2.45	2.39	2.35	2.28	2.20	2.12	2.08	2.04	1.99	1.95	1.90	1.84
21	4.32	3.47	3.07	2.84	2.68	2.57	2.49	2.42	2.37	2.32	2.25	2.18	2.10	2.05	2.01	1.96	1.92	1.87	1.81
22	4.30	3.44	3.05	2.82	2.66	2.55	2.46	2.40	2.34	2.30	2.23	2.15	2.07	2.03	1.98	1.94	1.89	1.84	1.78
23	4.28	3.42	3.03	2.80	2.64	2.53	2.44	2.37	2.32	2.27	2.20	2.13	2.05	2.01	1.96	1.91	1.86	1.81	1.76
24	4.26	3.40	3.01	2.78	2.62	2.51	2.42	2.36	2.30	2.25	2.18	2.11	2.03	1.98	1.94	1.89	1.84	1.79	1.73
25	4.24	3.39	2.99	2.76	2.60	2.49	2.40	2.34	2.28	2.24	2.16	2.09	2.01	1.96	1.92	1.87	1.82	1.77	1.71
30	4.17	3.32	2.92	2.69	2.53	2.42	2.33	2.27	2.21	2.16	2.09	2.01	1.93	1.89	1.84	1.79	1.74	1.68	1.62
40	4.08	3.23	2.84	2.61	2.45	2.34	2.25	2.18	2.12	2.08	2.00	1.92	1.84	1.79	1.74	1.69	1.64	1.58	1.51
60	4.00	3.15	2.76	2.53	2.37	2.25	2.17	2.10	2.04	1.99	1.92	1.84	1.75	1.70	1.65	1.59	1.53	1.47	1.39
120	3.92	3.07	2.68	2.45	2.29	2.18	2.09	2.02	1.96	1.91	1.83	1.75	1.66	1.61	1.55	1.50	1.43	1.35	1.25
∞	3.84	3.00	2.60	2.37	2.21	2.10	2.01	1.94	1.88	1.83	1.75	1.67	1.57	1.52	1.46	1.39	1.32	1.22	1.00

Degrees of freedom for denominator

Degrees of freedom for numerator

denom \ num	1	2	3	4	5	6	7	8	9	10	12	15	20	24	30	40	60	120	∞
1	4,052	5,000	5,403	5,625	5,764	5,859	5,928	5,982	6,023	6,056	6,106	6,157	6,209	6,235	6,261	6,287	6,313	6,339	6,366
2	98.5	99.0	99.2	99.2	99.3	99.3	99.4	99.4	99.4	99.4	99.4	99.4	99.4	99.5	99.5	99.5	99.5	99.5	99.5
3	34.1	30.8	29.5	28.7	28.2	27.9	27.7	27.5	27.3	27.2	27.1	26.9	26.7	26.6	26.5	26.4	26.3	26.2	26.1
4	21.2	18.0	16.7	16.0	15.5	15.2	15.0	14.8	14.7	14.5	14.4	14.2	14.0	13.9	13.8	13.7	13.7	13.6	13.5
5	16.3	13.3	12.1	11.4	11.0	10.7	10.5	10.3	10.2	10.1	9.89	9.72	9.55	9.47	9.38	9.29	9.20	9.11	9.02
6	13.7	10.9	9.78	9.15	8.75	8.47	8.26	8.10	7.98	7.87	7.72	7.56	7.40	7.31	7.23	7.14	7.06	6.97	6.88
7	12.2	9.55	8.45	7.85	7.46	7.19	6.99	6.84	6.72	6.62	6.47	6.31	6.16	6.07	5.99	5.91	5.82	5.74	5.65
8	11.3	8.65	7.59	7.01	6.63	6.37	6.18	6.03	5.91	5.81	5.67	5.52	5.36	5.28	5.20	5.12	5.03	4.95	4.86
9	10.6	8.02	6.99	6.42	6.06	5.80	5.61	5.47	5.35	5.26	5.11	4.96	4.81	4.73	4.65	4.57	4.48	4.40	4.31
10	10.0	7.56	6.55	5.99	5.64	5.39	5.20	5.06	4.94	4.85	4.71	4.56	4.41	4.33	4.25	4.17	4.08	4.00	3.91
11	9.65	7.21	6.22	5.67	5.32	5.07	4.89	4.74	4.63	4.54	4.40	4.25	4.10	4.02	3.94	3.86	3.78	3.69	3.60
12	9.33	6.93	5.95	5.41	5.06	4.82	4.64	4.50	4.39	4.30	4.16	4.01	3.86	3.78	3.70	3.62	3.54	3.45	3.36
13	9.07	6.70	5.74	5.21	4.86	4.62	4.44	4.30	4.19	4.10	3.96	3.82	3.66	3.59	3.51	3.43	3.34	3.25	3.17
14	8.86	6.51	5.56	5.04	4.70	4.46	4.28	4.14	4.03	3.94	3.80	3.66	3.51	3.43	3.35	3.27	3.18	3.09	3.00
15	8.68	6.36	5.42	4.89	4.56	4.32	4.14	4.00	3.89	3.80	3.67	3.52	3.37	3.29	3.21	3.13	3.05	2.96	2.87
16	8.53	6.23	5.29	4.77	4.44	4.20	4.03	3.89	3.78	3.69	3.55	3.41	3.26	3.18	3.10	3.02	2.93	2.84	2.75
17	8.40	6.11	5.19	4.67	4.34	4.10	3.93	3.79	3.68	3.59	3.46	3.31	3.16	3.08	3.00	2.92	2.83	2.75	2.65
18	8.29	6.01	5.09	4.58	4.25	4.01	3.84	3.71	3.60	3.51	3.37	3.23	3.08	3.00	2.92	2.84	2.75	2.66	2.57
19	8.19	5.93	5.01	4.50	4.17	3.94	3.77	3.63	3.52	3.43	3.30	3.15	3.00	2.92	2.84	2.76	2.67	2.58	2.49
20	8.10	5.85	4.94	4.43	4.10	3.87	3.70	3.56	3.46	3.37	3.23	3.09	2.94	2.86	2.78	2.69	2.61	2.52	2.42
21	8.02	5.78	4.87	4.37	4.04	3.81	3.64	3.51	3.40	3.31	3.17	3.03	2.88	2.80	2.72	2.64	2.55	2.46	2.36
22	7.95	5.72	4.82	4.31	3.99	3.76	3.59	3.45	3.35	3.26	3.12	2.98	2.83	2.75	2.67	2.58	2.50	2.40	2.31
23	7.88	5.66	4.76	4.26	3.94	3.71	3.54	3.41	3.30	3.21	3.07	2.93	2.78	2.70	2.62	2.54	2.45	2.35	2.26
24	7.82	5.61	4.72	4.22	3.90	3.67	3.50	3.36	3.26	3.17	3.03	2.89	2.74	2.66	2.58	2.49	2.40	2.31	2.21
25	7.77	5.57	4.68	4.18	3.86	3.63	3.46	3.32	3.22	3.13	2.99	2.85	2.70	2.62	2.53	2.45	2.36	2.27	2.17
30	7.56	5.39	4.51	4.02	3.70	3.47	3.30	3.17	3.07	2.98	2.84	2.70	2.55	2.47	2.39	2.30	2.21	2.11	2.01
40	7.31	5.18	4.31	3.83	3.51	3.29	3.12	2.99	2.89	2.80	2.66	2.52	2.37	2.29	2.20	2.11	2.02	1.92	1.80
60	7.08	4.98	4.13	3.65	3.34	3.12	2.95	2.82	2.72	2.63	2.50	2.35	2.20	2.12	2.03	1.94	1.84	1.73	1.60
120	6.85	4.79	3.95	3.48	3.17	2.96	2.79	2.66	2.56	2.47	2.34	2.19	2.03	1.95	1.86	1.76	1.66	1.53	1.38
∞	6.63	4.61	3.78	3.32	3.02	2.80	2.64	2.51	2.41	2.32	2.18	2.04	1.88	1.79	1.70	1.59	1.47	1.32	1.00

Degrees of freedom for denominator

Index

This book has been set VIP in 10 and 9 point Times Roman, leaded 2 points. Part numbers are 20 point Helvetica Light and chapter numbers are 24 point Helvetica light. Part titles are 18 point Helvetica Light italic and chapter titles are 18 point Helvetica Light. The size of the type page is 27 by 45½ picas.